The Enlightenment:
AN INTERPRETATION

The Science of Freedom

PETER GAY

WILDWOOD HOUSE

LONDON

First published Great Britain 1970 by Weidenfeld and Nicolson Ltd
Published by Wildwood House 1973
Copyright © 1969 by Peter Gay
Wildwood House Ltd, 1 Wardour Street, London W1Y 3HE
ISBN 0 7045 0018 3

Portions of Chapter One first appeared in slightly different form as
'The Enlightenment as Medicine and Cure' in *The Age of Enlighten-
ment: Studies Presented to Theodore Besterman*, edited by W. H.
Barber et al. (Oliver and Boyd, Edinburgh and London, 1967).

THE ENLIGHTENMENT

Volume 2—The Science of Freedom

FOR RUTHIE,
again

Aufklärung ist der Ausgang des Menschen aus seiner selbstverschuldeten Unmündigkeit. 'Unmündigkeit *ist das Unvermögen, sich seines Verstandes ohne Leitung eines Anderen zu bedienen.* Selbstverschuldet *ist diese Unmündigkeit, wenn die Ursache derselben nicht an Mangel des Verstandes, sondern der Entschliessung und des Mutes liegt, sich seiner ohne Leitung eines Andern zu bedienen.* Sapere aude! *Habe Mut, dich deines eigenen Verstandes zu bedienen! ist also der Wahlspruch der Aufklärung.*

—IMMANUEL KANT, Was ist Aufklärung?

But why is the experiment of an extended republic to be rejected merely because it may comprise what is new? Is it not the glory of the people of America, that whilst they have paid a decent regard to the opinions of former times and other nations, they have not suffered a blind veneration for antiquity, for custom, or for names, to overrule the suggestions of their own good sense, the knowledge of their own situation, and the lessons of their own experience? To this manly spirit, posterity will be indebted for the possession, and the world for the example of the numerous innovations displayed on the American theatre, in favor of private rights and public happiness.

—JAMES MADISON, The Federalist, *No. 14*

L'histoire des empires est celle de la misère des hommes. L'histoire des sciences est celle de leur grandeur et de leur bonheur.

—EDWARD GIBBON, Essai sur l'étude de la littérature

Preface

THIS VOLUME, the second, completes my attempt at defining the Enlightenment which I began with *The Rise of Modern Paganism*, published in 1966. Like the first, the present volume stands on its own: in *The Rise of Modern Paganism* I analyzed the philosophes' rebellion against their Christian world and their appeal to classical pagan thought; I dealt, in a word, with their education. In this volume I am analyzing the philosophes' environment—the economic and cultural changes that made the philosophy of the Enlightenment relevant and in fact inevitable, the position of writers and artists which gave substance to the philosophes' demands and to their expectations—and the philosophes' program, their view of progress, science, art, society, and politics. *The Science of Freedom*, as I have called this book in allusion to the philosophes' method and goal, may thus be read independently, as the social history of the philosophes' philosophy. At the same time, the two volumes belong together, and I have stressed this wholeness by embracing both in a common title, *The Enlightenment: An Interpretation*, and by constructing them in a dialectical triad: volume I includes the first two books, the thesis and antithesis; volume II includes book three, "The Pursuit of Modernity," which describes the synthesis—the philosophes' philosophy. At the same time, the two volumes belong together, and I have stressed this wholeness by embracing both in a common title, *The Enlightenment: An Interpretation*, and by constructing them in a dialectical triad: volume I includes the first two books, the thesis and antithesis; volume II includes book three, "The Pursuit of Modernity," which describes the synthesis—the philosophes' philosophy.

 The organizing principle of these two volumes is the Enlightenment taken in its narrow sense—the Enlightenment of the philosophes: I designed the three books, and their dialectical interplay,

as an archetypical definition of the philosophes' experience. But—
as I was aware from the beginning, said at the earliest possible
moment in the first volume, and reiterate in the present volume—the
narrow Enlightenment of the philosophes was embedded in a wider,
more comprehensive atmosphere, the atmosphere of the eighteenth
century, which may be called, without distortion, the Age of the
Enlightenment. It was from this age that the philosophes drew ideas
and support, this age which they partly led, partly epitomized, and
partly rejected. I have, especially in this volume, tried to specify
the relations between the two Enlightenments—the philosophic
movement and its environment. These relations were very complex,
and they were, as I have just suggested, partly hostile, partly
friendly. But complex as they were, an understanding of them is
essential to any full definition. To put it another way: Samuel Johnson and Voltaire, Pope and Hume, even Wesley and Lessing, had
much in common, even though much divided them; while I have
concentrated on Voltaire, Hume, and Lessing in these volumes, I
have not forgotten the others.

My enterprise has invited two misunderstandings, and I might
do well to take account of them here. I am committed to the proposition that we can write collective history, and need not be reduced
to the biography of single minds. At the same time, I know that
the Enlightenment, even the narrow Enlightenment of the philosophes, was rich, various, and sometimes contradictory. Both in the
first volume and in the present one, I have used the word "family"
to describe the philosophes, because that word seemed to me to do
justice at once to the affinities and the divergencies among the
philosophes. It is certainly of importance to record that the aesthetic ideas of Diderot and of Lessing were not the same; that Hume
and Voltaire differed in their political philosophy; that the philosophes' ideas on progress, science, education, and other matters
ranged across a fairly wide spectrum. I have recorded it—this is one
reason, indeed the main reason, why my two volumes are so long.
And this is why my general definition of "philosophe" makes no
specific reference to political or aesthetic ideas. In this fashion I have
tried to do justice to the wealth of history, to nuances, idiosyncrasies,
and, at the same time, to the clusters, the *Gestalten,* that make the
Enlightenment what it was.

In differentiating between the narrow and the wider Enlightenment—and this brings me to the second misunderstanding—I have invited some eighteenth-century figures into the club of philosophes and rejected others. In doing so, I have performed an act of definition, not of evaluation. I am not arguing that Voltaire is somehow "better" than Johnson; membership in the club is not a badge of merit—after all, the club included bores and mediocrities and excluded some of the most remarkable men of the time. As a historian, even when writing a work frankly labeled "An Interpretation," I made it my business to avoid value judgments of this sort; I sought instead to define, as clearly as I could, the interweaving of ideas and passions, beliefs and superstitions, and the clash of ideas with ideas that dominated a certain age.

To say this is not to say that I do not have certain sympathies. They lie, clearly enough I suppose, with the secular minds of the eighteenth century. But this should not affect—and I hope it has not affected—my appraisal of the Age of the Enlightenment. Despite these sympathies, in fact, I have avoided one large area of evaluation, important as it is: the possible relevance of the Enlightenment to our time. Obviously, I think that this relevance is considerable; greater by far than its critics and even its admirers acknowledge. If there is an age that desperately needs the humane aims and the critical methods of the Enlightenment, it is certainly our age. But I have refrained from pointing this moral here; I have thought it more important first to define the Enlightenment, for I think that before we can use the Enlightenment we must know what it was. This essay is dedicated to the effort of determining what it was.

But I am not letting the matter rest here. I have been studying the Age of the Enlightenment for twenty years, and it has given me persistent pleasure. Now, as I am moving to other fields of inquiry, I think it proper, even if not here, to express my convictions not as a historian but as a political man. I have therefore written a short polemic in behalf of the Enlightenment, *The Bridge of Criticism*, which will appear separately from this volume. I should like my readers to take it as a political epilogue to this long historical essay.

As with the first volume, I have incurred many obligations in this one. A fellowship from the Guggenheim Foundation in 1967–8, though mainly for other purposes, permitted me to do some essential rewriting; a travel grant from the American Council of Learned Societies gave me an opportunity to talk with a number of eighteenth-century scholars at a conference at St. Andrews, Scotland; the office of the Dean of the Graduate Faculties at Columbia University generously supported my applications for typing funds, particularly welcome in view of the bulky manuscript that this volume became. In this connection I want to express my particular gratitude to Ene Sirvet for her speed and accuracy in typing this manuscript, often under trying circumstances, and for her patience with me. The Procter & Gamble Gift for Progress in the Liberal Arts and Sciences, on which I could draw during 1967–8 and 1968–9, enabled me to buy some indispensable books and otherwise eased the burden of scholarship.

A number of my present and former students, notably Gerald J. Cavanaugh, Victor Wexler, William Keylor, Ronald I. Boss, Stephen Kern, Joan Karle, Theodor Brodek, among others, have generously assisted me in many welcome ways. At the University of Edinburgh and at the University of Virginia, at Vassar College, at Yale, at Cambridge University, and several other hospitable campuses, I have found critical listeners—many of whom I do not even know —who compelled me to recast my argument or change my mind. Two learned societies, the American Historical Association and the Society for French Historical Studies, have been just as patient with me.

In addition to these audiences, I tried out my ideas, much to my benefit, on the University Seminar on European Culture in the Eighteenth Century at Columbia University; it would be invidious to single out the assistance I have had from any one, and so I thank all the members for their patience and their generosity. I have had most helpful exchanges of letters with Herbert Dieckmann, Henry F. May, and Mary Peter Mack; in the difficult third chapter, on science, I had welcome criticism from Loren Graham. Charles C. Gillispie, with whom I have been talking eighteenth-century science for some years, sent me two magnificently circumstantial and enormously helpful letters which considerably changed that chapter. In addition, I thank Richard Hofstadter for his counsel.

I have saved my greatest debts to the last. Arthur M. Wilson,

Robert K. Webb, and my wife, Ruth (as always), read my drafts with
great care. I thank them for their readiness to take time off from
crowded schedules to share their views with me and to encourage me
in my long enterprise.

PETER GAY

New York City,
February 1969

TWO NOTES ON USAGE

As in the first volume, I have *refused to italicize the word "philosophe."* It is, of course, a French word and it has not yet been naturalized, but it is a French word for an international type for which there is no precise equivalent in English. To translate "philosophe" as "philosopher" is, in my view, to make a correct judgment, but the difference between the two words remains large enough to warrant an independent term. I should be pleased if my practice helped to domesticate this foreign word.

That part of a date of a letter appearing within parentheses, say the year or the month and year, was not in the manuscript but was added by the editor whose edition I used.

ABBREVIATIONS AND SHORT TITLES

WHAT I SAID in the first volume still holds true today: the writings of the philosophes are in a curious bibliographical limbo. The complete works of some philosophes are not available at all; the works of others, like Voltaire, are outdated and are now being superseded by critical editions of their major writings and their correspondence. In consequence, I have been compelled to cite from a variety of editions. I list the most important of these below, together with short titles wherever sensible, and with a few journals, frequently cited, the titles of which I have abbreviated as well.

Jean Le Rond d'Alembert: *Mélanges de littérature, d'histoire, et de la philosophie*, 5 vols. (1757). Cited as *Mélanges*.
————: *Œuvres complètes*, 5 vols. (1821–2). Cited as *Œuvres*.
American Historical Review (1895———): cited as *AHR*.
Annales de la Société Jean-Jacques Rousseau (1905———): cited as *Annales*.
Francis Bacon: *Works*, eds. James Spedding, R. L. Ellis, and D. D. Heath, 14 vols. (1854–74), which contain the Latin writings (vols. I–III), English translations and English writings (vols. IV–VII), the correspondence and a biography by Spedding (vols. VIII–XIV).
James Boswell: *Boswell's Life of Johnson, Together with Boswell's Journal of a Tour to the Hebrides and Johnson's Diary of a*

Journey into North Wales, ed. George Birkbeck Hill, rev. by L. F. Powell, 6 vols. (1934–50). Cited as *Life of Johnson*.

Étienne Bonnot, abbé de Condillac: *Œuvres philosophiques*, ed. Georges Le Roy, 3 vols. (1947–51). Cited as *Œuvres*.

Marie-Jean-Antoine-Nicolas Caritat, marquis de Condorcet: *Œuvres*, eds. A. Condorcet O'Connor and M. F. Arago, 12 vols. (1847). (I have abbreviated the long title of Condorcet's *Esquisse d'un tableau historique des progrès de l'esprit humain* as *Esquisse*).

Denis Diderot: *Correspondance*, ed. Georges Roth, 13 vols., so far, down to 1774 (1955———).

———: *Œuvres complètes*, eds. Jules Assézat and Maurice Tourneux, 20 vols. (1875–7). Cited as *Œuvres*.

———: *Œuvres esthétiques*, ed. Paul Vernière (1959).

———: *Œuvres philosophiques*, ed. Paul Vernière (1961).

———: *Œuvres politiques*, ed. Paul Vernière (1963).

———: *Œuvres romanesques*, ed. Henri Bénac (1951).

———: *Salons*, eds. Jean Seznec and Jean Adhémar, 4 vols. (1957–67). Vol. I (1957) covers the salons of 1759, 1761, and 1763; vol. II (1960) the salon of 1765; vol. III (1963) the salon of 1767; vol. IV (1967) the salons of 1769, 1771, 1775, and 1781.

The Encyclopédie of Diderot and d'Alembert: Selected Articles [in French], ed. John Lough (1954). Cited as *The Encyclopédie*.

Edward Gibbon: *Autobiography*, ed. Dero A. Saunders (1961).

———: *The History of the Decline and Fall of the Roman Empire*, ed. J. B. Bury, 7 vols. (1896–1902). Cited as *Decline and Fall of the Roman Empire*.

———: *Miscellaneous Works of Edward Gibbon, Esq., with Memoirs of his Life and Writings, Composed by Himself: Illustrated from His Letters, with Occasional Notes and Narrative*, ed. John, Lord Sheffield, 5 vols. (2d edn., 1814). Cited as *Miscellaneous Works*.

Johann Wolfgang Goethe: *Gedenkausgabe der Werke, Briefe, und Gespräche*, ed. Ernst Beutler, 24 vols. (1948–54). Cited as *Gedenkausgabe*.

Friedrich Melchior Grimm: *Correspondance littéraire, philosophique et critique par Grimm, Diderot, Raynal, etc.*, ed. Maurice Tourneux, 16 vols. (1877–82). Cited as *Correspondance littéraire*.

David Hume: *Dialogues Concerning Natural Religion*, ed. Norman Kemp Smith (2d edn., 1947). Cited as *Dialogues*.

———: *The Letters of David Hume*, ed. J. Y. T. Greig, 2 vols. (1932). Cited as *Letters*.

———: *New Letters of David Hume*, eds. Raymond Klibansky and Ernest C. Mossner (1954). Cited as *New Letters*.

———: *The Philosophical Works of David Hume*, eds. T. H. Green and T. H. Grose, 4 vols. (1882 edn.). Cited as *Works*.

Journal of the History of Ideas (1940———): Cited as *JHI*.

Journal of the Warburg Institute (1937–9); after April 1939 changed to *Journal of the Warburg and Courtauld Institute*. Cited as *Warburg Journal*.

Immanuel Kant: *Immanuel Kants Werke*, ed. Ernst Cassirer, with Hermann Cohen *et al.*, 11 vols. (vol. XI is Cassirer's *Kants Leben und Lehre*), (1912–22). Cited as *Werke*.

Gotthold Ephraim Lessing: *Sämmtliche Schriften*, eds. Karl Lachmann and Franz Muncker, 23 vols. (1886–1924). Cited as *Schriften*.

Charles de Secondat, baron de Montesquieu: *Œuvres complètes*, ed. André Masson, 3 vols. (1950–5). Cited as *Œuvres*.

Publications of the Modern Language Association of America (1884———): Cited as *PMLA*.

Jean-Jacques Rousseau: *Œuvres complètes*, eds. Bernard Gagnebin, Marcel Raymond *et al.*, 3 vols. so far (1959———). Cited as *Œuvres*.

Studies on Voltaire and the Eighteenth Century, ed. Theodore Besterman (1955———). Volume I appeared under the title *Travaux sur Voltaire et le dix-huitième siècle*. Cited as *VS*.

Anne-Robert-Jacques Turgot, baron de l'Aulne: *Œuvres de Turgot et documents le concernant*, ed. G. Schelle, 5 vols. (1913–23). Cited as *Œuvres*.

Voltaire (François-Marie Arouet): *Voltaire's Correspondence*, ed. Theodore Besterman, 107 vols. (1953–65). Cited as *Correspondence*.

———: *Lettres philosophiques*, ed. Gustave Lanson, 2 vols. (1909).

———: *Voltaire's Notebooks*, ed. Theodore Besterman, 2 vols., continuously paginated (1952). Cited as *Notebooks*.

———: *Œuvres complètes*, ed. Louis Moland, 52 vols. (1877–85). Cited as *Œuvres*.

———: *Œuvres historiques*, ed. René Pomeau (1957).

———: *Philosophical Dictionary*, ed. and tr. Peter Gay, 2 vols., continuously paginated (1962).

Vorträge der Bibliothek Warburg, 1921–1922 (1923) to *1930–1931* (1932): Cited as *Warburg Vorträge.*

Christoph Martin Wieland: *Sämmtliche Werke,* ed. J. G. Gruber, 50 vols. (Vol. L is a biography of Wieland by Gruber), (1824–7). Cited as *Werke.*

CONTENTS

BOOK THREE: THE PURSUIT OF MODERNITY

FINALE

BIBLIOGRAPHICAL ESSAY

BOOK THREE

The Pursuit
of
Modernity

CHAPTER ONE

The Recovery of Nerve

---

1. PRELUDE TO MODERNITY:
THE RECOVERY OF NERVE

I

IN THE CENTURY OF THE ENLIGHTENMENT, educated Europeans awoke to a new sense of life. They experienced an expansive sense of power over nature and themselves: the pitiless cycles of epidemics, famines, risky life and early death, devastating war and uneasy peace—the treadmill of human existence—seemed to be yielding at last to the application of critical intelligence. Fear of change, up to that time nearly universal, was giving way to fear of stagnation; the word *innovation*, traditionally an effective term of abuse, became a word of praise. The very emergence of conservative ideas was a tribute to the general obsession with improvement: a stationary society does not need conservatives. There seemed to be little doubt that in the struggle of man against nature the balance of power was shifting in favor of man.

Men had, of course, sometimes trusted their powers before, but never so justly as now; in the eighteenth century, for the first time in history, confidence was the companion of realism rather than a symptom of the Utopian imagination. The self-assurance of natural scientists, merchants, public servants—and philosophers—was not the boasting that conceals impotence; it was a rational reliance on the efficacy of energetic action. The philosophes played a strategic part in the construction of this new temper; they undertook to devise forms—a social, ethical, political, and aesthetic program—for the sake of freedom, rather than as a curb on anarchy. The Enlightenment may have been a consequence and expression of a revolution in men's minds; it was also one of its principal causes.

The old scourges persisted, though often in guises less terrifying than before. War, disease, starvation, insecurity, and injustice continued to darken men's lives and check their hopes. Progress itself called for new victims, and the very improvements that lightened the burdens of many intensified the sufferings of others: for the majority (to speak with Samuel Johnson) the eighteenth century remained a time in which there was little to be enjoyed and much to be endured. The new style of thought was in the main reserved to the well-born, the articulate, and the lucky: the rural and the urban masses had little share in the new dispensation. As in ideas, so in styles of life, Western society existed in several centuries at once: "Those," wrote the philosophe Duclos in 1750, "who live a hundred miles from the capital, are a century away from it in their modes of thinking and acting."[1] The poor, in England as in Sweden, France as in Naples, remained poor. Mothers continued to murder their illegitimate children; serfs in Prussia and Russia, under rulers who claimed to be guided by enlightened principles, continued to subsist under primitive, practically subhuman conditions; gin drowned the sorrows and shortened the lives of the poor in England—by its own admission the most civilized country in the world. "More than half the habitable world," Voltaire wrote as late as 1771, "is still populated by two-footed animals who live in a horrible condition approximating the state of nature, with hardly enough to live on and clothe themselves, barely enjoying the gift of speech, barely aware that they are miserable, living and dying practically without knowing it."[2]

For many, then, this age of improvement meant simply that their desperate, deprived existence assumed unexpected forms. Patterns of deference slowly changed, but deference itself persisted; while the propertied classes found new rationalizations for neglecting or exploiting the lower orders, neglect and exploitation survived the remonstrances of charitable Christians and humane philosophes. Tuberculosis took the place of the plague; humanitarian souls turned their attention from rural to urban destitution. There was less occa-

---

[1] *Considérations sur les mœurs de ce siècle* (1750; edn. 1939), 13.
[2] "Homme," *Questions sur l'Encyclopédie,* in *Œuvres,* XIX, 384.

sion for food riots, although they continued to disrupt the precarious public order all across Europe; more and more the victims of progress vented their frustrations and their helpless fury on defenseless Catholics or Huguenots, or on rapacious employers. The enclosure movement rationalized agriculture and in the long run benefited the bulk of the population, even the poor. But the hungry cannot wait for the long run. In England, displaced squatters infested or produced stinking slums, while in France the rural unemployed wandered about the countryside in begging, thieving bands. Misery followed economic improvement like a shadow. Practically all progress in the eighteenth century, whether in industry, agriculture, education, or government, was a doubtful blessing. Yet it *was* a blessing, and while passivity and pessimism survived, even among philosophes, those placed favorably enough to profit from the currents of the age were buoyed up by pleasing and unprecedented prospects.

I say "unprecedented," for while such states of mind are subtle in their manifestations, hard to detect, and perhaps impossible to prove, I am certain that the eighteenth-century mood I am describing was a genuine and far-reaching novelty in human affairs; it amounted to far more than a mere recapture of old positions, and it surpassed anything the most confident of antique rationalists could have imagined. It is not that in antiquity man was invariably unhappy or that he left all to chance: he studied medicine, built roads, and administered territories. He aspired to the life of reason. But he was aware that this aspiration was a vain hope in face of inescapable realities. Then, early in the Roman Empire, his passivity grew deeper, more pervasive. Christianity was both cause and symptom of an outlook more pathetic than the outlook it replaced. Gilbert Murray, who has chronicled this sapping of vitality and rationality, describes it in a famous paragraph as "a rise of asceticism, of mysticism, in a sense, of pessimism; a loss of self-confidence, of hope in this life and of faith in normal human effort; a despair of patient inquiry, a cry for infallible revelation; an indifference to the welfare of the state, a conversion of the soul to God." And, having described this "intensifying of certain spiritual emotions," he christened it a "failure of nerve."[3] The experience of the eighteenth century, to

---

[3] *Five Stages of Greek Religion* (edn. 1935), 123.

which I am giving the name "the recovery of nerve," was precisely the opposite: it was a century of decline in mysticism, of growing hope for life and trust in effort, of commitment to inquiry and criticism, of interest in social reform, of increasing secularism, and a growing willingness to take risks.

This—it is worth saying again—was new. Through the Renaissance, men had dramatized their impotence by portraying history as a tale of decline or as the playground of inexorable cycles. The Humanists had still alternated between moods of neo-Platonic resignation and alchemists' dreams of unmeasured power; fortune's wheel was their master metaphor—all is subject to change, states wax and wane, families rise and fall. At best, Machiavelli argued, vigor and ruthless energy may wrest half of existence from Fortuna's caprices, but the other half must always belong to the fickle goddess. It was Bacon and Descartes who broke with this historical fatalism. Toward the end of his *Discours de la méthode*, Descartes speaks in a moving passage of a practical science that would make men "masters and possessors of nature." That science, he thought, was "to be desired not only for the invention of an infinite number of devices that would enable us to enjoy without any labor the fruits of the earth and all its comforts, but above all for the preservation of health, which is doubtless the first of all goods and the foundation of all other goods of this life."[4] Shortly before, Bacon had pointedly revived the almost forgotten Roman saying, "Man is the architect of his fortune," and translated it into a program that was vastly ambitious for all its deliberate sobriety.[5]

By the time of the Enlightenment, this confident attitude had become commonplace among the devotees of the new philosophy. Locke noted in his journal that there was a "large feild for knowledg proper for the use and advantage of men," namely to "finde

---

[4] *Discours de la méthode*, part VI. *Œuvres*, eds. Charles Adam and Paul Tannery, 12 vols. (1897–1910), VI, 62.
[5] One of Bacon's precursors was the sixteenth-century French historian La Popelinière, who deliberately rejected Renaissance philosophy and insisted: "I cannot recognize any good or bad luck, chance, or fortune whatsoever in human actions; I should freely maintain we create our own fortune, good or bad, ourselves." Quoted by G. Wylie Sypher: "Similarities Between the Scientific and the Historical Revolutions at the End of the Renaissance," *JHI*, XXVI, 3 (July–September 1965), 359.

out new inventions of dispatch to shorten or ease our labours, or applying sagaciously togeather severall agents and patients to procure new and beneficiall productions whereby our stock of riches (i.e., things usefull for the conveniencys of our life) may be increased or better preservd." And, Locke added significantly, "for such discoverys as these the mind of man is well fitted."[6] Lord Shaftesbury, Locke's disciple, more inward than his master, applied the ancient saying to man's self-mastery: the "wise and able man," he wrote, "by laying within himself the lasting and sure foundations of order, peace, and concord" thus becomes "the architect of his own life and fortune."[7] Not surprisingly, both the proverb and the attitude spread to the English colonies in America: in 1770 Thomas Jefferson included "*faber suae quisque fortunae*" among his favorite maxims, while some years before Benjamin Franklin developed a plan for scientific cooperation among the colonies that would solve the mysteries of nature and enhance man's power, "over matter, and multiply the conveniences or pleasures of life."[8] In the German literary world, poets found new meaning in the grandiose myth of Prometheus, which Christians had piously reinterpreted for many centuries, and took it once again as a symbol of Bacon's proud pronouncement that knowledge is power. "I am under the impression," wrote the young Kant, a little cautiously, "that it is sometimes not useless to place a certain noble trust in one's own powers. A confidence of this sort gives life to all our efforts and lends them a certain verve, highly conducive to the investigation of the truth."[9] Later, in the *Critique of Pure Reason*, Kant was less tentative in his language: intelligence is an active force in the world. Reason, he wrote, with its principles in one hand and experiment in the other, approaches nature to learn from it, but not in the passive attitude of the pupil; rather, it acts like a judge who "compels the witnesses to

---

[6] Quoted in Maurice Mandelbaum: *Philosophy, Science, and Sense Perception* (1964), 50.
[7] "The Moralists," *Characteristics of Men, Manners, Opinions, Times, etc.*, ed. John M. Robertson, 2 vols. (1900), II, 144.
[8] Jefferson: *The Literary Bible of Thomas Jefferson*, ed. Gilbert Chinard (1928), 4; Franklin: quoted in Brooke Hindle: *The Pursuit of Science in Revolutionary America* (1956), 1.
[9] "Gedanken von der wahren Schätzung der lebendigen Kräfte," quoted in Ernst Cassirer: *Kants Leben und Lehre* (1918), 29.

answer questions which he himself has formulated."[1] Men of action
were of the same mind: in 1780, William Hutton, printer at Bir-
mingham and local historian, echoed Bacon with the engaging self-
assertiveness of his age. "Every man," he said, "has his fortune in
his own hands."[2]

II

The recovery of nerve was the product of many forces: the
spectacular career of the natural sciences, advances in medicine, the
improvement of manners and growth of humanitarian sentiment,
the slow crumbling of traditional social hierarchies, and revolutionary changes in the production of food, the organization of industry,
the pattern of population—all pointing in the same direction. It was
a time in which philosophers—most of them philosophes—invented
new sciences, all of them in the service of man's power over his
environment; the Enlightenment was the age of what David Hume
called "the moral sciences": sociology, psychology, political economy, and modern education.

The age demanded these new sciences: it was an age of administrative upheaval, when reforming public officials found themselves
in conflict with established bodies and traditional practices. Rational
public administration and rational statistics were in their infancy,
but they foreshadowed the modern welfare state. While the decay
of the guilds and the decline of clerical orders redounded mainly to
the advantage of industrial and commercial capitalism, behind the
troops of *laissez faire* marched the clerks of government regulation.
Medieval welfare society had been based on manageable units, un-
questioned social hierarchies, and the ideal of Christian charity. In
the eighteenth century, at least on the Continent, these charitable
bodies had been largely deprived of their economic base and their

---

[1] *Kritik der reinen Vernunft,* in *Werke,* III, 16.
[2] T. S. Ashton: *The Industrial Revolution, 1760–1830* (1948), 17. A
little earlier, Adam Ferguson had written: "We speak of art as distinguished from nature; but art itself is natural to man. He is in
some measure the artificer of his own frame, as well as his fortune. . . ." *An Essay on the History of Civil Society* (1767), ed.
Duncan Forbes (1966), 6.

emotional appeal; after a period of anarchy and sometimes quite unintentional brutality, the secular conscience was beginning to assert itself. The Hapsburg rulers confiscated the properties of expelled Jesuits and used them for public relief, while in other countries monarchs deprived the churches of their poorhouses, hospitals, foundling homes, and schools, either expropriating them outright or subjecting them to public supervision. All over the Continent the partial nationalization of relief was accompanied by the partial nationalization of education.

While this social technology remained rudimentary and advanced slowly against the stubborn resistance of entrenched habits, the application of reason to industry and agriculture had revolutionary consequences. By the 1760s, in fact, mainly in Britain and its American colonies, the rhythm of improvement had accelerated to such a dazzling pace that it alarmed almost as many as it gratified. In Philadelphia, the Reverend William Smith complained that "Building is one gulph of expense scarce fathomable. Additions, alterations, decorations are endless. 'Tis one eternal scene of pulling down and putting up."[3] He was far from alone in his bewilderment in the face of progress. Samuel Johnson, who was no reactionary, grumbled that "the age is running mad after innovation; all the business of the world is to be done in a new way; men are to be hanged in a new way; Tyburn itself is not safe from the fury of innovation."[4] But others rejoiced: in the 1770s the *Encyclopedia Britannica* proudly told its readers that "the discoveries and improvements" of eighteenth-century inventors "diffuse a glory over this country unattainable by conquest or dominion."[5]

The diffusion was rapid because it was organized and self-aware. Scientific academies, established in the seventeenth century to facilitate the exchange and propagation of reliable technical information, served as a model for the eighteenth century. The age of the Enlightenment was an age of academies—academies of medicine, of agriculture, of literature, each with its prizes, its journals, and its well-attended meetings. In the academies and outside them, in factories and workshops and coffeehouses, intelligence, liberated from

---

[3] Quoted in Carl Bridenbaugh: *Cities in Revolt: Urban Life in America, 1743-1776* (edn. 1964), 14.
[4] Boswell: *Life of Johnson* (under 1783), IV, 188.
[5] See Dorothy George: *England in Transition* (edn. 1953), 107.

the bonds of tradition, often heedless of aesthetic scruples or religious restraints, devoted itself to practical results; it kept in touch with scientists and contributed to technological refinements. While in the hundred years from 1660 to 1760, the number of patents granted in England averaged about 60 per decade, that average rose to 325 in the thirty years from 1760 to 1790. Only a few of the patent holders, romantic myths to the contrary, were inspired tinkerers or lonely geniuses; the representative inventor of the age was James Watt, who embodied to perfection the union between theory and practice, science and technology, that was such a favorite theme in the philosophes' homilies. In 1753, when Watt was a young man, Diderot had, as it were, drawn his portrait in his *De l'interprétation de la nature*. By repeating Bacon's metaphors, Diderot's little book makes explicit the connection between seventeenth-century fantasies and eighteenth-century realities, and between philosophy and social change. Theoretical and practical thinkers, Diderot urged, must unite against "the resistance of nature." Playful speculation has its place by the side of patient and systematic experimentation; together they make the philosopher of nature into a conqueror, rather than a spectator, into the bee which transforms what it acquires.[6] In Diderot's pages, art anticipates nature: Watt's steam engine—the decisive invention of the industrial revolution—is simply a superb illustration of Diderot's ideal; it is unthinkable without the work of Hooke and Newton, and without the work of contemporary scientists all over Europe. Nor did the idea of the steam engine leap to Watt's mind as he watched a kettle boil; he produced his model after conducting elaborate experiments and after systematic reflection.

The same practical philosophy that produced mechanical innovations produced the institutions that made their widespread use feasible and profitable. The factory, the minute division of labor, industrial discipline for workers and managers, improvements in credit and transport were all inventions as deliberate and as rational

---

[6] *De l'interprétation de la nature*, in *Œuvres philosophiques*, ed. Paul Vernière (1961), 178 ff. I have considered the importance of practice to thought in the philosophes' philosophy in the first volume of this two-volume essay; see *The Enlightenment: An Interpretation*, I, *The Rise of Modern Paganism* (1966), 127–59. I shall refer to this volume by its subtitle from now on.

as the steam engine or the flying shuttle. They were, precisely in the Enlightenment's sense of the word, *philosophical*: Adam Smith observed that some improvements in his time had been made by the ingenuity "of those who are called philosophers or men of speculation, whose trade it is not to do any thing, but to observe every thing";[7] and Samuel Johnson, for all the primitiveness of his own economic views, defended Adam Smith's right to philosophize on political economy; nothing, he argued, "requires more to be illustrated by philosophy than trade does."[8]

The recovery of nerve was ubiquitous and irresistible. In 1798, Thomas Malthus, no enthusiast and certainly no philosophe, could look back on a turbulent century and list as revolutionary forces, "the great and unlooked for discoveries that have taken place of late years in natural philosophy, the increasing diffusion of general knowledge from the extension of the art of printing, the ardent and unshackled spirit of inquiry that prevails throughout the lettered and even unlettered world, the new and extraordinary lights that have been thrown on political subjects which dazzle and astonish the understanding."[9] And even this list is far from complete. The production of food, the modernization of political and educational institutions, the diffusion of polite learning, the improved lighting, sanitation, and safety of the cities in which the men of the Enlightenment walked, even the roads offered contemporaries material for satisfying philosophical reflections. In 1789 Arthur Young praised the new turnpike to London for permitting the carrying of heavy loads, and for giving a "general impetus" to circulation; the highway, he wrote, brought "new people—new ideas—new exertions —fresh activity to every branch of industry," and, indeed, "animation, vigour, life and energy of luxury, consumption, and industry."[1] This prosaic rhapsody neatly captures the new spirit, with its emotional commitment to the mundane, its abundant love of life, and its sense of power. From our perspective, the technology of the

---

[7] *An Inquiry into the Nature and Causes of the Wealth of Nations* (1776), ed. Edwin Cannan (1937), 10.
[8] Boswell: *Life of Johnson* (under March 16, 1776), II, 430.
[9] *An Essay on the Principle of Population* ... (1798), in *On Population*, ed. Gertrude Himmelfarb (1960), 5.
[1] Quoted by H. L. Beales: "Travel and Communication," in *Johnson's England: An Account of the Life and Manners of His Age*, ed. A. S. Turberville, 2 vols. (1933), I, 128.

eighteenth century was crude, urban life uncomfortable, social welfare grudging and feeble, transport and communication cumbersome, diet inadequate, and medicine a gamble not worth taking. Even the philosophes, for all their radicalism, had not yet shed the mentality of a preindustrial age: modernity was still struggling to be born. But men saw life getting better, safer, easier, healthier, more predictable—that is to say, more rational—decade by decade; and so they built their house of hope less on what had happened than on what was happening, and even more on what they had good reason to expect would happen in the future.

Even eating was elevated from gluttony into an art and a science. Samuel Johnson, himself no mean feeder, boasted in 1778 that he could write a better cookbook than any written before: "It should be a book upon philosophical principles."[2] This was partly a jest, partly a trivial employment of elevated language, but it was also a symbol of cultural progress. When a mere commoner could approach dining as a philosophical problem, the recovery of nerve had indeed gone far.

2. ENLIGHTENMENT: MEDICINE AND CURE

I

THE MOST POWERFUL AGENT in the recovery of nerve was obviously the scientific revolution, with its radical attack on traditional ways of thought and its spectacular impact on technology and the moral sciences. But for observant men in the eighteenth century, philosophes as well as others, the most tangible cause for confidence lay in medicine—among the many clients of the Newtonian dispensation surely the most prosperous. Medicine was the most highly visible and the most heartening index of general improvement: nothing after all was better calculated to buoy up men's feeling about life than growing hope for life itself.

For the Enlightenment, medicine had more than visceral sig-

---

[2] Boswell: *Life of Johnson* (under April 15, 1778), III, 285.

nificance. It was in medicine that the philosophes tested their philosophy by experience; medicine was at once the model of the new philosophy and proof of its efficacy. And beyond that, medicine allowed philosophes to press as a realistic claim what men before them had only glimpsed as a shapeless, uncertain vision. "I love life," Diderot wrote to the famous surgeon Sauveur-François de Morand in 1748, "hence I want to live, at least as long as I continue to be happy; but there is no true happiness for the man who is not well."[3] This was an old idea, as old as Plato; what was new and characteristic of the recovery of nerve was Diderot's insistence that he had a right to hope for health and happiness together.

Medicine had been intimately linked to the scientific revolution —which was at bottom a philosophical revolution—from the beginning; the pioneers of that revolution saw themselves as physicians to a sick civilization. In his utopian commonwealth, the New Atlantis, Bacon paid assiduous attention to the safeguarding of health and the cure of disease; and Descartes, as we know, had ranked the preservation of good health as "the first of all goods." For even the mind, Descartes argued, "depends so much on the temper and disposition of the bodily organs that if it were possible to find some means of rendering men wiser and more competent than they have been up to now, I believe that we must seek it in medicine." Descartes's expectations of this medical science were boundless: "All we know is almost nothing compared to what remains to be known; we could be freed from innumerable maladies, of body and mind alike, and perhaps even from the infirmities of old age, if we had sufficient knowledge of their causes and of all the remedies with which nature has provided us."[4] Here was a program worthy of the new philosophy.

By the time of Locke, Bacon's and Descartes's ambitious claim —a brave hope disguised as a firm prediction—found echoes among practicing scientists. Medicine, it seemed, was transforming itself from a medieval mystery, from the furtive ally of alchemy and astrology, into a thoroughly philosophical science, and this association of the new philosophy with the art of healing proved to the thinkers of the day the strength of both. Leibniz forecast that new

---

[3] (December 16, 1748). *Correspondance*, I, 59.
[4] *Discours de la méthode*, part VI. *Œuvres*, VI, 62.

discoveries in natural philosophy and new precision instruments would result above all in "advances in medicine," that "important science,"[5] while John Locke experienced and articulated the alliance of medicine and philosophy both in his life and his thought. Locke was a physician before he was a philosopher, and a philosopher largely because he was a physician; medicine prompted his most philosophical reflections. "I perfectly agree with you," he wrote to Molyneux, "concerning general theories, the curse of the time and destructive not less of life than of science—they are for the most part but a sort of waking dream, with which when men have warmed their heads, they pass into unquestionable truths. This is beginning at the wrong end, men laying the foundations in their own fancies, and then suiting the phenomena of diseases and the cure of them, to those fancies. I wonder, after the pattern Dr. Sydenham has set of a better way, men should return again to this romance way of physics. What we know of the works of nature, especially in the constitution of health and the operation of our own bodies, is only by the sensible effects, but not by any certainty we can have of the tools she uses or the way she works by."[6] Thomas Sydenham, as this letter suggests, was Locke's model; he was also his friend. When Locke listed a select few "master-builders" who had revolutionized the sciences, he included Sydenham, "the English Hippocrates," and when he made "experience" into the final court of appeal, he was generalizing from his own, and Sydenham's, medical practice. In his turn, Sydenham collaborated with Locke and thought like him: the physician, he insisted, must avoid "speculations," and devote himself to the "industrious investigation of the history of diseases, and of the effects of remedies, as shown by the only teacher, experience."[7] Sydenham taught medicine on philosophical principles, Locke taught philosophy on medical principles.

As in so much else, Locke in this too set the pattern for the Enlightenment. The emotion the philosophes invested in medicine is as hard to appreciate today as their worship of Cicero, and as

---

[5] See Dr. Cabanès: *L'Histoire éclairée par la clinique* (n.d., c. 1920), 30.
[6] Quoted in G. S. Brett: *A History of Psychology*, II (1921), 257.
[7] Locke on Sydenham: "Epistle to the Reader," *An Essay Concerning Human Understanding*; Sydenham on method: Maurice Cranston: *John Locke: A Biography* (1957), 92.

revealing. Several of them were doctors: Daubenton, the naturalist, and Quesnay, the founder of physiocracy, were both physicians; Bernard Mandeville, the notorious freethinker who scandalized his century and influenced Voltaire and Adam Smith, was a practicing physician. The chevalier de Jaucourt, Diderot's prolific and indispensable associate in the *Encyclopédie*, studied at Leyden under the incomparable Boerhaave and took his medical degree, although he seems to have neglected his practice for his philosophy. La Mettrie, another student of Boerhaave, derived his philosophical materialism from medical principles and persistently alluded in his philosophical writings to his medical experience: "The great art of healing," he suggested in his most notorious book, *L'homme machine,* was man's noblest activity.

Other philosophes were well-informed amateurs. As a young man of letters, Diderot had been among the translators of Robert James's bulky *Medicinal Dictionary*; in his later years, he reaffirmed his conviction that medical science was strategic to all true knowledge: "It is very hard," he wrote, "to think cogently about metaphysics or ethics without being an anatomist, a naturalist, a physiologist, and a physician."[8] He secured the collaboration of more than twenty physicians for his *Encyclopédie,* notably his friends Théophile de Bordeu and Théodore Tronchin, who were minor philosophes in their own right. Bordeu, an urbane, skeptical empiricist, celebrated in his time for his brilliant polemical history of medicine as much as for his practice, used his *Encyclopédie* articles to diffuse medical information and unmask the pretensions of medical system-makers; his prominent role in one of Diderot's best dialogues, the *Rêve de d'Alembert,* is eloquent testimony to the intimate connection between medicine and philosophy in the Enlightenment. Tronchin, the fashionable Genevan physician whose practice reached as far as Paris and who attended Voltaire among many other famous patients, contributed a vigorous article on "Inoculation" which made propaganda for the new science and against medical superstitions.

The materialists among the philosophes had, of course, good reason to take medicine seriously; for them, disease, including men-

---

[8] *Réfutation de l'ouvrage d'Helvétius intitulé l'Homme* (1773–4), in *Œuvres,* II, 322; this important passage is also quoted in Arthur M. Wilson: *Diderot: The Testing Years, 1713–1759* (1957), 93.

tal disease, was a mere disorder in the human machine. But the deists and skeptics had as much regard for medical science as the atheists. Hume was on friendly terms with the greatest in a great generation of British physicians, including Sir John Pringle, president of the Royal Society and pioneer in military medicine, and William Hunter, the anatomist. Adam Smith and Edward Gibbon attended Hunter's lectures on anatomy. Benjamin Franklin, who was interested in everything, was also interested in medicine, especially in the establishment of medical societies. Voltaire, who enjoyed ill health for eighty-four years and knew as much about medicine as he knew about everything else (which is to say, a good deal), humorously distrusted but perpetually consulted physicians, and not as a patient alone. He went to Leyden to attend Boerhaave's lectures and discuss Newton with s'Gravesande; and all his life he read widely on medical subjects—he had read as many books on medicine, he said, as Don Quixote had read on chivalry. He campaigned on behalf of inoculation and inveighed against quackery, ridiculed such craft mysteries as secret ingredients in drugs, urged the application of common sense in the compounding of prescriptions and the appointment of hospitals, and represented, in all he wrote on the subject, advanced and rational scientific opinion.

Such medical preoccupations, philosophical rather than hypochondriacal, enabled the philosophes to employ medical language in their polemics without any sense of strain. The philosophes liked to argue that they must destroy in order to build, and their military metaphors—metaphors of aggression—dramatized their destructive activities.[9] Their medical metaphors, in turn, justified this destructiveness: with almost monotonous reiterations, the philosophes represented their campaign against Christianity as a campaign against disease. Christianity, they wrote, was an infection, a "sacred contagion," a "sick man's dream," a germ sometimes dormant but always dangerous, always a potential source for an epidemic of fanaticism and persecution. In the rhetoric of the Enlightenment, the conquest of nature and the conquest of revealed religion were one: a struggle for health. If the philosophes were missionaries, they were medical missionaries.

---

[9] See *The Rise of Modern Paganism*, 130–2, on the relation of destruction to construction, and for the philosophes' aggressive metaphors.

This rhetoric, like most rhetoric, was more than mere talk; it accurately reflects the philosophes' style of thinking, comically though it was sometimes expressed. In 1765, the Lombard *illuminista* Giuseppe Parini, a priest and radical satirist, wrote a poem on vaccination and dedicated it to Giovammaria Bicetti, a prominent Italian physician. Ordinary minds, so runs Parini's ode, always reject great new ideas as falsehoods, but an intrepid band of intellectuals in England, in France—and in Italy—were now standing bravely against the multitude; armed against murderous disease, they were protecting the lives of young children and defying relentless destiny with the healing art:

> Contro all'armi omicide
> non piu debole e nudo;
> ma sotto a certo scudo
> il tenero garzon cauto discese;
> e il fato inesorabile sorprese.[1]

These lines may strike us as droll in their earnestness, and they are droll; but philosophic literature abounds in solemn claims for the affinity—the near equivalence—of modern medicine with modern philosophy. Perhaps the most striking of these claims came toward the end of the Enlightenment, in 1798, in an extraordinary essay on medical enlightenment by the German physician Johann Karl Osterhausen. *Über medizinische Aufklärung*, with its title as in its content, is a deliberate imitation of Kant's *Was ist Aufklärung?* To make his imitation as ostentatious as possible, Osterhausen pointedly borrowed Kant's famous definition of Enlightenment for the medical profession: medical Enlightenment, he wrote, is "man's emergence from his dependence in matters concerning his physical well-being."[2] Nothing could be plainer than this: medicine was philosophy at work; philosophy was medicine for the individual and for society.

---

[1] *L'innesto del vaiuolo*, in Giuseppe Parini: *Poesie e prose* (edn. 1961), 197. In the same manner, Quesnay wrote to Mirabeau around the end of 1758: "We must not lose heart, for the appalling crisis will come, and it will be necessary to have recourse to medical knowledge." Ronald L. Meek: *The Economics of Physiocracy* (1963), 108.
[2] Quoted in Alfons Fischer: *Geschichte des deutschen Gesundheitswesens*, 2 vols. (1933), II, 8.

II

All this sounds extravagant, but in fact by the end of the seventeenth century the ideal of philosophical modern medicine was beginning to invade the most progressive among medical schools. Leyden, the best of them, was for decades dominated by Hermann Boerhaave, a philosophical physician of enormous range and energies. Boerhaave was clinician, methodologist, chemist, botanist, the most celebrated and most influential medical professor of his time; he taught generations of young physicians from all over the Western world, including the American colonies, and he left his mark on philosophes who came to listen even if they did not stay to matriculate. Boerhaave taught medical Newtonianism; he lectured on Newton and tried to embody Newton's empirical method in his theoretical work and clinical practice. His textbooks, promptly and widely translated, were models of Newtonian reasoning; they acquired almost scriptural authority and reached those who could not come to hear him. Doubtless, Boerhaave's ambition outran his performance, and his practice fell short of his preachments; he was more dogmatic than he knew. But his enlightened precepts reverberated throughout Europe and America, while at home his colleagues and successors, s'Gravesande, Nieuwentyt and Musschenbroek, carried on his medical practice and his philosophical teachings. They went to England, sought out Newton, and kept in touch with British science and British medicine; when they came home to assume their chairs, they lectured on the philosophy of Bacon and Locke, warned their students against occult principles, and urged them to eschew hypotheses, closely observe phenomena, pay attention to clinical experience, and design exact experiments. In gratitude, eighteenth-century physicians named the age after its Dutch preceptor. "The age of Boerhaave," an English observer wrote in 1780, "forms a memorable epoch in the history of physic. Theory, which before had been entirely conjectural, now assumed a more plausible and scientific appearance"[3]—that is to say, a Newtonian appearance;

---

[3] Henry Manning: *Modern Improvements in the Practice of Physic,* quoted in Richard Harrison Shryock: *The Development of Modern Medicine* (1947), 74 *n.*

William Cullen, probably the most famous surgeon and physiologist in Britain, was not the only one to pride himself on having "avoided hypothesis."[4]

All this stress on experience, on clinical study and experimentation, revolutionized medicine. Still, it is safe to speculate that in the eighteenth century a sick man who did not consult a physician had a better chance of surviving than one who did. There were troops of mountebanks who took their victims' money and abbreviated their lives; worse than that, responsible and knowledgeable physicians were often muddled and astonishingly ignorant. The medical guilds, crusty, doctrinaire, privileged, and exclusive, resisted the infusion of new ideas and the employment of new instruments; many drugs or surgical procedures reached the public from the hands of ill-trained but sensible and adventurous empirics—the bootleggers of science—who were often humane healers. Instruments like the fever thermometer or the machine for measuring blood pressure were neglected by a profession far too much taken up with squabbles over precedence to attend to its proper business: the prevalence of quacks was more a criticism of professional conservatism than a measure of popular gullibility. There was pressing need for renovating the profession. In France, the surgeons finally liberated themselves from the barbers' guild in 1731, and the English surgeons followed in 1745, but even after the reform, surgeons and physicians long remained antagonistic. Diderot picturesquely caricatured these hostile medical factions as two professional men, standing over his sick body and arguing, paying no attention to the suffering patient.

Diderot's satiric little scene shows a philosophe in a skeptical mood. Doctors have been the targets of wit ever since there have been patients, and the philosophes freely contributed to the treasury of caustic humor. Diderot put some rueful observations about the inefficacy of medical attention into the mouth of Dr. Bordeu. Voltaire scribbled into a notebook: "Men must have a religion and not believe in priests, just as men must have a diet and not believe in physicians." David Hume warned a friend: "I entreat you, if you tender your own Health or give any Attention to the Entreaties of those that love you, to pay no regard to Physicians: That is a

---

[4] Quoted in ibid., 37.

considerable part of your Distemper. You cannot pay a moderate
Regard to them; your only Safety is in neglecting them altogether."[5]
There was real point to this skepticism. Vital statistics were still
scanty and unreliable, and what was known was hardly reassuring.
Rousseau could estimate on one page of *Émile* that half of all children died before their eighth year, and, only a few pages later, that
about half reached adolescence—an indication not merely of continuing pessimism about life expectancy, but of continuing uncertainty about the precise figures. In the late 1760s, Voltaire calculated
that on the average men could expect to live to the age of twenty-
two, and, a few years before, Diderot, writing to his mistress from
his native town, Langres, pondered grimly on "the short existence
of those who entered life at the same time we did"—most of his
school fellows were dead, and when he wrote that letter, he was
only forty-six.[6] All the philosophes had oppressive memories of
capricious, early death. Voltaire was a young man when all of Louis
XIV's progeny died in rapid succession: the old King's only son
in 1711; his eldest grandson, the duc de Bourgogne, the duke's wife
and eldest son, all in 1712; his youngest grandson, the duc de Berry,
in 1714. "This time of desolation," Voltaire recalled, "left so profound an impression in men's hearts that during the minority of
Louis XV I saw numerous persons who spoke of these losses only
with tears."[7]

Every eighteenth-century family had its own horror tale to tell.
Goethe, in recalling his childhood, could not remember just how
many younger siblings had died in infancy, and Edward Gibbon,
recalling his childhood, coolly observed that "the death of a new-
born child before that of its parents may seem an unnatural, but
it is strictly a probable event: since of any given number the greater
part are extinguished before their ninth year." His own infantile
constitution, he added, had been so feeble, that "in the baptism of
my brothers, my father's prudence successively repeated the Chris-

---

[5] Voltaire: *Notebooks*, 352; Hume to John Crawford (July 20,
1767). *New Letters*, 175.
[6] Rousseau: *Émile* (1762; ed. Garnier, n.d.), 20, 61; Voltaire:
"A, B, C," in *Philosophical Dictionary*, II 590-1; Diderot to Sophie
Volland (August 4 or 5, 1759). *Correspondance*, II, 202.
[7] Voltaire: *Siècle de Louis XIV*, chap. XXVII. *Œuvres historiques*,
944.

tian name of Edward, that, in case of the departure of the eldest son, this patronymic appellation might still be perpetuated in the family."[8] This story has been discredited as a trick of Gibbon's memory, but it stands as touching testimony to the overriding concern of the century.[9] Infanticide, cruelty to orphans or illegitimate children, disease, and above all destitution, remained ravenous killers: "It is not uncommon, I have frequently been told," Adam Smith soberly noted, "in the Highlands of Scotland for a mother who has borne twenty children not to have two alive."[1] The poor died freely, in unrecorded numbers, but even men of means thought long life a stroke of unexpected luck.

But this was not all. Medicine was not merely the target of the philosophes' scorn and pessimism; it was also the object of their admiration. The philosophes could find cheer in signs of solid, often impressive achievements, and their hope for advances still to come was even more exhilarating than their satisfaction with results already achieved. It was gradually becoming obvious that the population of Europe was on the verge of a marked growth. In his essay "Of the Populousness of Ancient Nations," David Hume demonstrated that, contrary to widespread opinion, the Europe of his time was far more heavily populated than the Europe of antiquity, and that the three awful agents of wholesale destruction—"war, pestilence, and famine,"—which had with hideous impartiality desolated royal houses, bourgeois families, and ragged village clans, might finally be checked.[2]

Hume's case was reasonable: in England, the population grew from 6,500,000 in 1750 to 9,000,000 in 1800; France recorded an increase of four million in the eighteenth century; and Sweden, the first country to collect reliable vital statistics, reported that its popu-

---

[8] Goethe: *Dichtung und Wahrheit*, in *Gedenkausgabe*, X, 44–5; Gibbon: *Autobiography*, 53.

[9] D. M. Low checked the parish registers at Putney parish church, and found that the seven Gibbon children included only one "Edward" and one "Edward James," and that the most cherished name in the family, in fact, was James (the name of Mrs. Gibbon's father), which appears three times. Low: *Gibbon's Journal to January 28th, 1763* (n.d.), xxix.

[1] *The Wealth of Nations*, 79.

[2] *Works*, III, 383.

lation grew by seventy per cent between 1720 and 1815.[3] Malthus's alarm at the dramatic growth of population was a backhanded tribute to it, and—or so men thought in the late eighteenth century —to the progress of medicine. It is hardly surprising that by the end of the century philosophes should think Bacon's and Descartes's hopes near fulfillment.[4]

The history of medical progress in the eighteenth century, remarkable as it is, is not without its irony. Down to about 1750, a whole tribe of would-be medical Newtons obstructed progress with their search for a single cause of disease, for a final doctrinaire answer to all questions of health. It was not until mid-century, when the philosophes were at the height of their influence, and partly as a result of their propaganda, that pluralistic empiricism changed the course of medical research. It continued to suffer setbacks: the eternal struggle between rigidity and flexibility, the desire to conserve and the need to innovate, went on. But the results remained impressive, and some statistics at least, especially in the last decades of the eighteenth century, gave cause for optimism. The British Lying-In Hospital, for one, reported that while in the decade from 1749 to 1759 one baby in fifteen had died shortly after birth, by 1799 this dismal proportion had been reduced to one in 118. In the same period, in this hospital, the death rate for mothers declined from 26.7 to 2.4 per thousand. Epidemic diseases like typhoid and smallpox almost disappeared; surgeons like John and William Hunter vastly improved surgical techniques; physiology, obstetrics, materia medica, preventive medicine, and anatomy made great strides. And so, on January 1, 1801, "the first day of the

---

[3] Since precise statistics played a significant part in the recovery of nerve—precision was, after all, crucial to man's control over his environment—Voltaire's interest in Swedish record-keeping is instructive: in a public letter to the *Gazette littéraire* of October 1764 he praised the Swedes for undertaking "the useful enterprise of knowing the resources of their country thoroughly." *Correspondence*, LVI, 100.

[4] See Richard Harrison Shryock: *Medicine and Society in America: 1660–1860* (edn. 1962), 100, 115. Modern economic historians trying to make sense of incomplete and contradictory data are generally skeptical of advances in medicine as a cause of population growth. But eighteenth-century observers—and it is this that matters at this point—were inclined to see a drop in the death rate and give credit for it in large part to the medical advances of their day.

nineteenth century," Dr. David Ramsay, a prominent American physician, could review the "improvements, progress, and state of medicine in the eighteenth century" with undiluted pride. The eighteenth century, he said, had witnessed the birth of rational medicine, based on the principles of "Lord Bacon," the "father of all modern science," and on Boerhaave's teaching. It had been an age of major innovations in medical theory, astonishing advances in anatomy, proper midwifery, brilliant experimentation, sensible classification of diseases, the professionalization of surgery, an improved understanding of the role of fresh air and sound food in health, and, perhaps best of all, of attacks on superstition: "Many popular errors have been exploded; the common people have been accustomed to think and reason on medical subjects." And, he concluded, "I appeal to those who can look back on thirty, forty, or fifty years, whether a great reformation in these particulars has not taken place within the sphere of their own observation; and whether in consequence of more judicious treatment there are not more women safely carried through the perilous periods of pregnancy and child-birth; and whether there are not fewer instances of deformity, and a greater proportion of children raised at the present time, than formerly. In the same number of families, where our ancestors counted four or five, we can now show seven or eight. Our schools, our streets, and our houses are filled with straight, well formed children, most of whom have happily got over the smallpox, without any of those marks of it, which deformed their grandmother."[5] The recovery of nerve was visible on men's very faces.

---

[5] David Ramsay: *A Review of the Improvements, Progress, and State of Medicine in the Eighteenth Century* (1801), *passim*. Significantly the pamphlet is dedicated to Benjamin Rush, "the American Sydenham."

3. THE SPIRIT OF THE AGE

I

SOMETIME in the course of his visits to England in 1726 or 1727, Voltaire observed in his notebook, in his newly acquired English: "Where there is not liberty of conscience, there is seldom liberty of trade, the same tyranny encroaching upon the commerce as upon Relligion."[6] A few years later, probably not long after he had published *Lettres philosophiques*, his celebrated report on England, he noted, this time in French: "In a republic, toleration is the fruit of liberty and the basis of happiness and abundance."[7] The *Lettres philosophiques* is many things—a critique of bigotry in France, a popular summary of Newton's thought, covert deist propaganda—but above all it is an extended commentary on the sociological aphorisms I have just quoted. "The commerce that has enriched the citizens of England," Voltaire concluded, "has helped to make them free, and that freedom in turn has encouraged commerce; this has produced the greatness of the state."[8]

The point of these observations was not merely that England was rich, happy, and free, but that these characteristics depended upon and reinforced one another. Thus for Voltaire, as for the other philosophes, Anglomania and sociology were practically synonymous: besides embodying the recovery of nerve earlier and more completely than other countries, England exhibited the happy conjunctions that made this recovery possible. French philosophes other than Voltaire and German *Aufklärer* all made Voltaire's discovery for themselves. Montesquieu, who landed in England late in 1729, not long after Voltaire had left it, was deeply impressed by the coexistence of freedom and equality there; and the German poet Friedrich von Hagedorn, born and educated in liberal, cosmopolitan Hamburg, and thus ready to appreciate the quality of English

---

[6] *Notebooks*, 43.
[7] Ibid., 126.
[8] Lettre X, *Lettres philosophiques*, I, 120.

life, spent two years in England in the 1720s and came home impressed by a nation that applied its material abundance to the pursuit of reason. He even wrote a poem about it: it is in England, he said, that liberty and power protect and liberally reward the industrious, and there that men of wealth support the sciences:

> Wie edel ist die Neigung echter Britten:
> Ihr Überfluss bereichert den Verstand.
> Der Handlung Frucht, und was ihr Muth erstritten,
> Wird, unbereut, Verdiensten zugewandt;
> Gunst krönt den Fleiss, den Macht und Freyheit schützen:
> Die Reichsten sind der Wissenschaften Stützen.[9]

The lesson that England taught the philosophes, then, was that the recovery of nerve was infectious: progress in one sphere generated progress in others. The new sense of power seemed to be radiating out from scientists and physicians, merchants and civil servants, to civilization as a whole. There was nothing new in the philosophes' perception that society is a fabric with interdependent, interacting parts; what they did that was new was to take this perception as a justification for their own importance. After all, if progress is infectious, then to teach truth, expose error, and inculcate confidence—and all this, of course, the philosophes were sure they were doing—was to spread reason and shed light over large areas, even in unsuspected places. Thus the philosophes enlisted the enlightened atmosphere of their day in the service of their movement.

By mid-century, the philosophes had generalized their Anglomania into a sociological law. In the *Discours préliminaire* to the *Encyclopédie*, d'Alembert asserted that the arts and sciences are linked together as by a chain, and rise together;[1] in his article "Genève" he applied this dictum to a society that had grown rich "by its liberty and its commerce."[2] Diderot was also convinced that politics and society are inseparable—*la politique et les mœurs*, he told Sophie Volland, *se tiennent par la main*—and he composed his articles for the *Encyclopédie* in that spirit. "In the human under-

---

[9] Quoted in Hans M. Wolff: *Die Weltanschauung der deutschen Aufklärung in geschichtlicher Entwicklung* (2d edn., 1963), 179.
[1] *Mélanges*, I, 12.
[2] *The Encyclopédie*, 87.

standing," he wrote in "Bramines," "everything hangs together—
tout se tient." The "obscurity of one idea spreads over its neighbors.
An error throws shadows over surrounding truths." Fortunately,
he added, "the centers of shadow have never been fewer and smaller
than they are today; philosophy marches forward with giant steps,
and light accompanies and follows it."[3] Every day men were insti-
tuting new, useful things and discarding old, outmoded ways. It is
not extravagant to see the *Encyclopédie* itself—with its profusion
of articles on arts and crafts, philosophy and politics, theology and
language, and with its sly and informative cross references—as a
striking display of the recovery of nerve, of the variety, wealth,
and energy of eighteenth-century civilization.

In 1752 David Hume enumerated the ingredients of this civilization and defined its style. The cultivation and felicity of his age, he
suggested, depended on a conjunction of freedom in politics and
invention in industry: "Industry," he wrote, and "refinement in the
mechanical arts," generally "produce some refinements in the liberal;
nor can one be carried to perfection, without being accompanied,
in some degree, with the other. The same age, which produces great
philosophers and politicians, renowned generals and poets, usually
abounds with skilful weavers, and ship-carpenters. We cannot
reasonably expect that a piece of woollen cloth will be brought to
perfection in a nation, which is ignorant of astronomy, or where
ethics are neglected. The spirit of the age affects all the arts; and
the minds of men, being once roused from their lethargy, and put
into a fermentation, turn themselves on all sides, and carry improvements into every art and science." With refinement comes sociability, and both export their benefits to public life. "Thus, *industry,
knowledge,* and *humanity,* are linked together by an indissoluble
chain."[4] A man with few illusions, Hume knew that the chain was
often rather tangled: knowledge might lead to inhumanity; humanity often had irrational (that is to say, religious) roots; industry
sometimes encouraged, sometimes obstructed felicity. These were
complications, but the philosophes found them manageable. After
all, did not the currents of the times run in their direction?

---

[3] Diderot to Sophie Volland (October 12, 1760). *Correspondance,*
III, 120; "Bramines," in *Œuvres,* XIII, 511.
[4] "Of Refinement in the Arts," *Works,* III, 301–2.

II

The advance of knowledge, whether devout Christians liked it or not, meant the advance of reason. In the course of the eighteenth century, the world, at least the world of the literate, was being emptied of mystery. Pseudo science was giving way to science, credence in the miraculous intervention of divine forces was being corroded by the acid of skepticism and overpowered by scientific cosmology. The sacred was being hollowed out from within by the drying up of religious fervor, the call for good sense, the retreat from Augustinian theology, the campaign against "enthusiasm," and the advance of rationalism among the clergy of all persuasions.[5] In his early satires, Swift lampooned religious hysteria; in his *Spectator*, Addison ridiculed widely accepted superstitions; in Germany, Thomasius denounced the prosecution of witches as an irrational and brutal sport; while in Massachusetts, in 1700, Robert Calef raised his angry and sarcastic voice in the name of reason and true Christianity against the witchcraft trials. "Reason" became a potent word of praise, rather like "science"; architecture, and even poetry (much to its damage) were invaded by rationalist canons and forced under the rationalist yoke. More than ever before, Christian statesmen justified their policies as obedience to reason of state, while Christian philosophers elaborated rational and rationalistic philosophies of life: Wolff's *Vernünftige Gedanken von dem gesellschaftlichen Leben der Menschen*, published in 1721, was a characteristic product of the time—philosophers were agreeing that if one had thoughts about the social order, they might as well be reasonable thoughts. Disenchantment marked not merely the church and its doctrine; it marked all aspects of life.

The fate of touching, a venerable and remarkably tenacious superstition, is a striking instance of the new mentality. Sometime in the eleventh century, the belief rapidly spread across Europe that kings, blessed in some mysterious sense with divine attributes, were more than ordinary physicians: their touch was reputed to

---

[5] For a discussion of what I there call "the treason of the clerks," see *The Rise of Modern Paganism*, 336–57.

cure a variety of diseases, especially scrofula, "the king's evil." The king's touch soon became, and long remained, an awesome and cherished ceremony, and it survived into the age of absolutism as part of the baggage of royal prestige. But in the age of Newton and Locke faith in touching declined as precipitously as faith in astrology and alchemy. Robert Boyle, the "skeptical Chymist," still publicly expressed his confidence in the efficacy of the royal touch, and at the beginning of the eighteenth century, apparently in good faith, Sir John Floyer, the distinguished Lichfield physician, sent young Samuel Johnson to be touched by Queen Anne for his various ailments. But not long after, as political theorists came to treat kings as mere humans (just as Spinoza had offered cogent reasons for treating the Bible as a mere book), skepticism triumphed. When in his *Lettres persanes* Montesquieu dared to allude to the French king as "a great magician" who can make his credulous subjects believe he can cure them "of all sorts of diseases by touching them,"[6] his witticism annoyed the authorities, but it did not keep him out of the *Académie française*: too many highly placed personages agreed with him. Thirty years later, in Diderot's *Encyclopédie,* rationalism paraded as patriotism: in his article "Écrouelles," the chevalier de Jaucourt, no more a Christian than his editor in chief, questioned the medical powers of the British crown and left those of the French to the imagination of his readers. The Bourbons went on touching—in 1825, at his accession, Charles X once more revived the antique ceremony—but with little conviction and no results.

While Louis XV continued to act as *rex scrofularum medicus,* Voltaire, as usual, made irreverent and tendentious jokes, and— again as usual—held up the example of Great Britain for imitation; in a notebook entry that singles out the English for their philosophical character, Voltaire abruptly interrupts himself: "In a time of ignorance a king must cure scrofula; useless today."[7] Later, in his *Questions sur l'Encyclopédie,* he reminded his readers that William III had renounced this dubious prerogative; "When reason arrives," that is, in France, "that sacred fashion will disappear."[8] It is true that Queen Anne resumed what her predecessor had given

[6] "Lettre XXIV," *Lettres persanes. Œuvres,* I, 51–2.
[7] *Notebooks,* 98.
[8] "Écrouelles," in *Œuvres,* XVIII, 470.

up, but only half-heartedly; with the accession of the Hanoverian House in 1714, touching was finally abandoned. "The practice," wrote David Hume in his *History of England*, "was first dropped by the present royal family, who observed, that it could no longer give amazement to the populace, and was attended with ridicule in the eyes of all men of understanding."[9] This is a rare moment of excessive optimism for Hume: disenchantment, like enlightenment in general, was largely a matter of education, and hence of class; if many of the poor, especially in Protestant countries, were unchurched, this did not mean that they were free from superstitions or beyond myth. For many years the populace continued to be amazed by phenomena which men of understanding treated with ridicule. Reason prospered, but not everywhere.

III

The prosperity of reason in the eighteenth century was less the triumph of rationalism than of reasonableness. Reason and humanity were easily confounded, and an instance of one was often taken as an instance of the other. One of Diderot's spokesmen in his sentimental drama, *Fils naturel*, cheerfully pours rationality, refinement, and decency into the same container: "Certainly there are still barbarians. When won't there be? But the time of barbarism is past. The century has become enlightened. Reason has grown refined, and the nation's books are filled with its precepts. The books that inspire benevolence in men are practically the only ones read."[1] This is a little unrealistic; things were not so simple, and men not so decent, as Diderot suggests. But it remains true that the age of criticism was also an age of humanity. "Knowledge in the arts of government naturally begets mildness and moderation," David Hume observed, "by instructing men in the advantages of humane maxims

---

[9] *The History of England*, 8 vols. (edn. 1780), I, 189. Marc Bloch quotes this passage in his authoritative history of touching and comments that at this point Hume underestimates the persistence of this superstition among the lower orders: "For a long time, the popular mind did not abandon this belief." *Les rois thaumaturges* (edn. 1961), 395.
[1] Act IV, scene 3. *Œuvres*, VII, 68.

above rigour and severity." Hence rebellion becomes less likely, and
if it does occur, it is less likely to be prolonged by desperate men.
"When the tempers of men are softened as well as their knowledge
improved, this humanity appears still more conspicuous, and is the
chief characteristic which distinguishes a civilized age from times of
barbarity and ignorance." As rebellions grow less "tragical," so
foreign wars become less bestial, and warriors, after the battle, once
again become men.[2] This was not mere wishful thinking: Goethe,
like the philosophes convinced that in "every epoch everything is
connected," later fondly recalled this age of improvement. Young
lawyers, he remembered, and even elderly judges, came to be imbued
with humane convictions, and competed with one another not
merely to preach decency, but to practice it; the intolerance of
guilds, of the medical profession, and of religious bodies was effectively beaten down: "One dam after another was broken through."[3]
It seemed that in law courts, in politics, and on fields of battle alike,
reason begot humanity.

Men had been charitable before this time, obviously. They had
given alms to the poor and felt pity for the unfortunate. What was
new about eighteenth-century humanity was that it formed part of
the general recovery of nerve: its optimistic decency was grounded
in the rational foundations of scientific improvement as much as in
religious prescriptions. Generosity was a luxury a progressive society
could afford.

Like reason, humanity had strenuous partisans among devout
Christians. It was on the ground of decency that philosophes and
Christians could meet: they agreed, though from divergent motives,
that slavery should be abolished, illegitimate babies rescued, ferocious
punishments repealed, and the miserable relieved. Henry Fielding
was only one of many modern Christians to insist that "Christian
charity" was the most exalted of religious virtues, while Albrecht
von Haller, a deeply religious man for all his tormenting self-doubts,
confessed, "I should like, if possible, to have posterity consider me
a friend of man as much as a friend of truth."[4] Johnson and Voltaire,

---

[2] "Of Refinement in the Arts," *Works*, III, 301–2.
[3] *Dichtung und Wahrheit*, in *Gedenkausgabe*, X, 618–19.
[4] Fielding: see David Owen: *English Philanthropy, 1660–1960*
(1964), 11; Haller: a caption he wrote under one of his pictures in
1762, reproduced in Stephen d'Irsay: *Albrecht von Haller: Eine
Studie zur Geistesgeschichte der Aufklärung* (1930), following 98.

that incongruous pair, independently, for incompatible reasons but with equal vigor, denounced the trial and execution of Admiral Byng. Voltaire's intervention, culminating in his immortal witticism that it is good to shoot an admiral from time to time, *pour encourager les autres*, has achieved greater fame than Johnson's, but for an understanding of the eighteenth century, Johnson's intervention, which was more prosaic, is more significant. Voltaire, after all, making his joke after the event, was suspect as a mocker. Johnson had, or at least seemed to have, better reasons. He was not a radical but a representative man, and his credentials for respectability, unlike Voltaire's, were beyond question.[5]

Samuel Johnson's humanitarian impulses in fact closely resemble those of the philosophes: he, like them, did not affect a woolly-minded, indiscriminate pity for all creatures, but disapproved as he sympathized, hated as he loved—energetically. He detested slavery and had unwavering sympathy for the unlucky, the persecuted, and the poor. To be sure, with his suspicion of sentimentality and his nostalgia for old-fashioned authority, Johnson's humanity had to contend against contrary emotions, but at least some of his reservations were well taken. Eighteenth-century humanitarianism was afflicted with contradictions and disfigured by cant. Effusions went hand in hand with exploitation; men who piously lamented the lot of slaves abroad coolly sent children to the mines at home. Yet cynicism is unhistorical, at least here: this myopic humanity was the fumbling response to unprecedented social changes; it was the piecemeal, often painful attempt to construct a coherent attitude appropriate to a new society struggling to be born.

While humanity was incomplete and often illogical, it was nevertheless widespread. The old clean-cut social hierarchies retained much of their prestige, but they were on the defensive in the face of powerful social aspirations and a growing desire for social mobility. Especially in the middle ranges of Western European society, the father's power over his children and the husband's power over his wife markedly declined. The patriarchal family, still the pattern in the seventeenth century, was giving way to the nuclear family, with its well-defined boundaries against the community and

---

[5] I have briefly explored the affinity of this unlikely pair before, in *The Rise of Modern Paganism*, 21. For Johnson's opposition to slavery, see below, chap. viii, section 2.

its growing intimacy and equality. Within certain limits, still rather rigid but distinctly expanding, young girls were being permitted to choose their partners. Eighteenth-century fiction suggests that the tension between parental demands for obedience and young lovers' demands for freedom was unresolved, but—witness the novels of Richardson—it was becoming old-fashioned if not contemptible to force girls into an uncongenial connection for the sake of parental prestige or profit. Parents, supposedly experienced in the ways of the world, were to be consulted and their vetoes earnestly respected, but, as a writer put it in 1739, "the choice of a husband or wife more nearly concerns the happiness of the parties themselves than it does the parents; it is the young couple who are to abide by the choice; by consequence they ought to choose for themselves." The world of the family was changing, in the direction of freedom.

This change was possible largely because freedom was safe-guarded by reason. Rational love, the sober and well-considered mutual esteem of man and woman, was elevated to a social ideal: "There is," as one moralist put it in 1749, in perfect tune with his age, "an intellective, natural, sensible, and rational love," and this love, rather than insane infatuation or unbridled erotic passion, was the proper guide for the choice of a life partner. The English preached this doctrine first, and most articulately, but it made its appearance, if a little more timidly, in France and the more advanced German states as well. Rational love was idealized in sentimental fiction and dissected in moral periodicals; it was even discussed in the House of Lords. Speaking on the Marriage Act of 1753, which had been devised to prevent precipitate marriages, Lord Hillsborough observed that "a mutual love between the two parties contracting it" is indeed "a very proper ingredient," but he made clear that he meant "a sedate and fixed love, and not a sudden flash of passion which dazzles the understanding."[6] And so, in the delicate matter of love, as in other matters, an increased confidence in reason led to increasing humanity.

In consequence, marriage, which through the seventeenth century had been regarded as a sacred institution and as a legal device for the management of property and the regulation of inheritance,

---

[6] I owe these quotations to an unpublished paper on rational love in the eighteenth century, by J. Jean Hecht.

came to be spoken of in the age of the Enlightenment as a partnership, a contract, honorable and grave but secular in nature. Monogamy, long a Christian ideal, became for many a comfortable reality, and even those philosophes whose own marital experience was unhappy felt that they owed it to their philosophy to praise marriage as an institution. Lichtenberg, who was more miserable with his wife than he was with anything else (and that is miserable indeed), still reflected that what makes friendship, "and even more, the happy bond of marriage," so delightful is that both permit the Self, as it were, to expand "over a larger area than any individual could cover." When two souls unite, they do not lose their individuality, but retain the "advantageous differences" which make it so agreeable to live together. The man who laments his suffering, "laments it in the presence of a Self that may help, and is, indeed, already helping by its very sympathy. And the man who loves to hear his merits praised, will find in that Self a public which lets him boast, free from the fear that he is making himself ridiculous."[7]

In this atmosphere, which was clearer and less oppressive than the atmosphere of preceding centuries, women and children secured new respect and new rights. In the seventeenth century—as Milton's portrayal of Adam and Eve made plain to all—no one had doubted that women were inferior to men. But then, at the end of the 1690s, Daniel Defoe, who was always a pioneer, sharply took his fellow-men to task for their scurvy treatment of women: had women the education of men, he argued in his *Essay upon Projects*, their supposed inferiority would soon vanish. And it was Defoe, not Milton, whom the eighteenth century was to follow.

The philosophes were at home with intelligent women—one thinks of Diderot's Sophie Volland, Voltaire's Madame du Châtelet, and the cultivated Parisian ladies who played hostess to philosophes from all over the world—and they made attempts to treat them as equals, as well as an item on the agenda of reform. But while the philosophes were feminists in their way, they were feminists with misgivings: the age-old fear of women, the antique superstition that women were vessels of wrath and sources of corruption, was too deeply rooted to be easily discarded. David Hume insisted, in good

---

[7] Aphorism L 308, in *Aphorismen, 1793–1799,* ed. Albert Leitzmann (1908), 66-7.

progressive fashion, that "marriage is an engagement entered into by mutual consent," and he opposed the "male tyranny" which "destroys that nearness of rank, not to say equality, which nature has established between the sexes." Deeply appreciative of female company, he noted, rather winningly, that "our free commerce with the fair sex, more than any other invention, embellishes, enlivens, and polishes society."[8] Yet even Hume could not quite escape traditional prejudices: the essays he explicitly addressed to women have an unwonted coyness, and he could still resort to the well-worn platitude that women were a subject "little to be understood."[9] The *Encyclopédie* displays the same ambivalence: it delineated its womanly ideal as the pious, thrifty, gentle, orderly—and submissive—housewife, and described woman, rather as Hume had described her, as everything man was not: touching, charming, invaluable—and mysterious. At the same time, it vigorously criticized the legal disabilities on women for violating the natural equality of all human beings and for disregarding the well-established fact that women often proved more energetic, competent, and intelligent than men. Much of the supposed inferiority of women, the *Encyclopédie* argued, was merely the evil consequence of male dominance. In a sensible essay "Sur les femmes," Diderot expressed the same view.

The old attitudes might die hard, even with philosophes, but the enlightened public came to accept the educated woman as something other than a freak, a joke, or a sexual trap baited with the unnatural attribute of wit. Even the sentimental eroticism of the age, vulgar though it generally was, contributed to lifting the veils of woman's supposed "mysteriousness"—which was really a hidden fear of her sexual powers—and portrayed her as a human being. Laclos's magnificently malevolent marquise de Merteuil, who declares war on men to seek vengeance for centuries of suppression, suggests that there was much to be done until men would allow women to be fully human, but her sexual revolution, like many revolutions, was a symptom of improved morale among the victims.

Children, too, and in the very century in which they were being exploited on farms and in factories, were discovered as human beings in their own right. In the Middle Ages, through the sixteenth and

---

[8] "Of Polygamy and Divorce," *Works*, III, 231, 234, 234 *n*.
[9] Hume to William Mure of Caldwell, November 14 (1742). *Letters*, I, 45.

seventeenth centuries, adults had treated children as toys, strange animals, or small grownups. Children had mixed in adult company, played infantile adaptations of adult games, dressed in cut-down versions of adult clothing, overheard the grossest sexual allusions, and participated in overt sexual play. The precise age of the child was unknown, and if known, irrelevant; children mattered mainly in the economy, as sources of labor, and in law, as links in the chain of succession. All this changed very slowly. Near the end of the sixteenth century, Montaigne, who was not a notably cruel man and who recommended that children be treated with kindness, recalled that he had lost "two or three children in their infancy, not without regret but without great sorrow."[1] Montaigne's failure to mourn is less shocking than his inability to remember just how many of his children had died. It was beginning to be shocking in the eighteenth century: Rousseau, the archetypical vagabond, abandoned his off-spring to foundling homes, but at least he knew precisely how many he had given away—five. Locke's *Some Thoughts Concerning Education*, which was published in 1693 and enjoyed lasting influence in Britain and on the Continent, already displayed a new attitude, and the German moral weeklies of the 1720s campaigned against neglect and mistreatment of children and propagandized in behalf of sensible and humane educational reforms. But it is Rousseau's *Émile* that first fully stated the modern view of the child.

Like most intellectual innovators, Rousseau only articulated what many people had vaguely felt to be true: children have their own needs, their own rights, their own rhythm of growth. His *Émile*, which was widely read as a sentimental romance, encouraged, at least in those who admired Greuze's genre pictures, a cult of the child. To be sure, this cult, like most of the humanitarian notions of the time, was not free from paradox: many of its votaries carefully confined their humanity to their own children or to those of their social class. As society grew more complex—one of the prices exacted by modernity—class barriers grew steeper; mines and factories were voracious for the labor of children and the respectable classes resisted the aspirations of the lower orders. Many political radicals, therefore, concerned over the labor supply and the threat-

---

[1] "Que le goust des biens et des maux dépend ne bonne partie de l'opinion que nous en avons," in *Œuvres complètes*, eds. Albert Thibaudet and Maurice Rat (1962), 61.

ened decay of deference, began to display a streak of social conservatism. It is notorious that Voltaire objected to the education of
laborers' children, while in England the charity schools established
by generous Christians scrupulously refrained from teaching their
charges much more than the blessings of religion and the need for
obedience. Ambivalence was the rule, not the exception; Samuel
Johnson claimed he could perfectly understand why people were
not fond of children and flatly maintained that he, for one, had never
wanted a child of his own. Yet Boswell, who reports these remarks,
also reports that Johnson showed his "love of little children" on "all
occasions," a love that Boswell significantly cites as an "undoubted
proof of the real humanity and gentleness of his disposition."[2] Luise
Gottsched, the intelligent and ambitious wife of the moralist and
critic Johann Christian Gottsched, had been carefully educated by
her husband into an intellectual, and enjoyed it: she candidly confessed herself lucky to have had no children, for, she said, since a
mother should cherish and care for them, children would interfere
with a woman's scholarly pursuits.[3] Here even ambivalence testifies
to the discovery of the child: it was precisely the claims of the child
(which would have been incomprehensible to Montaigne) that made
him a nuisance in a scholar's household. The future clearly lay with
the resolution of this dichotomy in favor of the child; it lay with
consistent radicals like Condorcet, who never deviated from his
program for universal education.

In general, humanity was acquiring the status of a practical
virtue. The fashion of attending hangings or a good torture and the
applause for brutal measures against religious dissenters or sexual
deviates had been practically universal to the end of the seventeenth
century. Executions had furnished amusement to Madame de Sévigné
and to sympathetic characters in Molière's comedies. In the eighteenth century such gratifications were degraded into an entertainment
for the rabble and for men of special tastes. In 1699, in *Télémaque*,
Fénelon denounced war and brutality; in 1722, in *Colonel Jack*,
Defoe sympathetically portrayed a youthful thief as the victim of
his environment: these writers were pioneers in compassion. Only

---

[2] See Boswell: *Life of Johnson* (under April 10, 1776), III, 29; and
ibid., IV, 196. See below, chap. x, section 2.
[3] See Karl Biedermann: *Deutschland im achtzehnten Jahrhundert*,
2 vols. in 4 (1854–80), II, 520 n.

a few decades later their ideas were commonplace. The year 1746 was the last in which the British stuck the heads of traitors on Temple Bar and hawkers rented spy glasses at ha'penny a look, and in 1783 public executions gave way to executions in the privacy of prison (an innovation that Samuel Johnson, who respected them as a deterrent, rather regretted). In Prussia, Frederick the Great, for all his cynicism and consciousness of rank, curbed the savagery of punishments and aimed at a cautious diffusion of *Humanität* in his social policies. Laws, especially laws in defense of property, remained stringent throughout Europe and in some countries became more Draconian than before. But in England juries often refused to convict, and in France the *parlements*, despite occasional lapses into hysterical ferocity, generally meted out moderate sentences.

It became possible, and even stylish, to seek the causes of drunkenness and crime in social circumstances and to explain poverty neither as a divine dispensation nor as a just punishment for laziness, but as a stroke of misfortune or a failure of society. Still, such humane, utilitarian sociology remained controversial: in France, the abbé de Saint-Pierre, an indefatigable projector, invented the term *bienfaisance* and was praised for it by Voltaire, but pious conservatives, who disliked the secularization of charity, shook their heads. In England, Henry Fielding, as magistrate, displayed sympathy for the accused that appeared before him and was denounced for inventing "that cant phrase, goodness of heart."[4] In Prussia, Herr von Rochow, a prosperous Junker endowed with exceptional compassion, generously cared for the miserable peasants on his estates, founded schools, composed textbooks, and wrote pamphlets in behalf of popular education. In reply, Frederick's minister von Zedlitz, by no means a fossil, wondered out loud whether peasants really needed to learn anything but obedience: "The metaphysical education of peasants," he objected, "should not be driven too far." Only *"cosmopolites enthousiastes"* try to "convert peasants into philosophers."[5]

There were in fact many, and influential, *cosmopolites enthousiastes* in the eighteenth century, and their influence increased with their number. Montesquieu spoke for them in his aphoristic

---

[4] Sir John Hawkins quoted in Dorothy George: *England in Transition*, 74.
[5] Biedermann: *Deutschland in achtzehnten Jahrhundert*, II, 1145–9.

manner: "If I knew something useful to me," he noted, "but prejudicial to my family, I would reject it from my mind. If I knew
something useful to my family but not to my country, I would try
to forget it. If I knew something useful to my country but prejudicial to Europe, or useful to Europe and prejudicial to the human
race, I would regard it as criminal."[6]

All segments of society benefited from the new humanity; it became less fashionable to make victims than to succor them. Even
public servants found that the penalties for failure were less drastic
than they had been in the past. Through the seventeenth century a
fallen minister had generally been executed or imprisoned. In the
eighteenth century he lost neither life nor property; he might be
exiled to his estates, raised to the Peerage, or otherwise removed
from active politics. Horace Walpole noted that reason (by which
he meant sensible humanity) had begun to "attain that ascendant in
the affairs of the world" for which it had been granted to man.
Neither prejudices nor tyrannies had disappeared, but at least they
had produced no new "persecutors nor martyrs." Indeed, "no prime
ministers perished on a scaffold, no heretics in the flames: a Russian
Princess spared her competitor; even in Turkey the bowstring had
been relaxed." He forgot the political prisoners in Scandinavia
chained in their cells, the abandoned bastards in London dying of
hunger, the Jews in the Hapsburg domains tortured in pogroms and
expelled from Prague in 1745, but he forgot them not because he
was unfeeling.[7] The fate of these unhappy humans had been the fate
of many in the past, and was becoming the fate of the few. Later
critics have often wondered that men of the eighteenth century
should have been optimists; we should rather wonder how they
could have been anything else.

[6] *Pensées*, in *Œuvres*, II, 221-2.
[7] *Memoirs of the Last Ten Years of the Reign of George II*, 2 vols.
(1822), II, 111-12. It should hardly be necessary for me to add (but
I shall add it) that the age of the Enlightment was far from perfect;
the widespread sense of hope was induced by the general sense of
improvement. Not even the philosophes' attitudes can, after all, lay
claim to perfection: while, for example, Montesquieu and Lessing
were philosemites, other philosophes, with Voltaire in the lead,
never overcame or even tried to overcome, their prejudices against
the Jews. While at least some of the philosophes' "anti-Semitism"
was hostility to the fathers of Christianity, much of it was sheer
parochialism.

Even the laboring poor came to be regarded as human beings with real feelings and a right to subsistence. Adam Smith's advocacy of "the liberal reward of labor" was radical but in no way revolutionary.[8] Manufacturers like Josiah Wedgwood and David Dale organized model villages and provided a rudimentary form of social insurance for their workmen; and while their shrewd paternalist policies made humanity pay, they are hints at least of a new attitude toward a class of men traditionally beyond the bounds of humane concern. Duclos could write compassionately of the "*victimes du travail*" and expect his readers to understand him.[9] In Britain and France—less so elsewhere—hundreds of highly placed clerics, manufacturers, country squires, and literary men poured time, energy, and emotion into the campaign against the slave trade. Edward Gibbon, cool, sardonic, and self-centered as he was, found it repulsive that he should be carried across Alpine passes by porters, his fellow men—*mes semblables*. And, strolling about the gilded palaces of Turin, he was haunted by visions of "a village of Savoyards ready to die of hunger, cold and poverty."[1] In the same manner, and practically at the same time that Gibbon was depressed by the spectacle of destitution in the midst of luxury, Diderot discovered a humane revulsion against luxury as he walked about the royal château of Marly: "In the midst of the garden," he wrote to Sophie Volland, "in my admiration which I couldn't refuse Le Nôtre—it is, I think, his work and his masterpiece—I called Henri IV and Louis XIV back to life. Louis showed this magnificent edifice to Henri, and Henri said to him: 'My son, you're right; it's very beautiful. But I'd like to see the houses of my peasants in the village of Gonesse.' What would he have thought of finding all around these immense and magnificent palaces—of finding, I say, peasants without roofs, without bread, and on straw?"[2] Here, in these informal, troubled, private asides, we see the secular social conscience at birth.

Since the humanitarians were convinced that knowledge produced humanity, they took instances of callousness as evidence not

---

[8] Adam Smith: *The Wealth of Nations*, 78–9. See below, 363–8.
[9] *Considérations sur les mœurs*, 13.
[1] These striking sentiments have been noted by H. R. Trevor-Roper: "Edward Gibbon after 200 Years," *The Listener*, LXXVII (October 22, 1964), 618.
[2] September 23, 1762. *Correspondance*, IV, 164.

of innate cruelty but of surviving ignorance. Henry Fielding, who
had no pity for able-bodied beggars, thought that the needs of the
deserving poor were unattended because they were not known. He
recommended constructive slumming by members of Parliament
and other responsible persons. "If," he wrote, "we were to make a
progress through the outskirts of this town, and look into the habitations of the poor, we should there behold such pictures of human
misery as must move the compassion of every heart that deserves the
name of human. What, indeed, must be his composition who could
see whole families in want of every necessary of life, oppressed with
hunger, cold, nakedness, and filth, and with diseases, the certain consequence of all these: what, I say, must be his composition, who
could look into such a scene as this, and be affected only in his
nostrils?" He was sure that "such wretchedness as this" was "so little
lamented," because it was "so little known."³ This was a new tone,
sounded not by some unworldly soul, but by a competent observer,
an experienced judge.

Nothing seemed to be safe from the new, gentler spirit, Fielding's "glorious lust for doing good." The abbé Prévost denounced
war as a degradation of "reason and humanity," and, while war
went on, Prévost acquired a host of followers; pacifism remained
a utopian ideal, but hatred of war became a respectable sentiment.
Hertzberg, a minister of Frederick the Great, recommended that in
peacetime, at least, men should be moderate in their patriotism, while
Samuel Johnson, who loved England well, consistently placed the
interests of mankind above the interests of country, even his own.⁴
Mercantilism had been an economic policy subordinated to political
—or, rather, military—requirements: it had treated wealth, population, flourishing commerce as weapons in an unending struggle for
power in the international arena. In the dawning age of *laissez faire*,
competition was seen in advanced circles as the commercial equivalent of war: David Hume, in an essay significantly entitled "Of the
Jealousy of Trade," affirmed that "not only as a man, but as a BRITISH

---

³ Quoted by George Sherburn: "Fielding's Social Outlook," in
James L. Clifford, ed.: *Eighteenth Century English Literature*
(1959), 271.
⁴ For Hertzberg, see Hajo Holborn: *A History of Modern Germany, 1648–1840* (1964), 241; Johnson's remark, "Patriotism is the
last refuge of a scoundrel," is justly celebrated. See Boswell: *Life of
Johnson* (under April 7, 1775), II, 348.

subject, I pray for the flourishing commerce of GERMANY, SPAIN, ITALY, and even FRANCE itself."[5] Captain Cook, the greatest explorer of the century, concluded the account of his second voyage around the world by claiming glory not for his heroism or his geographical discoveries, but rather for having "discovered the possibility of preserving health among a numerous ship's company." This, he said, "will make this voyage remarkable in the opinion of every benevolent person, when the disputes about a southern continent shall have ceased to engage the attention, and to divide the judgment of philosophers."[6] No wonder conservatives looked about them and, like Romans longing for a mythical past, regretted the good old days. Sir John Hawkins, Samuel Johnson's friend and first biographer, petulantly observed in 1787 that prisoners were being treated with uncommon leniency, accused persons handled with respect in court, and guilty men likely to escape punishment. "We live in an age when humanity is in fashion."[7] It was, for men of Hawkins's temper, an unfortunate development.

The spread of good manners in the eighteenth century beyond restricted circles of courtliness shared in the ambiguities and the eventual triumph of humanitarianism. The meaning, the very territory covered on the linguistic map by such words as *manners* or *mœurs* (the translator's despair), was uncertain; it was, and continued to be, a hard struggle to diffuse standards of conduct. Incessant injunctions in behalf of courtesy suggest its scarcity, but also its importance as a new social ideal. True: for many, polish was bright because it was so new; refinement often barely concealed a fearful coarseness. Britain and France, the first centers of the Enlightenment, were also innovators in modern manners. By the time the traveler reached Prussia, he seemed to be approaching the state of nature: it was no surprise to see Frederick William I, the sergeant on the Prussian throne, behaving like a rustic barbarian early in the century; it was rather more dismaying to see his son, Frederick the Great, supposedly a cultivated man, merely sublimating his father's bestiality into crude practical jokes.

---

[5] *Works*, III, 348.
[6] *Captain Cook's Voyages of Discovery*, ed. John Barrow (edn. 1941), 228.
[7] Quoted in Dorothy George: *England in Transition*, 73.

Good manners extended their humanizing touch to all classes. Aristocrats, for centuries lordly, self-willed, and coarse, began to curb the insolence of birth and to practice, or affect, the maxims of *noblesse oblige*, or *Leutseligkeit*. The lower orders, too, especially the working poor in the cities, aspired to reputable forms of behavior: early in the nineteenth century, Francis Place, the celebrated radical ideologist who never lost his sense for harsh realities, looked back on the London he had known and acknowledged that the industrial revolution in England had benefited all classes at least in this respect. "The progress made in refinement of manners and morals," he wrote, including the whole population in his estimate, "seems to have gone on simultaneously with the improvement in arts, manufactures and commerce."[8] Manners were the drop of oil lubricating the machinery of life; in 1726 the chevalier de Rohan, decadent scion of an ancient noble house, avenged a fancied slight administered by Voltaire by having his footmen beat up Voltaire in public, but this was a survival from cruder times. For the most part, debates took the place of duels, and men were ready to talk rather than fight, in legislatures, in court, in the very streets. When young Samuel Johnson came to London he had witnessed unedifying scuffles over the right to walk next to the wall; a few decades later there was an end to these quarrels. "Now it is fixed," Boswell recorded in 1773, "that every man keeps to the right; or, if one is taking the wall, another yields it, and it is never a dispute."[9]

Precisely because they were new, eighteenth-century manners were marred by distortions and excesses. This was the age when Chesterfield could warn his son never to be caught laughing in good society, when the newly rich covered their vacuity by arch affectations, and when gracious sovereigns, forgetting that they were supposed to preside over a new age of social cordiality, invited and basked in nauseating compliments: Grimm wrote Catherine of Russia that he was happy to be counted among her dogs. Absurd conceits and false delicacy widely trivialized the very idea of good manners. "Every man of any education," Samuel Johnson noted,

---

[8] Quoted in Dorothy George: *London Life in the Eighteenth Century* (2d edn., 1930), 4.
[9] James Boswell: *Journal of a Tour to the Hebrides with Samuel Johnson, LL.D., 1773*, eds. Frederick A. Pottle and Charles H. Bennett (1962), 192.

"would rather be called a rascal, than accused of deficiency in *the graces*."[1] Such caustic comments were staples of eighteenth-century self-criticism.

They were as deserved as they were familiar, and critics of culture, like Rousseau, made the most of them. Yet triviality and artificiality were the inevitable by-product of far-reaching social changes; they were in themselves trivial compared to the civilizing effects of restrained conduct. Samuel Johnson felicitously defined "good breeding" as "fictitious benevolence,"[2] but by *fictitious* he meant not *false*, but *conscious* and *deliberate*. He knew, and he insisted, that breeding was "of great consequence in society." After all, hypocrisy is uncomfortable and in the long run, for most people, insupportable. What may have begun as an obeisance to fashion is likely to persist as a permanent mode of behavior; gestures become habits.

That much had already happened in the sphere of manners by mid-century is evident from Charles Duclos's urbane *Considérations sur les mœurs*. Duclos thought that the "science of manners"—the patient and critical observation of social conduct—established beyond doubt that the eighteenth century was witnessing a beneficent revolution in behavior; he had no sympathy with the nostalgia for more primitive times. Duclos recognized that politeness might be abused, but he preferred even false politeness to genuine brutishness: it reduced crimes, improved political life, and generally made men more civilized. "The taste for literature, science, and the arts," he concluded, "has insensibly increased, and has reached a point where those who do not have it, affect it."[3]

Half a century later, Immanuel Kant demonstrated in affecting circumstances how much terrain manners had conquered in the age of the Enlightenment. About a week before his death, eighty and already quite feeble, Kant received a visit from his physician. He rose to thank him, in disconnected words, for taking time from his busy schedule. The physician tried to persuade his patient to sit down, but Kant waited until his visitor was seated, and then, collecting his powers, said with some effort: "*Das Gefühl für Humanität hat mich noch nicht verlassen*—the feeling for humanity has not yet

---

[1] Boswell: *Life of Johnson* (under May 1776), III, 54.
[2] Boswell: *Tour to the Hebrides*, 57.
[3] *Considérations sur les mœurs*, 135.

left me." The physician, a witness tells us, was almost moved to tears.[4]

It was a moving moment, for Kant's courtesy was more than an empty formality; it was evidence that in his time civility had come to be recognized as part, and expression, of humanity. Diderot had been right to tell Sophie Volland that politics and manners hold each other by the hand.

It has frequently been observed, usually with some severity, that eighteenth-century vehicles for the diffusion of humanity—the novel, the tearful comedy, the domestic idyll, the genre painting— all too often pandered to the taste of a new public, which was bad taste. A half-educated bourgeoisie in search of cheap emotional satisfaction and prurient erotic thrills applauded heroes like Prévost's chevalier des Grieux for weeping because he sees his Manon sad, bought Greuze's most egregious family scenes, and cried freely over Richardson's novels. Sensibility all too often degenerated into sentimentality, and easy tears conveniently blinded the eyes of men and women reluctant to confront the realities of their times or their own lives.

The sentimentality and melodrama of the age deserve much of the criticism they have received, both on aesthetic and on social grounds. Yet even the sentimental productions of the time were agents in the humanization of man. Sentimentality is the expenditure of worthy emotions on unworthy objects, but it may act (and I think in the eighteenth century did act) to call attention to worthy objects as well. The *Empfindsamkeit* of the German writers encouraged readers to indulge their hypochondria, or to remain passive in life, but it taught, even if indirectly, the value of sympathy, pity, and love. These writers did not, perhaps, have a very exalted notion of what they called *wahre Menschlichkeit*, but even in its mediocrity, this "true humanity" was a turn away from brutality and the unmeasured indulgence of aggression. The hero of Henry Mackenzie's widely read novel, *The Man of Feeling*, weeps on almost every page, and is bound to bore or annoy the modern reader with sententious moralizing and maudlin melancholy. But his tears are often to the point; they are the harbingers of a rational, humane social policy.

---

[4] Cassirer: *Kants Leben und Lehre*, 440.

Mackenzie's hero pities miserable prostitutes (not all of whom have hearts of gold), and laments the lot of the poor insane wretches at Bedlam whom their callous keepers bring out on Sunday afternoons to entertain idle visitors. It would be pointless to complain that Mackenzie's *Man of Feeling* or Diderot's lachrymose dramas were a high price to pay for the humanization of man: humanity, to paraphrase Hegel, has its cunning; it uses many instruments—some pathetic, some grotesque, some even sordid—to realize its purpose.

IV

In his famous essay on the Protestant ethic, Max Weber argues that the spirit of capitalism (in which we may recognize Hume's "industry"), with its tight-lipped asceticism, its concentration on material things, its often rascally and usually ruthless search for profits, and its single-minded philistinism, was inimical to the smiling hedonism of the Enlightenment. Whatever the permanent value of Weber's thesis, which has been subjected to some telling criticism, it is true that the modes of life that characterized leading capitalists were far removed from the rococo grace of Wieland, the unbuttoned literary inventiveness of Diderot, or the serene classical learning of David Hume. At the same time, Benjamin Franklin, who is Max Weber's favorite exemplar of the eighteenth-century capitalist mentality, was Voltaire's brother in the masonic lodge, *Les trois sœurs,* and the two were brothers in much else besides. The spirit of capitalism questioned customary ways, despised tradition, and thus, precisely like the *Encyclopédie,* helped to change the general way of thinking and to point it, if not directly toward humanitarianism, at least toward the rationalization of life.

All over the West, in London as in Philadelphia, philosophers joined articulate businessmen in commending ceaseless activity and preached the postponement of immediate gratification for the sake of some higher and more enduring satisfaction. As preachers of practicality, the philosophes resorted to the virtue of action as a favorite text: it is significant that Locke, and Condillac after him, should regard restlessness or *inquiétude* as the mainspring of life. Other philosophes followed their lead. Hume regarded activity as essen-

tial to felicity: "There is no happiness without occupation."[5] Diderot
exalted Hercules, the man of action, over Antinoüs, the pretty
aesthetic object, and wryly called his *Encyclopédie*, the favorite
among his Herculean labors and his claim to immortality, "a labor
that has been the torment of my life for twenty years."[6] Voltaire
polemicized against the profusion of religious holidays, which kept
men from productive labor, preached the philosophy of energy—
"we do not want enough"—and told his mistress and niece that his
life was "to work and think of you."[7]

This doctrine has been sharply criticized as the ideology of a
rising bourgeoisie complacently presiding over the exploitation of
labor. There is some truth in this criticism. While facile allusions to
"the rising bourgeoisie" have fallen into disfavor, it is undeniable
that merchants, industrialists, bankers, attorneys, physicians, men of
letters, respectable shopkeepers, and *rentiers*—that social congeries
making up what we call, for short, the bourgeoisie—supplied the
new industriousness with its most zealous troops and most single-
minded advocates. Still, the term remains unsatisfactory: the philosophes applied the doctrine to themselves, and worked as hard as anyone. Furthermore, enterprising aristocrats and energetic members
of the lower orders strove for success side by side with the most
compulsive manufacturer. Just as there were Roman Catholics who
practiced the Protestant ethic, so men either beyond or beneath the
bourgeoisie held bourgeois values and led bourgeois lives. And, just
as not all industrious men were bourgeois, so not all bourgeois were
industrious. Large segments of the European middle classes were
as torpid as peasants, as wedded to tradition as aristocrats, too snobbish and too anxious for social advancement to destroy the status
ladder they themselves hoped to climb. The eighteenth century was
the age of the ossifying, as much as the age of the awakening,
bourgeoisie. "*Lo hicieron así mis padres*—That's how my forefathers did it," was not a slogan mouthed by Spanish grandees alone.

In city after city across Europe class barriers were growing
more rigid rather than less so. Oligarchies, in Amsterdam as in

[5] Hume to Dr. John Clephane, January 5, 1753. *Letters*, I, 170.
[6] Diderot to Guéneau de Montbeillard (June 30, 1765). *Correspond-ance*, V, 46.
[7] Voltaire to Madame Denis, September 3, (1753). *Correspondence*, XXIII, 166; see *The Rise of Modern Paganism*, 69.

Prague, became more oligarchical; patricians jealously guarded their privileges with carefully manipulated constitutions, adroitly arranged (though no longer forced) marriages, and sumptuary laws that delimited the prerogatives of each social stratum. As beneficiaries of recently acquired or inherited status, patricians attempted to close off the very avenues of ascent that they, or their grandfathers, had walked, and in their defensiveness they were often more reactionary than the old feudal families. Geneva, ruled by the descendants of Huguenot immigrants who had fled to the little republic early in the sixteenth century, late in the seventeenth century shabbily greeted French Protestant refugees from the persecutions of Louis XIV by discouraging their entry, taxing them heavily, and making it inordinately expensive for them to buy citizenship. Patricians married patricians, and a handful of families governed a republic of political pariahs. In Frankfurt, Goethe's city, a carefully nuanced *Kleiderordnung* rigidly separated social groups. In the Dutch cities small interlocking cliques of commercial aristocrats coopted new members, held on fiercely to the government of the United Provinces, and were so crabbed in their outlook and so avid in their lust for comfort and control that they forfeited most of the economic and diplomatic advantages their grandfathers had so laboriously acquired in the seventeenth century. In Strasbourg the governing legislative body "seemed to be a debating society for brothers, cousins, and brothers-in-law"—and Strasbourg was typical.[8]

The dynamism that is the capitalist spirit was, therefore, the property of a minority and to an impressive extent of outsiders. In England, the industrial revolution was almost proverbially in the hands of Protestant Dissenters and Scots in search of their fortune. In France, financial and industrial innovations were largely the work of foreign Protestants—Scots and Genevans—and Huguenot families who had survived the great purges of the 1680s. Prussia benefited immensely from those purges: the Great Elector intelligently invited Huguenot refugees into his domains, and thus acquired able administrators and inventive craftsmen. The great port city of Hamburg, one of many Free Cities in the German Empire, avoided the decay of most of the others by welcoming foreigners of all nationalities and giving them a share in civic and commercial affairs. The

---

[8] Franklin L. Ford: *Strasbourg in Transition, 1648–1789* (1958), 15.

Hamburg Constitution of 1712, perhaps the least oligarchical urban charter of the age, reflected this liberal spirit and promoted it. And in many European cities the Jews and the Lombards did the financial business that the new spirit demanded and the old religion condemned.

But whoever represented the spirit of industry—and clearly, so powerful and pervasive an attitude could not be the monopoly of outsiders alone—what matters here is that this spirit was, precisely like the reason employed and the humanity practiced by Christians, the surreptitious ally of the philosophes. By glorifying work, the bearers of the Protestant ethic substituted commercial for heroic, modern for medieval—bourgeois for aristocratic—ideals, which were, precisely, the ideals of the philosophes.

The celebration of industry, which is so prominent in eighteenth-century writings on morals and economic affairs, thus represents a radical criticism of the traditional ethical hierarchy. The criticism was, of course, not new. Proud, self-conscious commercial patriciates, like the great merchant and banking families of Renaissance Florence, had testified to the virtues of the trader's mind centuries before the Enlightenment, and by the end of the seventeenth century it was no longer rare to see the hero of legend, or the superb military aristocrat of medieval days, denounced as a villain: Dryden called the Homeric heroes "ungoldly man-killers," a "race of men who can never enjoy quiet in themselves, till they have taken it from all the world."[9] The pacific spirit of the Enlightenment had a dignified ancestry.

This was not simply, or not yet, the bourgeois spirit, which would merely rationalize the cowardice, the greed, and the philistinism typical of the trading mind. It was rather a spirit in which banker and squire, manufacturer, poet, and sensible aristocrat could participate. In 1705, Lord Shaftesbury, who was no bourgeois, wrote approvingly to a friend about the love of fame but added this caution: "All fame is not alike. There is as much difference as between noise and music. Mere fame is a rattle to please children, and the famousest people in the world are famous fools. But the fame that arises from the consent and harmony of wise and good men is music,

---

[9] Quoted in Reuben A. Brower: *Alexander Pope: The Poetry of Allusion* (1959), 89. See below, 50, and chap. viii, section 1.

and a charm irresistible to a heroic soul. The fame of nobility, high station, warlike feats or conquests, make not a single note in the symphony. What love was ever gained by these? What hearts were ever won in this manner?"[1]

With the growing popularity of these sentiments, the way to the glorification of the merchant classes was open, and it was taken early in the eighteenth century by British publicists. Daniel Defoe unblushingly characterized the "true-bred merchant" as a "universal scholar" who "understands languages without books, Geography without maps," who by his voyages and in his correspondence embraces the whole world and all nations and is therefore "qualified for all sorts of employment in the State."[2] The *Spectator* echoed Defoe in many papers. "Sloth," Addison gravely tells his readers, "has ruin'd more Nations than the Sword"; and again: "There are not more useful Members in a Commonwealth than Merchants. They knit Mankind together in a mutual Intercourse of good Offices, distribute the Gifts of Nature, find Work for the Poor, add Wealth to the Rich, and Magnificence to the Great." These mercantile statesmen-philanthropists, it would seem, did everything but make money for themselves.[3] In the light of these pronouncements, Addison's lyrical portrait of the London Stock Exchange comes as no surprise. "As I am a great Lover of Mankind," we read, "my Heart naturally overflows with Pleasure at the sight of a happy and prosperous Multitude, insomuch that at many publick Solemnities I cannot forbear expressing my Joy with Tears that have stolen down my Cheeks. For this reason I am wonderfully delighted to see such a Body of Men thriving in their own private Fortunes, and at the same time promoting the Publick Stock; or in other Words, raising Estates for their own Families, by bringing into their Country whatever is wanting, and carrying out of it whatever is superfluous."[4] Here Addison genially combines making money, trading shares, and loving humanity into a cheerful, sentimental, slightly cloying ideal.

In 1734 Voltaire appropriated this ideal for the Continent. The

---

[1] Shaftesbury to Lord Somers, October 20, 1705. *Life, Unpublished Letters, and Philosophical Regimen*, ed. Benjamin Rand (1900), 340.
[2] Quoted in James Sutherland: *Defoe* (2d edn., 1950), 46–7.
[3] *Spectator*, No. 2, ed. Donald F. Bond, 5 vols. (1965), I, 10; ibid., No. 69, I, 296.
[4] Ibid., No. 69, I, 294.

Lettres philosophiques is filled with tributes to the commercial spirit, which prefers peace to glory, opens high posts to men of talent, and converts the world into a market in which all traders tolerate one another. "Enter the London Stock Exchange," Voltaire writes, paraphrasing and improving upon Addison, "that place more respectable than many a court. You will see the deputies of all nations gathered there for the service of mankind. There the Jew, the Mohammedan, and the Christian deal with each other as if they were of the same religion, and give the name of infidel only to those who go bankrupt; there, the Presbyterian trusts the Anabaptist, and the Anglican honors the Quaker's promise. On leaving these peaceful and free assemblies, some go to the synagogue, others go to drink; this one goes to have himself baptized in the name of the Father, the Son, and the Holy Ghost; that one has his son's foreskin cut off and Hebrew words mumbled over the child which he does not understand; others go to their church to await the inspiration of God, their hats on their heads, and all are content."[5] This paragraph, which is often quoted, is not the description of commercial transactions; it is not even a candid statement of Voltaire's private convictions about brokers—he had enough dealings with them to know that they did not gather to serve mankind. It is, of course, a hit at religious ritual, a hint that the world of business is more reasonable than the world of faith. But it is also more than that. The marvelous, swift closing phrase—*et tous sont contents*—evokes a radically modern standard of excellence: a civilization that rewards social utility and cherishes the architects of peace and prosperity as its finest citizens. Who is more useful, Voltaire asks rhetorically, a powdered servile grand seigneur who has mastered all the intricacies of courtly ritual or the merchant who sends his ships across the seas and enriches his country?[6] The answer was obvious, and meant to be obvious. In 1735 Voltaire summarized the Enlightenment's transvaluation of values in a letter to a friend: "Great men I call all those who have excelled in the useful or the agreeable. Those who sack provinces are only heroes."[7]

---

[5] Lettre VI, *Lettres philosophiques*, I, 74.
[6] See Lettre X, ibid., I, 122.
[7] Voltaire to Thieriot (*c.* July 15, 1735). *Correspondence*, IV, 94. This may be another classical reminiscence: Seneca had called heroes mere killers, and scourges of mankind. If this is not an invisible quotation, at least it represents a kindred world view.

From the beginning, then, and in the course of its development in the Enlightenment, this new ideal had a positive and a critical component. On the one hand, it assigned high social value to merchants—in Hume's opinion, "one of the most useful races of men." On the other, it derided military men, the makers of war and desolation—"master butchers" was Diderot's name for them.[8] By mid-century, both these epithets were commonplace in advanced circles. Fielding heaped sarcasms upon "great men," the "sackers of towns, the plunderers of provinces, and the conquerors of kingdoms."[9] And: "I am far from intending to vindicate the sanguinary projects of heroes and conquerors"—thus runs a weighty paragraph published in 1754, voicing these convictions in the noblest manner, "and would wish rather to diminish the reputation of their success, than the infamy of their miscarriages: for I cannot conceive why he that has burned cities, wasted nations, and filled the world with horror and desolation, should be more kindly regarded by mankind than he who died in the rudiments of wickedness; why he that accomplished wickedness should be glorious, and he that only endeavoured it should be criminal. I would wish Caesar and Catiline, Xerxes and Alexander, Charles and Peter, huddled together in obscurity or detestation." This philosophic pronouncement, which sounds as though it were drawn from the pacific Hume or translated into ringing English from a passionate Voltairean broadside, is Samuel Johnson's, in the periodical *The Adventurer*.[1]

V

One of the most eloquent expressions of the new spirit at work, of reason, humanity, and industry celebrated by and for respectable Christians, was the periodical literature that began to flourish, first in Britain and then on the Continent, at the beginning of the eighteenth century. Everywhere, these weekly or daily periodicals, often frivolous, sometimes grave—secular homilies—found thousands

---

[8] Hume: "Of Interest," *Works*, III, 324; Diderot: *Pages contre un tyran* (1771), in *Œuvres politiques*, 147.
[9] Sherburn: "Fielding's Social Outlook," 266.
[1] No. 99, quoted in Donald J. Greene: *The Politics of Samuel Johnson* (1960), 151.

of buyers and almost rivaled printed sermons in popularity. The *Spectator* had a circulation of several thousand copies, and each copy had several readers, including women, in coffeehouses. Its bound volumes would be bought, displayed, and even read well into the nineteenth century. Defoe started his *Review* in 1704 and may claim to have been the first of the journalist-educators, but it was Addison and Steele, with their *Tatler* and *Spectator,* who set the style for all of Europe. These two periodicals lasted for only five years, intermittently from 1709 to 1714, but they were the most brilliantly written, intelligently varied, and hence assiduously copied journals of the age. They had dozens of imitators. In their later, lesser periodicals, Addison and Steele even imitated themselves, and as late as the 1750s Samuel Johnson wrote his *Rambler* and *Idler* with the *Spectator* as his model. On the Continent, dozens of moral weeklies tried themselves in the tone and temper of the *Spectator*: in Sweden, such a journal was started in 1732; after 1760 Italians could aim at moral improvement by reading Count Caspar Gozzi's *Osservatore Veneto*, a sheet that explicitly, if rather timidly, imitated Addison and Steele; in France, Marivaux published *Le Spectateur français*, and the abbé Prévost copied the *Spectator* with his *Le Pour et le Contre*. Most of these high-minded periodicals did not last, but even in their brief life spans they reflected and to some extent satisfied a widespread craving for instructive secular reading material. The *Spectator* and its epigones were attempts to confirm the Socratic maxim that virtue can be taught, if on a less exalted level than the virtue Socrates had tried to inculcate.

It was, of course, precisely their blandness, their confounding of common sense with strenuous philosophizing, their concentration on improving manners and clarifying taste while avoiding political acrimony, that made these journals the civilizing agents they were. Addison was perfectly candid about the character of his readers: "I shall spare no Pains," he declared in the famous tenth number of the *Spectator*, "to make their Instruction agreeable, and their Diversion useful. For which Reasons I shall endeavour to enliven Morality with Wit, and to temper Wit with Morality." He even found occasion to invoke the first of moralists, Socrates, and thus lend his essentially modern enterprise the prestige of a classical ancestry. "It was said of *Socrates*, that he brought Philosophy down from Heaven, to inhabit among Men; and I shall be ambitious to have it said of me, that I have brought Philosophy out of Closets and Libraries, Schools and Colleges, to dwell in Clubs and Assemblies, at Tea-tables, and in Coffee-Houses." Addison knew, as all educators know, that one does not cultivate new segments of society without stooping.

It must be said, however, that Addison and Steele and most of their followers stooped with dignity. Their very tone—their sweet reasonableness, their decent language, their gentle wit—was a rebuke to coarseness, an appeal to lay aside party spirit, an invitation and a guide to gentlemanly conduct. The content of their periodicals matched their tone to perfection. Their choice of expression, the calculated abstraction from technical or philosophical jargon, made them accessible to men and women with a modicum of learning. In part they created their audiences, but in large measure they found them; each country got the periodicals it could absorb.

In the German states, where the reading public was still small and timid, the *moralischen Wochenschriften* tried to instill their bourgeois public with confidence and self-respect. They drew pleasing profiles of *Bürger*, who worked hard and accumulated capital by austere living but not through greed. Those idealized merchants were good Christians and submissive subjects even more than they were machines for accumulation: the weeklies specialized in advocating unquestioning piety and unquestioning obedience to constituted authority. At the height of the *Aufklärung*, there were journals edited by prominent German philosophes like Nicolai and Wieland that ventured into discussions of art and literature: the moral weeklies had accomplished their mission. But in the early years, the most successful of these weeklies, the *Patriot*, launched in 1724 in the prosperous and liberal Free City of Hamburg by a group of poets, publicists, and scholars, departed from reiterating the lessons of worldly, mercantile asceticism only to teach polite manners: it scolded its readers for coquetry and affectation, recommended the education of women and the purification of family life. The *Bildung* envisioned by the writers of the *Patriot* was trivial and feeble compared with the rounded humanism to which Goethe and Humboldt could make their readers aspire almost a century later, but it should be taken for what it was—the first sign of a new mentality among people still groping for a cultivation that others already had firmly in their possession.

In contrast to the Germans, the British periodicals could count on a public at least partly prepared for culture and schooled in self-confidence. Few readers could have missed—certainly all later commentators have observed—the skill with which the *Spectator* captured the variety of its potential audience with its happy invention, the "Spectator Club," which makes its appearance in the second number and whose activities are reported by a single voice, the "Spectator of mankind," urbane, perceptive, and generous. The most prominent member of the club is Sir Roger de Coverley, a lovable eccentric without enemies, a Tory who regularly sleeps in the church he faithfully attends, a squire who is, like all members of the club, cheerful and humane. His fellows include a courageous and honorable captain; a man of the world well versed in the ways of women; a clergyman distinguished by latitudinarian piety ("a very philosophick Man, of general Learning, great Sanctity of Life, and the most exact good Breeding"); an attorney, bookish but witty, competent to understand his times precisely because he is a classicist ("his Familiarity with the Customs, Manners, Actions, and Writings of the Antients, makes him a very delicate Observer of what occurs to him in the present World"); and—a prominent figure—Sir Andrew Freeport, the merchant. This company is shrewdly chosen: learning and good temper, worldliness and industry, rational piety, good breeding, and firm confidence combine into a collective portrait of the beneficent, active, modern, rational Christian, the perfect spokesman for the recovery of nerve.

Many of Mr. Spectator's topics are trifling; many of his targets safe; some of his strictures, especially those touching on women, patronizing. He gently ridicules hypochondria, amuses himself at the expense of vain women and envious men, censures viciousness of speech and commends, in its place, wit "tempered with Virtue and Humanity." He inveighs against frenzy and "enthusiasm" in all their forms: significantly, most of the mottos that decorate each number are drawn from Horace, the poet of the middle way. He prescribes calm cheerfulness almost like a medicine. But even this tepid moralizing has a serious point: it is intended to polish man's behavior and purify his intentions. The *Spectator*'s ideal is the civilized man who practices virtue and recognizes his duties; the man who makes it his business "to advise the Ignorant, relieve the Needy, comfort the Afflicted." The human man is the humane man.

He is also an industrious and rational man. The *Spectator* celebrates the virtues of the capitalist in the person of Sir Andrew Freeport, "a merchant of great eminence in the city of London, a person of indefatigable industry, strong reason, and great experience." His "Notions of Trade are noble and generous"; he holds that "true Power is to be got" not by arms, but by "Arts and Industry," and that "Diligence makes more lasting Acquisitions than Valour."[2] Thus the *Spectator* anticipates Samuel Johnson's injunction that trade deserves philosophical consideration and the sort of mercantile pacifism later advocated by David Hume and Adam Smith.

This rational humanity—and here too the *Spectator* fitly represents the spirit of the age—is suffused with religion, the bland, polite religion of the latitudinarians. The *Spectator* lamented the asceticism of the Puritans—clearly the only asceticism it appreciated was worldly—and included some pioneering papers on literature and wit; but it also lamented the irresponsible, malicious irreligion of the libertines, and preached instead a sober religion, short on theology and long on philosophical worship. The *Spectator* is Newton for the average man: it offers the new physics and astronomy as arguments for the beneficence of the Creator; it suggests a look through the telescope and microscope to produce "rational admiration in the soul" closely akin and little inferior to devotion. "The Spacious Firmament on High," Addison's famous hymn, in which rationalist Christianity and constructive deism converge, was first printed in the *Spectator*. Clearly, life was good to the cultivated reader. God was in His heaven, but He rarely, if ever, left it. Man, *Spectator* in hand, was enlightened man. The Enlightenment of the philosophes would be no shock to him.

---

[2] For the preceding quotations see the *Spectator*, Nos. 10, 2, 23, 93, 2; I, 44, 10–13, 99, 395, 10.

CHAPTER TWO

Progress: From Experience to Program

For the spokesmen of the Enlightenment, progress was an experience before it became a program. The recovery of nerve was a matter of concrete, often homely realities, directly perceived, and as professional empiricists, as theorists infatuated with practicality, the philosophes were prepared to translate that recovery into the basis and a call for action. Just as artists learn less from nature than from other artists, reformers often learn to formulate the problems of their society largely from books: rumors of war or the sights, sounds, and smells of cities are rarely converted directly into a social philosophy. But the philosophes basked in experience and drew their program, far more than idealists in earlier ages, from the laboratory, the workshop, and the political arena. Ideas are often little more than mirrors or masks; in the age of the Enlightenment they became actors.

The philosophes, after all, were men of ideas in the world hungry for the real thing. Some of their ventures into the jungle of reality (as one of their cohorts, Laurence Sterne, put it in an immortal metaphor) smelled too strong of the lamp: Helvétius's faith in education, say, or Voltaire's naïve ambition to play the diplomat with Frederick the Great were triumphs of wishful thinking over good sense. But for the most part the philosophes were something better than coffeehouse gossips or imitation-Aristotles educating imitation-Alexanders: they were hard-headed public servants, like Turgot; tough-minded economists, like Adam Smith; omnivorous consumers of experience, like Diderot; theoreticians of the practical reason, like Kant. Even Rousseau—I say, "even," for if any philosophe has been written off as a dreamer, it is Rousseau—was often at the edges and sometimes at the center of Genevan politics: while his *Contrat social* reads like an exercise in abstract reasoning, the Attorney General of Geneva condemned the book as seditious less for its theoretical formulations than for its all-too-specific criticisms that echoed the language and reflected the program of the middle-class reformers who had been active in the Republic for half a century. And, just as Rousseau does not deserve the reputation of a mere utopian, Gibbon was far from being a bookish recluse; in his *Autobiography*, he pays explicit and deserved tribute to his encounters with life: "The captain of the Hampshire grenadiers (the reader may smile) has not been useless to the historian of the Roman empire."[1] No need for the reader to smile: there are many roads to reality.

I. THE REPUBLIC OF LETTERS

I

THE PHILOSOPHES took most available roads to reality, but the road they traveled most often was their experience as poets, novelists, editors, and polemicists. They experienced the recovery of nerve both as reformers and as men of letters, for since the seventeenth century, men of letters had begun to enjoy a recovery of nerve of their own. Bayle had claimed dignity for the literary craft by calling his periodical *Nouvelles de la république des lettres*; a quarter of a century later, Addison's announced purpose of bringing philosophy to tea tables and coffeehouses suggested that writers had achieved both a respected and an influential position in their society. It was a position the philosophes enjoyed, celebrated, and exploited.

The unprecedented prestige and prosperity of literary men thus brought the recovery of nerve home to the philosophes in the most intimate manner, and provided them with a secure base of operations. Both as writer and as reformer the philosophe required a wide audience, free expression, and respectable status. The eighteenth century provided him with all three; the growing independence of the literary profession greatly facilitated the philosophes' self-

---

[1] Gibbon: *Autobiography*, 134.

imposed task to be the preceptors of the modern world. The interests of the republic of letters and the Enlightenment were identical.

II

The first precondition for a flourishing republic of letters was a wide reading public; it alone could give the writer freedom from capricious and overbearing patrons, freedom to choose his subject matter and find his own tone of voice. Reading habits are notoriously hard to gauge; statistics are scarce and resist interpretation, but it seems evident that such a public was being formed in the Age of the Enlightenment. Calvinist states like Geneva and the Dutch Republic were avid for learning, and England, with its vigorous Puritan strain, already had developed a substantial reading public in the seventeenth century. In these countries the habit of reading took hold of wider and wider circles in the time of Hume and Voltaire. When Samuel Johnson, in 1781, called the English "a nation of readers,"[2] his exaggeration was pardonable because it was moderate; a year later, the Swiss traveler Carl Philipp Moritz, a great Anglomaniac, was pleased to note that the English classics were being republished in numerous and inexpensive editions read by everyone; his landlady, a tailor's widow, read Milton, and read him, it seemed to Moritz, with proper understanding.[3]

Literacy made strides in other countries as well. In France (to judge from signatures on marriage certificates) the percentage of literate adults rose from about four in ten in 1680 to more than seven in ten a century later. Bourgeois pretensions to cultivation, which had furnished Molière with ripe comic material, came to be taken for granted. Lending libraries—an eighteenth-century invention— flourished in provincial French towns as much as in Paris: in the reign of Louis XVI the public library at Lyon proudly displayed a collection of more than fifty-five thousand volumes. In other cities, ambitious town fathers bought great private collections and placed them at the public's disposal; universities and provincial academies

---

[2] Johnson: *Lives of the Poets,* quoted in Ian Watt: *The Rise of the Novel* (1957), 37.
[3] James Sutherland: *A Preface to Eighteenth Century Poetry* (1948), 47.

threw open the doors of their libraries several days a week to satisfy the insatiable demand for reading matter. Literary societies proliferated, especially after the 1760s; cultivated provincials rented reading rooms, subscribed to advanced journals, and bought sets of Diderot's *Encyclopédie*. German cultivation moved more ponderously, but it did move: in 1762, Wieland optimistically observed that "the number of readers" was "growing steadily."[4] There were still some illiterate noblemen in Russia and Lombardy late in the century, but in western Europe illiteracy was reserved to the lower orders.

To be sure, literacy often meant little. Millions of Frenchmen who could write their names often could write little else, and rarely read popular periodicals, let alone philosophic propaganda. In 1762 —the year of Rousseau's *Émile* and *Contrat social*—an anonymous work on public education (perhaps by Diderot) estimated that only 180,000 boys of school age, less than ten per cent of all French boys between the ages of seven and eighteen, had any sort of academic education, while a small number among the rest got some rudimentary training that permanently kept them beyond the pale of serious literature. In Germany, a handful of prosperous commercial cities like Hamburg and Leipzig had a reading public of some consequence and supplied its modest needs with the publications of small houses. But these cities were exceptional: in other German states, readers remained a numerically insignificant if socially prominent minority. German publishers made money with cookbooks, almanacs, and French grammars, but they rarely printed more than five hundred copies of books on history, science, and philosophy. While popular encyclopedias sold by the hundreds of thousands, the first edition of Goethe's works in the late 1780s found only six hundred subscribers. As the German writers themselves were the first to insist: civilizing the Teuton was a slow, disheartening business.

The situation in England was rather more auspicious, but many English poor were illiterate, while those who had attended the charity schools were prepared mainly to read religious tracts or sentimental novels. For all the coffeehouses and all the lending libraries, only a small minority of Englishmen ever saw a newspaper or read a book: at the time of the French Revolution, Burke esti-

---

[4] Friedrich Sengle: *Wieland* (1948), 166.

mated the serious reading public to be not much larger than eighty thousand. Most of Johnson's "nation of readers," it seems, consumed mainly uplift or melodrama.

But whatever the quality of reading in the eighteenth century, its quantity grew, and the reading public changed its composition and its tastes. The contest between the scholar and the general reader, which had first been fought out in the Italian Renaissance, now widened to all of western Europe and to its cultural outpost, the American colonies, and the scholar lost. The plain style—the mark of Puritan and Methodist preachers as much as the mark of philosophic propagandists—won out over the ornate Mandarin style; reasonableness and clarity became the accepted standards of good writing. English and French poets and playwrights reached the exalted status of classics: in the course of the eighteenth century, literary scholars edited their works with the same piety that classical scholars had lavished, and continued to lavish, on the Greek and Roman masters. In the same century the English and French languages acquired a finish and complexity that made the compilation of authoritative dictionaries not merely desirable, but practically inevitable.

One drastic consequence (and hidden cause) of these irreversible developments was the decay of Latin. Early in the sixteenth century two books out of every three published in France were in Latin (the corresponding figure in Germany was somewhat higher), but by the 1780s, these proportions were reversed: only one book in twenty in France, and one in eleven in Germany, was still in Latin. The *érudits* themselves contributed to this shift: while in the sixteenth century most historians and philosophers addressed themselves to an exclusive learned audience, in the seventeenth century Hobbes and Descartes wrote their greatest books, beautifully, in the vulgar tongues of their countries. The philosophes completed this linguistic revolution. Christian Thomasius shocked contemporary opinion in 1688 when he lectured at the University of Leipzig in German and later compounded his heresy by founding German journalism with his literary and moral periodical, the *Monatsgespräche*. He wrote an ugly German, pockmarked with French words and pedantic constructions, but he made an essential beginning. Thomasius's successors, the German *Aufklärer*, like their counterparts in England and France, wrote in their own language as though they enjoyed it—without condescension, and, by the time of Lessing, with distinction.

The growth, the changing contours, and, ironically, the persistent limitations of the reading public all served the philosophes well. They were pleased, and had every right to be pleased, with its growth: Voltaire delighted in seeing Genevan workmen eating their lunch intent on a book—by him. That is why the philosophes welcomed the victory of the modern languages. Since they all handled them with vigor and elegance, they found a new audience for their polemics—the civilized reader who inhabited the middle range of society, the man who would read Hobbes's English but not his Latin works and was less erudite than the scholar but more discriminating than the consumer of trash. Finally, the very limits of the serious public made it possible for the philosophes to educate their readers without resorting to excessive simplifications or crudities. They could presuppose what Samuel Johnson called a "community of mind."[5] Their *vulgarisation* was rarely vulgar.

While this restricted aristocratic character of the reading community had its advantages, the philosophes did not find it an unmixed blessing. The taste of the majority for mediocre novels, fanciful travel tales, and libelous political scandal—their staple food, which they showed no inclination to abandon for more refined fare—meant that there were thousands of readers whom the philosophes could never hope to reach. Hence they deplored the general taste, as cultivated men always have and always will. Voltaire spoke with contempt of French journalists as the "canaille" of literature, while Diderot complained in the *Encyclopédie* that most periodicals were the "fodder of ignoramuses, the resource of men who want to talk and make judgments without reading"[6]—that is, without reading the philosophes.

What doubtless irritated the philosophes most was the undiminished popularity of religious literature on all levels, from abstruse theology and literate sermons to crude catechisms or brightly illustrated saints' lives. In his much publicized and much overrated campaign to "westernize" Russia, Peter the Great directed the Russian presses to print a handful of technical manuals, but the bulk of

---

[5] Boswell: *Life of Johnson* (under May 8, 1781), IV, 102.
[6] "Hebdomadaire," *Œuvres*, XV, 77.

Russian books remained religious tracts. In France, a quarter of all books published in the sixteenth and seventeenth centuries had been on theological subjects, and in the eighteenth century the figure was still one in six—hardly a serious decline. Even in England, where secular literature flourished, the best seller of the century was Bishop Sherlock's *Letter from the Lord Bishop of London to the Clergy and People of London on the Occasion of the Late Earthquakes,* of which over a hundred thousand copies were sold and given away.[7] Sermons and devotional manuals went into edition after edition, year after year. And yet, while the eighteenth century remained a widely if perhaps not deeply religious century, the philosophes poured out against it an ever-growing quantity of antireligious propaganda and found that demand kept pace with supply. *"Ignorance is the mother of Devotion,"* is a saying which, Hume reminded his readers, had become proverbial in his time.[8] In contrast, knowledge would be the mother of incredulity—or so the philosophes devoutly hoped. The stake of the Enlightenment in the expansion of literacy was therefore high.

While the eighteenth-century reading public was smaller in number and more vulgar in taste than men of letters liked to see, it was large, prosperous, and discriminating enough to support literary establishments in several countries: in the 1760s Oliver Goldsmith, though at other times by no means free of bitterness, cheerfully observed that writers no longer depended on the great for subsistence: "They have now no other patrons but the public, and the public, collectively considered, is a good and generous master."[9] His optimism was a little premature, even for Britain. But in Britain as on the Continent writers were seeking independence through the men and women who bought books, for higher income brought greater dignity. True, the status of writers improved in part because more and more aristocrats abandoned their supercilious consciousness of caste for pretensions to the literary life, in part because the

---

[7] This was the famous pastoral letter of 1750 to which David Hume referred with such wry amusement. While this devout tract was in all hands, Hume's own essays were being held back by the publisher. See *The Rise of Modern Paganism,* 253–4.
[8] "Natural History of Religion," *Works,* IV, 363.
[9] Letter LXXXIV, *The Citizen of the World,* in *Collected Works of Oliver Goldsmith,* ed. Arthur Friedman, 5 vols. (1966), II, 344.

spread of commercial values reflected credit on men who earned a living by their talents. But as men of letters discovered over and over again, in private salons and royal courts alike: their respectability seemed to grow mainly with, and through, their wealth. Most writers, said Voltaire, are poor, and poverty "weakens courage; every philosopher at court becomes as much a slave as the first official of the crown." As for himself, he added with engaging candor, "I have seen so many writers who were poor and despised, that I decided long ago not to increase their number."[1] Voltaire's testimony deserves to be taken seriously: with Samuel Johnson, Voltaire was the most passionate and effective representative of the writers' interest in the eighteenth century.

The first country to offer men of letters social respectability and adequate financial rewards was Great Britain. Alexander Pope, a cool, unsentimental craftsman, cast about for various ways to make his talents pay and finally hit upon the device of selling his books by subscription: he sold his translations of the *Iliad* and the *Odyssey* by this method and realized over nine thousand pounds— a respectable sum in his day. A little later, in the 1720s, John Gay, whose *Beggar's Opera* had been the scandalous hit of the decade, was refused a license to stage its sequel, *Polly*; instead he printed it and earned twelve hundred pounds. Samuel Johnson was as tough-minded about the literary profession as Pope, and more eloquent; he completed what Pope had begun. Johnson acknowledged—indeed confidently asserted—that his, and, he thought, anyone's, single motive for writing was money.[2] But while he was crass, he was not vindictive. When James Boswell commiserated with him for receiving only £1,675 for his great *Dictionary*—a work he had planned to complete in three years, and completed in nine—Johnson refused to blame the publishers: "The booksellers," he allowed, "are generous liberal-minded men."[3] In fact, rascally as they usually were, publishers sometimes took chances: David Hume, young and still unknown, got fifty pounds for his *Treatise of Human Nature*; it seems a contemptible sum, but then, with the total failure of the book, even this small advance lost the publisher money. Later, when

---

[1] *Mémoires*, in *Œuvres*, I, 39, 44.
[2] See Boswell: *Life of Johnson* (under April 5, 1776), III, 19.
[3] Ibid. (under 1756), I, 304.

Hume was famous, he commanded more substantial returns: he was paid a thousand pounds and more for each volume of his *History of England*.

Publishing was a secular business, and in the eighteenth century mainly benefited secular authors, but writers of popular sermons did not have to wait for heaven to claim their reward: Hume's friend Hugh Blair, minister of the High Church of Edinburgh, realized over seventeen hundred pounds on his four volumes of sermons. William Strahan, his publisher, had given him a hundred pounds for the first volume, but its sales brought higher bids for the succeeding volumes from rival publishers, and Strahan quickly amended his contract with Blair; free enterprise did not bring profits to merchants alone. By the 1770s Gibbon, who could afford to wait and appeared to be a lucrative property, dictated his own terms and claimed a share of the publisher's profits. Many writers remained what they had always been—impecunious hacks, the victims of ruthless booksellers. The most popular authors, too, were often victims, but of success rather than failure: the clandestine book industry did much for the new ideas all across Europe, but publishers turned against authors the fearlessness and unscrupulousness required to outwit customs officials and bribe censors; underground publishers stole manuscripts, pirated editions, and defaulted on their payments. Yet, while in the eighteenth century (as in ours) few writers made a comfortable living by their writing alone, it had at least become possible, and the very possibility was an inducement to action, a signpost on the road to independence.

British men of letters took this road tentatively at first, later with confidence. They were sped on by sympathetic aristocrats and an elite of responsible publishers like Strahan and Andrew Millar: "I respect Millar, Sir," Samuel Johnson said, "he has raised the price of literature."[4] It had been customary to solicit the financial support of wealthy noblemen through cringing dedications; even Dryden had not been able to escape servility. But early in the eighteenth century Alexander Pope pointedly dedicated his translation of the *Iliad* to a fellow-writer, Congreve, a mere commoner, and remarked (it has often been repeated) that he liked "liberty without a coach." So, evidently, did David Hume; when he was a young man, he laid

---

[4] Ibid. (under 1755), I, 288.

down a plan of life that he ever after "steadily and successfully pursued": to "make a very rigid frugality supply my deficiency of fortune" and thus "to maintain unimpaired my independency."[5] When Samuel Johnson repudiated the patronage system with his immortal letter to Lord Chesterfield (surely one of the haughtiest letters ever addressed by a commoner to a nobleman), he uttered what his predecessors had kept to themselves: a patron, he wrote, was a man who "looks with unconcern on a man struggling for life in the water, and, when he has reached ground, encumbers him with help."[6] The patron, callous to the needy and parasitic on the successful, was losing his social utility.

Samuel Johnson's letter was an admirable bravura piece, though it did not quite kill patronage; Johnson himself accepted a pension from George III. But the relation of author to patron had been reversed: noblemen were now pleased to be known as the friends of writers. The royal pension, Bute told Johnson after he had decided to accept it, "is not given you for any thing you are to do, but for what you have done."[7]

On the Continent, writers envied their English colleagues and tried to follow them. Voltaire's book on England reports with glowing adjectives that English men of letters—Addison, Congreve, Prior, and Swift—had all held public posts and enjoyed private fortunes as well as public esteem. Voltaire was so sensitive to the status of writers that he took it upon himself to criticize Congreve for telling him (casually and probably as a joke) that he, Congreve, despised his own literary work and the profession of letters in general.[8] When it came to the situation of literary men, Voltaire the wit was absolutely humorless.

He had some right to his solemnity, since on the Continent the position of writers remained precarious. Literary life in Lombardy, Tuscany, and all the Hapsburg domains was unthinkable without noble patronage. German society was inhospitable to the formation of an esteemed and prosperous literary profession; through the 1750s, authors were generally poverty-stricken and pathetic scribblers, clerics with a taste for polemics, or university professors

[5] "My Own Life," *Works*, III, 2.
[6] Boswell: *Life of Johnson* (under February 7, 1755), I, 261.
[7] See ibid. (under 1763), I, 374.
[8] Lettre XIX, *Lettres philosophiques*, II, 108–9.

doubling as moralists. Until the time of Klopstock, Goethe recalled, German literary men "did not enjoy the slightest standing" in their society. "They had neither protection, position, nor esteem" and acted a melancholy part in the world as "jesters and parasites"; it was only with the writings of aristocrats like Hagedorn and scholars like Haller that they began to acquire some dignity.[9] Then, as their prestige slowly rose, their income rose with it, but neither the size of their public nor the political institutions of their states ever gave them the wealth or the influence of British and French writers. None of the *Aufklärer* could afford to be a full-time polemicist or even a full-time playwright: Kant and Lichtenberg were professors, Nicolai a publisher; Wieland and Lessing (the first an assiduous flatterer, the second proud and austere) sought independence through their writings and failed. The Germans' veneration of the old Goethe, Olympian, aloof, more than human and just a little unreal, symbolized not the power of German literary men in their society, but their impotence.

In France, the writer's bid for self-determination and self-respect was more successful than it was at Weimar, but the struggle was long and exhausting. In the seventeenth century, independence was out of reach, for both financial and social reasons. Descartes had disposed of his *Discours de la méthode* for two hundred free copies, and he depended most of his life on royal largesse. Molière received the princely sum of two thousand *livres* for his *Tartuffe*, but his royal master and his aristocratic audiences never allowed him to forget his lowly parentage. Later, in the beginning of the eighteenth century, the highly regarded poet J.-B. Rousseau frequented high society, but his patrons condescended to him as to an entertainer and maliciously reminded him of his petit bourgeois origins.

This contempt was slow to fade, and the old system of patronage survived the long reign of Louis XV. At the very time that English lords deferred to poets and dabbled in poetry themselves, French noblemen with a passion for literature generally indulged that passion in private, almost as though it were a vice. There was, it seemed, something common about literature; the days of the French Renaissance, when princes had written poetry, were in the distant past. As late as the 1750s, Grimm drew a depressing sketch

---

[9] *Dichtung und Wahrheit*, in *Gedenkausgabe*, X, 436–7.

of the average author's life: "For some time now," he wrote, "wit has been so fashionable in Paris that the house of the most insignificant financier is filled with members of, or aspirants to an academy. Still, despite this eagerness, the financier is no less stupid than he was, and the author no less poor. The latter's role is a real torture. If he wants to hold on to his place, he is compelled to applaud the master's dull conversation, and the lady's bad taste. He must think like the one and talk like the other; he must suffer the haughtiness of the first and the caprices of the second." Worse, "he must fawn on everybody, even the most menial of the servants: on the porter, in order to be allowed into the house at mealtime; on the flunkies, in order not to be kept waiting at table when he asks for something to drink; on the waiting maid, because the fate of a book often depends on the judgment she forms of it when she read it during her mistress's toilette. This, truth to tell, is the situation of an author who frequents the elegant houses of Paris."[1]

Voltaire changed much of this, but at a high price to himself. He came from a well-placed family that consorted with wealthy bourgeois and powerful aristocrats, but after he chose a literary career in defiance of his father he had to claw his own way to recognition, and he always bore the scars of his travails. While for the most part the philosophes disliked snobs and frowned on servility, Voltaire snubbed Grub Street hacks—his brothers—and dearly loved a lord. It was not an edifying spectacle, and other writers claimed to be shocked by it, with the sovereign ingratitude that the second generation is likely to display toward the first. When Voltaire launched his unscrupulous campaigns for admission to the *Académie française*, even hardened worldlings professed to find his self-abasement distasteful, and when he tried to consolidate his connections with the Russian court by writing *Pierre le grand*, a collection of gross compliments disguised as history, d'Alembert said that the book made him want to vomit.

But it was easier to deplore Voltaire's tactics than to avoid them; many of his critics practiced them in disguised form. D'Alembert liked to proclaim his independence and to think of himself as a "slave of freedom";[2] in 1753, he expressed these sentiments in an aggressive *Essai sur la société des gens de lettres et des grands,*

---

[1] See David T. Pottinger: *The French Book Trade in the Ancien Régime, 1500–1789* (1958), 89–90.

[2] Ronald Grimsley: *Jean d'Alembert, 1717–83* (1963), 126.

which neither superb aristocrats nor servile men of letters much liked. And in fact, d'Alembert guarded a measure of autonomy by his frugal style of life, a style distinct enough to win the praise of David Hume. But d'Alembert supplemented his income by several royal pensions; besides (and the celebrated incident underlines the relevance of Voltairean methods to eighteenth-century France), when the *Encyclopédie* came under fire for d'Alembert's own article on Geneva, d'Alembert simply deserted his post. In the same manner, Rousseau scorned to flatter the great who protected him from the police and paid his rent, but he might have reflected that his ostentatious, bearish refusal to be grateful was perhaps the subtlest form of flattery of all. He might also have reflected that if he made money on some of his books—the publisher Duchesne paid him 5,400 *livres* and an annuity of 660 *livres* a year for his *Dictionnaire de la musique,* while *Émile* brought him more than 7,000 *livres*—such sums had been fought for by some of the very writers he detested. It was doubtless possible for literary men to behave better than Voltaire did: although he was not rich and deeply in her debt, Diderot addressed Catherine the Great with more spirit and less duplicity than the wealthy Voltaire. But it was still Voltaire, more than any other literary man of his century, who freed French writers from servitude and enabled them to speak with at least some candor about political and religious questions. In 1750 Duclos noted that "Of all empires, that of the intellectuals—*gens d'esprit*—without being visible, is the most extensive";[3] a dozen years later, the abbé Voisenon told the *Académie française* in his reception speech that "courtiers have learned to reason, men of letters, to converse. The former have ceased to be bored, the latter, to be bores."[4] In moments of self-pity writers continued to lament their perilous lot, even in the 1760s. In the *Dictionnaire philosophique,* Voltaire compared the man of letters to flying fish: "If he raises himself a little, the birds devour him; if he dives, the fish eat him up."[5] But this was more picturesque and pathetic than just; surely Voltaire had dived, and dived in order to raise himself up, and survived. Hume visited Paris about the time that Voltaire voiced

---

[3] *Considérations sur les mœurs,* 136.
[4] Quoted in Roger Picard: *Les salons littéraires et la société française, 1610–1789* (1943), 150.
[5] "Letters, Men of Letters, or Literati," *Philosophical Dictionary,* II, 349.

his complaint, and found the status of literary men so secure that it aroused his envy for a moment, although he was not an envious man. In London, he wrote, a writer was little respected, but in Paris, "a man that distinguishes himself in Letters, meets immediately with Regard & Attention."[6] This social distinction perverted perhaps as many talents as it fostered: Rameau, in Diderot's *Le neveu de Rameau*, is such a parasite; it is the "I" in the dialogue, the solitary moralist, who is truly free. But what really mattered after all was not the social strategies of literary men, not the choice of solitude or sociability for their own sake, but their consequences. When wealth, brilliant company, public recognition became ends in themselves, they enslaved men of letters in glittering chains. When they were used as means, they were instruments of liberation. "The first step," says the "I" in *Le neveu de Rameau*, "is to secure the means of life without servitude."[7] And this was Voltaire's larger purpose. "I have always preferred freedom to everything else,"[8] he claimed in his *Mémoires*, and there is no reason to dispute his claim: Voltaire did not lie, or flatter, or hoard money because he was mendacious, servile, or miserly by nature. His motives were mixed; motives usually are. But in part he sacrificed his personal pride for the sake of his professional dignity. Goethe, who was inclined to be a little severe with Voltaire precisely because he admired his work, saw this shrewdly: "Rarely," he said, "has anyone made himself so dependent for the sake of independence."[9] This may be taken as a criticism, but it was also something else; it was the tribute one writer paid another for seeking what writers needed most of all —freedom.

III

While escape from poverty and dependence was essential to a writer's freedom, it was by itself not enough. The republic of letters subsisted in a world of oligarchies that protected their positions of privilege and power by controlling the flow of new ideas

---

[6] Hume to Rev. Hugh Blair and others, April 6, 1765. *Letters*, I, 497–8.
[7] *Le neveu de Rameau*, ed. Jean Fabre (1963), 44.
[8] *Mémoires*, in *Œuvres*, I, 39.
[9] *Dichtung und Wahrheit*, in *Gedenkausgabe*, X, 531–2.

and the latitude of critical comment. In many places, the authorities choked off meaningful public discussion altogether. "It's a real pity," Voltaire complained to Diderot, "that we cannot tell the truth whenever we touch on metaphysics, or even on history." Writers "are compelled to lie, and then they are still persecuted because they did not lie enough."[1] Voltaire was complaining about France, but to some degree his complaint held true all over the Continent: censors harassed, humiliated, and intimidated writers everywhere.

In the large tracts of territory controlled by the Hapsburgs, repression reached comical proportions. In 1765, the government at Vienna issued a *Catalogue of Forbidden Books*, which it periodically revised and kept up to date until, in 1777, it felt compelled to include this very *Catalogue* in its *Catalogue*: adventurous spirits, it seemed, were using the Hapsburg Index as a guide to interesting reading. It is true that when Joseph II came to the throne in 1780, he reformed things for a time: "Good German books," Nicolai reported from Vienna in 1783, "are now all permitted here," and this was a great improvement over the 1750s, when it was dangerous to betray even a casual familiarity with Montesquieu's *De l'esprit des lois*.[2] But then in 1790, not long before his death, Joseph retreated from his liberalism, and under his successors, with the specter of the French Revolution haunting Europe, repression returned with the old force and the old methods, with the old results—the paralysis of productive literary forces.

Most European states regarded politics, religion, and the ruling house as forbidden subjects. When Count Francesco Dalmazzo Vasco dared to translate the *De l'esprit des lois* of his "hero" Montesquieu, the Piedmontese authorities hounded him mercilessly, while other *illuministi*, like the Neapolitan historian Giannone, were excommunicated, exiled, or imprisoned. In the German states, political censorship was so oppressive that Lessing, in 1751, found the newspapers dull and dry.[3] The best of the journalists exercised some influence and manipulated their new weapon—the appeal to public opinion—with some skill, but even the newspapers published

---

[1] June 26 (1758). *Correspondence*, XXXIII, 278.
[2] This, at least, was Sonnenfels's recollection. See Biedermann: *Deutschland im achtzehnten Jahrhundert*, I, 128–38.
[3] See Lessing to his father, Johann Gottfried Lessing, February 8, 1751. *Schriften*, XVII, 24.

in Hanover and Hamburg, the freest spots on the German map, were largely innocuous. A. L. von Schlözer, professor and political journalist, published journals at Göttingen that princes professed to fear, but while Schlözer was without doubt the most outspoken journalist writing in the German language, his targets were chiefly administrative abuses crying out for reform, or petty princelings who took care not to strike back. Schlözer suavely professed submission to his own ruler and the deepest respect for all others, and escaped the censor's hand by selecting his victims with care and exercising rigorous self-censorship. Frederick II of Prussia professed horror at imposing fetters on free expression, and in the first years of his reign he checked the censors' pencils; but after 1749, when he restored the traditional controls, freedom of thought in Prussia (as Lessing put it with the humor of the helpless) came to consist mainly of anticlerical jokes. Appearances were belied by realities: "Sometimes," Nicolai wrote, "it seems as though we enjoyed freedom of the press in Germany, and scholars, who like to think that their writings have some influence, talk themselves into believing it. But in reality it's not so."[4]

The *Aufklärer* could testify to the accuracy of Nicolai's observation. When Lessing dared to publish fragments from Reimarus's deist treatise, he was silenced, and a few years later Kant was silenced as well under humiliating circumstances. Whatever constricted freedom writers had enjoyed in the long reign of Frederick the Great was choked off under his flighty but pious successor, and in 1794, Frederick William II himself severely reprimanded Kant for his *Religion innerhalb der Grenzen der blossen Vernunft*. Kant, to be sure, never recanted the religious views that had aroused his king, but after the incident he published nothing more on this sensitive subject. Eight years before, in 1786, the year of Frederick II's death, Kant had warned that without freedom of thought the unfolding of genius would come to an end; now, in 1793, the year of his little book on religion, he put it even more pointedly. "Freedom of the pen," he insisted, "is the sole safeguard of the rights of the people."[5] Kant was right, yet, as he sadly knew, freedom of the pen existed nowhere in Germany, not even in the self-proclaimed havens of freedom, Hanover and Prussia.

---

[4] Biedermann: *Deutschland im achtzehnten Jahrhundert*, I, 153.
[5] Cassirer: *Kants Leben und Lehre*, 393.

But compared to most of the other German states, Hanover or Prussia was a writer's paradise. Most princes were or wanted to be like Duke Charles Eugene of Württemberg, who in 1777 lured the Swabian publicist Schubart to his territory and kept him incarcerated for ten years, without trial and without charges. In his early years, Schubart had timidly aspired to become the Schlözer of southern Germany—in vain; his caution and servility failed to protect him from the authorities. In 1774 Schubart had started a journal, the *Deutsche Chronik*, in the Free City of Augsburg, and in the first number casually commented on the freedom enjoyed by Englishmen. The city government immediately suppressed the paper. Schubart moved elsewhere and began, a little more boldly, to bait the small princes, and to satirize the "tedious scribblings" offered up to "grand seigneurs" by fawning hacks.[6] But his experience in prison drove him, at least for some time, into the slavery he had so acidulously condemned: he became a hired scribbler for the duke who had incarcerated him. One cannot blame him; solitary confinement, dank cells, years without books or writing implements are not the soil in which independent spirits flourish.

Freedom was precarious everywhere. In June 1762 the Genevan government banned Rousseau's *Émile* and *Contrat social*, ordered the seizure of copies at booksellers, prohibited the importation of further copies, and called for Rousseau's arrest should he dare to enter Genevan territory. Even England, around whose freedom Continental philosophes wove such pleasing myths, encouraged writers to restrain themselves. Hume professed no surprise when he heard that Rousseau's books were banned in Geneva and elsewhere. Rousseau, he wrote, "has not had the precaution to throw any veil over his sentiments; and as he scorns to dissemble his contempt of established opinions, he could not wonder that all the zealots were in arms against him. The liberty of the press is not so secured in any country, scarce even in this, as not to render such an open attack of popular prejudices somewhat dangerous."[7]

In his own writings, Hume threw few veils over his sentiments, but he did take some precautions: in 1757 he told Adam Smith, who

---

[6] I am indebted for these quotations to an unpublished paper on Schubart by Mr. Theodor Brodek.
[7] Hume to the Comtesse de Boufflers, January 22, 1763. *Letters*, I, 374.

had read his "Natural History of Religion" in manuscript, that he would find the printed version "somewhat amended in point of Prudence,"[8] and he exercised even greater prudence with his *Dialogues Concerning Natural Religion.* Hume had completed the *Dialogues* in the early 1750s, and circulated them among a few intimates, who, to his dismay, all urged him to suppress the book. Hume reluctantly complied. In 1763 he comically appealed to his friend Gilbert Elliot: "Is it not hard & tyrannical in you, more tyrannical than any Acts of the Stuarts, not to allow me to publish my Dialogues? Pray, do you not think that a proper Dedication may atone for what is exceptionable in them?"[9] Hume's friends won out; the *Dialogues* were not published until after his death. In his last lingering illness, Hume laboriously corresponded with his publisher, William Strahan, and several times rewrote his will, which left the manuscript to Adam Smith; finally, two days before his death, he dictated the last of his letters, entrusting the *Dialogues* to his nephew, young David Hume. His heir followed his instructions, and the *Dialogues* appeared in 1779. They aroused no scandal and caused little comment. David Hume, who had wanted to live quietly and avoid "clamour"; Adam Smith, who had hoped to protect him from harassment; William Strahan, who backed out of his contract at the last moment—all had misjudged the temper of the times and the intentions of the authorities.

Since these were hardly timid men, their caution testifies to the uncertainties that beset writers even in Great Britain. Unquestionably, Britain, as Hume had been one of the first to assert, was the freest country in Europe. The panegyrics of French and German writers to English freedom were not groundless, since writers in England could say much without any fear: Sir Robert Walpole boasted that he had sent no scribblers to prison although many had deserved it. There was no formal censorship; the government had allowed the Licensing Act to lapse in 1695. But the authorities had other means of imposing restraint. Writers and publishers could be called before the bar of both Houses of Parliament for breach of privilege; stringent laws of libel, loosely interpreted by the courts, made the expression of unorthodox opinions rather risky; plays

---

[8] (February or March 1757). Ibid., I, 245.
[9] March 12, 1763. Ibid., I, 380.

were subject to the licensing power of the Lord Chamberlain. The pillory, the fine, or the prison were used rarely, but they were there, and British authors prudently protected themselves by voluntary self-censorship, deriding as license the liberty that would have made a real difference. "In a free country," wrote Henry Fielding in 1747, "the people have a right to complain of any grievance which affects them, and this is the privilege of an Englishman; but surely to canvass those high and nice points, which move the finest wheels of state, matters merely belonging to the royal prerogative, in print, is in the highest degree indecent, and a gross abuse of the liberty of the press."[1] But it would be too cynical to say that the British government did not employ censorship because there was so little to censor: David Hume, after all, excepting the *Dialogues*, felt little constraint at publishing his radical views on religion, and Gibbon felt none. The situation was not perfect, but from the other side of the Channel, especially from France, it looked like perfection.

The conflict between French writers and the French authorities were the noisiest, most protracted, and most inconclusive in Europe. On the one hand, not all censors censored, not all penalties penalized; some only aroused radicals to greater efforts. Censors were embroiled with one another over areas of jurisdiction, and they were too inconsistent, too venal, often too lazy to enforce the Draconic laws against blasphemous, heretical, and seditious writings. Besides, if a writer had some influential friends, he might find the Bastille a relatively comfortable residence, and in general, bribery and connections did much to ease the writer's lot. During the critical years of 1750 to 1763, the years when most of the *Encyclopédie*, Helvétius's *De l'esprit*, and Rousseau's major works were published, Malesherbes was in charge of censorship; and Malesherbes, a decent, cultivated public servant, thought it his duty to encourage talent rather than repress opinion. He did more to protect writers from the government than to protect the government from writers. If the old ordinances dating back to Francis I had been literally enforced, they would have stifled all but the most innocuous fairy tales and devout homilies: every piece of writing from

---

[1] Quoted in Laurence Hanson: *Government and the Press, 1695–1763* (1936), 2.

the weightiest treatise to the flightiest broadsheet was supposed to secure the official approval of a government censor, and to obtain the imprimatur, *Avec permission et privilège du Roi*, only if it contained not a single word offensive to Religion, State, or Morality. But they were not enforced; in practice, publishers concluded informal agreements with the censors. They would obtain an unofficial promise—a *permission tacite*—to exempt a book from prosecution even though it contained matter that prevented a censor from passing it. Most of the best-known books of eighteenth-century France— most of Voltaire, most of Montesquieu—reached the public under a *permission tacite*, in the twilight of semi-legality. But, one might add, they did after all reach the public.

All this is true, but it is not the whole truth. The government's small army of censors—there were 76 in the year 1741 and 178 in the year 1789—was staffed with stupid and fearful clerks, anxious to please their superiors. Not all censors were lax or corrupt; some were devoted to their repressive task. Besides, there was less risk in erring on the side of severity than on the side of leniency: one never knew what allusion might seem offensive to a bishop, a minister, or a royal mistress. Therefore, censors often held up manuscripts for months and engaged publishers in tedious, exhausting negotiations. "It is easier for me to write books," Voltaire said in some exasperation in 1744, "than to get them published."[2]

To make the writer's life even more unpredictable, the censors were not the only authorities to be pleased or placated. Powerful institutions like the church and the *parlements* had never wholly accepted the royal monopoly on censorship, and a book that had secured the *privilège* might still be condemned by magistrates, universities, or bishops. Time and again these vested interests were more watchful than the government and compelled the censors to do their duty. It was the concerted protests of the Sorbonne, the archbishop of Paris, and the Paris *parlement* that induced the government to renege on its tacit agreement to let Rousseau's *Émile* appear. Four years earlier, in 1758, a royal censor gave his approval to Helvétius's Utilitarian tract, *De l'esprit*, but then alert Christians read the book, were horrified, and aroused the cumbersome state machinery to

---

[2] Voltaire to Chevalier d'Espinasse (*c.* May 1, 1744). *Correspondence*, XIII, 221.

exert itself with unaccustomed energy. The censor was fired, the archbishop of Paris, the Attorney General, and the Pope himself joined the chorus of condemnation. Nothing much happened to Helvétius; he lost a lucrative court appointment and remained silent for a while. Yet all this uncertainty and inefficiency and caprice bred confusion among writers, anxiety, and often fear.

There was no way of stopping the new ideas. Forbidden books were printed at night in provincial towns, or smuggled into France from abroad. But these were Pyrrhic victories: clandestine editions were scarce and expensive. They increased their readership with their air of mystery, but their circulation remained limited: legal censorship became, in effect, economic censorship. In 1768 Diderot furiously told Falconet, "The intolerance of the government is growing day by day. One might think it's a deliberate plan to exterminate literature in this country, to ruin the book trade, and reduce us to beggary and stupidity. All the mss. are fleeing to Holland, and authors won't long delay in joining them. They're producing a trade in contraband books where one can make ten times as much profit as in cotton, tobacco, and salt. They're spending immense sums to make us buy brochures at insane prices—a sure way of ruining the state and the citizen. Le Christianisme dévoilé is selling for as much as four louis"—an enormous price.[3] Writers boasted that the public burning of a book—its fate decreed by law, and a favorite spectator sport—was only an advertisement for it. But when tempers ran high, writers saw the danger of the situation, not its humor. Publishers of books officially declared obscene or blasphemous were harassed by police raids, ruined by prohibitive fines, and sometimes condemned to the galleys. Without powerful protection, an author's career—in law, in the government, at the university—was in constant peril. Under Louis XIV and Louis XV, over a thousand booksellers and authors were incarcerated in the Bastille, and there were more harrowing places of detention for hundreds of others. Many of these were Voltaire's "literary canaille," pirates of manuscripts or purveyors of pornography, but some were serious literary men. In 1745, one Dubourg, the obscure editor of a satirical gazette, was put into a tiny cage at Mont Saint-Michel and died there in a fit of madness. As late as October 1768

---

[3] (May 1768.) Correspondance, VIII, 44–5.

Diderot reported that a book peddler, a *colporteur* named Lescuyer, who had sold copies of Holbach's *Christianisme dévoilé* and Voltaire's *L'Homme aux quarante écus*, had been arrested with his wife and his apprentice, and that all three were pilloried, whipped, and branded, the men sent to the galleys, and the wife to prison.[4] Dubourg and Lescuyer are forgotten now; they emerge from the shadows of history only in the correspondence of their more famous and more fortunate contemporaries, but prominent writers also suffered gross indignities. In 1749, Diderot, already on the way to acquiring a reputation as a philosopher, was condemned to solitary confinement in the fortress at Vincennes for his *Lettre sur les aveugles*. His room was airy and his food edible, but his solitude and his anxiety over the disposition of his case nearly drove him to a collapse. To his immense relief, he was freed a few weeks later, but the circumstances of his liberation were as humiliating as his incarceration had been wearing: he abjectly confessed to writing his bold little book, used the influence of his publishers, and agreed to dedicate the first volume of the *Encyclopédie* to comte d'Argenson, then director of publications. True, especially after mid-century, the best-known writers found themselves playing a harmless charade with the authorities: as long as Voltaire denied that he had written a book which was marked, by its incomparable style, as unmistakably his, the government was unlikely to prosecute him. But in an age of nervous bishops, unpredictable officials, and malicious courtiers, even Voltaire could not be wholly secure. Not all his fits of panic can be dismissed as hypochondria: when in July 1766 the French government burned the adolescent chevalier de La Barre at the stake for acts of blasphemy, one of the books thrown into the flames with him was Voltaire's *Dictionnaire philosophique*—a book, Diderot said later, La Barre had not owned. Nor was Voltaire alone in his anxiety. In 1768, Diderot, who was neither timid nor hysterical, told Sophie Volland, "I'm afraid that despite all the esteem, all the protection he enjoys, despite all his rare talents, all his fine works, those fellows will play our poor patriarch some bad trick"[5]—and by *mauvais tour* Diderot meant nothing less than burning at the stake. To say that the philosophes won their

---

[4] Diderot to Sophie Volland (October 8, 1768). Ibid., VIII, 186–7.
[5] Ibid., 187.

war with the French authorities is not to say that the battles were bloodless or the victory easy.

In this war, the philosophes used every weapon that came to hand—their connections, judicious outlays of money, and above all, lying. These tactics are familiar; I shall only add that they did not trouble the philosophes' consciences. They lied freely, with abandon, and often, I think, with pleasure. But whatever their deeper motives, the philosophes never had any doubt that they were doing the right thing. Rousseau, the solitary exception, only confirmed the uses of mendacity: Rousseau, who signed all he wrote, spent much of his life wandering from refuge to refuge. As early as 1709, Shaftesbury, living in much freer surroundings than the French philosophes, had noted that "if men are forbid to speak their minds seriously on certain subjects, they will do so ironically. If they are forbid to speak at all upon such subjects, or if they find it really dangerous to do so, they will then redouble their disguise, involve themselves in mysteriousness, and talk so as hardly to be understood."[6] This of course was not precisely what the philosophes wanted; they wanted above all to be understood by the public. But they did feel, as Shaftesbury had felt, that if they were mysterious, they were forced to be so by the authorities. In the eighteenth century, honest men like d'Alembert and Condorcet, Buffon and Diderot, defended lying on the grounds of self-defense. "A lie is a vice only when it does harm," was Voltaire's dictum in 1736, "it is a very great virtue when it does good. So, be more virtuous than ever. You must lie like a devil, not timidly, not for a while, but boldly, and persistently. . . . Lie, my friends, lie, I shall repay you when I get the chance."[7]

Voltaire repaid his friends later, in the 1750s and after, when he made himself into the chief strategist of the little flock, giving directions from Ferney on how to lie, and to whom: "I never want it said," he wrote in 1764 to his Paris correspondent Damilaville about his *Dictionnaire philosophique*, "that I wrote this book; I have written to M. Marin in this vein, since he spoke to me about it in his last letter. I flatter myself that the true brethren will back

---

[6] "An Essay on the Freedom of Wit and Humour," *Characteristics*, I, 50.
[7] Voltaire to Thieriot, October 28 (1736). *Correspondence*, V, 286-7.

me up. This work must be regarded as a collection from several writers put together by a Dutch editor. It is extremely cruel to name me: it would deprive me henceforth of the freedom to render services. The philosophes must make the truth public and hide their persons."[8] This, of course, was precisely the point. The philosophes lied in order to tell the truth; they discovered that duplicity is inescapable in a society that denies criticism free range, especially if its literary men, lacking the missionary's taste for martyrdom, burn with the missionary's zeal for making converts.

IV

For the most part, the republic of letters was a casual association, held together by friendly suppers, informal club meetings in taverns and coffeehouses, and extensive correspondence. But in France, it was severely and rationally organized into the *Académie française*, and its control was therefore a political question of some importance. Since 1634–5, when Richelieu had founded the *Académie française* to guard the purity and supervise the development of the French language, literary men had aspired to belong to its exclusive circle. It had traversed brilliant periods and dull stretches; it had been dominated by deserving literary men and supple courtiers. But prosperous or mediocre, the *Académie française* was a symbol of esteem and therefore a source of power. To be elected meant to join a select group, the Forty Immortals, to speak as an equal to all other members, be he duke or cardinal, and to obey no veto but that of the royal protector himself. In the course of the eighteenth century the philosophes set about to capture the institution, not with any preconcerted plan—they were a family, not a cabal—but from a shrewd sense of social and political realities mixed with literary ambitions.

It is a platitude at least as old as Aesop that men often affect to despise what they cannot hope to obtain, and so, early in the French Enlightenment, the philosophes ridiculed an *Académie* that was reluctant to elect them. When Montesquieu characterized it in 1721 as a tribunal that no one respects, as a club whose members

---

[8] September 19, 1764. Ibid., LVI, 31–2.

chatter without end but do nothing else, nothing seemed further from his mind than his own candidacy; yet he, like practically every self-respecting writer in France, aspired to it.[9] Indeed, after 1727, his witticisms against the *Académie* ceased: he had been elected. A few years later, Voltaire expended his satiric talents on the traditional discourse delivered by each new member to inaugurate his tenure. By rigid custom these addresses were flowery panegyrics on the member's predecessor and on the Academy's supreme patron, and they lent themselves to ridicule: "After the new member has asserted that his predecessor was a great man, that Cardinal Richelieu was a very great man, chancellor Séguier a passably great man, and Louis XIV a more than great man, the chairman replies in the same vein and adds that the new member might well be a kind of great man too." Voltaire suggested that these eulogies not be printed: the awkward character of the opening speech made even witty men appear absurd.[1] This was in 1734. In 1736, Voltaire was making some flowery speeches of his own, for he had ventured to offer himself as a candidate. It was a long, arduous candidacy, and Voltaire paid penance for his early irreverence. He had made too many prominent enemies to be elected promptly, and was passed over, for all his international fame and indisputable distinction. His ordeal did not end until 1746, and after that, after he had safely joined the Immortals, he began to discover virtues in the institution he had so mercilessly lampooned before.

With the election of Voltaire, the *Académie* began to change its composition and improve its intellectual style: Duclos was elected in the same year, Buffon in 1753, d'Alembert in 1754. At first the new members behaved simply as loyal and intelligent Academicians. Buffon delivered his celebrated *Discours sur le style*, Voltaire a widely applauded address on the *Universalité de la langue française*, d'Alembert a variety of interesting papers, and with these performances, the new Immortals enhanced the reputation of the Academy with the literate public. But then, in the late 1750s, as new member succeeded new member, and as the philosophes acquired notoriety, the Academy was inescapably drawn into the ideological struggle for the mind of France.

The conflict erupted in 1760. On March 10, a new member,

---

[9] See *Lettres persanes*, in *Œuvres*, I, part 3, 152–3.
[1] Lettre XXIV, *Lettres philosophiques*, II, 173–4.

Lefranc de Pompignan, a nobleman of the robe, brother of a bishop, and a hopelessly minor poet, used his opening discourse as a forum to denounce the threat of impiety. "The true philosopher," he declaimed, "is a wise and virtuous Christian," a dictum offensive to pagans who thought they were the only true philosophers. Modern men of letters, Lefranc warned, were undermining the time-honored hierarchy of birth and destroying respect for throne and altar.

This was inflammatory talk, for the year was 1760, and the atmosphere had already been poisoned by the controversy over Helvétius's *De l'esprit* and the government's suppression of the *Encyclopédie*. Unfortunately—for Lefranc de Pompignan—he had committed some philosophical indiscretions in earlier years and left deist sentiments on the public record, and now Voltaire took it upon himself to deliver a rebuttal in the name of the philosophes, outside the sacred precincts of the Academy. In his curt polemic, *Les quand*, Voltaire laid down a barrage of reminders: "*When* one has the honor of being received into a respectable company of literary men, one should not turn one's inaugural speech into a satire against men of letters . . . *when* one has translated, and 'improved,' Pope's Deist Prayer; *when* one has been suspended for six months from one's provincial post for translating that deist creed and making it more poisonous . . . then it is an insult to good manners to give oneself airs in speaking of religion; *when* one delivers to an Academy one of those discourses people talk about for a day or so, but which might be carried to the foot of the throne, then, if one dares to say in that discourse that the philosophy of our time undermines throne and altar, one has committed an offense against one's fellow citizens . . ." and so on, through a catalogue of *whens*, which are telling, irrefutable—and, in their pointedness, really untranslatable.

Les quand was admired and widely imitated. Morellet wrote the *Pourquoi*, others the *Quis* and the *Quois*—Voltaire was often a setter of literary fashions. Unwisely, Lefranc de Pompignan chose to reply. In May he sent a boastful address to Louis XV, claiming to have vanquished irreligion, and to be the king's favorite reading matter. This was provocative and, to Voltaire, irresistible; in June he replied with a collection of satires in which Pompignan appears as a poor devil, a mediocrity bloated with self-importance and misguided zeal:

> Et l'ami Pompignan pense être quelque chose!

It was the end: Pompignan never went back to the Academy, and in the years that followed, his allies gradually shrank to a minority.[2] When d'Alembert was elected perpetual secretary in 1772, the *Académie française* was securely in the philosophes' hands.

All of this controversy seems like a mock battle in a burlesque war, too trivial, indeed too ludicrous, to belong into the realm of serious politics. But graver issues have been settled by slighter means; the French philosophes' avidity to dominate the Academy cannot be dismissed as a commentary on the fallibility of reformers —the stakes were high. In the turbulent sixties, control of the *Académie française* meant relative immunity from persecution and privileged access to a new and still rather mysterious power—public opinion. Persecution had grown more sporadic, but it had not wholly lost its sting. When young La Barre was decapitated and his body burned at the stake, Voltaire fled from Ferney to Geneva, and tried to form a colony of French writers abroad. "The scene which has just taken place in Paris," he wrote to Morellet, "conclusively proves that the brethren must carefully hide their mysteries and the names of their fellows. . . . In such baneful circumstances sages must keep quiet and wait."[3] Diderot was inclined to wait rather than emigrate, but he agreed with Voltaire that there was reason for alarm. "My friend," he wrote to Falconet in August 1766, a little more than a month after La Barre's execution, "men of letters are not as free as you think. They too have their despots, without whose permission it is forbidden to appear and to succeed."[4] And he also agreed with Voltaire that the recent dissolution of the Jesuit order in France, far from weakening the forces of persecution, had merely strengthened the anti-Jesuit fanatics and would permit them to concentrate their rage on the new ideas. I know, he told Voltaire in October 1766, using Voltaire's language, that this "ferocious beast" —the *parlements*—"lacks nourishment, and now that it has no more Jesuits to eat, it will throw itself on the philosophes."[5] And a year later, after the excitement over the La Barre case had died down, he still felt the old constraints: "Literature languishes," he wrote.

---

[2] For the whole incident, see Voltaire: "Les quand," *Œuvres,* XXIV, 111–13, and 111 *n.*
[3] July 7 (1766). *Correspondence,* LXII, 14–15.
[4] *Correspondance,* VI, 259.
[5] Ibid., 334.

Writers are forbidden to discuss "government, religion, and morals.
What else should they subsist on? The rest isn't worth the effort."[6]

Yet in the midst of these anxieties, the philosophes came increasingly to express, and to dominate, the forces of progress. In
1787, the French historian Rulhière told a receptive *Académie française* that it had been in 1749—precisely in 1749, not a year earlier,
or later—that philosophy had liberated itself from polite literature
and Paris had liberated itself from the Court: "It was then that there
arose among us what we have come to call *the empire of public
opinion*."[7] The philosophes themselves had a strong sense of the
changing atmosphere: Voltaire confidently claimed that just at the
time that public opinion was beginning to rule France, the philosophes were beginning to rule public opinion; and other philosophes
reiterated that mid-century marked, in d'Alembert's firm conviction,
an epoch in the history of ideas.[8]

It marked an epoch because the growing radicalism and increasing freedom of the Enlightenment reflected and produced irreversible, if often subterranean, changes in Western politics, economy,
and society. As democrats and atheists took the lead in the family
of philosophes, radicals rebelled against constituted authority all
over the Western world; as the industrial discipline and the invention of new techniques in manufacturing, in agriculture, in medicine, and in government grew at an accelerating pace, Voltaire came
out into the open with his campaign to *écraser l'infâme*, Rousseau
brought out his two revolutionary books, *Contrat social* and its
companion piece, *Émile*, Diderot completed his *Encyclopédie* and
composed, even if he did not publish, some of his most subversive
dialogues, Lessing published his literary criticism, Beccaria his *Dei
delitti e delle pene*, Holbach his first materialist broadsides. If mid-
century marked an epoch in the history of ideas, it was the philosophes' ideas that marked it, and the philosophes, anxious or not,
were happy to note the fact. The Enlightenment and its world
moved toward modernity together, with the philosophes, goading
and guiding, a single but decisive step ahead.

---

[6] Diderot to Falconet, May 15, 1767. Ibid., VII, 56.
[7] Arthur M. Wilson quotes a long passage from Rulhière's address
in *Diderot: The Testing Years*, 94–5.
[8] For d'Alembert's pronouncement, which has often been quoted,
see Ernst Cassirer: *The Philosophy of the Enlightenment* (1932;
tr. Fritz Koelln and James P. Pettegrove, 1951), 3–4.

2. FROM PAST TO FUTURE:
THE GREAT REORIENTATION

I

IN INCORPORATING THE RECOVERY of nerve into their program, the philosophes resolved their ambivalence toward antiquity and accomplished their emancipation. The ancients had felt helpless before the forces of nature and man's irrationality, and the philosophers of antiquity had rationalized this impotence in systems pervaded by a profound pessimism. To philosophize was to learn how to die; to study history was to trace the decline of mankind from some golden age of innocence, honor, and virility. Even the ambitious political constructions of Plato and Aristotle, which rested on the assumption that man can manage his own affairs, were largely designed as measures of defense against the ubiquitous threat of tyranny or the savage power of the passions. With all their admiration for classical thought, the philosophes could not remain content with such resigned philosophizing; instead, with their activism and their practicality, they completed the great reorientation in man's view of life under way since the Renaissance.

Gloom had prevailed even in the Enlightenment's favorite classical philosophers: Lucretius' *De rerum natura*, which the philosophes liked to read as a model of aggression, a plan of campaign to *écraser l'infâme*, was dominated by a melancholy that the eighteenth century did not share, and did not even see. It is a somber mood, which a twentieth-century reader would be tempted to describe as existentialist despair. Goethe saw it: Lucretius, he told von Müller in 1821, had fallen into extremism, embittered by prevailing superstitions. "Through the whole didactic poem," he said, "we sense a dark, grim spirit."[9] More recently, George Santayana discovered more than melancholy in the poem; he describes Lucretius' attack on the fear of death as a fear of life: "The force of the great passage against the fear of death, at the end of the third book . . ."

---

[9] February 20, 1821. *Gespräche*, in *Gedenkausgabe*, XXIII, 121-2.

he writes, "comes chiefly from the picture it draws of the madness of life."[1]

Santayana's paradox deserves exploration. Philosophers of antiquity sought to free men from the fear of death, for, once freed from this fear, men would be beyond superstitious terrors and morbid preoccupations. A tyrant had no leverage on the man who enjoyed this freedom, for what did threats, extortions, tortures mean to him? In the light of the political situation in ancient Rome—and it was from Rome, after all, not from Greece, that the philosophes drew most of their classical intellectual nourishment—freedom from the fear of death was a reasonable philosophical aim, since the political freedom of philosophers usually amounted to little more than the freedom to endure. Sometimes the accomplices, more often the victims of decadent governments and capricious dictatorships, philosophers lived in a world of ruinous insecurity and a ruthlessness that stopped quite literally at nothing. Their insistence on man's right to suicide was thus the recognition of a terrible reality in which dignified life was sometimes impossible. As Voltaire noted, Caesar objected to the death penalty for his friend Catiline because, "to put a criminal to death is not to punish him." After all, death "is nothing"; it is the end of our ills, "more a happy than a dreadful moment."[2] For the ancients, the right to choose one's moment to depart was sacred and undeniable. The free man, they said sententiously, will always find the door open.

The philosophers of antiquity were divided by irreconcilable differences in doctrine; they flung disdainful invectives at one another, called each other pedant, fanatic, bigot, or sensualist. But on this one issue they agreed; fear of death is the supreme enemy of life. Cicero, who thought it his business to reconcile philosophical systems, makes this consensus explicit in the first of his *Tusculan Disputations*, where he echoes Socrates. Death is not an evil, he argues, no matter what philosophical school one may adopt. If the soul is immortal (as the Stoics taught and as Cicero liked to believe) it will not suffer eternal pain in the nether regions; Hades is the foolish fancy of superstitious men. If the soul is mortal (as the Epicureans maintained, braving charges of impiety) immediate dis-

---

[1] *Three Philosophical Poets* (edn. 1953), 53.
[2] "Atheist, Atheism," *Philosophical Dictionary*, I, 101–2.

solution means complete insensibility—and who needs to fear that which he does not feel?

It was this ubiquitous preoccupation that made Socrates the folk hero of pagan antiquity. Socrates had conquered the problems of life by confronting and defeating death. The story of Socrates' final hours had moved the ancients to heroism as it moved moderns to awe. Death was worth admiring only if it resembled the death of Socrates. One such death was that of Julius Canus, a Roman aristocrat, whose last days were celebrated by Seneca. After an altercation with Caligula, the Emperor ordered Canus executed. The condemned man spent the ten days before the sentence was carried out without any anxiety whatever, mainly playing *latrunculis,* an antique form of chess, with his friends. He was in the middle of a game "when the centurion who was dragging a column of condemned men to their death ordered Canus summoned too. Having been summoned, he counted the pieces and said to his companion: 'See that you don't lie after my death and claim that you won.' Then, nodding to the centurion, he said, 'You're witness that I'm one piece ahead.' " When his friends lamented the loss of such a man, Canus urged them not to be sad, and promised to report back on the condition of souls after death if they should after all turn out to be immortal. He maintained his Stoical courage to the very end. "*Ecce in media tempestate tranquillitas, ecce animus aeternitate dignus,*" Seneca exclaims: "Here, in the midst of the storm, is tranquillity! Here is a mind worthy of immortality!" Such tales became conventions in Latin literature—the *Annales* of Tacitus, for example, break off with an account of two Stoic suicides—but Seneca appears deeply engaged in Canus' fate: "*Non raptim relinquetur magnus vir et cum cura dicendus. Dabimus te in omnem memoriam!*" he concludes. "Such a great man should not be hastily given up, and we must make a point of speaking about him. I shall hand you down to the memory of all ages!"[3]

For philosophical minds in antiquity, then, death was the capstone of life; it was the supreme opportunity for demonstrating that one's philosophy was authentic and that it could withstand the final, most severe test. And death was (through posthumous biographies and funerary monuments) an occasion to glance back at life, to

---

[3] *De tranquillitate animi,* XIV, 7–10.

recount glorious deeds done. Christianity retained the preoccupation with death but changed its spiritual significance and reversed its meaning. Death became an opportunity for repentance, if one was fortunate enough to die in the full possession of one's faculties; and it was, for everyone, the porch to the future life: the Christian conceived of death not as the last act of a heroic drama, but as the first act of an eternity of bliss or torment, to which earthly existence had been mere prologue. For over a thousand years priests chided their errant flocks for loving life too much: the good Christian ought to love God and pray for salvation. The only conduct in this world that deserved to be remembered, and celebrated in retrospect, was the martyrdom of saints.

In the Renaissance and the seventeenth century, the Christian view of death came to be complicated by growing admixtures of classical thought. Elaborate monuments celebrated human greatness, flattered family vanity, and made death appear truly horrible—as the enemy, not the deliverer of man. Death was now portrayed as a hideous skeleton, emphasizing, by its very horror, the new value of life. For rigorous Christians mindful of the great tradition, seventeenth-century ways of dying appeared singularly impure: to die with fear seemed like a criticism of the Divine arrangements; to die without fear seemed all too often like a pagan, philosophical acceptance of the universe. The devout all over Europe found harsh old lessons on the art of dying replaced by gentler lessons on the art of Christian living. Christians still understood that to die was (as Cardinal Newman would say in the nineteenth century) "going home," but the contours of the Christian's eternal home grew dim as believers, under the benign guidance of Arminian pastors and modern priests, sought to reconcile their duty to God with their duty to polite society.

But while the pompous monuments to Renaissance princes or the bland sermons of Anglican divines display a passionate attachment to life, it was the philosophes who expressed the new worldliness most clearly, without pious circumlocutions. As usual, the philosophes appealed from Christianity to classical thought and then, having made their polemical point, they mitigated their classicism with a modern confidence in this world.

The exploitation of antiquity, then, is simply another example of the philosophes' characteristic attitude to their past. Diderot retells Seneca's own account of Canus' heroism, and adds his account of Seneca's own philosophical suicide; thus Diderot borrows the prestige of antique philosophizing for his own polemical purposes. Seneca had said that he "must make a point of speaking" about Canus; by speaking about him he will rescue him from oblivion. By bearing witness, the philosopher gives immortality to the man of courage, and breathes this courage into others. Now, by quoting Seneca at length, Diderot justifies Seneca's confidence that Canus will be long remembered, and by celebrating Seneca's own brave death, Diderot immortalizes another Roman who died well. More than any other discipline, Diderot implies, philosophy repairs the ravages of time and defies the calendar: "O Seneca!" he exclaims, "you are and will always be, with Socrates, with all the illustrious unhappy men, with all the great men of antiquity, one of the sweetest links between my friends and me, between the educated men of all ages and their friends. You have remained the subject of our frequent conversations; and you will remain the subject of theirs."[4] Our century, uncomfortable with the subject and inclined to attribute a brave death to luck or temperament rather than philosophy, may find this enthusiasm a little strained and even embarrassing. But for men seeking to vindicate the autonomy of philosophy and its superiority to all other guides to life, philosophical bravery in the face of death was simply another argument against the need for religion.

Death, then, was in the largest sense of the word a political issue in the eighteenth century. If there was a good pagan way to die, this threw doubts on some of the most cherished of Christian beliefs. Just as St. Jerome had attempted to discredit Lucretius by dismissing him as a madman and a suicide, so eighteenth-century Christians waged an undignified debate over Voltaire's last moments. The evidence was and must remain incomplete, but the devout entertained two possibilities: they either gleefully reported that Voltaire had died a repentant Catholic, or they charged, just as gleefully, that the old devil had died in horrible torment. Many years later, Flaubert revived the old stories: in *Madame Bovary* the abbé Bournisien edifies the faithful every other Sunday with tales of Voltaire's last agony. On their side, the philosophes, as unfeeling

---

[4] *Essai sur les règnes de Claude et de Néron*, in *Œuvres*, III, 12.

as their adversaries, invented details to prove that Voltaire had
maligned Jesus in his last breath. The controversy seems callous
to us, and irrelevant, but it enlisted the passions of the eighteenth
century.

While there was some question about the manner of Voltaire's
end, there could be none about Hume's: it was reported too fully
to admit of any controversy.[5] Hume had died, as he had lived, with
cool, ironic courage, as a complete pagan; and he was not an isolated case. When Rousseau, adopting the magisterial Spartan manner
that is such a persistent and troublesome undertone in his writings,
pronounced that in his day men no longer knew how to die, he was
giving way to unwarranted nostalgia.

Hume, like other philosophes, had defended man's right to
suicide, aligning himself with the classical writers and making light
of Christian prohibitions. Yet it is worth noting in passing that
while the philosophes explored the subject of suicide at some length
and approved of it on principle, none of them—with the unlikely
exception of Condorcet, who in any event faced certain death—
resorted to it, no matter what their private sufferings. Life, with all
its tedium, all its disappointments and misery, was worth living.
As cheerless a subject as death brought out Hume's cheerfulness,
and surely Voltaire, however he died, clung to life with the tenacity
of a man who loved it and had no expectation of anything beyond
it. In his treatise, *The Brevity of Life*, Seneca had sententiously articulated what nearly all thoughtful ancients, in Greece and Rome,
believed: "Learning how to live is learning how to die." His precursors had prepared the way for this Stoic maxim with dialogues
on the nothingness of existence, on the serene condition of death,
and on the absurdity of fearing what one should greet with joy.
It was the kind of maxim a classicist like Diderot could appreciate;
he quoted it, and then turned it around, somewhat brightening its
tone in the process. "To learn how to die," he wrote, "is to learn
how to live well."[6] But the rest of Diderot's work, with its variety,
its abundant vitality, its stubborn hope in the midst of discouragement and occasional weariness, suggests that his preoccupation with
learning how to die was mainly a classical reminiscence. For the

[5] For a short account of Hume's stoical death, see *The Rise of
Modern Paganism*, 356–7.
[6] *Essai sur les règnes de Claude et de Néron*, in *Œuvres*, III, 339.

eighteenth century in general, and for the Enlightenment especially, the issue was not so much to die well—one did this at the end, as best as one could—but to live to the point.

II

The philosophes' love of the world had one ironic aspect: it was directed toward the future, and thus rather oddly resembled the Christian concern with salvation. But while the resemblance is striking, it is rhetorical rather than substantive. The eighteenth-century Christian, to the extent that he thought of it at all, hoped to live so that he might deserve heaven; the philosophe on the other hand hoped to live so he might deserve the applause of posterity— to the extent that *he* thought of it at all, for there is little evidence that the philosophes were much preoccupied with their posthumous reputations. But there were times when they visualized themselves as they might appear to future ages, and then they wanted to be remembered for their labors in behalf of humanity.

As so often in the Enlightenment, it was Diderot who probed the question most energetically. Beginning late in 1765, and through the following year, he exchanged a dozen letters with his friend, the sculptor Falconet, in which he analyzed and defended man's longing for the applause of future generations. They are long letters, some of them long enough to make up a sizable pamphlet; they are learned, voluble, and extravagant. But with all their repetitiveness, all their occasional bombast and obtrusive classical allusions, they offer valuable evidence for the distance separating Christians from philosophes. Diderot made that distance explicit in an epigram: "What posterity is for the philosopher," he wrote, "the other world is for the religious man."[7] Posterity and heaven, Diderot told Falconet, are mental constructs that may serve the same psychological purpose; both may satisfy a craving for some sort of survival after death, for *le sentiment de l'immortalité et le respect de la postérité*.[8] Nevertheless, the two notions have different origins and produce very different forms of conduct.

---

[7] Diderot to Falconet (February 15, 1766). *Correspondance*, VI, 67.
[8] See Diderot to Sophie Volland (November 21, 1765), ibid., V, 190, and elsewhere—this formulation is evidently a favorite with him.

In fact, Diderot's argument is throughout strenuously secular and aggressively anti-Christian. Mankind, he argues, is by nature too ambitious for glory to be content with renown in its own sphere: "If our productions could go to Saturn, we should like to be praised on Saturn."[9] This craving for applause is best satisfied by an appeal to the future: the praise of contemporaries is distorted by jealousy and the ambitions of others; the praise of future generations may rise to disinterested admiration for historic deeds or great works of art, for good taste, the supreme arbiter, is a being that never dies. To be sure—Diderot insists on this—posterity is a present, not a future, reality. It appears in the imagination while men are performing the actions which, they hope, will bring them immortality; men like to visualize just how later generations will appreciate a noble speech, a fine piece of sculpture, or a generous act like, say, Voltaire's efforts in behalf of the Calas family. "Posterity is only the echo of the present corrected by experience."[1] And, just as posterity materializes, as it were, only in living men, so it exists solely for their sake; men achieve immortality only through works remembered, but never in their bodies or their souls. Most men, Diderot wrote, perish like dumb beasts; only a few men of virtue and talent die with glory, and it is "their sweetest reward to count on the gratitude of posterity."[2]

Diderot was so sure of the psychological efficacy of this reward that he was ready to support it even if it should turn out to be an illusion. He did not think it an illusion, but even if it were, he insisted, men should live by it, for it would lift up their souls and strengthen them against the sense of loss and impermanence that often afflicts fathers as they contemplate their children, or artists as they contemplate their works. Diderot was willing to preach a myth for the sake of its utility, much as Rousseau a few years before had defended the social uses of a profession of faith. But Diderot's myth was secular; it demanded no supernatural mysteries, claimed no religious sanctions. To allow men to hope for the respect of posterity was to give them a motive for virtuous action, and so Diderot's very myth becomes a characteristic expression of the Enlightenment's passion for effectiveness.

---

[9] Diderot to Falconet (January 10, 1766). Ibid., VI, 15.
[1] Diderot to the same (February 15, 1766). Ibid., VI, 84.
[2] Diderot to the same (January 27, 1766). Ibid., VI, 37.

III

The Enlightenment's concentration on the future as a realm of unrealized possibilities invited a corresponding depreciation of the past. The philosophes did not repudiate history; they found it amusing, instructive, and intensely interesting. But they could not take it as an authoritative guide. The past—especially the classical past—was a storehouse of glorious, unsurpassable achievements, especially in literature and morals, and a museum of appealing figures. But the past was also, and for the most part, a tragic pile of error and crime, to be studied for mistakes to avoid and injustices to repair, not for models to imitate. Of all arguments in behalf of an idea or an act, the argument from tradition struck the philosophes as the most treacherous and least cogent: "At best," Locke had laid it down, "an argument from what has been, to what should of right be, has no great force,"[3] and the philosophes agreed with him.

In agreeing with Locke, the philosophes were on this point at odds with the ancients. As the ancients had looked to death as the confirmation of life, they had looked to the past for their ideals; Diderot's admiring remark that the ancients had no ancients of their own may have been witty, but it was wrong. In fact, the Romans, and to some degree the Greeks before them, had been steeped in nostalgia; as urbane, civilized men they had celebrated rustic heroes and Arcadian shepherds.

Nostalgia runs deep in the human psyche; it is almost irresistible, all the more so because it generally masquerades as rational criticism of the present (where there is always much to criticize) and rational praise of the past (where there is always much to praise). But nostalgia drives reasonable criticism and reasonable praise to unreasonable lengths: it converts healthy dissatisfactions into an atavistic longing for a simpler condition, for a childhood of innocence and happiness remembered in all its crystalline purity precisely because it never existed. Nostalgia is the most sophistic, most deceptive form regression can take.

The Greeks invented this regression by inventing the pastoral

---

[3] John Locke: *Second Treatise of Civil Government*, para. 103.

—a rustic genre that only an urban civilization could have produced. The Romans were haunted by it: it was Cicero, a man of the world and presumably a tough-minded politician, who exclaimed, *O tempora, o mores!* Nothing moved him or, after him, Seneca so deeply as the recollection of the simple manners practiced by the early republicans, their plain fare and unadorned clothing, the legendary courage of the men and the unspotted virtue of the women. Regulus, who returned to Carthage to face certain torture and death rather than break his word, touched men many centuries before, and men much less sentimental than, Rousseau. Horace, urbane and disillusioned, devoted a moving ode to Regulus, and in the midst of fame and pleasures wrote other odes lamenting the decay of Roman virtue and the corruption of his own time. Even Juvenal, usually too busy denouncing the vulgarity and decadence on the contemporary scene to indulge in backward glances, wondered out loud in his second Satire what the Scipios and the brave young men who died at Cannæ would have thought of the perfumed dandies and lascivious ladies who were infesting and misgoverning the Rome of his day.

Such mythmaking—the primitivism of time—was accompanied by the glorification of Rome's neighbors—the primitivism of space. Noble savages lived not only in Rome's past, but also on Rome's borders: the heroic legends of the Greeks and Romans were projected on Germans or Persians. Tacitus was not merely writing a primitivist Utopia in his *Germania*, but the note of idealization is unmistakable; and other Roman writers professed to find the good man, unspoiled by luxury or vain philosophizing, in the tribes and nations that surrounded them.

Not all of this primitivism deserves to be taken seriously. Some of it was political propaganda. It served the purposes of an emperor like Augustus, who (as Gibbon was to recognize) made a revolution in the name of a restoration, and built a new state with the rhetoric of the old; it served to cloak in dignified words the resistance of reactionaries to the reform of class relations and the improvement of social habits. Besides, in antiquity nostalgia often had a critical function: it was usually the only form of criticism repressive governments would permit. Nor did this nostalgia itself go uncriticized; Greeks and Romans alike countered it with healthy doses of common sense. The poets urged their readers to live in the present, and

Seneca, whose essays are filled with primitivist preachments, still recognized that most talk of decadence was merely literary convention. Tacitus could check himself in the midst of a long critique of Rome's decay to observe with remarkable objectivity that, after all, "Not everything was better in the past; our own age, too, has produced many specimens of excellence and culture for posterity to imitate."[4] In the same vein, Petronius deplored the stifling of poetic talent by the rhetoricians of his age and professed to long for the days of Euripides, but he advised young poets to study the past with diligence and then free themselves from their precious burden to give voice to their own genius. It was only in the age of the Antonines, when cultural decay, or at least civilized weariness, could no longer be arrested, that an antiquarian rage seized the educated. They celebrated the feats of long-neglected heroes, worshipfully visited ruins like so many ancient Winckelmanns, and strained to restore the purity of republican manners in the midst of an aging cosmopolitan empire.

Nostalgia survived the Roman Empire, and through the centuries, poets, novelists, and essayists experimented with many forms of primitivism. They idealized happy Indians, wise Chinese, decent aborigines, and even affectionate beasts—all good, pure, and brave, and better, purer, and braver the larger their distance from the artifices of urban culture. Montaigne's wry praise of cannibals, and Dryden's felicitous term, "the noble savage," retained their popularity in the age of the Enlightenment. While most philosophers, and most philosophes, celebrated cultivation, a minority of cultural critics eloquently voiced their disgust with civilization and exploited the paradox that the very acquirements polite men valued most were most baneful.

Yet, at least among the philosophes, this cultural criticism was primitivist mainly in its trappings, not in its aims. Like other radicals, the philosophes also occasionally indulged in nostalgic fantasies; they sympathetically read poets who thought night thoughts, or novelists who constructed imaginary cultures. But their own "primitivist" writings—Rousseau's first two *Discours*, and Diderot's *Supplément au Voyage de Bougainville*—were critical rather than sentimental. Rousseau, it is true, has long had the reputation of a

---

[4] *Annales*, III, 3.

primitivist, and that reputation had its origins among the philosophes themselves. Diderot described Rousseau's famous *Discours sur les sciences et les arts* as "an old warmed-over quarrel," an "apologia for ignorance," which exalted the "savage over the civilized state."[5] And Voltaire wittily thanked Rousseau for sending him the *Discours sur l'origine de l'inégalité*, that "new book against the human race."[6] But both Diderot's strictures and Voltaire's wit, often so accurate, were misplaced here. For all his rhetorical extravagance and love of paradox, all his genuine revulsion against the sophistication and mendacity of modern culture, Rousseau directed his energy toward discovering not a state of nature without culture but a culture that would realize man's true nature. "Human nature," he insisted, "cannot turn back. Once man has left the time of innocence and equality, he can never return to it."[7] Rousseau idealized simplicity, affection, family life, bucolic feasts, legendary Roman and equally legendary Spartan heroes. But his nostalgia was never for a primitive state of nature. Rousseau's natural savage is an amiable, amoral, and fundamentally uninteresting beast.

In this analysis, Rousseau was at one with most writers who have appealed to nature as a judgment on civilization. There are few true primitivists. And obviously—as Diderot's response to Rousseau shows—one man's primitivism is another man's cultivation. It

---

[5] *Essai sur les règnes de Claude et de Néron*, in *Œuvres*, III, 95.

[6] Voltaire to Rousseau (August 30, 1755). *Correspondence*, XXVII, 230. It is interesting to note that this misreading of Rousseau was quite popular. Thus the English novelist, Mrs. Frances Brooke, said of Rousseau's second *Discours:* "Rousseau has taken great pains to prove that the most uncultivated nations are the most virtuous: I have all due respect for this philosopher, of whose writings I am an enthusiastic admirer; but I have a still greater respect for the truth, which I believe is not in this instance on his side. . . . From all that I have observed, and heard of these people, it appears to me an undoubted fact, that the most civilized Indian nations are the most virtuous; a fact which makes directly against Rousseau's ideal system." Quoted in Lois Whitney: *Primitivism and the Idea of Progress in English Popular Literature of the Eighteenth Century* (1934), 124–5.

[7] *Rousseau Juge de Jean-Jacques*, in *Œuvres*, I, 935. Another useful work in which to observe Rousseau's supposed primitivism is his *Considérations sur le gouvernement de Pologne* (1772), in which he commends to the Poles an increased emphasis on agriculture, encouragement of simple customs, and wholesome tastes—all goals to be achieved within the frame of civilization.

is amusing to read Diderot's *Supplément au Voyage de Bougainville* in the light of his critique of Rousseau, for Diderot offers an idealized Tahitian tribe whose elders are deist natural philosophers and whose members affirm life, enjoy sex, and always tell the truth. But the *Supplément* is not in the main a primitivist tract. It is in some respects a minority report, a dissent from the prevailing infatuation with the refinements of Western civilization. It is, besides, a playful exploration of alternative moral positions, so typical of Diderot's experimental method. It is also what I have called a cross-cultural dialogue, designed to expose the poisonous consequences of Christian hypocrisy about sexual relations. But with all this, the *Supplément*, precisely like Rousseau's *Discours*, seeks not to destroy but to purify and perfect Western civilization. Dryden's noble savage follows no law and knows no restraint:

> I am as free as nature first made man,
> Ere the base laws of servitude began,
> When wild in woods the noble savage ran.[8]

But the point of Rousseau's prepolitical men and Diderot's Tahitians is precisely that they are not savages though they are noble, and that they do not run wild. They live by rules and restrain some of their impulses; it is only that their art is in accord with what is good in nature. For Rousseau, as for Diderot, the cure for the sickness of civilization is more, and authentic, civilization. The philosophes' primitivism, in a word, served not the purposes of escape but those of reform.

The philosophes were in general suspicious of nostalgia and directed against it some of their most sustained criticisms. Montesquieu, writing in the shadow of the seventeenth-century quarrel between ancients and moderns, still betrays a certain ambivalence. He was inclined to accept the ancients' own estimates of their literary greatness and economic prosperity, but at the same time he ridiculed St. Cyprian's much-quoted lament that nature herself is decaying, that summers are less hot, winters less cold, mines less rich in yield, and friendships less affectionate than in former times; and he could even criticize, a little tartly, his beloved ancients:

---

[8] *The Conquest of Granada*, part I, act I, scene 1.

"Horace and Aristotle have already spoken to us about the virtues of their forefathers and the vices of their own times, and through the centuries, authors have talked the same way. If all this were true, we would be bears today."[9] Hume called attention to the "fallacy" that drives men "to declaim against present times, and magnify the virtue of remote ancestors," and thought it a "propensity almost inherent in human nature."[1] Even the educated rarely escaped it: "The humour of blaming the present, and admiring the past, is strongly rooted in human nature, and has an influence even on persons imbued with the profoundest judgment and most extensive learning."[2] And Voltaire spoke with some asperity against "man's natural inclination to complain about the present and boast about the past," to imagine vanished ages of gold and denounce the present age of iron. This nostalgia, he said, had infected the best of the Romans; Horace had found kind words for "those barbarians," the Tartars, but perhaps this was only natural: it is easy for satiric poets to "exalt foreigners at the expense of their own country." Tacitus, Voltaire thought, was even worse: he "wears himself out praising the German barbarians, who pillaged the Gauls and sacrificed human beings to their abominable gods. Tacitus, Quintus Curtius, and Horace resemble those pedagogues who lavish praise on the pupils of others, however boorish, in order to spur on their own pupils to emulation."[3] The reasons why "men have always deplored the present and extolled the past" lay in men's desire to escape their misery. Overburdened by work, depressed by their lot, men like to construct imaginary days of happy idleness—"hence the idea of the golden age," hence those old tales, like the story of Pandora's box, "of which some are amusing, and none is instructive."[4] To be sure—Voltaire was the first to assert it—the world is filled with "horrible misfortunes and crimes"; but then, "the pleasure of complaining is so great that at the slightest scratch you cry out that the world is running with blood."[5] For Voltaire, nostalgia is nothing more than a lyrical, sustained mode of complaining, and complaining,

[9] *Pensées,* in *Œuvres,* II, 153.
[1] "Of Refinements in the Arts," *Works,* III, 307.
[2] "Of the Populousness of Ancient Nations," ibid., III, 443.
[3] *Essai sur les mœurs,* I, 51.
[4] "Genesis," *Philosophical Dictionary,* I, 294.
[5] "Evil," ibid., II, 380.

unlike criticism, paralyzes man's will to action. That is why it was so dangerous, and why the philosophes persisted in exposing it, even though it seemed to them rooted deeply in human nature: the unsparing analysis of nostalgia would lay bare its psychological roots, neutralize it, and thus free men's energies for progress.

3. THE GEOGRAPHY OF HOPE

I

WE CANNOT DETERMINE to what height the human species may aspire in their advances towards perfection," wrote Gibbon in *The Decline and Fall of the Roman Empire*, "but it may safely be presumed that no people, unless the face of nature is changed, will relapse into their original barbarism." Gibbon thought he had no illusions about man, but he was confident that the inestimable gifts of civilization, which had been diffused even among savages, "can never be lost." Hence men may "acquiesce in the pleasing conclusion that every age of the world has increased, and still increases, the real wealth, the happiness, the knowledge, and perhaps the virtue of the human race."[6] And John Adams, probably the most caustic critic of fatuous optimism that the age of Enlightenment produced, pointed with unreserved pride to the advances man had made in recent times. "The arts and sciences, in general," he wrote in 1787, "during the three or four last centuries, have had a regular course of progressive improvement. The inventions in mechanic arts, the discoveries in natural philosophy, navigation, and commerce, and the advancement of civilization and humanity, have occasioned changes in the condition of the world and the human character which would have astonished the most refined nations of antiquity. A continuation of similar exertions is every day rendering Europe more and more like one community, or single family."[7] Nor was this merely the euphoria of victory; after the

---

[6] *Decline and Fall of the Roman Empire*, IV, 167–9.
[7] These are the opening words of the Preface to *A Defence of the Constitutions of Government of the United States of America* (1787–8), in *The Works of John Adams*, ed. Charles Francis Adams, 10 vols. (1850–6), IV, 283.

traumas of the French Revolution, the Napoleonic Wars, and the travails of establishing a new nation, Adams could still write, "I have no doubt that the horrors We have experienced for the last forty Years, will ultimately, terminate in the Advancement of civil and religious Liberty, and Ameliorations, in the condition of Mankind. For I am a Believer, in the probable improvability and Improvement, the ameliorabi[li]ty and Amelioration in human Affairs."[8] If such optimism seized even John Adams, the realist who ridiculed Helvétius's egalitarian dreams and Rousseau's theory of perfectibility, then the idea of progress must indeed have been irresistible in his time.

Gibbon's and Adams's hopes were the common property of educated men in the eighteenth century, and they became more familiar as time passed: optimism grew more pronounced decade by decade. But, although the confident belief in progress was in the air, the philosophes' predictions as to the progress mankind had a right to expect—its speed, its extent, its character—varied with their view of human nature, their reading of history, and their experience of the world. They did agree that progress was supremely desirable, eminently possible and, in fact, a significant political reality in their own time. *Le monde avec lenteur marche vers la sagesse*—in this much quoted line, Voltaire summed up the consensus among the little flock;[9] some of the philosophes emphasized the fact of movement, some its slow speed, but nearly all saw the world moving in measured pace toward good sense.

In a mood of high expectancy, the philosophes reasoned, with Gibbon and John Adams, that the study of history revealed progress through the centuries, or claimed, with Bentham and Diderot, that progress would take place if the world adopted a program of action —their program. A few of the philosophes, fascinated by developments in the biological sciences, were even willing to dream of the

---

[8] Adams to Thomas Jefferson, July 16, 1814. *The Adams-Jefferson Letters*, ed. Lester J. Cappon, 2 vols. (1959), II, 435.
[9] *Les lois de Minos*, act III, scene 5. *Œuvres*, VII, 213. That the emphasis in this line should be put on the *lenteur* is evident from Voltaire's own use of it. In 1778, the last year of his life, as he made some final revisions in his *Essai sur les mœurs*, he quoted the line again, reflecting rather grimly that in this very year there were still "slaves" in France, and, what was most absurd of all, the "slaves of monks." Progress was indeed a laborious business! (See *Essai*, I, 777.)

possible evolution of the human species into higher forms. But these claims and speculations, no matter how utopian their formulation might sometimes be, were grounded in reality. They were expectations derived from experience, organized into a program designed to articulate and sustain high morale, and controlled by an ineradicable strain of pessimism.

A program for progress, it is worth insisting, is not a theory of progress. Theologians, historians, and philosophers developed true theories of progress, before, during, and after the age of the Enlightenment, but despite exceptions like Turgot, the philosophes' mentality was not hospitable to them. For centuries, Christian optimists had described man's pilgrimage on earth as the education of humanity from sin to purity—we see traces of it in the secular ecstasy of Lessing's *Erziehung des Menschengeschlechts*. For centuries, Christian enthusiasts had preached an apocalyptic version of the theory of progress in their predictions for the millennium. After the Enlightenment, Hegel, Ranke, and their vulgarizers were to offer modern versions of these Christian speculations; they viewed improvement as constituent of the universe, indispensable in its very nature and thus inevitable, whether realized through the workings of biological Evolution, engineered by the cunning of History, or decreed by divine Providence. There were rationalists among these prophets of progress, but at least until the nineteenth century it was easier for a Christian than for a philosophe to construct a theory of progress. Christians could call on the millennial utopianism that was never far below the level of their consciousness, but the philosophes were, for all their lapses into optimistic fantasies, bound by the exigencies of this world. The pilgrim's progress was rather more direct, it seems, than the philosophes' progress.

Far from basking in cheerful certainty, then, the philosophes qualified their hopes with reservations. They were haunted by antique metaphors which they thought they had discarded; they pictured civilizations as individuals, with a distinct life cycle ending in decay and death. They suspected the very advance of civilization: Voltaire's *Le Mondain*, a glowing hymn to luxury and to his own marvelous "iron age," was distinctly unrepresentative, even of Voltaire; most of the philosophes feared luxury as a dark shadow following the growth of cultivation. They preached abundance and distrusted it. Montesquieu, who had early expressed his pessi-

mism about human nature in his *Lettres persanes,* put the two antique commonplaces about the cycle of civilizations and the menace
of luxury into a single sentence: "Almost all the nations of the
world travel this circle: to begin with, they are barbarous; they
become conquerors and well-ordered nations; this order permits
them to grow, and they become refined; refinement enfeebles
them, and they return to barbarism."[1] D'Alembert restated this view,
appropriately enough, in his eulogy to Montesquieu: "Empires, like
men, must grow, decay, and die"—this, d'Alembert insisted, is a
"necessary revolution" in the history of states.[2] Condillac flatly
asserted that "sooner or later, luxury ruins those nations into which
it has insinuated itself,"[3] and David Hume laid it down as a "well
known" law of politics, "that every government must come to a
period, and that death is unavoidable to the political as well as to
the animal body."[4] The affairs of men were like an irresistible tide.
"It is remarkable," Hume observes, "that the principles of Religion
have a kind of flux and reflux in the human mind, and that men have
a natural tendency to rise from idolatry to theism, and to sink
again from theism to idolatry."[5] And what was true of religion
was true of all civilization; a high culture is a peak from which
civilized men may glimpse both the long ascent they have made
and the long descent they must make in the future: "*When the
arts and sciences come to perfection in any state, from that moment
they naturally, or rather necessarily decline, and seldom or never
revive in that nation, where they formerly flourished.*"[6] Hume had
no hesitation in celebrating the summits of civilization and his own
civilization as a summit, but he had no room in his philosophy for
the claim that the future guarantees man even higher peaks.

In fact, the philosophes saw progress not merely as circumscribed and impermanent, but also, even at its best, as a highly
ambiguous blessing. All progress, they insisted, exacted its price.
"No advantages in this world," Hume asserted, "are pure and un-

---

[1] Quoted in Henry Vyverberg: *Historical Pessimism in the French
Enlightenment* (1958), 155.
[2] *Éloge de M. le Président de Montesquieu,* in *Mélanges,* II, 103.
[3] Vyverberg: *Historical Pessimism,* 129.
[4] "Whether the British Government Inclines More to Absolute
Monarchy or to a Republic," *Works,* III, 125–6.
[5] *The Natural History of Religion,* ibid., IV, 334.
[6] "Of the Rise and Progress in the Arts and Sciences," ibid., III, 195.

mixed." Just as "modern politeness, which is naturally so ornamental, runs often into affectation and foppery, disguise and insincerity," so "ancient simplicity, which is naturally so amiable and affecting, often degenerates into rusticity and abuse, scurrility and obscenity."[7] The risks of progress are not always obvious, but they are always there. To take but one instance: "According to the most natural course of things, industry and arts and trade increase the power of the sovereign as well as the happiness of the subjects,"[8] so that men might pay for their flourishing literature by slavery. A little grimly, d'Alembert called this law of compensation "the misery of the human condition." We men, he argued, "hardly acquire any new knowledge without undeceiving ourselves about some agreeable illusion, and our enlightenment is almost always at the expense of our pleasures. Our simple ancestors were perhaps moved more strongly by the monstrous plays of our old theatre than we are moved today by the finest of our dramas; nations less enlightened than ours are not less happy, for with fewer desires they also have fewer needs, and coarse or less refined pleasures are good enough for them. Still, we would not want to exchange our enlightenment for the ignorance of those nations, or for the ignorance of our ancestors. If this enlightenment does reduce our pleasure, it flatters our vanity at the same time; we congratulate ourselves on having become sophisticated, as though this is some sort of merit."[9] It is a revealing passage: like his brethren, d'Alembert refused to equate progress with happiness; but he also refused to abandon civilization simply because it makes men unhappy. Cultivation itself, though always precarious, is a value.

For the historian of the Enlightenment, Voltaire's shifts of mood are particularly instructive. It is true that Voltaire lived long and wrote much, and had ample opportunity to contradict himself. It is true as well that he was quick to take courage and quick to despair. But Voltaire was more than a capricious and irresponsible publicist; he was supremely responsive to the deeper currents of his age and his movement, and hence supremely representative of the Enlightenment as a whole. In his capacity as self-appointed guardian to

---

[7] Ibid., 191.
[8] "Of Commerce," ibid., 292–3.
[9] "Réflexions sur l'usage et sur l'abus de la philosophie dans les matières de goût," *Mélanges*, IV, 318–19.

the philosophic family, Voltaire was a professional optimist; periodically he cheered up the brethren, and himself, with hopeful bulletins from Ferney. There were moments when he permitted his ebullience full flight; in a famous letter of 1764 he wrote: "Everything I see scatters the seeds of a revolution which will definitely come, though I won't have the pleasure of being its witness. Frenchmen discover everything late, but in the end they do discover it. Enlightenment has gradually spread so widely that it will burst into full light at the first right opportunity, and then there'll be a fine uproar. The young people are lucky: they will see some great things."[1] At the same time, Voltaire often joined the philosophic chorus of resignation and gloom. He had moments of cheerful, sardonic pessimism—his short stories testify to them—but beyond this, in full seriousness, he often insisted that evil is pervasive, persistent, and unconquerable, that man is powerless against the caprice of fortune, and that his most strenuous efforts to progress are held in check by cycles of growth and decay. "Everything has its limits," he wrote in *Le siècle de Louis XIV*, in a paragraph that is well known but deserves to be better known than it is. "One should not think that the great tragic passions, the great emotions, can be infinitely varied in new and striking ways. Everything has its limits." Comedy, pulpit oratory, all reach a certain perfection and then become commonplace. "After that one is reduced to imitation or eccentricity." Once a La Fontaine has written his fables, later fabulists can only point the moral he had pointed before them. "And so genius has but one century; after that, everything must degenerate—*après quoi il faut que tout dégénère*."[2] The decline of culture was an obsessive theme with Voltaire, and it lent his most optimistic pronouncements a touch of Stoic resignation. He was convinced that the century of Corneille and Molière had scored such stunning triumphs that it left its successor a Silver Age: the age of Louis XIV had cleared a vast field, so vast that the age of Louis XV could

---

[1] Voltaire to Bernard Louis Chauvelin, April 2, 1764. *Correspondence*, LIV, 231. But on the same day he could write: "Good men—*les honnêtes gens*—should profit from the war among the wicked. The only thing that troubles me is the inaction of the brethren. . . . The brethren do not understand one another, do not get stirred up, do not have—do not have—any rallying place; they are isolated, dispersed." To Damilaville, ibid., 232.

[2] *Œuvres historiques*, 1016–17.

cultivate only a small part of it. Even the growth of population, the source of so much confidence in the age of the Enlightenment, gave Voltaire occasion for some melancholy observations. "For several years now people have talked a great deal about population," he wrote in 1764, the very year that he had indulged in his famous optimistic outburst. "I'd like to venture some reflections. Our great interest is to see that the men who exist should be as happy as human nature and the extreme disparity among different conditions of life permit. But if we haven't yet been able to secure this happiness to men, why all this desire to increase their numbers? Is it to produce new miserable beings?" Governments, to be sure, want an increase in population, but "most fathers are afraid of having too many children."[3] *Candide* marks the low point of Voltaire's mood, and he never wholly overcame it. Candide's despairing exclamation, "If this is the best of all possible worlds, what are the others like?"[4] was and remained Voltaire's own.

These pronouncements are hard to reduce to a consistent position. The same man who castigated life as a shipwreck and the world as a miserable pile of mud, who described history as a depressing tale and valued peaks of cultivation as rare and precarious moments, also predicted a far-reaching, beneficent revolution and the inevitable triumph of philosophy. But while Voltaire's predictions fluctuated, they circled around a hard core of conviction: life is, has always been, and will always be, hard; man needs courage, patience, and luck to survive at all; but reason, often flouted, often defeated, is a tough and aggressive force in the world, and it was now at last making progress slowly, painfully, with many setbacks but also with good prospects of ultimate success. The history of the human spirit, Voltaire wrote in 1763, in a considered statement of his position, "shows us errors and prejudices succeeding one another in turn, and driving out truth and reason. We see the clever and the lucky enslaving the stupid and crushing the unfortunate; and yet, these clever and lucky people are themselves the playthings of fortune as much as those whom they dominate. In the end, men enlighten themselves a little through this account of their misfortunes and their stupidities. As time goes by, societies manage

---

[3] Voltaire to *Gazette littéraire* (October 1764). *Correspondence*, LVI, 102.
[4] *Candide*, chap. 6. *Œuvres*, XXI, 149.

to amend their ideas; men learn to think."[5] Here was a paradox that modern pagan philosophers could appreciate: only the honest recognition of harsh truths might enable men to make the future less harsh; open-eyed pessimism was the precondition for sensible optimism. "If this is the best of all possible worlds, what are the others like?"—no man, no movement committed to a theory of automatic progress could have invented such a question.

The mixture—grim, programmatic optimism controlled by frank pessimism—that dominated the British century of philosophy and the French *siècle des lumières* also dominated the German *Aufklärung*. In some tentative, hypothetical essays on history, Kant postulated the inevitable unfolding of human capacities, with mankind guided forward by the invisible hand that benefits the species while it crushes the individual. Progress simply *must* take place; it is too important, too deeply enmeshed in man's very existence, to be denied. Like his admired Rousseau, who defended his belief in Providence against Voltaire's skepticism as necessary to his well-being, Kant, desperately wishing for progress, surrendered his philosophical detachment to his will to believe. But not for long; considering the condition of the world, he wrote, "I should blame no one," if he should "begin to despair of the salvation of mankind, and of its progress to better things." Prophets of progress reminded Kant of a physician who specialized in consoling his patients by finding them improved every day; then, ill himself one day, he received a visit from a friend. "How is your illness?" the friend asked the optimistic doctor, and the doctor replied: "How should it be going? *I'm dying from sheer improvement!*"[6] And when improvement was not illusory, it was wretchedly slow and far from obvious. The belief in progress, Kant rightly saw, was a modern belief, and applied most accurately to the progress of civilization. Moral progress was another matter altogether: if a man should claim that moral progress has in fact taken place, one must reply that he has not deduced his claim from experience: "The history of all times testifies too powerfully against it."[7] The conquest of moral goodness is, to be sure, not impossible; it is even a great duty,

---

[5] *Remarques pour servir de supplément à l'Essai sur les mœurs* (1763), in *Œuvres*, XXIV, 548.
[6] *Der Streit der Fakultäten*, in *Werke*, VII, 406-7.
[7] *Religion innerhalb der Grenzen der blossen Vernunft*, in *Werke*, VI, 158.

but it demands an inner revolution, and this revolution can take place only "in continuous activity and growth."[8] Man's viciousness, foolishness, childish vanity, and sheer destructiveness are an antidote to conceit and easy self-confidence.[9]

Kant's fellow *Aufklärer* were even more explicit than he, and for the most part did not trouble with speculations about future progress. Lichtenberg lamented man's self-destructive mania for opposing what he needs most: "People talk a great deal about Enlightenment and ask for more light. My God! What good is all this light if people either have no eyes or if those who do have eyes, resolutely keep them shut!"[1] Wieland persistently made the same point. Man is a "silly animal"; the exercise of reason may be the road to progress, but if it is taken at all, it is taken slowly; enlightenment will come only "slowly, step by step," with an "almost imperceptible increase of light."[2] And it is so difficult and slow because in this world one pays for everything, especially for progress. "You would as easily turn a Negro into a white man by washing him, as inoculate a man with the advantages of culture without giving him, with every skill a fault, every truth an error, every virtue a vice." There are prophets who talk of the continuing expansion of reason, and its final victory over "ignorance, mental sloth, caprice, and egotism," but they are utopians: "Has it not always been obvious that the time of highest refinement is precisely the time of the most extreme moral rottenness? that the epoch of brightest enlightenment is always the very epoch in which all sorts of speculations, madness, and enthusiasm, flourish most?"[3] Wieland did not regard this law of compensation as a mechanical law of history or a divine dispensation; its origins are only too human. It springs from the sinister interests of the powerful and the stupid resistance of the impotent: "Just think: as against one man who actively advances true enlightenment, there are a hundred who work against it with all their might, and ten thousand who

---

[8] Ibid., 188.
[9] I am using Kant's harsh words; see *Idee zu einer allgemeinen Geschichte in weltbürgerlicher Absicht* (1784), ibid., IV, 152.
[1] This aphorism is quoted in the Grimms' German dictionary as an illustration of the world "Aufklärung." See Jacob and Wilhelm Grimm: *Deutsches Wörterbuch* (1854) I, 675.
[2] *Gespräche unter vier Augen*, in *Werke*, XLII, 32.
[3] Quoted in Sengle: *Wieland*, motto.

neither desire nor miss his services." There can be no doubt that
universal enlightenment will "never take place."[4] The world is a
theater in which actors and spectators alike are fools and knaves;
the world is so ridden with misery and absurdities that man does
well to divert his attention from the depressing spectacle by dreaming philosophical dreams about universal happiness. Most men are
like the legendary citizens of Abdera, about whom Wieland wrote
some of his most sardonic tales: they are silly beyond belief, pedantic
to the point of mania, gullible and dishonest. Wieland concludes his
Geschichte der Abderiten with a line from Horace: *Sapientia prima
est stultitia caruisse*—to have shed stupidity is the beginning of
wisdom. But the advice sounds wistful and sarcastic after a recital
of so many idiocies: the effort to shed stupidity—this after all is the
burden of the tales—will never be made, certainly not by the many.

Some of this gloom, to be sure, is the superb disdain of the
urbane Epicurean philosopher for his swinish fellow men; some of
it is literary license: the praise of folly had entertained writers and
readers for centuries before Wieland. It also reflects Wieland's
disappointment with the course of the French Revolution. Yet even
though the pessimistic formulations may be derived from literary
models and mirror a momentary disappointment, their general tone
and message represent Wieland's sense of life; his very sarcasm seems
like an effort to master or to mask despair through literary discipline
and liberating humor. "Our Enlightenment?" he asks. "Oh how our
descendants will laugh in a hundred years—that is, if they can laugh
for weeping—when they read how conceited we were with 'our
Enlightenment.'" Looking back at his century in 1798, Wieland
denied that mankind had in any essential way progressed since the
sixteenth century. "If by Enlightenment you mean the twilight
gradually brought forth by the ever-progressing cultivation of the
sciences," then indeed "I gladly concede that, on the average, things
look a little less gloomy than they did in the sixteenth century."
But if one understands by "Enlightenment" the true light that
"allows men to think and act rationally and consistently," then "we
shamefully flatter our age, if we claim for it the smallest real advance
over all earlier centuries, with the single exception perhaps, that in
most European countries neither witches nor heretics are any longer

---

[4] *Gespräche unter vier Augen*, in *Werke*, XLII, 32–3.

being burned to the greater glory of God." It is true as well that
the sciences have greatly advanced; we speak "a more graceful and
more adroit language, write more books, read more, and have infinitely refined the art of lying to ourselves. But that we have become
on the whole wiser, better, and happier—I don't see that. Just
mention a single vice, a single folly, that is less pronounced in our
day than in our forefathers'; a single virtue in which we surpass
them; a single pleasure in life we have over them, and which we
do not buy more dearly, out of all proportion, than they did." Is it
really true, Wieland asks, that the people are better cared for than
before? less oppressed? robbed less viciously by the mighty? do we
have fewer wars now? are they by any chance more just, more
necessary than earlier wars? are they being conducted more hu-
manely than before?[5] These are rhetorical questions.

II

The Enlightenment's hesitations, its unconquerable outbursts of
pessimism and resignation mark even Turgot's *Discours sur les
progrès successifs de l'esprit humain* and Condorcet's *Esquisse d'un
tableau historique des progrès de l'esprit humain*. It is worth insisting
once again that these essays, revealing as they are, are exceptional
rather than typical creations of the philosophes' spirit. In fact, in
their calmer moments, Turgot and Condorcet themselves would
have qualified the emphatic simplicities of these dramatic productions. But beyond this, it is remarkable that they too, for all their
metaphysics of hope, are stamped by realism and downright anxiety.

Turgot was a promising, precocious intellectual of twenty-three
when he delivered his *Discours* in 1750, as one of two Latin discourses, to the Sorbonne. He had just been elected a prior to the
Sorbonne, a tribute to his brilliance or his connections, but the
scanty surviving correspondence of this time shows a young man
tormented by doubts about his religious vocation, if conscious of his
intellectual powers. For months before he delivered his lectures he
had been prey to vacillations and depressions, and not long after his
triumphant performance he deserted his clerical career for public

---

[5] See ibid., 333-5.

service, moved from speculative philosophy to practical activity as
a provincial intendant and royal minister, and never filled in the
outlines of his theory of history: the famous law of the three stages
of mental development remained hidden among his manuscripts.[6]
Turgot opens his *Discours* by distinguishing the phenomena of
nature, "enclosed in a circle of revolutions that are always the same,"
from the civilizations of man, "offering an ever varied spectacle,
from century to century." Man can break the cycle of nature, for
he has "reason, passions, liberty," and the priceless gift of language,
which permits him to grasp his knowledge firmly and to transmit
it to others. Yet civilizations have a cycle of their own; since circumstances vary enormously from place to place and time to time,
barbarism alternates with cultivation, empires rise and fall. Laws,
forms of government, the arts and sciences improve, but "in turn
checked and accelerated in their progress, they move from climate
to climate." Vice coexists with virtue. "Self-interest, ambition, vain-
glory perpetually change the face of the world, inundate the earth

---

[6] In part of an undatable and unpublished draft, Turgot postulated
three stages through which mankind had passed in its history: first,
the religious stage in which men deified their rulers and anthropo-
morphized natural events; second, the metaphysical stage so familiar
from the philosophes' assaults on system-making—this was the stage
in which philosophers, having unmasked religious fables without
truly understanding nature, thought they could explain the world
by abstractions like "essence" or "faculties," new divinities in the
place of old; and third, the recent stage in which men observe the
mechanical actions of bodies and make reasonable hypotheses—the
positive or scientific phase. (See "Plan du second Discours sur les
progrès de l'esprit humain," *Œuvres*, I, 315–16). This ladder of
ascent has been much criticized, and justly so, but it should be read
as a reflection of the recovery of nerve, a tribute to man's sense of
mastery over the world. There is an interesting anticipation of
Turgot's stages in Roger Cotes's preface to the second edition
of Newton's *Principia*. Cotes argues that there are natural philosophers who have "attributed to the several species of things specific
and occult qualities, on which, in a manner unknown, they make
the operations of the several bodies to depend"—these are the Aristotelians. Then there are philosophers who have rebelled against
this, regard matter as homogeneous, and speculate on the simple
foundations of the world: "Those who fetch from hypotheses the
foundation on which they build their speculations, may form,
indeed, an ingenious romance, but a romance it will still be." And
finally there are philosophers who "profess experimental philosophy." Turgot's discovery was in the air. *Newton's Philosophy
of Nature*, ed. H. S. Thayer (1953), 117.

with blood; and, in the midst of their ravages, *mœurs* grow milder, the human mind is enlightened, isolated nations approach one another; finally, commerce and politics unite all parts of the globe; and the totality of mankind, through alternations of calm and agitation, good and evil, marches continuously, though with slow steps, toward a greater perfection."

Progress, then, exacts its tribute—it is an idea familiar to the philosophes, but it is startling here, in a discourse on inevitable progress. Progress is slow, costly, uncertain. Evil often produces good, but it remains evil just the same; the miserable instruments of general progress are not the less miserable for that. In fact, in the great combat of truth and error, it is often the error that survives and the truth that is crushed. Even science sometimes resists progress by developing an institutional conservatism.

Despite these reservations, Turgot's tone is confident; he paints the gloomy side of his sketch with serenity. But that side is prominent. In barbarism, men are equal; civilization brings commerce, arts, travel, and it binds cultures together, but it also produces inequality and fosters the unchecked passions of ambitious men. Writing—"precious invention!"—gives mankind wings, but a survey of man's opinions remains appalling: "I seek the progress of the human spirit there and see practically nothing but the history of its errors." In mathematics, progress is certain, but elsewhere it is continuously threatened. Mankind wavers between wisdom and foolishness, although it does advance: man's invincible restlessness slowly overcomes conservatism, blind passion, stupidity. "Always restless —*toujours inquiète*—incapable of finding rest anywhere but in the truth, always excited by the image of that truth which he fancies he touches and which flees before him, man in his curiosity multiplies questions and disputes." Turgot's intellectual masters, Locke and Condillac, had singled out restlessness as man's distinctive quality; Turgot now detects it as the secret spring of man's advance toward reliable scientific knowledge.

But, Turgot suggests, restlessness by itself is not enough. It has to be harnessed to a critical spirit and to systematic methods of inquiry. That is why the Greeks are so important in the history of mind: they invented philosophy. Earlier cultures, like the Egyptians, were crippled by superstition; the Phoenicians had at least cultivated trade and spread new ideas along their routes. But the Greeks were the first to develop a language made for progress—it was euphonious, rich, and varied; they invented civic freedom, moral codes, high culture, and systematic thinking: "Happy age! When all the arts spread their light on all sides! When the fire of a noble emulation rapidly communicated itself from one city to another: painting, sculpture, architecture, poetry, history developed everywhere, and at the same time." After this, Rome was an anticlimax; the Christian religion grew and conquered in centuries of depressing cultural decay. Yet the Christians held high their sacred faith and cultivated the seeds of renewal: "Do men rise only to fall?" It would seem so, yet it cannot be true: it took many centuries to cure the plague that had afflicted mankind since the days of the Roman Empire, but the cure came at last with the revival of the arts in the immortal hands of the Medici, Leo X, and Francis I, and with the invention of printing. Yet Turgot finds it striking to observe "how slow is the slightest progress in every genre!" It is only in recent times that progress has become unmistakable and irresistible—in the glorious century of Galileo and Newton, of "great Descartes" who at least destroyed the tyranny of error even if he did not always find the truth, the glorious century of Louis XIV, "century of great men, century of reason."

The adroit patriotism of these references to the age of *Louis le grand* is only a transition to the adroit courtliness of Turgot's peroration: now at last men live in the light; the shadows have been dissipated; the reign of Louis XV sheds its brilliance over all culture; great men are no longer rare but crowd upon one another; and true religion, always pure, always complete, freely contributes to progress. "O Louis! What majesty surrounds you! What bright magnificence has your beneficent hand not spread over all the arts! Your happy people has become the center of cultivation. Rivals of Sophocles, Menander, Horace, assemble around his throne! Learned academies, arise! Unite your labors for the glory of his reign! What a multitude of public monuments, productions of genius, new arts invented, old arts perfected! Who would be adequate to paint them! Open your eyes and see! Century of Louis the Great, may your light embellish the precious reign of its successor! May it endure forever, may it extend over the whole world! May men steadily take new steps in the career of truth! May they, even more, steadily grow better and happier!"[7] Turgot believed in inevitable progress—I am not inclined to dispute it—and he believed in the progressive character of his own age, at least as a young man. But the courtier's rhetoric of his conclusion reads like a sardonic commentary on his hopes: Turgot's language was the accepted language of the day, his flattery the flattery a man of letters was expected to lavish on the powers of church and state, but standing as it does at the end of his bold exercise in optimism, it served as a reminder that the age of unaided reason and free criticism had not come—not yet.

Condorcet wrote in hiding from the Jacobins, too much in haste to correct obvious slips of the pen, compelled to rely on his fine memory and a handful of books smuggled in by reliable associates. Scribbling in fear of death, Condorcet is a far more poignant figure that Turgot, delivering his orations to an appreciative audience. Unlike Turgot, Condorcet writing on progress had no one to please but himself. "I shall perish," he noted down, appealing at once to a favorite classical and a favorite modern martyr to philosophy, "I shall perish like Socrates and Sidney."[8] Condorcet had started his career as a mathematician, if anything more precocious and more brilliant than Turgot, his mentor; his extraordinary scientific talents had opened the doors of leading academies to him, including, in 1782, the *Académie française*, and his unwearied devotion to the philosophes' cause had secured him the friendship of Voltaire. But, then, by the 1780s it was his devotion rather than his scientific talents that engrossed his time, and during the Revolution his passion for devising schemes of constitutional and educational reforms only served to estrange him from the politicians. He was an anachronism, a philosophe who had known the giants—Voltaire, d'Alembert, Turgot—in whose name the Revolution was carrying on its business, respected for his memories and his intelligence but pathetically unsuitable to the sanguinary party battles of the Year II; principled, humane, in his way unworldly, Concorcet was a natural victim of the Revolution. Proscribed in 1793, he went into hiding and

---

[7] *Discours sur les progrès successifs de l'esprit humain*, in *Œuvres*, I, 214–35 *passim*.
[8] A fragment from the last days of his life. *Œuvres*, I, 608.

wrote his essay on progress, a prospectus for a vast history of the human mind, between July 1793 and March 1794, watching his Revolution going the way of violence, and brooding on his own almost certain death. It would be unjust to dismiss the *Esquisse* as the desperate entertainment of a doomed man; it sums up Condorcet's convictions and hopes. But it is not coolly reasoned or cautiously circumscribed; it is dashed off, not without reflection, but with an anxious haste to get it all down before it is too late, an urgency that left no room for subtleties or modulations.

Condorcet divided his *Esquisse* into ten epochs, and while his periodization appears arbitrary, it is not meaningless. Both the space he devoted to each epoch and the events he used to divide one epoch from another serve as dramatic illustrations of his central theme: the career of the human mind in world history. Thus, Condorcet opens and closes epochs not with royal reigns, but with such cultural events as Aristotle's introduction of the division of labor into philosophy, the triumph of Christianity over paganism, the invention of printing. For the same reason, Condorcet allocates the bulk of his essay to modern history, when man's spirit had made its most spectacular advances, and to the period of classical Greece, Alexandrian Hellenism, and ancient Rome, which produced rational inquiry and all the cultural and natural sciences. Condorcet forces even prehistory—the formation of tribes, the development of pastoral settlements, and the rudiments of agricultural civilization, for which, he concedes, his information is highly speculative—into his general scheme; these first three epochs, brief as they are, amount to an overture that states two major concerns of the *Esquisse*: the reactionary power of privilege and the dialectical nature of progress.

It was a commonplace among philosophic historians that the world had always been divided between critics and believers, philosophy and superstition, and that the combat of reason and unreason had provided at once the ground of conflict and the impetus for progress.[9] But, strongly tempted as they were, the philosophes had not simply identified the clergy as the supreme obstacle to reason. Turgot, whom Condorcet admired as much as he admired anyone, and Lessing as well, had assigned to Christianity a progressive role in the drama of man's evolution. Even Gibbon had been objective

---

[9] See *The Rise of Modern Paganism*, 31–8.

enough to associate the incursions of the barbarians, the long peace, the extent of the empire, and the corruption of manners and institutions with the triumph of religion as the causes of the decline and fall of the Roman Empire. Gibbon and Voltaire and Hume were as anticlerical and anti-Christian as Condorcet, and their histories suffer from a narrowing of sympathy, a distortion of perspective whenever they deal with religious matters. But these three historians had the historians' sense for the variety, the complexity, the sheer value of the past, and in consequence their histories are richer, more detached, and more objective than their political stance might have led one to expect. Gibbon and Voltaire and Hume did not scruple to exploit history for polemical purposes, but they controlled their spleen; they wrote history.

Condorcet did not follow his masters in this, certainly not in the *Esquisse*. He wrote polemics, not history, and, since the *Esquisse* purports to be a historical essay and an ambitious one, the flaw is fatal. Condorcet simply elevated his anticlericalism into his philosophy of history. He concedes that castes of philosophers and other secular elites may set their faces against human advancement, but his ideal type of the true reactionary, the great enemy, is the religious man operating from the protected sanctuary of a sacred institution. We may observe in the first epoch, he writes, "the first traces" of "a class of men who are depositaries of scientific principles or craft procedures, of mysteries or religious ceremonies, of the practices of superstition, often even of the secrets of legislation and politics." This "separation of the human species into two parts; one destined to teach, the other made to believe; one proudly hiding that which it boasts of knowing, the other respectfully receiving what one deigns to reveal to him; one wishing to elevate itself above reason the other humbly renouncing its reason"[1]—this separation, established before recorded history, still exists in the eighteenth century, and is still being defended, naturally by priests of all sects.

Not unexpectedly, Condorcet devotes generous space to the activities of privileged establishments, clerical and lay, through the ages. Quite early in the history of human society, in the second epoch, some shrewd observers developed sound ideas about astronomy, but "at the same time," they perfected "the art of deceiving

---

[1] *Esquisse*, in *Œuvres*, VI, 30.

men in order to plunder them."[2] Again, in the third epoch, the rulers of agricultural peoples gained some insights into natural history, but they regarded "the progress of the sciences as only a secondary goal, as only a means of perpetuating or extending their power." They "sought the truth only to spread errors"; and while they discovered a certain amount of knowledge, "one should not be astonished that they found the truth so rarely."[3] Even the glorious fourth epoch, the time of classical Greece, displays the tragic spectacle of the persecution of reason by superstition; this is the period when Socrates, that first martyr to philosophy, is brought to his death by "preachers" who, alarmed to see men perfecting their autonomous reason, determine to subvert this dangerous progress by censoring philosophy and, if necessary, killing philosophers.[4] Here clerical villainy is manifest and prophetic: Condorcet presents the death of Socrates as the opening skirmish in the great war between philosophy and superstition that still rages. Thus distant events may serve the present as an inspiration and a warning. If the fourth and fifth epochs did show remarkable, almost unimpeded progress, that was only because priests were not powerful enough to establish their tyranny; Hellenic and Hellenistic society was too cosmopolitan, too eager for new experience, too open for them. But the rise of Christianity finally gave the priesthood the power they had long sought, a power they did not fail to exploit to the full. The Christian millennium is an impressive demonstration of what energetic reactionaries can do to spread superstition, demote the intellect, prolong stagnation, secure tyranny, degrade man as a reasoning being, and thus hold back the march of mind for centuries. And even in the seventh epoch, after their time of supreme power was over, as the sciences began to restore themselves, entrenched reactionaries continued their machinations. This was not the end. In the eighth epoch the churches, a wounded but still formidable colossus, launched a terrifying series of persecutions; in the midst of magnificent scientific discoveries and unprecedented improvements in general cultivation, they mounted articulate opposition to the principles of toleration and the most obvious of scientific truths, like the Copernican astronomy. Even now, Condorcet

---

[2] Ibid., 34–5.
[3] Ibid., 54.
[4] Ibid., 66–7. See *The Rise of Modern Paganism*, 82.

concludes, in the ninth epoch, as the new dispensation is at hand and men have at last broken the chains that so long bound them to tyranny and superstition, the forces of reaction remain alive and retain some power.

But then—and Condorcet argues that this historical principle too can be observed as early as the first epoch—the pernicious institution of an organized clergy has had surprisingly beneficent results for the human mind. At the same time that it diffused error, it "accelerated the progress of enlightenment"; at the same time that it plunged the common people into "ignorance and religious servitude" it "enriched the sciences with new truths."[5] Historical causes, in other words, obey a dialectical law; history is the battleground of unintended consequences. The forces of evil may lead to good; the forces of good may lead to evil. Reasoning, itself a good, may produce error as easily as it produces truth; in turn error, itself an evil, may become an unwitting tool of progress. Civilization has its discontents which become manifest as early as prehistoric times, when primitive cultures, and with some justice, view their civilized contemporaries as models of doubtful value—"more powerful, wealthier, better informed, more active, but also more vicious and above all less happy than they are themselves."[6] Later, enlightenment led to exploitation: in ancient Greece the enlightened, who were also the rich, used their superiority to oppress the ignorant, who were, and remained, the poor. Still later, superstition involuntarily invited its overthrow. From the moment of its establishment in the Roman Empire, Christianity, this deplorable system of superstition, produced "a disastrous epoch, in which the human spirit rapidly descends from the height to which it had risen, and ignorance drags after it in one place ferocity, in another refined cruelty, everywhere corruption and perfidy."[7] For centuries, under Christian leadership, manners and customs retained "their corruption and ferocity," religious intolerance grew worse than ever in history, and warfare, petty and large, was perpetual.[8] But at last,

---

[5] Ibid., 29–30.
[6] Ibid., 37–8.
[7] Ibid., 109.
[8] Ibid., 137. Perhaps the only unambiguous positive value Condorcet was willing to allow Christianity was its preachment of human brotherhood. This preachment, though violated and often wholly ignored, did in modern times contribute to the campaign for abolition of slavery (ibid., 111).

the priests' lust for power, their intolerance, scandalous greed, bad morals, and unabashed hypocrisy "aroused against them pure souls, healthy minds, courageous characters," who led a general rebellion against clerical domination. In the same manner, the Crusades, hideous offspring of religious enthusiasm, widened the horizons of the crusaders, and, "undertaken for the sake of superstition," they "only serve to destroy it." Finally, the Scholastics served a hostile cause, a cause they did not even recognize: "Scholasticism did not lead to the discovery of truth; it did not even serve for the discussion or thorough appreciation of scientific proofs, but it sharpened men's minds; and that taste for making subtle distinctions, that need endlessly to subdivide ideas, to seize their fugitive nuances, and represent them by new terms, the apparatus designed to embarrass an opponent in a disputation, or escape its traps—all these were the first origins of that philosophical analysis which has since become the fertile source of our progress."[9] Scholastic rationalism the mother of the scientific method: the irony of the historical dialectic could hardly go further than this.

History, then, in Condorcet's view, is an oddly inconclusive affair. Indeed, for a prophet of progress, Condorcet was remarkably uncheerful. His *Esquisse* is a striking mixture of exaltation, gloom and serenity; beyond arguing that the instruments of progress are ambivalent. Condorcet also insists that history in general is not merely a record of progress but also a tale of suffering, and of suffering in the midst of brilliant civilization and breath-taking innovations. Progress has not been continuous; civilization shows "sometimes advance, sometimes decay."[1] In fact, at least twice in the past the cause of reason has been resoundingly defeated—once in Europe, when Christianity routed paganism, and once among the Arabs, when the religious despots who had permitted some feeble attempts at independent philosophizing finally stifled them. In primitive times—Condorcet mentions this as a matter of course—and in the darkness of the Christian Middle Ages, misery had been the lot of most men. But it remained a significant and widespread experience even in times of glorious respite from barbarism. Greece witnessed imperialism, exploitation, slavery, contempt for women. The marvelous sixteenth and seventeenth centuries were "sullied,

[9] Ibid., 125, 130, 133.
[1] Ibid., 281.

more than any other, by great atrocities." This was the "period of
religious massacres, sacred wars, the depopulation of the new world,"
and the re-establishment of that antique institution, slavery, in
America, "more barbarous, more fertile in crimes against nature,"
than it had ever been. "Mercantile avidity trafficked in men's blood,"
human beings were sold as though they were merchandise after
they had been bought through "treason, brigandage, and murder."
Meanwhile, in Europe, hypocrites covered country after country
"with stakes and assassins." The "monster of fanaticism, irritated by
its wounds, seemed to redouble in ferocity, hastening to pile up its
victims because reason was about to tear them from its hands."[2]
Even the ninth epoch—the time of scientific, moral, political, and
religious enlightenment, of Newton and Locke, Adam Smith and
Voltaire, of the new social sciences, the triumph of moderns over
ancients, the great American Revolution, of the greatest demonstration in history of progress in practice, in the midst of the
amelioration of man's lot through the application of science—compels Condorcet to say "but"—like Zadig, one of Voltaire's most
felicitous, least optimistic creations. "But," writes Condorcet, "if
everything tells us that mankind should no longer fall back into
its former barbarism; if everything must reassure us against that
pusillanimous and corrupt system that condemns mankind to eternal
oscillations between truth and error, liberty and servitude, we see
at the same time that the light occupies only a small part of the
globe, and the number of those who really possess light disappears
before the mass of men delivered over to prejudices and ignorance.
We see vast countries groaning in slavery, and offering a spectacle
of nations, in one place degraded by the vices of a civilization
whose corruption slows down its march, in another place still
vegetating in the infancy of its first epochs. We see that the labors
of these last ages have done a great deal for the progress of the
human spirit, but little for the perfection of the human species;
much for the glory of man, something for his freedom, but still
almost nothing for his happiness. In a few areas our eyes are struck
with a dazzling light; but heavy shadows still cover an immense
horizon. The soul of the philosopher rests with consolation on a
small number of objects; but the spectacle of stupidity, slavery,

---

[2] Ibid., 157–8.

extravagance, barbarism, afflicts him still more often, and the friend of mankind can taste unmixed pleasure only by surrendering to the sweet hopes of the future."[3] It is a powerful and instructive passage. Earlier in the same epoch, Condorcet had inveighed against modern philosophies born, he thought, of philosophers' pride and vanity, philosophies that taught the wickedness of culture and the futility of knowledge; but here, looking at the world with open eyes, Condorcet sounds like Rousseau at his most critical, Voltaire at his most cynical. Optimism, the closing phrase reveals, is a form of therapy; to surrender to the sweet hopes of the future is the only way to make life bearable.

Still, Condorcet's vision of the future—the last, tenth, epoch—is more than therapy. Condorcet was writing the history of the human mind for the sake of prophecy; the very study of that history, he said, like Voltaire, made men face grim and promising truths alike, and would thus become an instrument of progress. It might be that there are "vices necessarily attached to the progress of civilization,"[4] it might be that some civilizations have remained hopelessly arrested in infantile stages, it might be, finally, that most agents of progress are unreliable; still, much had happened to reduce ignorance and misery and brutality, much that gave men the right to hope. The French Revolution itself was like a leap into the future; it had proved how much men could do in a little time; the further perfection of the social science, pacific technology, and modern education might be expected to do the rest.

Condorcet launched into his predictions with some trepidation. He said modestly that he wished merely to "hazard some *aperçus*," to offer speculations based on the extrapolation from previous performance, "with some probability."[5] What may men hope? That inequality among nations will disappear, that equality will increase within each nation, and that mankind will really perfect itself. The sober study of history gives men "the strongest reasons for believing that nature has put no limits on our expectations." Nature—on this Condorcet has insisted from the beginning of his book—"has set no limit to the perfection of human faculties"; the "perfectibility of

---

[3] Ibid., 231–4.
[4] From an unpublished fragment intended for the Fourth Epoch. Ibid., 463.
[5] Ibid., 24, 236.

man" is capable of indefinite extension.[6] There will be no retrogression until our world comes to an end. "The moment will come, then, when the sun will shine only on free men on this earth, on men who will recognize no master but their reason; when tyrants and slaves, priests and their stupid or hypocritical instruments will exist only in history or on the stage; when men will study the efforts and sufferings that characterized the past only to guard vigilantly against any recurrence of superstition and tyranny," and stifle them under the weight of reason—should they ever dare to reappear![7] Moral, political, and above all social science will progress and point the way to happiness: the colonies will be freed, the slaves will be emancipated, women will at last become the equals of men, barbarous nations will civilize themselves. As the productivity of the soil increases and medicine improves, the population will increase as well, but the world will be hospitable to it. Men will grow more beneficent, just, and virtuous; family life will be happier; war will become obsolete; the arts and literature will participate in the general renaissance. Men's very faculties will refine and perfect themselves; with sounder food and habitations, with sensible exercise, high living standards, preventive medicine, men will live longer and healthier lives. Is it absurd, now, to suppose that this perfection of the human species should be regarded as susceptible of indefinite progress, that a time must come when death will be nothing more than the effect of extraordinary accidents or the slower and slower destruction of vital forces, and that, finally, the average duration of the interval between birth and that destruction will itself have no assignable limit? Doubtless, "man will not become immortal"; but cannot the length of life "grow ceaselessly?" It is such contemplation, the contemplation of man the master, freed from the tyrannies of accident and superstition alike, that "presents to the philosopher a spectacle which consoles him for the errors, the crimes, the injustices with which the world is still sullied, and whose victim he often is!"[8]

The future, Condorcet promised, would realize the possibilities

---

[6] Ibid., 237–8, 13.
[7] Ibid., 244.
[8] Ibid., 275–6.

of man; it would give his capacity for perfectibility full play. But, with all these heady prospects before him, Condorcet remained wary. The term "perfectibility," which he used with abandon and imprecision, aroused the skepticism of John Adams and of Malthus, but for Condorcet perfectibility meant capacity for growth rather than a guarantee of perfection. He did not think it necessary to reiterate the self-evident: man would always remain a mere mortal, subject to the limitations of the human condition, victim of the problems that progress inevitably brought into the world. Even in the glorious future man will become only "as happy as it is permitted him to be in the midst of sufferings, needs and losses, which are for him the necessary consequences of the general laws of the universe."[9] Even the term "indefinite" in Condorcet's confident prediction for the range of improvement subsisted in an aura of uncertainty and ambiguity that he took care not to dispel. Condorcet's optimism was not the facile cheerfulness of the man who ignores realities, but the stern, almost Roman determination of the man who has looked suffering in the face and taken it into his philosophy.

I need not labor the pathos of Condorcet's position—the victim of the world's injustice permitting himself this one oblique reference to his own situation, the prophet of progress prophesying in the shadow of the guillotine. It is perfectly obvious that many of Condorcet's hopes turned out to be misplaced. Subsequent history reads like a sardonic commentary on the *Esquisse;* the future was to falsify many of its predictions, and to fulfill others almost as though to show, with heavy irony, that men were no happier now that they had what Condorcet had wanted them to have—freedom, long life, affluence—than they had been without it. But the limitations of the *Esquisse* lie neither in its pathos (Condorcet's quixotic faith in the future is in its way admirable), nor in its optimism, a feeling, as I have insisted, that seemed appropriate to Condorcet's century and that infected even Condorcet's most determined critics. The limitations of the *Esquisse* lie rather in Condorcet's crude conception of historical causation.

Condorcet was a decent man, a humanitarian distressed by the

[9] From an unpublished fragment intended for the Tenth Epoch. Ibid., 595.

spectacle of suffering, a believer in good causes who wished mankind well. And he was an intelligent and learned man; his range of allusion in the *Esquisse*, considering his working conditions, is nothing less than impressive. But, as I have said, he failed to control his historical vision with historical discipline. Even his dialectical principle that the instruments of progress may be instruments of reaction and instruments of reaction the instruments of progress is a naïve, mechanical device. Worse than that, Condorcet took what one might call the polemical psychology of the philosophes to absurd lengths. The Enlightenment had divided the world into heroes and villains and attributed to their villains considerable insight into their villainy. Condorcet's tribal chiefs, primitive priests, and barbaric kings, to say nothing of popes and scholastic theologians, know precisely what they are doing when they encourage superstition: they want to keep themselves in power. Their own reason is clear and disenchanted; they do not believe in the mysteries they retail to their credulous subjects. Condorcet's villains, therefore, are simple men who can be characterized by simple epithets—they are tyrants, bigots, persecutors, frigid cynics. And, just as the misery of the past can be largely explained as the clash of interests, the marvels of the future can be safely predicted as flowing from improved education and social science, rational forces that serve to clarify men's true interests and thus reduce or eliminate their clash. The *Esquisse*, we must conclude, is as much a caricature of the Enlightenment as its testament; it is rationalism run riot, dominated by a simple-minded faith in science that confuses, over and over again, the improvement of techniques with advances in virtue and happiness.

But while this is an accurate reading of the *Esquisse*, it is not complete. The *Esquisse* testifies, if obliquely, to the mature self-confidence of a movement of which Condorcet was among the last representatives. The *Esquisse* selects the progress of the human mind as a central theme in history, and selects the eighteenth century as a period of strategic importance in that history. This meant that the philosophes were, more than philosophers in the past, and more than merchants or generals in their day, privileged agents of the historical process. The self-doubt and false modesty that had marked the philosophes of an earlier generation were gone; in Condorcet's *Esquisse* we can see the Enlightenment taking the burden of progress on its shoulders.

III

His naïve exuberance did not prevent Condorcet from differentiating among types of progress—had he not asserted that the labors of good men had done "much for the glory of man, something for his freedom, but still almost nothing for his happiness"? He would claim that "the progress of virtue has always accompanied that of enlightenment,"[1] but then his own history documented a rather more pessimistic conclusion: men might use, and often had used, science that they might dominate and exploit others.

The other philosophes were equally discriminating. They recognized that progress in one area did not automatically produce progress in all others. Diderot explicitly noted that to be virtuous and enlightened was not the same thing; and that, while error is always bad, enlightenment can be abused.[2] Voltaire carefully referred to his admired seventeenth century as a century "of great talents much more than that of enlightenment,"[3] and he sprinkled his historical works with painful examples of great art, great wealth, great cultivation producing neither virtue nor happiness.[4] I have already described Rousseau's conviction that cultivation brings sophistication and a sterile artificiality, and Wieland's law of compensation. Gibbon made the central distinction almost painfully plain in the open-

---

[1] Ibid., 78.

[2] See Diderot to Sophie Volland, September 22, 1761. *Correspondance*, III, 313. Again, in May 1769, he wrote to Madame de Maux: "It is quite certain that we are not so barbarous as our forefathers. We are more enlightened. Are we better? That is another question." Ibid., IX, 61. And it was in this vein that Diderot thought Voltaire had started out as a great man and become a good man (to Falconet, [May 15, 1767], ibid., VII, 63.) Diderot's correspondence is eloquent witness to the complexities of the idea of progress in the philosophes' minds. On the one hand, Diderot could grimly say, "I am convinced that it is a thousand times easier for an enlightened people to return to barbarism than for a barbaric people to take a single step toward civilization," and on the other, hopefully, "Enlightenment can move from country to country, but it cannot be extinguished." Diderot to Princess Dashkoff (April 3, 1771), ibid., XI, 21; and to Falconet, (February 15, 1766), ibid., VI, 65.

[3] *Épître à Boileau, ou mon testament* (1769), in *Œuvres*, X, 398.

[4] See for instance, *Essai sur les mœurs*, II, 865.

ing words of his *Essai sur l'étude de la littérature:* "The history of empires is that of men's misery. The history of the sciences is that of their grandeur and happiness."[5]

Everything could be abused, even science. But while there was much about progress that remained shrouded in uncertainty, there were two things of which the philosophes remained confident: if there was one area of human experience in which progress was reliable it was science, and if there was any real hope for man, it was science that would realize it. Turgot spoke for them all. With his usual gift for defining logical categories, he gave science a distinctive place in culture: "The knowledge of nature and of the truth are as infinite as they are. The arts, whose object it is to please us, are limited as we are. Ceaselessly, time hatches new discoveries in the sciences; but poetry, painting, music, have a fixed point determined by the spirit of language, the imitation of nature, the limited sensitivity of our organs; they reach this point with slow steps and cannot go beyond it. The great men of the century of Augustus reached it, and they are still our models."[6]

I have said that by incorporating the recovery of nerve into their program, the philosophes emancipated themselves from their beloved ancients. This emancipation was possible precisely because in science the great men of Augustus' century were no longer appropriate models. In the seventeenth-century quarrel between the ancients and the moderns the moderns had rested their case precisely on the superiority of modern over ancient science: "The Beautiful Bosom of Nature," Sprat wrote in 1667, in his *History of the Royal Society,* "will be expos'd to our view: we shall enter into its garden, and taste of its Fruits, and satisfy ourselves with its plenty; instead of Idle talking, and wandering, under its fruitless shadows; as the Peripatetics did in their first institution, and their successors have done ever since."[7] And Sir William Temple, who defended the ancients against Wotton, acknowledged that it was the rise of "the new philosophy" that had given the moderns their arguments for progress.[8] In the eighteenth century the philosophes

---

[5] *Miscellaneous Works,* IV, 15.
[6] *Discours sur les progrès,* in *Œuvres,* I, 214–15.
[7] Quoted in Richard Foster Jones: "The Background of 'The Battle of the Books,' " in Jones *et al.: The Seventeenth Century,* 17.
[8] See ibid., 33.

adopted their modern position without reserve, and with new arguments. The ancients, wrote Voltaire, were magnificent in all things, in fact unsurpassed, except for their natural science, which was nothing less than silly.[9] Consequently, "there isn't a little book in science today that isn't more useful than all the books of antiquity."[1] True, it was refreshing to see men returning to sound antiquity after languishing so long in the barbarism of the schools, but they had not returned to ancient science for much more than entertainment and a few ideas: in the natural sciences at least, Voltaire wrote, the quarrel between the ancients and moderns has definitely been settled, in favor of the moderns. This had some rather odd consequences: "A simple mechanic like the abbé Nollet, who knows nothing but recent experiments, is a better physicist than Democritus and Descartes. He is not as great a man as they were, but he knows more, and knows it better."[2] I have defined the Enlightenment as a mixture of classicism, impiety, and science, and the philosophes as modern pagans; what made the pagans modern and gave them hope for the future was that they could use science to control their classicism by establishing the superiority of their own, second age of criticism over the first, and thus keep their respect for their ancestors within proper bounds.

---

[9] See "Philosopher," *Philosophical Dictionary,* II, 420.
[1] "Job," in ibid., II, 336.
[2] *Notebooks,* 221.

CHAPTER THREE

The Uses of Nature

THE ENLIGHTENMENT'S ENTANGLEMENT with science is pervaded with ironies. The philosophes celebrated the scientific revolution, accepted its findings, and imitated its methods. They pushed its philosophical implications far beyond what the scientists themselves would have thought warranted. They tried to apply the scientific style of thinking to the regions of aesthetic, social, and political theory. But they discovered that, having eliminated the problem of God, they had burdened themselves with new difficulties, almost as intractable as the old.

In the age of the Enlightenment, that great time of discovery, consolidation, and triumphant popularizing, it did not take unusual perspicacity to recognize the scientific revolution as an extraordinary event. It was plain that this revolution was the most far-reaching upheaval the West had experienced since the Protestant Reformation, indeed more far-reaching: the discoveries of Galileo and Boyle and Newton were changing the world more drastically than it had been changed by the doctrines of Luther and Calvin. The spectacular intellectual conquests of astronomers and physicists made science interesting to many, and not to philosophes alone: the philosophes might think themselves privileged admirers, but in fact science had many other courtiers in the age of the Enlightenment; indeed, when Rousseau denigrated the sciences in his first *Discours*, it was the Jesuit *Journal de Trévoux* that defended them against this eloquent slanderer.

The philosophes welcomed the widespread passion for science —the mass of popular explanations of abstruse theories, the new scientific journals—but, as men of letters, they were also a little uneasy about it. In 1735 Voltaire, on a short visit to Paris from Cirey, complained that "verses are hardly fashionable any longer." Now "everybody has begun to play at being the geometer and the physicist," and as a result, "sentiment, imagination, and the graces have been banished. Someone who had lived under Louis XIV and returned to the world would no longer recognize the French; he'd think that the Germans had conquered this country. Literature is perishing before our very eyes."[1] Obviously literature was far from perishing—Voltaire was seeing to keeping it alive—and the graces were still in their place, but Voltaire's comical lament testifies to a widespread and often serious interest in the sciences.

In fact, the scientific revolution, far from challenging poetry, enriched it; it invaded Western languages and literature with its terms, metaphors, and themes. Critics of the new learning were no less obsessed with scientific language than its admirers; Pope and Swift at the beginning, Blake at the end of the eighteenth century tried to damage the new "mechanistic philosophy" by punning on its technical terminology and ridiculing its practitioners. In vain: their Humanist's fear of science was eclipsed by the confidence of its supporters. James Thomson's *Seasons*, a comprehensive celebration of the metaphysical and aesthetic virtues of the new science, is only the best known of a host of poetic tributes to natural philosophy. Far from dismaying eighteenth-century poets, science stabilized their philosophy, enlarged their vocabulary, and opened unexplored regions for their talents. "Voltaire's knowledge of physics," Condorcet asserted, "served his poetic talent"; his "study of the sciences widened the sphere of his poetic ideas, and enriched his verses with new images."[2] And what was true of Voltaire was true of other poets: theological allusions and metaphysical conceits gave way to "philosophic" language, with little loss and much gain to poetry. If poetry in the eighteenth century was indeed in decline, as some of the poets themselves regretfully acknowledged, it was not science that was the cause.

The philosophes seized upon the new science as an irresistible force and enlisted it in their polemics, identifying themselves with sound method, progress, success, the future. They had a certain right to their acquisitiveness. We are inclined to think of the scien-

---

[1] Voltaire to Cideville (April 16, 1735). *Correspondence*, IV, 48–9.
[2] *Vie de Voltaire*, in Voltaire: *Œuvres*, I, 214. Some scholars, including Gustave Lanson, have objected that this is a doubtful assertion (see Lanson: *Voltaire* [1906], 73-4), but it is not wholly without merit.

tists among the philosophes as literary men with a scientific avocation, but, in fact, practically all the philosophes with serious scientific interests—Maupertuis, Buffon, d'Alembert, Lichtenberg, Franklin, Kant, Condorcet—began with science before they turned to philosophy, and the intelligent amateurs and popularizers among them —Voltaire and Diderot among others—did not have far to go to consult the experts; some of their best friends were mathematicians, physicists, and astronomers.

But the philosophes' seizure of science was a far from untroubled affair. As the sciences grew more technical, more professional, they developed autonomously, and confronted the philosophes, eager as they were to turn knowledge into politics, with linguistic, ethical, and metaphysical difficulties they had not anticipated and for which most of them were ill-prepared. Hume and d'Alembert, Condillac and Kant thought about the philosophical implications of the sciences fruitfully and constructively; they set the terms on which the debate over the nature of science is still conducted today. But there were other philosophes who, as the eighteenth century progressed, found science to be not a servant or an ally but an embarrassment.

1. THE ENLIGHTENMENT'S NEWTON

I

THE SCIENTIFIC REVOLUTION was a voyage into abstraction and specialization, but, fortunately for their cause, the philosophes found it possible to dramatize that revolution by deifying one of the revolutionaries. While science was surrendering old mysteries, the men of the Enlightenment constructed a new mystique: they satisfied their need for a representaive figure, their craving for a hero, through Isaac Newton.

Newton was a congenial kind of hero for the philosophes: when Voltaire set the fashion for the Enlightenment by calling Newton the greatest man who ever lived, he contrasted him, significantly, with the heroes that had served earlier, more bellicose ages: "If true greatness consists of having been endowed by heaven with powerful genius, and of using it to enlighten oneself and others, then a man like M. Newton (we scarcely find one like him in ten centuries) is truly the great man, and those politicians and conquerors (whom no century has been without) are generally nothing but celebrated villains."[3]

Everything cooperated to make Newton into a fitting object of a mystique. He was eccentric and fallible enough to provide memorable stories—like the imperishable anecdote about Newton meditating on fruit dropping from his trees which Voltaire brought back with him from England. Equipped with penetrating vision where others had seen nothing, unsurpassed and unsurpassable in his achievement, too preoccupied and too aloof to conduct his own polemics, Newton had unified disparate phenomena, laid bare age-old secrets, and, with one almost incredible intellectual effort, compelled nature to order. He had been a visionary disciplined by the appeal to experience, an empiricist illuminated by profound vision, a pioneer who employed all weapons in the scientific arsenal—mathematics, experiment, observation—with equal ease. Such a giant did more than invite assent to his theories; he commanded submission. By mid-century, d'Alembert noted, Newton's system was "so generally accepted, that people were beginning to dispute their author the honor of having discovered it," and in 1776 Voltaire surprised no one when he announced, quite simply, "We are all his disciples now."[4] Even the Cartesians were irresistibly drawn into the circle of admiration: Fontenelle composed his eulogy for the *Académie des sciences* on the occasion of Newton's death as though he were in the presence of a towering natural force: what a marvelous mathematician, he exclaimed, to have unraveled the mysterious complexities of the universe![5]

Not surprisingly, the philosophes' celebrations of Newton all bear a certain family resemblance: Beccaria was delighted to hear his friends calling him "little Newton"; d'Alembert and Jefferson

---

[3] Lettre XII, *Lettres philosophiques*, I, 153. And see Voltaire's letter to the abbé d'Olivet, October 18 (1736): Newton, he writes there, was "the greatest man who ever lived." *Correspondence*, V, 281.

[4] D'Alembert: *Discours préliminaire*, in *Mélanges*, I, 137. Voltaire: to the *Académie française*, in *Œuvres*, VII, 335.

[5] It would, of course, be oversimplifying his thought to call Fontenelle simply a Cartesian; while he never abandoned Descartes's physics and his famous *tourbillons*, he was sympathetic to Newton's method and, as his eulogy makes plain, aware of Newton's stature.

displayed his portrait in their studies; all of them, following Voltaire, included him in their trinity of the greatest men in history, placing him beside Bacon and Locke or (if they were Germans), Locke and Leibniz. Hume gave Newton a glowing paragraph in his *History of England*, portraying him simply as thinking man incarnate: "In Newton this island may boast of having produced the greatest and rarest genius that ever rose for the ornament and instruction of the species. Cautious in admitting no principle but such as were founded on experiment; but resolute to adopt every such principle, however new or unusual: From modesty, ignorant of his superiority above the rest of mankind; and thence, less careful to accommodate his reasonings to common apprehensions: More anxious to merit than acquire fame: He was, from these causes, long unknown to the world; but his reputation at last broke out with a lustre, which scarcely any writer, during his own lifetime, had ever before attained. While Newton seemed to draw off the veil from some of the mysteries of nature, he shewed at the same time the imperfections of the mechanical philosophy; and thereby restored her ultimate secrets to that obscurity in which they ever did and ever will remain."[6] It was this magnificent specimen of enlightened man—the philosophe idealized, purified, as he aspired to be—that Kant celebrated and sought to serve in his major philosophical writings. And when Kant suggested that Rousseau deserved to be called the Newton of the moral world, he was at once assigning Newton a place in the intellectual atmosphere of the Enlightenment and giving Rousseau the highest praise he could imagine.

In the deification of Newton, the Enlightenment of the philosophes and the age of the Enlightenment were at one. Devout literary men and philosophers who would have little to do with the philosophes' radical notions shared, and in fact anticipated, the philosophes' worship of Newton. At the time of Newton's death, James Thomson composed a *Poem Sacred to the Memory of Sir Isaac Newton*, whose hyperbole appeared to its contemporaries as a sober, truthful report—and not to its contemporaries alone. When Thomson had occasion to rethink his verses on Newton and revise his eulogy, he took nothing back, and a quarter of a century later

---

[6] *History of England* . . . (edn. 1780), VIII, 326.

Lessing would note that by itself Thomson's *Zum Andenken des Isaac Newtons*, even if he had written nothing else, would have secured him "an outstanding place among poets."[7] Pope's famous couplet about Newton, which saw him as a divinely inspired bringer of light, became a master metaphor, almost a master cliché, and the adjectives "divine" and "immortal" became practically compulsory. Sometime around 1730, Voltaire put his own version into his notebook: "Before Kepler, all men were blind, Kepler had one eye, and Newton had two eyes."[8] As late as 1750, the publicist Benjamin Martin composed a *Panegyrick on the Newtonian Philosophy*, in which he described *"Natural Philosophy"* as a "Mystery that has been hid from Ages, and from Generations; but is now made manifest, to all Nations, by the divine Writings of the immortal Sir Isaac Newton."[9]

Interestingly enough, the originator of this literary convention was not a poet but a scientist: when the astronomer Edmond Halley saw Newton's *Principia* through the press, he took the opportunity to express his admiration with some prefatory Latin hexameters, and concluded: *nec fas est proprius Mortali attingere Divos*—it is not lawful for mortals to approach divinity nearer than this. The English scientific community, in fact, despite the professional disputes that disturbed Newton's later career, and the English crown, despite its intellectual mediocrity, elevated Newton into a major national asset. In 1703, the Royal Society, for years in the hands of aristocratic amateurs, made Newton its president, and in 1705, Queen Anne knighted him—the first time in English history, it seems, that a scientist had been thus honored for his scientific work. When Newton died, he was buried in splendid pomp at Westminster Abbey among the great men of the nation, "like a king," said Voltaire, who was there, "who had been good to his subjects."[1]

With Voltaire as its chief propagator, the mystique of Newton traveled from England to the Continent with little delay. In the 1730s, at the height of his preoccupation with natural science, Vol-

---

[7] "Leben des Herrn Jacob Thomson," *Theatralische Bibliothek* (1754), in *Schriften*, VI, 61.
[8] *Notebooks*, 63.
[9] Quoted in Brooke Hindle: *The Pursuit of Science in Revolutionary America, 1735-1789* (1956), 80.
[1] Lettre XIV, *Lettres philosophiques*, II, 2.

taire composed some stirring poems in praise of Newton, and in
1738, when the Maupertuis-Clairaut expeditions were producing
mathematical proofs of Newton's claims that the earth is flattened
at the poles—a claim that Cartesian astronomers had denied—Voltaire depicted the spirit of Newton exhorting his faithful followers
from the empyrean to produce empirical confirmation for his theories. And in the second half of the eighteenth century, nearly half
a century after Newton's death, the abbé Jacques Delille adapted
Pope's famous couplet for his French readers:

> O pouvoir d'un grand homme et d'une âme divine!
> Ce que Dieu seul a fait, Newton seul l'imagine,
> Et chaque astre répète en proclamant leur nom:
> Gloire à Dieu qui créa les mondes et Newton![2]

In the same manner—that is, with remarkable poverty of invention
and equally remarkable dependence on English models—Helvétius,
Marmontel, Saint-Lambert offered versified celebrations of Newton
the demi-god, the discoverer of universal attraction and the true
theory of colors. While in England Newton's *Opticks* had aroused
the poets' interest from the moment of publication, in France it was
Voltaire, some decades later, who claimed to have been "the first
poet to have drawn a comparison from the refraction of light,"[3]
and once Voltaire had drawn it, others followed.

German men of letters in their turn dutifully copied British
and French rhetoric. Albrecht von Haller, groping for an appropriate apostrophe to his fellow student the mathematician and physicist Johannes Gessner, felt compelled to remind him that he was
about to follow in Newton's footsteps and thus enter nature's secret
councils, led by the Newtonian art of measurement, the infallible
bridle of the imagination:

> Bald steigest du auf Newtons Pfad,
> In der Natur geheimen Rath,
> Wohin dich deine Mesz-Kunst leitet;
> O Mesz-Kunst, Zaum der Phantasie!

---

[2] Delille: *Œuvres*, (1824), IX, 7, quoted in Ruth T. Murdoch:
"Newton and the French Muse," *JHI*, XIX, 3 (June 1958), 324.
[3] Quoted in Murdoch, 326.

Wer dir will folgen, irret nie;
Wer ohne dich will gehn, der gleitet.[4]

Lessing introduced some variation into the accepted pattern by comparing Newton to Homer and imposing on him the burden of representing the moderns against the ancients: if such a divine man as Newton had chosen to equal Homer in poetry, he would have succeeded. But the variation was insignificant: obedient to prevailing fashion, Lessing punned on the theory of attraction and dragged out the image of Newton, the heavenly visitor:

Die Wahrheit kam zu uns im Glanz herabgeflogen,
Und hat in Newton gern die Menschheit angezogen.[5]

From country to country and decade to decade, the tributes to Newton changed little. They were always fervent, usually sincere, but in the long run mechanical and monotonous. But then it was precisely this monotony—one poet, usually more well-intentioned than well-informed, rewriting another poet—that gave the literary deification its cultural significance. The poets, after all, claimed neither to solve scientific difficulties nor to provide scientific information; their task was to reflect and diffuse a new attitude toward nature, toward knowledge, toward the world.

II

The poetic celebration of Newton would have been impossible without the serious exploration of his work that accompanied it, undertaken, first in England and then elsewhere, by mathematicians, physicists, and chemists intent on clarifying the Newtonian system for themselves, for the professional student, and for intelligent but bewildered amateurs like John Locke who wanted to grasp Newton's system without troubling to learn Newton's mathematics.

This exploration was essential because Newton, in offering some

---

[4] Haller: *Versuch schweizerischer Gedichte* (11th edn., 1777), 157.
[5] "Aus einem Gedicht an den Herrn Mxxx" (fragment of 1748), *Schriften*, I, 243, 245.

large answers, had raised some large questions. Newton left some ingenious hints concerning chemistry, but their real meaning and possible fertility remained to be explored; and a number of his most interesting ideas in mechanics were obscurely expressed or incompletely worked out. Newton had expounded, and in his practice triumphantly demonstrated, a method, but its implications for the human sciences, and even the natural sciences, were by no means settled. If audacious propagandists like Voltaire offered relatively simple solutions to Newton's methodological difficulties, this simplicity was deceptive—a function less of scientific thinking than of polemical skill. In fact, the very direction that science would have to take after Newton remained in doubt. Newton's own attitude was perspicuous and consistent: he had disclaimed any knowledge of the nature of gravity and humbly deprecated his contributions by reviving the medieval commonplace of "standing on the shoulders of Giants"; late in life he had compared himself to a boy discovering pretty pebbles on the seashore "while the great ocean of truth lay all undiscovered before me." The philosophes liked to repeat these remarks as valuable support for the Enlightenment's campaign against system-building and in behalf of "philosophical modesty."[6] Yet, while Newton's disciples honored Newton's modesty—did not d'Alembert and Hume and Kant repeat Newton's injunctions on that score?—some of his more impetuous followers used Newton's very triumphs as an argument against Newton's self-restraint and revived the age-old claim for universal knowledge. The history of eighteenth-century science is far more than the history of assimilating Newton's ideas, confirming Newton's guesses, generalizing Newton's conceptions beyond his own expectations, and wrestling with Newton's philosophical puzzles; especially in the field of mechanics, the Bernoullis, Euler, Lagrange, and d'Alembert did much fruitful work on their own. But "Newtonianism" dominated even those who struck out on new and untried paths so that it incorporated, with its capacious prestige, scientific explorations that had little to do with Newton's work.

Whatever the difficulties Newton had left, whatever the work of independent researchers, the informal and unorganized troop of

---

[6] See *The Rise of Modern Paganism*, 127–59.

Newton's popularizers did their work quickly and effectively, in England and on the Continent alike. The appetite for expositions and commentaries seemed inexhaustible: Algarotti's *Newtonianismo per le dame* was promptly translated into English, as though the English had not yet produced enough popularizations of their own. By mid-century, such books were all over the Western world.

The rapid spread of Newton's ideas on the Continent only underlines Newton's towering authority. Many continental scientists knew English, and came to England to visit Newton or his followers; others read the Latin lectures of Newton's expositors and became Newtonians at a distance. A center—for years, *the* center— for the assimilation and propagation of Newtonianism on the Continent was the University of Leyden. Boerhaave, the great chemist, botanist, philosopher, and physician who presided over the school of medicine there, was one of Newton's most faithful and most effective allies. In his published lecture of 1715, the *Oratio de comparando certo in physicis,* Boerhaave laid down the line that he and his pupils were to follow for decades: Newton's theory of attraction is the true explanation of celestial and terrestrial phenomena, while Newton's modest declaration of ignorance concerning its cause and nature is the true method of scientific inquiry; other great natural philosophers, Boerhaave argued, even his compatriot Huyghens, had fallen into erroneous theories through the *esprit de système;* yet, he added, consistent in this too with Newton's spirit, this kind of principled caution should not lead to "pyrrhonism in physics"—a proper reliance on experience as point of departure and continuous control, and on reason and mathematics, should lead the inquirer to reliable knowledge of the world of nature.[7]

Boerhaave reiterated these arguments with the persistence of the pedagogue seized by a persuasive system; his younger colleagues, an impressive group of investigators and publicists, reiterated them in their own lectures and writings, in their own manner. S'Gravesande, who had met Newton and kept in close enough touch with the English scientific fraternity to be elected to the Royal Society, published his treatise *Physices Elementa Mathematica,* in 1715, "to

---

[7] Pierre Brunet: *Les physiciens hollandais et la méthode expérimentale en France au XVIIIe siècle* (1926), *passim.*

make good the *Newtonian* Method, which I have followed in this
Work"[8]; and he continued to make it good in his later writings.
Musschenbroek and Nieuwentyt, Boerhaave and s'Gravesande's
younger colleagues, like their elders, corresponded with English
scientists, experimented in the hope of confirming Newton's theories, and publicized their findings and their procedures to a wide
audience.

Their influence was nothing less than astonishing. In 1736
Musschenbroek noted with pardonable pride that "Physical science
has never been cultivated in Holland so much as it is today," and
that physical science, it was clear, was Newtonian in temper. Physics,
he added, "makes new conquests every day, and is insensibly spreading into most professions." In consequence, the new consumers of
science "have formed societies in several of the principal cities,
where they occupy themselves with making experiments, using a
large number of expensive instruments, and where they spend their
time agreeably in research into the properties and operations of all
sorts of bodies."[9] This passion for Newtonianism was not confined
to the United Provinces; Leyden was a gathering place for foreign
students, including Haller and La Mettrie, and foreign visitors, including Voltaire. Books by Dutch scientists were translated as readily as books by English scientists, and carrying the same message
they won the same influence. In 1738, upon Boerhaave's death,
Fontenelle acknowledged in his eulogy, "All states of Europe supplied him with disciples, principally Germany and even England,
proud though it is—justly—of the flourishing state of its sciences."[1]

It was perhaps no coincidence that Fontenelle should have
omitted France from his list, for by 1738 the impact of Newton
on France was still problematical. But it was beginning to be real
enough: in 1732, nearly half a century after Newton's *Principia*,
Maupertuis, a member of the Royal Society who had for years
goaded the *Académie des sciences*, finally published his *Discours
sur les différentes figures des astres*, the first book by a Frenchman
fully to accept and clearly to expound Newton's theory of gravita-

[8] E. W. Strong: "Newtonian Explications of Natural Philosophy,"
JHI, XVIII, 1 (January 1957), 68.
[9] Brunet: *Les physiciens hollandais*, 93.
[1] Ibid., 103.

tion. In 1756, when that theory had triumphed in France, two years before Maupertuis's death and several years after he had quarreled with him, Voltaire claimed that *he* had been "the first man in France to explain Newton's discoveries."[2] In view of the help that Maupertuis had given Voltaire with his chapters on Newton in the *Lettres philosophiques*, the claim was ungracious in the extreme. Voltaire's anxiety to participate in Newton's prestige in France was partly literary vanity, partly an attempt to show himself competent in a difficult and popular pursuit. But it also showed, once again, how strong a hold the mystique of Newton had on its propagators.

III

Voltaire's claim was overstated, but it hints at his share in the appropriation of Newton from the enlightened atmosphere of his time for the Enlightenment of the philosophes. It was Voltaire, with his quick intelligence, who was the first of the philosophes to grasp the uses to which Newton's theories could be put. By no means all of Voltaire's Newtonianism was manipulative: his excursions to Leyden, his dogged reading of scientific monographs, his conversations with French scientists, his solemn experiments in physics performed at the château and in the company of Madame du Châtelet all display the disinterested side of his passion for scientific understanding. At the same time, first in his *Lettres philosophiques*, and then, four years later, in 1738, in his *Éléments de la philosophie de Newton*, Voltaire demonstrated the political utility of a culture hero. Newton was right, and hence the Enlightenment, basing itself on Newton's method as much as on Newton's discoveries, must be right as well—it was as simple as that.

In the *Lettres philosophiques*, Voltaire still held his aggressive-

---

[2] In a note of 1756, added to his *Épître à la Madame du Châtelet sur la philosophie de Newton* (1736), in *Œuvres*, X, 302 *n*. Interestingly enough, Voltaire's malicious estimate of Maupertuis survived Maupertuis, and even Voltaire. In his biography of Voltaire, published in 1787, Condorcet perpetuated the old slanders by calling Maupertuis an intelligent man but a "mediocre scientist and even more mediocre philosopher." In Voltaire: *Œuvres*, I, 231.

ness in check. Here, Voltaire's Newton is a fascinating and admirable historical personage, the source of anecdotes, the appropriate subject of hero worship. But—as a last concession to the reigning Cartesianism in France and perhaps to his own uncertainty—Voltaire refuses to commit himself wholly to Newton's theory of gravitation, and takes refuge in a witty comparison: "A Frenchman arriving in London finds things much changed, in philosophy as in all the rest," he writes in a characteristic passage that has been much quoted. "He has left the world full; he finds it empty. In Paris, one sees the universe composed of vortices of subtle matter; in London, one sees nothing of the sort. In our country, it is the pressure of the moon that causes the tides in the sea; in England, it is the sea that gravitates toward the moon." Indeed, "with your Cartesians, everything happens through an impulsion which is hardly understood; with Mr. Newton, it happens through an attraction whose cause one does not know any better. In Paris, you think that the earth is shaped like a melon; in London, it is flattened at the two poles. For a Cartesian, light exists in the air; for a Newtonian, it comes from the sun in six and a half minutes. Your chemistry performs all its operations with acids, alcalis, and subtle matter; English chemistry is dominated by attraction."[3] The contradictions between these systems, Voltaire says evasively, are fierce indeed. But whatever the scientific complexities, one thing was perfectly clear to Voltaire, and he did not hesitate for a moment to point it out to his French readers: while Descartes was reviled, intimidated, and hounded from his country, Newton was left in peace, honored, and rewarded. Here was one use of Newton for the Enlightenment: he was a demonstration of the advantages of freedom, and, conversely, of the stupidity of repression.

But even at this early stage, Voltaire's Newton was not simply a representative figure in the struggle for intellectual freedom; in some pioneering passages of the *Lettres philosophiques*, Voltaire noted the virtues of Newton's disciplined empiricism—that famous

---

[3] Lettre XIV, *Lettres philosophiques*, II, 1. As early as 1730, Voltaire had added some Newtonian verses to a revised version of his epic, the *Henriade*, but hedged his position with a disclaimer in the footnotes: "Whether we accept Mr. Newton's attraction or not, it is still certain that the heavenly spheres seem to attract or repel each other." *Œuvres*, VIII, 170, quoted in Murdoch: "Newton and the French Muse," 325.

"philosophical modesty" which was to become such an effective slogan for the philosophes' assault on Christian theory and on dogmatic metaphysics. Descartes's physics, Voltaire wrote, was too facile, too dogmatic to be convincing; Newton, in contrast, respected the facts, heroically faced obscure phenomena, and refused to make systems.

From such general approval it was only a short distance to a firm commitment to Newton, and, encouraged by years of research, reflection, and conversations with persuasive Newtonians like Maupertuis, Voltaire made this commitment in his *Éléments de la philosophie de Newton*. There are no evasions in this book, and few anecdotes. Newton is quite simply the discoverer of the true system of the world, and, quite simply, the destroyer of Cartesian vortices, of subtle matter and the plenum. "This philosopher," Voltaire wrote in his dedication to Madame du Châtelet, "gathered in during his lifetime all the glory he deserved; he aroused no envy because he could have no rival. The learned world were his disciples, the rest admired him without daring to claim that they understood him."[4]

The Éléments is a venture in making Newton understood. "The author of the *Éléments*," Voltaire wrote a year after the book appeared, "tried to make these new truths available to minds with little practice in these matters."[5] The book proceeds, in sober, classical logic and with superb lucidity, through three sections, beginning with Newton's religion, continuing with Newton's optics, and concluding with Newton's physics. With a great measure of success, without recourse to mathematics, Voltaire seeks to explain such difficult matters as the nature of perception, the character of colors, the orbits of the planets, the laws of gravitation.

Voltaire's *Éléments*, then, is an exercise in high popularization, but it functions in a wider cultural context, as a participant in a great debate. It is not an accident that Voltaire begins his exposition with a series of chapters on Newton's religious convictions, and calls the whole a book on Newton's "philosophy." In the late seventeenth century, and throughout the eighteenth, when the character, the methods, the very territory of the sciences were still unsettled, debates over science were debates over religion, and religion was a

---

[4] *Éléments de la philosophie de Newton*, in *Œuvres*, XXII, 402.
[5] "Réponse aux objections principales qu'on a faites en France contre la philosophie de Newton" (1739), in *Œuvres*, XXIII, 72.

subject in which everyone was vitally concerned. Voltaire's *Éléments*, therefore, at least touches on issues that agitated educated men—and, as Voltaire's Madame du Châtelet was not the only one to prove, educated women—in the eighteenth century. The debates between Newtonians and Leibnizians and between Newtonians and Cartesians were debates that Voltaire, alert to controversy, knew to be no mere quarrels over laws of physics. They were, often implicit, sometimes explicit, acknowledgment that the triumph of Newtonian science was transforming the contours of religious belief in the century of the Enlightenment.

2. NEWTON'S PHYSICS WITHOUT NEWTON'S GOD

I

THE SCIENTIFIC REVOLUTION of the seventeenth century had marked no break with the Christian view of the world. The discoveries of natural philosophers threatened the grosser forms of superstition, enlarged the bounds of naturalistic explanation, and lent authority to those proofs for the existence of God that relied on the divine work in nature rather than on the divine word to man. It frightened only a few exceptional spirits. "Whatever God himself has been pleased to think worthy of making," wrote Robert Boyle, as firm in his personal piety as he was bold in his scientific inquiries, "its fellow creature Man should not think unworthy of knowing." Indeed, "If the omniscient author of nature knew that the study of his works tends to make men disbelieve his Being or Attributes, he would not have given them so many invitations to study and contemplate Nature."[6] Few scientists in the time of Boyle and Newton predicted that true religion and true science would some day be at war; few of them so much as acknowledged that religion and science might belong to two potentially hostile camps. There were border skirmishes, no more, and even these were less

---

[6] "Some Considerations Touching the Usefulness of Experimental Philosophy" (1663), quoted in Martha Ornstein: *The Role of Scientific Societies in the Seventeenth Century* (3rd edn., 1938), 58-9.

between theology and science than between theology and some extreme philosophical consequences drawn from scientific discoveries. It is true that churchmen condemned certain scientific views as heretical, but this was a familiar story, and seventeenth-century Christians disagreed, as Christians had always disagreed, on the wisdom of particular condemnations. To side with Galileo was not to side with infidelity. Throughout the seventeenth century it was the rare scientist who repudiated Providence or miracles, even obliquely; Galileo's spirited polemics, which had frightened the papacy, had been directed mainly against Aristotelian metaphysics, crude Biblical literalism, and the claim that theology was the master science; the polemics of later scientists aimed at similar targets.[7] Newton thus pursued his researches into Biblical chronology in the best of scientific company. Although they were all revolutionaries, natural philosophers solemnly and sincerely announced their discoveries as demonstrations that Christianity was true and in fact divine; most of them would have been outraged to see the philosophes in the eighteenth century abuse these discoveries to demonstrate that Christianity was in fact all too human and false.

For Newton, God was an active being: he is Creator and watchful master, wise, just, good, and holy. This "Being," Newton argued, "governs all things, not as the soul of the world, but as Lord over all"; he is a "powerful, ever-living Agent" who prevents the fixed stars from falling upon one another—perhaps by natural, perhaps by miraculous, means—and occasionally corrects the irregularities introduced into the solar system by the eccentric orbits of the planets and the incursions of comets.[8] The laws of nature, themselves the creation of God, must be supplemented by special acts of his Providence. Like other modern Christians of his day, Newton was inclined to read the Pentateuch not as a literal report but as a convincing account of creation and man's earliest history adapted

---

[7] See *The Rise of Modern Paganism*, 314–17: Thomas Sprat, whose famous *History of the Royal Society* (1667) was a vigorous defense of the new philosophy, later became a bishop; Robert Boyle left £350 in his will endowing lectures defending Christianity; Joseph Glanvill and after him Cotton Mather were at once champions of modern science, Fellows of the Royal Society, and believers in witchcraft.
[8] See *Newton's Philosophy of Nature*, 41.

by the narrator to the limited understanding of his audience. Yet Newton did not doubt that while Moses had used metaphors and images, he had told the essential truth: whatever God's precise mode of procedure, whatever the precise number of days he had taken to make the universe, God, Newton believed, had created the world and every living creature. In an age and in a country sensitive to the threat of infidelity, Newton kept his fellowship at Cambridge and enjoyed profitable preferment in the government service. He was a Unitarian, but not a deist: no deist, no matter how brilliant, could have had Newton's public career.

Yet, two generations of philosophes, anxious to poison relations between science and religion, found that, whatever Newton's own religious convictions, they could do without them. "I have not seen a Newtonian," Voltaire claimed in the 1730s, "who was not a theist in the strictest sense of the word." All of "Newton's philosophy necessarily leads to an awareness of a supreme Being, who has created everything, arranged everything freely."[9] But Voltaire was speaking only for the first generation, which eliminated the distinctly Christian element from Newton's thought. The second generation would go beyond even this and eliminate the religious element altogether.

It is one of the minor ironies in the larger ironic pattern that Voltaire's insistence on a stable, lawful universe as the only basis for true natural religion placed him in the company of Leibniz, the great compromiser, with whom Voltaire thought he was disagreeing. Beginning in 1705, Leibniz had been embroiled with Newton—or, rather, since Newton refused to be drawn, with Newton's spokesmen—first over the invention of the calculus, then over the character of gravity, and finally, beginning in 1715, over the theological consequences of Newton's God. The debate, conducted in Newton's behalf by Samuel Clarke, a skillful and well-informed controversialist—"a veritable thinking machine," Voltaire called him[1]—ranged widely over many theological and metaphysical questions raised by Newton's system, but for the philosophes the nature of God and the influence of Newton's beliefs on the status of natural religion remained the critical questions. "Natural religion itself," so Leibniz began his assault, "seems to decay (in England) very much," and

---

[9] Éléments de la philosophie de Newton, in Œuvres, XXII, 403–4.
[1] Lettre VII, Lettres philosophiques, I, 72.

much of this seemed to him the fault of Locke's and Newton's doctrines: "Sir Isaac Newton, and his followers," Leibniz argued, have a "very odd opinion concerning the work of God. According to their doctrine, God Almighty wants to wind up his watch from time to time: otherwise it would cease to move. He had not, it seems, sufficient foresight to make it a perpetual motion." In Leibniz's sarcastic caricature, Newton's God is a clumsy watchmaker, "obliged to clean" his creation "now and then by an extraordinary concourse, and even to mend it." On the contrary, Leibniz insisted, "the same force and vigour remains always in the world, and only passes from one part of matter to another, agreeably to the laws of nature, and the beautiful preestablished order." God's miracles are acts not of repair, but of grace. "Whoever thinks otherwise, must needs have a very mean notion of the wisdom and power of God."[2]

Much to Leibniz's annoyance, Clarke in his reply turned the charge of subverting natural religion against the aggressor: "The notion of the world's being a great machine, going on without the interposition of God, as a clock continues to go without the assistance of a clockmaker; is the notion of materialism and fate, and tends, (under pretence of making God a *supra-mundane intelligence*,) to exclude providence and God's government in reality out of the world."[3] Stung, Leibniz sent a rejoinder, and the correspondence moved through many fields of controversy: Leibniz charged that Newton had reintroduced the old, discredited notion of the scholastic, occult qualities, with his mysterious doctrine of gravitation; that Newton had converted the physical career of the world into a perpetual miracle; and that Newton (and with him Clarke) had failed to understand the principle of sufficient reason, which would have taught them that God "wills only to produce what is the best among things possible"[4]—a principle to which Voltaire would return as late as the mid-1750s, in his *Candide*.

The correspondence was published in 1717, translated into German and French in 1720, and widely read; when Voltaire used it in the first book of his *Éléments*, its arguments on the nature of space and time, the vacuum, and the role of God in the physical

---

[2] Leibniz to Caroline, Princess of Wales, November 1715. *The Leibniz-Clarke Correspondence*, ed. H. G. Alexander (1956), 11–12.
[3] Clarke's first reply to Leibniz (November 26, 1715). Ibid., 14.
[4] Leibniz's fifth paper. Ibid., 81.

universe, were familiar. "It is perhaps," Voltaire noted, "the finest
monument we have of literary combat."[5] Voltaire found himself in a
strange situation. He sided with Clarke and Newton against Leibniz,
without hesitation: God had the freedom to make the world he
chose to make, and in any event, Newton's ideas, far from destroying
natural religion, guaranteed it. But without conceding, perhaps without seeing it, Voltaire found himself constrained to accept Leibniz's
central contention: the universe is regular and needs no miracles.

The awkwardness of Voltaire's argumentation suggests that the
protagonists in the great literary combat were in a false position.
They were partly vindicated, partly contradicted by the course of
natural philosophy in the eighteenth century. Leibniz was proved
right in defending the regularity of the universe, wrong to think
that his view would preserve natural religion; Clarke was wrong
to insist on divine intervention, proved right in seeing the Leib-
nizian view as an invitation to materialism. And Voltaire, for his
part, was right to insist on regularity, on Newtonian grounds, wrong
to think he could stem the tide of atheism, even though for several
decades it was Voltaire's particular brand of Newtonian deism that
dominated the Enlightenment.

Doubtless Voltaire contributed to this complex development by
pitting science against Christianity, though not against religion.
Whatever scientists themselves might believe, as Newtonian physics
secured its hold in the age of the Enlightenment, the philosophes
found much cause for satisfaction: for them at least, the developments in science offered confirmation for their secular philosophy.
The scientific community itself long kept a religious cast; while
there were some tensions between science and religion in the eighteenth century, the conflict did not reach the stage of war to the
death until a hundred years later, with Darwin. The worshipful
study of God's work, which had inspired Christians for many centuries, retained its vitality for many, perhaps most, scientists throughout the age of the Enlightenment. Stephen Hales, the distinguished
English chemist and physiologist, was an Anglican divine; Leonhard
Euler, perhaps the greatest mathematician of the eighteenth century,
always remained a devout Calvinist; Joseph Priestley, a versatile
and inventive scientist and philosophical materialist, combined his

---

[5] *Éléments de la philosophie de Newton*, in *Œuvres*, XXII, 408.

radical notions with Unitarian Christianity and a firm confidence that the Second Coming was at hand; Albrecht von Haller was tormented by his bouts of unbelief, but never ceased to defend Christianity against Voltaire and other impious philosophers.

Yet, however much devout scientists might object, it became obvious that God had constructed the world with fewer irregularities than God's sublime interpreter, Newton, had imagined; as d'Alembert put it, theological explanations of mechanical laws turned out to be not merely false but irrelevant. But most philosophes argued that they were, above all, false, and the scientists offered them good evidence in behalf of their arguments. The astronomical irregularities which, Newton had insisted, required divine intervention in the running of the universe, proved to be part of larger, hitherto incomprehensible regularities. By the 1770s and 1780s, brilliant mathematicians like Lagrange and Laplace had offered naturalistic explanations for planetary perturbations and had established the essential stability of the solar system. It was scientists like these who moved Kant to praise the sound quality of natural philosophy in his time. In 1692 Newton had told Richard Bentley that he had labored to establish "such principles as might work with considering men for the belief of a Deity"[6]; a hundred years later, while there were many scientists who were Christians, their discoveries no longer worked for the same purpose. The work of scientists and the ideology of philosophes were by no means the same thing, but at the very least the direction of science could give deists and atheists great comfort and supply them with what they wanted—Newton's physics without Newton's God.

II

In this development, Descartes played an even stranger role than Leibniz. As the professed followers of Newton, constructing their secular philosophy of science—and their secular philosophy *through* science—the philosophes ostentatiously joined the camp of the anti-Cartesians, for since the late seventeenth century the main burden of scientific controversy had fallen on Cartesians and

---

[6] See *The Rise of Modern Paganism*, 316.

Newtonians. It is true that the ideas, and perhaps even more, the literary and intellectual style of Descartes, retained their power over some of the philosophes—especially in France, where Montesquieu and Diderot and the others acquired their Descartes, as they acquired their classics, at a most impressionable age, in school; but these philosophes were ungenerous in acknowledging and hasty to minimize that power. Descartes ranks among the teachers of the Enlightenment and among its victims.

The Enlightenment's victimization of Descartes was never wholly unambiguous: his thought was too rich, he was too useful either as a cardboard hero or, far more often, cardboard villain, to permit the philosophes to agree on his real stature; he was, as d'Alembert rightly observed, an "extraordinary man" whose reputation had "varied greatly in less than a century."[7] Even his seventeenth-century readers who were, after all, close to him in time, had argued over him as they had never argued over Spinoza or Newton.

Descartes's first admirers had accepted him at his own valuation—as the lonely, self-impelled hero of the *Discours de la méthode*, the bold, persistent skeptic who liberates himself from the dead hand of traditional philosophy and rigid theology to stand forth as a model to his fellow men. Later, long after he was dead, historians anxious to simplify a complicated situation arranged a duel between Bacon the empiricist and Descartes the rationalist, but to their contemporaries the two were firm allies, prophets of a new scientific age that would improve the lot of man.[8] Indeed, in the middle of the seventeenth century, Descartes's most prominent followers were in England rather than in France. The theologians at Cambridge read Descartes with profound admiration; Henry More, opening his correspondence with the master in 1648, rather grandiloquently hailed Descartes as a giant who made all other philosophers, even great philosophers, appear as mere pygmies. More and his fellows were never uncritical Cartesians—they were, in their own highly in-

---

[7] *Discours préliminaire*, in *Mélanges*, I, 130. One distinguished scientist, at least, Albrecht von Haller, demurred: there is no evidence, he argued, that Newton or Locke learned anything from Descartes or that Descartes "opened the way to true philosophy." *Tagebuch*, 2 vols. (1787), I, 112, 381–2.
[8] See above, 6, and *The Rise of Modern Paganism*, 310–13.

dividual Anglican way, Platonists—but for a time they were intensely stimulated by Descartes's ideas, and felt safe with them: "There is no philosophy, indeed, except perhaps the Platonic," Henry More asserted, "which so firmly shuts the door against Atheism."[9] Some years later, More and Cudworth regretted their infatuation and denounced the philosophy of Descartes as an invitation to godless materialism. But that was later, in the 1660s; Descartes died in 1650, well before his Cambridge supporters became his antagonists. His fame in France, on the other hand, was almost wholly posthumous; it had to await the assimilation of his philosophy to Catholic orthodoxy, for from the beginning there had been critics like Pascal who feared Descartes as a glib tempter who would seduce men away from belief in the active Christian God. But Descartes became fashionable in high society and valuable to highly placed apologists; gradually, in the hands of philosophers like Malebranche and Fénelon and biographers like Baillet, there emerged a pious, safe, modern but wholly reliable Descartes, young Henry More's Descartes—not an invitation to, but a bulwark against, atheism.

With the appearance of Newton's *Principia* other aspects of Descartes's thought, his physics and his scientific method, became embroiled in controversy, and this later at once simplified and complicated the philosophes' polemical task. It simplified it by permitting them to construct a Descartes who was the ideal type of the rash metaphysician; complicated it by compelling them to make a complex judgment of him. Descartes the physicist, it seemed, was not the same man as Descartes the critical philosopher, and the performance of that philosopher, in turn, varied radically in quality from task to task.

Newton himself contributed to the caricature of Descartes by treating him as his supreme, almost sole opponent. Hence Newton could not—or at any rate did not—acknowledge, even to himself, the great debt he owed to Descartes: *"Error, error, non est Geom"* he scribbled over and over again in the margins of his copy of Descartes's *Geometry*, while in public, in the *Principia*, he scolded Descartes for his mistakes and passed over his contributions to the new science in silence.

---

[9] John Tulloch: *Rational Theology and Christian Philosophy in England in the Seventeenth Century*, 2 vols. (1872), I, 373; see ibid., II, 369.

This pettiness, though deplorable, was perhaps inescapable; controversy is not an atmosphere calculated to produce disinterested judgments on the merits of one's antagonist. Besides, the construction of a simplified Descartes enlarged the public for the new science by encouraging the kind of vivid teaching that would make Newtonianism memorable: in 1697 Samuel Clarke cleverly offered the English public a new Latin translation of Jacques Rohault's immensely influential Cartesian textbook, *Traité de physique*, first published in 1671, and haunted the text with Newtonian annotations and footnotes which, to the amusement and instruction of its many readers, made the original text appear ridiculous.[1]

Doubtless, much of that text was, if not ridiculous, wholly untenable. Descartes's logical arguments proving that the universe was a plenum and that the planets were dragged around the sun in vortices could not stand the rigorous scientific examination they received at the hands of Newton and his followers. And all the philosophes knew enough about physics and astronomy to ridicule Descartes's hostility to the void and ignorance of gravitation. Yet clearly what really mattered to them was less the content of Descartes's astronomical notions than the method that had led him to arrive at them. The question of Descartes in the Enlightenment, therefore, resolved itself into two related questions: what was the impact of his skeptical philosophy on theology? and what was the nature of his scientific method? The Enlightenment, which was seeking at once for arguments against Christianity and a basis for reliable knowledge must therefore give Descartes a mixed reception; Diderot, who knew his Descartes well, spoke for his French brethren when he characterized him epigrammatically as an "extraordinary genius born to mislead and to lead."[2]

While the philosophes continued to debate details of Descartes's meaning, their image of him became as conventional as the poets' image of Newton. Voltaire, who furnished literary models for so many of the Enlightenment's ideas, offered a series of convenient metaphors for the little flock. "Descartes," Voltaire wrote, "gave sight to blind men; they saw the errors of the ancients and his own";

---

[1] Alexandre Koyré: *Newtonian Studies* (1965), 54 *n.*, 79 *n.*
[2] *Œuvres*, XIII, 371, quoted by Aram Vartanian as the motto to his *Diderot and Descartes: A Study of Scientific Naturalism in the Enlightenment* (1953), 2.

his radical skepticism, in other words, had helped to destroy the pernicious metaphysics of the Scholastics and offered a method capable of destroying the rather less pernicious metaphysics of seventeenth-century philosophers, including his own. "The path he opened has, since his time, become immense"; we owe him what we owe to all pioneers respect for being first. It may be true, Voltaire thought, that Descartes "deceived himself, but at least he did it with method and in a consistent spirit; he destroyed the absurd chimeras with which young minds had been filled for two thousand years; he taught the men of his time to reason, and to employ his own arms against him." And so, "it is not too much to say that he was estimable even in his mistakes."[3]

Other French philosophes accepted this estimate without question. However admirable Descartes had been in his assault on medieval nonsense, his method remained a fertile source of new nonsense; Newton had never suffered from Descartes's *esprit de géometrie et d'invention*. In his brilliant *Traité des systèmes*, Condillac included Descartes among the four great system-makers of the seventeenth century, and criticized him both for his deductive method—"which has bred nothing but errors"—and for his boast that he could construct the world with matter and movement. Newton had been content with observing the world, "a project less beautiful than Descartes's, or, rather, less daring, but wiser."[4] D'Alembert agreed. In his *Discours préliminaire* to the *Encyclopédie*, he generously sketched Descartes's troubled career and courageous philosophy: Descartes, he said, was brave, a victim of persecution, an inventive philosophical mind who brilliantly applied his method with impressive results to a variety of sciences; if he was wrong, as he was especially in astronomy, he remains a leader in the liberation of the human mind. He showed men the way "to throw off the Scholastic yoke, of opinion, of authority," and by leading the revolt himself, "performed greater services to philosophy than, perhaps, any of his successors." He may, indeed, be thought of "as the leader of a conspiracy with the courage to rise up against despotic and arbitrary power," and to put down the foundations of a "juster and happier government which he himself did not live to see."[5]

---

[3] Lettre XIV, *Lettres philosophiques*, II, 1–6.
[4] *Œuvres*, I, 199–200 (see *The Rise of Modern Paganism*, 139–40).
[5] *Discours préliminaire*, in *Mélanges*, I, 130–6.

Grudging as they were, then, the philosophes recognized Descartes as a John the Baptist in the long struggle against superstition, an admirable but tragic pioneer. The materialists among the philosophes—La Mettrie, Holbach, and Diderot in his later years—went beyond this. They were especially indebted to Descartes's geometric conception of God and materialistic interpretation of animal existence; by delineating a God who withdraw once he had built his machine, and creatures that were mere soulless automatons, Descartes permitted his radical successors to construct a wholly materialist world view. Like the disillusioned Cambridge Platonists before them, the deists among the philosophes accused Descartes of preparing the way for atheism—"I have known many persons," wrote Voltaire, "whom Cartesianism has led to admit no God other than the immensity of things"[6]—an accusation that the materialists among the philosophes converted into praise. Descartes's role in the Enlightenment varied, but this much is clear: the philosophes exploited him, as they exploited Newton, in the service of secularism. The antireligious implications of the scientific revolution obviously did not trouble them. Science did become a problem for the Enlightenment, but the problem lay elsewhere.

3. NATURE'S PROBLEMATIC GLORIES

I

LATE IN 1753, in his aphoristic *Pensées sur l'interprétation de la nature*, Diderot made a striking, if slightly hedging, prediction. "In less than a hundred years," he wrote, "there will not be three great mathematicians left in Europe." Mathematics will come to a standstill "at a point where the Bernoullis, where Euler, Maupertuis, Clairaut, Fontaine, d'Alembert, and Lagrange have left it. They will have erected the columns of Hercules. We shall not get beyond them."[7] Time proved Diderot's prediction to be worthless; even in

---

[6] *Éléments de la philosophie de Newton*, in *Œuvres*, XXII, 404.
[7] *Œuvres*, II, 11.

his own time mathematicians continued to do significant work. But it suggested, though only by implication, the emergence of some new interests. By mid-century, natural scientists were discovering some relatively unexplored fields. With Newton's physics, astronomy, and optics entrenched everywhere, even in France, ambitious young men found room for their energies in the study of the earth, of life, of substances—often in the name of Newton.

Newton's prestige was untouched. If effusions about him grew rarer it was simply because poets had said as much about him as could be said about any man. Newton's name remained as magical and his ideas as commanding as ever, and the sciences peculiarly associated with him continued to advance on a broad front of agreement. The newer sciences, on the other hand—geology, biology, chemistry—continued to generate new puzzles; they compensated for their lack of authority with sheer excitement. John T. Needham, a priest whom Voltaire derisively dismissed as an "Irish Jesuit," even though he was neither Irish nor a Jesuit, "proved" the existence of spontaneous generation, but the Italian priest Lazzaro Spallanzani repeated and refined Needham's experiments and discredited Needham's discoveries. Two schools of biologists—one, the preformationists, arguing that the embryo is wholly formed at conception, the other, that the embryo begins with mere undifferentiated potentialities which are realized in the course of development—confronted one another with incomplete and inconclusive evidence. In 1744 Abraham Trembley achieved instantaneous though rather short-lived celebrity when he published his observations on the fresh water polyp, which could regenerate itself into new complete polyps when cut to pieces by the experimenter. His work opened heady if rather dim vistas into nature's powers to repair itself without outside aid, and it gave intellectual support to materialists. Subjects such as the classification of plants, the age of the earth, the relations of animal species to one another engaged the earnest attention of natural philosophers—the philosophes among them.

The ambition of these biologists was clear: to become the Newton of living nature. Maupertuis, as gifted a naturalist as he was physicist, whose contributions to biology have been overlooked in the dazzling light of Voltaire's malicious and comical attacks upon him, aroused widespread debate with his brilliant, prescient hypotheses on the nature of heredity and the character of species. As Newton's name was often in Maupertuis's writings, Newton's theories and methods were always in his mind: he thought it possible that Newton's theory of gravity might have its counterpart in biology, and his investigations into genetics were models of the kind of scientific care that eighteenth-century scientists, not unjustly, connected with the name of Newton.

Among the aspirants to Newton's mantle there was one, Buffon, who was widely thought to deserve it; in 1751, when only a few volumes of his vast *Histoire naturelle* had appeared, d'Alembert hailed him as a sage who rivaled Plato and Lucretius.[8] Buffon was not inclined to dispute d'Alembert's estimate; though a genial man, he was vastly ambitious and did not scruple to exploit his post as keeper of the *Jardin du roi*, or a stable of associates willing to work under his direction, to improve his opportunities for glory. But Buffon's career was a career in the service of science as much as of himself. His magnificent, expansive *Histoire naturelle* was an epic effort to write the biography of the world, the work of a man who was at once a skillful mathematician and meticulous stylist, Newtonian in thought and Cartesian in clarity, comprehensive methodologist and diligent empiricist, bold polemicist in behalf of autonomous science and tactful courtier anxious to escape trouble with the authorities. His work had something for everyone interested in nature, which, in eighteenth-century France, meant practically every literate adult. He encompassed the history of the earth from the moment it had first been shaken loose from the sun by a comet, blazing hot, to a time of universal death on a frozen planet; he wrote about the formation of the continents, the nature of man, about animals, plants, rocks. The profusion of his work mirrored the lavish wealth of nature.

The pages of Buffon's vast and varied production testify to his deep, passionate attachment to nature; he had an almost religious enthusiasm for it, controlled only by his respect for method and care for literary style. "Natural History," he wrote in 1749, "taken in its full extent, is an immense History, embracing all the objects that the Universe presents to us. This prodigious multitude of Quadrupeds, Birds, Fish, Insects, Plants, Minerals, etc., offers a vast spectacle to the curiosity of the human spirit; its totality is so great

---

[8] *Discours préliminaire*, in *Mélanges*, I, 158.

that it seems, and actually is, inexhaustible in all its details." It seems, Buffon goes on, "that everything that can be, is; the hand of the Creator seems not to have opened to give being to a certain fixed number of species; rather, it seems that it has thrown out, all at once, a world of beings related and unrelated, an infinity of harmonious and unharmonious combinations, and a perpetual destruction and renewal."[9] Nature is not a thing, or a single being; it should be regarded as "a living power, immense, which embraces everything, animates everything," created, and given its marching orders, by "divine Power." Nature is "a work perpetually alive, a worker ceaselessly active, who knows how to employ everything." It is inexhaustible: "Time, space, and matter are its means, the Universe its object, movement and life its goal."[1]

Faced with such immensity, such variety, such inexhaustible energy, the natural scientist, Buffon argued, must combine two apparently incompatible qualities, the "large vistas of an ardent genius who encompasses everything with a single glance, and the small attentions of a laborious instinct which attaches itself to a single point."[2] Like Falconet in the arts, Buffon had nothing but contempt for amateurs who lack both vision and patience, and pleaded for the professional scientist who disciplines his speculations with his firm grasp on scientific method and animates his knowledge with the kind of imaginative insight that only the thoroughgoing grasp of facts can produce. "Sensible people will always recognize that the only and true science is the knowledge of facts."[3] Himself a noted stylist and student of style, Buffon thought clarity one of the distinct contributions of the eighteenth century: after the immense, unreadable compilations of earlier ages, he wrote, their stylistic faults "have been corrected in our century; the order and precision with which we write today have made the Sciences more agreeable, easier," and, he added, "I am convinced that this difference of style contributes perhaps as much to their advancement as the spirit of research that reigns today."[4] Buffon's love of nature was lyrical, but he did not permit his passion to muddy his thinking.

---

[9] Buffon: *Histoire naturelle*, in *Œuvres philosophiques*, ed. Jean Piveteau (1954), 7, 9.
[1] Ibid., 31.
[2] Ibid., 7.
[3] Ibid., 15.
[4] Ibid.

This commitment to clarity was of great importance in a time of dizzying advances in the natural sciences. As Buffon saw—and, as the vagaries of romantic scientists after his death would demonstrate, saw rightly—the gravest menace to correct scientific understanding was the failure to separate objective inquiry from subjective wishes, the insistence on importing ethical or aesthetic considerations into scientific inquiry. With a generosity rare in his time, Buffon praised the ancient Greeks for being the first naturalists; in offering "faithful histories" of natural objects, he noted, the ancients were perhaps superior to the moderns. But the ancients had failed to perform the second half of scientific inquiry, "the exact description of everything," because they had insisted on the utility of philosophizing and despised "vain curiosity."[5] Hence they had neglected botany and physics alike. The implication was clear: only inquiry directed exclusively to the pursuit of truth could be adequate to the questions scientists sought to answer.

But truth, as Buffon also recognized, was a complex word, used in confusing ways. Much like Hume, though for different purposes, Buffon divided objects of knowledge into two parts—mathematical truths, which depend on definitions and are therefore abstract, intellectual, arbitrary; and "physical truths," which are, in contrast, not arbitrary at all; "they do not depend on us and, instead of being based on suppositions we have made, they rest only on facts."[6] To say this was not to despise logic and mathematics, but to define their proper function and warn against their abuse. "The most delicate and most important point in the study of the Sciences is here: to know how to distinguish clearly what is real in a subject from what we put into it arbitrarily, to recognize clearly the properties that belong to it and those we lend to it, seems to me the foundation of the true method for guiding one's conduct in the Sciences."[7]

These methodological cautions in no way impeded Buffon's expansive will to theory. He developed theories of the earth and the heavens, speculated on the organization of the human animal— for man, as he said, must be recognized to be an animal—participated prominently in eighteenth-century debates on perception, generation, and species. His energy was remarkable even in an age rich

---

[5] Ibid., 22.
[6] Ibid., 24.
[7] Ibid., 26.

in energetic men; his encyclopedia of animate and inanimate nature was comprehensive.

It was also subversive of established Christian belief. Buffon himself might have demurred at being called a philosophe: his relations with Voltaire, d'Alembert, and Diderot, though generally amiable, were rather reserved. But the Encyclopedists had no hesitation in claiming him for the good cause, and foreign visitors like Horace Walpole and David Hume included him among the philosophes without hesitation and with perfect justification.[8] Buffon, for his part, made obeisances to established authority—he wanted, above all, to get his work done. When the Faculty of Theology at the Sorbonne complained, in 1751, that his geological writings permitted impious inferences and threw doubts on Scriptural statements, Buffon promptly retracted and proclaimed his complete faith in the Bible: "I declare," he wrote piously, "that I had no intention whatever of contradicting the text of Scriptures; that I believe, with complete firmness, everything that it says about Creation, whether it concerns the order of time or the circumstances of the facts; and that I give up everything in my book, dealing with the formation of the earth, and in general everything else, that could be contrary to Moses' narration—I had presented my hypothesis concerning the formation of the planets, after all, as a pure philosophical supposition."[9] No retraction could be more complete or less sincere: Buffon continued his investigations into the formation of the earth with complete disregard of the dates to which the devout felt compelled to subscribe. He was a radical in what he wrote, in what he merely implied, in the general direction of his work. He was an Anglomaniac for the reasons Voltaire was an Anglomaniac, an admirer of Locke, an advocate of experimentation and a critic of metaphysics, all for the philosophes' reasons and with the philosophes' rhetoric. Indeed, the figures on the age of

---

[8] Horace Walpole thought Buffon the only philosophe who was amiable and agreeable (see *The Rise of Modern Paganism*, 10); on his visits to Paris, David Hume numbered him among his group of philosophic friends, which included d'Alembert, Helvétius, Holbach, Suard, Marmontel, Diderot, Duclos, and Galiani (see Hume to Hugh Blair [December 1763]. *Letters*, I, 419; and Hume to Morellet, July 10, 1769. Ibid., II, 205).

[9] March 12, 1751; in Buffon: *Œuvres*, 108.

the world that he permitted himself to publish, suspicious as they were to orthodox Christians, were bland compared to his private guesses, which would have scandalized them completely: "When I counted only 74,000 or 75,000 years for the time passed since the formation of the planets," he noted in one of his manuscripts, "I gave notice that I constrained myself in order to oppose received ideas as little as possible."[1] He was convinced that to account for the palpable facts of geology, the earth must be assigned an age not of thousands, but of millions of years. In the same way, his geological speculations offered alternatives to the Christian creation myth, his biological speculations alternatives to the Christian view of man. Beyond all this, the bulky authority of his work confirmed his philosophical tendency to the most casual reader: his history of nature concentrates with ostentatious singlemindedness on the creation rather than on the creator. Whatever his private religious views, Buffon's temper was the temper of the Enlightenment: his explanation of astronomical, geological, archaeological, and biological phenomena was wholly naturalistic, his style of thinking wholly secular.

II

In the light of Buffon's magisterial effort and Maupertuis's pioneering investigations, both widely known by 1753, Diderot's refusal to grant mathematics a future acquires a certain plausibility. But, plausible or not, its deepest meaning does not lie here; like many predictions, Diderot's prediction concealed a wish. Diderot was anxiously seeking to keep alive a dying ideal, and his anxiety suggests that with all their noisy affection for science, far from taking their ease in the world that Newton's researches had disclosed, some of the philosophes at least were greatly troubled by it. The pursuit of a scientific world view evidently imposed a strain on some of its most articulate devotees. Diderot, after all, had the competence of the well-informed amateur in mathematics; his sus-

---

[1] Francis C. Haber: "Fossils and the Idea of a Process of Time in Natural History," in *Forerunners of Darwin, 1745-1859*, ed. Bentley Glass *et al.* (1959), 236.

picion of it was something other than the resentment of the ignorant against an intellectual instrument he could never master.

One aspect of Diderot's uneasiness lies on the surface; it was the resistance of the versatile man of letters to the professionalization of science. Mathematics symbolized the threat that the radical philosophes, with their scientific propaganda, had raised to themselves; the triumph of their cause threatened the extinction of their type.

The philosophes should not have been surprised to see that scientific progress exacted its price. But surprised or not, some of them did not like to pay it. Scientists were coming to rely increasingly on the language of mathematics—exact and objective but abstract—and to discover the advantages of the division of labor, which made intelligent participation in the scientific process increasingly difficult. In the seventeenth century scientists had been "natural philosophers": Boyle had been chemist, physicist, theologian, man of letters all at once, and a member of an international community in which amateurs mixed freely with professionals. His versatility was characteristic of his fellows. In the eighteenth century, "natural philosophers" became scientists, general scientists became specialists. "Physics" was first used in its modern sense, excluding chemistry and biology, in 1715, and while the new usage established itself slowly—at mid-century d'Alembert could still say that the phenomena of chemistry as well as electricity were in the domain of the *physicien*[2]—its eventual triumph was inescapable. It was in this period also that astronomy was first explicitly separated from astrology, that Hartley first used the word *psychology* as we use it today, and that *chemistry* and *chimie* acquired their restricted, current meaning; this growing precision in terminology mirrored the growing specialization of the scientist.

In this new professional atmosphere, the gentleman-scientist survived—I have said that the passion for science spread more widely than ever—but he withdrew into the private sphere or, if he competed with professionals, cut a pathetic figure. As late as 1764 the Anglican cleric Richard Watson could still be appointed professor of chemistry at Cambridge even though, as he later conceded, he "knew nothing at all of chemistry, had never read a syllable on

---

[2] "Expérimental," in *The Encyclopédie*, 79. The Cartesians, it seems, were rather slower than the Newtonians in adopting the new usages.

the subject, nor seen a single experiment in it."[3] But such an unpro-
fessional career was becoming an anachronism, even in the English
universities. The age of universal knowledge was over; and the
philosophes, for all their scientific bent, could not help but lament
its passing. "It's not," Voltaire wrote, "that I'm angry to see
philosophy cultivated, but I don't want it to become a tyrant who
excludes all the rest."[4] It was an understandable but no longer very
tenable position, as Voltaire himself felt compelled to admit in
private. "Literature," he noted rather sadly, "has become immense,
the number of books innumerable, universal knowledge—*science*—
impossible."[5] Around the time that Voltaire confided this disappointment to his notebook, Wieland complained that the sciences
had split up into "a thousand sects,"[6] and Diderot, in helpless longing
for the old comprehensible scientific style, denounced the austere
mathematical language of Newton's *Principia mathematica* as "*the
affectation of the great masters*," as "the veil" which scientists "are
pleased to draw between the people and nature."[7] And he wistfully
reiterated the old ideal of the universal cultivated man: "Happy the
geometer in whom a consummate study of the abstract sciences
has not weakened the taste for the fine arts; to whom Horace and
Tacitus will be as familiar as Newton; who could discover the properties of a curve and sense the beauties of a poem."[8] Diderot, like
Voltaire and Wieland, understood that the realization of a new and,
to the philosophes, desirable ideal—the man who understands and by
understanding, masters nature—was driving out the old and equally
desirable ideal: Renaissance man.

This was bad enough, but Diderot's malaise went deeper than
this. Precisely at the moment when the time for amity seemed to
have come, the new philosophy threatened to render man's relation
to nature problematical once again. Eighteenth-century thought had

---

[3] Richard Watson: *Anecdotes of the Life of R. W. written by himself at different intervals, and revised in 1814* (1817), quoted by F.
Sherwood Taylor: "The Teaching of the Physical Sciences at the
End of the Eighteenth Century," in *Natural Philosophy Through
the 18th Century and Allied Topics*, anniversary number of the
Philosophical Magazine (1948), 162.
[4] Voltaire to Cideville (April 16, 1735). *Correspondence*, IV, 49.
[5] *Notebooks*, 361.
[6] Sengle: *Wieland*, 41.
[7] *Pensées sur l'interprétation de la nature*, in *Œuvres*, II, 38.
[8] Ibid., 11.

liberated man from his filial dependence on God and made him part of nature, but the philosophical anthropology of the philosophes, which promoted man from servitude, ironically enough demoted him at the same time—from his position little lower than the angels to a position among the intelligent animals. While man seemed on the point of conquering his worldly domain through his critical intelligence, he was faced with a second expulsion from his terrestrial paradise, and this time the avenging angel was man himself.

The threat, as I have said, was not chiefly to man's aesthetic enjoyment of the world about him: far from being anxious over Newton's universe, the poets thrived upon it. "Although I'm in commerce with Newton-Maupertuis and Descartes-Mairan," Voltaire wrote to his old teacher, the abbé d'Olivet, "this does not prevent Quintilian-d'Olivet from being always in my heart." He could not see, Voltaire insisted, "why the study of science—*la physique*—should crush the flowers of poetry. Is the truth such a poor thing that she cannot stand the ornamental?" Sound thinking and eloquent speech, deep feelings and good expression, are not enemies to science: "No, certainly not; to think that would be to think like a barbarian." After all, Voltaire pointedly reminded his Jesuit teacher, "*Multae sunt mansiones in domo patris mei*," and a person like Madame du Châtelet, who understands "Newton, Vergil and Tasso," far from being a freak or a survival, was characteristic of her time.[9]

The apologetic tone in Voltaire's assertions is faint, but audible —here is, after all, a pupil addressing a former preceptor, a deist, a priest, an embattled literary man another embattled literary man; and Voltaire's denial that science and poetry are at war, like the denials by pious scientists late in the seventeenth century that science and religion were at war, only suggests that the war was real enough. But Voltaire, and his mistress, even if they saw a problem, also embodied the solution: in their work, in their whole mode of life, they bridged the threatened separation of science and art, science and culture, in a personal union. The threat of science to life lay elsewhere: it lay in its neutrality, its chilling objectivity. The irresistible propulsion of modern scientific inquiry was toward positivism, toward the elimination of metaphysics, and the

---

[9] Voltaire to d'Olivet, October 20, 1738. *Correspondence*, VII, 412.

clean separation of facts and values, foreshadowed by Bacon, implied by Newton, triumphantly announced by Hume, taken for granted by the leading scientists of the late eighteenth century. Scientific thinking exacted the stripping away of theological, metaphysical, aesthetic, and ethical admixtures that had been a constituent part of science since the Greeks; scientific philosophers of the eighteenth century, with justice, treated these admixtures as impurities, as survivals from earlier stages of consciousness. Every scientific discovery weakened the hold of theological explanation, metaphysical entities, and aesthetic considerations: the orbits of planets were neither beautiful nor ugly; the law of gravitation was neither cruel nor kind; observed irregularities in the skies proved nothing about divine activity. And every improvement in scientific terminology or mathematical formulation further liberated scientists from old anthropomorphic conceptions of the world and reduced to irrelevance many of the old questions that philosophers had addressed to nature.

It was an exhilarating development. After a millennium of the reign of fancy, the reign of fact was at hand; but, as the philosophes' treatment of nature shows, it was a confusing and at times frightening development as well. Nature had always been a word rich in comforting associations, a profuse, almost inexhaustible metaphor, and the philosophes were reluctant to surrender all these comforts without a struggle. In the age of the Enlightenment, therefore, nature continued to supply norms for beauty and standards for conduct—at least to some philosophes; and the philosophes continued to treat nature rhetorically as a bountiful mother, a treasure house lying open to be raided, a servant waiting for orders, a treacherous opponent requiring constant vigilance. The deists admired nature as a storehouse of lessons and evidence of divine skill; the materialists celebrated it as the origin of all things which, therefore, made the constructions of theology wholly unnecessary. Optimists and pessimists among the philosophes debated just how ready nature was to be dominated, how shrewd or vicious in its resistance, but they agreed that whether man's relation to nature must be viewed as a collaboration or as a duel, that relation was intimate, inescapable, and exclusive. And some philosophes, Diderot being prominent among them, saw nature as a refuge from science.

The result was a curious set of contradictory attitudes toward science that troubled the philosophes' clarity of thought and mitigated their pleasure in the process of scientific investigation. Having made man master in his own house, some of the philosophes felt like strangers in it, and they could not quite suppress their longing for ancient simplicities. This nostalgia was by no means universal among them; on the whole one can say that the philosophes who knew science best feared it least. Hume, d'Alembert, and Kant are the fathers of three divergent modern philosophies of science —the first of empiricism, the second of positivism, the third of critical idealism—but their general attitude toward science was one of warm welcome. Each in his own way sought to work out the epistemological and metaphysical meaning of science, and sought to establish reliable standards for ethical and aesthetic judgments outside the confusing tangle of meanings clustering around the word "nature," but each did his work in the name, and without fear, of Newton. Similarly, Voltaire showed in his celebrated popularizations how thoroughly he had entered Newton's world and how fearlessly he was ready to draw its philosophical implications. At the same time, Voltaire's scientific philosophy harbored a rather surprising survival from the prescientific view of nature—final causes. Voltaire had ridiculed as naïve the claim that "rocks were created to build houses" and "silkworms born in China that we might have satin in Europe." But unlike Buffon, who firmly rejected final causes as a metaphysical abstraction, Voltaire insisted that when the effects were invariable, nature's purposes could be discerned through the idea of final cause: we should be "mad to deny that stomachs were made to digest, eyes to see, ears to hear"—a refinement on an antique, anthropomorphic notion only slightly less naïve than the naïve version Voltaire felt bound to dispute.[1] It was a symptom of an unresolved confusion in Voltaire's mind, of a yearning for a palpable connection between science and purpose that even he could not quite shake off. But it was nothing more than that; it did not shape, and thus ruin, Voltaire's philosophy of nature.

Diderot was in a rather more compromising position. He was

---

[1] "End, Final Causes," *Philosophical Dictionary*, I, 271. Voltaire was not alone: Adam Ferguson thought the evidence for final causes in nature obvious and overwhelming (Gladys Bryson: *Man and Society*, 36–7). For Buffon's rejection, see *Œuvres*, 258.

reluctant to accept the cruel verdict of Newtonian science; he refused to believe in a nature largely empty, populated by cold, colorless corpuscles, and wholly indifferent to moral questions. "Man," Diderot exclaims in an impassioned plea in his article "Encyclopédie," "is the single place from which we must begin and to which we must refer everything"; remove "my existence and the happiness of my fellowmen, and what do I care about the rest of nature?" Man is, and must be, at the center of all things: "If we banish man, the thinking or contemplating being, from the face of the earth, this moving and sublime spectacle of nature will be nothing more than a sad and mute scene. The universe will cease to speak; silence and night will seize it. Everything will be changed into a vast solitude where unobserved phenomena take place obscurely, unobserved. It is the presence of man which makes the existence of beings meaningful."[2] All philosophes agreed that man is important; in fact, they insisted on it. Hume and d'Alembert, cool precursors of modern scientific objectivity, were wryly willing to concede that man is indeed nature's masterpiece. But Diderot wanted more than that: he wanted man to merge into nature, and draw from it answers to his most pressing questions—What must I do? and, even more significant, Who am I? Diderot found it impossible to live with the teaching, implied by Newton and elaborated by eighteenth-century scientists, that science discloses what is and says nothing about what should be, that truth and beauty, truth and goodness, are wholly distinct. Nature, he insisted, in his *Pensées sur l'interprétation de la nature*, in his major articles in the *Encyclopédie*, in *Le rêve de d'Alembert*, is one vast interconnected organic whole in which the steps from matter to life, from science to ethics, from observation to admiration are not merely possible but proper and indeed essential. And so Diderot, looking back to the Stoics and ahead to the *Naturphilosophie* of the German Romantics, united what scientific philosophy was separating and asked of it what it could not give. "The distinction between a physical and a moral world," he wrote about Jacques the Fatalist, and himself, "seemed to him empty of meaning."[3]

---

[2] "The Encyclopédie," 56.
[3] See Charles C. Gillispie: *The Edge of Objectivity: An Essay in the History of Scientific Ideas* (1960), 181.

III

For all these alarms and evasions, the drift of scientific philosophy toward moral neutrality created some anxiety among the philosophes but no panic; Diderot's distrust of mathematics remained a relatively temperate minority report from the camp of progress.

Science failed to take the monstrous spectral shape it has taken since because, first of all, the really destructive possibilities of technology were still far in the future and almost beyond the imaginative reach of reasonable men. What is more, the philosophes—*all* philosophes—had an enormous investment in science as an ally in their war against religion; it was a commonplace among them that when science advances, superstition retreats. But beyond this, the philosophes found science genuinely admirable for its own sake. It was, with its unprecedented method, vastly superior to the alternative ways of seeking knowledge—the methods of theology and of metaphysics—that men had devised before. Not all new discoveries, especially in the biological sciences, stood above controversy. But that did not matter. They were subject to rules that permitted the testing of proposals, the confirmation and refinement of theories; scientific progress silenced disputes. Decade by decade, sometimes it seemed year by year, the area of agreement grew larger.

Educated men who had grown up amidst the clamor of philosophers and theologians found this astounding. The history of thought, as they well knew, was a history of discord, of endless, fruitless wrangles among the doctrinaire representatives of schools and sects, all claiming possession of infallible truth and denouncing their adversaries as fools or agents of the devil. Skeptics in ancient Alexandria had offered these pointless disputes as advertisements for their own school, which taught a courageous suspension of judgment. Some centuries later, Christian theologians in turn had exploited the quarrels of philosophical sects, and asked men to give up the vain games of reason and embrace the certainties of Christ. But, as the history of dogma proved over and over again, the theologians had been no better than the heathen philosophers: dispute and mutual abomination was everywhere, progress and certainty in knowledge nowhere. And now the sciences of nature promised a way to knowledge, and an accumulation of knowledge, to which all reasonable men could assent.

This is why the scientific method struck the eighteenth century as an invention unprecedented in its sheer magnificent effectiveness. In this new atmosphere, Voltaire suggested, the survival of the epithets "Newtonian" or "Cartesian" was misleading; scientific groupings were not contesting parties of hate-filled theologians: "What do names matter? What do the places matter where the truths were discovered? We are concerned with experiments and calculations, not with party chieftains."[4]

The momentous manifestation of the scientific method—one of the most significant, most heartening realities in the world of the Enlightenment—promised a momentous consequence. If the scientific method was the sole reliable method for gaining knowledge in a wide variety of contexts, from the phenomena of the heavens to the phenomena of plant life, it seemed plausible and in fact likely that it could be profitably exported to other areas of intense human concern where knowledge was as primitive now, and disagreement as vehement, as it had been in physics a century before—the study of man and society. Even if facts and values were distinct, even if science was not the source of all past values, a bridge could be built between facts and values and the scientific method might become the instrument for the creation of future values.

As the men of the Enlightenment knew, Newton himself had seen this heady possibility. In the last of the famous queries with which he concluded his *Opticks*, he had noted that "if natural Philosophy, in all its parts, by pursuing this method, shall at length be perfected, the bounds of moral philosophy will also be enlarged." It was a hint from the lips of the master, which the philosophes had every intention of exploring. J. T. Desaguliers, whose popularizations of Newton had wide circulation, proclaimed the imperial possibilities of Newton's work shortly after Newton's death in a poem winningly entitled "The Newtonian System of the World, the Best Model of Government."[5] Voltaire, with remarkable prescience, hoped to transfer the methods of the sciences to history:

---

4 "Réponse aux objections principales qu'on a faites en France contre la philosophie de Newton," in *Œuvres*, XXIII, 74.
5 See W. K. Wimsatt, Jr.: *Philosophic Words* (1948), 100.

"Perhaps, soon," he wrote, still a little tentatively, "what has already happened in physics will happen in the writing of history. New discoveries have led us to proscribe ancient systems. We will want to know mankind in the interesting detail which today forms the basis of natural philosophy."[6] Rousseau defended his procedure in his *Discours sur l'inégalité* by likening his speculative history of culture to the acceptable type of hypothesis current in modern physics. Lichtenberg made the significant observation that scientific method was even more important than a specific scientific discovery: "Inquiring into truth, we should always proceed so that some day even more enlightened ages will be able to take for their model not our beliefs but our procedure."[7] Much like d'Alembert, Condillac, whose methodological program is at the heart of Enlightenment philosophizing, proposed a reconstruction of philosophy on the model of the natural sciences. "Today," he wrote—the year was 1749—"a few physical scientists, above all the chemists, are concentrating on collecting phenomena, for they have recognized that one must possess the effects of nature, and discover their mutual dependence, before one poses principles that explain them. The example of their predecessors has been a good lesson to them; they at least wish to avoid the errors that the mania for systems has brought in its train. If only all the other philosophers would imitate them!"[8] For Condillac, scientific thinking was a model and a warning to all other kinds of thinking, the critical mind at its best and most effective, a potent objective instrument that good men could turn to good results.

Significantly enough, it was David Hume, the very philosopher who had insisted on the strictest possible separation of facts and values, who also insisted on the social relevance of scientific enquiry. It is well known that Hume advertised his *Treatise of Human Nature* to be "An Attempt to introduce the experimental Method of Reasoning into Moral Subjects," and his Introduction to the *Treatise* is a manifesto of the Enlightenment's critical positivism,

---

[6] "Nouvelles considérations sur l'Histoire" (1744), in *Œuvres historiques*, 46.
[7] J. P. Stern: *Lichtenberg: A Doctrine of Scattered Occasions* (1959), 37.
[8] *Traité des systèmes*, in *Œuvres*, I, 127. It is this temper that permitted philosophes in Europe (and, as the writings of Madison show, America as well) to speak of the science of morals or the science of politics. See below, chap. vii and chap. ix, section 1.

a call to have objective knowledge serve human ends. " 'Tis evident," Hume argues, "that all the sciences have a relation, greater or less, to human nature; and that however wide any of them may seem to run from it, they still return back by one passage or another." After all, even "*Mathematics, Natural Philosophy, and Natural Religion*" are to some degree "dependent on the science of MAN"; they "lie under the cognizance of men, and are judged of by their powers and faculties." If this holds for these abstruse disciplines, how much more must it hold for the "other sciences," like logic, ethics, aesthetics, and politics, "whose connexion with human nature is more close and intimate"? Human nature is the capital or center of the philosophical sciences, which "being once masters of, we may every where else hope for an easy victory. From this station we may extend our conquests over all those sciences, which more intimately concern human life." Hume conceded that the establishment of a reliable science of man was a difficult task; it depended on the accumulation of "experience and observation," and, unlike the natural sciences, the science of man could not artificially multiply its observations through experiment. Still, it was possible to "glean up our experiments in this science from a cautious observation of human life, and take them as they appear in the common course of the world, by men's behavior in company, in affairs, and in their pleasures." The modern philosopher had every right to be confident: "Where experiments of this kind are judiciously collected and compared, we may hope to establish on them a science, which will not be inferior in certainty, and will be much superior in utility to any other of human comprehension."[9] Even if he did not always say what he meant, Hume always meant what he said: the science of man was possible and would be immensely useful. That is why the men of the Enlightenment were ultimately not afraid of science; it was not merely their best, but their only, hope for the knowledge that would give man both abundance and freedom. More than a century before Freud—the greatest scientist of man the world has known and the philosophes' most distinguished disciple in our century—the philosophes believed, as he would put it later: "No, science is no illusion. But it would be an illusion to suppose that we could get anywhere else what it cannot give us."

---

[9] *A Treatise of Human Nature* (1739–40; edn. 1888), xix-xxiii.

CHAPTER FOUR

The Science of Man

I. ENLIGHTENMENT MAN

T HE SCIENCE OF MAN," wrote David Hume in his *Treatise*, "is the only foundation for the other sciences." And "the only science of man" is "Human Nature." Yet, important as it was, that science had been "hitherto the most neglected." Therefore, Hume thought, it was his special task and the task of his age to "bring it a little more into fashion."[1]

On this point, as so often, Hume was both modest and right. What had passed for the science of man in earlier centuries was interesting and often penetrating speculation—philosophical reflection on the passions, orderly classification of temperaments, urbane aphoristic wisdom about human conduct, or candid autobiography: Rousseau and Lichtenberg were the eighteenth-century heirs of a long tradition. But the age of the Enlightenment made the study of man into a science. Before Locke, wrote Voltaire, "great philosophers had positively"—that is to say, boldly and wrongly—"determined the nature of the soul"; they had written its "romance" —*le roman de l'âme*. But then Locke, a true sage, "had modestly written its history."[2] The philosophes intended to do no more than occupy the territory that Locke had discovered.

Not content with making psychology into a science, the Enlightenment made it, among the sciences of man, into the strategic science. It was strategic in offering good, "scientific" grounds for the philosophes' attack on religion; it was strategic in the broader sense of radiating out to other sciences of man, to educational,

---

[1] *Treatise of Human Nature*, xx, 273.
[2] Lettre XIII, *Lettres philosophiques*, I, 168–9.

aesthetic, and political thought—"general psychology," Dugald Stewart wrote, is "the center whence the thinker goes outward to the circumference of human knowledge"[3]—and strategic, finally, because it was the groundwork, the empirical base, of the Enlightenment's philosophical anthropology, its theory of man.[4]

In repudiating Christianity, the philosophes gave the question of human nature new poignancy. Christians, to be sure, had not wholly agreed among themselves. There had been Christian optimists and pessimists, Christian rationalists and irrationalists, but the broad outlines of their view of man had been authoritatively laid down by the opening myth in Genesis: man's place, lower than the angels, higher than the beasts, had been determined by the great hierarchy of being established, and governed, by God, but man's godlike reason had been dimmed and his character degraded by his sin of disobedience. But if, as the philosophes asserted, the myths of God's fatherhood and man's fall from grace were so much nonsense, man's true nature and place in nature became truly problematic; if the old answers would not do, the old questions must become more insistent than ever.

It was in this spirit that the philosophes inquired into human nature, and asked whether it was uniform through time and space, the same in ancient and modern man. For all their loose terminology, all their inclination for burdening their conjectures with fantastic travelers' reports, the philosophes on the whole thought that there was such a nature, and that, although individual character and differences in environment produced wide, often astounding variations, nature had built a certain uniformity into man's basic patterns of growth and behavior. Even extreme environmentalists like Helvétius, who thought that education could make man into almost anything, saw all men as endowed with the same bundle of potentialities. "It is universally acknowledged," David Hume wrote in a famous passage, "that there is a great uniformity among the actions of men, in all nations and ages, and that human nature remains still the same, in its principles and operations. The same motives always

---

[3] Quoted in Bryson: *Man and Society*, 21.
[4] For the use of psychology in the philosophes' attack on Christianity, see *The Rise of Modern Paganism*, chap. vii, especially 407–12; for its relation to aesthetics, see below, 290–318; to education, 510–15; and political thought, 522–8.

produce the same actions." The passions of "ambition, avarice, self-love, vanity, friendship, generosity, public spirit," mixed "in various degrees, and distributed through society, have been, from the beginning of the world, and still are, the source of all the actions and enterprizes, which have ever been observed among mankind." Indeed, "Mankind are so much the same, in all times and places, that history informs us of nothing new or strange in this particular."[5] At the same time, Hume wondered at the display of human variety: "Mighty revolutions have happened in human affairs," he noted, and "those, who consider the periods and revolutions of human kind, as represented in history, are entertained with a spectacle full of pleasure and variety, and see, with surprize, the manners, customs, and opinions of the same species susceptible of such prodigious changes in different periods of time."[6] The other philosophes sounded much like Hume: the uniformity of human nature permitted some sound philosophizing about man, and even some well-founded predictions, but it was not so rigid as to induce boredom in the observer or the student.[7]

This conception of human nature was vague enough to leave adequate room for dispute. The Scottish school argued that man is equipped with an instinct of generosity or sociability, the Utilitarians rejoined that man is by nature self-regarding; similarly, the philosophes never reached full agreement on the power—even if there was near-unanimity on their high estimation—of the passions.[8] And behind their debates there stood the fundamental question of the value the philosopher should place on man's nature: Diderot epitomized the question in the title of his enigmatic play, *Est-il bon? Est-il méchant?* He was analyzing a single individual, the antihero of his play who is transparently Diderot himself, but this analysis barely conceals Diderot's unsettled, and unsettling, question about the nature of man in general. "The heart of man," Diderot said

---

[5] *An Enquiry Concerning Human Understanding*, in *Works*, IV, 68.
[6] "Of Civil Liberty," ibid., III, 157; "Of Eloquence," ibid., 163, although Hume here goes on to say that in the course of "civil" history the variety of human experience is rather less marked than in what we would today call cultural history.
[7] I shall return to this question in the section on history; see below, 380–5.
[8] See below, section 3.

elsewhere, sententiously but seriously, "is by turns a sanctuary and a sewer."[9]

This epigram was conventional eighteenth-century moralizing, striking only in its choice of metaphors, but it confirms the impression that the philosophes' paganism in no way committed them to optimism about man's nature. The very issues of the debate were far from clear; one man's vice was another man's virtue. The Utilitarians were in general men of hope, but Helvétius thought man often lower, more ferocious than beasts, while Bentham, a patient realist, conceded that man was more a pugnacious than a rational animal. Helvétius's notorious faith in the omnipotence of education is a reflection not of optimism about human nature, but of stark pessimism about his starting point. The cool realism of the *Federalist* was a characteristic Enlightenment attitude; Holbach's extravagant cynicism about human nature was far more prevalent than Diderot's warmhearted, if intermittent, confidence.[1] Doubtless, a number of philosophes were perfectly ready to accept, and even to celebrate, man's inborn egotism, but they looked to some countervailing power, either restraining institutions or sociable feelings, to keep this egotism within the bounds of innocence and productivity. "It seems that nature has given us *l'amour propre* for our preservation," Voltaire noted, "and *la bienveillance* for the preservation of others, and, perhaps, that without these two principles (of which the first should be the stronger) there could have been no society."[2] The philosophes were certain that man is born innocent—"No, dear friend," Diderot exclaimed to Sophie Volland, "nature has not made us evil; it is bad education, bad models, bad legislation that corrupt us"[3]—but they were inclined to dwell on his capacity for evil. Even Rousseau, who shocked and delighted thousands of readers with his reiterated claims for man's essential goodness, regarded that goodness as a mere collection of possibilities, an absence of original corruption, and a mere hope—a rather slim hope—that in

---

[9] Diderot to Falconet (May 15, 1767). *Correspondance*, VII, 59.
[1] For the confrontation between Diderot and Holbach, see Diderot: ibid., III, 195–6, 320; for Helvétius's pessimism, see ibid., 281.
[2] *Notebooks*, 219.
[3] Diderot to Sophie Volland (November 2 to 6 or 8, 1760). *Correspondance*, III, 226.

the right circumstances, with the right education and the right society, man might become a decent citizen.

Yet, despite these reservations, the philosophes' insistence on man's original innocence was a decisive break with Christian anthropology. To the Christian, man is, in Pascal's splendid imagery, a fallen king, a galley slave; for all his initial resemblance to his creator, man is incapable of securing happiness in this life or salvation in the next without divine aid. Voltaire readily conceded in his polemic against Pascal that man's nature is a mixture of good and evil, and man's life a mixture of pleasure and pain, but, he argued, just as man's difficulties have natural causes, so his solutions must arise from natural actions.[4] Submission to organized religion is a betrayal of man's true estate, hope for eventual salvation is a childish dream. Man, dreadful though this may often appear, is on his own.

This rebellious pagan spirit dominates the philosophes' proud declarations of man's dignity. Even Christian pessimists, of course, had asserted that dignity: if man was now corrupt, he was still the son of God, and it was a matter of great moment that Christ, God's only begotten son, should have come to earth to rescue man from himself. If, to Pascal, man was mired in his sin, he was also a fallen king—fallen, but with the memory of his former high estate alive in him. But the philosophes, including those philosophes who punctuated their writings with despairing witticisms on man's stupidity and cruelty, found Christian assertions of human dignity to be worthless cant—insignificant concessions that did nothing to correct the Christian hatred of this world and of nature and the Christian doctrine of man's abjectness and servility. The language the philosophes used was often the language that pious men had used before them, but in their writings the words had new meaning. When Kant asserts that it is man's chief task to discover his proper place, his "distinctive station," in the universe, and resist all temptations to rise above or sink below his true level, he was expressing that mixture of secular confidence and philosophical modesty characteristic of the Enlightenment rather than arguing, in traditional Christian fashion, that man was lower than the angels and higher

---

[4] For Voltaire's one-sided "debate" with Pascal, see *The Rise of Modern Paganism*, 388–90.

than the beasts.⁵ The evils man is inclined to commit only man is capable of preventing or curing. "One should say to every individual," wrote Voltaire, denying that man is born evil, in a curt and radical injunction: " 'Remember your dignity as a man.' "⁶ Both Christians and philosophes recognized that the Enlightenment's anthropology was revolutionary. When in his *Religion innerhalb der Grenzen der blossen Vernunft*, Kant asserted man's "natural propensity" to wickedness, Goethe, fearful that his favorite philosopher had relapsed into the old faith, was deeply offended: Kant, he wrote, had "slobbered" on his "philosopher's robe" and left on it "the shameful stain of radical evil," seeking thus to lure Christians "to kiss its hem."⁷ It was an interpretation as intemperate as it is doubtful, but it shows, with its very vehemence, how precious the Enlightenment's denial of original sin was to a perceptive contemporary.

Thirty years before Goethe's outburst, an equally perceptive observer had drawn just as drastic a conclusion, only from the other camp. When Christophe de Beaumont, archbishop of Paris, or—as is more likely—an intelligent cleric in his office, wrote a Pastoral Letter against Rousseau's *Émile* for its impiety, he recognized the core of that impiety to be Rousseau's denial of original sin, and Rousseau's own sin to be the old pagan sin of pride. "No understanding or reconciliation," Ernst Cassirer has written, was possible here: "In the seventeenth and eighteenth centuries the dogma of original sin stood in the center and focus of Catholic and Protestant theology. All great religious movements of the time were oriented toward and gathered up in this dogma. The struggles over Jansenism in France; the battles between Gomarists and Arminians in Holland; the development of Puritanism in England and of Pietism in Germany—they all stood under this sign. And now this fundamental conviction concerning the radical evil in human nature was to find in Rousseau a dangerous and uncompromising adversary. The Church fully understood this situation: it stressed, at once, the

---

⁵ See Kant: *Sämmtliche Werke*, ed. G. Hartenstein, 8 vols. (1867–8), VIII, 624 ff., as quoted in John E. Smith: "The Question of Man," in Charles W. Hendel, ed.: *The Philosophy of Kant and Our Modern World* (1957), 24.
⁶ "Evil," *Philosophical Dictionary*, II, 378.
⁷ Goethe to Johann Gottfried and Karoline Herder, June 7, 1793. *Gedenkausgabe*, XIX, 213.

decisive issue with full clarity and firmness."[8] And it stressed the issue, one might add, with a wit that might have been learned from Voltaire; the author of the *Mandement* belabored Rousseau with a series of energetic antitheses—"From the heart of error there has arisen a man filled with the language of philosophy without being truly a philosopher; his mind endowed with a mass of knowledge which has not enlightened him, and which has spread darkness in the minds of others; his character given over to paradoxical opinions and conduct, joining simplicity of manners with ostentatious displays of ideas, zeal for ancient maxims with a rage for innovation, the obscurity of seclusion with the desire for notoriety: we have seen him thunder against the sciences he was cultivating, crying up the excellence of the Gospels whose dogmas he was destroying, paint the beauty of virtues he was obliterating in the souls of his readers. He has made himself the preceptor of the human race only to deceive it, the mentor of the public only to mislead everyone, the oracle of the century only to secure its ruination"— invective designed to discredit once and for all a pagan who dared to preach man's original innocence. Significantly, the *Mandement* against Rousseau takes as its text a Pauline epistle warning against "perilous times" in which there would be men who loved themselves, who were haughty, boastful, blasphemous, impious, bloated with pride, lovers of pleasure rather than of God; men corrupt in spirit and perverted in faith—a catalogue of failings in which the sin of pride predominates. Indeed, Rousseau, the *Mandement* insists, speaks for a party of unbelief that thinks itself empowered to "throw off a yoke which, it argues, dishonors mankind and God himself," the yoke—once again—of original sin; does not this party hold that "the first movements of nature are always good," that "there is no original perversity in the human heart"? This view, and the plan of education built upon it, the *Mandement* reasons, and reasons justly, are "far from being in accord with Christianity." They are, rather, evidence of the spirit of "rebellion" and, significantly, of "independence," the spirit of "audacious men" who refuse to subject themselves to the authority of God and of men alike. Rousseau, the *Mandement* complains, appeals to the words that God has

---

[8] Ernst Cassirer: *The Question of Jean-Jacques Rousseau* (1932; tr. Peter Gay, 1954), 74.

written in the hearts of men, but he misreads them: they are not incitements to rebellion and autonomy, but to submission. "Ah! My very dear brethren, be not thrown off the track on this matter. True faith—*la bonne foi*—is worthy only when it is enlightened and docile." Christianity is indeed the religion of reason, but that reason leads man to the door of revelation, to humble acceptance of the mystery of his faith and acknowledgment of his evil heart, to an understanding of the "weakness and corruption of our nature," and the history of the "lamentable fall of our first fathers."[9]

These strictures, for all their hysterical tone and conventional rhetoric, are not empty formulas; they are a recognition of an unappeasable conflict, perhaps more palpable here, in the struggle over man's nature, than anywhere else. Whatever the Christians thought of man—capable or incapable of participating in his salvation, likely to be doomed or likely to be saved—the point of Christian anthropology was that man is a son, dependent on God. Whatever the philosophes thought of man—innately decent or innately power-hungry, easy or hard to educate to virtue—the point of the Enlightenment's anthropology was that man is an adult, dependent on himself.

2. NEWTONS OF THE MIND

I

IN CONSTRUCTING their secular philosophy of man, the philosophes did not wholly abandon "romance" for science; or, rather, they often took for science what was really romance. Diligently, sometimes credulously, they studied travelers' reports about savage tribes, or accounts of lost creatures roaming the forests in Europe, to discover essential man. Like others in their time—for this was by

---

[9] See *Mandement de Monseigneur l'Archevêque de Paris portant condamnation d'un livre qui a pour titre, Émile, ou de l'éducation, par J. J. Rousseau, citoyen de Genève*, in Rousseau: *Œuvres complètes*, 4 vols. (1835), II, 747–54 *passim*. The author of the *Mandement*, whoever he is, draws on II Timothy 3, verses 1, 2, 4.

no means characteristic of the philosophes alone—the men of the Enlightenment sought clues to the universal in the unique, the typical in the extraordinary.[1] This was the age of "Wild Peter," the autistic idiot who had been found wandering about on all fours in the woods of Hameln in Hanover, and was brought to England to be cared for and studied by Dr. Arbuthnot.[2] It was the age of Nicholas Saunderson, the blind professor of mathematics at Cambridge, whose perceptual universe fascinated the pious commonsense philosopher Thomas Reid as it fascinated the rather less pious Diderot.[3] It was the age also of enthusiastic investigations into comparative anatomy, eked out with study of travel literature, which together encouraged Monboddo and Rousseau to formulate their theory that the advanced primates, notably the orangutan, were consanguineous with men, stunted, undeveloped, potential human beings.[4] It was an age of thought experiments: Diderot, in his *Lettre sur les sourds et muets*, imagined a "mute by convention," a construction that would permit the psychologist to exhibit the

---

[1] "Diderot was experimenting with . . . the method of trying to find out about the nature of the normal by studying the abnormal, of learning about the nature of the well through studying the diseased." Wilson: *Diderot*, 98.

[2] See Jonathan Swift to Thomas Tickell, April 16, 1726. *Correspondence*, ed. Harold Williams, 5 vols. (1963-5), III, 128, 128 *n.*; and the sensible observation by Adam Ferguson: "A wild man . . . caught in the woods, where he had always lived apart from his species, is a singular instance, not a specimen of any general character." *An Essay on the History of Civil Society* (1767; ed. Duncan Forbes, 1966), 3.

[3] Diderot's scientific interest here has a malicious edge: if all of men's ideas come through the senses, the moral experience of a blind man might well exclude God.

[4] Once again, Adam Ferguson is worth quoting. "In opposition to what has dropped from the pens of eminent writers, we are obliged to observe, that men have always appeared among animals a distinct and superior race; that neither the possession of similar organs, nor the approximation of shape, nor the use of the hand, nor the continued intercourse with this sovereign artist, has enabled any other species to blend their nature or their inventions with his; that in his rudest state, he is found to be above them; and in his greatest degeneracy, never descends to their level. He is, in short, a man in every condition; and we can learn nothing of his nature from the analogy of other animals." *History of Civil Society*, 5-6. In other (familiar) words, the proper study of mankind is not the apes, but man. It was from such discussions that the modern social sciences were to develop.

nature of each separate sense; Buffon had earlier proposed a perfectly formed, perfectly equipped human shape awakening to the world around him; and in 1754, much to the annoyance of his fellow-philosophes, Condillac, with a certain air of novelty, used the device of a statue "organized internally like us, and animated by a spirit deprived of all sorts of ideas" to display the structure and growth of mental activity.[5] It was, finally, an age of unsparing self-examination: Rousseau's *Confessions* and Laurence Sterne's *Tristram Shandy* and *Sentimental Journey* offered unprecedented insights into human motives.

The scientific value of these intellectual games was questioned even in the Enlightenment. While in nearly every instance, Adam Ferguson complained in 1767, "the natural historian thinks himself obliged to collect facts, not to offer conjectures," in "what relates to himself, and in matters the most important, and the most easily known," he "substitutes hypothesis instead of reality, and confounds the provinces of imagination and reason, of poetry and science."[6] At the same time, the scientific intention behind these conjectures was unimpeachable, their share in the construction of a scientific psychology decisive. With such games eighteenth-century psychologists redefined and partially clarified their relations with epistemology, and, by moving into the orbit of organized observation, deliberate experiment, and controlled generalization, they distanced themselves from their old alliance with imaginative literature and casual worldly wisdom. Locke, at the very beginning of his *Essay Concerning Human Understanding*, was the first to articulate the new direction the science of man was to take: while inquiries into the "essence" of mind, or the ultimate causes of sensation, were admittedly "speculations" at once "curious and entertaining," he proposed to concentrate on the activity of the mind, on "the discerning faculties of a man, as they are employed about the objects which they have to do with." And in considering these employments, Locke proposed to use the "historical, plain method,"[7] the scientific method of Bacon and Newton.

---

[5] *Traité des sensations*, in *Œuvres philosophiques*, I, 222. On the controversy over this device see ibid., 222 *n*. Condillac did give credit to an obscure friend, a Mademoiselle Ferrand, for giving him some ideas, but this acknowledgment seemed to his exasperated colleagues inadequate.

[6] *History of Civil Society*, 2.

[7] *Essay Concerning Human Understanding*, I, i, 2.

Locke's empirical psychology—at least its aims and methods, if not all its doctrines—became the psychology of the Enlightenment. In 1746, half a century after Locke's *Essay*, Condillac announced in the Introduction to his *Essai sur l'origine des connoissances humaines*: "Our first object, which we should never lose sight of, is the study of the human mind—*l'esprit humain*—not in order to discover its nature, but to understand its operations, to observe in what manner they are combined and how we should employ them that we might acquire all the intelligence of which we are capable. It is necessary to go back to the origin of our ideas, to work out their generation, follow them up to the limits nature has prescribed to them, and thus establish the extent and the limits of our knowledge, and renew all of human understanding." We can conduct "successful research" into the understanding "by way of observation alone."[8] And both David Hume and Adam Ferguson, the one in the 1730s, the other in the 1760s, put the weight of the Scottish Enlightenment behind Locke's systematic unpretentiousness. Hume disclaimed any intentions of explaining the "*original* qualities of human nature"; nothing, he wrote, "is more requisite for a true philosopher, than to restrain the intemperate desire of searching into causes."[9] And Ferguson took the same position: the student of man is more interested in the "reality" of a psychological disposition "and in its consequences," than in "its origins, or manner of formation."[1]

One motive for this ostentatious limitation of concern and insistence on the primacy of experience in mental life was, of course, that it permitted the philosophes to attack the Cartesian notion of innate knowledge. But it was also part of the philosophical modesty which, according to the philosophes, lay at the heart of all fruitful inquiry. In psychology, as everywhere else, to turn one's back on the unknowable permitted—almost enforced—a salutary concentration on what could be known; it was compatible with enormous ambitions for the science of man.

This aggressive modesty, and this emphatic empiricism, drove the philosophes into writing some rather perverse intellectual history. D'Alembert claimed that the sensationalist maxim to which

---

[8] In *Œuvres philosophiques*, I, 4. For the impact of this view on d'Alembert, see his *Discours préliminaire*, in *Mélanges*, I, 12.
[9] *Treatise of Human Nature*, 13.
[1] *History of Civil Society*, 25-6.

they all subscribed—there is nothing in the intellect that had not previously been in the senses—was an antique truth taken up, of all people, by the Scholastics, not because it was true but because it was old. Then came the great liberator, Descartes, who discarded, along with all the Scholastic nonsense, this truth as well. And now the time had come to discard Descartes's nonsense in turn.[2] Of such history-writing—which blithely passes over Descartes's contributions to physiological psychology and the contributions of many others —one can only say that it served the cause of the day. As I have noted before, like other revolutionaries the philosophes were anything but just to their adversaries or their ancestors. "Immediately after Aristotle comes Locke," wrote Condillac summarily, "for we should not count the other philosophers who have written on this subject."[3] As Locke had turned the mind, Condillac turned the history of its study into a *tabula rasa,* and endowed Locke with the eminence of the lonely pioneer.

This cannibalism says more about Condillac's intellectual ancestry than about the evolution of psychology. Condillac was a professional Lockian, more Lockian in his final system even than Locke himself.[4] The mind, Locke had argued, beginning as "white paper," is furnished with its "vast store" of ideas from a single source, experience, but this source has two branches, "our observation employed either about external sensible objects, or about the internal operations of our minds, perceived and reflected on by ourselves"—sensation and reflection.[5] But then, in the characteristic manner of the scientist, Locke's successors sought to simplify and beautify the psychological theories they had learned from him: "The development of empirical psychology from Locke to Berkeley and from Berkeley to Hume," Ernst Cassirer observes, "represents a series of attempts to minimize the difference between sensation and reflection, and finally to wipe it out altogether. French philosophical criticism of the eighteenth century hammered at this

---

[2] *Discours préliminaire,* in *Mélanges,* I, 13–14.
[3] *Extrait raisonné du Traité des sensations,* in *Œuvres philosophiques,* I, 324; the same passage struck Ernst Cassirer: see *Philosophy of the Enlightenment,* 99 n.
[4] See *The Rise of Modern Paganism,* 321.
[5] *Essay Concerning Human Understanding,* II, i, 2 and subsequent sections.

same point also in an attempt to eliminate the last vestige of independence which Locke had attributed to reflection."[6] In the *Essai sur l'origine des connoissances humaines*, his first treatise on psychology, Condillac ambitiously announced that he planned to "reduce everything that concerns the understanding to a single principle."[7] But the book kept the promise imperfectly. It retained Locke's dual scheme: "At the first moment" of a man's existence, "his mind first undergoes different sensations, like light, colors, pain, pleasure, movement, rest—these are his first thoughts"; then he "begins to reflect on what the sensations produce in him," and "forms ideas about the different operations of his mind, like perceiving and imagining—these are his second thoughts."[8] But in his *Traité des sensations*, published in 1754, Condillac offered a radical simplification, converting what he had treated as a temporal sequence into a causal one: reflection, which in the *Essai* had followed sensation, now became its effect. Rigorously carrying through the device of the inanimate, perfectly equipped statue, Condillac demonstrated that each single sense permits man to develop all his faculties. To "remember, compare, judge, discern, imagine, be astonished, have abstract ideas, ideas of number and duration, know general and particular truths," are after all nothing but "different ways of being attentive"; and to "have passions, love, hate, hope, fear and wish," are nothing but "different ways of desiring." Now, to be attentive and to desire are "in their origins nothing but feeling," and so it follows "that sensation comprehends all the faculties of the soul."[9] Condillac did not despise or deny the enormous complexity of mental life or the intricate structure of the mind, but he insisted that it is possible to trace this complexity and this structure to essentially simple elements. All mental activity arises from attention: thought is the child of need, for—and here, too, Condillac takes a position of Locke's to its conclusion—man's first and decisive experience is uneasiness. For Locke uneasiness—the desire to gain absent good or flee present evil—"determines the will,"[1] for Condillac *inquiétude*,

---

[6] *Philosophy of the Enlightenment*, 100.
[7] This is the subtitle of the first edition of the *Essai*; in *Œuvres philosophiques*, I, 1.
[8] Ibid., I, 6.
[9] *Traité des sensations*, ibid., I, 239.
[1] *Essay Concerning Human Understanding*, II, xxi (this is the famous chapter on "Power"), especially sections 31 *ff.*

or *tourment*, determines everything: "Locke," Condillac gratefully records, "was the first to note that the uneasiness caused by privation of an object is the principle of our determinations." Yet as far as Locke had gone, he had stopped short. He "had uneasiness arise from desire, and precisely the opposite is true." Condillac therefore thought that it remained to him to "demonstrate that this uneasiness is the first principle which gives us the habits of touching, seeing, hearing, feeling, tasting, comparing, judging, reflecting, desiring, loving, hating, fearing, hoping, wishing; that, in a word, it is through uneasiness that all the habits of mind and body are born."[2] And with this demonstration, Cartesian rationalist psychology had been refuted, and scientific empiricist psychology triumphantly held the field alone: "The will"—this was Condillac's conclusion—"is not founded on the idea, but the idea on the will."[3]

II

Ambitious to secure the status of empirical scientists, the psychologists of the eighteenth century, though openly, even effusively, grateful to Locke, found it necessary to place him second to another, still more admirable model. They acknowledged Locke as the father of modern psychology, but they made Newton into its hero —a desertion that would hardly have wounded Locke, who was himself Newton's enthusiastic admirer. Just as Buffon aspired to be called the Newton of nature, there were philosophers who aspired, more or less openly, to be called the Newton of the mind. They prided themselves on following his method, adapted some of his physical concepts to the mental world, and hoped to emulate his success in establishing a securely scientific system. In 1750 the Italian psychologist F. M. Zanotti published a fragment with the striking title, *Della forza attrativa della idee*. And David Hume, deliberately employing and emphasizing a term borrowed from the master himself, posited in the *Treatise* that man's simple ideas are

---

[2] *Extrait raisonné du Traité des sensations*, in *Œuvres philosophiques*, I, 325; see Cassirer: *Philosophy of the Enlightenment*, 103 *n*.
[3] As Cassirer notes, this was also the general conclusion of the Enlightenment. Ibid., 103.

united in the memory by "a kind of ATTRACTION, which in the mental world will be found to have as extraordinary effects as in the natural, and to shew itself in as many and as various forms."[4]

In these instances, Newton's influence on psychology was implicit, though obvious. In the work of David Hartley—perhaps the most inventive and certainly, despite intermittent periods of eclipse, the most influential psychologist of the eighteenth century—it became explicit. In his masterpiece, *Observations on Man, His Frame, His Duty, and His Expectations,* Hartley offered two connected psychological theories, of "vibration" and of "association," the first developed "from the hints concerning the performance of sensation and motion, which Sir Isaac Newton has given at the end of his *Principia,* and in the Questions annexed to his *Optics,*" the second, "from what Mr. Locke, and other ingenious persons since his time, have delivered concerning the influence of *association* over our opinions and affections."[5] While the theory of associations turned out to have a longer life than the theory of vibrations, it was Newton, far more than Locke, who presided over Hartley's system. Newton gave Hartley the impetus for his physiological psychology, supplied him with evidence on the persistence of sensations or the organization of the nervous system, and shaped his entire style of scientific thought. "The proper method of philosophizing," Hartley pronounced, and his pronouncement did not offer, and was not meant to offer, any surprises to a reader familiar with the *Principia* or the *Opticks,* is "to discover and establish the general laws of action, affecting the subject under consideration, from certain select, well-defined, and well-attested phaenomena, and then to explain and predict the other phaenomena by these laws." This, Hartley concluded, "is the method of analysis and synthesis recommended and followed by Sir Isaac Newton."[6] It is significant that when Thomas Reid criticized Hartley, he criticized him not simply for being wrong, but for being a bad Newtonian. It was, in an indisputably Newtonian universe, the most telling *Schimpfwort* Reid could find.[7]

---

[4] *Treatise of Human Nature,* 12–13.
[5] *Observations on Man, His Frame, His Duty, and His Expectations* (1749; 6th edn., 1834), 4.
[6] Ibid., 4–5; see also 8, 11–12.
[7] *Essays on the Intellectual Powers of Man* (1785; ed. A. D. Woozley, 1941), 60–9.

In the hands of his ruthless followers, Hartley's theory of vibrations was otiose, worthy of being excised, so that the theory of associations might gain the prominence it deserved. But for Hartley's own system, and for its place in eighteenth-century speculation, the theory of vibrations is essential.[8] It helps to define both Hartley's private ambition and his intellectual universe: whatever Hartley's religious convictions and apologetic intentions—and I shall return to them presently—his theory of vibrations placed man securely into the world of nature, invited secular explanations of human conduct, and thus made the old Christian conception of the active God, man's father and untiring guide, more remote, more irrelevant than ever.

Hartley's theory of vibrations is simple, and its simplicity is its virtue. Sensations and ideas, which are both "internal feelings," are "presented to the Mind" by the "white Medullary Substance of the Brain," which, with "the spinal Marrow, and the Nerves proceeding from them," acts as the "immediate Instrument" of "Sensation and Motion."[9] As a loyal Newtonian, Hartley conceived of the medullary substance as a collection of infinitesimally small particles, especially equipped to act as transmitters of stimuli. The nerves respond to sensations by vibrating, and produce vibrations among the medullary particles. "External objects, being corporeal, can act upon the nerves and brain, which are also corporeal, by nothing but compressing motion on them."[1] The relation of sensation to response—that is, vibration—is constant and predictable; as sensations change, ideas change with them. Whatever the limitations of such a theory—and they gradually became obvious with the progress of psychology—the purpose and formulation of such a straightforward physiological psychology opened new prospects to the science of man.

Hartley's theory of associations points in the same scientific direction. It had a long history, dating back beyond Locke and "other ingenious persons since his time" to a passage in Aristotle's

---

[8] Several historians of psychology, including George Sidney Brett, have rightly criticized Priestley's abridgment of Hartley's *Observations,* published in 1775, for omitting the theory of vibrations.
[9] *Observations on Man,* 6.
[1] Ibid., 8.

De Memoria et Reminiscentia, and, in modern times, to the materialist psychology of Hobbes. Locke, oddly enough, had treated the principle casually, as a truth familiar to all observant men, and useful only for the explanation of extravagant and even mad thoughts, but, at the same time, Locke gave the principle the name—"association of ideas"—under which it made its fortune in the age of the Enlightenment.[2] John Gay, a devout Anglican whose Utilitarian ideas came to exercise wide influence especially on English thought, and David Hume, were only two—there were others—to take association seriously.

For Hume, the theory of association offered a solution to a problem he himself had posed; association explained man's sense of confidence in the world in which, strictly speaking, nothing outside of mathematics is certain. The materials of experience, Hume argued, are sensations, and no sensation can guarantee the appearance of another sensation. Yet man does see the world as an ordered pattern, and "the common subjects" of his "thoughts and reasoning" are "complex ideas." Now this order and complexity, both indispensable, yet both in a sense artificial, are the products of the association of ideas. Sensations are repeated, sensations are like one another, sensations appear to have certain invariable effects, and it is from these three "principles of union"—contiguity, resemblance, and causation—that man constructs his mental world; association alone makes possible relations, modes, complex structures—in a word, organized thinking and rational discourse. With his customary caution, Hume conceded that his three principles were doubtless neither the "infallible" nor the "sole" principles of association, but he was certain that they were the "general principles" basic to mental life.[3]

Hume's psychology, with its atomism, its naturalism, its appeal to experience, its mixture of comprehensiveness and simplicity, and its modesty, was strikingly similar to Hartley's, but Hartley, although his *Observations* appeared in 1749, a decade after Hume's *Treatise,* had been at work on his own. Hartley was thoroughly familiar with the philosophical literature, and around 1730 he was told that "the Rev. Mr. Gay, then living, asserted the possibility of

[2] This chapter was only added to Locke's *Essay* in its fourth edition, in 1700: II, xxxiii.
[3] *Treatise of Human Nature*, 10–13, 92–3.

deducing all our intellectual pleasures and pains from association."
It was this hint that put Hartley "upon considering the power of
association,"[4] and late in the 1730s his system, if not his book, was
ready.

Like Condillac, Hartley was intent on simplifying Locke. "Excellent" as Locke's *Essay* was, he noted, it had wrongly taken reflection as a "distinct source" of ideas;[5] in fact, all ideas come from
sensations, and simple ideas are gathered into complex ideas by
association alone. As Hartley puts it schematically: "Any sensations
A, B, C, etc., by being associated with one another a sufficient
number of times, get such a power over the corresponding ideas
a, b, c, etc., that any one of the sensations A, when impressed
alone, shall be able to excite in the mind, b, c, etc., the ideas of the
rest."[6] Association is, for Hartley, the great, indeed the sole, principle of construction; it is built into the organism and indispensable
to man's physical and mental life. And its connection with vibrations is intimate and indissoluble: "One may expect, that *vibrations*
should infer *association* as their effect, and *association* point to *vibrations* as its cause."[7] Indeed, Hartley restated the law of associations
as the fundamental law of vibrations: "Any vibrations A, B, C, etc.,
by being associated together a sufficient number of times, get such
a power over a, b, c, etc. the corresponding miniature vibrations,
that any of the vibrations A, when impressed alone, shall be able
to excite b, c, etc., the miniatures of the rest."[8]

Hartley's system was neat and audacious: the theory of vibrations explains the action of sensation in the human organism, the
theory of associations, which is its twin, explains the construction
of simple sensations into man's total experience. Nothing else is
necessary: there are no epicycles in Hartley's psychology. "Simple
ideas will run into complex ones, by means of associations,"[9] and
simple muscular motions are built up into man's most complex physical activity in the same manner. Thus, vibration and association
together account for all that needs accounting for: the activity of

---

[4] *Observations on Man*, "Preface," a2.
[5] Ibid., 226–7.
[6] Ibid., 41.
[7] Ibid., 4.
[8] Ibid., 43.
[9] Ibid., 46.

the senses and of memory, the varieties of pleasures and pains, involuntary actions like breathing or the beating of the heart, the flights of the imagination, speech from the simplest to the most philosophical, the sexual appetite—the sexual organs are, after all, particularly sensitive both to vibrations and to the association of ideas, to the "numberless things" that "young people hear and read" in this "degenerate and corrupt state of human life, which carry nervous influences of the pleasurable kind (be they vibrations, or any other species of motion) to the organs of generation"[1]—and even the truths of religion.

Inevitably, Hartley's enterprise, which sought to explain with two simple interlocking physical principles the infinite variety of man's experience from his dimmest awareness of shapes and colors to his most exalted perception of God, from his most animal-like sensuality to his most abstruse cogitations, aroused a variety of responses. A little late, Dugald Stewart would censoriously dismiss Hartley's work as unscientific, as a "metaphysical romance"[2]—perhaps the most devastating pair of words a critic could utter in that age, while Joseph Priestley, Hartley's most assiduous and most effective popularizer, thought that Hartley had done more for psychology than Locke, and "thrown more useful light upon the theory of the mind than Newton did upon the theory of the natural world."[3] Clearly, both critic and disciple were wrong. To be a Newtonian did not make Hartley into a Newton, but to be a Newtonian in the study of man was, in itself, a good thing to be.

III

Considering the relatively primitive state of eighteenth-century physiology, Hartley's psychology was a major achievement. But it is also an instructive cultural artifact of the age of the Enlightenment; it unwittingly reveals the irresistible pressure of the Newtonian method on traditional religious convictions. Hartley's intentions were

---

[1] Ibid., 151.
[2] Quoted in Maria Heider: *Studien über David Hartley (1705–1757)*, (1913), 67.
[3] Quoted in Élie Halévy: *The Growth of Philosophic Radicalism* (tr. Mary Morris, 2d edn., 1934), 9.

apologetic: in his letters as in his *Observations*, his piety is transparent and affecting; he built his system, with constant, fervent prayer, to "show," as he wrote to a friend, "that the Christian revelation has the most incontestable marks of truth and certainty,"[4] and was compatible in all respects with the findings of the natural philosopher. The entire second part of his book is devoted to "Observations on the Duty and Expectations of Mankind" designed to demonstrate the relation of natural religion to Scripture and the truth of Christianity, and to offer rules for the conduct of the Christian life.

But, as Hartley was the first to recognize, his theories of vibrations and associations seemed to deny the free will that Christians of all persuasions except the Calvinist deem essential to salvation, and seemed instead to point toward a materialistic determinism that not even Calvinists could accept. "I think," wrote Hartley in the Preface of his *Observations*, defiantly but a little pathetically, that "I cannot be called a system-maker, since I did not first form a system, and then suit the facts to it, but was carried on by a train of thoughts"—shall we say, persuasive associations?—"from one thing to another, frequently without any express design, or even any previous suspicion of the consequences that might arise." Hartley knew that this was sound scientific procedure, but he found the results disturbing, especially "in respect of the doctrine of *necessity;* for I was not at all aware, that it followed from that of association, for several years after I had begun my inquiries; nor did I admit it at last, without the greatest reluctance."[5] His friends were not convinced, but Hartley himself, once having developed his deterministic system, could not abandon it, and set himself instead to reconcile it with the immateriality of the soul, the truth of revelation, and man's eventual happiness. Hartley himself seemed to be persuaded by his compromise between Anglicanism and materialism; it satisfied his scientific probity and Christian optimism. But most of his followers dropped the Anglicanism and retained the materialism. Joseph Priestley was, to be sure, an odd sort of materialist: he was the kind of pious scientist with which eighteenth-century England was so richly endowed—a Christian optimist much like Hartley; a ma-

---

[4] Hartley to Rev. John Lister, December 2, 1736. Quoted in Heider: *Studien über Hartley,* 44.
[5] *Observations on Man,* iv.

terialist, a Unitarian, and a political radical; a Voltairian scourge of "superstition" and the "corruptions of Christianity" who believed in the miracles of Christ and in His resurrection. But other partisans of the new psychology were less complicated: Helvétius in France and Bentham in England incorporated its doctrines into a naturalistic materialism that made no compromises with theology. When some time around 1800 the German philosopher Friedrich August Carus wrote an essay on the history of psychology, he characterized Hartley's *Observations* as offering the "principles of modern materialism" and said nothing about Hartley's religion.[6] And so Hartley, like other enlightened Christians of the day, was victimized by the growing tensions between science and theology and lent involuntary aid to the radical Enlightenment, which was bent upon understanding man without recourse to God.

3. THE REVOLT AGAINST RATIONALISM

I

T HE PHILOSOPHES WELCOMED and explored psychology as a rational discipline, but in their hands reason was not its central object of study. The metaphysicians of the seventeenth century had allowed their urgent desire for rationality to govern their conclusions: had not Descartes claimed, "There is no soul so weak that it cannot, if well directed, acquire absolute power over its passions"?[7] The philosophes thought such a claim preposterous. As David Hume noted in one of his memoranda, tendentiously pitting antique pagan

---

[6] *Geschichte der Psychologie* (posthumously edited and published by Ferdinand Hand, 1808), 746. That Hartley's ideas were thought to lead to infidelity is shown by Coleridge who, as a young man, much admired Hartley, but then records in a letter to Poole, March 16, 1801: "I . . . have completely overthrown the doctrine of association as taught by Hartley, and with it all the irreligious metaphysics of modern infidels—especially the doctrine of necessity." Quoted in I. A. Richards: *Coleridge on Imagination* (2d edn., 1950), 15.

[7] *Les passions de l'âme*, article 50; *Œuvres*, XI, 368.

against modern Christian philosophers, "The Moderns have not treated Morals so well as the Antients merely from their Reasoning turn, which carry'd them away from Sentiment."[8] This was a dubious interpretation, characteristic of the philosophes' manner of reading—or, rather, misreading—the history of psychology. But, however indefensible as history, Hume's observation directs attention to a fallacy that the philosophes did not intend to perpetuate: reason, Hume insisted, neither influences the will nor gives rise to morality; nor does reason have any part in producing those associations of ideas by which men think and live. "Is it likely," he asked rhetorically, "that reason will prevail against nature, habit, company, education, and prejudice?"[9] He put it more formally in the *Treatise:* "We speak not strictly and philosophically when we talk of the combat of passion and of reason. Reason is, and ought only to be the slave of the passions, and can never pretend to any other office than to serve and obey them."

It is a harsh aphorism, rather more energetic than Hume's own philosophy required it to be—Hume would have been the first to insist that there are some passions whose tyranny man should, and could, shake off—and he deprecated it as "somewhat extraordinary."[1] But it was only extreme, not at all extraordinary: the limits of rational inquiry into ultimate mysteries, the impotence of reason before the passions, were after all themes that haunted the Enlightenment. "People ceaselessly proclaim against the passions," wrote Diderot in the opening paragraph of his first philosophical work, "people impute to the passions all of men's pains, and forget that they are also the source of all his pleasures. It is an element of man's constitution of which we can say neither too many favorable, nor too many unfavorable things. But what makes me angry is that the passions are never regarded from any but the critical angle. People think they do reason an injury if they say a word in favor of its rivals. Yet it is only the passions, and the great passions, that can raise the soul to great things."[2] It was a position that, once taken, he would surrender only with reluctance. In 1762 he told Sophie

---

[8] Quoted in Mossner: *Life of David Hume,* 76.
[9] Hume to John Clephane, February 18, 1751. *Letters,* I, 149.
[1] *Treatise of Human Nature,* 415.
[2] *Pensées philosophiques,* in *Œuvres,* I, 127.

Volland: "I forgive everything that is inspired by passion."[3] And seven years later he wrote to another correspondent: "The language of the heart is a thousand times more varied than that of the mind, and it is impossible to law down the rules of its dialectics."[4] In its treatment of the passions, as in its treatment of metaphysics, the Enlightenment was not an age of reason but a revolt against rationalism.

This revolt was at once substantive and methodological. It opposed not merely excessive claims for man's power to control his emotions, but also the arid, schematic, often unworldly constructions and classifications of earlier philosophers of the mind. But the philosophes' revolt in psychology was also—and here its delicacy lies—a revolt against antirationalism, against that devout psychology which meekly served Christian theology by denying man's capacity to find his own unaided way in life. It is no accident that the philosophes chose as their intellectual ancestors, in the study of man as elsewhere, those modern writers who had distrusted reason without exalting unreason: Montaigne, Hobbes, Spinoza—and Locke. The pious Christian, the Enlightenment conceded, had been right to explore the limits of reason and the range of passion, but he had misconceived them both. In response, the philosophes saw psychology as a dual escape—from unreasonable rationalism and superstitious antirationalism.

The issue between the Enlightenment and its adversaries, therefore, was less the power of the passions than their value, although the new psychology made that power appear greater than ever before. Tentatively, even playfully, often drawing no consequences from their own discoveries, the philosophes had intimations of the unconscious, the superego, of rationalization and sublimation. Swift had already called attention to the earthy, passionate sources of abstract thinking; Diderot, treating it as almost a commonplace, told Damilaville: "There is a bit of testicle at the bottom of our

---

[3] (July 31, 1762). *Correspondance*, IV, 81. In the same paragraph Diderot insists—it is an important point—that the passions make man human and that lack of passion is, really, beastly: "The mediocre man [which must here be taken to mean the man without passion] lives and dies like an animal."
[4] To Madame de Maux (?), (November 1769). *Correspondance*, IX, 204. See also below, 194–200.

most sublime sentiments and most refined tenderness."[5] Behind and
beneath reason the philosophes glimpsed a large undiscovered country, strange and terrifying. "The sleep of reason begets monsters,"
wrote Goya under one of his Caprichos, showing a man asleep, with
his head on his arms, while batlike apparitions swirl about him.
"Deserted by reason," Goya commented, "imagination begets impossible monsters. United with reason she is the mother of all arts
and the source of their wonders."[6] Picture and commentary together
embody the wisdom of a century.

It was in this climate that Diderot tersely formulated what
Freud was to acknowledge as a remarkable anticipation of the Oedipus complex: "If your little savage were left to himself," Diderot's
spokesman says to Rameau's nephew, "keeping all his childish foolishness—imbécillité—and joining the bit of rationality of the infant
in the cradle to the violent passions of the man of thirty, he would
strangle his father and sleep with his mother."[7] And it was in this
climate that Lichtenberg commended the study of dreams to solve
the secrets of the soul: "A philosophical dream book could be written." Lichtenberg distinguished, and regretted that others had failed
to differentiate, between the scientific "interpretation of dreams" and
superstitious "dream books." "That's the way it usually is. I know
from undeniable experience that dreams lead to self-knowledge";
after all, "we live and feel as much dreaming as waking."[8] If, in the
philosophes' hands, the universe of the mind became wholly natural,
its nature gained in depth and mystery.

For most of the philosophes, the analysis of passion became a
celebration. Diderot was convinced that without passion nothing
could be done either in the arts or in civilization as a whole. Hume

---

[5] (November 3, 1760). Ibid., III, 216. A little later Diderot attributes
this idea—"it is impossible to analyze the most delicate of feelings
without discovering a bit of filth in them"—to Madame d'Aine,
Holbach's mother-in-law. It seems, then, to have been well known
in advanced circles (see ibid., 236).
[6] The etching has often been reproduced and commented upon;
conveniently in Michael Levey: *Rococo to Revolution: Major
Trends in Eighteenth-Century Painting* (1966), 8, 10-12, 210-14.
[7] *Le neveu de Rameau*, 95.
[8] *The Lichtenberg Reader*, tr. and ed. Franz Mautner and Henry
Hatfield (1959), 70.

argued that all effort, all activity, all work spring from passion.[9] Mendelssohn asserted that "reason acts as a kill-joy (*Störerin*) to sentiment and pleasure."[1] Lessing, writing to Mendelssohn, offered the paradox that even the most disagreeable passion is agreeable to man, since each heightens his self-awareness.[2] Vauvenargues, Voltaire's protégé, praised the instincts in a series of aphorisms that were much quoted and widely admired in his time: "The great thoughts come from the heart"—"Reason does not know the interests of the heart"—"Reason misleads us more often than nature."[3] And Voltaire, though more moderate than Vauvenargues, anticipated him and the others when he called the passions "the principal cause of the order we see today in the world."[4]

Yet the philosophes' celebration of passion inevitably had its wry aspect. Wieland and Voltaire, David Hume and John Adams joined in regretting man's susceptibility to irrational impulse; they were complacently amused by his love of wonder, sardonic about the ease with which his noble philosophizing was subverted by appeals to baser passions, and horrified by his inclination to violence. Like progress, the passions seemed to the philosophes an uncertain blessing: Voltaire speaks of them as a divine but dangerous gift; Diderot, whose commitment to the emotions was wholehearted and almost hysterical, nevertheless thought them an untrustworthy ally and a capricious master: "The passionate man would like to control the universe," he wrote, and evidently found this desire at once admirable and terrifying.[5] Love, he wrote, is a tyrant who dominates man's moods and corrupts his judgment: "Where is the lover

---

[9] "Our passions are the only causes of our labour." "Of Commerce," *Works*, III, 293.
[1] *Briefe über die Empfindungen*, quoted in Robert Sommer: *Grundzüge einer Geschichte der deutschen Psychologie und Aesthetik* (1892), 116.
[2] See Lessing to Mendelssohn, November 13, 1756. *Schriften*, XVII, 69–70; and Lessing to the same, February 2, 1757, ibid., 90.
[3] "Réflexions et maximes," in *Maximes et réflexions*, ed. Lucien Meunier (1945), 43, 44.
[4] *Traité de métaphysique* (1734), ed. H. Temple Patterson (1937), 53.
[5] Diderot to Sophie Volland (July 14, 1762). *Correspondance*, IV, 39.

who allows himself to be told, patiently, that his mistress is ugly?"[6] Obviously reflecting on his own experience, he wrote to Vialet, engineer and Encyclopedist: "In men like you and me, my friend, passion often speaks the language of reason, but we all act like the other madmen."[7] Even Rousseau—and this in his great homage to sentiment, the *Nouvelle Héloïse*—warned against the perils of the passions: "With the help of good sense," so runs the device on the frontispiece for the novel, "we save ourselves in the arms of reason."[8]

II

Revolutionary for all its hesitancy and equivocations, the Enlightenment's rehabilitation of the passions was essential to its rehabilitation of man as a natural creature. Two sentiments in particular—pride and lust—which Christians for centuries had condemned as mortal sins, acquired in the philosophy of the philosophes a new, high, and, to the devout, offensive status.

As the Pastoral Letter condemning *Émile*, and a thousand other texts, make plain, Christians found few mysteries in pride and few intellectual difficulties; some theologians proposed it as an ingenious divine device to spur men into activity, but in general, they treated it as simply and vastly sinful. For the philosophes, pride was much more problematical. In its passage through time, the term had gathered up a cluster of diverse and not wholly consistent meanings— self-love, boastfulness, sober confidence, desire for the approval of one's soul or one's fellow men—and the philosophes' evaluation of it was as varied and unstable as its meanings. This much seemed evident: pride appeared in some egregious forms—conceit, vanity, lust for power—and in these forms it had done good only, if at all, unintentionally or by indirection. Rousseau, in his two *Discours*, was inclined to hold pride responsible for civilization with all its glaring flaws; Mandeville, more wryly, argued that "the Moral Virtues are the Political Offspring which Flattery begot upon

---

[6] Diderot to Falconet (June 15, 1766). Ibid., VI, 220.
[7] (End of April or early May, 1766). Ibid., 179.
[8] See F. C. Green: *Jean-Jacques Rousseau: A Critical Study of His Life and Writings* (1955), 182.

Pride."[9] When Voltaire, *méchant* and sardonic, commended pride for being "the principal instrument with which men have built this fine edifice, society,"[1] he was following Mandeville's doctrine that private vices confer public benefits. But this seemed feeble consolation for the harm conceit and egotism had done: they had seduced philosophers to waste their lives constructing comprehensively foolish systems, statesmen to sacrifice ordinary men to their schemes, aristocrats to wound their fellow men with their arrogance, Stoics to attempt, nobly but in vain, to exercise control over their passions, and men of good hope to suffer grievous disappointments. Wieland's and Voltaire's fables are filled with cautionary figures who fell low because they reached too high. The philosophes' inconclusive debates over the true character of *amour propre* show their suspicion of self-regarding sentiments; their repetitive injunctions against system-making and against intolerance were warnings against philosophical and theological pride.

At the same time, it was important for the philosophes' reformist style of thought to assert that pride also took beneficent forms; in the guise of serene, realistic self-confidence, they argued, or the philosophical sentiment of inner worth, pride was a passion appropriate to enlightened men. This was the kind of pride Voltaire had in mind when he asked men to remember their human dignity, and Kant, when he suggested that man should put "a certain noble trust" in his powers.[2] It was David Hume who made the pagan implications of this view explicit. Those, he wrote pointedly, "accustom'd to the style of the schools and pulpit" treated pride simply as a vice; but Hume thought it "evident" that, just as humility is not always virtuous, pride "is not always vicious."[3] Even more pointedly, Hume suggested that men who "judge of things by their natural, unprejudiced reason, without the delusive glosses of superstition and false religion," will firmly reject "celibacy, fasting, penance, mortification, self-denial, humility, silence, solitude, and the whole train of monkish virtues." These so-called virtues are

---

[9] "An Enquiry into the Origin of Moral Virtue," *The Fable of the Bees, or, Private Vices, Publick Benefits* (1714; ed. F. B. Kaye, 2 vols., 2d edn., 1957), I, 51.
[1] *Traité de métaphysique*, 53.
[2] Both, see above, 172, 177.
[3] *Treatise of Human Nature*, 297–8.

really vices, making man neither rich, nor good company, nor a sound citizen, nor happy; they "stupify the understanding and harden the heart, obscure the fancy and sour the temper."[4] Christian and Enlightenment anthropology could hardly be contrasted more sharply than this.

The philosophes' "rescue" of sensuality was, if anything, more daring than their rescue of pride, though less conclusive. The strategies for their campaign are familiar enough; they defined the issue and their aims by writing tendentious history. In their polemics, the Christian view of the body appears as a debased Stoicism: like Stoicism it made inhuman demands on man's nature; unlike Stoicism, its promised rewards for asceticism were fictitious, infantile, insulting to self-respecting men. La Mettrie saw the priesthood as the sworn enemy of man's passionate nature; Diderot, for all his detestation of La Mettrie's *Anti-Sénèque*, agreed with him on this point. Describing an abbé to Sophie Volland—in fact, his brother—Diderot regretted his flawed humanity: "He would have been a good friend, a good brother, if Christ had not ordered him to trample under foot all these trifles." What these Christians "call evangelical perfection," he added, "is nothing but the deadly art of stifling nature."[5] This criticism became a commonplace in Holbach's circle. "The proper object of Christianity," wrote Damilaville in the *Encyclopédie*, "is not to populate the earth; its true aim is to populate heaven. Its dogmas are divine, and one must concede that this holy religion would achieve its goal if the belief were universal, and if the impulses of nature were not unfortunately stronger than all dogmatic opinions."[6] And Holbach himself asserted, "If we examine matters without prejudice, we will find that most of the precepts which religion, or its fanatical and supernatural ethics, prescribe to man, are as ridiculous as they are impossible to practice. To prohibit men their passions is to forbid them to be men; to advise a man carried away by his imagination to moderate his desires is to advise him to change his physical constitution, to order his blood to run more slowly." Holbach offers several instances of such in-

---

[4] *Enquiry into the Principles of Morals*, in *Works*, IV, 246–7.
[5] (August 16, 1759). *Correspondance*, II, 218.
[6] "Population," in *D'Holbach et ses amis*, ed. René Hubert (1928), 192.

sensate counsel: shun the pursuit of wealth, give up the desire for fame. But he reserves his climactic, most telling illustration for the erotic sphere: "To tell a lover of impetuous temperament that he must stifle his passion for the object that enchants him is to make him understand that he should renounce his happiness."[7] This, to Holbach, was the utmost in folly; but he witnessed it with a mixture of the worldling's resigned amusement and the reformer's purposeful fury. After all, he was certain that religions—all religions, not Christianity alone—demand, practice, and impose some form of self-mutilation. And he was equally certain that the philosophes must rescue the body from the castrating zeal of pious men.

This clear-cut, unrelieved condemnation of the Christian attitude toward sensuality was a malicious caricature of a complex reality. It was plausible and popular: professing to worship Priapus, the earl of Pembroke said late in the eighteenth century: "So superb a deity ought always to have been treated with every possible mark of religion and respect but, from the natural perverseness and exclusive monopoly of the Christian faith, he has been neglected for too long a series of ages."[8] And it contained a core of truth. Christian asceticism had arisen at least in part as a response to pagan indulgence. In Rome, as Stoic philosophers noted with disgust, pleasure, when it was available, was orgiastic: internal restraint was weak and life cheap. Pleasure meant gluttony, ruinous spending, blood sports, sexual experimentation, and murder. Christianity offered the ideal of restraint and the threat of an all-seeing God; it redirected pleasure on all levels, from eros to agape, from uninhibited lust to sexual abstention, from the self to the divine. And so, in Freud's words, "Religious credulity stifled the neuroses" of antiquity.[9] Catholic Christianity, Heinrich Heine observed more than a century ago, "was necessary as a salutary reaction against the horrible colossal materialism that had developed in the Roman Empire and threatened to destroy all the spiritual splendor of man." Flesh had become "so impudent in this Roman world that doubtless it needed Christian

---

[7] *Système de la nature*, I, 357.

[8] Quoted in Nina Epton: *Love and the English* (edn. 1963), 276.

[9] Sigmund Freud to Oskar Pfister, February 9, 1909. *Sigmund Freud, Oskar Pfister, Briefe 1909–1939*, ed. Ernst L. Freud and Heinrich Meng (1963), 12.

discipline to correct it." After Trimalchio's dinner what was needed was a "starvation diet like Christendom."[1]

But, despite sermons against the flesh, philosophical deprecation of love, monasticism, the cult of virginity, Christian civilization was not solely a starvation diet. The sexual appetite did not vanish behind a wall of discreet silence after the triumph of Christianity; medieval literature was often coarsely direct. Not all praise of sensuality was the private property of heretical sects or exclusive privileged castes; others, too, sang the love of man for woman, or man for boy. Even the Puritans, whom the Enlightenment liked to malign as dour, fanatical enemies of life, were refreshingly unpuritanical in their sexual behavior. Yet, when all corrections have been made in the philosophes' portrait, when all the liberality in practice, and all the erotic passages in medieval literature have been remembered, it remains true that Christianity officially condemned sexual desire, and sexual pleasure, as sinful—at least since the Fall.[2] It was not the philosophes' intention to deny that sexual intercourse, or sexual enjoyment, had been widespread before they came on the scene, or that erotic literature had been stifled by piety until their century: they had read Chaucer and Boccaccio, Aretino and Bembo, and, for all their tendentiousness, they were men of sense. Their intention was, rather, to reassert the innocence of sexuality, and to celebrate it as an integral and praiseworthy part of man's nature.

It is this intention that controls one of the most striking polemics of the Enlightenment, Diderot's *Supplément au Voyage de Bougainville*. Its procedure is perfectly simple: it is to contrast, invidiously, Christian sexual morality with Tahitian sexual morality by contrasting corrupt, superstitious, and above all hypocritical Christian civilization with pure, free, honest Tahitian civilization. Diderot's Tahitians, though noble, are not savages, and the contrast Diderot wishes to draw is the more effective for it.

Tahitian society, as reported by the world traveler Bougain-

---

[1] *Die Romantische Schule*, in *Heinrich Heines sämtliche Werke*, ed. Oskar Walzel *et al.*, 10 vols. (1910–15), VII, 8–9.

[2] For St. Augustine, "lust" came into being after Eve's disobedience; without that, he believed, Adam and Eve should have copulated without sin, commanding their sexual organs by their wills rather than being driven on by concupiscence. *The City of God*, book XIV, chaps. xviii–xxiv.

ville and then reconstructed for his own purposes by Diderot, is a reasonable order, close to man's nature. Its institutions are modeled on and make proper use of the deepest promptings of the passions. There is no private property in land or women, but this communism leads to a sense of abundance: "Everything that is good and necessary for us, we possess." When "we are hungry, we have enough to eat. When we are cold, we have enough to wear."[3] The Tahitians' wants are simple, but this simplicity is not a virtue imposed by necessity—it is a rational code of conduct.

Christian morality, on the other hand, strikes the Tahitians as "useless knowledge," as "fetters disguised in a hundred different shapes," which "can only arouse the indignation and contempt" of men in whom "the love of liberty—*le sentiment de la liberté*" is the deepest of feelings.[4] Tahitian indignation is aroused by Western greed and bellicosity, but it is aroused most fiercely by the Christian sexual code. Diderot, composing an angry oration for his spokesman, an aged Tahitian, eloquently pleads for the pagan sensuality he thinks proper for the Enlightenment: "Only a little while ago, the young Tahitian girl blissfully abandoned herself to the embraces of a young Tahitian man; she impatiently awaited the day when her mother, authorized by the girl's nubility, would lift her veil and show her naked breasts. She was proud to be able to excite the desires and attract the amorous looks of strangers, of her relatives, of her brother; she accepted the caresses of the one whom her young heart and the secret voice of her senses had pointed out to her— accepted them without fear and without shame, in our presence, in the midst of a crowd of innocent Tahitians, to the sound of flutes and amid dancing. The idea of crime and the fear of disease entered among us only with you. Our enjoyments, once so sweet, are attended with remorse and dread. That man in black standing near you, listening to me, has spoken to our boys; I don't know what he said to our girls, but our boys hesitate, our girls blush. Go bury yourself in the dark woods, if you like, with the perverse companion

---

[3] *Supplément au voyage de Bougainville,* ed. Herbert Dieckmann (1955), 14. While at least one speaker in this essay-review-dialogue refers to the Tahitians as "savages," the overwhelming and intended impression is that they are a civilized people.

[4] Ibid., 10.

of your pleasures, but let the good, simple Tahitians reproduce
themselves without shame under the open sky, and in broad daylight."[5]

It is hardly necessary to emphasize that this improbable discourse contradicts the Christian condemnation of lust point for
point. In the paradise of Tahiti's innocence, Christian morality acts
the part of the serpent. Diderot, one might say, wryly accepts the
Fall by transferring the burden of responsibility: it is not man, but
Christianity that is guilty of bringing sin—the sin against nature—
into the world. Diderot relates that after Bougainville's landing, the
ship's chaplain is invited to stay in one of the natives' huts. The
Tahitian and his family make their guest comfortable, and when
he is about to go to sleep, his host appears by his bedside with his
wife and three daughters, all naked, and makes him a little speech:
"You have had dinner, you are young, you are in good health; if
you sleep alone you will sleep badly; at night a man needs a companion by his side. Here is my wife; here are my daughters. Choose
the one that pleases you, but if you would do me a favor, you
would give preference to the youngest of my daughters: she has not
yet had any children." The chaplain declines, pleading "his religion,
his holy orders—état—morals and decency," a refusal that sends
his host into a lyrical defense of nature: "I don't know what this
thing is that you call 'religion,' but I can only think ill of it, since
it keeps you from enjoying an innocent pleasure to which nature,
our sovereign mistress, invites us all." The chaplain's refusal, he
suggests, is offensive alike to the demands of hospitality and the
needs of nature in search of offspring. The only acceptable excuse
is physiological: "I am not asking you to harm your health. If you
are tired, you should rest." With this he leaves the chaplain to fight
out the conflict between unnatural self-denial and natural desire.
It ends as it must end: the chaplain spends the night with the girl,
objecting to the last: "But my religion! My holy orders!" And in
succeeding nights, the chaplain performs the same service for the
other girls and finally, "out of politeness," sleeps with his host's wife,
punctuating the nocturnal silence with his repeated exclamations,
"But my religion! But my holy orders!"[6]

---

[5] Ibid., 16–17.
[6] Ibid., 22–4, 49.

The chaplain's manly if reluctant compliance emboldens his host to question him about a religion that exacts such conduct. The Christian God appears to the Tahitian an irrational and vicious master: his precepts, which totally prohibit his priests from enjoying sexual activities, and prevent other men from diversifying them, are "opposed to nature, contrary to reason." In demanding an impossible constancy, the laws regulating morality in Christendom are simply "contrary to the general laws of being." They certainly have no relation to true morality: "Would you like to know what is good and evil in all times and places? Cling to the nature of things and actions, to your relations with your fellow-creatures, to the influence of your conduct on your personal welfare and the public good. You are raving if you think that there is anything in the universe, high or low, which could add to or subtract from the laws of nature." Christianity—and this is the heart of Diderot's indictment and of his pagan psychology—multiplies crime and misery, depraves the conscience and corrupts the mind: "People will no longer know what they must do or not do; guilty in the state of innocence, tranquil in the midst of crime, they will have lost the north star that should guide their course."[7]

But for Diderot, even in this Tahitian fantasy, sexual liberty is not sexual license: Diderot scoffs at celibacy, monogamy, and the fear of incest, and insists that the sexual impulse, being natural, is as innocent as it is essential for the survival of society. But Diderot defines "natural" not as primitive- or animal-like, or as everything that is possible; the natural, for him, is the appropriate. He places distinct limits on permissible sexual activity: Diderot's Tahitians impose strict taboos on intercourse before maturity has been reached, and the enforcement of these taboos "is the principal object of domestic education, and the most important point in public morality."[8] Bigamy, fornication, adultery, incest are imaginary crimes foisted on a supine humanity by religion, but nature itself sets boundaries which, since they emerge from nature rather than violate it, are truly sacred.

Since Diderot was among the most passionate men—or, in any

---

[7] Ibid., 26, 28, 28–9. As Diderot wrote to Falconet: "The first step toward becoming wicked" is "to see wickedness where it is not" (August 21, 1771). *Correspondance*, XI, 128.
[8] *Supplément au voyage de Bougainville*, 33.

event, among the most uninhibited writers—of the eighteenth century, his defense of lust is exceptional in its vivacity. While La
Mettrie celebrated *volupté*, and Rousseau made his masochism public
property, the other philosophes were more restrained, or at least
less candid: Voltaire enjoyed the obscene Restoration poems he
learned in England, but he kept them in the privacy of his notebooks, and when he wrote impassioned love letters to his niece, he
kept them utterly secret and kept, in a sense, his passion from
himself by putting the most erotic passages into Italian. Yet there is
an indication, and from an unexpected quarter, that the philosophes
were preparing the way for a rational analysis, and thus for a less
hostile view, of sexuality: David Hume suggests that sexual taboos
or the sense of shame are by no means natural, let alone God-given,
but are valuable only because they are deemed to perform a social
function.

As Hume sees it, civilization does not express the sexual instinct
but represses it. In 1743, he argued, against Francis Hutcheson, that
social institutions arise not from natural inclinations but from the
fear of natural inclinations. "You are so much afraid to derive any
thing of Virtue from Artifice or human Conventions, that you have
neglected what seems to me the most satisfactory Reason, viz lest
near Relations, having so many Opportunities in their Youth, might
debauch each other, if the least Encouragement or Hope was given
to these Desires, or if they were not early represt by an artificial
Horror, inspired against them."[9] Even chastity and fidelity, those
Christian virtues, are artificial, and are virtues only because they
have social uses: "The long and helpless infancy of man requires
the combination of parents for the subsistence of their young; and
that combination requires the virtue of CHASTITY or fidelity to the
marriage bed. Without such a *utility*, it will readily be owned, that
such a virtue would never have been thought of."[1] This is scandalous, even revolutionary, doctrine, resembling Christian social thought

---

[9] January 10, 1743. *Letters*, I, 48.
[1] *Enquiry Concerning the Principles of Morals*, in *Works*, IV, 198.
How difficult it was even for Hume to maintain this posture is
illustrated by his observation—on the following page—in which he
describes incest as "pernicious"; not as seeming, or being widely
thought, but as actually, pernicious. Cultural relativism, which
flourished in the Enlightenment, was still too new to be complete.
(See also below, chap. vii, *passim*.)

only on the surface. Christians, too, had asserted that men must bear the yoke of social institutions to control the Old Adam, but Christian speculation moralized and theologized this psychological insight. Hume's analysis, in contrast, is cool, secular, and relativistic: why is it, Hume inquires, that the bounds of incest are drawn widely in one society and narrowly in another, that uncles and nieces, half-brothers and sisters, could marry at Athens but not at Rome? "Public utility is the cause of all these variations."[2] The manner of Hume's question, and the character of his answer, reduce the very notion of sin and salvation to irrelevance, and bring the passion of the sexes within the boundaries of nature and the control of science.

III

The philosophes' drastic revaluation of the passions was a hope, a forecast, a critique of prevailing pieties and, to some extent at least, a report on subtle developments in their own time. That the Enlightenment's defense of pride reflects the widespread and growing confidence in man's capacity to master his world is plain enough; it was the psychological and anthropological counterpart of the recovery of nerve. Its defense of lust reflects some changes as well, but these changes are by no means plain. In the eighteenth century, sexuality was still surrounded by coy circumlocutions or embarrassed secrecy, and by striking diversities between professions and performance; most men, even the most philosophical, were still reluctant to engage in a philosophical discussion of sexual behavior.

Therefore, and not unexpectedly, eighteenth-century culture gave its philosophers—as it has given its historians—fragmentary, confusing, and contradictory information on this delicate subject. Libertinism coexisted with modesty, high exaltation with cynicism. There was a distinct improvement in the status of women, and increasing emphasis, especially among bourgeois circles, on marital fidelity. Young Christian rakes, like James Boswell—who took his women where he found them, in the streets, against walls, in parks—forgot the preachments of their faith in the gratification of their

---

[2] Ibid., 199.

desires, but they were haunted by self-reproaches. Aristocrats, as
the letters of Lord Chesterfield testify, continued to be, as they
had long been, wholly utilitarian in their treatment of women, coldly
sensual, exploitative and gross, in stark, shocking contrast to the
refinement of their tastes in other matters. Prostitution was widespread and open—another tribute the lower orders paid to their
betters—while moralists extolled rational love, the mature, sober
affection of two reasonable adults superior to the seductions of un-
reasoning erotic attractions.[3] A few set sensible rules by distinguishing between private indulgence and public reserve: in 1755, Lady
Mary Wortley Montagu confessed to her daughter, Lady Bute,
that she had wept over Richardson's *Clarissa*, but thought it on the
whole "miserable stuff." Clarissa, she wrote, "follows the maxim
of declaring all she thinks to all the people she sees, without reflecting that in this mortal state of imperfection, fig-leaves are as necessary for our minds as our bodies, and 'tis as indecent to show all
we think as all we have."[4] Others were wholly cynical: perhaps the
century's most celebrated aphorism on sensuality is Chamfort's definition of love as "nothing but the contact of two epidermises," a
definition anticipated by Diderot ("the transitory rubbing of two
intestines"[5]) and doubtless by others. But then, such aphorisms,
though easy to quote, are hard to interpret: just whom, besides a
few worldlings, do they speak for? Again, what is one to make of
Mozart's Don Juan, at once a compulsive libertine desperately afraid
of impotence, and a courageous, free man who defies the repressive
gods? Or of *Fanny Hill*, which appeared in 1749—the year of Hartley's *Observations on Man*—and the rest of the pornographic tribe,

---

[3] See above, 31–3.
[4] October 20 (1755). *Complete Letters*, ed. Robert Halsband, 3
vols. (1965–7), III, 97.
[5] To Sophie Volland (August 29, 1762). *Correspondance*, IV, 120.
While Diderot here is speaking of sexual intercourse rather than
love, this callous, medical tone is doubtless Chamfort's ancestor.
See also Diderot to Sophie Volland (July 31, 1762), where he
speaks of "the voluptuous loss of a few drops of fluid." (Ibid., 84.)
Both of these remarks are combined in his *Supplément au voyage
de Bougainville*: "Write as much as you like, on tablets of brass,
to borrow Marcus Aurelius' expression, that this voluptuous rubbing of two intestines is a crime; man's heart will be bruised between the threat of your inscription and the violence of his inclinations" (59).

much on the increase in the age of the Enlightenment? With its impudent disregard of law, convention, and that greatest of tyrants, good taste, and with its advocacy of the forbidden, pornography was doubtless liberating; but with its monotonous subliterate style, its brazen appeal to adolescent fantasies, its endless repetitiveness, its lack of realism and hence lack of relevance to the world, it was less an ally than an enemy of Enlightenment, an inducement to conformism and apathy.

It is not surprising that the philosophes found it hard to make their way through this jungle: the road to honesty leads through the swamp of half-truths. And this, I think, explains Diderot's extravagant admiration for Greuze, which has long embarrassed his biographers. I have elsewhere defined sentimentality as the expenditure of worthy emotions on unworthy objects; we may also define it as an attempt to disguise indecent thoughts—that is, what prevailing morality holds to be indecent thoughts—in decent dress. Greuze always advertised his pictures, whether large narrative compositions or single figures, as moral, but his painting of young girls is always erotically suggestive: he catches, as it were by surprise, and in *déshabille*, simpering, barely nubile adolescents, with upturned eyes and sumptuous half-revealed figures. Greuze paints one such girl being assaulted by an affectionate puppy (he calls it *Fidélité*); another just sitting showing off her finer points (*L'Innocence*); still another, kneeling, partly nude, by her bed (*Prière de matin*). Yet for Diderot, Greuze had spirit and sensibility, he was the first of moral painters, indeed, "my painter."[6] All this did not keep the observant Diderot from noticing and enjoying Greuze's eroticism: in one of Greuze's most famous paintings, showing a peasant paying the dowry of his daughter (*L'Accordée de village*), Diderot sees that the girl has "a charming figure"; she is "very beautiful." And even though she is modest, and her bosom is concealed, "I bet that there is nothing there lifting it up, it holds itself up by itself."[7]

---

[6] See below, 275–6.

[7] Salon of 1761; *Salons*, I, 142. It is instructive to consider the probable response of a twentieth-century reader to Diderot's report on *L'Accordée de village* and compare it with the nineteenth-century view of John Morley. In his biography of Diderot, which was authoritative, at least in the English-speaking world, for generations, Morley quotes from Diderot's description of the painting at great length but stops precisely when he reaches the phrase I have quoted. See *Diderot and the Encyclopaedists*, 2 vols. (1878), II, 74–6.

Diderot did not see that *his* painter, the first of the moral painters, was a sly pornographer.

Yet, while such lapses in taste illustrate the risks attached to the philosophes' groping toward a free appreciation of sensuality, their problems were less desperate than those of their predecessors. All civilizations, as the philosophes recognized, have had trouble managing the passions, trouble escaping their disruptive consequences and harnessing them to useful and approved activity. Savage, primitive, and antique cultures assuaged their fears of the passions by controlling and justifying them through elaborate rituals, obsessive rites, highly developed rules against incest, and threats of dreadful divine punishment. The Greeks, who invented so much else, also invented rational speculation on the place of sensuality; Plato's classic analysis of the endemic discord and possible harmony among the three parts of the soul—reason, passion, and appetite—is only the most notable and most ingenious attempt to bring Dionysus to terms with Apollo. Greek playwrights and philosophers toyed with libertinism but favored, for the most part, rigid control and even asceticism: in the great battle between Dionysus and Apollo, Apollo was the inevitable victor. And his peace terms were harsh: of the two ways to felicity—detachment or involvement—ancient thinkers were compelled to choose detachment. Leaving aside the Greek Stoics, the Roman Stoics, for all their cosmopolitanism and calls to public service, prized inner detachment in the midst of activity; and even the Epicureans, for all their later reputation, taught that the avoidance of pain was superior to the pursuit of pleasure. There was little else the ancients could do: their philosophy was simply responsive to the realities of their life.

But the growth and diffusion of conscience, the gradual decline of the violence that had so troubled the Middle Ages and the Renaissance, the piecemeal construction of moral equivalents for unbridled impulsive action—with, in a word, the domestication of pleasure—the philosophes were in a position to construct a philosophy of involvement, a passionate naturalism. The dialectics of history confronted the Enlightenment with an apparent paradox which was, in actuality, a magnificent opportunity; as the power of conscience had grown, the passions had become safer; as reason tightened its hold, sensuality improved its reputation. It was precisely the growth of the superego in Western culture that made greater sexual freedom possible.

The most perceptive among the philosophes, as modern pagans, seized this opportunity, if not always with complete candor or full clarity. In the life of the senses, as in politics, aesthetics, and general morality, the Enlightenment sought to reconcile form and freedom, to increase the range of permissible action by discovering within nature the rational rules to guide it: form without freedom, they thought, was dead, freedom without form, brutish. And so the philosophes moralized sexuality in a double sense, by endowing lust with moral purity and attempting to purify lust by an appeal to its own inner logic. La Mettrie assimilated the pleasures of philosophy to sexual pleasure: he speaks of "the sublime voluptuousness of study," and hints that he had found it necessary to lead a life of sensual dissipation for the sake of finding philosophical truth.[8] Gibbon, without straining for paradox, could speak of the "rational voluptuary," the man who "adheres with invariable respect to the temperate dictates of nature."[9] Wieland thought that sensuality and rationality were united in *Humanität*, and took pride that his *Oberon* had been conceived "by his heart and head together."[1] James Boswell characterized the intellect as "vigorous"[2]; William Godwin maintained that "passion is so far from being incompatible with reason, that it is inseparable from it,"[3] and while Boswell's remark is a commonplace, and Godwin's a facile aphorism that evades as many problems as it solves, both suggest the prevalence of the growing prestige and simultaneous taming of pleasure.

Once again, this double process is realized most completely in Diderot. "Head and heart are such different organs," he wrote,

---

[8] See La Mettrie's satirical dedication of *L'Homme machine* to Albrecht von Haller, in the critical edition by Aram Vartanian (1960), 143–8.

[9] Quoted in Arnaldo Momigliano: "Gibbon's Contribution to Historical Method," *Historia*, II (1954), 463, now in *Studies in Historiography* (1966), 55.

[1] Sengle: *Wieland*, 372.

[2] *Life of Johnson* (I cannot now trace this reference).

[3] *An Enquiry Concerning Political Justice*, 2 vols. (3rd edn., 1798), I, 81, quoted in Burton Ralph Pollin: *Education and Enlightenment in the Works of William Godwin* (1962), 38.

but not without hope: "Should there not be some circumstances that would allow us to reconcile them?"[4] Diderot himself reconciled them playfully: in his *Paradoxe sur le comédien*, Diderot proposes that the most profound actor is the actor who knows precisely what he is doing at all moments; he must have all rational art and no spontaneous emotion. "I claim," he wrote to Grimm, "that sensibility makes mediocre actors; extreme sensibility, limited actors; cold sense and head, sublime actors."[5] Another way to reconciliation for Diderot was to employ sexual metaphors and imagery for intellectual or moral activity; thus Diderot lent passions to ideas and status to lust. In the opening of *Le neveu de Rameau*, "Moi" describes his customary afternoon walks around the Palais Royal, his ruminative strolls during which he permits his mind to wander, abandoning it to free *libertinage*, granting it leave to follow any idea, wise or foolish, just as "our young libertines follow the steps of a courtesan," picking up one and leaving the other: "My thoughts are my strumpets."[6] Similarly, Diderot could experience a moral act as though it were a satisfying sexual experience: "The spectacle of equity," he told Sophie Volland, inflamed his ardor: "Then it seems to me that my heart expands beyond me, that it swims; an indescribably delicious and subtle sensation runs through me; I have difficulty breathing; the whole surface of my body is animated by something like a shudder; it is marked above all on my forehead, at the hairline; and then the symptoms of admiration and pleasure come to mingle on my face with those of joy, and my eyes fill with tears."[7] There was a rank order for this sensual Stoic—"The man who despises the pleasures of the senses," he wrote, "is either a lying hypocrite or a crippled creature; but the man who prefers a voluptuous sensation to consciousness of a good action is a debased

---

4 To Falconet (February 15, 1766). *Correspondance*, VI, 98–9.
5 Diderot to Grimm (November 14, 1769). *Correspondance*, IX, 213. The editor, Georges Roth, suggests (ibid., 213 *n*.) that this is the passage from which the *Paradoxe sur le comédien* took its rise. See below, 283–6.
6 *Le neveu de Rameau*, 3.
7 (October 18, 1760). *Correspondance*, III, 156. I have quoted this instructive passage at somewhat greater length in *The Rise of Modern Paganism*, 187–8.

creature"[8]—but in general Diderot had the best of both by joining lust and ethics.

Diderot's confidential correspondence is a record of this experimental morality. To his mistress he can describe the joys of sexual excitement in the most graphic terms—the burning lips, the delicious shudders, the torrents of tears that come with satiety[9]— but he also treats love as an exalted human experience: "It is four years ago now," he ardently tells Sophie Volland, "that you seemed beautiful to me; today I find you more beautiful still. That is the magic of constancy, the most difficult and the rarest of our virtues."[1] Love is extreme or it is nothing: "Love, friendship, religion" are among "the most violent enthusiasms of life,"[2] and this startling juxtaposition, which groups love with religion and burdens it with the epithet *enthusiasm*, which was, for the philosophes, a term of disapproval, is a sign of Diderot's uneasiness. Obviously even for Diderot, sexual gratification was not the highest of all goods, though all of it that was within the bounds set by nature was good. For Diderot, and with him for the Enlightenment in general, the passions were coming into their own, but they remained a touchy problem.

---

[8] Diderot to the Princess of Nassau-Saarbruck (May or June 1758). *Correspondance*, II, 56.
[9] See for an example Diderot to Sophie Volland (May 15, 1765). Ibid., V, 35.
[1] (October 14, 1759?). Ibid., II, 277.
[2] To Sophie Volland (July 14, 1762). Ibid., IV, 42. It should be obvious, but remains worth remarking, that there was no agreement among the philosophes on the proper manner of expressing the passions, even if they on the whole agreed that they were valuable. Voltaire particularly objected to Diderot's effusions; what he called *"exclamations à la Jean-Jacques"* struck him as "supremely ridiculous." Voltaire to Charles Joseph Panckoucke (October–November 1768). *Correspondence*, LXX, 129.

4. THE CAREER OF IMAGINATION

I

Around 1808, looking back at more than a century of Enlightenment, William Blake struck at one of its most vulnerable spots—its treatment of the imagination. "Burke's Treatise on the Sublime & Beautiful," he wrote, with his customary vehemence, "is founded on the Opinions of Newton & Locke; on this Treatise Reynolds has grounded many of his assertions in all his Discources. I read Burke's Treatise when very young; at the same time I read Locke on Human Understanding & Bacon's Advancement of Learning; on Every one of these Books I wrote my Opinions, & on looking them over find that my Notes on Reynolds in this Book are exactly similar. I felt the same Contempt & Abhorrence then that I do now. They mock Inspiration & Vision. Inspiration & Vision was then, & now is, & I hope will always Remain, my Element, my Eternal Dwelling place; how can I then hear it Contemned without returning Scorn for Scorn?" "Meer Enthusiasm," he added decisively, "is the All in All! Bacon's Philosophy has Ruin'd England," and destroyed "Art & Science."[3]

Blake's assertion that the creative imagination had atrophied in the eighteenth century implied essentially three things: that religion had decayed, that art had declined, and that the new philosophy, especially its epistemology and psychology, had been responsible for this lamentable state of affairs. Had he looked into the matter, Blake would have been astonished to find that the very men he despised as knaves and destroyers did not wholly reject the facts he

---

[3] "Annotations to Sir Joshua Reynolds' Discourses," in *The Complete Works of William Blake,* ed. Geoffrey Keynes (2d edn., 1966), 476–7, 456, 470. To be sure (as one of my students rightly objected) Blake's view is a very particular one and cannot be treated as a typically Romantic response to eighteenth-century views of reason. Blake was certainly not a typical Romantic; in most respects he was not a Romantic at all. But his vehement assault on Newton and Reynolds remains instructive.

offered, although they naturally interpreted the evidence quite differently. All philosophes were of course delighted to think that religion had receded in their time and that their assault on fictions had contributed to this favorable turn of events. And there were some philosophes, most notably Voltaire though not he alone, who regretted the decline of poetry in an age of Enlightenment. But none of the philosophes would have conceded that it was their philosophy of the imagination that had caused this decline: their respect for that faculty, they would have insisted, had been perfectly adequate.

It was, in fact, less than adequate. But Blake's sweeping diagnosis was inadequate as well. In actuality the relations between art and philosophy, poetry and psychology, were by no means clearcut. Not all prosaic men were philosophes, not all philosophes were prosaic. If the philosophes on the whole felt more comfortable in the realm of fact than in the realm of fiction, eighteenth-century believers were inclined to share their preference: it was an age of prose for Christians and pagans alike, and, as we know, well-educated Anglicans or Roman Catholics shared the philosophes' impatience with enthusiasm or Gothic fancy. Samuel Johnson was as disdainful of the "ebullitions" or "digressive sallies of imagination," or the "wild diffusion of the sentiments"[4] as, say, d'Alembert. Besides, if artists and writers came to feel that the veins which neoclassicists had explored or newly tapped in the seventeenth century, had been exhausted in the eighteenth, this exhaustion had nothing to do with the teachings of the new psychology. They were an aspect of a cycle familiar in the history of art. And finally, although it would be as extravagant to call the philosophes singleminded rescuers of poetry as it is unjust to call them its determined enemies, the very men who tried to revive the imaginative arts and free them from dryness, conventionality, and commonplace moralizing—Diderot and Voltaire, Lessing and Wieland—were philosophes. In the 1730s Voltaire regretted the ascendancy of science and prosaic philosophy over "sentiment, imagination, and the graces" and hoped

---

[4] Quoted in René Wellek: *A History of Modern Criticism, 1750–1950*, I, *The Later Eighteenth Century* (1955), 97. Chapter xliv of Johnson's *Rasselas* is a sermon against the disorders of the intellect and the evils of imagination.

that this would be only a passing fashion.[5] The other philosophes shared Voltaire's regret and his hope.

The complexity that marks the cultural situation of the time also marks the Enlightenment's philosophical analysis of the imagination. The philosophes freely repeated hoary Platonic platitudes about the frenzied poet and uncritically accepted the old saying that every genius has his touch of madness. And the philosophes never disputed—it was one tradition they did not care to overturn —that the imagination is the most precious instrument the creative artist can possess. Shaftesbury, whose writings reverberate throughout the eighteenth century, proposed that the artist creates beauty through his aesthetic intuition, and Addison laid it down, perhaps a little mechanically, that a poet "should take as much Pains in forming his Imagination, as a Philosopher in cultivating his understanding."[6] La Mettrie commended this passion less coolly. The "soul" and all its functions, he writes in a characteristic passage in which analysis and eroticism become one, can be reduced to the faculty of imagination: "Through it, through its flattering brush, the cold skeleton of reason takes on lively, carmine colors; through it, the sciences flourish, arts beautify themselves, the woods speak, echoes sigh, rocks weep, marble breathes, all takes on life among inanimate bodies"; in fact, "the more one exercises the imagination, or the meagrest talent, the more it takes on plumpness, so to speak; the more it grows, becomes vigorous, robust, enormous and capable of thought. The best physical constitution needs this exercise."[7]

While La Mettrie's metaphor is unusually lush, especially for a philosophe, most of the phrases about mad geniuses and the uses of the imagination were little more than clichés; they could be found in the most academic of academic treatises. But for the philosophes they were, so to speak, the right kind of cliché. They did not impede, in fact they were gestures toward, a favorable estimate of the role that inner freedom plays in life and art.

Unanimous in uttering benign generalities about the imagination, the men of the Enlightenment were nevertheless divided on

[5] Voltaire to Cideville (April 16, 1735). *Correspondence*, IV, 48–9. I have quoted from this letter before; see above, 158.
[6] *Spectator*, No. 417, in *The Spectator*, ed. Donald F. Bond, 5 vols. (1965), III, 563.
[7] *L'Homme machine*, 165–6.

its precise nature. Some, a distinct minority, saw it as creative; the majority, disciples of Locke's psychology, saw it as merely constructive. Leibniz, whose most incisive criticism of Locke, the *Nouveaux Essais sur l'entendement humain*, came to light only in 1765, too late to touch the Enlightenment anywhere outside of Germany, had asserted that all consciousness is spontaneous and creative: perception is not passive receiving; it is an act through which the perceiver grasps, orders, reconstructs and, in a sense, creates the world. German psychologists generally followed Leibniz on this point: feelings, ideas, concepts, they held, are never simply rearrangements of material furnished through the senses by external forces. The creative imagination, Johann Nicolas Tetens said, always makes its own contribution: "Psychologists usually explain poetic creation as a mere analysis and synthesis of ideas which are recalled in memory after having been acquired through sense perception." But they are wrong; if they were right, poetry would be "nothing but a transposition of phantasms." And this would be doing an injustice to poets like Milton or Klopstock, whose imagery is more than "an accumulated mass of perceptual ideas," and can be understood only by postulating the "plastic power of the imagination."[8]

In France, largely—probably wholly—independent of Leibniz, Diderot analyzed the imagination in similar fashion, concluding it to be a special kind of active, shaping memory. "The imagination," he argued, as a good Lockian, "creates nothing," but he argued at the same time that while ordinary memory is "a faithful copyist," the imagination is "a colorist"; it "imitates, it composes, combines, exaggerates, it makes things larger or smaller." For the painter or poet the imagination organizes an "internal model" which he realizes in his production, which, in turn, stirs the imagination of his audience.[9] This doctrine adroitly combined the notions of genius and imagination: the genius was simply the artist in whom the creative imagination acted most vigorously and flowed most freely.

But most of the philosophes held that the imagination, as Diderot had dutifully noted, creates nothing. Still, it was persistently active. It combined perceptions into complicated and remarkable shapes: the centaur—a mythical beast which, with the unicorn,

---

[8] Cassirer: *Philosophy of the Enlightenment*, 128–9.
[9] See below, 279–80.

served eighteenth-century psychologists as faithfully as did the blind man endowed with sight—was a being that the imagination had made. In his famous papers on the pleasures of the imagination, which were enormously influential in the eighteenth century, leaving their mark on Hume and Voltaire and Kant, Addison celebrated the imagination with some explicit Lockian reservations. "We cannot indeed," he wrote, "have a single Image in the Fancy that did not make its first Entrance through the Sight; but we have the Power of retaining, altering and compounding those Images, which we have once received, into all the varieties of Picture and Vision that are most agreeable to the Imagination."[1] The pleasures of the imagination are magnificent and almost infinitely various; Addison devotes eleven numbers of his *Spectator* to enumerating them, and sometimes, in his excitement, he almost loses sight of his central philosophical position: imagination is "the very Life and highest Perfection of Poetry," indeed, it "has something in it like Creation; It bestows a kind of Existence, and draws up to the Reader's View, several Objects which are not to be found in Being";[2] it "makes new Worlds of its own."[3] Yet Addison—he is, after all, trying to educate his readers by educating their passions—always returns to sobriety: the imagination, "once Stocked with particular Ideas," can "enlarge, compound, and vary them"[4]; it works, in a word, with raw material it has not made.

David Hume took substantially the same position, but, since he was more interested than Addison in technical philosophical questions, he was more moderate in his tone. Addison had praised fancy, Hume felt compelled to distinguish in the imagination "betwixt the principles which are permanent, irresistible, and universal," and "the principles, which are changeable, weak, and irregular." The former are "the foundation of our thoughts and actions"; they are the basis of memory, the senses, causal inference, and the understanding, and without them "human nature must immediately perish and go to ruin." The latter principles, in contrast, "are neither unavoidable to mankind, nor necessary, or so much as useful in the conduct of life; but on the contrary are observ'd only to take place in weak

---

[1] *The Spectator*, No. 411; III, 537.
[2] Ibid., No. 421; III, 578-9.
[3] Ibid., No. 419; III, 573.
[4] Ibid., No. 416; III, 559.

minds"[5]; these are "the frivolous properties of our thought," the "bright fancies" and "trivial suggestions of the fancy," which "very often" degenerate "into madness or folly." Imagination sober is not only essential to life but to philosophy, imagination drunk is pernicious to both one and the other. "Nothing is more dangerous to reason than the flights of the imagination, and nothing has been the occasion of more mistakes among philosophers." But whichever activity the imagination may be pursuing, Hume, unlike Addison, did not waver in his allegiance to Locke's sensationalism: the imagination converts ideas into impressions, it "transposes and changes" ideas "as it pleases," and can "join, and mix, and vary" them, but it never can go beyond "original perceptions."[6] The French philosophes—most prominently Condillac and Voltaire and even, as we have seen, Diderot—adopted the same line of reasoning: The imagination is valuable and troublesome, infinitely varied and therefore in appearance a creator. But only in appearance: the imagination—this was the firm majority view of the Enlightenment—was a builder, not a god.

II

From the perspective of the Romantics, this sort of faculty seemed a receptive, essentially passive thing. The philosophes did not see it that way: just as their conception of a uniform human nature did not prevent them from seeing enormous variety among human actions, so their conception of the imagination as dependent on given materials did not prevent them from reshaping those materials with astounding vigor. Yet, whatever the philosophes' pleasure in the work and play of the imagination, the Romantics were not wholly misguided to suspect the Enlightenment's dominant theory of knowledge, its sensationalism and psychological atomism culminating in what Coleridge would tartly call "the monstrous puerilities of CONDILLAC and CONDORCET."[7] For in fact the philosophes

---

[5] *Treatise of Human Nature*, 225.
[6] Ibid., 504 *n.*, 267, 123, 267, 427, 629, 85. That Hume fully recognized the difficulties in the way of using the term precisely is evident from his analysis on 117–18 *n.*
[7] Quoted in Richards: *Coleridge on Imagination*, 51 *n.*

had grave misgivings about man's employment of fantasy, particularly after the uses to which it had been put by religious men. Christianity, in their eyes, was after all the enemy of passion and reason at once; it simultaneously overvalued and undervalued them both, denigrating the natural passions of pride and sensuality while it encouraged the unfortunate passions of credulity and love of wonder, stifling man's critical activity while it prized the cancerous growth on man's reason. It was behind this multiple misreading of man's nature and possibilities, the philosophes thought, that the imagination had luxuriated, constructing those monstrous lies that had so long governed the world.

In 1754 the abbé Nicolas Trublet gave voice to these misgivings in an extraordinary prediction: "As reason is perfected," he wrote, "judgment will more and more be preferred to imagination, and, consequently, poets will be less and less appreciated. The first writers, it is said, were poets. I can well believe it; they could hardly be anything else. The last writers will be philosophers."[8] What Trublet is suggesting here is, in effect, that the art of poetry is the art of pleasing and instructing, but it only instructs when it is truthful, when it portrays the blessings of virtue or the need for composure amid the vicissitudes of life, in fitting epigrams, through appropriate imagery, with lucid allegories. But poetry is also an art of lies—charming lies, to be sure, but lies just the same—and lies, as Plato had recognized long ago, that were effective and dangerous. Poets, said David Hume, are "liars by profession," who "always endeavour to give an air of truth to their fictions."[9] Whether poetry was truthful or mendacious depended on whether it sprang from disciplined, clear-eyed, if passionate, invention—imagination at its best, or wild, fanciful musing—imagination at its worst.

Now the most dangerous lies that poets have generated, or have propagated by giving pleasing and memorable shape to the prosaic lies of others, are myths, which is to say, religion. The imagination of the poets embroidered the policies of statesmen or superstitions of priests and, in turn, inflamed the imagination of their audiences.

---

[8] Quoted in Margaret Gilman: *The Idea of Poetry in France from Houdar de la Motte to Baudelaire* (1958), 1. In 1820, in one of his witty essays, "Four Ages of Poetry," Thomas Love Peacock took precisely the same line.
[9] *Treatise of Human Nature*, 121.

Enthusiasm, that much-despised ebullition of religious sentiment unchecked by reason or decorum, was one fruit of diseased imagination; theology was another. The poetic mentality, indeed—with its logic not of argument but of intoxication, a logic in which beauty is taken for truth, and proof offered through images and metaphors rather than demonstration—was therefore nothing other than the religious mentality. Hence it became the task of the critical philosopher to keep poetry from contaminating philosophy, to enjoy pleasing fictions without taking them for truths.

Some of the Romantics rebelled precisely against this separation; the philosophes, I think, would have been appalled, and felt justified, could they have read Novalis's extravagant claims for poetry as the hero of philosophy, as more truthful than history, and as the highest form of wisdom. Shelley's claim that "Poets are the unacknowledged legislators of the world," would have struck them as an invitation to disaster. Not that there were no poets among the philosophes who liked to play at being legislators, but it was not in their capacity of poet that they played it. Nor were the philosophes strangers to the figure of the learned poet—Diderot had, after all, told Catherine of Russia that Voltaire was a good poet precisely because he was an intellectual[1]—but it seemed to the philosophes that the poets, at least of the Christian era, knew all the wrong things: Dante and Milton were two prize specimens of learned myth-makers, or myth-merchants. And, since it was the task of the critical mentality to unmask lies and myths, to render superstition harmless, the poetic mentality, much more than poetry itself, became the target of the philosophes' most unsparing assaults. Embattled as they were, they saw the matter quite simply—too simply: poetry, the fruit of unchecked fancy, produces myth; prose, the fruit of disciplined understanding, leads to truth. However intemperate and partial Blake's indictment of the Enlightenment's psychology proved to be, it pointed to a certain ambivalence about the imagination; and it remains true that while this psychology did much for the study of man and the advancement of science, it did little for the arts of the day.

---

[1] For Diderot's comment, see *The Rise of Modern Paganism*, 197, and below, 510.

CHAPTER FIVE

The Emancipation of Art: Burdens of the Past

I. ART AND ENLIGHTENMENT

THERE WAS NO DISTINCTIVE Enlightenment style in the arts. The eighteenth century lived amid a profusion of tastes, techniques, and subject matter; aesthetic ideas and ideals changed and traveled, amalgamating with traditional and foreign styles to produce hybrids and new species. "There is at present," Hogarth said in the early 1750s, a "thirst after variety."[1] The mixture ranged from late baroque to nascent romanticism, each style with its domestic coloring and differing from art to art and decade to decade. It was further enriched by the invasion of bourgeois sentimentality, fads for Chinese or Gothic motifs, and repeated neoclassical revivals, differentiated one from the other by the models it appealed to and the individuality it permitted itself. And none of these styles was the domestic, or privileged, style of the Enlightenment.

The taste of the philosophes was as varied as the taste of their age. Voltaire admired Racine and detested Richardson; Diderot admired Racine and Richardson, and Voltaire as well; Lessing attempted to free himself from Racine and Voltaire, but not from Diderot. Lessing and Diderot wrote dramas in the naturalistic manner of their contemporaries, while Voltaire persisted in writing tragedies in the neoclassical manner of the seventeenth century. Hume and Jefferson had highly developed, if conventional neo-

---

[1] William Hogarth: *The Analysis of Beauty* (1753; ed. Joseph Burke, 1955), 62.

classical tastes; but while Jefferson hailed "Ossian" as a great poet, Hume exposed him as a fraud. Kant, who, like almost everyone in the Enlightenment, loved the Latin classics and Alexander Pope alike, found music irritating and painting boring—an engraving of Rousseau was the only picture in his house. Neoclassicism, rococo, naturalism, indifference to, and even, with Rousseau, a certain Spartan suspicion of, the arts, were all possible aesthetic positions for philosophes to adopt, and were all compatible with the philosophy of the Enlightenment.

While the philosophes did not agree on what they liked, they agreed on what they disliked—the Gothic—but even this did not markedly differentiate them from other civilized men of their day. Lessing and Winckelmann, Montesquieu and Turgot, Hume and Rousseau detested Gothic as disorderly, capricious, affected, overloaded with detail, rigid, graceless, dull, and barbarous. Diderot, who was, after all, surrounded by some of its finest productions, could ask rhetorically, "How can one admire a Gothic tapestry after one has seen a Raphael?"[2] But half a century before, Addison had employed the name "Gothick" in his *Spectator* as a general term of abuse signifying "tasteless," and distinguished between ancient writers, with their "majestick Simplicity" and "Strength of Genius," and lesser writers, compelled to "hunt after foreign Ornaments"—"*Goths* in Poetry."[3] A distaste for Gothic early in the eighteenth century, therefore, was no mark of radicalism; men who did not equate "Gothick" with Christians disliked it as much as those who did. If anything, the philosophes' consistent rejection of Gothic finally placed them, rather awkwardly, in a reactionary position: while, at mid-century, a growing historical awareness and a new readiness to find beauty in the unfamiliar permitted Thomas

---

[2] For Lessing and Winckelmann see Justi: *Winkelmann und seine Zeitgenossen*, 3 vols. (5th edn., Walther Rehm, 1956), I, 21; for Montesquieu: "De la manière gothique," in *Œuvres*, III, 276–82, and "Essai sur le goût," in ibid., I, part 3, 620; for Turgot: *Tableau philosophique des progrès*, in *Œuvres*, I, 234; for Hume: "Of Simplicity and Refinement in Writing," *Works*, III, 241; for Rousseau: "Lettre sur la musique françoise," in *Œuvres complètes*, ed. G. Petitain, 8 vols. (1839), VI, 144. See also Diderot to Falconet (beginning September 1766?). *Correspondance*, VI, 320–1; and to the same (June 15, 1766). Ibid., 213, 214, 219.

[3] *Spectator*, No. 62; I, 268. See also No. 70; ibid., 297–303.

Warton and Thomas Percy to rescue medieval romances from contempt, and Horace Walpole in England, Jacques Germain Soufflot in France, and, a little later, Goethe and Herder in Germany, to reverse the current appraisal of Gothic, the philosophes never permitted themselves to see what the new defenders of Gothic saw—lightness, boldness, inventiveness, and, hidden behind fantastic incrustations, a splendid order. Ironically enough, then, their philosophical radicalism seduced the philosophes into aesthetic conservatism. It never occurred to them that one might appreciate the art of Christians without surrendering to their myth. The Enlightenment's incurable aversion to Gothic, therefore, illustrates not the connection between art and enlightenment but the baleful influence of dogmatism on taste.

To be sure, traffic between the Enlightenment and the arts was heavy and unimpeded. The philosophes did not hesitate to turn their fictions into vehicles for their program: Voltaire wrote his *Mahomet* and Lessing his *Nathan der Weise* to dramatize the horrors of fanaticism and to inspire tolerant sentiments; Wieland and Diderot wrote stories and novels that, more than expressing, candidly preached the virtues of pagan sensuality. And in return, artists reflected enlightened ideas in their work. Handel composed his music in the confident spirit of the secular craftsman, as remote from religious fervor as any philosophe; he preferred pagan to Christian, and worldly to religious subjects. Gluck reformed the opera in the name of reason and nature, and Mozart, whatever his precise religious ideas, imported Masonic notions into his compositions. Hogarth, hostile to the religious enthusiasm of the Methodists and sympathetic to the rationalistic Whiggish Anglicanism of Bishop Hoadly, popularized in his celebrated cycles of engravings the enlightened values of industry, sobriety, and humanity. Januarius Zick paid his tribute to modern science with a complicated allegorical painting celebrating *Newton's Service to Optics*. And Goya painted his Caprichos to "banish harmful vulgar beliefs"; he was a rationalist who hailed Voltaire as an immortal.[4] None of these artists was

---

[4] Zick's painting has been reproduced in Michael Levey: *Rococo to Revolution: Major Trends in Eighteenth-Century Painting* (1966), 155. For Goya see ibid., 202.

a philosophe, all had learned much from the enlightened ideas current in their day.

This interplay documents the obvious: the philosophes were embedded in the antique tradition that held art to be a moralizing and civilizing force, and eighteenth-century artists, far from being recluses or illiterate artisans, lived in the world; many of them were bound to share its more advanced ideas. There were, after all, many artists who had other, rather less revolutionary, ideas: for every deist Handel there was a devout Bach, and while Hogarth could not stop improving the public, Fragonard and Boucher obviously felt no obligation to purify the morals of their contemporaries.

At the same time, while metaphorical descriptions of rococo as "free" and the sonata as "rational" are merely facile, parallels between the ideas of the philosophes and the productions of the artists are clues to a new temper. The connection between art and enlightenment was close, the relevance of enlightenment to art enormous. Artists, art criticism, and art theory were, like the civilization of the eighteenth century and its philosophy, under great strain; they were in search of self-awareness, of new ground on which to stand. This was the century in which philosophers first undertook really systematic inquiries into the philosophy of art; the very word "aesthetics" entered the language in the age of the Enlightenment, with Baumgarten's writings. It was the century that, although it lived in the shadow of sixteenth- and seventeenth-century masters, found it necessary to question what it admired. The Christian myth, once and until recently a fertile source for plays, paintings, and poems, now appeared less credible, and less creditable, than before. Conflicting boundary claims and new genres were threatening accepted categories in poetry and drama, in painting, sculpture, and architecture. A new interest in the psychology of artistic creation and taste was confronting traditional canons of beauty. The whole neoclassical machinery, in other words, was under attack. Neoclassicism had taught that art is scientific, moral, orderly, and refined, capable of developing objective standards, and improving, as it entertained, its public. It required strict separation of genres, the three unities of time, place, and action in the drama, obedience to hierarchies in painting, with historical painting at the top and still lifes at the bottom, and the imitation of nature without coarseness. These ideals continued to find support, and even their opponents treated them with marked respect. But at the very least, neoclassicism required clarification and redefinition in the light of the new philosophy. In aesthetics, as in all areas of thought, the age felt the need to be clear, to reconcile the desire to conserve with the desire for independence, to synthesize freedom and discipline. "The philosophical spirit which has made such progress in our times and has penetrated all the domains of knowledge," Algarotti observed in 1756, "has in a certain manner become the censor of all the arts."[5] In raising urgent questions about itself, in leaving nothing untouched by criticism, the arts were moving toward intelligent self-appraisal, toward enlightenment—in the Enlightenment's company.

2. PATRONS AND PUBLICS

I

THE ENLIGHTENMENT developed its ideas on the arts not in some secluded realm of abstract speculation, but amid social struggles and social change. The interplay between the artists' efforts to escape the need for deference and the aestheticians' efforts to construct a modern philosophy of art was often obscure and unexpected —a conservative dramatist like Voltaire, for instance, had radical plans for raising the status of literary men; and in contrast an innovating composer like Haydn served his lordly patrons with becoming docility—but the interplay was there, and it was important.

The most eloquent witness to this connection between social ideals and philosophical inquiries is probably the sculptor Falconet, for many years Diderot's friend; no artist joined more closely than

---

[5] Quoted in Remy G. Saisselin: "Neo-Classicism: Virtue, Reason and Nature," in Henry Hawley: *Neo-Classicism: Style and Motif* (1964), 5. While Algarotti here singles out architecture, his observation applies to all the arts.

he the campaign for new dignity to the campaign against old theories. Falconet served the cause of Enlightenment more disagreeably than anyone else, but his morose energy reflects not simply his neurosis but quite as much the frustrations facing eighteenth-century artists.

If, then, Falconet had more enemies than he needed, most of them were the right ones: snobs, presumptuous amateurs and connoisseurs, and "anticomaniacs"; his writings and activities read like a point-by-point refutation of them all. While Falconet rose to fame and prosperity, and found royal favor in France and Russia, he paraded his lowly origins, his hard-won erudition, and his philosophical friends ostentatiously and humorlessly, as if to prove that anyone, even a Falconet, could become a learned artist. This learning was of a special kind: the artist, he insisted, is a scholar in his own way, and not in the scholar's way—in the course of his arduous apprenticeship he acquires arcane information inaccessible even to benevolent outsiders, and this should protect him from the dictates of the rich and the derision of the well-educated: when someone dared to suggest that the ancient Romans had esteemed works of art but despised the artist, Falconet found the man's "arrogance and pedantry" simply "contemptible," and answered that the ancient Romans, as a civilized people, had of course honored arts and artists alike.

Much to his dismay, Falconet discovered that there were men of letters—his obvious potential allies—who enjoyed their own improved status so much that they refused to share it, and instead mercilessly ridiculed painters and sculptors for their illiteracy. And wealthy art lovers, it seemed, persisted in treating artists as lowly workmen whose fate they could decide, whose subjects they could dictate, and whom they could buy with their commissions. In reply, Falconet argued that artists are not mere artisans who work by rote and for money, but civilized men who work for their pleasure and glory. And he reinforced his position with some grand gestures: when the Russians negotiated with him about a statue to Peter the Great, they offered him a number of possible designs, but Falconet took the risk of losing his commission by rejecting them all and by insisting on freedom of action which, he said, was wholly indispensable to him. And when he finally secured the commission and was offered four hundred thousand livres, he demanded that he be paid only half that sum.[6]

The most devastating enemy of modern artists and modern art, Falconet believed, worse than the ignorant amateur or the selfish *littérateur*, was the anticomaniac—the politics and the philosophy of art join hands at this point. Anticomaniacs, in Falconet's savage portrait, were rich amateurs in whom stupidity was reinforced by arrogance; idlers who returned from Italy laden with bits of antique sculpture, or expensive drawings of ancient temples, anxious to outdo their social rivals with their collections. They sought to bring modern art into contempt, but succeeded only in arousing contempt for the antiques they worshipped. "Modern artists," Diderot observed, agreeing with Falconet, "have rebelled against the study of antiquity because it has been preached to them by amateurs."[7] In ostentatious contrast, fighting his private version of the battle between ancients and moderns, Falconet claimed the right to worship as a free man: "I want to look at the idol before I kneel down." There were some praiseworthy ancient sculptures, doubtless, but most ancient art was inferior to the best modern work: "We owe Greece," he wrote, "so many masterpieces and so many foolish things." And the anticomaniacs overlook these *sottises*, and, blind to the defects of antique art—its lack, in most instances, of variety, grandeur, harmony, grace, intelligence, correctness in proportions and perspective—impose false standards on modern artists and blight their productivity.[8]

Even philosophes sympathetic to Falconet's causes did not think that the burdens of deference and of the past could be cast off by inflammatory rhetoric alone. At the same time, the philosophes, many of them artists and friends of artists, found themselves by and large in Falconet's camp: the artist's claim to dignity as well as artistic freedom was a kind of test case for their ideal of an open society, in which low birth did not matter and talent was rewarded for its own sake. This is the meaning of Voltaire's passionate lament for his former mistress Adrienne Lecouvreur, France's leading tragedienne, who had died young in 1730 and was, as an actress,

---

[6] Anne Betty Weinshenker: *Falconet: His Writings and His Friend Diderot* (1966), chap. iii.
[7] Salon of 1765; *Salons*, II, 207.
[8] Weinshenker: *Falconet*, chap. iv.

refused the last rites and buried in unhallowed ground. The verses Voltaire insisted on publishing after her death and the letters he wrote to his friends are, in the highest degree, political: "Whoever has talents is a great man in London," while in France he is despised. In England, where the actress "Mlle Oldfield" had been buried in Westminster Abbey, Adrienne Lecouvreur would have found her tomb "among wits, kings, and heroes," but in France her "body was thrown into the sewer."[9] Voltaire drew the largest possible conclusions from this contrast: England is free, France a land of slaves, England is bold, France the victim of superstition. Though personal in feeling and hysterical in tone, Voltaire's rage exemplifies the close ties between the arts, the artist, and the Enlightenment.

Yet the incident was more a survival than a foretaste. Rather like eighteenth-century men of letters, eighteenth-century artists enjoyed their own recovery of nerve, which was, on the whole, unprecedented.[1] I say, "on the whole," for while the artists' struggle took the same direction as that of the writers, and had the same goal, it was much less decisive. Alexander Pope's and Samuel Johnson's declarations of independence had the trumpetlike clarity of a revolutionary manifesto; in the arts, independence was declared more often and less firmly, and besides, there were artists who persisted in preferring dependence to autonomy.

While the social emancipation of the artist had begun in the Renaissance, and while seventeenth-century artists had made contributions to it, the social revolution initiated in the Italian cities early in the sixteenth acquired irresistible momentum only in the eighteenth century. Renaissance artists had revived antique notions about divine madness and the privileged position of the creative process. They had exacted respect for their individuality, which they defined as respect for their creative genius, their financial needs, and their oddities: late in the sixteenth century there were even complaints that painters who were by nature neither melancholic nor eccentric came to affect both melancholy and eccentricity, because these were the trademarks of the fashionable artist. The combat be-

---

[9] "La mort de Mlle Lecouvreur, célèbre actrice," in *Œuvres*, IX, 370; Lettre XXIII, *Lettres philosophiques*, II, 159; Voltaire to Thieriot, May 1, 1731. *Correspondence*, II, 174.
[1] See above, chap. i and chap. ii, section 1.

tween Michelangelo and his patron, Pope Julius II, had the epic stature of a battle of giants; in the seventeenth century, Bernini re-enacted Michelangelo's career on a somewhat lower level, patronizing his highly placed patrons, while Salvator Rosa assiduously cultivated his prickly genius and claimed, in language anticipating late-eighteenth-century artists, that he painted solely for his own satisfaction and only when he was seized by creative rapture. And from the beginning of the seventeenth century, artists had tried to stabilize their situation; they showed their works to call attention to their particular talents, and organized themselves into academies that would free them from medieval guild restrictions, raise their prices, enhance their social status, and honor their claim to be practicing a "liberal art." But these efforts were fitful and relatively futile. The legendary careers of the divine Michelangelo and the only slightly less divine Bernini could furnish no guides for more mortal artists: these men were too extraordinary to invite emulation. Rubens, diplomat, humanist, entrepreneur, a genius of legendary energy and versatility, was similarly beyond envy; he seemed more like a natural force than a practical model. Rosa, with his outspoken cranky campaign for artistic independence, was a lonely and admittedly eccentric outsider, with little influence and no direct descendants. Exhibitions were few, unorganized, and usually held to celebrate a saint's day or a historic local event rather than an artist. Dealers were for the most part exploiters of lesser talents. As soon as he could afford to do so—that is, as soon as he found a patron—a promising painter or sculptor left his dealer, never to return. By the 1650s, the French *Académie Royale de Peinture et de Sculpture* was well organized, generously endowed, and under august protection, but it substituted a new slavery in place of the old; the Paris Academy defeated the restrictive guilds in the name of royal authority, established a monopoly for selected artists, trained students in one style—the style approved at Court—and tied the artist to absolutism. "While dignity and freedom were the motto of the struggle in the Cinquecento," writes Nikolaus Pevsner, "it was now dignity and service."[2] Academies were not enough; what

---

[2] Nikolaus Pevsner: *Academies of Art, Past and Present* (1940), 109.

was needed was a shift in ideals and conditions, and both were provided in the age, and partly through the efforts, of the Enlightenment.

II

The relations of the eighteenth-century artist to his publics, much like his relations to ideas, were extraordinarily diverse. They depended not solely on the wealth of potential customers, dominant social attitudes, the vagaries of taste, or the efficiency of the censor— though they depended on these as well—but on the very medium in which he worked: the painter of humble genre scenes or the craftsman who built furniture in a small shop was in a sense freer than the church architect or the ambitious muralist, who had to find extensive commissions and was often enslaved for years to a single customer. And freedom was by no means an unambiguous advantage. As Dutch painters discovered to their pain a century before the others, the artist without a regular patron was usually indentured to unscrupulous dealers, and dependent not on the whims of one man, but on the whims of many. It is notorious that Jan Steen had to make his living as an innkeeper, that Hobbema got an income from buying a privilege on the wine excise, and that Rembrandt prospered only so long as his style coincided with the taste of the wealthy burghers who were his customers. When he moved into his magnificent last phase, he saw desirable commissions go to other, lesser painters and went bankrupt. If anything, the market was more capricious than, say, an art-loving cardinal. Dr. Richard Mead, a pioneer in public health in London and among the most generous and discriminating bourgeois patrons in the eighteenth century, owned Rembrandts, Poussins, Titians, all in quantity, and commissioned Watteau, when he was in England in 1719, to paint two pictures for him. But when Mead's collection was sold upon his death in 1754, a historical painting by Carlo Maratti realized £183, while Alderman Beckford picked up the two Watteaus for £42 and £52/10 respectively—hardly confirmation of the commonplace that the free play of the market was favorable to the prosperity of artists and the purification of taste.

While freedom was always risky, servitude was often rewarding. Not all patrons were tyrants, and it was possible to find room for maneuver within the system of patronage. Popes, dukes, religious orders, and wealthy amateurs often paid artists munificently and often, if not always, gave them satisfactory latitude. Besides, a patron with good taste and sufficient funds could initiate an aesthetic revolution; he could, quite literally, afford to be adventurous. English eighteenth-century architecture perhaps owes more to Lord Burlington's infectious enthusiasm for Palladianism as to the speculative builders who threw up houses in the major cities after the 1760s, more intent on making immediate profits than architectural history.

It is therefore not surprising that patronage should survive into the eighteenth century and find outspoken defenders. Giambattista Tiepolo spent his long and productive life in the service of great patrons, including the prince-bishop of Franconia and the king of Spain, and each of his major commissions kept him occupied for extended periods: he spent three years decorating the *Residenz* in Würzburg and eight years doing frescoes for Charles III's palace in Madrid. Handel was one of the few artists to benefit from the taste of the Hanoverian kings. And Franz Joseph Haydn was handed from one princely Esterhazy to another almost as though he had been a favorite horse—and was, for the most part, happy and prolific. It was only when he first visited London, a free man and a social lion, that an alternative presented itself to him: "How sweet is some degree of liberty!" he wrote from England in 1791. "I had a kind prince, but was obliged at times to be dependent on base souls. I often sighed for release and now I have it in some measure. . . . The consciousness of being no longer a bond servant sweetens all my toil."[3] But the habit of submission was hard to break: Haydn did not settle in London, as he might have, but returned to his masters.

Just as it is impossible to draw a line between slavery and freedom, or to define unambiguously the environment congenial to artistic enterprise, so it is impossible to distinguish clearly between a patron and a customer. There were many types of patrons: kings,

---

[3] Karl Geiringer: *Haydn: A Creative Life in Music* (edn. 1963), 121.

courtiers, bishops, and speculators; local aristocrats or visiting Englishmen; sacred institutions that could exact loyalty through spiritual
pressure, and private individuals who had no inducement but
money[4]; imperious magnates who practically owned an artist for
some years, and rather less wealthy amateurs who commissioned a
few works and then kept a tenuous hold on the artist they patronized
by recommending him to their friends. Nor was it simply a matter
of rank or class; while bourgeois art lovers took an increasingly
commanding part in the world of eighteenth-century painting and
theater that part was neither new nor exclusive. Wealthy commoners had bought paintings and sculptures and commissioned
buildings in sixteenth-century Florence and seventeenth-century
Paris, and in the age of the Enlightenment clerics and aristocrats
often competed with merchants or physicians for the same work of
art, in the same market. What happened in the eighteenth century
was not that the patron was replaced by the public, or the aristocratic by the bourgeois customer, but that wealthy and acquisitive
amateurs traveled more than ever, that artists finally established
their claim to be differentiated from mere artisans, and that their
opportunities for displaying their works—in a few private houses
thrown open to the public, in rudimentary museums, and in exhibitions sponsored by the French and English academies—greatly
increased. And, as the artists' public multiplied and their social
visibility increased, their status improved. In Rome, in 1750, the
academy officially laid it down that artists were subject to no guild,
since their work belonged among the *"artes liberales,"*[5] and a few
years later the Venetian official and patron Andrea Memmo
reminded himself in a private memorandum that painters were eccen-
trics who must be freed from all subservience: "It is right that the
imaginative side of painting should be exercised freely and with
nobility; genius should not be fettered in the practice of the fine

---

[4] "Two different types of patron, one with the spiritual authority
that came from having a saint as founder, the other with money."
Francis Haskell: *Patrons and Painters: A Study in the Relations
Between Italian Art and Society in the Age of the Baroque* (1963),
65.
[5] Pevsner: *Academies of Art*, 114. This rhetoric, though hardly the
reality, goes back to the seventeenth century.

arts. That is why they were called liberal."[6] This was the new tone, soon to become dominant. Whatever the artists' preference in style of life—and they varied in the age of the Enlightenment as they had varied before—the realities of the century pointed, ambiguously yet firmly enough, toward independence. Much unlike writers, to whom the advantages of freedom were almost self-evident, many painters, sculptors, and architects had to be dragged into the marketplace of modernity.

3. BURDENS OF THE PAST

I

THE MODEL OF MODERNITY—partly idealized by the philosophes, partly a reality—the first country to offer public concerts and grant knighthoods to mere face painters, was England. It was England's liberalism to actresses, after all, that had made Voltaire ashamed of his France, England's lionizing a mere musician that had shown Haydn an alternative to serfdom.

The openness of Englishmen to the arts was not new. For centuries the English had freely imported styles and artists, adapting what they borrowed and rewarding what they enjoyed. It was a virtue born of necessity: through the seventeenth century, England did not produce enough talented or fashionable musicians and sculptors to satisfy domestic demand. But the English transformed foreign styles so skillfully that after a time they were widely taken, and proudly displayed, as characteristically English. Wren and Vanbrugh translated Continental into English baroque in their buildings, Sir James Thornhill employed French and Italian techniques in his majestic murals celebrating the Glorious Revolution.

The domestication of foreign artists matched the domestication of foreign styles. Van Dyck, born in Antwerp and schooled in Italy, settled in England in 1632 and was knighted; a little later,

---

[6] Haskell: *Patrons and Painters*, 330 (the document from which this passage is quoted is reprinted in full, in the original Italian, in ibid., Appendix I, 386–7).

Pieter van der Faes, a Dutch painter, re-emerged in England with a new name and new dignity as Sir Peter Lely; the German portraitist Gottfried Kniller, who followed Lely in power, honors, and strategy, became Sir Godfrey Kneller. And there were many others—sculptors, composers, and architects as much as painters—who settled in England and made their fortunes there.

Beginning early in the eighteenth century, with the emergence of native-born talents in painting and increasing willingness to employ native-born architects, this openness changed its character. But it did not diminish. Foreigners continued to come to England to prosper and to become more English than the English: George Frideric Handel never regretted his transplantation; and the leading English sculptors of the age, who populated colleges and Westminster Abbey with busts of distinguished scientists and poets, were all foreign-born. Scheemaker and Rysbrack were from Antwerp, and the famous Roubiliac, who sculpted Newton for Trinity College, came from Lyon. And what the English did not learn from the foreigners, whom they welcomed and assimilated, they learned on their travels or by studying foreign works of art that had found their way to England. Gainsborough, that most English of painters, was influenced by the French engraver Gravelot, the landscapes of Ruisdael, and the stately portraits of Van Dyck; Reynolds's three-year stay in Italy was decisive in shaping his taste. Lord Burlington's elegant buildings, which for some years dominated English architecture, were tributes not merely to Roman antiquity and the English genius of Inigo Jones, but also to Palladio's cool villas—Burlington's English Palladianism was English, but it was Palladian as well. Even Hogarth, with all his xenophobic railing and all his spirited denials, patterned his highly successful conversation pieces on Dutch genre paintings. English talent continued to need, and to be fertilized by, foreign inspiration. "The ENGLISH are, perhaps, greater philosophers," David Hume noted, with the detachment of the Scot and the cosmopolitanism of the philosophe, "the ITALIANS better painters and musicians; the ROMANS were greater orators: But the FRENCH are the only people, except the GREEKS, who have been at once philosophers, poets, orators, historians, painters, architects, sculptors, and musicians."[7]

---

[7] "Of Civil Liberty," *Works*, III, 159.

By the time this was published—in 1742—Hume's judicious generosity, like the British willingness to borrow and capacity to absorb, was a sign not of backwardness but of confidence. Early in the century, when that confidence was still untried and uncertain, English writers had felt compelled to make some improbable claims for the relationship between England's liberties and England's supposed pre-eminence in the arts: in 1710 Lord Shaftesbury had denied the French, "that airy neighbouring nation," the "high spirit of tragedy"; that spirit, Shaftesbury maintained in defiance of all evidence, "can ill subsist where the spirit of liberty is wanting." England, on the other hand, where the muses still "lisp as in their cradles," is destined to greatness in the arts because it has undergone the glorious revolution and secured its "hitherto precarious liberties."[8] Two years later the *Spectator* noted with sublime self-importance that "No Nation in the World delights so much in having their own, or Friends or Relations Pictures"—a boast (or complaint) that was being made in other countries at the same time. But beyond that, the *Spectator* claimed that "Face-Painting is no where so well performed as in *England*," because, it seemed, of the "beautiful and noble Faces with which *England* is confessed to abound," and the "Encouragement, the Wealth and Generosity," that the "*English* Nation affords."[9] Continental philosophes like Voltaire, Anglomaniacs from policy as much as from conviction, were inclined to be indulgent with such English conceit, if only to goad their own countries into improving the artists' lot. But in the 1740s, when David Hume examined the question again, such cultural chauvinism was mainly in the hands of truculent patriots like Hogarth. Hume, in addition to stating flatly that foreigners excelled Englishmen in the arts (which was disturbing enough), could argue (and this was even more disturbing) that artistic excellence often emerged in unfree nations. Modern France, he wrote, "scarcely ever enjoyed any established liberty, and yet has carried the arts and sciences as near perfection as any other nation," while modern Rome "carried to perfection all the finer arts of sculpture, painting,

8 "Advice to an Author," *Characteristics*, I, 141–3.
9 *Spectator*, No. 555; IV, 496. A little more sardonic than this, Hogarth thought that portrait painting was particularly popular in England because the English united vanity with selfishness. Basil Williams: *The Whig Supremacy, 1714–1760* (edn. 1952), 374.

and music, as well as poetry, though it groaned under tyranny, and under the tyranny of priests," and Florence "made its chief progress in the arts and sciences, after it began to lose its liberty by the usurpation of the family of MEDICI."[1] His candor suggests that the British no longer needed to boast. Their country was, after a century of turmoil, at last enjoying political stability, religious peace, international security, and economic expansion. The governing oligarchy —a loose coalition of peers, squires, and a few leading merchants, their power based on land and exercised in local and national government—found that they could now turn their attention to peaceful pursuits; they built magnificent houses, and adorned them. Sir Robert Walpole, responsible more than anyone else for this tranquillity, was himself a collector of discriminating taste, generous habits, and unquenchable appetite: his Titians, Rembrandts, and Poussins rivaled those of Dr. Mead's collection in London.

This oligarchy, immensely wealthy and ready to pour its wealth into houses, gardens, paintings, and sculpture, assumed leadership in guiding taste, and produced a cultural revolution—less by design than by default. The influence of the Court on the arts markedly declined, mainly through royal indifference. If the king did not say, "I hate bainting and boetry"—it has been variously attributed to George I and George II—the Georges by and large acted as if they did. The artists themselves did not repudiate the Court; when Frederick Prince of Wales died on March 20, 1751, Reynolds, with unashamed egotism, professed himself "extremely afflicted" because, he wrote, the "Prince of Whales," certainly "would have been a great Patron to Painters."[2] And when George III agreed to lend his

---

[1] "Of Civil Liberty," *Works*, III, 158–9. In the face of this conclusive argument, artists who were also ideologists in behalf of freedom continued to link times of artistic greatness with political liberty. And Winckelmann insisted that the Egyptians had produced bad art because the country was unfree and artists degraded; Greece had produced great art as soon as, and only as long as, it was free: "Art, which as it were had been given life by freedom, must necessarily droop and fall after its loss"—which came with the death of Alexander the Great. *Geschichte der Kunst des Altertums* (1764; edn. 1934), 332.

[2] Reynolds to Miss Weston (1750). *Letters of Sir Joshua Reynolds*, ed. Frederick W. Hilles (1929), 12. That Reynolds was not above flattering a patron is evident from his correspondence; see for one instance his letter to the Hon. William Hamilton, British ambassador to Naples, March 28, 1769. Ibid., 20–3.

name to the Royal Academy in 1768, and endowed it with five thousand pounds, Reynolds, its first president, was neither proud enough nor stupid enough to refuse.

But whatever prestige still attached to royal patronage, it was no longer indispensable, while the ruling oligarchy—which *was* indispensable to artists—was, by eighteenth-century standards, remarkably open, almost democratic, and left the road to independence unobstructed. At a time when there were neither museums nor public galleries, Dr. Mead opened his splendid collection of paintings to students, and liberally entertained visiting artists—including foreigners. Lord Burlington was at once the munificent patron and egalitarian associate of the artists he supported: William Kent, whom he met on his first visit to Italy and converted from a mediocre painter into a fine architect, became Burlington's intimate friend, for all his low origins, limited education, and provocative impudence to his betters. Lord Chesterfield, it is true, criticized Burlington for rather lowering himself "by knowing the minute and mechanical parts of architecture too well,"[3] but then Chesterfield was a snob.

In this new atmosphere, artists soon learned to deal with their most highly placed patrons with ease and dignity. When Thomas Gainsborough refused, in the 1760s, to execute a commission for Lord Hardwicke, he did so with some polite and even obsequious phrases, but he refused[4]; and Capability Brown, who came from a Northumbrian hamlet and began as a humble gardener on a local estate, knew before long what the world owed him: "He writes Lancelot Brown, Esquire, *en titre d'office*," Lord Chatham wrote of him, he "shares the private hours of the King, dines familiarly with his neighbor of Sion"—that is, the Duke of Northumberland—"and sits down at the table of all the House of Lords."[5] Not even Hogarth—the bellicose social critic who never forgot, and never

---

[3] Quoted in Peter Quennell: *Hogarth's Progress* (1955), 44.
[4] "Mr. Gainsborough presents his humble respects to Lord Hardwicke, and shall always think it an honour to be employed in anything for his Lordship, but with respect to real views from Nature in this country he has never seen any place that affords a subject equal to the poorest imitations of Gaspar or Claude. . . . Mr G. hopes that Lord Hardwicke will not mistake his meaning, but if his Lordship wishes to have anything tolerable of the name of Gainsborough, the subject altogether, as well as figures &c., must be of his own brain." Ellis Waterhouse: *Gainsborough* (1958), 15.
[5] Dorothy Stroud: *Capability Brown* (2d edn., 1957), 43.

let anyone else forget, his modest origins and his great merits—found it possible to start a class war in England. Hogarth vigorously satirized the "connoisseurs," the wealthy, often titled amateurs who spouted neoclassical commonplaces and adored the French and Italian masters; and this self-proclaimed "war"[6] was doubtless part of his battle for independence. But he did not disdain painting conversation pieces for the rich and the noble, or accepting lucrative commissions for altarpieces; in 1746 he offered to dedicate his *March to Finchley* to King George II, and most of his life he showed grudging respect for neoclassical hierarchies by trying his hand at grand historical subjects—"very impudently, or rather presumptuously," as Sir Joshua Reynolds, who did not much care for Hogarth, rather severely put it.[7] Even Hogarth, the radical, continued to have some respect for the traditional social and artistic hierarchies. The burdens of the past, it seemed, were not merely pains but also pleasures.

II

The perfect specimen of the new man in English art was Joshua Reynolds—Sir Joshua Reynolds after 1769. He is of special interest here because he was, as Falconet was a philosophe among sculptors, a philosophe among painters. True, devotion to work, social ambitions, literary aspirations, a shrewd sense of money were not the monopoly of the little flock. But in Reynolds they had an emotional intensity, took an intellectual form and acquired a social significance that gave them the meaning they had, say, in Voltaire. Reynolds associated with Christians more easily than Voltaire ever could; when he, with Dr. Johnson, founded his Club in 1764, he eventually included among its members modern pagans like Edward Gibbon and Adam Smith, although most of its members were firm Christians like Samuel Johnson himself, Bishop Percy, and Edmund Burke, and uneasy believers like James Boswell. But then, in eighteenth-

---

[6] This is the word Hogarth himself used to Hester Lynch Piozzi; see Joseph Burke: "Introduction," to William Hogarth: *The Analysis of Beauty*, xiii.
[7] Sir Joshua Reynolds: "Discourse XIV," *Discourses on Art*, ed. Robert R. Wark (1959), 254.

century England the little flock was less firmly organized than elsewhere, less visibly differentiated from the larger culture, and in-
tegrated into the enlightened atmosphere of the day: it was this in
part, after all, that made England into the model for envious philosophes from France or Prussia. Yet, on the supreme question of
religion, Reynolds quite clearly belonged with Adam Smith and
Edward Gibbon: much to Boswell's regret, he was not a Christian
but a Stoic. And the dialectic that defines the other philosophes—
loss of religious faith, admiration of the ancients conquered by a
decisive assertion of independence—defines Reynolds as well. Much
as he respected the grand style, much as he accepted the hierarchies
in painting, which placed historical subjects above portraits and
representative above individualized figures, Reynolds knew that he
excelled in the last of these genres and that his countrymen, in any
event, preferred it to all else. Fuseli, who knew his Englishmen
well, remarked that there was "little hope of Poetical painting finding encouragement in England. The People are not prepared for it.
Portrait with them is everything. Their taste and feelings all go
to realities."[8] Reynolds's taste and feelings, whatever his theory,
also went to realities. He derided the "moderate attempts" he had
made, as instances not of what he thought best, but of what he
could do best, and late in life he scolded himself for failing to
imitate his favorite master, Michelangelo: "I have taken another
course, one more suited to my abilities, and to the taste of the
times in which I live."[9] To choose to exercise one's profitable talent
rather than to obey an exalted tradition was, despite Reynolds's self-
critical undertone, a willful, even proud choice, characteristic of
enlightened men in the eighteenth century and revolutionary in its
implications.

We can read Reynolds's life, then, as an intelligent and persistent attempt to realize the ideals of the artist as philosophe, a life
carefully planned and wholly successful. Born in 1723 into a respectable but notably unprosperous family of clergymen and school-
masters, Reynolds displayed and developed his talents early, studied
portrait painting with Thomas Hudson and rapidly rose to become

---

[8] Quoted in Nikolaus Pevsner: *The Englishness of English Art*
(edn. 1964), 31.
[9] Reynolds: "Discourse III," *Discourses*, 52; "Discourse XV," ibid.,
282.

the most sought-after portrait painter in England: by 1755, he had
more than a hundred sitters, and by 1759, he raised his prices to
keep his work within bounds. He could afford to: he was already
making six thousand pounds a year. Much like Voltaire, he had a
marked capacity for earning, enjoying, and using money; as soon as
he could, Reynolds bought a coach, which symbolized the status
he had gained through his talents. As his pupil James Northcote
suggests, Reynolds's "chariot," splendidly ornamented and ostentatiously driven about, was intended to "give a strong indication of
his great success, and by that means to increase it."[1] Yet work had
intrinsic value for him as well; like the other philosophes, Reynolds
made a cult of work and derived profound satisfaction from it.
When he was still a young painter he discovered that he was "the
happiest creature alive" at the easel[2]; and later he put his discovery
into a piece of advice, sententious perhaps but wholly sincere:
"Whoever is resolved to excel in painting," he wrote, "or indeed
any other art, must bring all his mind to bear upon that one object,
from the moment he rises till he goes to bed."[3] But he was
not without a certain rebellious humor: in 1751, during his all-
important Italian stay, he painted a group of *English Connoisseurs
in Rome,* which satirized at once the English amateur on the grand
tour—a creature about whom Reynolds felt much as Hogarth did—
and one of his favorite classics, Raphael's *School of Athens.* And
in 1776 he parodied the grand style—his own—with a portrait of
Master Crewe as Henry VIII, showing a four-year old boy dressed,
and posturing, in imitation of Holbein's celebrated portrait.[4] Such
lighthearted parodies should not be made to bear too much weight,
but they suggest forcibly enough that neoclassicist though he was,

---

[1] Quoted in Sir Joshua Reynolds: *Portraits,* ed. Frederick W. Hilles
(1952), 149.
[2] Reynolds to his father, Rev. Samuel Reynolds (July 1742).
Letters, 3.
[3] Reynolds to James Barry (1769)—the two painters were obviously still on good terms then. In the same letter, Reynolds urged
Barry to go to Rome and see the Sistine Chapel: "It is *there* only
that you can form an idea of the dignity of the art, as it is there only
that you can see the work of Michael Angelo and Raffael"—evidently the quality and the status of art were inseparable in Reynolds's mind. Ibid., 16–18.
[4] These paintings are reproduced in Pevsner: *Englishness of English
Art,* 69, 70.

Reynolds was a free man. In his later years he was to put his freedom to good use, in his writings on aesthetics.

For Reynolds was more than a painter. Fulfilling a characteristic Enlightenment ideal, an ideal the Enlightenment had borrowed from the Renaissance, Reynolds was eminently sociable, and
tried to be eminently literary. No flattery flattered him more than
to be told that he was a good writer. As soon as he was established,
he sought out prominent politicians, actors, and literary men, to
shine in their circle as he shone, effortlessly, in his own. When
James Boswell dedicated his *Life of Johnson* to Reynolds—it was
only one of the many books dedicated to him, for Reynolds was
an assiduous patron of writers—Boswell singled out Reynolds's temper, politeness, conversation, and "that enlarged hospitality which
has long made your house a common centre of union for the great,
the accomplished, the learned, and the ingenious."

Doubtless his "enlarged hospitality" gave Reynolds real pleasure.
But it was also a social strategy, part of his effort to secure his
dignity as an artist, and with this, the dignity of all artists. The very
shape of his sociability was an assertion of self-esteem and a demand
for the esteem of others. He did not want to be known as a pedant
—and he defined a pedant as a man who can profitably associate
only with his fellow craftsmen because he can talk only about his
own craft—but as a man of the world, a learned artist, a philosopher.
His literary friends were his friends for disinterested reasons, but
they were also proof of his respectability; his literary productions,
in which he took great and just pride, were another. When, after
several false starts, the Royal Academy was finally founded late in
1768, Reynolds was its logical, indeed its inescapable first president:
under his presidency the Academy became a fortress of respectability. Exclusive, prosperous, and from 1780 adequately quartered
in its own rooms at Somerset House, it organized fashionable exhibitions, sought out deserving talent, and between 1769 and 1790
gave Reynolds an attentive audience for his Discourses.

Reynolds's Discourses were the formal counterpart to his sociability. They urged students of art to learn the principles of neoclassicism, take the road to independence through hard work and
alera observation, keep respect for the great masters—Reynolds melodramatically ends the last of his Discourses with "the name of—

MICHAEL ANGELO"[5]—and, perhaps most important of all, remember the dignity of their calling. Painting, he insisted, belonged to the "Polite Arts"; it had "beauty for its object," and a beauty that was "general and intellectual." It has been "my uniform endeavour, since I first addressed you from this place," Reynolds begins his Seventh Discourse, "to impress you strongly with one ruling idea. I wished you to be persuaded, that success in your art depends almost entirely on your own industry; but the industry which I principally recommended, is not the industry of the *hands*, but of the *mind*. As our art is not a divine *gift*, so neither is it a mechanical *trade*. Its foundations are laid in solid science: and practice, though essential to perfection, can never attain that at which it aims, unless it works under the direction of principle."[6] The association between the intellectual and social aspects of the artist's life and the distinction between rational art and manual artisanship could not be drawn more clearly than this.

English artists could only prosper in such a climate; Reynolds's influence radiated out from painting to other arts as well. His friend Dr. Burney was among the first musicians to be admitted to polite company as an equal; Reynolds marked this social conquest when he called Burney "both a Philosopher & a Musician."[7] And his friend Garrick found it possible, as Reynolds and Dr. Johnson were happy to note, to make acting respectable. But the painters profited most: in the 1780s Gainsborough could confidently ask, and expect to get, 160 guineas for a full-length portrait, and Romney was earning over 3,500 guineas a year. And Reynolds outdid them all: in the last dozen years of his active career he asked 50 guineas for a head, 100 guineas for a half-length, and 200 guineas for a full-length portrait. When he died in 1792, he left a fortune of well over a hundred thousand pounds, and was buried in splendid ceremony at St. Paul's, with three dukes, two marquesses, three earls, and two barons as his pallbearers. It was a funeral to impress any philosophe, even a French philosophe: no Frenchman practicing the liberal arts in the eighteenth century, except possibly Voltaire, had amassed such a

[5] "Discourse XV," *Discourses*, 282.
[6] "Discourse VII," ibid., 117.
[7] See Roger Lonsdale: *Dr. Charles Burney: A Literary Biography* (1965), 479–80.

fortune and commanded such prestige; no Frenchman, not even Voltaire, had been laid to rest with such pomp.

III

In France, the burden of the past was more magnificent, and, through its very magnificence, more oppressive, than anywhere else. The Golden Age of Louis XIV loomed, a gigantic presence, over the Silver Age of his successor. The habits that had governed it— authoritarianism, centralization in the Court, condescension of patron to artist—were tenacious, and its dominant aesthetic tradition proved to be as persistent as the social attitudes. Artists responded by resigning themselves to the system, by cynically bending it to their purposes, or by sullen revolt.

The revolutionaries themselves conceded that no one could hope to rival the masterly tragedies of Corneille and Racine; Voltaire, who tried, knew better than his most enthusiastic admirers that his own work was inferior to its models. Molière's comedies had no eighteenth-century rivals; even Rousseau, who deplored their effect on their audience, found them admirable and thought that Molière's successors lacked his "genius and his probity."[8] Contemporary plays, Diderot said late in life, are "detestable," and cannot compare with the theater of an earlier day.[9] The fables of La Fontaine, the libretti of Quinault, the eloquence, if not the theology, of Pascal, Bourdaloue, and Bossuet, remained unattainable, ideal, luminous ornaments of a culture whose richness was a reproach to the eighteenth century. "The time will not come again," Voltaire wrote, "when a duke de La Rochefoucauld, author of the *Maximes*, upon leaving the conversation of a Pascal and an Arnauld, goes to the theatre of Corneille."[1] Voltaire's overwhelming popularity, even among those who distrusted his character and disliked his ideas, is in a sense a symptom of French cultural pessimism: the cultivated public was thirsty for at least one living giant.

---

[8] *Lettre à M. d'Alembert sur les spectacles*, ed. M. Fuchs (1948), 60.
[9] See *Est-il bon? Est-il méchant?*, ed. J. Undank (1961), 172, 180, and editor's introduction, 65.
[1] *Siècle de Louis XIV*, in *Œuvres historiques*, 1012.

In the arts in which the rococo style dominated—in painting and, to a lesser degree, in architecture, sculpture, and poetry—the old models were less forbidding, but the situation, more fluid, was also less clear. Voltaire, who almost singlehandedly sought to rescue French poetry from its prosaic phase, conceded that "the *beaux-arts*, which had given France such superiority over other nations, have badly decayed," and he was compelled to offer, as an instance of "a small number of works of genius," Saint-Lambert's mediocre and derivative *Saisons*.[2] Other observers, like d'Alembert, agreed with him: the need for poetic reform was as glaring as the absence of reformers.

The state of French painting was, if anything, even more muddled than that of poetry, and self-appraisals alternated between unjustified satisfaction and unjustified despondency. At the end of the seventeenth century, the French Academy of Painting had witnessed its own version of the battle between the ancients and the moderns, in which one misunderstood seventeenth-century master, Rubens, had been used to discredit another seventeenth-century master, Poussin, equally misunderstood. This triumph of color over design produced, at least for a while, a certain painterly freedom, and brought forth one real master, Watteau. But in the hands of second-rate academicians the new freedom soon became the new orthodoxy. "We have not had a great painter since we have had an *académie de peinture*," Voltaire wrote in 1735 to the abbé d'Olivet, and while the observation ill conceals the tremulous insecurity of an aspirant to the *Académie française* addressing a member, Voltaire's diagnosis was not without point.[3] True, the philosophes had moments of euphoria: in 1765, Diderot claimed that the brilliant collection of paintings displayed in the Salon of that year could have been assembled only in France, and two years later he still thought it easy enough to find "about twenty" talented painters in France. But also in 1767, contemplating the French scene from a wider perspective, he lost his buoyancy: if one looks at the paintings

---

[2] See *Précis du siècle de Louis XV*, in ibid., 1570–1; see also above, 103–4.

[3] November 30, 1735. *Correspondence*, IV, 192. But he sounded that way even after he was a member of the Academy; see the catalogue of painters appended to his *Siècle de Louis XIV*, in *Œuvres historiques*, 1217.

of "Rubens, Rimbrand, Polembourg, Teniers, Wovermans," he told
Falconet glumly, one must mourn their art as lost, and find the
decadence of contemporary painting depressing.[4]

Of course, as solemn reformers, willing to sacrifice even their
sensuality to their moralizing urge, the French philosophes were better equipped to deplore the failings than to enjoy the virtuosity of
contemporary painting. Rococo struck them as irresponsible and
immoral; it was court art, and, though some of them were assiduous
courtiers, courtly art offended the philosophes' professed social
ideals. Thus they could not take pleasure in Fragonard, even though
Fragonard's greatest patron, the abbé de Saint-Non, was a radical
intellectual who admired Voltaire and Rousseau, and though some
of his other patrons, far from being courtiers, were wealthy and
discriminating *roturiers*. Nor could they appreciate Watteau, whom
they mentioned only to dismiss. Instead, they concentrated their
scorn on Boucher, whom they saw as a panderer feeding the jaded
sensuality of Louis XV. "Well, my friend," wrote Diderot to Grimm
in 1765, "it is at the moment when Boucher has stopped being an
artist, that he has been named *premier peintre du roi*."[5] The implication was inescapable: in France, the best were being neglected, while
the servile were gathering honors and commissions.

Their diagnoses, far from paralyzing the philosophes, stirred
them into action. Voltaire, whose pessimism about the cultural
possibilities of his day and concern for the social aspirations of his
fellow artists were almost obsessive and became almost proverbial,
matched his gloom with his energy, and did all he could in his life
and in his art to falsify his predictions.[6] And the other French
philosophes followed Voltaire in this, as in so much else. Eighteenth-
century art was like eighteenth-century politics: the English, who
had had their revolution, consolidated it, and thus appeared, in the
age of the Enlightenment, to be more conservative than they were;
the French, who were moving toward revolution, failed to see it
clearly, and were therefore more radical than they knew. And the
Germans, who could not even dream of revolution, had to begin
at the beginning.

---

[4] See "Introduction" to *Salons*, I, 20; and letter to Falconet (May
15, 1767). *Correspondance*, VII, 57.
[5] Salon of 1765; *Salons*, II, 76.
[6] See below, 250–1.

IV

Germany found the burdens of the past more poignant and often more distasteful than they were for Englishmen or Frenchmen, for they were not domestic burdens. German artists and writers suffered under a double slavery: they were yoked to a rigid social system and to a foreign neoclassicism. "That multitude of polite productions in the FRENCH language, dispersed all over GERMANY and the NORTH," David Hume observed in 1742, two years after Frederick II had ascended the Prussian throne, and while Lessing was a schoolboy, "hinder these nations from cultivating their own language, and keep them still dependent on their neighbours for those elegant entertainments."[7] Hume was right, but he took effect for cause: Germans remained dependent not because the French had invaded them, the French had invaded them because the Germans were dependent. And, much to the artists' disadvantage, German society imitated not merely French styles, but French authoritarianism as well. While philosophers grumbled and great princes sneered, petty princes postured as little Louis XIVs; they built French castles, kept mistresses in the French style, imitated French fashions, and borrowed prestige by importing French painters and actors. Francomania was the anticomania of eighteenth-century Germany.

France was everywhere, in large matters and small. When Balthasar Neumann, the most gifted German architect of the age, had completed his drawings for the *Residenz* of the prince-bishop of Würzburg, his patrons obliged him to take his plans to Paris that he might secure the approval, and incorporate the suggestions, of two leading French architects. When Germany princes built their châteaux, they organized them in the French fashion, placing their bedrooms at the end of a long flight of rooms, to make themselves accessible only to favorites at their *levées*. When German states founded academies of art, they gave them French names, imposed on them French rules, and associated with them as many

---

[7] "Of the Rise and Progress of the Arts and Sciences," *Works*, III, 196.

Frenchmen as they could find. Obviously, to be German was low, unfashionable, barbarian.

This conduct was less voluntary than it appeared to be. Even more than Italy, Germany in the age of the Enlightenment was a geographical expression, with its three thousand Imperial Knights and its three hundred often tiny states. These units were in general too small, too poor, and too ill-governed to sustain any kind of domestic culture, too hostile to one another, for religious or dynastic reasons, to make up a common cultural territory. Cities were small—even flourishing Frankfurt had only thirty-five hundred inhabitants at mid-century, when Goethe was born there—and in general dependent on some ruling family. There were too few squires and financiers able, and too few princes willing, to form independent centers of taste or sources of commissions. Some of the larger states in southern Germany, like Bavaria, found themselves powerless to prevent, and in fact invited, the invasion of baroque culture from neighboring Hapsburg territories. And the state dominating the north, Prussia, was crippled by severely limited resources: its soil was barren, its raw materials were scanty, its territories were scattered and indefensible. Much of Prussia's national income, therefore, went to the army and, after the Seven Years' War, to rural and urban reconstruction. There was no place in eighteenth-century Prussia for any taste but the king's taste.

That taste was French. To a large extent, Frederick was less the shaper of his culture than its symptom and its victim; Lessing, for one, candidly admitted in 1760 that if the German drama was in desperate straits, this was "perhaps not wholly and simply the fault of the great, who fail to give protection or support. The great do not like to busy themselves with things in which they anticipate little or no real progress."[8] Yet, however restricted Frederick's choices might have been, he did nothing to foster and everything to stifle domestic talents. If, for some reason, a Frenchman or a French style lost favor with him, he was replaced by another foreigner or another foreign style. When Voltaire came to Prussia in 1750, ostensibly to stay, he did not find it necessary to revise any of the current clichés about the poverty of the culture around him. "The

---

[8] Letter LXXXI, February 7, 1760, *Briefe, die neueste Litteratur betreffend*, in *Schriften*, VIII, 218.

language least spoken at court is German," Voltaire observed in August 1750. "Our language and literature have made more conquests than Charlemagne." And two months later, he revived a cruel old joke: "German is for soldiers and horses."[9] In fact, at Potsdam, Voltaire was witness to and an instrument of the realization of a self-fulfilling prophecy: King Frederick II, a perverse patriot who loved his country but despised its civilization, eloquently deprecated German culture and did nothing to invalidate his verdict. He insisted on the French language for his entourage, his academy, and his poetry—his denunciations of German culture were, of course, in French. True, music, in which the king took an abiding interest, was enjoying a minor domestic renaissance: visitors testified to the king's proficiency on the flute, to Carl Philipp Emanuel Bach's talents as a composer and as the king's accompanist on the clavier, and to the competence of local chamber groups, orchestras, and opera companies. But music was unique: Frederick's most famous building, the charming *palais* in Potsdam which Knobelsdorff built after the king's designs, was pure rococo, mainly French in inspiration, and bore the appropriate name *Sans-souci;* when, after Knobelsdorff's death, Frederick's taste in architecture shifted, it moved from the French to Italian neoclassicism and English Palladianism. The same was true in painting: Frederick amassed an impressive collection of modern French painters—Watteau and Boucher, Lancret and Chardin—and then, in later years, collected other masters, also foreign, Rubens and Correggio. And his court painter was Antoine Pesne, a Frenchman who had settled in Berlin in the days of Frederick William I. No German school of architecture or painting could grow in such a chilly climate.

Prussian literature and learning faced the same cold hostility. Again the king set the tone. He loved Racine above all other poets: he once told d'Alembert that he would have preferred writing *Athalie* to winning the Seven Years' War,[1] an unexceptionable sentiment for an enlightened monarch, but also the pathetic confession

---

[9] Voltaire to Madame Denis, August 24 (1750). *Correspondence*, XVIII, 131; and to the Marquis de Thibouville, October 24 (1750). Ibid., 188. My attention was drawn to these passages by Adrien Fauchier-Magnan: *The Small German Courts in the Eighteenth Century* (1947; tr. Mervyn Savill, 1958), 30–1.

[1] See Wilhelm Dilthey: *Das Erlebnis und die Dichtung: Lessing, Goethe, Novalis, Hölderlin* (4th edn., 1957), 103.

of a Prussian who could never quite repress the wish that he had been born a Frenchman. Not surprisingly, the Prussian theater consisted in the main of low farces, feeble occasional pieces celebrating a wedding or a victory, or translations from the French. When in the 1770s enterprising producers put on plays by Lessing and the young Goethe, the king responded to these efforts with an essay, *De la littérature allemande,* in which he foresaw the day when Germany would have its own classics, but warned that the day had not yet come, remained pointedly silent about some of the best German writers of his time, and maligned Goethe's bold *Goetz von Berlichingen* as a "revolting imitation of bad English plays"[2]—the deadly verdict of a belated French neoclassicist.

It was in full accord with these tastes that Frederick surrounded himself with French men of letters, some distinguished, some mediocre, all French. He invited more to his court than were willing to come—Diderot, deeply suspicious of the "tyrant," would not stop on his way back from his visit to Catherine II; and d'Alembert, though willing to enter into an active correspondence with Frederick, refused to become director of the Prussian Academy. Had they all accepted his call, Prussia would have become, not the modern Athens (as Voltaire called it in some of his more complaisant moments) but a German Paris. When Frederick II quarreled with Voltaire in 1752, the irreparable breach was, despite all of Frederick's much-publicized contempt for Voltaire, a great defeat, not for the poet, but for the king. Naturally enough, visiting French *littérateurs* made no effort to correct Frederick's bias; among his closest associates was the marquis d'Argens, an agile and versatile literary errand boy, who had said in print that France had for many years produced the greatest artists in the world, so superior to the Italians that Italy envied France.[3] He did not find it necessary to say that Frenchmen were superior to Germans; that went, literally, without saying.

D'Argens was, among other things, director of the philosophical section of the Prussian Academy. For decades, certainly until the 1770s, that Academy was dominated by Frenchmen: its first permanent president was Maupertuis, its first prize-winner was d'Alembert,

---

[2] *De la littérature allemande . . .,* in *Œuvres de Frédéric le grand,* ed. J. D. E. Preuss, 31 vols. (1846–57), VII, 125.
[3] Weinshenker: *Falconet,* 31 *n.* For Frederick and the philosophes, see below, 483–7.

its chief concerns were set by French philosophy. This was not an accident: the Academy—or *Académie*—was the king's creation and creature; he took a persistent interest in its lectures, prizes, and members. Revived and reorganized in 1744, after it had been allowed to lapse under Frederick William I, the *Académie des sciences et des belles lettres de Prussie* was, therefore, aptly named; it was designed to foster literature and learning in Prussia, but it seemed perfectly plain, at least to the king, that it was not Prussians who would foster them. Moses Mendelssohn—whose application to the Academy the king had vetoed on the sole ground that he was a Jew—spoke not from spite, but from intimate knowledge of the Prussian cultural scene, when he lamented in 1767: "The unfortunate love for French literature robs German literature of all hope for a better future."[4] It was ironic: the king who had captured the imagination of German poets with his cultivation and his victories did nothing for his real admirers and instead courted venal flatterers. He permitted Klopstock to emigrate to Denmark, and refused to employ Winckelmann and Lessing, although both were eager to be employed. In 1751, Klopstock noted in the Introduction to his *Messias* that "The King of the Danes has given the author of the *Messias*, who is a German, the leisure he needed to complete his poem." Lessing quoted these pointed words in a review, and added, even more pointedly: "An excellent testimony to our time, which will doubtless reach posterity. We do not know if everyone sees as much satire in it as we do."[5] But as the years went by, Frederick continued to furnish as much material for this kind of remark— the savage sarcasm of the rejected lover—as he had at the beginning of his reign.

But this, whatever self-satisfied French travelers might think, was not all one could say about German culture. Germany experi-

---

[4] Quoted in Ludwig Geiger: *Berlin: 1688–1840. Geschichte des geistigen Lebens der preussischen Hauptstadt*, 2 vols. (1892–3), I, 464.

[5] *Das neueste aus dem Reiche des Witzes*, May 1751, *Schriften*, IV, 401. Some time in his early years, Lessing wrote a prose draft for a satire (never completed), which is as political as anything he ever wrote. It is addressed "To Maecenas," and laments the disappearance of great and literate patrons; modern patrons (which is to say, Frederick of Prussia) fall short. "A king may indeed govern me; let him be more powerful than I am, but let him not imagine that he is better." *Schriften*, I, 149.

enced other foreign influences—Dutch genre painting, Italian frescoes, English poetry—and besides, some small courts, too sensible or too poor even to try imitating the French, like some prosperous Free Cities, encouraged indigenous art. Frankfurt's patrician art collectors—bankers and lawyers and men of leisure—accumulated splendid private collections of antique coins, seventeenth-century etchings, and, most significant of all, the works of living local painters. Leipzig, where Lessing attended the university, was a lively city with an active (if, fearful of the censor, cautious) intellectual life, with enterprising publishers and wealthy art-loving bourgeois. And yet, in 1740, the French *littérateur* Mauvillon, who was observing the German scene from Brunswick, impolitely challenged his hosts to name a single German endowed with creative spirit, a single poet worthy of an international reputation—*Nommez-moi un esprit créateur sur votre Parnasse; c'est-à-dire, nommez-moi un poète allemand qui ait tiré de son propre fond un ouvrage de quelque réputation! Je vous en défie.*[6] When Lessing set about to respond to this challenge, he was not without domestic resources, but the difficulties in his way, as he knew, would be daunting.

V

For Lessing and his associates, the greatest and most infuriating obstacle was the servile attitude of German patrons, German artists, and German critics to their foreign, especially their French, masters. But this servility had greater uses than the impatient and imperious reformers of the high *Aufklärung* could imagine. It was a matter of giants standing on the shoulders of dwarfs, and ruthlessly trampling them: in the 1730s, the academic aesthetician Johann Christoph Gottsched had poured out lectures, periodical articles, and learned treatises dedicated to the purification of the German language and the German theater through one panacea—the imitation of French neoclassicism; in the 1750s, Lessing could afford to adopt Gottsched's aims while denigrating his methods and derivative phi-

---

[6] Erich Schmidt: *Lessing: Geschichte seines Lebens und seiner Schriften*, 2 vols. (2d edn., 1899), I, 58-9.

losophy as the work of a "learned charlatan."[7] Gottsched's rigid and unimaginative neoclassicism—its tiresome insistence on rules and hierarchies, and its equally tiresome refusal to rescue anything from the rude popular drama or speech of his time—doubtless deserved the ridicule it received. Gottsched was a pedant—the epithet has forced itself on more than one historian; his naïve confidence that masterpieces could be constructed from prescription as though they were machines built from plans marks him as a stranger to the conditions for artistic creativity. At the same time, Gottsched's earthbound, energetic crusades aimed at the right target: as a true *Aufklärer*, he wanted Germans to use their own reason; he wanted them to develop a pure and flexible language; he wanted them to take the theater seriously. Persistently attacking and persistently attacked, he prepared the public for controversy over aesthetic principles; he prepared the public, in other words, for Lessing. As there were philosophes who found it convenient to deny the contributions of Christians to their thought, so Lessing denied Gottsched. But without him, Lessing's task would have been even more difficult than it was.

In her *De l'Allemagne* of 1811, Madame de Staël would characterize Germany as the land of poets and thinkers. Seventy-five years before, it was a land of thinkers who hoped to stamp poets out of the ground. The problems of practice—the absence of a real German theater, the small size of the German reading public, the relative impotence of German art lovers—drove writers into theory: "The comparative isolation of German critics from concrete literature," René Wellek has observed, "goes a long way to account for their intense preoccupation with general aesthetics."[8] In 1730, Gottsched published his *Kritische Dichtkunst*, a doctrinaire collection of prescriptions for the writers of poetry and plays that foundered under the weight of moralizing, philistine readings of the classics, and lifeless rules; it annoyed, among others, two bellicose Swiss critics, Bodmer and Breitinger, who came forward as the champions of imagination against reason, metaphor against prosiness, Milton

---

[7] Letter LXV, November 2, 1759, *Briefe, die neueste Litteratur betreffend*, in *Schriften*, VIII, 178.
[8] *A History of Modern Criticism, 1750–1950*, I, *The Later Eighteenth Century*, 144.

against Boileau, and who in 1740 incorporated their views in a counter-manifesto provocatively entitled *Kritische Dichtkunst.*

The confrontation of these two parties produced a noisy but not a great debate. Since the adversaries had much in common— the Swiss, like Gottsched, rejected bombast and the German baroque, and both sides had an excessively high opinion of the effects of theory on practice—their controversies were often marginal, often confused, and wholly inconclusive. Yet Bodmer and Breitinger called attention to the inadequacy of Gottsched's system and the limitations of his taste, and, by stigmatizing his Cartesianism, offered respectability to sentiment and to imagination in a culture united in a worship of reason that France and England had outgrown. In their defense of the passions, the Swiss critics were sensitively responding to new forces that would further confuse, but also enrich, the German literary scene: the yearning nature poetry of Haller, the pathetic, sentimental, mystical poetry of Klopstock, the versatile work of Gellert, fabulist, novelist, poet, part rationalist, part pietist —the German galley slave (as Voltaire might have said) was rattling at his chains. "The literary epoch into which I was born," as Goethe felicitously put it, "grew from its predecessor by means of contradiction."[9]

Lessing knew this from the beginning. "A just and well-founded criticism," he wrote as a very young man, "is an indispensable office in the world of learning. It frightens the miserable scribbler away from his pen, it compels the mediocre writer to make an effort, it warns the great man not to spare himself, and to publish nothing imperfect, nothing in haste. It spreads good taste across the land." And he added: "Without criticism the arts would not flourish so greatly in France."[1] As a true philosophe Lessing was perfectly willing to struggle, without resentment or embarrassment, for the emancipation of German culture with the aid of the French, or, more precisely, one Frenchman: as long as the Frenchman was Diderot, Lessing could regard the French invasion of Germany as a good thing. It was a reasonable judgment; both, after all, were engaged in the same task—to rescue the best of the past, and throw off its burdens.

---

[9] *Dichtung und Wahrheit,* in *Gedenkausgabe,* X, 285.
[1] Schmidt: *Lessing,* I, 184.

CHAPTER SIX

The Emancipation of Art:
A Groping for Modernity

I. DIDEROT AND LESSING:
TWO RESPECTFUL REVOLUTIONARIES

I

DIDEROT AND LESSING have often been treated as kindred spirits. The pairing is apt; in aesthetics even more than in other matters, they confronted similar problems and offered similar solutions, in a similar spirit. And their affinity went deeper than a certain convergence of concern and temperament: they directly influenced one another. Diderot, impressed by Lessing's bourgeois tragedy, *Miss Sara Sampson*, thought of having it translated; Lessing translated Diderot's first two plays and his discourses on the drama, reflected upon—and reflected—Diderot's aesthetics, and advertised him to German readers in lyrical language, all the more striking for Lessing's notorious aversion to hyperbole: "After Aristotle," he wrote in 1760, "no more philosophical spirit has concerned himself with the drama than he."[1] Other Germans thought as Lessing did: they found Diderot's atheism shocking, but they were receptive to his novels, his dramatic theories, and his bourgeois plays; *Aufklärer* and *Stürmer und Dränger* alike prized him as a fascinating and fertile thinker, and drew courage as well as ideas from his rebelliousness. But when Lessing said, near the end of his life, "Diderot appears to

---

[1] "Vorrede des Übersetzers," to *Das Theater des Herrn Diderot*, in *Schriften*, VIII, 286.

have had far greater influence on the German theatre than on the theatre of his own nation," he was speaking about himself even more than others.[2]

The affinity between Lessing and Diderot is very close and highly instructive. Both were intent upon independence and dignity for the estate of letters, both were contentious and inquisitive, both were learned and cultivated critics of Christianity and modern lovers of antiquity. "Let us go to school to the ancients," Lessing wrote to Moses Mendelssohn in 1756. "What better teachers, after nature, could we choose?"[3] And in the following year, Diderot exclaimed: "I shall not get weary of shouting at Frenchmen: Truth! Nature! The Ancients! Sophocles! Philoctetes!"[4] Here were two revolutionaries who never lost their respect for tradition.

No one bore the burdens of the past more heavily, and suffered them more publicly, than Diderot. He exacted admiration for antiquity and, at the same time, freedom of action for himself, and combated with equal eloquence the anticomaniacs who adored the old for the sake of its age, and the modern barbarians who did not know, or affected to despise, the classics.[5] Diderot himself understood the classics—both Homer and Racine—too thoroughly to imitate them blindly, and he loved them too well—at this point he parted company with Falconet—to be easy about the overthrow of artistic canons that had made them possible.

While Diderot for many years experienced these two attitudes as an unresolvable tension, and paid for his irresolution with a certain vacillation, an unsureness of touch, Voltaire's persistent lucidity proves that there was nothing inherently inconsistent about loving the classics and independence at the same time. As Voltaire saw it—and the contrast with Diderot, who admired Voltaire's work, is instructive—the proper task of the eighteenth century was to rescue neoclassicism from deadly academicism, to preserve in it what was valuable and discard what could be spared. The product of the age of Louis XIV, and its most distinguished spokesman in the Enlightenment, Voltaire consistently advocated decorum, clarity, obedience

---

[2] "Vorrede des Übersetzers," to the second edition of *Das Theater des Herrn Diderot*, ibid., 288.
[3] November 28, 1756. Ibid., XVII, 73.
[4] *Entretiens sur le Fils naturel*, in *Œuvres esthétiques*, 120.
[5] See *The Rise of Modern Paganism*, 70–1.

to rules. Yet, nourished by his wide reading, his linguistic facility, and a passionate if selective alertness to literary excellence, he also permitted his taste to modify and modernize his doctrine: if he found Addison's *Cato* correct and elegant, he was constrained to admit that it was frigid and dull; if he condemned Shakespeare's irregularities, vulgarity, and mixture of styles, he was haunted by the force and sublimity of his genius[6]; if Racine's *Athalie* was filled with the kind of "fanaticism" Voltaire most abhorred, its poetry compelled him to call it a masterpiece. And in his own plays he subjugated his principles to dramatic necessities: he introduced action that closely skirted the edges of pathos and melodrama, though, he hoped, without overwhelming traditional decorum: "One must be novel," he wrote, "without being bizarre, often sublime, and always natural."[7] But in defiance of his own injunction, Voltaire resorted to stage business that startled his audiences; he brought ghosts onto the stage, cannon shots and howling mobs, ideas in tragic combat, exotic personages and remote ages—Chinese, Muslims, medieval Frenchmen. And as his plays explored territory unknown or unpleasant to his seventeenth-century predecessors, his philosophical tales, which he professed to take lightly and passed over in his correspondence with almost complete silence, were, in their own unobtrusive way, innovations. Voltaire, the self-proclaimed conservative, began an aesthetic revolution that others, younger than he, would carry further.

In comparison, Diderot long was unadventurous, content to leave most of the neoclassical structure untouched. He explicitly defended, and in his first two plays strictly observed, the unities of time, place, and action, accepting them as "difficult" but "sensible."[8] He accepted, if a little uneasily, the hierarchy of subject matter in painting. He drew on classical doctrines for his early ideals of art as imitation and art as moral. And he justified his experiments in the bourgeois drama by insisting that they owed less to the modern

---

[6] Voltaire's attitude toward Shakespeare was far from simple; he took pride in being among the first to appreciate him on the Continent (see Lettre XVIII, *Lettres philosophiques*, where he also expresses himself about Addison's *Cato*), but in his later years Voltaire became more defensive about French neoclassical drama and more hostile to Shakespeare.

[7] *Candide*, in *Œuvres*, XXI, 192.

[8] *Entretiens sur le Fils naturel*, in *Œuvres esthétiques*, 81.

Lillo than to the ancient Terence. It was not until the 1760s—
always remaining himself, or, rather, becoming himself more and
more—that he discarded inherited ideas and began to grope for a
modern aesthetic.

It was a groping, no more, a series of fitful though not fruitless
raids. As he was aware, his ideas on the arts were anything but systematic: in 1767, he compared himself to an undisciplined hunting
dog who chases whatever wild game rises before him[9]—not without
justice: his preoccupation with aesthetic questions was as unorganized
as it was persistent. He began to theorize early and ended late. He
moved, with his characteristic ease, from a response to a particular
painting to a general inquiry into beauty. He wasted some of his
most interesting ideas in private letters, hid others in unpublished
dialogues, and never wrote the treatise that he sometimes thought
he should write.

Yet his explorations ended with the victory of independence
over memory; the sum of his writings stamps him as one of the
fathers of modern aesthetics. For his very failings—his early dependence, his uncontrolled profusion, his irreducible inconsistencies—
were only the shadow side of his infatuation with experience. Diderot's empiricism is all of a piece: he was committed to experience
on principle and by temperament, through the philosophical style
he shared with the other philosophes and in the aesthetic ideas he
developed on his own. His best plays, novels, and dialogues—I am
thinking especially of *Est-il bon? Est-il méchant?* and *Jacques le fataliste* and *Le neveu de Rameau,* all dating from the sixties and later—
are conscious experiments. The mobility of his moods and ideas, his
alertness, his restlessness, his powerful sensuality—all of which he
cultivated so energetically that his ease sometimes seems forced and
his spontaneity strenuous—kept him from bookishness and rigidity.
That is why his later pronouncements are almost invariably superior
to his earlier pronouncements: as he saw, and read, and listened, and
wrote, the pressure of experience enlarged his perspective, deepened
his taste, and clarified his ideas.

There was nothing passive about Diderot's encounter with life
and art. Just as he had prepared himself—or announced that he had
prepared himself—for his *Encyclopédie* by consulting "the ablest

---

[9] Salon of 1767; *Salons,* III, 56.

craftsmen of Paris and the kingdom," visiting "their workshops, interrogating them, taking down their dictation, developing their thoughts," so he prepared himself for his vocation as critic and theorist by going to school to the artists themselves.[1] He shared Falconet's contempt for contemporary art critics—for the venal reviewers, timid and superficial, who compiled lists and lavished praise, and for arrogant and capricious connoisseurs, who underscored their preferences with purchases: a "cursed race."[2] Artists needed protection from both, but they also needed, for their own sake as much as the public's, informed criticism. When in 1747 La Font de Saint Yenne had dared to claim the right to exercise his taste on the paintings of the day, his little book, cautious though it was, had called forth outrageous slanders and a painters' strike; the artists behaved like guildsmen invaded by unlicensed outsiders. This far Diderot was not prepared to go—had he not laid it down that everything is subject to criticism?[3] Fortunately, Falconet had admitted that while the best judge of art is an artist, there were a few—a very few—experienced, sensitive men whose aesthetic judgment had some merit, and he graciously included Diderot among these "*vrais connoisseurs.*"[4] And Diderot did his best to deserve Falconet's good opinion; he at least would judge works of art drawing on reliable technical knowledge. He frequented painters' studios to watch them at work, sat for his portrait asking a stream of questions, and walked through the Salons with discriminating painters like Chardin—"perhaps no one," he said, "talks about painting better than he does"[5]—and with the opinionated, articulate Falconet. He studied the language of the studio, borrowing, as he put it, the painters' "very eyes." And all this made him magnificently independent after a time, and thoroughly professional: "If I happen to wound the artist," he wrote in 1765, "it is often with the weapon he himself has sharpened; I have questioned him."[6]

---

[1] "Prospectus" for the *Encyclopédie*, in *Œuvres*, XIII, 140. I have already quoted this passage in *The Rise of Modern Paganism*, 183. See Jean Seznec: "Introduction" to *Salons*, I, 10–11; and Vernière in Diderot: *Œuvres esthétiques*, 440.

[2] Salon of 1767; *Salons*, III, 55.

[3] "Fait," in *Œuvres*, XV, 3; see *The Rise of Modern Paganism*, 149.

[4] Weinshenker: *Falconet*, 71.

[5] Salon of 1761; *Salons*, I, 125.

[6] Quoted by Seznec, Introduction in ibid., 11.

As he practiced he preached. Again and again he would justify his views by an appeal to his experience—to paintings or plays he had seen. He often regretted that he had not seen more; it would have helped him make pertinent comparisons, detect plagiarisms, and further improve his taste. And he commended his own education to others: "Do you want to make reliable progress in your knowledge of the techniques of art, which is so difficult? Stroll through a gallery with an artist, have him explain to you, and show you on the canvas, the meaning of technical words. Without this you will never have anything but confused notions."[7] Later, in the *Paradoxe sur le comédien*, he extended this principle to actors. Nature only laid down the foundation on which experience must build: "It is up to nature to supply the qualities of the person—face, voice, judgment, sensitivity. But the study of great models, knowledge of the human heart, exposure to the world, assiduous labor, experience, and the habit of the theater will perfect the gift of nature."[8] The artist and his judge alike must forget theories and plunge instead into experience—to look, to listen, to act, and it was experience itself that had taught Diderot this lesson.

In his first pronouncements on the arts, his first plays and *Salons*, his experience—largely of books and some great examples— committed Diderot to an almost unrelieved moral naturalism: only perfect imitation can produce the proper aesthetic effect on the public; "only the true pleases and moves."[9]

The idea was antique, commonplace, and in this simple formulation, ambiguous. Aristotle had held that the work of art is a work of imitation, although to him this had meant rational selection, the elimination of the fortuitous and the particular, in a word, the idealization of the actual as it could or should be. But from the Renaissance on, a number of Aristotle's interpreters had read his dicta as injunctions to literalism: the artist is the ape of nature; the better the artist, the more complete the realism; the greatest painter is the

---

[7] Ibid. In 1761, Diderot suggested that Richardson, that greatest among novelists, must have had a "prodigious head"—*la prodigieuse étendue de tête*—but also an "astonishing knowledge of laws, customs, habits, manners, the human heart, life," and an "inexhaustible fund of morality, experiences, and observations." *Éloge de Richardson*, in *Œuvres esthétiques*, 40.

[8] *Paradoxe sur le comédien*, ibid., 303.

[9] *Les bijoux indiscrets*, in *Œuvres romanesques*, 142.

one who can induce birds to peck at his grapes in a still life. Yet literalism never wholly displaced idealization: the celebrated story of Zeuxis, who captured Helen's incomparable beauty by choosing the most beautiful single features of several lovely virgins, argued for a kind of selective, intelligent naturalism—and educated men in the age of the Enlightenment, including Diderot, were fond of this anecdote.

Yet, with the choice of several versions of mimesis open to him, Diderot selected the crudest. Doubtless it never occurred to him— it would have embarrassed him greatly if it had—that in those years his criterion for judging the merit of a play was in perfect agreement with the uninformed judgment of the most uneducated playgoer. "The perfection of a play," he wrote, "consists in the imitation of an action so accurate that the spectator, continuously deceived, imagines himself to be present at the action itself."[1] Dramatic speech should reproduce the authentic accents of passion, the hesitations, exclamations, incomplete sentences characteristic of real speech. And, transferring this reasoning to his first essays in art criticism, Diderot reserved his highest praise for painters who could evoke nature itself.

In his own dramas, Diderot took his own advice, and searched for ways to insure verisimilitude. His first play, *Fils naturel*, published though not performed in 1757, is an experiment in *trompe l'œil*, and the *Entretiens sur le Fils naturel*, published with it, is its apology: the *Fils naturel*, Diderot insists, is "not a fiction but a fact," a report designed "to preserve the memory of an event" and to "represent it as it took place."[2] Criticism of improbabilities in the action or the speeches of individual personages is therefore beside the point. If Dorval, the hero, drinks a cup of tea on stage, why not? He has traveled, and adopted the habit of drinking tea from the Dutch. "But on stage?" The question is irrelevant: "My work must be judged in the salon."[3] In fact, Diderot makes Dorval into the chief spokesman of his *Entretiens*, a device that in no way anticipates the metaphysical mystifications of Pirandello: it permits Diderot to ad-

---

[1] Ibid. Diderot was, of course, not alone; for a crude statement of the imitation theory see Voltaire's casual references in *Le siècle de Louis XIV*, in *Œuvres historiques*, 1216–17.
[2] "Introduction," to *Fils naturel*, in *Œuvres*, VII, 20. *Entretiens sur le Fils naturel*, in *Œuvres esthétiques*, 92.
[3] *Entretiens*, in *Œuvres esthétiques*, 86.

vertise not the ambiguities haunting reality but the truthfulness of
his "report."

It is this concern with journalistic verisimilitude that moved
Diderot boldly to place the action of his drama in the present and
in a realistic setting. More: he exacted realistic acting (less declama-
tion, more pantomime), prescribed realistic settings, and wrote realistic speeches, or, rather, speeches he thought were realistic.[4] Far
from mastering experience, Diderot in this phase of his career became its servant, confounding art and life, to the detriment of art.

Diderot's next play, Le père de famille, of 1758, and the Discours sur la poésie dramatique that accompanied it show no deepening of aesthetic perception. Diderot drew the action, with almost
embarrassing fidelity, from his own life, and loaded down the stage
business with sentimental tableaux. Precisely like its predecessor,
Le père de famille strives for realism in every possible way: it contains pointed references to contemporary events and social problems,
its dialogue is naturalistic rather than elevated, and its stage directions prescribe settings and movements drawn from nature. And
Diderot pressed the point that his efforts at naturalism constituted
a deliberate program: "My good friend," he wrote to Madame
Riccoboni, actress and novelist, "I believe that you have not read
me well. My first and second play form a system of theatrical action;
one should not quibble about a point here or there, but accept or
reject it in its entirety."[5]

Diderot had no doubt that the highest, ultimate purpose of his
"system" was ethical. One of his characters in Fils naturel—clearly
a spokesman—comments favorably on the prevalence of moral books
and moral plays: "These are the lessons with which our stage re-
sounds, and cannot resound too often."[6] What, he asks, is the object
of a dramatic composition? and replies, "It is, I think, to inspire men

---

[4] One of Diderot's aims (as Vernière points out in ibid., 112 n.)
was to clear the stage of spectators, a reform that Voltaire the dramatist also wanted to see undertaken in those years.
[5] (November 27, 1758). Correspondance, II, 98.
[6] Fils naturel, act IV, scene 3. Œuvres, VII, 68. By the side of this
line I found in the Columbia University copy of this book a curt,
despairing penciled comment: "Et Hitler?"

with love of virtue and horror of vice."[7] His simplistic view that art directly imitates reality was matched by his expectation that the spectator directly applies in his own life the lesson he has learned from the play.

Nothing could have been more conservative. The idea that art has a didactic purpose is almost as ancient as the idea that it consists of imitation. It goes back to two much-quoted passages from Horace's *Ars poetica* asserting that art must be useful as well as delightful, and it had been continually reiterated since the Renaissance. The claim that art was useful was useful to the artist; it justified his existence. By the seventeenth century, it had been firmly embedded in neoclassical theory; allowing artists wide latitude in practice, it underlay familiar demands that in drama, as in poetry, and as much as possible in painting, the good be rewarded and the bad punished, and that artists choose elevated actions and avoid repellent ones. Decorum demanded, as Horace had said long ago, that Medea kill her sons offstage.

Late in the seventeenth century, Boileau once again insisted on the moral purpose of art in his influential *Art poétique,* and so did La Bruyère and many others. The most vicious Restoration playwrights piously proclaimed that it was their purpose to hold up mirrors to corrupt society; their pretensions were ironic, cynical, or self-protective, but they suggest that the old doctrine had lost none of its power. In the eighteenth century neoclassicists bravely said it again: in art, virtue should attract and vice disgust, rewards and punishments be properly distributed in accord with merit, degraded persons or actions not be shown. But gradually it became clear, even to neoclassicists, that this was doubtful philosophy, and they appealed, in Samuel Johnson's words, "from criticism to nature."[8] Johnson himself conceded that an artist might properly portray reality even if it violated poetic justice. Nicolai, with his pedestrian good sense, introduced these doubts into Germany: a poet, he reasoned, could be a lawgiver only among barbarians, while in civilized modern Europe he had a different function; the very idea, in fact, that the stage is a school of morals is a "fad" refuted "daily" by

---

[7] *Entretiens,* in *Œuvres esthétiques,* 152. A year later he reiterated this point in the *Discours sur la poésie dramatique,* ibid., 196.

[8] Quoted in Hilles: *Literary Career of Joshua Reynolds,* 102 *n.*

experience.[9] And in the latter part of the century, Sir Joshua Reynolds bluntly broke with the whole system: "The business of art is rationally to amuse us and not send us to school. If it is, we should go unwilling to school. We must be recreated with variety."[1] In his thirteenth Discourse, Reynolds laid it down quite formally: "The end of art," he told his listeners, is "to produce a pleasing effect on the mind"[2]—not a word about instruction.

This was a welcome relaxation of the old strenuousness, opening new vistas on art, but the philosophes, who visibly longed to join the radicals, could not easily bring themselves to yield up their cherished schoolmasterly role. "Forget your rules," Diderot exclaimed in 1758, "put technique aside: it's the death of genius."[3] It was a heartfelt cry, but there was simply too much work to be done—too many injustices to be righted, superstitions to be exposed, tastes to be improved, to permit the philosophes to abandon their poses as modern Socrateses, or modern Catos; with their humorless didacticism they continued to find the old doctrine appealing and even offered some new rationalizations for it. Most of what they wrote, after all, whether it was history, fiction, or art criticism, was designed to improve the reader as it persuaded him, and they saw no reason why art should be left out of the great venture of changing the general way of thinking. What was surprising about Diderot's moralizing was its naïveté, the triviality of its lessons—what *are*, when one thinks of it, the lessons imparted by Greuze?—and its singleminded neglect of aesthetic considerations.

It is only this highly saturated atmosphere that could have produced Rousseau's famous *Lettre à d'Alembert sur les spectacles*, written and published in 1758, the year of Diderot's *Père de famille*. It is Rousseau at his most Platonic, most Genevan, and most paradoxical: he argues, in essence, that Horace is right in principle—art should inculcate virtue and discourage vice—but since this has become impossible in corrupt modern civilization, there should be no theater, at least in Geneva. Rousseau's *Lettre à d'Alembert* is, to be

[9] Letter 201, *Litteraturbriefe*, quoted by Joan Karle: "The Early Writings of Christoph Friedrich Nicolai" (unpublished M.A. thesis, 1967), 35.

[1] Reynolds: *Portraits*, 117.

[2] *Discourses*, 241.

[3] Diderot to Madame Riccoboni (November 27, 1758). *Correspondance*, II, 100.

sure, more than an attack on the theater and a criticism of d'Alembert; it is part of Rousseau's break with his old associates and a veiled attack on Voltaire. But it explicitly insists on the intimate relation of art and morality: the modern theater is essentially French, that is to say, Parisian, and to import the theater into Geneva would be to poison a simple manly society with effeminate spectacles. Rousseau offers the *Misanthrope* as a significant example: in this famous play, Molière encourages vice by ridiculing virtue, for he portrays Alceste, an "upright, sincere, estimable, truly good man," as an absurd creature whose courageous, independent conduct the spectator is induced to despise.[4] If Geneva wants spectacles, let it conduct public festivals, carefully supervised balls, and edifying gymnastic shows, where young people can meet openly, where the aged are respected, and honest marriages encouraged.

The *Lettre à d'Alembert* tempted the philosophes into cheap jokes about an unsuccessful playwright who has turned against the theater in which he has failed, and it infuriated Diderot,[5] but not because Rousseau had mistaken social for aesthetic criticism, misread Molière, and connected action on the stage with action in life—Diderot had after all done much of this himself.[6] The issue was not Rousseau's principle, but his prescription.

Indeed, three years after Rousseau's *Lettre à d'Alembert*, late in 1761, Diderot restated his doctrine, in his *Éloge de Richardson:* "Richardson is no more. What a loss for letters and for humanity!" —a significant conjunction. If pressing need should ever compel him to sell his library, Diderot exclaimed, "You would be left to me, you would be left on the same shelf with Moses, Homer, Euripides, and Sophocles." And Richardson deserved to be in this distinguished company because he was the subtle psychologist who had "carried the torch into the bottom of the cavern," an eloquent rhetorician who had known "how to make the passions speak," and above all

---

[4] *Lettre à M. d'Alembert sur les spectacles*, 48. I have dealt with the origins of this quarrel—d'Alembert's visit to Geneva—in *The Rise of Modern Paganism*, 336–8.

[5] In his letter to Sophie Volland (June 2, 1759), Diderot accuses Rousseau of being, among other things, a "great sophist" avid for paradox. *Correspondance*, II, 144–8.

[6] In point of fact, as late as 1765, Diderot argued that art should encourage virtue; see *Essais sur la peinture*, in *Œuvres esthétiques*, 718.

because he was a moralist, a writer who had taught Diderot to love his fellow men and his duties better than before, who had taught him pity for villains and new sympathy for the unhappy, greater veneration for good men, contempt for life, and love of virtue. To read Richardson, it seems, was less a literary experience than an ethical one: "All that Montaigne, Charron, La Rochefoucauld, and Nicole have put into maxims, Richardson put into action."[7] Historians falsify; Richardson has made his readers spectators to hundreds of real situations: "O painter of nature, you never lie!"[8]

II

None of this was new; much of it, reactionary. But Diderot drew one radical conclusion from the naïve neoclassicism of these years, a conclusion that links him directly to Lessing. "I like to see the sphere of our pleasures enlarged," he wrote in 1757,[9] and what he had in mind, quite specifically, was a reform of the theater that would permit dramatists to treat the lives of ordinary people as seriously as neoclassical tragedy had treated kings and aristocrats. The last century, he suggested, had left the eighteenth century much work to do, notably a need for reform in acting, staging, and the dance, but, most urgently, the need to create "the domestic and bourgeois tragedy."[1]

Diderot held up his own two plays as moral dramas belonging to this new genre, the *genre sérieux*, and as moving with ease from it to tragedy and comedy. This relaxation, Diderot thought, would permit the modern dramatist to expand traditional notions of *vraisemblance* and raise the bourgeoisie to dramatic acceptability.

---

[7] *Éloge de Richardson*, ibid., 41, 33, 32, 38, 29. This last phrase seems to have been a commonplace: on October 28, 1759, Madame du Deffand told Voltaire that Richardson's novels were "moral treatises in action" (quoted by Vernière in ibid., 29 *n*.).

[8] Ibid. 40. This too was a commonplace: Voltaire used it, and so did Rousseau. Reynolds called Shakespeare a "faithful and accurate painter of nature," Discourse VIII, *Discourses*, 148.

[9] *Entretiens sur le Fils naturel*, in *Œuvres esthétiques*, 155.

[1] Ibid., 167. Samuel Johnson, incidentally, also thought that the "mingled drama" was a reasonable theatrical genre.

Genres, after all, he argued, are not the product of nature but of a single genius whose invention is then repeated, hardened into rules by imitators and imprisoned in habit. But times change and forms must change with them: "Nothing prevails against the truth."[2] And the truth of Diderot's time was patently larger, wider, deeper than could be comprehended in the neoclassical genres. Certainly the initial pressure on Diderot to loosen his rigid theory of imitation came from his experience, which was teaching him that there was more to be worthily imitated than Poussin or Racine had imagined.

It must be admitted that there was more bourgeois ideology in his writings on the drama than in the dramas themselves; Diderot was more radical in his program than in his practice. The central figures in his first two plays are highly placed, wealthy, and probably noble as well, and the morality they preach, or represent, is a decency, a family loyalty, a sentimentality that was as available to aristocrats as it was to commoners. The ambiguity that shadows the status of some of Diderot's characters testifies to the novelty of his social ideal and his uncertainty, and reflects the persistence of aristocratic tastes, and aristocratic audiences, in the theater of Diderot's time.

The young Lessing was prodded by the same uncertainties—and others: in Germany's French culture he found it essential first to discover who he was before he could determine what he must do. As he muses in an instructive early poem: I have neither honor nor wealth, nor would it matter if an ignorant posterity tramples me underfoot. All that matters is self-knowledge—

> Wie lange währt's, so bin ich hin
> Und einer Nachwelt untern Füssen;

[2] *Entretiens sur le Fils naturel*, in *Œuvres esthétiques*, 189–90. Reynolds took precisely the same line: "If the rules of epic poetry are formed from the practice of Homer, and those of tragedy from Sophocles and Euripides, and of comedy from Menander and Terence, and if a new and great genius has arisen equal to any of them and superior for universality of powers, with success superior to what was ever before seen, and upon a plan in the general construction totally different, it is time for a new code of laws, or at least for the old to be fairly and candidly revised." *Portraits*, 122.

Was braucht sie, wen sie tritt, zu wissen?
Weiss ich nur, wer ich bin.[3]

He knew soon enough that he was a critic. He discovered later that
he was a critic at the expense of creativity. "I am neither actor nor
poet," he confessed in the *Hamburgische Dramaturgie*, at the height
of his powers. Those who generously thought him a genius, he insisted, did not know him. What he had done well was to criticize;
that living source that bubbles up in the *Dichter* in a pure stream
and by its own inner power—that, he admitted, he lacked.[4] But this
capacity for recognizing his limitations liberated his real powers:
being ruthless with himself permitted him to be ruthless with others,
without qualms. He was not as great a critic as he himself, and a
grateful posterity, thought; he was often hasty in his judgments,
obsessive in his polemics, and a little pedantic in his struggle against
pedantry. But he was as courageous and honest as he was intelligent—and he was very intelligent. Like Reynolds, Lessing was not
the first to think his thoughts, but he thought them at the right time
and pronounced them in the right words. He used candor at a time
when German culture needed it above all else, clear when there
was only muddle.

The first thing candor exacted was the recognition that French
culture was vastly superior to German culture. Let Diderot criticize
his country's drama, Lessing wrote; it is sobering to reflect that "at
least the Frenchman has a stage, when the German has barely a few
booths." In France, the king, his court, and distinguished citizens
flock to the theater, while in the German states a playwright must
be grateful if a few honest bourgeois "timidly steal into the booth."[5]
"Give me the names of the spirits," Lessing exclaimed, sounding
precisely like Mauvillon, "of whom the comic muse of Germany
could be proud!"[6] The muse had no cause for pride: "We have no
theater. We have no actors. We have no audience."[7]

But, while France had a civilization, much of it was vicious.

---

[3] "Ich," dated October 11, 1752. *Schriften*, I, 131.
[4] "101st to 104th Number" (the last), *Hamburgische Dramaturgie*,
ibid., X, 209.
[5] Letter LXXXI, February 7, 1760, *Briefe, die neueste Litteratur
betreffend*, ibid., VIII, 217.
[6] "Vorrede" to part III of Lessing's *Schriften* (1754), ibid., V, 269.
[7] Letter LXXXI, *Briefe . . .*, ibid., VIII, 216–17.

"How fortunate France would be," Lessing wrote in 1751, reviewing Rousseau's first *Discours*, "if it had many such preachers."[8] It
had far too few, and in consequence, irreligion and lasciviousness
ruled. This was one reason why German adoration of France was so
misplaced, so stifling. "What dominates our purified theatres?" Lessing asked, with a glance at Gottsched, the leading purifier. "Is it
not all foreign wit which, as often as we admire it, makes a satire
on our own?"[9] When he was barely twenty, Lessing had pitted the
"creative spirit" against Gottsched's rules, and in 1759, in a widely
quoted article, he said it again, with brusque finality. The German
stage, he argued, has no reason to be grateful to Gottsched. "'It
would have been desirable if Herr Gottsched had never meddled
with the theater." His supposed improvements were either trivial or
actually damaging. Granted, when Gottsched began to write, the
German theater was full of "nonsense, bombast, filth, and mob-
humor." Anyone could have improved such a situation. But what
did Gottsched do? "He understood a little French and began to
translate; he encouraged everyone who could rime and could understand *Oui, monsieur*, to translate, too"; he compiled a mediocre play,
Der sterbende Cato, with scissors and paste; he cursed the harlequin,
he damned improvisation and wished, "not merely to improve our
old theater, but be the creator of a new one." But what kind of
theater? "A frenchifying theater," and this without asking whether
the *französierende* theater was as appropriate to the German mentality as the English.[1]

   Lessing was being less than just, but it must be said for him that
he was both ambitious enough and fair-minded enough to invite
criticism in his turn. If he was to succeed where Gottsched had
failed, he must not merely make telling points in reviews or essays,
but write memorable poems and plays. This proved to be difficult.
Lessing's lyrics, odes, epigrams, fables, and narratives, though lucid
and economical, were little more than rationalistic exercises which
others performed as well or better. His early plays, on the other
hand—though they, like the poems, were strained, and visibly embodied a literary or social program—effectively translated Lessing's
desire for reform into actuality. As early as 1749, when he was only

---

[8] *Das neueste aus dem Reiche des Witzes*, April 1751, ibid., IV, 395.
[9] "Vorrede" to part III of Lessing's *Schriften*, ibid., V, 269–70.
[1] Letter XVII, *Briefe . . .*, ibid., VIII, 41–2.

twenty, he joined the *Aufklärer* with his philosemitic drama, *Die Juden*, explicitly designed to cut the ground from prevailing prejudices against the Jews' supposed racial characteristics; and with the rhetorical fragment *Samuel Henzi*, based on a contemporary event, the brutal torture and hasty execution of a radical *littérateur* in Berne for alleged sedition. These were brave essays in the Germany of Lessing's day, Enlightenment dramas in which the critical served the reforming spirit. And then, in 1755, Lessing scored his first real triumph with *Miss Sara Sampson*, a bourgeois tragedy—"*bürgerliche Tragödie*"—drawn largely from Lillo and Richardson: the affinity of Lessing and Diderot extended to their borrowings.

Miss Sara Sampson is derivative, sentimental, lachrymose, but its cultural significance is decisive. It is a feeble effort in nearly all respects: for a revolutionary drama it is all too obedient to the neoclassical rules; for a bourgeois tragedy its characters are too highly placed in the world; and its safe English locale appears to compromise its radical intentions. Yet Lessing's choice of an English title, English subject, English names was not mere timidity; it was also programmatic—a declaration of independence from French, or French-inspired German neoclassicism. "I would infinitely prefer being the author of the *London Merchant*," he wrote a year after his play had first been performed, "than of *Der sterbende Cato*"— an ambition, one is tempted to observe, that *Miss Sara Sampson* almost wholly realized. The reason for Lessing's preference was that the comparative yield of tears was greater in one play than in the other. "In a single performance" of the *London Merchant*, he wrote, "more tears were shed, even by the callous," than could "conceivably be shed in all possible performances" of *Der sterbende Cato*, "even by the most sensitive."[2] As he confessed to Moses Mendelssohn in 1756: "I hate French tragedies; they wring a few tears from me at the very end of the fifth act. The true poet distributes sympathy through his whole tragedy."[3] Lessing's efforts to evoke these tears seem laughable today, as do similar efforts by Diderot. But contemporary audiences, from the premiere on, cried steadily for the whole length of the play or broke into fits of hysterical laughter when their weeping became unbearable. And in any event, the glory

---

[2] "Vorrede," to the translation of "Des Herrn Jacob Thomsons sämtliche Trauerspiele," ibid., VII, 68.
[3] Lessing to Mendelssohn, December 18, 1756. Ibid., XVII, 80.

of *Miss Sara Sampson* soon faded, even for its author. It remained a landmark, if in the long run an inconspicuous one, in Lessing's struggle against rationalism, against the neoclassical genres, against France. In 1760, Lessing left Berlin for Breslau, his long apprenticeship behind him, ready for the work that would be his real claim to a share in the aesthetic revolution of his time.

III

Laocoön, the most celebrated product of Lessing's years in Breslau and still Lessing's best-known work of criticism, was a decisive contribution to a widespread debate. Since the Renaissance, Horace's laconic pronouncement that painting and poetry are sister arts—*ut pictura poesis*—had evoked reiterated references to the painterly virtues of poetry and the poetic value of painting and innumerable paintings that told stories and poems that painted scenes. Then, in the eighteenth century, English and French writers on aesthetics began to throw doubt on the doctrine, and sought to clarify the nature of each art by clarifying their relations to one another. Among these writers was Diderot, although his speculations on the question were for years characteristically tentative and ambiguous. On the one hand he had cheerfully applied terms of one art to others; he had called Richardson a painter of nature and his novels, dramas,[4] and had sought for painterly effects in his plays. As more than one critic has noticed, the edifying tableaux that populate Diderot's *Fils naturel* and *Père de famille*—stagy groupings in which he took great pride—closely resembled the sentimental gatherings in Greuze's moralizing canvases. On the other hand he had thrown out casual, tantalizing hints as early as 1751 that the painter has only a single moment at his disposal, while the poet and musician deal with successive moments, and in 1757—while Lessing was debating the question in his correspondence with Moses Mendelssohn—he had suggested that while all the arts imitate nature, they do so in accord with their inner laws: "Each art imitates in the manner ap-

---

[4] See above, 260; and "O my friends! *Pamela, Clarissa,* and *Grandison* are three great dramas!" *Éloge de Richardson,* in *Œuvres esthétiques,* 33.

propriate to it."[5] And in his *Salon* of 1767 he finally made a frontal attack on the doctrine of *ut pictura poesis*, which he thought had caused endless mischief: painting is *not* like poetry: "*Ut pictura poesis non erit.*"[6]

By this time, Lessing's *Laocoön*, written explicitly to determine "the boundaries of painting and poetry," had been before the public for a year. It remains uncertain whether Lessing's brilliant essay was directly indebted to Diderot.[7] But Lessing did not need Diderot's fugitive hints; the question was in the air. As he observes in the preface to *Laocoön*, the attempt to classify the arts, if only by epigram, went back to the Greeks; perhaps its first pungent expression was the "brilliant antithesis" of the "Greek Voltaire," Simonides of Ceos: "Painting is mute poetry, and poetry speaking painting." Lessing found much truth in the saying, truth so obvious that it had induced critics to neglect what is "uncertain and untrue" in it[8]; he cites the Renaissance critic Dolce, and such contemporary critics as Joseph Spence and the comte de Caylus in evidence that the old *bon mot* has survived into the eighteenth century to confuse criticism and cripple both painting and poetry: poets, Lessing said severely, had fallen victim to a mania for description—*Schilderungssucht*—while painters suffered from the disease of allegory-making—*Allegoristerey*. He knew that he was not alone in his disapproval; thirty years before Diderot, the abbé Dubos had already suggested that painters and poets each have subjects they can do best. Lessing claimed that he was merely collecting notes—Germans, he sarcastically suggested, did not suffer from any shortage of systematic works. But his intention was more ambitious than that; it was to give Mendelssohn's ideas, and his own, a lucid and persuasive form, and to "counteract" the "false taste" and the "unfounded judgments" dominating the arts in his time.[9]

The argument of Lessing's *Laocoön* is thoroughly familiar. In

---

[5] *Entretiens sur le Fils naturel*, in ibid., 168; see also *Lettre sur les sourds et muets*, ed. Paul Hugo Meyer (1965), 84.

[6] Salon of 1767; *Salons*, III, 108.

[7] Lessing had certainly read Diderot's *Lettre sur les sourds et muets* with care—he had, in any event, reviewed it, and he had translated Diderot's *Entretiens sur le Fils naturel*.

[8] "Vorrede," to Lessing: *Laocoön*, ed. Hugo Blümner (2nd edn., 1880), 146-7.

[9] Ibid., 147-8.

his essay of 1755, *Gedanken über die Nachahmung der griechischen Werke in der Malerei und Bildhauerkunst*, Winckelmann had argued that Greek painting and sculpture are characterized by "noble simplicity and quiet grandeur—*edle Einfalt und stille Grösse*," qualities evident even in the sculpture depicting the Trojan priest Laocoön and his two sons being attacked by two snakes—that celebrated group first rediscovered in Rome in 1506 and widely admired since, though, Winckelmann argued, for the wrong reason: for its alleged vivid portrayal of extreme horror and violent torment. In the *Aeneid* Vergil has his Laocoön screaming; the sculptor, in full accord with the Greek ideal, has him emitting a sigh. Laocoön suffers, as Sophocles' Philoctetes suffers, with soul-piercing anguish, but with enviable nobility and endurance.

Lessing quotes this passage from Winckelmann at length—it is his text—and does not dissent from Winckelmann's view of the statue and praise of its sculptor. But he rejects Winckelmann's reasoning and his general interpretation of Greek literature: Philoctetes shouts and curses and disrupts sacred rites; Homer's bravest warriors cry as they fall; Mars screams; "Venus, barely scratched, shrieks aloud." The Greeks, in a word, far from always displaying quiet grandeur, gave voice to their feelings with a freedom we no longer enjoy. The lost *Laocoön* of Sophocles surely would have shown the Trojan priest as no more Stoical than Philoctetes. "All Stoicism is undramatic"; admiration for greatness of soul is cool indeed. It follows that if the statue of Laocoön does not show him screaming, this cannot be (as Winckelmann had claimed) because screaming is incompatible with the Greek character. "There must be another reason" why the sculptor "differs on this point from his rival, the poet."[1] To seek this other reason is Lessing's self-imposed problem; to find it is its solution.

For the ancients, Lessing begins, "beauty was the highest law for the visual arts." The sculptor of the Laocoön group was therefore obliged to moderate the priest's sufferings; a bellow of pain, which can only be depicted by a wide-open mouth and a contorted face, would have made the statue repulsive. Hence, in the visual arts, the Greeks reduced rage to seriousness, anguish to sadness. This, as the ancients understood, is necessary particularly because the spec-

---

[1] "I," ibid., 149–54.

tator's imagination completes the impression the work of art must only suggest: a man shown broadly smiling will soon turn into a grinning fop, a Laocoön shown screaming will soon become unbearable to look upon. That is why, since they must select a single moment, the painter and the sculptor must avoid the climax of an action: to judge from descriptions, the Greek painter Timomachus had portrayed Medea not in the act of murdering her children, but a few moments before, when maternal love still struggled with the lust for revenge. And Timanthes had painted the sacrifice of Iphigenia with each witness expressing his appropriate measure of sadness, but he had veiled the face of Agamemnon, distorted as it must be by a father's anguish; this, Lessing insists, demonstrates not the painter's incapacity, but his recognition that Agamemnon's face properly painted would have made the picture hideous. "Timanthes knew the limits that the Graces had set for his art." His subject did not permit him to pass over ugliness; "what then was left to him but to veil it? What he was not permitted to paint he allowed to be guessed."[2]

But while the sculptor cannot permit Laocoön to scream, Vergil has every right to show him in all the violence of his last moments. For the possibilities of poetry, and its tasks—and here Lessing approaches his solution with the characteristic bias of the man of words—differ in their very essence from those of painting or sculpture. Poetry has a wider range than painting, "it has at its disposal beauties that painting can never reach."[3] While their sense of decorum should keep poets from depicting the extremely repellent, like Dante's Ugolino, they *can* fully describe a Venus angry, something the painter cannot do without turning his goddess into someone else. Painting, Lessing holds, in complete disregard for the deep emotions and hidden qualities a great portraitist suggests on the canvas, can only show visible action, in only one way, and only at one moment. The superiority of poetry lies chiefly in this: "The poet conducts us through a whole gallery of paintings."[4]

Here, then, is Lessing's solution. "I argue as follows: if it is true that painting and poetry use for their imitations completely different means or signs, namely, the one figures and colors in space, and

---

[2] "II," ibid., 155–63.
[3] "VIII," ibid., 211.
[4] "XIII," ibid., 244.

the other articulated sounds in time," it must follow that signs which coexist in time can only express objects that coexist, while signs that follow one another can only express objects that are consecutive. The former objects are bodies—the proper subject of painting; the latter are actions—the proper subject of poetry. Of course, since bodies persist in time, a painting may suggest an action; and since actions require actors, poetry can suggest bodies—for all his legislative intentions, Lessing is not wholly dogmatic. But he insists that each art has its distinct center of gravity. "Painting in its simultaneous compositions can utilize only a single moment of an action, and must therefore choose the most suggestive—*prägnantesten*," while "poetry in its progressive imitations can utilize only a single property of bodies, and must therefore choose the one that calls up the most sensuous image—*sinnlichste Bild*—of the body."[5]

A little apologetically, Lessing calls this a "dry chain of reasoning"[6]—dry but, he claims, far from abstract; it draws on a specific model, Homer, and aims at specific vices, at contemporary poetic practice like Haller's *Die Alpen*, which seeks to evoke the spectacle of a flower-strewn alpine meadow by listing each flower in turn and describing each with vivid metaphor. Haller's word painting, Lessing argues, is, as it must be, a failure: the poet has invaded the painter's domain. In contrast, Lessing invites the reader to admire the shrewdness and tact of Homer: trying to persuade his readers that Helen is the most desirable woman in the world, he does not trouble to picture her trait by beautiful trait; rather, he makes the reader experience her beauty by describing the ecstatic response of the Trojan elders to her appearance—here is a woman worth fighting a war over! Once again, modern folly and confusion are reproved by antique intelligence and moderation.

Lessing's *Laocoön* thus exemplifies the familiar dialectic; it is an appeal from a misunderstood antiquity to antiquity read right, for the sake of clarity in modern criticism and modern art. *Laocoön* is distinctly the work of an anticophile, if not an anticomaniac. Only a critic who has concentrated his attention on the ancients—a critic, I might add, who has read many classical texts but seen little modern art—could have wondered, as Lessing wondered, "whether it would

[5] "XVI," ibid., 250–1.
[6] Ibid., 252.

not have been desirable if the art of oil painting had never been invented"[7]—a depressing thought that could never have occurred even to a fanatical classicist like the comte de Caylus. "The count," Lessing says in Laocoön, "understood painting better than poetry."[8] It is appropriate to turn this patronizing judgment against its author: the critic understood poetry better than painting.

He did not even fully understand poetry. For Laocoön is a curiously constricted book, reflecting the limitations of Lessing's aesthetic opportunities, of his taste, and of his age. He wrote about Laocoön without ever having seen it. Just as Winckelmann, the discoverer of Greece, never went to Greece, Lessing, who based his whole argument on the appearance of a statue, never went to Italy; in fact, he never even saw plaster casts, but relied on inaccurate engravings that rather underplayed its unclassical Hellenistic distortions. He wrote about painting having seen few paintings—after all, most of the pictures he discusses in Laocoön had disappeared, and survived only in descriptions—and he was remarkably obtuse to purely painterly values—color, composition, expression, and those subject matters that, like landscape or still life, failed to glorify the human figure. He wrote about poetry without a feeling for the lyrical genre. His soundest judgments reflect his grasp of classical principles, his most disappointing ideas his failure to sympathize fully with contemporary artistic developments.

At the same time, Lessing's most perceptive contemporaries saw Laocoön as a bold blow for modernity. Goethe was only the most eloquent of Lessing's readers: "One must be a young man," he wrote, "to recognize what effect Lessing's Laocoön had upon us. It carried us from the region of poverty-stricken notions to the open country of thought."[9] They were right: with all its obvious defects, Laocoön is a splendid representative of the constructive criticism— "creative criticism," as Dilthey calls it—that was one of the special achievements of the Enlightenment. As Goethe and others noted,

---

[7] Notes from the Nachlass in ibid., 469; Wellek (History of Modern Criticism, I, 166) has also noted this passage.
[8] "XI," Laocoön, 229.
[9] Dichtung und Wahrheit, in Gedenkausgabe, X, 348. Ernst Cassirer quotes this passage on the last page (360) of The Philosophy of the Enlightenment.

Laocoön ruined once and for all the doctrine of *ut pictura poesis* and opened new vistas for poets and sculptors and painters by assigning to each their own field of strength.

But while *Laocoön* is a document of the Enlightenment, it is remarkably disinterested, aloof from the battlefields of religious and political disputation on which the philosophes customarily displayed their forensic talents. It was only with the *Hamburgische Dramaturgie*, which is in a sense a continuation of *Laocoön*, that Lessing returned to familiar territory. The *Dramaturgie* is the *Laocoön* of the drama, but it is more than that. The *Hamburgische Dramaturgie* is explicitly directed against France and against neoclassicism, two targets which, in Lessing's polemic, coalesce into a single menacing figure: an incubus from which the German theater must be freed.

Much like Diderot's criticism, the *Hamburgische Dramaturgie* is unsystematic but enormously suggestive, an occasional work that rises above its occasion. Lessing produced it, as most philosophes produced their writings, amid the pressure of work and in response to a demand. In 1766, the year of *Laocoön*, the city of Hamburg had founded a "German National Theater"—the ambitious title represented a cherished fantasy—and in 1767 Lessing joined the venture as *Dramaturg*, a mixture of literary adviser to playwrights, critical observer of actors, reviewer and public educator. The enterprise was a failure. For a time Lessing reviewed current productions, but he found German actors, and, worse than that, German actresses, so avid of praise and sensitive to criticism that, at first irritated and then disillusioned, he soon retreated from reviewing to general principles. It was just as well: the theater failed late in 1768. Lessing then collected his papers and published them in two volumes in 1769. Hamburg's loss was the Enlightenment's gain; in the *Dramaturgie* Lessing extends his search for clarity to the theater, with impressive vigor and, in welcome contrast to his writings on the plastic arts, animated by the breath of experience.

Lessing's task in the *Dramaturgie* was precisely the task he had faced in *Laocoön*: he felt compelled to rescue the classics from the neoclassicists. His appeal to antiquity was strategic. It was necessary to demonstrate that the French neoclassical drama had reduced the theater to a cold, mechanical spectacle—Lessing's denunciations of Corneille and Voltaire, the two French playwrights most influential in Germany, are almost unrelieved hysteria; but beyond that it was necessary to rescue the Germans from the brink of another disaster—"We were on the verge of mischievously discarding all experience of the past, and of asking each poet and playwright to discover the art anew for himself."[1] Lessing saw the *Stürmer und Dränger* of his day as children, almost as savages, who wished to blot out the past rather than study and transform it; this was a barbarism from which any philosophe, no matter how much in love with the future, must, as a good classicist, recoil. "Thank Heaven," Lessing wrote sarcastically, "we now have a generation of critics whose best criticism consists in—bringing suspicion on all criticism. They scream, 'Genius! Genius!' "[2] Lessing himself had once or twice screamed "Genius! Genius!" in the *Hamburgische Dramaturgie*, but his admiration for the artist who depends solely on his own creative resources was always controlled by his respect for intelligence and craftsmanship. Freedom, the *Dramaturgie* implies in chapter after chapter, is not the enemy but the product of form; that is why the two heroes of the book are Aristotle and Shakespeare, the legislator and the poet, portrayed as grievously misread by Frenchmen and Germans alike.

Lessing interpreted the teaching of Aristotle and the practice of Shakespeare as proof that rules are essential, but they must be organic to the art from which they are evolved; they must codify its inner laws rather than impose external legislation. Much like the mature Diderot, Lessing accepted most of the canons of neoclassicism. But he thought that neoclassical dramatists had taken sensible prescriptions into absurdity: in their search for truth they had converted the playwright into a historian, in their slavish imitations they had tried to reproduce reality instead of appearance, in their obedience to propriety they had driven real characters from the stage, in their passion for morals they had devised dry didactic dramas, and in their rage for order they had imposed the three unities, which are mechanical, ridiculous, and in any case rarely observed. Again like Diderot, in addition to defending neoclassicism against itself, Lessing called for reforms in the neoclassical scheme: in good

---

[1] "101st to 104th Number," *Hamburgische Dramaturgie*, in *Schriften*, X, 215.
[2] "96th Number," ibid., 190.

hands—that is, certainly in Diderot's and perhaps in Lessing's own hands—the bourgeois tragedy, which according to neoclassical doctrine is a hybrid, is a perfectly acceptable genre. Indeed, Lessing insists that tragedy is about ordinary men whose fate the spectator observes with pity, and from which he derives moral and even a kind of religious edification.

It is easy to show, and critics have long complained, that this analysis is inconclusive, incomplete, and often inconsistent. Lessing fails to deal justly with the French, whose theater he treats highly selectively, with a view to its flaws rather than its accomplishments; he robs tragedy of its grandeur; and he can never decide whether the drama creates a world of its own or mirrors, enters, and improves the real world. And Lessing's own later plays—the charming comedy *Minna von Barnhelm*, the influential but rather earth-bound tragedy *Emilia Galotti*, and his famous *Nathan der Weise*, that enlightened sermon on toleration—underscore, for all their merits, the limitations of his talent. But the limitations were not Lessing's alone; the failure of the Hamburg theater was a symptom of a wider malaise. What Lessing had sadly noted in the 1750s he noted once again in the late 1760s, with abundant experience behind him: "Let me say it right out": compared to the French, the Germans "are still true barbarians, more barbarian than our most barbarian forefathers." To provide the Germans with a national theater is "a good-natured," that is to say, a well-meaning but slightly ludicrous idea: the Germans are not yet a nation. "I am speaking not of a political constitution but only of our moral character. And that, one might almost say, consists of not wanting to have one. We are still the sworn imitators of everything foreign, especially the servile admirers of the never-to-be-enough-admired French; whatever comes to us from beyond the Rhine is beautiful, charming, delightful, divine."[3] Lessing was tired when he wrote these words, tired and angry, and, just as he had earlier been inclined to overestimate, he now underestimated his own influence. In any event, under the circumstances of his Germany a certain measure of failure was foreordained. Had Lessing lived beyond 1781 he would have found consolation: after all, had he not helped to create the atmosphere in which Goethe could breathe?

---

[3] "101st to 104th Number," ibid., 213.

IV

The 1760s were as decisive for Diderot as they were for Lessing, though for different reasons. They were years of education through adversity. Diderot was visibly depressed by the failure of his *Père de famille* in 1761, harassed even beyond his endurance by his editorship of the *Encyclopédie*, disappointed by the desertion of d'Alembert and shaken by his estrangement from Rousseau. He thought he was getting old: he was nearing fifty, with little to show for his pains but some fugitive successes and an uncertain fame. But his resiliency served him well. Late in 1762 he discovered *Tristram Shandy*, by "Mr. Stern," the "English Rabelais,"[4] and he permitted the novel to work in him, unconsciously. In the deepest privacy he began to write *Le neveu de Rameau*. Perhaps most beneficial of all, he discovered art criticism.

In 1759, Diderot's friend Grimm, who had been reviewing the biennial Salons in his *Correspondance littéraire* since 1751, had asked Diderot to relieve him of this burden. It proved to be a piece of luck that Diderot's talents deserved; his *Salons*, probably even more than Laurence Sterne, became the agents of his aesthetic liberation. As early as 1751, in his *Lettre sur les sourds et muets*, Diderot had dismissed Batteux's attempt to reduce all aesthetics to an imitation of *la belle nature*, but his own aesthetic ideas had been in some respects as simplistic as Batteux's, in others, more confused. Now, in the course of testing his ideas in a new field, he revised them in all fields.

His first three *Salons*, it is true, were still under the sign of his uncompromising moral realism. But as he moved from 1759 to 1761, and from 1761 to 1763, his reports swelled in volume, grew in brilliance, and displayed more and more touches of his passionate and problematic individuality. In 1759, he was still in search of veracious imitation; he singled out Chardin—not for the last time—for embodying "nature and truth": one is tempted to "take his bottles by the neck"; his "peaches and raisins awake the appetite and invite the

---

[4] Diderot to Sophie Volland (October 7, 1762). *Correspondance*, IV, 189.

hand."[5] And he praised a head of the sculptor Le Moyne by his pupil Pajou for the same reason: "What a beautiful bust! It lives, it thinks, it looks, it sees, it hears, it is about to speak."[6] In contrast, Carle Van Loo's *Medea* is a bad painting because it is theatrical and false: "This painter neither thinks nor feels."[7] Yet in this very first *Salon*, his sensibility contended with his principles. Boucher, whom he despised as corrupt, courtly, and lascivious, in a word, immoral, exhibited a nativity scene that Diderot found offensive in many respects: its color is wrong, its brilliance is out of place—and yet, how gratifying to the senses: "The Virgin is so beautiful, so loving and so touching." And he confessed, "I would not be displeased to have this picture. Every time you came to see me, you would criticize it, but you would look at it."[8] Diderot the critic was trying to be honest with himself.

In the *Salons* of 1761 and 1763, Chardin remains Diderot's favorite for his extraordinary realism: "O Chardin! It is not white, red, black you grind on your palette: it is the very substance of objects, it is air and light which you put on the tip of your brush and attach to your canvas." Chardin paints nothing less than "nature itself"; his subjects are "of a veracity that deceives the eye"[9]—as though successful *trompe l'œil* were the highest form of art. Vien, too, is admirable because his pictures are truthful, free from exaggeration[1]; while Le Bel's *Soleil couchant* arrests the attention for its skillful imitation of the atmosphere.[2] And Diderot's contrast between Greuze and Boucher remains on the ground of morality: Boucher is wasting his valuable time and ruining his remarkable talent with his lasciviousness: "What colors! What variety! What wealth of objects and ideas! That man has everything, except the truth."[3] Greuze, on the other hand, whom Diderot compliments with detailed descriptions, is magnificent because he is moral. His *Paralytique* is a *tableau de mœurs;* his celebrated *Accordée de village* is a wholly successful scene, full of pathos, crowded without being dis-

---

[5] Salon of 1759; *Salons*, I, 66.
[6] Ibid., 69.
[7] Ibid., 64.
[8] Ibid., 68–9.
[9] Salon of 1763; ibid., 222.
[1] Salon of 1761; ibid., 118–20.
[2] Ibid., 127.
[3] Ibid., 112.

orderly, and touching: "His choice of subjects is a mark of sensibility and good morals."[4]

But this is not all. As Diderot's perceptions sharpen, his praise and his criticisms reach for new subtlety. Boucher is repellent in part because his realism is too explicit: "When one writes, must one write everything? When one paints, must one paint everything? Please, let my imagination supply something"[5]—a real advance over the literalism of his early plays. Yet Greuze, the moralist, is appealing in part because he is erotic: the young girl in the *Accordée de village*, though decently dressed, displays—or rather, lets the onlooker suspect—a lovely bosom.[6] Besides, Diderot is beginning to introduce criteria other than verisimilitude and morality. He finds Deshays's painting of *Saint Victor* impressive because it is at once simple and grand; Amédée Van Loo's *Deux Familles de satyres* gives him pleasure because it has "poetry, passion, naked flesh, character."[7] Visibly, Diderot was introducing new complications into his judgments.

Complication did not mean conversion; Diderot's continued admiration of Greuze and detestation of Boucher alone suggest the persistence of his tastes. Greuze's sly eroticism masquerading as didactic morality never wholly lost its power over him: "Here is your painter and mine," Diderot exclaimed in 1765, repeating an exclamation of 1763, "the first among us who dared to give morals to art."[8] In fact, Diderot failed to see in 1765 what he had seen in 1761: that Greuze's plump young mother surrounded by her adoring children, and his nubile young girl mourning her dead bird, are "charming" and "delicious" largely because they display their abundant physical charms in sentimental poses. And, as Greuze remained the beneficiary, Boucher remained the victim of Diderot's sentimentality: in 1765, he decisively disposed of Boucher, candidly and severely, as a whoremaster, a depraved courtier whose vices, the counterparts of his gifts, are on a grand scale. "I don't know what to say about that man. The degradation of taste, color, composition, characters, ex-

---

[4] Ibid., 135, 144.
[5] Salon of 1763; ibid., 205.
[6] Salon of 1761; ibid., 142; see above, 203.
[7] Ibid., 121, 123.
[8] Salon of 1765; *Salons*, II, 144. In 1763, Diderot had already called Greuze "my painter," *Salons*, I, 236.

pression, design, have followed the depravation of morals step by step. What do you want this artist to throw on the canvas? What he has in his imagination. And what can a man have in his imagination who spends his life with prostitutes of the lowest possible birth?"—a daring rhetorical question, since the *prostituées du plus bas étage* Diderot had in mind were not merely Boucher's models but Louis XV's mistresses—"I venture to say that that man does not really know what grace is; I venture to say that he has never known the truth; I venture to say that the ideas of delicacy, decency, innocence, simplicity, have practically become strangers to him," the man is mincing, affected, unacquainted with "severe art." Nor are his faults only moral: his colors are wrong and his compositions confused and busy: "He is the most mortal enemy of silence I know." He is not even a successful sensualist: "That man takes brush in hand only to show me tits and bottoms. I am delighted to see them, but I don't want them to be shown to me." In a word, Boucher is "a false good painter."[9]

While Diderot's cast of heroes and villains remained substantially unchanged, the *Salons*, like his other writings of the sixties, reach beyond the easy simplicities of melodrama to the problematic ambiguities of true drama. Had he ceased to write about art in 1763, he would be remembered mainly as a lively, often perceptive though rather unoriginal neoclassicist who had strained to force even his novel ideas into traditional patterns.[1] But, to everyone's benefit, he went on writing.

He knew that his work was better than ever. In November 1765, after two exhausting weeks of writing the great *Salon* of that year, he reported to Sophie Volland that Grimm was stupefied, con-

---

[9] Salon of 1765; *Salons*, II, 75–6. For the political meaning of his allusion to "prostitutes" see Vernière in Diderot: *Œuvres esthétiques*, 453 n.

[1] Thus he had argued that the three unities are the product of "the observations and experiences of centuries," a claim that was itself traditional; he had carefully placed his own dramas in the serious genre within the orderly hierarchy of the neoclassical canon; and he had, finally, praised Greuze by suggesting that he was, for all his genre paintings, practically a history painter. See *Entretiens sur le Fils naturel*, in *Œuvres esthétiques*, 82; Wellek: *History of Modern Criticism*, I, 53; Jean Seznec: "Diderot and Historical Painting," in Earl R. Wasserman, ed.: *"Aspects of the Eighteenth Century* (1965), 141.

vinced that "no man under heaven ever had made, or would make, a work like it." Engagingly, Diderot confessed that he was secretly vain enough to agree with him. Certainly, he told his mistress, "this is the best thing I've done since I began to cultivate literature." He admitted that at times he was torn apart by contradictory ideas, and assailed by guilt for his severity, but on the whole he was proud of his essay.[2]

He had every right to be. The *Salon* of 1765, like its successor of 1767 and, to a lesser degree, that of 1769, eloquently testifies to the evolution of Diderot's sensibility. He continued to moralize, but with more wit, more discrimination, and more control than before. Thus, in 1767, he lectured Baudouin for his *Coucher de la mariée*, a painting of a young bride being urged to enter the marriage bed. Her husband is imploring her on his knees, and a maid whispers to her—one can imagine what. The bride is *en déshabille*, crying; the bed, a looming affair with an enormous canopy, is open, and several other maids busy themselves about the room, unpacking, extinguishing candles. The whole picture, as Diderot instantly recognizes, breathes lubricity. "Monsieur Baudouin," he writes, "kindly tell me where in the world this scene took place. Certainly not in France. Here you have never seen a well-born, well-brought up young lady half nude, one knee on the bed, being solicited by her husband in the presence of her women who tug at her." Even "without the base, low, and dishonest faces the painter has given them, the role of these servants would be of an intolerable indecency." This is not a conjugal bedroom; it is a house of assignation: "All that's missing is an old crone." Diderot insists that he is not a bigot or a religious man, and that he has little taste for censorship: "I know that the man who suppresses a bad book, or destroys a voluptuous statue, resembles an idiot who is afraid to piss in a river for fear he might drown someone." Yet Baudouin's painting, with its improbability, its ill-chosen moment, its suggestiveness, unwittingly proves that morality and taste are inseparable. "Artists, if you are anxious for your work to last, I advise you to stick to decent subjects. Everything that urges men toward depravity was made to be destroyed; and destroyed all the more surely the more perfect the work."[3] This, like most of

[2] Diderot to Sophie Volland (November 10, 1765). *Correspondance*, V, 166-8.
[3] Salon of 1767; *Salons*, III, 197-8.

Diderot's art criticism, concentrates on the subject matter, the message of the painting, at the expense of purely aesthetic considerations, but Diderot is at last ready to present morality as a problem, with a lighter hand than before.

Diderot now offers better reasons for his continuing enthusiasm for Chardin. "Chardin is not a history painter," he writes in 1769, "but he is a great man"—and what could be higher praise from a critic who still respected the old hierarchies?[4] He continues to call Chardin truthful, but his truth—Diderot sees this now—is the truth of the creative artist: he achieves it through the energy and precision with which he lays on his colors, the sure taste with which he disposes of his masses. Chardin's is the harmony only an "old magician" can produce—and it is notorious that magicians achieve their effects not by slavishly copying but by persuasively suggesting an illusion of reality.[5]

That Diderot could admire Chardin, painter of humble domestic scenes and even humbler still lifes, had suggested from the outset the possibility that Diderot's taste might be superior to his principles. In the mid-1760s, his principles rose to meet his taste, and in the introductory pages to his *Salon* of 1767, a minor masterpiece of autobiographical musings, aesthetic theorizing, and invective against amateurs, Diderot at last seriously confronted the question of just where the artist is to find his model. A portrait, no matter how lovely, does not depict general beauty; by imitating the individual, it is only a copy of a copy. "Your line will not be the true line, the line of beauty, the ideal line, but a line somehow altered, deformed, portrait-like, individual."[6] (This, parenthetically, is why a history painter is likely to be a poor portraitist.[7] Where, then, the painter asks, is my true model? It is not in nature: "This model is purely ideal, and is not directly borrowed from any individual image in Nature." That, the painter objects, is embarrassing, it is metaphysics. Well, replies Diderot, anxious to share his newly found clarity: "You blockhead—*grosse bête*—doesn't your art have its metaphysics?"—and the most sublime metaphysics at that? In rebuttal,

[4] Salon of 1769; *Salons*, IV, 82.
[5] See ibid.; this formula had appeared as early as 1765 and reappeared in 1767: *Salons*, II, 111; and *Salons*, III, 128.
[6] Salon of 1767; *Salons*, III, 57.
[7] Ibid., 67, 339.

the painter offers Zeuxis' example: if I want to make a statue of a
lovely woman, I shall have a large number of girls undressed and
then choose the most beautiful parts of each. But Diderot rejects
even this compromise: "And how will you recognize beauty?" By
conforming to the ancients. Once again, Diderot, in full flight, refuses to accept what he would have taken for granted in earlier
years. "And if there were no antiquity, what would you do? You
don't answer. Then listen, for I'll try to explain to you how the
Ancients, who had no ancients, proceeded." Aware that every individual they could choose was somehow imperfect, in some way
remote from the ideal, the ancients advanced through "long observation, consummate experience, with exquisite tact, with a taste, an
instinct, a sort of inspiration given to a few geniuses," gradually,
slowly, laboriously erasing false lines, rising above the individuality
of the portrait to find the true line of beauty. We moderns can
follow them, not by correcting our view of nature by looking at
the ancients, for that would be to reverse their procedure, but by
looking at nature as the ancients did.[8]

In these fiery and inconclusive pages, Diderot attempts to define
the "ideal model" at which he had only hinted earlier. Grimm, to
whom they were addressed, was puzzled by them: his epithet for
Diderot, "our modern Plato,"[9] is half-ironic, half-admiring—and
half-mistaken. For Diderot did not merely correct his misreading of
Aristotle by appealing to Plato; his ideal model was beyond nature
only in the sense that no individual, no matter how beautiful, wholly
embodied it, and that no collection of individuals could, by a simple
process of combination, produce it. The ideal model was the product
of the artist's creative, inspired imagination, but it was, far from
being laid up in heaven, the fruit of labor and experience. In 1769,
Diderot summed up his new empirical Idealism with epigrammatic
economy: "In your place," he pointedly told Baudouin, "I'd rather
be a poor little eccentric—*original*—than a great copyist."[1] He
could not have written that sentence ten years before.

---

[8] Ibid., 57–64.
[9] Ibid., 57. Diderot had already referred to an "interior model," if
rather tentatively, as early as 1758; see *Discours sur la poésie dramatique*, in *Œuvres esthétiques*, 286.
[1] Salon of 1769; *Salons*, IV, 94.

V

While Lessing was breaking the grip of French neoclassicism in *Laocoön* and the *Hamburgische Dramaturgie*, Diderot was writing stories and dialogues in which he translated his private experience into fictions that could appeal to a circle wider than his intimates, a public that knew nothing of him. He was transforming biography into art. He was also returning, with new confidence and finer perceptions, to his first interest, the theater, and his writings of these years often read like answers to the *Entretiens* and the *Discours* of the 1750s. If his last *Salons* lack the fire and inventiveness of his masterly, profuse productions of the mid-sixties, this was not (as he put it, with excessive self-denigration) because he was burned out. Rather, he was turning his attention to a supremely difficult problem, central to his own aesthetics, as it was to the Enlightenment as a whole: the management of man's most magnificent and most dangerous endowment—the passions.

Diderot, as we know, praised the passions more freely and more frequently than his fellow philosophes. He celebrated them in his first philosophical essay, in his early writings on the theater, in his letters to Sophie Volland.[2] He dared to prize enthusiasm—a mental state that all philosophes, including Diderot, viewed with deep suspicion as a source of religious fanaticism—as a quality essential for the creation of sublime works of poetry, painting, eloquence, and music.[3] And as late as 1765 he could praise man's irrational, amoral powers regardless of their consequences: "I hate all those sordid little things that reveal only an abject soul; but I do not hate great crimes: first, because one makes beautiful paintings and fine tragedies of them; and besides, because great and sublime actions and great crimes have the same quality: energy."[4]

---

[2] See above, 186–9.
[3] See "Éclectisme," in *Œuvres*, XIV, 322.
[4] Salon of 1765; *Salons*, II, 144. Sir Joshua Reynolds has a very similar formulation: "It is undoubtedly true that the same qualities, united with virtue or with vice, make a hero or a rogue, a great general or a great highwayman." *Portraits*, 96.

Diderot never made a secret of the sexual roots nourishing his enthusiasm for enthusiasm. In his early *Entretiens* he had portrayed Dorval carried away by nature as though he were experiencing orgasm: "Enthusiasm is born of an object in nature." If the poet's spirit "has seen it in striking and diverse phases, it is absorbed, agitated, tormented. The imagination heats up; passion is stirred." It is in turn "amazed, moved, shocked, irritated." The moment of enthusiasm, which arrives after the poet has meditated, announces itself to him "by a shudder that starts from his chest and moves, deliciously and rapidly, to the extremities of his body. Soon it is no longer a shudder; it is a strong and enduring heat that inflames him, makes him pant, consumes him, kills him, but which gives spirit, life, to everything he touches. If this heat were to increase further, phantoms would multiply before him. His passion would rouse itself almost to madness. He would know relief only by pouring out a torrent of ideas which crowd, jostle, and chase one another."[5] Reason plays no part in artistic creation, and so, Diderot quite consistently concludes, "Poets, actors, musicians, painters, first-rate singers, great dancers, tender lovers, truly religious men—all that enthusiastic and passionate troop feels vividly and reflects little."[6]

This outburst was simply another instance of Diderot's early confusion of life and art. But his experience with both taught him the inadequacy of this facile equation. He retreated neither from his affection for spontaneity and imagination nor from his admiration for the genius who is sublimely indifferent to rules, but came to see that feelings must be subjected to the control of reason, and acquired new respect for the technical mastery of the craftsman. Sensibility alone, he now argues, is not enough; in fact, sensibility alone is likely to be unproductive and even dangerous. The creative artist cursed with extreme sensibility, he wrote, evidently and painfully using himself as an example, must make a real effort to dominate that sensibility and master his impulses. The unitarian priest of sensibility had become the trinitarian priest of sensibility, work, and intelligence.

Diderot long hesitated before his new, cooler aesthetic doctrine

---

[5] *Œuvres esthétiques*, 98. For another instance of what I have called Diderot's voyeurism of virtue, see *The Rise of Modern Paganism*, 187–8; and see above, 206.

[6] *Entretiens*, in *Œuvres esthétiques*, 104.

and felt visibly uncomfortable with it. As late as 1767, when he analyzed La Tour, one of his favorite painters, he uneasily mingled praise and criticism in almost undefinable quantities. "There is no poetry here; there is only painting. I have seen La Tour paint; he is calm and cold; he does not torture himself; he does not suffer; he does not pant." La Tour is simply a genius in technique, a "marvelous mechanic—*machiniste merveilleux*."[7]

Whatever Diderot's residual uneasiness, the theoretical gain of all this is considerable. In conceding that in art inspiration must be controlled by skill and sensibility by judgment, Diderot finally abandoned his simplistic view of art as a sheer outpouring of feeling, the direct translation of enthusiasm into tangible forms, and recognized that if the academic rationalism of his day had induced a deadly monotony, the naked emotionalism to which he had long been committed must induce an art as chaotic and private as it was self-indulgent. Diderot saw deeper and farther than this. He saw that the collaboration of reason and passion, or craftsmanship and enthusiasm, was at best uneasy and produced unending tensions, unstable compromises, and unresolvable ambiguities.

Diderot's *Paradoxe sur le comédien*, which he began to write in 1769, the very year he started on his *Rêve de d'Alembert* and began to lose interest in the *Salons*, is therefore an instructive document. It is, as is usual with Diderot's writings, autobiographical. Diderot portrays himself burdened by his sensibility, and makes himself into the victim of some self-lacerating anecdotes in which reflective intelligence wins out over the kind of uncontrollable spontaneity that he, with obvious regret, finds typical of himself. The anecdotes do not quite make the point they are intended to make: in the very telling, Diderot shows himself superior to the self-caricature he has drawn. But they relate, once again, Diderot's experience to his philosophy. And the *Paradoxe* is autobiographical in still another way: just as it had been his study of painters that helped him to refine his art criticism, it was his study of actors that helped him to refine his drama criticism: Garrick did for the *Paradoxe* what Chardin had done for the *Salons*.

But it is the objective rather than the biographical meaning that gives the *Paradoxe* its importance. With great dialectical skill, Di-

---

[7] Salon of 1767; *Salons*, III, 168–9.

derot confronts his doctrine of experience with his doctrine of artfulness, in language familiar to, and often drawn directly from, his *Salons*. The great actor, like the great painter, performs with his ideal model in his mind's eye, a model he has purified, step by step, in long practice. Chardin had proved that great genre painting is possible only to old men or men who are born old; similarly, only an actor who "has trod the boards for long years" is likely to do justice to a part calling for the first youth.

This argument, though important, is only a preface to the central problem of Diderot's dialogue: the successful actor, who must convincingly portray emotions, must himself be cool. Diderot wants the actor to have "much good judgment," and to be a "cold and tranquil spectator." He must have "penetration and no sensibility, the art of imitating everything or, which comes to the same thing, an equal aptitude for all sorts of characters and roles." No sensibility—essentially the *Paradoxe* is a debate rehearsing variations on this single point. The actor who feels the passions he portrays can never give the same performance two days running: even if he feels them at the premiere, routine must take over: everything must be "measured, combined, learned, ordered in his head." It is the task of "*sang-froid* to temper the delirium of enthusiasm." This is why the good actor leaves the tragedy tired, while the spectator leaves it sad. This is why the actor who portrays himself—the miser playing a miser, the voluptuary playing a voluptuary—must miss the essence of his role, and descend to satire: "Satire is about a tartuffe, and the play is about Tartuffe." This is why the actor finds sensibility a liability rather than an asset. "Sensibility is scarcely the quality of a great genius"; inborn or cultivated, sensibility is, after all, nothing more than a "disposition that accompanies the weakness of the organs, a consequence of the mobility of the diaphragm, the vivacity of the imagination, the delicacy of the nerves, which inclines a person to sympathize, shiver, wonder, fear, become agitated, weep, faint, help, flee, shout, lose his reason, exaggerate, despise, disdain, have no precise idea of the true, the good, and the beautiful, be unjust, be mad." Such a quality can only lead to bad acting. "The tears of the actor descend from his head; those of the sensible man rise from his heart." A good actor has listened to himself, and "his whole talent consists not of feeling, as you suppose, but of rendering as scrupulously as possible the external signs of sentiment." His "cries of pain are noted down in his ear." In a word, "great poets, the great actors, and perhaps all the great imitators of nature in general, whoever they are, endowed as they are with a fine imagination, excellent judgment, fine tact, absolutely sure taste, have less sensibility than anyone. They are equally well equipped for too many things; they are too busy looking, recognizing, and imitating, to be vividly affected within themselves. I see them ceaselessly with their portfolios on their knees and their pencil in their hand."[8] Sir Joshua Reynolds, who, like Diderot, had learned much of what he knew about acting from Garrick, said the same thing in his own way: he rejected "the vulgar opinion" that the artist, whatever his art, is "possessed himself with the passion which he wished to excite." This was certainly true of the great actor. "Garrick's trade was to represent passion, not to feel it." Clearly, "Garrick left nothing to chance. Every gesture, every expression of countenance and variation of voice, was settled in his closet before he set his foot upon the stage."[9] The English and the French Enlightenments discarded the naïve theory of imitation at about the same time.

Some years before he wrote the *Paradoxe*, Diderot had told a young friend, the actress Mlle. Jodin, dogmatically enough: "An actor who has only good sense and judgment is cold; the one who has only verve and sensibility is mad."[1] But the *Paradoxe* itself is free from this paradox. It is, rather, a forceful claim in behalf of intelligence in artistic creation and the autonomy of art. This is Diderot's great insight of the 1760s: the truth the actor obeys is the ideal model that he acquires—wrests, as it were, from experience—through patient practice and long refinement, fully aware that even when he seems to be imitating nature he is really obeying art, for art and nature are not the same. The actor who dies must die dramatically, following certain rules, just as the ancient gladiator did. "How could nature form a great actor without art, since nothing happens on stage precisely as it does in nature, and since dramatic works are all composed on a certain system of principles? And how could a role be acted in the same manner by two different actors, since in the clearest, the most precise, the most energetic writer the words

---

[8] *Paradoxe sur le comédien*, in *Œuvres esthétiques*, 322, 306, 307, 309, 313, 338, 310, 343, 313, 312, 310.
[9] Reynolds: *Portraits*, 51–2, 104–5.
[1] (1766?). *Correspondance*, VI, 168.

are only, and can only be, signs approached by a thought, a sentiment, an idea?"[2] With this rhetorical question, Diderot has wholly
overcome naturalism.

There is one respect in which acting reaches down to the deepest ambiguities of creativity. The actor is the accomplished craftsman, but he enters, at the same time, into his character; that great
actress, Mlle. Clairon, whom Diderot and Voltaire so much admired,
remains, yet transcends, herself: "In that moment, she is double: the
little Clairon and the great Agrippina."[3] Diderot had observed this
inner split before, in his own person; in 1758, he had told Madame
Riccoboni that he was not a wit but a deeply sensitive being, ready
to smile, weep, admire freely, and at the same time, capable of step-
ping outside himself. "*Je sais aussi m'aliéner.*"[4]

As Diderot's aesthetics grew more rigorous, more disciplined,
this capacity for detachment, which gave him inner distance and
permitted him to analyze and to check passion without freezing it
to death, came to occupy an ever more prominent part of his thinking. In the early 1770s it even invaded a strategic stronghold—
Diderot's view of genius.

The most conservative neoclassical theorists had made room for
the untrammeled originality of the genius. Even a rationalist like
Boileau acknowledged the elemental force of genius, and Pope
spoke, in measured tones but with full approval, of "a grace beyond
the reach of art."[5] For these writers, as for reformers like Dubos,
genius was the highest form of talent, it was originality, great power
of invention and execution, a happy natural endowment for finding
aesthetic forms and making aesthetic impressions that differed from
ordinary craftsmanship merely in degree. This was the view of

---

[2] *Paradoxe sur le comédien,* in *Œuvres esthétiques,* 304. Once again
Reynolds is worth quoting: "Theatrical representation" has "its
mode of imitating nature. The best acted scene, the most pathetic
and what we call the most natural, will be found on examination
very affected, and is really very different from a similar scene in
real life." *Portraits,* 157.
[3] *Paradoxe sur le comédien,* in *Œuvres esthétiques,* 309.
[4] (November 27, 1758). *Correspondance,* II, 96–7. Italics mine.
[5] "Great wits sometimes may gloriously offend, / And rise to
faults true critics dare not mend; / From vulgar bounds with brave
disorder part, / And snatch a grace beyond the reach of art. . . ."
Essay on Criticism, I, 152–5. Reynolds, among others, quotes the
crucial line in the first of his Discourses.

Reynolds as it was the view of Voltaire. "Fundamentally," Voltaire rhetorically asked in the early 1770s, "is genius anything else but talent?"[6] Genius is great talent, intelligently recognized and assiduously cultivated.

Diderot found this prevalent view dry and rationalistic; it gave too little play to individuality. As a good disciple of Shaftesbury, as an advocate of the passions and of enthusiasm, the young Diderot strictly differentiated the talented craftsman from that unusual, highly individualistic creature, the genius: he is nature's gift to art; others are laborious, he is quick; far from imitating, he finds imitators—he is original in the best sense of this word. Diderot never gave up his admiration for such an extraordinary being, and he pursued this train of thought into the 1770s. When he wrote his refutation of Helvétius's posthumous *De l'Homme* in 1773 he insisted that Helvétius had spoken of genius in the way "a blind man speaks of colors": the "tyrannical impulsion of genius is alien to him."[7]

At the same time, in full accord with his later emphasis on reason and control, Diderot refused to drive his irrationalism to the length it was being driven by the *Stürmer und Dränger*, and would be driven by the Romantics. In a fragment, probably of 1772, Diderot defined genius as a mysterious but not wholly inexplicable quality in which alertness and detachment were as important as sheer inner irrational potency: Men of genius, he writes, poets, philosophers, painters, musicians, have a certain secret, indefinable quality of mind without which nothing great or beautiful can be produced. What is this quality? It is not imagination, or judgment, or wit, or warmth, or sensibility, or good taste. Diderot is willing to accept the common view that it consists of a certain "conformity of head and viscera," but he insists that nobody knows the precise character of that conformity, and insists, in addition, on adding another quality to it, the *esprit observateur*, a gift for effortless seeing and self-instruction, a rare form of judgment which is a kind of prophetic spirit. It does not guarantee success, but the failures of the genius are never contemptible: "The man of genius knows what

---

[6] "Génie," *Questions sur l'Encyclopédie*, in *Œuvres*, XIX, 245. On the page just preceding, however, Voltaire insists that not all great talent may lay claim to the name of genius; only "inventive" talent may, and the inventiveness must "seem to be a gift of the gods."
[7] *Réfutation de l'ouvrage intitulé de l'Homme*, in *Œuvres*, II, 341.

he stakes, and he knows it without having weighed the chances for and against; that calculation was all made in his head."[8] The fragment is short and incomplete, as elusive as the quality it seeks to define. But its attempt to combine rationalism with irrationalism, its insistence that the quality of genius, though rare, mysterious, and nonrational, is still human, amenable to analysis, and allied to reason, is typical of the later Diderot. It makes Diderot's last works—the long defense of the Stoic Seneca and, even more important, his last play, *Est-il bon? Est-il méchant?*—wholly comprehensible.

Est-il bon? Est-il méchant?, Diderot's best play—it has been badly neglected—was written out of Diderot's capacity for detachment and analysis; its protagonist, Hardouin, conducts a public examination of his innermost motives. It has all the characteristics of a late work; it is an autumnal comedy, light and yet curiously grave, and its tone perfectly matches the time of its composition: Diderot began to write it in the early 1770s, revised it several times and completed it around 1783, when he was seventy. It was precisely in these years—1776 to 1779—that Lessing worked out the final version of his *Nathan der Weise;* the two most striking representatives of Enlightenment theater, one psychological, the other didactic, belong to its last period.

Est-il bon? Est-il méchant? is a kind of belated criticism of *Le Fils naturel* and *Le père de famille;* it demonstrates that these earlier plays had to fail because they had not been, for all their supposed realism, realistic enough: they had put on stage caricatures rather than characters and offered, with their prosaic speeches and naturalistic stage settings, the mere surface of reality. *Est-il bon? Est-il méchant?* is, in its own way, a realistic play; it draws most of its characters, and most of its incidents, from life. Yet it leaves the realm of anecdote to explore the mysteries of character and of moral action. An air of resignation hangs over it: *Est-il bon?* reads like the last word of a pagan sage who expects little from the world and, indeed, from himself.

Le Fils naturel and *Le père de famille* were nothing if not obvious; *Est-il bon? Est-il méchant?* is a puzzle, almost a mystification. Diderot forces an unconventional action into a conventional setting:

8 "Génie," in *Œuvres esthétiques*, 19–20.

the play is like a French provincial room hung with abstract paintings. Hardouin acts on the surface like a stock figure of comedy. With unbelievable ease, and within an unbelievably short time, he solves the problems of his friends and of strangers who happen to come his way. He persuades a temperamental mother to let her daughter marry the man she loves. He obtains a pension for the beautiful young widow of a captain drowned in the line of duty. He settles a lawsuit to everyone's satisfaction. But he employs unconventional, shabby, even vicious means to accomplish his purposes: he intimates that the young widow—whom he has only seen once—is his mistress and her son his bastard; he wins the mother's consent by claiming—falsely—that her daughter is pregnant. While all ends well and everyone forgives Hardouin, his beneficiaries are often angry at him and not likely to be grateful.

The action of the play is slight, but Hardouin—that is, Diderot—is thoroughly modern in his complexity. He is daemonic, almost diabolical, but he is no Mephistopheles: it is not that he wills the evil and does good; he wishes to do good, but with evil—or at least with his own—means. Hardouin is puzzled, gravely troubled, by himself; he knows his capacity for making mischief and regrets the pleasure he takes in playing games with the lives of others: "I, a good man, as people say? I'm nothing of the kind. I was born essentially hard, bad, perverse. I'm practically moved to tears by the tenderness of that mother for her child, her sensibility, her gratitude; I might even develop a taste for her; and despite myself I persist in the project that may make her miserable . . . Hardouin, you amuse yourself with everything; nothing is sacred to you; you're a regular monster . . . That's bad, very bad . . . You must absolutely get rid of this bad inclination . . . and renounce the prank I've planned? . . . Oh, no . . . But after this one, no more, no more. It will be the last one of my life."

The play is a psychological drama, an unsparing self-exploration, partly serene in its acceptance of life, partly heavy with world-weariness. But it is also a morality tale about the meaning of freedom. Hardouin is tired of the world, "very tired," largely, it seems, because he is not his own master. A dramatist well supplied with friends, but poor and unrecognized, he has spent his life working too hard, depending on others, and making compromises that disgusted him. His restlessness is a critique of his passivity. "I was born, I think, to do nothing that pleases me, to do everything that others demand, and to satisfy nobody—no, nobody—not even myself." In his disappointment with himself and his persistent desire for autonomy, Hardouin feels compelled to resist what he really wishes to do, and to refuse to do—or at least do in his strange and solitary way— what he thinks he really should do. The question, Is he good, is he bad?, baldly asked in the title, is asked again in the last scene, and answered with commonplaces that solve nothing:

"Is he good? Is he bad?"
"One after the other."
"Like you, like me, like everybody."[9]

Diderot has deepened the meaning of realism while, indeed precisely because, the mystery of the play remains intact. And he has connected both the realism and the mystery to the overriding question of the eighteenth century: how to find the proper sphere and justified boundaries of freedom. The modernity of Diderot's aesthetics lies here.

2. THE DISCOVERY OF TASTE

I

IN 1781, now old and often tired, Diderot compiled his last *Salon* and made his last discovery: David's severe neoclassical composition showing the aged general Belisarius, blind, destitute, asking for alms and being recognized by a shocked soldier. "That young man," he wrote in some excitement, "shows great style in his handling of the work. He has sensibility—*de l'âme*. His heads have expression without affectation. His attitudes are noble and natural."[1] After all

---

[9] *Est-il bon? Est-il méchant?* act III, scene 9, ed. Undank, 289; act IV, scene 9, p. 397; act IV, scene 18, p. 463.
[1] Salon of 1781; *Salons*, IV, 377.

these years of searching, Diderot had at last found a painter who had the good taste of antiquity, the *grand goût*—Diderot's taste.

Diderot's discovery is not without its irony. David's painting was part of a wider movement: Western civilization was experiencing one of its neoclassical revivals. Architects, painters, sculptors borrowed antique forms, revived antique myths, adapted antique motifs; they built pantheons, painted Socrates, sculpted Perseus. Yet, while they sufficiently controlled the classical vocabulary, they lacked the classical spirit; like many revivals, the classical revival of the late eighteenth century was not a genuine renaissance. It was an outburst of antiquarian nostalgia, a mania for decoration, and a response to developments outside the arts—mainly to archeological discoveries in Italy and Greece. The contradictions and instability of this revival have been neatly captured in the label "romantic classicism"; one can speak, with equal cogency, of the rococo classicism, the mannerist classicism of the late eighteenth century. A certain moralizing strain continued to inform the art of these decades, but it was curiously adaptable and thus essentially immoral: David's early paintings, which extol the virtues of the Roman Republic in stark, tightly controlled compositions, were in no way subversive of the monarchy in which they were produced; during the Revolution, David did Jacobin propaganda without changing his classicism, and under Napoleon he placed his characteristic style into the service of the Emperor.[2] The classical revival to which Diderot responded in his last years was little more than a caricature of the appeal to antiquity that had played such an essential part in the Enlightenment.

If traditional neoclassicism did not survive, that was largely the responsibility of men who knew the ancients well and loved them sincerely: neoclassicism was dismantled by classicists. As we know, Diderot, Reynolds, Lessing, and their associates—knowledgeable classicists to a man—had discredited the idea of imitation, hier-

---

[2] In the same manner, Claude-Nicolas Ledoux, the greatest architect of the age, was an artist with "strong royalist sentiments" which "did not prevent his revolutionary projects and executed works of the 1780s from embodying visual ideals that could be absorbed by literally Revolutionary artists and commissions." Robert Rosenblum: *Transformations in Late Eighteenth Century Art* (1967), 120.

archies in painting, and the separation of styles in the drama. But beyond that—and this was the most damaging attack of them all— they sought to demolish the theory of objective beauty.

The search for the laws of beauty goes back to the ancient Egyptians, to the Pythagoreans, to Plato, and survived into, and even beyond, the eighteenth century; number mysticism, it seems, is buried deep in the human psyche and resists the most convincing refutations. From the beginning it was evident that these laws were elusive, but the obstacles to discovery only proved to humble searchers that God was secretive, reluctant to reveal his legislation. Pagan and Christian alike believed that God had made everything with numbers, even though the numbers he had used were not known. It was accordingly to mathematics that practitioners and philosophers turned: Egyptians constructed their bas reliefs on a theory of human proportions, St. Augustine found divine harmonies in musical ratios, medieval architects built these same ratios into their cathedrals. Alberti, Leonardo da Vinci, Dürer all accepted some musical-mathematical theory of proportions; they agreed that the artist does not create beauty but discovers it.

This doctrine was at once antihistorical and authoritarian: it was the existence of a masterpiece that mattered, not its provenance, and, since the standards of beauty are objective, everyone—artist, critic, consumer of art—could, indeed must, arrive at the same evaluation of a certain work of art.

With all their passion for scientific generalizations and all their horror of anarchy, the philosophes could not leave this theory undisturbed. The suspicion of objective laws of beauty was, to be sure, in the air: the philosophes only confirmed and systematized what others had begun. Since the sixteenth century, Pyrrhonist skeptics had persuasively argued that we can know nothing certain of the past; later their followers extended this historical skepticism into the arts—one man's taste, they repeated one after the other, was as good as another's. Besides this, travelers had for centuries nourished the impulse for cultural relativism with their reports; while the philosophes used these largely for anti-Christian propaganda, they had their use also in raising doubts about the precise status and unique value of Western art. The rationalism of Boileau, with his famous dictum that only the true is beautiful, continued to hold the field, but relativism found an ever wider hearing. When in the late

1760s Piranesi recommended that artists study Etruscan and Egyptian as well as Greek and Roman art, this precept surprised few readers. The Enlightenment's skepticism concerning laws of beauty was thus embedded in a wider cultural movement. But it was also characteristic of its philosophical style, a natural outgrowth of its irresistible urge toward historical and psychological explanation. In aesthetics, as elsewhere, the Enlightenment was a consistent revolt against rationalism. Even Voltaire, who believed in the simplicity and objectivity of moral values, was compelled to concede that the search for objective laws in aesthetics was metaphysical, that is to say, pointless. And—more significant and more poignant—even Winckelmann, who argued that "there is only one beauty as there is only one good,"[3] and who firmly believed that he had found objective beauty realized in a particular historical moment, did much to undermine the very neoclassical doctrine he cherished.

II

All men harbor contradictions; Winckelmann was their embodiment and ultimate victim. A propagandist in behalf of men's dignity and artists' freedom, he abased himself all his life before his patrons in language that was servile even for the eighteenth century. A discoverer and enormously influential interpreter of ancient Greece, he never reached Greek soil; all the Greece he saw was in Italy, and in his mind. An unbeliever from his schooldays on and a follower of French philosophes despite his pronounced Francophobia, he allowed himself to be converted to Roman Catholicism that he might find helpful patronage in Italy: he turned Catholic without becoming a Christian. An advocate of the classical theory that beauty is an objective phenomenon, he discovered his own preferences through the most subjective of all passions—his erotic impulses. A pioneering historian of ancient art, he judged art as a sovereign and opinionated judge, dealing out praise and censure in the most unhistorical manner possible; his conception of style, though a remarkable diagnostic instrument, was at the same time impregnated with value judgments.

---

[3] Quoted in Friedrich Meinecke: *Die Entstehung des Historismus,* 2 vols. continuously paginated (1936), II, 318.

Only a genius could have harnessed these tensions and converted them to productive work.

Perverse and pitiful, Winckelmann *was* a genius, and his life, though unedifying, sordid, and pathetic, the triumph of that genius over his neuroses. Winckelmann was dominated by a single longing, inadequately sublimated, for male affection, which burst out in repeated, always disappointing, and in the end fatal attachments to men whom he loved more passionately than they loved him. But while his homoerotic inclinations ruined his life, they sharpened, concentrated his perceptions. If masculine friendship and masculine beauty were forever unattainable to him, or at best imperfect, they had existed in pure form in ancient Greece, and it was on ancient Greece that he expended all his imagination, all his hard-won learning, all his abnormally developed sensibility. Had he been rich, it might have mattered little; he would have been a superb dilettante, a greater Caylus. But he was abysmally poor, and thus he begged and lowered himself for the sake of getting the education, the books, the environment he needed. He served as a private tutor, as a village schoolteacher, as a librarian in a cultivated aristocratic household. It was an abject life, and he hated it, but it gave him time to read the classics and to see in Potsdam and Dresden a good deal of antique and Renaissance art. Little though this was, it permitted him to develop the principles underlying his history of art. He wrote his pamphlet of 1755, *Gedanken über die Nachahmung der griechischen Werke*, without ever having been to Italy.

Understandably, he longed for Rome and Athens, and, after long hesitations and with visible regrets, he took the step that might get him there. Rome was worth a mass, and at last, in 1755, at the age of thirty-eight, he entered Rome. This, finally, was enough: in 1764 he published his *Geschichte der Kunst des Altertums*, for which all his life had been a preparation. When he was murdered in 1768 for the sake of a few gold coins by a dubious acquaintance he had picked up, he was mourned in the learned world as a giant who had been toppled before his time by a jealous fate.

For he had lived long enough to become the founder of the modern history of art. The late Renaissance, marked by high consciousness of individuality and by artists' struggles for social recognition, produced biographies of painters and some rudimentary schemes of periodization: in the middle of the sixteenth century,

Vasari, whose great lives found wide response and retained wide influence, visualized the history of art as the story of a rise to perfection in the arts of Greece and Rome, followed by a disastrous decline with the advent of Christianity, and a magnificent rebirth beginning with Giotto and culminating in the incomparable Michelangelo. Vasari's followers in the seventeenth century elaborated his biographical method and his historical scheme, and in the eighteenth century a number of antiquarian enthusiasts, like the comte de Caylus and Winckelmann's friend, the German painter Mengs, hinted at a developmental view of styles. It was left to the philosophe Winckelmann to transform their hints into history.

Winckelmann himself publicly testified to the tension that polarized his ideas—between description and legislation, history and philosophy—and to the leitmotiv that governed his life, by dedicating his *Geschichte der Kunst des Altertums* to the ideal, to history, and to friendship: "to art," as he put it, "and to time, and especially to my friend, Herr Anton Raphael Mengs."[4] The historic import of his book lies in the fertility of its suggestions rather than the unity of its conception. Winckelmann argues that the history of art is the history of the culture in which it lives: "The sciences, indeed wisdom itself," he writes, "and art even more than they, depend upon their age and its vicissitudes."[5] The proper subject of art history must therefore be the birth, growth, maturity, and decline of art in conjunction with the history of the "styles of nations, epochs, and artists." These principles could be generalized to apply to all art, but Winckelmann's primary concern was, of course, the art of Greece. The splendor of Greek art, he argued, in full observance of his principles, must be explained by a multiplicity of historical, physical, and sociological causes: a beneficent climate, a fertile soil, peaceful competition among city states, the high social status of artists, and— the principal cause—political freedom. Environment, status, freedom: it is obvious that Winckelmann had read his Montesquieu and his Voltaire to good effect.

As the biological metaphor suggests, Winckelmann believed that in addition to fitting art organically into its culture, the historian of art can chart a certain life cycle in the history of art itself. "The

[4] *Geschichte der Kunst des Altertums*, 22.
[5] Ibid., 295.

arts which depend upon drawing," he writes in the beginning of
the *Geschichte der Kunst*, "started, like all inventions, with the
necessary; after that men sought for beauty, and at the end came the
superfluous: these are the three principal stages of art."[6] Whatever
the merits of this time-worn notion—it goes back to Vasari, and
behind Vasari stands Cicero—it gave Winckelmann the decisive clue
for his history of styles: crude workmanship, for instance, and simple
naturalism reveal stylistic immaturity; refinement of handling and
idealization, stylistic maturity. On the basis of such criteria it is possible to date works of art precisely, fit them into their proper niche,
and thus learn to know them, instead of merely appreciating them.
To his contemporaries, this kind of thinking was a revelation:
Goethe called Winckelmann a new Columbus who had discovered
art as a living thing, as a member of a developing cultural organism.

But Winckelmann's master metaphor also points in the opposite
direction: to speak of growth, maturity, decay is not merely to place
works of art but to judge them. In fact, as Herder was perhaps the
first to notice, even in his history of art Winckelmann was "more
concerned to produce a historical metaphysics of beauty" than "a
history proper."[7] It could not be otherwise: beauty, so inadequately
exhibited in his young men, was Winckelmann's principal object of
study, and beauty, he insisted, was one and eternal. To penetrate
into the essence of beauty, as Winckelmann sought to do by omnivorous reading and rapturous contemplation, was to penetrate into
the essence of art. And it was the Greeks who had found beauty
and immortalized it. They had experienced, like everyone, the inescapable cycle of growth and decay, moving from the naïveté of
the heroic age to the effeminate decadence of Hellenism; but in their
glorious periods, embracing the austere grandeur of Phidias and the
grace of Apelles, they had made divine beauty human. They had
discovered taste and left it a legacy to a world that could do no
better than to imitate them. In comparison, all other efforts at reach-
ing beauty must seem appalling failures: the Egyptians, for example,

---

[6] *Ibid.*, 25. These are the opening words of the first chapter. Reynolds dedicated his lectures to the Royal Academy to King George
III, and his dedication begins: "The regular progress of cultivated
life is from necessaries to accommodations, from accommodations
to ornaments." *Discourses*, 3.
[7] Quoted in Carl Justi: *Winckelmann und seine Zeitgenossen*, III,
129–30.

who had degraded their artists into low artisans, could show in their statues only one virtue—diligence; their faces, with their slanting eyes, high cheek bones, small chins, and their bodies, with their rigid stances, were simply ugly.

This is normative, unhistorical thinking pure and simple—anticomania, as Diderot noted,[8] though on a high level. It was overtly hostile to neoclassicism only because Winckelmann judged neoclassicism to have failed in its chosen enterprise: it had not imitated the ancients well enough. Especially in Germany, Winckelmann's anticomania did much harm: while it inspired some splendid poetry, it also inspired a great deal of wooly-minded utopianism, a longing for a perfection that had never been and could never be. Yet on balance, and against his own intentions, Winckelmann's system of ideas powerfully contributed to the liberation of taste. Anticipating Goethe's dictum that we come to know only what we love, Winckelmann's erotic epistemology—obvious enough to have been remarked upon by all his commentators—drove him to empathize with a long-dead culture, to see it and its great works of art much as its contemporaries had seen it. Winckelmann's historical *Einfühlung*, to be sure, was exceedingly narrow; it failed with Egyptian statuary much as all the philosophes' historical empathy failed with Christians. Yet, though narrow, his passionate empiricism could serve as a model for wider perceptions. His love of art, he wrote, was an "inner calling," but his judgment did not depend on intuition alone. Much like Diderot, he insisted that he had taken infinite pains to inform himself, and infinite care to pronounce only on what he had observed: "Everything that I am offering in evidence I have seen myself, often, and have been able to contemplate."[9] This happy mixture of disciplined observation and warm feeling offered the way out of rationalist neoclassical aesthetics into authentic history.

Winckelmann's stress on style was another path to the same destination. For to think about style is to think about history; style reaches out horizontally and vertically at once, into the culture in which it exists, from which it draws and on which it imprints its characteristic shape, and into the past, to its antecedents. A style is a coherent pattern with its own course of life; it develops and de-

---

[8] See Salon of 1765; *Salons*, II, 207.
[9] "Vorrede," *Geschichte der Kunst des Altertums*, 16.

cays, acquires and discards, and calls, by the insistent fact of its evolution, for periodization. Styles have histories and by having histories compel historical thinking. Winckelmann, the first modern student of style, was far more of a historian than he knew.

III

In 1764, the year Winckelmann's masterpiece appeared, Voltaire defended the relativistic view of beauty in a trivial article, "Beauté," all the more instructive for its superficiality. "Ask a toad what beauty is, the supreme beauty, the *to kalon*. He will tell you it is his lady toad with her two big round eyes coming out of her little head, her large flat snout, yellow belly, brown back." In the same way, the Negro will call beautiful a "black oily skin, sunken eyes, and flat nose"—an insight which Winckelmann could well have used in his consideration of Egyptian statues—while the devil will admire "a pair of horns, four claws, and a tail." Then, Voltaire recommends with a sneer, ask the philosophers what beauty is: they will reply with jargon. Pleasure clearly depends on environment and culture: once, Voltaire relates, he saw a tragedy in France in the company of a philosopher, who thought it beautiful; then the two men traveled to England to see the same tragedy, and there it made all the spectators yawn. "Oh, oh!" said the philosopher. "The *to kalon* is not the same for the English as for the French," and he concludes (obviously it is Voltaire's own conclusion) that "the beautiful is often quite relative, so that what is decent in Japan is indecent in Rome, and what is fashionable in Paris is not so in Peking."[1] This is hardly profound, but it is arresting doctrine from the pen of a neoclassicist, and proof that rationalism had lost a great deal of ground.

It had in fact been under attack for more than half a century, and philosophes had been among its leading assailants. Perhaps its most effective early opponent was the abbé Dubos, whose *Réflexions critiques sur la poésie et la peinture* of 1719, a pioneering, widely quoted, and highly appreciated book, celebrated the imagination, creative genius, and taste without denigrating knowledge and re-

---

[1] "Beauty," *Philosophical Dictionary*, I, 111-12.

straint. "The theoretician of sentiment," A. Lombard, his biographer, has well said, "was not a sentimentalist."[2]

Dubos was an empiricist, a follower of Locke and Addison, all the more rigorous in his empiricism for being a reformed Cartesian. Art, he holds, can be analyzed only through the aesthetic experience rather than by predetermined rules. This analysis will displace art from its position as moral teacher or adjunct to religious worship, and show it to be an all-too-human satisfaction whose principal function is to offer relief from boredom and a cure for restlessness. Antiintellectualism here is liberating; Dubos denies that art must instruct, or that its effect arises from rational comprehension: its particular and peculiar pleasure springs from the inner movement of taste.

It is his analysis of taste that constitutes Dubos's real originality. Men, Dubos argues, are equipped with an immediate sentiment, an invisible "sixth sense," which acts spontaneously. The action of the heart "anticipates all reasoning, as the action of the eye and the ear precede it in their sensations." It will "move on its own," when "the object presented to it is truly a touching object—*Le cœur s'agite de lui-même, et par un mouvement qui précède toute délibération, quand l'objet qu'on lui présente est réellement un objet touchant.*"[3] Man's heart was made, explicitly constructed, for this purpose; it is as rare to find a man without this sense as a man born blind. Since pleasure is primary, the rules become secondary; and pleasure is irrational—we know what we like before we know why.[4]

Despite all of Dubos's hesitations—as a neoclassicist he could, for example, find no beauty in genre or landscape painting—this was radical doctrine, and his book acquired high authority among advanced thinkers throughout France and Germany: Voltaire and Helvétius, Mendelssohn and Lessing, were Dubos's disciples. Just as important, perhaps more: Dubos's *Réflexions critiques* aroused Montesquieu's interest in aesthetic questions, and propelled him toward a subjectivist, relativist philosophy of art.[5]

Montesquieu's article "Goût" in Diderot's *Encyclopédie* ap-

---

[2] *L'Abbé Du Bos, un initiateur de la pensée moderne (1670–1742)* (1913), 188.
[3] Ibid., 226–7.
[4] Ibid., 227.
[5] For Dubos's influence on Montesquieu's theory of climate and Montesquieu's theory of government, see below, 328–30, 467–8.

peared in 1757, two years after his death, but its origins go far back to the 1720s, when Montesquieu was directly engaged with Dubos's ideas. Though like everyone else a loyal classicist and fervent admirer of ancient literature, Montesquieu found those ideas congenial and stimulating, for he was also a cultural relativist—one of the first, and certainly the most conscientious in the Enlightenment—who showed his capacity for appreciating the moral and aesthetic standards of alien nations in his earliest writings; his relativism underlies his social criticism in the *Lettres persanes,* and it was deepened and enriched by his travels. "Goût" is incomplete and unrevised, but its central argument is plain enough: "The sources of the beautiful, the good, the agreeable" are "in us," activated by such stimuli as a poem or a piece of sculpture.[6] Taste, which is wholly subjective, is the "measure" of the pleasures that men experience, and these experiences depend wholly on man's constitution: "Our manner of being," Montesquieu argues, in good Cartesian fashion, but drawing unclassical, un-Cartesian conclusions, "is wholly arbitrary; we could have been made as we were, or differently. But if we had been made differently, we would see differently; one organ more or less in our machine would have given us another kind of eloquence, another poetry; a different structure of the same organs would have produced still another poetry: for instance, if the constitution of our organs had made us capable of longer attention, all the rules which proportion the disposition of the subject to the measure of our attention would disappear."[7] The relativistic consequences of this materialism are far-reaching.

Having laid down his principles, Montesquieu surveys the stimuli that arouse pleasure. They are both internal and external: the soul has its autonomous pleasures, independent of self-knowledge, such as awareness of its existence, its greatness, and its capacities. In the same manner, *esprit*—wit and talent in their various connotations—enjoys exercising itself, as does curiosity. And in addition, man takes pleasure from the world, from many and apparently contradictory experiences: he enjoys variety, order, symmetry, contrast, surprise, sensibility, delicacy, the *je ne sais quoi,* and a certain intensification which moves from the expected to the unexpected.

---

[6] *Essai sur le Goût,* in *Œuvres,* I, part 3, 612.
[7] Ibid., 613–14.

All this sounds like chaos, but Montesquieu insists that the action of taste is anything but chaotic. In the first place, the stimulus must be somehow "right"; it must respond to some inner need: the soul that craves variety will not be satisfied by order; too much order induces monotony, too much variety, bewilderment. Taste therefore regulates, as it were tames, experience by its selective approval. Moreover, Montesquieu argues that "what gives us pleasure should be founded on reason."[8] Taste can be refined; natural inclinations can be corrected, so that caprice yields before a kind of educated subjectivity. Like Dubos, Montesquieu offers room to sentiment without being sentimental: "All works of art have general rules which are guides that should never be lost sight of. But, as the laws are always just in their general being, yet almost always unjust in their application, so the rules, always true in theory, can become false in hypothesis."[9] Hence the great artist must know, remember—and violate—the rules. Freedom arises from the thorough knowledge and intelligent use of form.

IV

The ideas of Dubos rapidly circulated all over Europe; they had reached England long before 1748, when Thomas Nugent, who would also translate Montesquieu's *De l'esprit des lois*, translated the *Réflexions critiques*. Burke's *Enquiry Into The Sublime and Beautiful* was deeply in Dubos's debt; David Hume knew his Dubos thoroughly and quoted him with evident approval. Yet Dubos was less necessary to England than to France, for England had its own antirationalist tradition. The psychological school of philosophy had turned the attention of English critics from the laws to the effects of art before the eighteenth century. In 1688, upon crossing the Alps, John Dennis had noticed and appreciated an odd mixed feeling of exaltation and fear: "A delightful Horrour, a terrible Joy," he noted. "At the same time that I was infinitely pleas'd, I trembled."[1]

---

[8] *Essai sur le Goût*, fragment, *Œuvres*, III, 531.
[9] Ibid.
[1] Quoted in Marjorie Hope Nicolson: *Mountain Gloom and Mountain Glory: The Development of the Aesthetics of the Infinite* (1959), 277.

And in the 1690s, the great combative classicist Richard Bentley argued that "All Pulchritude is Relative": when men look at irregularly shaped mountains and claim to see deformities in them, this response is wholly subjective: *"This objected Deformity is in our Imaginations only, and not really in the things themselves."*[2]

In the first half of the eighteenth century, more and more English critics discovered the profits that art derives from the passions. Addison, in addition to analyzing the pleasures of the imagination in the *Spectator*, offered his readers a brief disquisition on taste, which he defined as a discriminating *"Faculty of the Soul, which discerns the Beauties of an Author with Pleasure, and the Imperfections with Dislike."*[3] Like most neoclassicists, Addison vacillated. Someone who reads without emotion the finest works of the ancients, "which have stood the Test of so many different Ages and Countries," or those of the moderns, "which have the Sanction of the Politer Part of our Contemporaries," invites reflection not upon the works he has failed to enjoy, but on himself. Doubtless, taste "must in some degree be born with us"—in its origins, then, it is subjective.[4] It can, however, be cultivated and improved by reading, conversation, knowledge of critical writings; the man of taste makes sure judgments not by recognizing some mathematical law but by appreciating the agreement of the well-bred. Subjectivity here is still tame, and timid.

In the 1720s, Francis Hutcheson, a lucid and independent-minded disciple of Shaftesbury, who left his mark on David Hume and a whole school of Scottish philosophers, took Addison's tentative ideas further. In his lectures at the University of Glasgow and in a series of essays, he postulated an inner sense for beauty, analogous to the inner moral sense. This aesthetic sense is part of man's original nature; it may be cultivated or distorted by external influences, but it is inborn and it responds, immediately and without admixture of the will, to stimuli provided by natural beauty or by works of art. In its essence, then, Hutcheson argues, man's response to art is nonrational.

By mid-century, Locke had largely replaced Boileau in English criticism. In a well-known essay in the *Idler*, Sir Joshua Reynolds

---

[2] Quoted in ibid., 262–3.
[3] *Spectator*, No. 409; III, 528.
[4] Ibid., 529.

argued that taste springs "from custom or some association of ideas." The man who calls a swan more beautiful than a dove really means to say that "he has more pleasure in seeing a swan than a dove, either from the stateliness of its motions, or its being a more rare bird," while the man who makes the opposite choice, "does it from some association of ideas of innocence which he always annexes to the dove." Habit, custom, association, Lockian qualities all, determine man's idea of beauty. To be sure—and here is a characteristic neo-classical compromise—the essence of beauty is objective. But its perception follows inner laws. "I have no doubt," Reynolds asserted, "but that if we were more used to deformity than beauty, deformity would then lose the idea now annexed to it, and take that of beauty."[5] Anticipating Voltaire, Reynolds was certain that if Europeans preferred light-skinned people, and Ethiopians dark-skinned ones, both were guided by custom alone: the Ethiopian would paint the goddess of beauty black, with thick lips, flat nose, and woolly hair, and no one would have the right to dispute him. This was written in 1759; much later, in 1782, when Lockian psychology was already under attack, Reynolds persisted in it: "May not all beauty proceeding from association of ideas," he wrote to Beattie, "be reduced to the principle of habit or experience?"[6]

Reynolds's essay had been a casual performance. But in the same decade, in the 1750s, the case for subjectivity received serious philosophical support in Edmund Burke's *Philosophical Enquiry into the Origin of our Ideas of the Sublime and Beautiful*, which subjected traditional arguments for objectivity to a thoroughly destructive, and thoroughly convincing, analysis. Burke shows that the claims for a theory of proportion must lead to unresolvable contradictions, and that all attempts at basing aesthetic legislation on the utility of an object, or its moral goodness, are just as futile. Proportion, fitness, perfection, he asserts, are all valuable qualities, but they are not aesthetic qualities. Beauty arises from passion alone; it is as independent of intellect as it is of volition—"Beauty is, for the greater part, some quality in bodies, acting mechanically upon the

---

[5] *The Literary Works of Sir Joshua Reynolds*, 2 vols., ed. Henry William Beechy (1892–1901), II, 132–4. On the subjective and "arbitrary" nature of beauty, see Reynolds's draft for No. 82 of the *Idler*, in *The Literary Career of Sir Joshua Reynolds*, 19–21.

[6] March 31, 1782. *Letters*, 93.

human mind by the intervention of the senses"; it is "no creature of our reason."[7] True, the operations of taste follow ascertainable laws; the principles of taste are the same in all men, "the standard both of reason and Taste is the same in all human creatures."[8] But these are psychological, even physiological standards. For Burke, as for other eighteenth-century aestheticians, subjectivism and antirationalism did not mean anarchy or chaos.

It is significant that the central theme of Burke's *Enquiry* should be the sublime. The notion of sublimity was a safety valve for the pressures of neoclassical legislation. It originated in ancient Roman works on rhetoric, mainly from "Longinus' " *On the Sublime*, a very popular work in the late seventeenth and early eighteenth centuries, which treated the sublime mode of speech—grandiose, elevated, ornate, pathetic—as one of the principal styles of oratory; modern treatises on aesthetics boldly generalized this element in rhetoric to aesthetic experiences as a whole. The sublime became a rule for evading rules. It gave good reasons for unreasonable preferences, objective sanction to subjective sentiments, legitimate justification for breaking the law. It explained why men could admire that which was not beautiful—storms at sea, ruined castles, terrifying earthquakes. It found room for the irregular, literally unruly, productions of genius. It permitted Addison to prefer Milton, with all his faults, to lesser writers, faultless though they might be. It gave respectability, in Thomson's words, to "fancy—enthusiasm—rapturous terror."[9] It recognized the admixture of sensuality in aesthetic appreciation: "In all cases," wrote Diderot to Sophie Volland, with his characteristic mixture of psychological penetration and brutal imagery, "great effects are born from voluptuous ideas intertwined with terrible ideas; for instance, beautiful, half-naked girls who present us with a delicious brew in the bloody skulls of our enemies. *There* is the model of all sublime things."[1] The sublime even brought back into favor that least enlightened of all qualities, obscurity:

---

[7] *A Philosophical Enquiry into the Origin of our Ideas of the Sublime and Beautiful* (1757; ed. J. T. Boulton, 1958), 112.
[8] "On Taste" (added to the second edition of the *Enquiry* in 1758), ibid., 11.
[9] Quoted in Samuel H. Monk: *The Sublime: A Study of Critical Theories in XVIIIth-Century England* (edn. 1960), 90.
[1] (October 14, 1762). *Correspondance*, IV, 196.

"The obscure idea," wrote Burke, is "more affecting than the clear,"[2] more likely, with its intimations of infinity and eternity, to do the work of poetry, which is to arouse the passions. "A clear idea is therefore another name for a little idea."[3]

Burke's intention in his *Enquiry* was to make obscurity not merely respectable, but clear. Neither he, nor anyone else, he noted, had anything "like an exact theory of our passions, or a knowledge of their genuine sources," and the definition of beauty and of the sublime, as well as their mutual relation, was in great confusion. Burke now attempted to define both, and to separate them sharply; the book was his *Laocoön*. The fundamental categories of his aesthetics are pain and pleasure, "simple ideas, incapable of definition."[4] The idea of beauty is aroused by the pleasure men take in the small, the smooth, the delicate, the colorful, the graceful, the shape or tone that undergoes gradual change. The idea of the sublime, on the other hand, is a pleasure men take from pain; it is aroused by terror, by power, vastness, obscurity, difficulty, magnificence. Obviously, as Burke well knows, there are forms of terror that cause nothing but suffering; terror gives pleasure only when it has been anesthetized by remoteness, by a certain unreality. Yet, while not all terror is sublime, all sublime experiences spring from terror: "Indeed terror is in all cases whatsoever, either more openly or latently the ruling principle of the sublime."[5]

Burke's *Enquiry* is a young man's book, energetic, facile, a little irresponsible, and sometimes embarrassing. His idea of beauty, as modern critics have not failed to observe, is simply a generalization of his sensuality. Smoothness, softness, delicacy, smallness, are the qualities of a pretty woman, rather than of beauty in a larger signification: "All bodies that are pleasant to the touch," Burke writes, and we seem to be in the presence of Diderot in one of his moments of sexual excitement disguised as moral exaltation, "are so by the slightness of the resistance they make. Resistance is either to motion along the surface, or to the pressure of parts to one another; if the former be slight, we call the body, smooth; if the latter, soft. The chief pleasure we receive by feeling, is in the one or the other of these

---

[2] *Enquiry*, 61.
[3] Ibid., 63.
[4] Ibid., 32.
[5] Ibid., 58.

qualities; and if there be a combination of both, our pleasure is greatly increased."[6] And, just as Burke trivializes the idea of beauty, he oversimplifies the idea of the sublime: in comparing sublime things to beautiful things, he seems to rely mainly on differences in size. Yet Burke's influence, for all his shortcomings, was pervasive, on aestheticians and poets alike; he caught the mood of his time. Long before Romanticism, and without the aid of Romantics, the age of the Enlightenment discovered and managed to gratify a taste for pathos, for graveyards, for moonlight, for the dark and the infinite. In giving the public good reasons for its tastes, Burke became a leader in the great eighteenth-century revolt against theories of imitation and proportion. It was the study of man's passions, he insisted, not the study of nature or aesthetic tradition, that leads to recognition of artistic excellence. Others had argued it before him, and would argue it after him; few had argued it so lucidly, so glibly. "The true standard of the arts is in every man's power,"[7] Burke said, and his dictum, democratic in its implications where traditional aesthetics had been uncompromisingly aristocratic, reads like an epitaph to neoclassicism.

V

In 1757, the year of Burke's *Enquiry*, David Hume published an important essay, "Of the Standard of Taste," which is deep where Burke is shallow, measured where Burke is impetuous. It is, despite its brief compass, a landmark of Enlightenment thought. "There are many different Kinds of Certainty," Hume had written in 1754, "and some of them as satisfactory to the Mind, tho perhaps not so regular, as the demonstrative Kind."[8] His essay on taste attempts what the Enlightenment at its best always attempted: to substitute the authentic if relative certainty of experience for the absolute but spurious certainty of metaphysics or tradition.

Hume begins with what he himself calls an "obvious" fact: there is great variety in matters of taste. Everyone pronounces with

---

[6] Ibid., 120.
[7] Ibid., 54.
[8] Hume to (John Stewart), (February 1754). *Letters*, I, 187.

confidence, even with rudeness, yet all disagree. "We are apt to call *barbarous* whatever departs widely from our own taste and apprehension: But soon find the epithet of reproach retorted on us."[9] In fact, disagreement is even deeper than men perceive, for while all praise the same qualities, like decorum, they do not define these qualities in the same way. In the face of this discord it is "natural" to "seek a *Standard of Taste;* a rule, by which the various sentiments may be reconciled; at least, a decision, afforded, confirming one sentiment, and condemning another."[1] There are skeptics who proclaim that such a rule cannot be found; since taste depends on sentiment, these philosophers reason, and since "no sentiment represents what is really in the object," all sentiments must be equally right. "Beauty," the skeptics say, "is no quality in things themselves: It exists merely in the mind which contemplates them; and each mind perceives a different beauty. One person may even perceive deformity, where another is sensible of beauty; and every individual ought to acquiesce in his own sentiment, without pretending to regulate those of others."[2]

This relativism is not Hume's own view: Hume always insisted, and was right to insist, that he was a moderate skeptic, not a Pyrrhonist. It is precisely his point that the subjectivity of beauty should not lead to relativism, for subjectivity does not necessarily imply arbitrariness. Hume allows the skepticism he has so lucidly expounded the merits of good sense and realism: it is an intelligent response to experience. But he proceeds to reject it, on precisely the grounds on which it has been asserted. "Though this axiom"— that tastes differ—"by passing into a proverb, seems to have attained the sanction of common sense; there is certainly a species of common sense which opposes it, at least serves to modify and restrain it." In fact, debates about works of art and literature often end in agreement. "Whoever would assert an equality of genius and elegance between OGILBY and MILTON, or BUNYAN and ADDISON," would be thought as extravagant as if he maintained a pond to be as extensive as an ocean. "Though there may be found persons, who give the preference to the former authors; no one pays attention to such a taste; and we pronounce without scruple the sentiment of these pre-

---

[9] "Of the Standard of Taste," *Works*, III, 266.
[1] Ibid., 268.
[2] Ibid., 268-9.

tended critics to be absurd and ridiculous. The principle of the natural equality of tastes is then totally forgot."[3] It is an unfortunate choice of examples, illustrating, better than Hume's explicit arguments, the relativity of taste. While no one today will pit Ogilby against Milton, many would rank Bunyan with, or above, Addison without fear of appearing extravagant. But Hume's point remains valid: some reputations are secure, some painters or poets would appear on any responsible list of masters. Hume's own instance of such a poet, Homer, is unimpeachable: "The same HOMER," he writes, "who pleased at ATHENS and ROME two thousand years ago, is still admired at PARIS and at LONDON. All the changes of climate, government, religion, and language, have not been able to obscure his glory" [4]—and, we might add, two centuries after Hume, Homer is admired still and his glory remains lustrous.

There is hope, then, for the discovery of general principles, but Hume insists that they can never emerge from some metaphysical rule or some objective mathematical law. To construct a work of art by "geometrical truth and exactness" would violate the laws of criticism and result in a "most insipid and disagreeable" production.[5] In fact, "none of the rules of composition are fixed by reasonings *a priori*"; their "foundation is the same with that of all of the practical sciences, experience." They are "general observations,"[6] no more, and, as Hume's general epistemology has made plain, such observations can no more claim universal validity than any other inductive generalization.

Yet to Hume's mind the history of taste offers sufficient instances, and the unity of human nature sufficient guarantees, to permit at least empirical generalizations. "It appears, then, that, amidst all the variety and caprice of taste, there are certain general principles of approbation or blame, whose influence a careful eye may trace in all operations of the mind. Some particular forms or qualities, from the original structure of the internal fabric, are calculated to please, and others to displease."[7] Hume was in general a careful writer; when he spoke of "certain general principles of ap-

---

[3] Ibid., 269.
[4] Ibid., 271.
[5] Ibid., 270.
[6] Ibid., 269.
[7] Ibid., 271.

probation or blame"[8] he had in mind no more than a few rules that would set boundaries to legitimate disagreement without destroying legitimate diversity. In aesthetics, certainty came from the observed consensus of cultivated men.

It remained to construct the conditions for such a consensus. To begin with, Hume argues, good health and spirits are essential to sound aesthetic observation, as essential as daylight is to accurate sight. "In each creature, there is a sound and a defective state; and the former alone can be supposed to afford us a true standard of taste and sentiment."[9] Secondly, the good judge of art must possess a "*delicacy* of imagination,"[1] a virtue all claim and few possess. This quality, whose importance is discovered in experience, can be cultivated through experience alone. "The same address and dexterity, which practice gives to the execution of any work, is also acquired by the same means, in the judging of it."[2] The primitivist cult of ignorance, which was to be widely preached only a few decades after Hume's death, found no place in Hume's system; on the contrary, he insisted that the practice he had in mind was hard work: no one can really judge a work of art after seeing, or hearing, or reading it only once, or without making suitable comparisons—he may miss its architecture, its finer parts, its true merit. "It seldom, or never happens, that a man of sense, who has experience in any art, cannot judge of its beauty; and it is no less rare to meet with a man who has a just taste without a sound understanding."[3] Thirdly, the judge of art must "preserve his mind free from all prejudice,"[4] for prejudices lead to stubbornness, distort the judgment with extraneous matter, and corrupt the sense of beauty. Hume concedes that such critics are rare, but he is confident that they exist, that they can be identified and distinguished from pretenders by the ascendancy they gain over their civilization and the guidance they provide to those willing to learn. Hume's good critics form an assembly of civilized men—men like himself.

---

[8] Ibid. For Hume, though a skeptic, it was clear that there were (as he said, ibid., 280) "general principles of taste" that were "uniform in human nature."

[9] Ibid., 271–2.

[1] Ibid., 272.

[2] Ibid., 275.

[3] Ibid., 278.

[4] Ibid., 276.

But Hume does not end on this note. Despite all efforts to "fix a standard of taste, and reconcile the discordant apprehensions of men," two "sources of variation" will always remain, "not sufficient indeed to confound all the boundaries of beauty and deformity," but sufficient to "produce a difference in the degrees of our approbation or blame."[5] One of these is "the different humours of particular men," the other, "the particular manners and opinions of our age and country." A passionate young man is likely to make Ovid his favorite author, at forty he will have reached Horace, and at fifty, Tacitus. "We choose our favourite author as we do our friend, from a conformity of humour and disposition."[6]

VI

From the perspective of Kant's *Kritik der Urteilskraft*, the aesthetic writings of his precursors appear to be encumbered with irrelevancies, with social, moral, political, and religious concerns that diminish the importance and obscure the meaning of art. It has its own glaring limitations, but the vitality of Kant's aesthetics is in fact nothing less than astonishing: his practical criticism is scanty in quality and negligible in insight, the narrow compass of his taste in art is reflected in his failure to deal adequately with the aesthetic significance of poetry or music, the rigor of his philosophizing, though often a decisive advantage, leads him into making sharp distinctions—between beauty and sublimity, interested and disinterested pleasure—that do violence to aesthetic experience. Yet Kant saw the issues others had raised before him more clearly than they, and he saw them through; compared to him, even Hume, for all his logical rigor, appears irresolute: with his belief in the uniformity of human nature, and hope for ultimate agreement in aesthetic questions, he seems to take back or at least render ineffective his exhilarating doctrine that taste is subjective. It is true that the aesthetic thought of the Enlightenment freed itself from neoclassicism with the greatest reluctance. As I have said, even revolutionaries like

---

[5] Ibid., 280.
[6] Ibid., 281.

Diderot and Lessing had great respect for the past. The politics of eighteenth-century aesthetics showed a distinct conservative, aristocratic, authoritarian strain. Hume had argued that "few are qualified to give judgment on any work of art, or establish their own sentiment as the standard of beauty."[7] Lest there be any doubt, Lord Kames had made it plain that this kind of restriction, characteristic of all eighteenth-century discussions of taste, was a matter of class: "Those who depend for food on bodily labor, are totally void of taste, of such taste at least as can be of use in the fine arts. This consideration bars the greater part of mankind; and of the remaining part, many by a corrupted taste are unqualified for voting."[8] But this conservatism was realistic rather than snobbish: a consistent aesthetic democrat in the eighteenth century would have been a utopian, and the philosophes were not utopians. In any event, small and select as the republic of criticism was in the philosophes' eyes, it was a functional aristocracy, open to anyone whom hard work or good luck should grant the prosperity and the leisure necessary to cultivate his sensibilities. In art criticism, as elsewhere, the philosophes were thoroughly committed to the ideal of careers open to talent. Besides, the legislation of the critics was the fruit of discussion, not of fiat; it was provisional and experimental rather than eternal and mathematical. Nor was this all: despite their refusal to adopt the skeptical argument that all beauty is relative and that all can judge art with equal competence, the philosophes, with their critique of the idea of imitation, of hierarchies in painting and rules in the drama, were ruthlessly subversive of the long and powerful tradition that had governed European aesthetics for many centuries. Like another celebrated bid for freedom in the eighteenth century— the revolt of the American colonies—the emancipation of art was a long, arduous, but single struggle, a historic whole: as Jefferson's Declaration of Independence is unthinkable without the preliminary work of Samuel Adams and Benjamin Franklin, Kant's declaration of the independence of art—for Kant was the Jefferson of aesthetics— is unthinkable without Addison or Burke or Mendelssohn. If, with-

---

[7] Ibid., 278.
[8] *Elements of Criticism* (1762), quoted in Wellek: *History of Modern Criticism*, I, 109.

out Kant, the emancipation of art would have been incomplete, without his precursors Kant could not have done his work. Kant's debt to his century was as obvious to him as it is to us. He worked through the *Aesthetica* of Baumgarten with great care, criticized it but found it useful. He defined the role of the genius— "the inborn talent (*ingenium*) through which nature gives art its rules"[9]—in formulations that Diderot would have found admirable and in no way strange. He analyzed the phenomenon of sublimity perhaps more rigorously and more eloquently than others, but his exposition—the odd mixture of horror and attractiveness, the power that has no power over the beholder, the magnificence of natural phenomena that transcend man's imagination, which all characterize the sublime—offered few surprises to readers of Addison and Burke. Significantly, Kant acknowledged Burke as the foremost representative of the physiological school of aesthetics. In appreciating Burke, Kant noted his dependence on eighteenth-century thought; in setting limits to that appreciation, he staked out what he regarded as his own distinctive contribution.[1] For Kant always insisted that his primary concern was philosophical rather than practical; he sought the *a priori* laws, not the empirical rules, of taste: he had undertaken the analysis of taste, he said, "not to educate and cultivate" it,[2] but to lay down its general principles.

True enough: besides being a typical product of the Enlightenment, Kant's *Kritik der Urteilskraft* is also characteristic of his own thought; it is highly abstract, utterly uncompromising in its universality, intimately linked to his earlier two Critiques—it is the culmination and completion of a vastly ambitious piece of philosophical architecture. In fact, the book has an air of relief about it: "With this," Kant writes in the Preface, and the note of satisfaction is evident, "I end my whole critical business."[3] It had taken him twenty years: in 1771 he had written to Markus Herz that he intended to analyze the principles underlying "the theory of taste, metaphysics, and ethics"[4]; in 1790, with the publication of his third

---

[9] *Kritik der Urteilskraft*, in *Werke*, V, 382.
[1] See ibid., 349–50.
[2] Ibid., 238.
[3] Ibid.
[4] June 7, 1771. *Werke*, IX, 97.

Critique, after enormous intellectual difficulties and despite prolonged doubts, the program was complete.

As was appropriate to his orderly, almost obsessive style of thinking, Kant took considerable pains to emphasize the architectonic unity of his "critical business." In his letters and his highly explicit Prefaces, he made it plain that each of his Critiques addressed itself to a distinct branch of philosophy: the *Critique of Pure Reason* to metaphysics, the *Critique of Practical Reason* to ethics, the *Critique of Judgment* to aesthetics. Each considered a different cognitive faculty: the first, understanding; the second, reason; the third, judgment. And, to make obvious what was already plain, Kant tied his Critiques to the terminology of faculty psychology: the first Critique, he said, concerned itself with the nature of knowledge, the second with the faculties of desire, the third with the feelings of pleasure and pain. This was a great deal, but it was not enough: Kant's three Critiques do not merely stand side by side, in sturdy symmetry; they are systematically related to one another. As Kant saw it, philosophy was both theoretical and practical. Theoretical philosophy studied nature—the realm of necessity; practical philosophy studied morals—the realm of freedom, and he had devoted his first two Critiques to each of these realms. But there must be a way of reconciling the two, of harmonizing determinism and freedom, appearance and reality, law and action, the universal and the particular. And Kant's last Critique expounds this reconciliation. The *Kritik der Urteilskraft* deals with two apparently quite disparate subjects, biology and aesthetics. This pairing is neither accidental nor perverse: Kant saw the phenomena of life and of art as closely related, indeed analogous processes. Both exist for their own sake, both display a harmony, a design, that make them something better than mere instruments or mere products; both possess, in Kant's famous formula, "purposeless purposiveness." It is this quality that heals the dualisms that divide the world. The artist (for this is our concern here) is at once bound and free: the genius, who is the artist at his highest potential, combines within himself imagination and understanding, mind and taste. Genius is "a talent for art, not for science, in which distinctly understood rules take precedence and must determine its activity"; it "represents the imagination as free from all guidance of rules, yet as purposeful in presenting a given concept"—its imagination is free while its understanding is lawful. Genius, in a word, is "the exemplary originality of natural gifts" in the "free employment of its cognitive faculties."[5]

But, while art is like nature, it is different as well. In one of his most important chapters, Kant distinguishes art from nature, science, and handicraft. Art differs from nature in that it must be a "production through freedom," the work of "a will which makes reason the basis of its actions"—we call beehives "works of art" only through analogy. Art differs from science because it is a skill, a practical faculty which acts, rather than a theoretical faculty which knows. And art differs from handicraft because it is "free" rather than mercenary; it is "play," that is, "an activity agreeable for its own sake." But he emphasized—it is a point he made over and over again—that "in all the free arts something compulsory is still necessary." Without what he calls "a *mechanism*," the spirit, "which must be *free* in art and which alone animates the work," would be without body and would simply evaporate: "It is not inadvisable to recall this—for example, in poetry, accuracy and wealth of language, as well as prosody and measure—since some recent educators think they can best advance free art by freeing it of all constraint and by translating it from labor into mere play."[6] Kant was doubtless glancing at the untrammeled "geniuses" of the *Sturm und Drang*, but he was speaking to posterity as well. Art is originality channeled by craftsmanship, passion guided by reason: there was, for Kant and for his Enlightenment, no higher praise than this.

Kant's exalted estimation of art and the artist is his contribution to the aesthetic thinking of the Enlightenment. The problem of eighteenth-century aesthetics had been to shake off a dying tradition and to place rules on the firm new ground of reason. This was a very difficult task: Kant, more than anyone, was aware just how daunting it was. Like his predecessors, though with greater rigor, he confronted the current cliché that "every man has his own taste"—taste, that is to say, is wholly relative, subjective, and not subject to correction by others. This is a "commonplace," he said severely, "with which every man without taste thinks he can escape criticism." But, he noted, there was also a "second commonplace,"

---

[5] *Kritik der Urteilskraft,* in *Werke,* V, 393.
[6] Ibid., 377–9.

equally current: "There is no disputing about tastes"—there are objective laws of taste with universal validity, but since they do not refer to determinate concepts, argument about them is futile.[7] These two clichés lead to an antinomy: a pair of irreconcilable conclusions that leaves the question of aesthetic judgment in a dangerous muddle. But a clash of doctrines, Kant knew long before Whitehead, may be an aid to progress.[8] The antinomy of taste offered the recognition that art has its distinct realm and its own logic.

In the debate between the classicists, who held to objective laws of art, and the moderns, who argued for its subjective status, Kant had no hesitation: "The judgment of taste," he wrote, is not a cognitive judgment, and *"cannot be anything but subjective."*[9] But this, Kant makes clear, does not imply relativism and will not lead to anarchy; rather, it demands new and special laws for the aesthetic judgment. And it is with the enunciation of these laws that Kant consummates the liberation of art. The judgment of taste is determined by "a pure disinterested satisfaction—*dem reinen, uninteressierten Wohlgefallen.*" Suppose "someone asks me," Kant writes, "if I find beautiful the palace I see before me. I might reply: I do not like things of this sort, made only to be gaped at; or, like that Iroquois Sachem: what he liked best in Paris were the eating houses. Beyond that, I can, like a good Rousseauian, declaim against the vanity of the great who expend the sweat of the people on such superfluous things. Finally, I can easily convince myself that if I should find myself on an uninhabited island, without hope of ever meeting men again, and could conjure up such a splendid building through my mere wish, I should not even take the trouble to do it if I already had a hut that was sufficiently comfortable. All this may be conceded to me, and be approved of—only, we are not speaking of this now."[1]

Davon ist jetzt nicht die Rede—here, in this curt phrase of dismissal, is the essence of Kant's case. To speak of morality or psychology, politics or religion, is not to speak of aesthetics. "Everyone must concede that judgment about beauty in which the slightest

---

[7] Ibid., 414.
[8] Alfred North Whitehead: *Science and the Modern World* (1925), 266: "A clash of doctrines is not a disaster—it is an opportunity."
[9] *Kritik der Urteilskraft*, in *Werke*, V, 271-2.
[1] Ibid., 273.

interest interferes is highly partisan and not a pure judgment of taste."[2] This is radical doctrine, wholly appropriate to the Enlightenment in its consequent secularism; who, before the philosophes would have dared to define aesthetic judgment as "disinterested satisfaction"? Although "the art-lover of our day may succeed in contemplating the Sistine Madonna with 'disinterested pleasure,' " Max J. Friedländer rightly observes, "the pious-minded in the sixteenth century certainly did not glance up at the altar-piece with anything of the sort."[3] But Kant did not waver. Men take satisfaction in morality, he wrote, calling it good; but this is a satisfaction in which interest—the desire for its existence—plays a part. Similarly, men take satisfaction in the pleasant, calling it lovely, enjoyable, agreeable; but this is a satisfaction in which interest—the desire for sensual gratification—plays a part. Neither is therefore a pure aesthetic judgment.

This distinction permits Kant to find a place for relativism. In the judgment of the pleasant, relativism is not merely legitimate but inescapable, for that judgment is arbitrary and personal, and therefore cannot serve as the basis of general legislation. A man who finds something agreeable may say, " 'Canary dry wine is pleasant,' " but then, if someone else corrects him and reminds him "that he ought to say, 'It is pleasant *to me*' " he will be perfectly content.[4] The expression "this pleases me," is logically distinct from the expression "this is beautiful." What is distinctive about the latter is its disinterestedness, which implies a claim to universality. If a man is aware that his satisfaction is wholly disinterested, he can only think that his judgment contains "a ground of satisfaction for everyone." For "since it is not grounded in any inclination of the subject, nor upon any other considered interest," but, rather, since the man making the judgment "feels himself quite *free* in view of the satisfaction he attaches to the object," he can "discover no private conditions as grounds for his satisfaction" and must therefore "see it as grounded in what he can presuppose in everyone else." He must believe that

---

2 Ibid.
3 *Landscape, Portrait, Still Life: Their Origin and Development* (1947; tr. R. F. C. Hull, 1949), 12.
4 *Kritik der Urteilskraft*, in *Werke*, V, 281.

he has good reason to "attribute a similar satisfaction to everyone."[5] This, Kant suggests, often leads to a difficulty: sensing this universality, men tend to speak as though beauty were an objective quality. But while they are right in their claim to universality they are wrong in their claim to objectivity: the universality is, in fact, a "subjective universality."[6] Kant has thus avoided aesthetic chaos without honoring the traditional legislation.

As a moralist and an empiricist, Kant was fully aware of the dangers in his libertarianism. He never conceived of art as amoral; the animus against bourgeois philistinism implied in the doctrine of art for art's sake was wholly alien to him. The aesthetic judgment, with its claim to universality and its elevation above pleasure and interest, is highly moral; indeed, "the beautiful is the symbol of the morally good."[7] The point is only that art is not the result or the dependent of morality; art is not a satellite but its own master.

It is precisely this claim that reconciles the truths of aesthetic experience with the demands of Kant's aesthetic system. Experience shows that disagreements on artistic matters are widespread and often unresolved, and that fashions in artists change. But this diversity only points once again to the unique logic of art. Kant's aesthetics claims universal validity for the statement "this is beautiful." But this statement is universally valid not because men actually agree—they do not agree. Nor does it imply that men must be forced to agree—they cannot really be compelled to like or dislike anything, and in any event, to try compulsion in such matters is to deny man's autonomy. Rather, the statement "this is beautiful" *imputes* universal agreement; it acts as if all men of reason would assent to it once they had fully grasped it. Thus aesthetic judgment is a call to seriousness and responsibility; it burdens the critic with the highest possible obligation—to make judgments that *deserve* universal acceptance.

This is a severe system and a decisive step. By assigning to art its own sphere and its own logic, and by liberating it from irrelevant concerns just as scientists of his day were freeing science, Kant car-

---

[5] Ibid., 280.
[6] Ibid., 281.
[7] Ibid., 430.

ried a century-old revolution to its logical conclusion. "*Élargissez l'art*—set art free!" Mercier had exclaimed in 1773, in his *Nouvel Essai sur l'art dramatique*, and Kant did nothing less. It was, at least in one respect, an amusing and paradoxical act: in its aspirations, art took the same course as the social and political thought of the Enlightenment, but it could encompass its aim only in one way—by separating itself from them.

CHAPTER SEVEN

The Science of Society

I. THE FIRST SOCIAL SCIENTISTS

I

In AESTHETICS, the philosophes wrote brilliant and fertile essays; in the social sciences they did more—they laid the foundations and wrote the classics. They were the pioneers in sociology, political economy, and history; we can still read Montesquieu's *De l'esprit des lois*, Adam Smith's *Wealth of Nations*, and Gibbon's *Decline and Fall of the Roman Empire* with real pleasure, and more than pleasure, with the sense that they are part of our world. With them, and with other classics like Voltaire's *Essai sur les mœurs* and Ferguson's *Essay on the History of Civil Society*, the prehistory of the social sciences gives way to its history.

The prehistory of the social sciences had its beginning in the emergence of cultural relativism, the bittersweet fruit of travel. Whether realistic, embroidered, or imaginary, whether on ships or in libraries, travel was the school of comparison, and travelers' reports were the ancestors of treatises on cultural anthropology and political sociology. It led to the attempt on the part of Western man to discover the position of his own civilization and the nature of humanity by pitting his own against other cultures. The essence of social science, like that of any science, is objectivity, and in the study of society, the search for objectivity was materially aided by the conviction, at first tentative and timid but growing more confident with time, that no culture, not even Christian culture—and, in the philosophes' view, especially not Christian culture—was the privileged standard of perfection by which other, lesser cultures could be measured and patronized.

One did not need to be a philosophe to find travel literature instructive. Once again, the philosophes were sustained by a widespread attitude. In 1735, in the Preface to his translation of *père* Jerome Lobo's *Voyage to Abyssinia*, Samuel Johnson praised the Jesuit traveler for his refusal to feed his readers "romantic absurdities," and for staying instead within the realms of probability: "Here are no Hottentots without religion, polity, or articulate language; no Chinese perfectly polite, and completely skilled in all sciences."[1] One could wish that Montesquieu and Voltaire had always been as tough-minded as Samuel Johnson; the philosophes, seeking to discredit Christianity by exalting Oriental philosophers or Tahitian savages, could be credulous on principle. However, these lapses apart—and they are disturbing rather than crippling to the philosophes' enterprise of founding the science of society—the philosophes used the abundant travel literature intelligently, keeping both their sentimental regard for the stranger and their polemical purpose within bounds. While the discovery of well-organized cultures that knew not Christ was a trauma to many, it was an opportunity for the philosophes, and not simply an opportunity for scoring points. For the social scientists of the Enlightenment, travel reports were a valued source of information, a "museum, in which specimens of every variety of human nature may be studied,"[2] and, with that, a basis for general theories. Montesquieu's inquiries into foreign civilizations, which he noted down among his *Pensées*, published in short essays, and wove into the texture of his masterpiece, *De l'esprit des lois*, was an influential instance of this new relativism: other social scientists of his time, and after him, absorbed his teachings and imitated his method. Montesquieu, in his jottings and asides, demonstrates that cultural relativism consists in part of separating what had been united: the Chinese theater may offend Western sensibilities, he writes, but not reason; the use of certain techniques

---

[1] "Preface" to Father Jerome Lobo: *Voyage to Abyssinia*, quoted from James L. Clifford: *Young Sam Johnson* (1955), 147.

[2] Sir James Macintosh: *The Law of Nature and of Nations* (1798), quoted in J. W. Burrow: *Evolution and Society: A Study in Victorian Social History* (1966), 12. While Sir James has history in mind here, for the social scientists of the eighteenth century what applied to history applied to all other social sciences as well.

in the modern drama may be contrary to custom, but not to nature.[3] For Montesquieu, and for the other philosophes, the world turned out to be larger, more interesting, more varied than it had ever been; travelers proved that the range of possible beliefs, customs, institutions, and defensible human behavior was enormous. The spectacle moved Montesquieu to observe, most unclassically: "The true is not always probable."[4] This was radical, even shocking doctrine, but indispensable to the establishment of a truly comprehensive science of man and society. It is through such science alone, Condillac suggested that the statesman and the reformer can move from writing a *roman* to understanding and mastering reality.[5]

The lust for improvement was never far from the philosophes' consciousness. Facts and theories existed for the sake of values. Doubtless the philosophes found the world interesting for its own sake; their inquiries into comparative institutions or the history of religion are pervaded by the pure air of sheer curiosity. They delighted in the new, and found the steady enlargement of their world nothing less than exhilarating. But they could rest content with private pleasure as little as with scientific detachment; in this engagement with reform, they were different from many social scientists in our own day.

They were different from twentieth-century sociologists and economists in another respect as well. Like other professions, the social sciences of the eighteenth century were beginning to define their areas and refine their methods, and to undergo a process of specialization. But even by the end of the Enlightenment, the division of labor among intellectuals was not yet very much advanced; perhaps nothing places the philosophes quite so much as the fact that they were not specialists but men of letters with classical training and philosophical competence. The versatility of their productions is testimony to their aspiration to universality. Montesquieu was a historian, political scientist, social critic, and political theorist

---

[3] For instances of this kind of relativism, see Charles Jacques Beyer: "Montesquieu et le relativisme esthétique," *VS*, XXIV (1963), 171–82, especially 178–9.

[4] *Pensées*, in *Œuvres*, II, 158.

[5] *Traité des systèmes*, in *Œuvres*, I, 208-9.

as well as a sociologist; Adam Smith a student of rhetoric and a moral philosopher as well as an economist; Voltaire a playwright, popularizer of science, and a religious and political publicist as well as a historian. And the other things these social scientists were shaped the way they wrote sociology, economics, and history. Their most technical performances are highly literate, and, in the end, utilitarian. The philosophes were relativists to a degree unthinkable before them, but neither their professional situation nor their philosophical convictions permitted them to erect their relativism into an absolute principle. Their absolutes were freedom, tolerance, reason, and humanity.

The philosophes' conception of social sciences, then, was dual, and in potential inner tension. The dilemma they faced in the natural sciences pursued them to the social sciences. Knowledge itself—of this they were certain—was a value; ignorance was certainly always an evil. But—and of this they were certain also—if knowledge was always a value, it was not always used well. To be sure, scientific truths, whether in physics or economics, were only themselves. Wishes were not truths; in fact, wishes often obscured the search for truth. But unfortunately, truths could be used for evil ends in evil hands: Gibbon's analysis of the manner in which Roman statesmen manipulated popular credulity and kept their power by preaching superstitions they did not share was one instance of it; Bentham's analysis of "sinister interests," which explained why politicians who knew the truth failed to apply it in their policies, was another.[6] The philosophes' refusal to construct a theory of progress now turns out to be a refusal to be complacent about the effects that the accumulation of knowledge might have on the shape of life. The harmony between knowledge and improvement was not automatic, or inevitable; it was a demand that runs through the philosophes' conception of what social science must be. In their eyes, scientific detachment and reformist involvement belonged together; the application of reason to society meant that knowledge and welfare, knowledge and freedom, knowledge and happiness must be made into inseparable allies. The philosophes were the ancestors of modern positivism, but their positivism, as Herbert Marcuse has rightly said,

---

[6] See *The Rise of Modern Paganism*, 154–9.

was "militant and revolutionary"[7]; it was, on principle and in practice, critical.

2. SOCIOLOGY: FACTS, FREEDOM, AND HUMANITY

I

WHATEVER MAY HAVE BECOME OF sociology in the nineteenth century, when the discipline got its name and took a distinctly conservative and nostalgic turn, in the Enlightenment, when it was invented, it was a science designed to advance freedom and humanity. "The philosophy of the eighteenth century," wrote Saint-Simon, "has been critical and revolutionary; that of the nineteenth century will be inventive and constructive."[8] Like other intellectual instruments devised or perfected in the eighteenth century, sociology suffered from bouts of self-confidence that its practitioners could not suppress. There were times when moral philosophers rose with unseemly haste from statements of fact to general laws, or, eager to cast their net as widely as possible, accepted facts with a credulity they would have spurned in Christians, or, imitating mathematicians, rashly imposed quantitative methods on qualitative experience. But theirs were venial rather than mortal sins, the missteps of scientists groping for the methods and the boundaries of their new science. For all this lack of clarity and lack of modesty, the aims of eighteenth-century sociology were clear enough: to substitute reliable information and rational theory for guessing and metaphysics, and to use the newly won knowledge in behalf of man.

Montesquieu, the first and the greatest sociologist in the Enlightenment, embodies this scientific reformism perhaps more strikingly than anyone else. As he insisted in the Preface to his *De l'esprit des lois,* he was indeed a scientist: "I have not drawn my principles

---

[7] *Reason and Revolution: Hegel and the Rise of Social Theory* (1941), 341.
[8] Quoted in "Introduction," *Henri de Saint-Simon: Social Organization, The Science of Man and Other Writings,* ed. Felix Markham (1952), xxi.

from my prejudices, but from the nature of things"; and he reassured his readers that he was merely a reporter: "I do not write to criticize whatever is established in any country." At the same time, and in the same place, he made it plain that facts, for him, were in the service of values: "I should think myself the happiest of mortals if I could help men to cure themselves of their prejudices"; indeed, "it is not unimportant to have the people enlightened."[9] His intentions, at least, were clear and pure.

His execution was something else again. *De l'esprit des lois* is a flawed performance; even contemporaries who admired its originality and shared its pagan philosophy tempered their praise with reservations. It is the most unkempt masterpiece of the century: short chapters, some only one sentence in length, alternate with long disquisitions, and, especially in the later books, topics appear and reappear in bewildering sequence. The work has a certain coherence imposed on it by its author's passion for finding law behind the apparent rule of chance and general themes in the fragmented mosaic of particular facts, but the order is concealed behind digressions, abrupt shifts of theme, and rhetorical outbursts. Roughly the first third of *De l'esprit des lois*—doubtless the most important deals with the nature and forms of government and the rights of subjects; the book then turns to an analysis of the impact of environment on politics and concludes with a potpourri which contains, among other things, discussions of political economy, French politics, and legal theory. No wonder Voltaire called the book "a labyrinth without a clue, lacking all method" and thought that its strength lay in particular ideas, in its "true, bold, and strong things." Moreover, as Voltaire also complained, not without cause, Montesquieu was uncritical of the facts he had drawn from histories and travelers' reports, and his citations were often inaccurate: "He almost always mistakes his imagination for his memory."[1] Finally, Montesquieu, no doubt unconsciously, smuggled ideology into his science: his definition of political freedom, his analysis of the British Constitution, and his advocacy of powerful aristocracies made him into a partisan in the great struggle that divided the French state in the eighteenth century rather than a neutral observer transcending his

---

[9] "Préface," *De l'esprit des lois*, in *Œuvres*, I, part 1, lx–lxi.
[1] "A,B,C," in *Philosophical Dictionary*, II, 500, 502.

time and class. His claim that he had freed himself from his prejudices was not borne out by his performance.[2]

Yet whatever his ambiguous role in French politics, whatever the limitations on his vision and the defects in his scholarship—and I make this assertion after due deliberation and with due consideration for the claims of potential rivals—Montesquieu was the most influential writer of the eighteenth century. Horace Walpole, who read *De l'esprit des lois* as soon as it became generally available, in January 1750, called it without hesitation "the best book that ever was written—at least I never learned half so much from all I ever read"[3]; when he heard that Montesquieu's reputation in France had suffered, he declared his contempt for French "*literati*" and reiterated his initial response: "In what book in the world is there half so much wit, sentiment, delicacy, humanity?"[4] The world agreed with Walpole. The men of the Scottish Enlightenment studied *De l'esprit des lois* with great care and great profit. The book was read, clandestinely, in Vienna and, more openly, in the Italian states, where Genovesi, Beccaria, Filangieri, and other *illuministi* confessed themselves the disciples of "the immortal Montesquieu."[5] In the Germanies, Lessing and the Göttingen historical school admired and imitated Montesquieu's cultural relativism while political thinkers absorbed his views on the British Constitution. The leading revolutionaries and Founding Fathers in America used the writings of "that great man" —the epithet is Hamilton's[6]—probably more than they used anyone else's. And it is instructive to see Catherine of Russia, who was, after all, relatively untouched by his comprehensive liberality, finding it useful to borrow Montesquieu's prestige by proclaiming herself his devoted follower. Even the French could not finally refuse him their esteem—had not Voltaire written that Frenchmen discover everything late, but, in the end, do discover it? Diderot's *Encyclopédie*, which enlisted Montesquieu among its most distinguished contributors, did much to disseminate his ideas, and Rous-

---

[2] See below, chap. ix, section 2.
[3] Walpole to Horace Mann, January 10, 1750. *The Letters of Horace Walpole*, ed. Mrs. Paget Toynbee, 16 vols. (1903–5), II, 419.
[4] Walpole to the same, February 25, 1750. Ibid., 433.
[5] This is Beccaria's name for him; see *Dei delitti e delle pene* (1764; ed. Franco Venturi, 1965), 10.
[6] *The Federalist*, No. 9 (ed. Jacob E. Cooke, 1961), 52.

seau's *Contrat social* is unthinkable without Montesquieu's political
sociology.

To judge from the response of his contemporary readers, much
of Montesquieu's immediate appeal lay in the quality that Horace
Walpole had listed last—his humanity. The polemic against the slave
trade in *De l'esprit des lois*, for one, struck Walpole as "glorious"[7];
and Voltaire found the same glory in the same polemic: "The chapters on the Inquisition," he wrote, "and on Negro slaves, are far
better than Callot. Throughout he battles despotism, makes financiers
hateful, courtiers contemptible, monks ridiculous."[8] The book was,
for the philosophes, a feast of reason and decency.

The real originality and lasting importance of *De l'esprit des
lois*, however, lie in the particular relation it established between
reason and decency. Montesquieu's argument is fairly simple,
and its materials are old; what was complex, and new, was his manner
of combining what others had known. His system is imperfectly
perspicuous, for it depends on intellectual procedures—deduction
and induction—that Montesquieu neither clarified nor reconciled.
On the other hand, he professes to deduce his sociological laws from
first principles; on the other, his laws group particular experiences
into intelligible wholes—in Montesquieu's sociology the great
contest between rationalism and empiricism was never settled. It
was "Descartes and Malebranche far more than Locke," Franz
Neumann has written, "who determined Montesquieu's scientific
method"[9]—but the importance of Locke was not negligible. The two
principles on which he constructed his system—the uniformity of
human nature and the diversity produced by environment and
culture—have an independent validity. But they are also at times
in tension.

Whatever these tensions, his argument was, as I have said, plain
enough. There are, Montesquieu reasons, certain laws of nature that
apply to all men, since they are derived from "the constitution of our
being."[1] But these laws find different expression in different situa-

---

[7] To Horace Mann, February 25, 1750. *Letters*, II, 433.
[8] "A,B,C," in *Philosophical Dictionary*, II, 500. For a more detailed
discussion of Montesquieu's humanitarianism, especially as embodied in book XII of *De l'esprit des lois*, see below, 410–13, 427–33.
[9] "Introduction," Montesquieu: *The Spirit of the Laws* (edn.
1949), xxxiv.
[1] *De l'esprit des lois*, book I, chap. ii, *Œuvres*, I, part 1, 5.

tions; they are bent into individual shape by physical causes like climate, soil, size of the country, and by what Montesquieu calls "moral" causes like customs and religion. The task of social science is to find both the universal laws and their appropriate application to each situation. The logic of Montesquieu's social science is the logic of cultural relativism: "There is, he believes, no universally applicable solution. There are only types of solutions."[2]

The configuration of laws appropriate to a certain nation is "the spirit of the laws,"[3] and Montesquieu's book is an attempt to discover and define that spirit in all its multiformity. He begins, conventionally enough, with a classification of government by types of rulership—an enterprise as old as Plato and Aristotle, although his classification differs from theirs. He finds essentially three forms of government: republics, monarchies, and despotisms. This classification caused some dissent in his day; but it is only a prelude to what really matters: the "principles" actuating each of these forms.[4] The history of political sociology begins at this point. The principle of republics, Montesquieu argues, is "virtue," and, as there are two kinds of republics, there are two kinds of virtue: democratic republics rest on public spirit; aristocratic republics on the moderation and self-restraint of the ruling families. Monarchies for their part are animated by what Montesquieu calls "honor"—a keen awareness of status, accompanied by aspiration to preferment and titles. Despotism, finally, is actuated by fear. Montesquieu knows perfectly well that there is an admixture of each of these elements in all states; what matters is which predominates. When one principle powerfully invades a state to which it is not suited, pernicious consequences are inescapable: the right principle will be corrupted, then collapse and revolution must follow.

This is a fertile scheme. It permits Montesquieu to penetrate

---

[2] Franz Neumann: "Introduction," *The Spirit of the Laws*, xxxii.
[3] See *De l'esprit des lois*, book I, chap. iii, *Œuvres*, I, part 1, 9.
[4] As most commentators have noted, Montesquieu's classification differs from the classical model. Montesquieu groups together aristocracies and democracies under republics, while Plato and Aristotle had separated them; and he lists despotism as a separate form, while to the classical theorists it was a corruption of a good form of government. But what is essentially new about Montesquieu's classification is his introduction of the principles that underlie the forms.

beyond forms to substance; to discover, behind institutions, the forces that make them cohere, persist, or falter. It permits him, further, to find the institutions appropriate to each state: a monarchy needs schools, or a family organization, quite different from those needed in a republic. And finally it permits him to address himself to the dynamic of social change: "The corruption of every government," Montesquieu writes, in one of those one-sentence chapters that so amused Voltaire, "begins almost always with the corruption of its principles."[5] *De l'esprit des lois* takes a comprehensive view of political sociology: it finds room for the sociology of law and of education, and suggests a sociological view of history.

Up to this point, Montesquieu has taken the diversity of governments as given; now, in his most celebrated and most controversial chapters, he turns to the physical causes that have made this diversity possible, indeed inevitable: size, geographical situation, and climate. For all the apparent abruptness with which Montesquieu moves from the principles of government to the physiology of man, the two sections are closely related: the one supplies the ideal categories—that is, the various forms of government; the other accounts for their origins. It is here that Montesquieu depends most openly on travelers like Chardin, whose writings he had already exploited in his *Lettres persanes;* they now reappear to supply him both with facts and theories.

Montesquieu's famous chapters on climate, which borrow extensively from the ubiquitous abbé Dubos, generalize a notion from physiology into a theory of human conduct. "Cold air contracts the extremities of the external fibres of the body; this increases their activity, and facilitates the return of the blood from the extremities to the heart." On the other hand, "warm air relaxes and lengthens the extremities of the fibres, and thus reduces their force and their activity." It follows that in cold climates, where the blood moves freely, men are courageous, generous, candid, insensitive to pain: "One must skin a Muscovite alive to make him feel." In hot climates, on the contrary, men are timid, sensitive to pleasure, amorous: "In northern climates, sexuality—*la physique de l'amour*—can scarcely

---

[5] *De l'esprit des lois,* book VIII, chap. 1, *Œuvres,* I, part 1, 149.

make itself felt; in temperate climates, love, accompanied by a thousand accessories, makes itself agreeable with things that seem at first to be, but are not yet, love; in warmer climates, love is loved for itself; it is the only cause of happiness; it is life." These physiological differences leave their mark in the most astonishing places: "I have heard operas in England and in Italy, the same pieces with the same singers, but the same music produced very different effects in the two nations: one was so calm, the other so carried away, that it seemed inconceivable."[6] The consequences are far-reaching: different climates produce different wants, different wants different styles of life, different styles of life different laws.[7] Institutions like slavery, or polygamy, or parliamentary government arise in response to climatic requirements, and some of them, like polygamy or monogamy, should actually be "left to the climate"[8]—here speaks the relativist. Even the Englishman's love of liberty, which Montesquieu so admired, had its roots in the environment; it is the fruit of the impatience produced by disagreeable cold weather.

Montesquieu considers environment in a comprehensive sense: it is not merely the prevailing temperature that creates the prevailing temper, but also the geographical configuration of a country—the presence of vast plains or high mountains, the relative fertility of its soil, or the size of its territory. The wise legislator understands all these physical causes and undertakes to make laws in accordance with them. Man need not be wholly dominated by climate—he is governed, after all, by moral as well as by physical causes. But there is wisdom in restraint, and the environment sets limits beyond which the intelligent politician must not go. Bacon's injunction that we master nature by obeying her acquires new vigor in Montesquieu's sociology.

Montesquieu's physiology is of mere antiquarian interest today. Even in his own time, there were some skeptics. In his essay "Of National Characters," published in 1748, the year that *De l'esprit des lois* first appeared, Hume expressed his "doubt altogether" that "*physical causes*" have any effect on man; he did not think "that

---

[6] Ibid., book XIV, chap. ii, *Œuvres*, I, part 1, 305–9.
[7] Ibid., book XIV, chap. x, *Œuvres*, I, part 1, 315–17.
[8] Ibid., book XVI, chap. xi, *Œuvres*, I, part 1, 360.

men owe any thing of their temper or genius to the air, food, or climate."[9] Voltaire for his part explicitly denied at least part of Montesquieu's theory: "The influence he claims for climate on religion is taken from Chardin, and is no truer for all that."[1] Yet, in 1767, Adam Ferguson almost despaired of having any sociological work left to do: "When I recollect what the President Montesquieu has written, I am at a loss to tell, why I should treat of human affairs."[2] In the same year, after much reflection, Hume judged that *De l'esprit des lois*, though "considerably sunk in Vogue," was still a book with "considerable Merit, notwithstanding the Glare of its pointed Wit, and notwithstanding its false Refinements and its rash and crude Positions."[3] What mattered then, and matters now, is not Montesquieu's physiology—his false refinements and rash positions—but the nature of his enterprise, his method, and his purpose.

That purpose flowed directly from a will to understand, which was the will to give reasons for what appeared irrational, to find order in apparent chaos, and unity in variety without denying that variety. Montesquieu's purpose, Raymond Aron has said, "was to make history intelligible," and he realized that purpose, if incompletely, by seeking causes rather than ascribing everything to inscrutable fortune, and by grouping causes into small, manageable groups. The road to positivist sociology was thus open.[4]

It is worth repeating that Montesquieu was never satisfied to formulate general laws and leave value judgments to others; he was too much the classicist, too much the humanist, too much the philosophe for that. He recognized that his commitment to facts and values sometimes involved him in paradoxes and contradictions. It is touching to see him struggling with himself: thus he speaks at length, and quite coolly, about slavery, and argues that in the West at least slavery is useless and uneconomical—then he adds a little

---

[9] "Of National Characters," *Works*, III, 246.
[1] "A,B,C," in *Philosophical Dictionary*, II, 502.
[2] *History of Civil Society*, 65.
[3] To Hugh Blair, April 1, 1767. *Letters*, II, 133.
[4] See Raymond Aron: *Main Currents in Sociological Thought*, I, *Montesquieu, Comte, Marx, Tocqueville* . . . (1960; tr. Richard Howard and Helen Weaver, 1965), 14–16.

pathetically, "I do not know if this chapter was dictated to me by my mind or my heart."[5] The distinction between causal and normative inquiry was hard to maintain, even for him.

His analysis of despotism reveals both his ambivalence and his intentions. On the one hand, Montesquieu lists despotism among forms of government and assigns to it a principle as he has assigned principles to others. On the other hand, he sets off despotism from all other forms: monarchies, aristocracies, and democracies are legitimate forms, despotism is always bad. It is a "monstrous" form of government; it "takes glory in despising life." Despotism may aim at tranquillity, but its tranquillity is only terror: "It is not peace; it is the silence of towns the enemy is ready to occupy." Despotism enlists religion in the regime of fear—"fear added to fear"—depoliticizes its subjects, and treats men like animals by subjecting them to corruption and police brutality under capricious and unknown laws. As a sociologist, Montesquieu found it appropriate to analyze the phenomenon of despotism, to acknowledge its plausibility in vast empires and hot climates, but as a moralist he found nothing worthy in a regime whose principle was fear, whose policy was tyranny, and whose consequence was inhumanity. "Nothing I have said here," Montesquieu suddenly and passionately bursts out in the midst of a detached analysis of the spirit of nations, "should diminish in any way the infinite distance between vice and virtue: may God forbid it!"[6] The analysis of despotism was meant as a warning against it.

It is, as I have suggested, this mixture of curiosity and decency that impressed even his critics among the philosophes. *De l'esprit des lois*, Voltaire said, was "full of admirable things," which "should always be precious to men," precious because everywhere Montesquieu "reminds men that they are free; he shows mankind the rights it has lost in most of the world; he combats superstition, he inspires good morals."[7] Adam Ferguson put Montesquieu's admirable search for harmony between science and ethics quite economically:

---

[5] *De l'esprit des lois*, book XV, chap. viii, *Œuvres*, I, part 1, 334.
[6] Ibid., book III, chaps. ix, viii; book V, chap. xiv; book XIX, chap. xi, *Œuvres*, I, part 1, 34–6, 78–84, 418.
[7] "A,B,C," in *Philosophical Dictionary*, II, 508–9.

Montesquieu, he wrote, was a "profound politician and amiable moralist."[8]

II

Like another French philosophe—Diderot—Montesquieu was more influential abroad than at home. I have indicated the range of his empire—from America to Russia, from the Scotland of Ferguson to the Naples of Filangieri—but among all his dependencies Scotland must rank first. Hume, though critical of Montesquieu's "abstract theory of morals" and sparing with hyperbole, thought him an "author of genius, as well as learning."[9] Ferguson treated him as a modern classic: he lectured on Montesquieu, recommended him to his students, quoted him without criticism and paraphrased him without acknowledgment; indeed, acknowledgment would have been otiose: *De l'esprit des lois* was the common coin of learned discussion.

There was good reason for Scotland's receptivity to Montesquieu: his particular mixture of philosophy and science was wholly congenial to the Scottish Enlightenment, which had been developing its own tradition of secular sociological inquiry since the beginning of the eighteenth century. Francis Hutcheson, moral philosopher and student of society, had many disciples, a brilliant assembly of intellectuals—David Hume, John Millar, Adam Ferguson, Lord Kames, Lord Monboddo, William Robertson—followed, in the next generation, by Adam Smith and Dugald Stewart. All were to a degree moral philosophers, all turned under the pressure of their inquiries to the scientific study of society. The problems these Scots addressed became the classical problems of sociology: the origins of civilization, man's place in society, the development of language, the relations of classes, the rise and fall of population and their interplay with cultivation and prosperity, and the forms of government. Their inquiries led them into the commonplace and the remote: Lord Monboddo, perhaps the most learned and certainly the

---

[8] *History of Civil Society*, 65.
[9] *Enquiry Concerning the Principles of Morals*, in *Works*, IV, 190, 191 *n*.

most eccentric member of the clan, took a persistent and sometimes comical interest in the place of apes in the chain of created beings. But Monboddo, too, was serious: he studied apes so that he might understand man. However much their researches varied in effectiveness and direction, the intentions of the Scottish school were united in a single pursuit: to place moral philosophy on a sound, that is to say, a scientific, basis. By mid-century, the Scots could equate morals and science—Hume spoke of "Moral philosophy, *or* the science of human nature."[1] Scientific metaphors were always in their minds: "The great Montesquieu pointed out the road," wrote John Millar in acknowledging the debt he owed to Adam Smith, his teacher and friend. "He was the Lord Bacon in this branch of philosophy. Dr. Smith is the Newton."[2] The comparison was trite when Millar made it in the 1780s, and its application doubtful, but it confirms the aspiration of the Scottish school toward a science of society.

The strategic figure in translating that aspiration from a philosophical fantasy to a realistic possibility was, as usual, David Hume. "There is no subject," he warned with his characteristic skepticism, "in which we must proceed with more caution, than in tracing the history of the arts and sciences; lest we assign causes which never existed."[3] He was willing to claim that "politics admits of general truths"[4]; there are certain universal axioms that scholars can derive from history and observation. But these truths are provisional, and the axioms few and uncertain, for the materials of the social sciences are difficult to control—even more difficult than the materials of the biological sciences: "It affords a violent prejudice against almost every science, that no prudent man, however sure of his principles, dares prophesy concerning any event, or foretel the remote consequence of things. A physician will not venture to pronounce concerning the condition of his patient a fortnight or month after; And

---

[1] These are the opening words of Hume's *Enquiry Concerning Human Understanding*, in ibid., IV, 3 (italics mine).
[2] *An Historical View of the English Government from the Settlement of the Saxons in Britain to the Revolution in 1688*, 4 vols. (1787; 4th edn., 1818), II, 429–30. I owe this reference to my former student David Weissbrodt.
[3] "Of the Rise and Progress of the Arts and Sciences," *Works*, III, 176.
[4] "That Politics May be Reduced to a Science," ibid., III, 101.

still less dares a politician foretel the situation of public affairs a few years hence."[5]

Hume's cautious disclaimer was at the same time an ambitious claim. "Moral philosophy has, indeed, this peculiar disadvantage, which is not found in natural," he noted in his first work, "that in collecting its experiments, it cannot make them purposely, with premeditation, and after such a manner as to satisfy itself concerning every particular difficulty which may arise." Men can "glean up" experiments in the science of society only "from a cautious observation of human life, and take them as they appear in the common course of the world, by men's behavior in company, in affairs, and in their pleasures." But while this disability was specific to the social sciences, the problem of knowledge in the social and the natural sciences was in principle precisely the same. It was after all a central tenet of Hume's epistemology that man can attain absolute certainty only through deduction, in what he called "relations of ideas," in definitions and in mathematics, but he must remain content with high probability in all inquiries employing induction, in matters of fact. The distinction between physics and sociology, therefore, was only one of degree, involving the recalcitrance of the material. "If this impossibility of explaining ultimate principles should be esteemed a defect in the science of man," Hume wrote, "I will venture to affirm, that 'tis a defect common to it with all the sciences, and all the arts, in which we can employ ourselves, whether they be such as are cultivated in the schools of the philosophers, or practised in the shops of the meanest artizans. None of them can go beyond experience, or establish any principles which are not founded on that authority." The certainty men could secure in the natural sciences was smaller, the certainty they could secure in the social sciences was greater than they had hoped for. Hume's skepticism is really a prescription for confidence: "Where experiments," he concludes, "are judiciously collected and compared, we may hope to establish on them a science, which will not be inferior in certainty, and will be much superior in utility to any other of human comprehension."[6]

---

[5] "Whether the British Government Inclines More to Absolute Monarchy, or to a Republic," ibid., III, 122.
[6] "Introduction," *Treatise of Human Nature*, xxii–xxiii. See above, chap. iii.

The temper of Hume's social science thus represents the critical temper of the Enlightenment: man must unmask pleasing dreams for the sake of realistic programs, fictions for the sake of reality. As his respectful but devastating critique of Locke's political thought shows, Hume is ready to sacrifice even a beneficent fiction: the idea of an original social contract may have useful consequences, but it is unfortunately unfounded. "Reason, history, and experience shew us, that all political societies have had an origin much less accurate and regular."[7] Hume seeks to convert not merely moral philosophy, but political philosophy, into sociology.

I need hardly add that as a man of the Enlightenment, Hume, for all his skepticism and for all his inclination toward positivism, was never the merely neutral observer. Hume was not the man to get excited about social reform; if (to paraphrase Lessing) he had been offered a choice between truth and improvement, he would have chosen truth. Yet he made no secret of his preferences for cultivation, cosmopolitanism, and decency, his distaste for superstition, enthusiasm, and barbarism, and his hopes that his philosophizing would aid the one and oppose the other. "Indulge your passion for science," he has Nature say to man, "but let your science be human, and such as may have a direct reference to action and society. . . . Be a philosopher; but amidst all your philosophy, be still a man."[8] It is a sententious sentiment, but, since Hume was not a sententious man, it deserves to be taken seriously. It is of great interest to see Hume explicitly disputing Pope's relativistic couplet—"For forms of government let fools contest/Whate'er is best administer'd is best." "Though a friend to moderation," Hume objects, "I cannot forbear condemning this sentiment." Pope is wrong in fact: human affairs depend on more than the "casual humours and characters of particular men."[9] He is undiscriminating in theory: absolute monarchies are far more exposed to the caprice of individuals than constitutional regimes. Finally—although this is implicit rather than

---

[7] "Of the Original Contract," *Works*, III, 450.
[8] *An Enquiry Concerning Human Understanding*, ibid., IV, 6.
[9] "That Politics May be Reduced to a Science," ibid., III, 98 *n.*, 98. In one of his political dialogues, Wieland takes issue with the same couplet. *Gespräche unter vier Augen*, in *Werke*, XLII, 166. It is quoted in *The Federalist*, No. 68 (ed. Jacob Cooke), 461; and see below, 494.

explicit—Pope's extreme relativism obstructs an understanding of political laws which permit the construction of a good government. "In every respect," whatever its form, "a gentle government is preferable, and gives the greatest security to the sovereign as well as to the subject."[1] Science, precisely by being science rather than metaphysics, creates and preserves values.

III

In 1767, Hume's friend Adam Ferguson, a former chaplain, lapsed Christian, Professor of Moral Philosophy and Pneumatics at Edinburgh, published his first and, it was to turn out, his most important book, *An Essay on the History of Civil Society*. For some reason, still obscure, Hume did not like the *Essay;* perhaps its ponderous, often tedious manner reminded him a little uncomfortably of the Scottish provincialism he himself had barely escaped. But whatever the reason, his disapproval should not obscure Ferguson's affinity with Hume: the *Essay* embodies and occasionally improves upon the style of sociological thinking that Hume had defined and exemplified in his essays. Like Hume, Ferguson was an enemy to fictions, and like Hume, he undertook the scientific study of society for moral reasons. Men shall know the truth—this, in sum, is Ferguson's motive and program—and the truth shall permit them to break the traditional cycles of civilization and decay. But the truth is elusive: Ferguson punctuates his *Essay* with warnings against rash conjectures, easy generalizations, and mere book learning. The warnings are repetitious and seem a little insistent, but they were not without point: only five years before, Adam Smith had told his students that "the practical sciences of Politics and Morality or Ethics have of late been treated too much in a Speculative manner."[2] The very obscurity of man's origins, Ferguson argues, has seduced modern investigators into that supreme intellectual vice—system-making. "The desire of laying the foundation of a favourite system, or a fond expectation, perhaps, that we may be able to penetrate the

---

[1] "That Politics May be Reduced to a Science," *Works*, III, 105.
[2] Adam Smith: *Lectures on Rhetoric and Belles Lettres*, ed. John M. Lothian (1963), 37.

secrets of nature, to the very source of existence, have, on this subject, led to many fruitless inquiries, and given rise to many wild suppositions." After all, Ferguson complains, other scientists do not follow such dubious methods: "In every other instance . . . the natural historian thinks himself obliged to collect facts, not to offer conjectures." But, it seems, when he studies himself, "in matters the most important, and the most easily known," the student of society "substitutes hypothesis instead of reality, and confounds the provinces of imagination and reason, of poetry and science"; he selects a few human characteristics, abstracts from current experience, and invents feeble fictions like the state of nature or the noble savage. "The progress of mankind from a supposed state of animal sensibility, to the attainment of reason, to the use of language, and to the habit of society, has been accordingly painted with a force of imagination, and its steps have been marked with a boldness of invention, that would tempt us to admit, among the materials of history, the suggestions of fancy, and to receive, perhaps, as the model of our nature in its original state, some of the animals whose shape has the greatest resemblance to ours." The sarcasm is heavy and its target obvious, but Ferguson does not permit his readers a moment's uncertainty: a footnote refers them to Rousseau's *Discours sur l'origine de l'inégalité parmi les hommes*. Rousseau's way, Ferguson insists, is not the way of science; the student of society must rest his case on "just observation." Human nature cannot be discovered by stripping away the contributions of culture to arrive at the naked, original being: "Art itself is natural to man."[3] So, significantly but not surprisingly, Ferguson begins his *History of Civil Society* with an attempt to arrive at a realistic appraisal of human nature—not its origins but "its reality" and "its consequences."[4] Two years later, in his published lecture notes, Ferguson would utter the same warnings and follow the same procedure: moral philosophy must rest on a scientific basis, an empirical natural history of man, which finds its evidence in geography, psychology, the history of language, culture, and population, and rises from facts to values, from science to morals, by slow steps. Ferguson was an independent disciple; he distilled his principles from Montesquieu's and Hume's sociological

---

[3] *History of Civil Society*, 1–5, 5 *n.*, 3, 6.
[4] Ibid., 26. See above, chap. iv, section 1.

ideas, but he was more severe, more chaste in its pursuit of ascertainable fact, that Montesquieu and even Hume had been.

The first victim of Ferguson's empiricism is the state of nature, the second is the legislator who supposedly transforms the horde into a society. "Man is born in society," Ferguson writes, quoting Montesquieu, "and there he remains." There can be no doubt: "Mankind have always wandered or settled, agreed or quarrelled, in troops and companies." The study of man and the study of society are thus wholly interdependent. What they show at the outset—here Ferguson turns to Hume—is both the unity and the diversity of man's nature. "The occupations of men, in every condition, bespeak their freedom of choice, their various opinions, and the multiplicity of wants by which they are urged; but they enjoy, or endure, with a sensibility, or a phlegm, which are nearly the same in every situation. They possess the shores of the Caspian, or the Atlantic, by a different tenure, but with equal ease." The claim that man has changed fundamentally by moving from the state of nature to the civil state is a total misreading of his history. If we ask, "Where the state of nature is to be found?" the answer must be, "It is here; and it matters not whether we are understood to speak in the islands of Great Britain, at the Cape of Good Hope, or the Straits of Magellan." And, just as travel in space offers the spectacle of uniformity, so does travel in time: "The latest efforts of human invention are but a continuation of certain devices which were practised in the earliest ages of the world, and in the rudest state of mankind."[5]

This uniformity is the expression of certain "universal qualities" in man, certain "instinctive propensities," which are "prior to the perception of pleasure or pain." Most notable among these propensities is man's instinct for self-preservation, which expresses itself in automatic self-protection, in sexuality, and in his sociable traits. Man's reason is equally composite: God—a singularly shadowy figure in Ferguson's philosophy—has endowed man with reason to permit him to know and to judge. But neither the urge for self-preservation nor the capacity to reason makes man essentially into a calculating and selfish animal: hedonistic psychology is, in Ferguson's judgment, shallow at its best and in general contrary to experience. Man is a creature of habit as much as of reason, the prey to

_____

[5] Ibid., 7–9.

ambition as much as the victim of conformity, and, above all, he is an active being, happiest when he exercises his powers. "Man is not made for repose," Ferguson writes, sounding much like Diderot. "In him, every amiable and respectable quality is an active power, and every subject of commendation an effort. If his errors and his crimes are the movements of an active being, his virtues and his happiness consist likewise in the employment of his mind." Happiness, writes Ferguson, in words that Lessing might have written, "arises more from the pursuit, than from the attainment of any end whatever."[6] The human animal is above all strenuous.

While Ferguson insists on the uniformity of man's nature, he insists just as emphatically on the diversity of institutions and ideals, and it is here—in accounting for this diversity—that social science finds its proper employment. It is a difficult task, for "the multiplicity of forms" that the social scientist must take into account "is almost infinite." After all, as Montesquieu had recognized, "forms of government must be varied, in order to suit the extent, the way of subsistence, the character, and the manners of different nations." Paradoxically enough, it is precisely the propensities of human nature—the principles, that is, of its unity—that lead to the diversity of human experience. For the urge to ally oneself with some implies the urge to divide oneself from others. "They are sentiments of generosity and self-denial that animate the warrior in defence of his country; and they are dispositions most favourable to mankind, that become the principles of apparent hostility to men." This is not a perverse pleasure in paradox: the dialectical character of human experience is for Ferguson an overwhelming fact. Civilization is natural; all civilizations are natural. But—and here we seem to hear the language of Freud's *Civilization and its Discontents*—all civilizations exact their price, all are a mixture of cooperation and conflict, of decay implicit in progress. To condemn all conflict indiscriminately is to read out of court half of human nature—"He who has never struggled with his fellow-creatures, is a stranger to half the sentiments of mankind."[7]—and to misunderstand, and misunderstand disastrously, the positive function of conflict in culture.

Ferguson's analysis of the nature and function of conflict is

---

[6] Ibid., 10–11, 210, 49.
[7] Ibid., 64, 62, 24.

well known; it deserves to be, for its cool detachment is as impressive as it is chilling. Man, Ferguson argues, positively enjoys hostility: "Mankind not only find in their condition the sources of variance and dissension; they appear to have in their minds the seeds of animosity, and to embrace the occasions of mutual opposition, with alacrity and pleasure." Friendship acquires its meaning from enmity; in fact, the stronger the hostility to outsiders the closer the bond of fellowship. Nor is it mere self-interest or rational calculation that brings aggression into play; here, as everywhere, hedonistic psychology fails. Aggression is natural, supremely human; it is—and this, for Ferguson, is high praise—invigorating: "To overawe, or intimidate, or, when we cannot persuade with reason, to resist with fortitude, are the occupations which give its most animating exercise, and its greatest triumphs, to a vigorous mind." Ferguson is a minority voice in the pacific consensus of the Enlightenment, but his admiration of heroic virtues is more than a reminiscence of classical ways of thinking or a personal prejudice; it is grounded, at least to his satisfaction, in his observation and his anthropological reading. Is it not true, after all, that man's very "sports are frequently an image of war"?[8]

Conflict—Ferguson returns to this point again and again—is not merely natural and pleasurable; it is also useful, in fact essential. "Without the rivalship of nations, and the practice of war, civil society itself could scarcely have found an object, or a form." In the light of Ferguson's psychology, the conclusion is inescapable: "It is vain to expect that we can give to the multitude of a people a sense of union among themselves, without admitting hostility to those who oppose them." States, like individuals, need enemies: "Athens was necessary to Sparta, in the exercise of her virtue, as steel is to flint in the production of fire."[9]

Ferguson's science of man does not end here. It is not enough to analyze and then fold one's hands, watching tyrants or corrupt politicians misuse one's work. Precisely like the other social scientists of his time, Ferguson refuses to equate objectivity with neutrality. Whether we are "actors or spectators," we perpetually "feel the difference of human conduct," and are "moved with admiration and pity, or transported with indignation and rage." These emo-

---

[8] Ibid., 20–4.
[9] Ibid., 25, 59.

tions, "joined to the powers of deliberation and reason," constitute "the basis of a moral nature."[1]

It is with this sense of being an engaged scholar that Ferguson delineates his virtuous man and describes the threats to flourishing civilizations. Fortunately, private happiness and public prosperity are consonant; benevolence gives pleasure not solely to the receiver but to the giver as well, and the vigorous exercise of one's public spirit is at once a source of personal gratification and of national well-being. Activity is praiseworthy, but it "may be carried to excess," and then it deserves censure. Similarly, while conflict is valuable, not every conflict is creditable in origins or beneficial in consequences—"the quarrels of individuals, indeed, are frequently the operations of unhappy and detestable passions; malice, hatred, and rage"[2]—and it should be possible to devise a kind of moral equivalent for detestable quarrels by sublimating them into praiseworthy competition.[3] This kind of discrimination that the student of society should apply to activity and conflict he must apply to other forms of social experience, all for the sake of moral judgment and sound public policy.

This policy, Ferguson believed, faced one awesome difficulty: the dialectic of progress. Civilization was preferable to rudeness—of this Ferguson had no doubt. The litanies against luxury, classical in inspiration and commonplace in the eighteenth century, struck him as indiscriminate, humorless, and on the whole reactionary. One man's luxury, he suggested reasonably enough, was another man's necessity; what might be the source of corruption in a simple culture might well be a pleasing and even essential quality in an advanced culture. Luxury, like every other aspect of highly civilized nations, must be seen as an ambiguous gift: "The boasted refinements, then, of the polished age, are not divested of danger. They open a door, perhaps, to disaster, as wide and accessible as any of those they have shut." A cure may bring a new disease, an advance in one field a retreat in another. The city that builds ramparts and walls protects itself but at the same time saps the martial energy of its citizens; the nation that forms disciplined armies may be safe from

---

[1] Ibid., 33.
[2] Ibid., 24.
[3] Forbes: "Introduction" to ibid., xix.

external aggression, but at the same time it prepares the way for a military dictatorship at home. Efficient administration may bring personal security and public honesty, but, by killing public spirit, it makes subjects "unworthy of the freedom they possess." Again, the pursuit of wealth produces the kind of civilized refinement that makes life pleasant, advances politeness, and helps the arts to flourish, but it also turns citizens into selfish hunters after wealth, destroys all sense of community, introduces false values—"we transfer the idea of perfection from the character to the equipage"[4]—and, indeed, spawn the kind of moral confusion that is both sign and cause of decay.

To Ferguson's mind, perhaps the most extraordinary instance of the paradox of progress is the division of labor. On the one hand, the division of labor is essential to social advance. Savages and barbarians are men of all trades, too worn out from their labors to improve their fortune, too scattered in their pursuits to acquire commendable skill in any single occupation. As the manufacturer, the merchant, the artist, the consumer discover, "the more he can confine his attention to a particular part of any work, his productions are the more perfect, and grow under his hands in the greater quantities." But just as the division of labor in public affairs brings efficiency in administration and alienation from politics, the division of labor in industrial or mercantile or artistic matters brings skill and prosperity—and alienation as well. Man (as Ferguson's admirer Karl Marx would put it) is alienated from his community, his labor, and himself; he is fragmented and mechanized: the community falls apart, divided between lowly mechanics and proud practitioners of the liberal arts, and the general increase in wealth is unevenly distributed, to the benefit of an elite and at the expense of the mass: "In every commercial state, notwithstanding any pretension to equal rights, the exaltation of a few must depress the many."[5] Thus the division of labor produces conceit and selfishness in some, envy and servility in most; it is a blessing and a curse, creating vast possibilities and great dangers. The economic problem is, for Ferguson, a social and, even more, a political problem.

Ferguson's pages on the division of labor are a minor triumph

---

[4] Ibid., 231–3, 221, 252.
[5] Ibid., 180–6.

of eighteenth-century sociology. True, they are scanty and incomplete, even for their own day—only a few years later, Ferguson's friend Adam Smith, who had been lecturing on this subject since the 1750s, would show in his *Wealth of Nations* just what could be done with it. Moreover, they are hesitant: Ferguson refused to draw all the revolutionary implications of his analysis. Yet they are in their own way admirable; they are alive with the critical energy that is intent on moving beyond the formal analysis of legal rights or constitutional arrangements to social and economic realities, and courageous enough to discard bland satisfaction with modern civilization and explore its discontents. He was unwilling to become a consistent radical reformer, but he pointed to action. "An extension of knowledge," he wrote, "is an extension of power," and the point of power was to exercise it.[6] States are not like individuals; the metaphor that likens the life of society to that of an individual is an invitation to irresponsibility. "When we are no longer willing to act for our country, we plead in excuse of our own weakness or folly, a supposed fatality in human affairs." The fact is that the life of institutions is not fixed, and the word "fatality" is only a self-fulfilling prophecy; if men say that decay is irresistible, they will cease to resist it, and decay will follow. But "men of real fortitude, integrity, and ability" will understand not merely the limits, but the extent of their powers. "While they are destined to live, the states they compose are likewise doomed by the fates to survive, and to prosper."[7] So, in the end, Ferguson converts analysis into prescription. It was a conversion wholly characteristic of sociological thinking in the Enlightenment.

---

[6] See David Kettler: *The Social and Political Thought of Adam Ferguson* (1965), 132.
[7] *History of Civil Society*, 279–80.

3· POLITICAL ECONOMY: FROM POWER TO WEALTH

I

IN THE AGE of the Enlightenment, the science of sociology consisted mainly of attempts at objectivity and at making laws from
comprehensive comparative surveys. The conquest of quantity,
which was then, as it is now, the very symbol of science to many,
was a bright fantasy among eighteenth-century sociologists, little
more. Beccaria suggested the application of probability theory to
finding the proper punishment for convicted criminals;[8] and Condorcet sought to develop what he called a "social mathematics"[9] in
pursuit of a reliable system of suffrage. "The social art," he wrote
in his last book, significantly confounding art and science in a single
phrase, "is a true science based, like all the others, on experiments,
reasoning, and calculation."[1] Condorcet made explicit what the
others believed: the more precise the information, the more effective the reform.

But sociologists found quantity elusive. Political economists, on
the other hand, confidently manipulated figures and scanned tables.
The eighteenth century was the age of political arithmetic; economists exploited parish registers and bills of mortality, reports on
navigation and trade, with new methods and new imagination, to
satisfy the "demand for precise information in numerical form."[2]
But the origins of the search for precision in economic questions go
back into the seventeenth century. Sir William Petty, the brilliant
and versatile statistician, gave the search its name—Political Arithmetic—in the 1670s, and supplied it with a rationale. "Sir Francis
Bacon," Petty wrote, happily combining an appeal to Bacon and to
medical science, "in his *Advancement of Learning*, has made a judi-

---

[8] See *Dei delitti e delle pene*, chap. xxix, on imprisonment.
[9] Quoted in Gilles-Gaston Granger: *La Mathématique sociale du
Marquis de Condorcet* (1965), 2.
[1] *Esquisse*, 255.
[2] T. S. Ashton: *An Economic History of England: The Eighteenth
Century* (1965), 1.

cious parallel in many particulars, between the Body Natural and Body Politic, and between the arts of preserving both in health and strength: and as its anatomy is the best foundation of one, so also of the other: and that to practice upon the politic, without knowing the symmetry, fabric, and proportion of it, is as casual as the practice of old women and empirics."[3] Not all of Petty's followers were Baconians; some of the early political arithmeticians, like Roger North, advocated clear and distinct ideas in the name of Descartes, and it was not until the end of the seventeenth century that they came to develop, or at least to urge, a cautious empiricism in the name of Newton. Among the sciences of man and society, political economy was doubtless the first to deserve the name of science, quick to leave its pioneers behind. By 1776, Adam Smith could coolly dismiss the work of a century: "I have no great faith in political arithmetic," he announced in *The Wealth of Nations*.[4] He, and with him the science of economics, had moved beyond it.

The ascendancy of economics over other disciplines is anything but mysterious: the raising of taxes, the value of money, the relation of trade to power were supremely practical matters that had exercised the ingenuity of statesmen for centuries. The seventeenth century was the age of reason and mathematics, and nothing was more natural than to apply reason and mathematics to pressing public questions. The "mercantile system," the economic theory developed and systematized in that century, was partly superficial, partly wrong, partly of limited applicability, but its intent and its procedures at least approached the scientific spirit.

Mercantilism was a conglomerate of economic ideas flexible enough to satisfy the requirements of statesmen in the most varied circumstances. Its most widely practiced techniques, designed to secure what significantly came to be called a "favorable balance of trade"—the bounties for exports and duties on imports, the hoarding of bullion, the placing of restrictions on the emigration of skilled workmen, the supervision of the quality of products and the compe-

---

[3] Quoted in Paul F. Lazarsfeld: "Notes on the History of Quantification in Sociology—Trends, Sources and Problems," in Harry Woolf, ed.: *Quantification: A History of the Meaning of Measurement in the Natural and Social Sciences* (1961), 155.
[4] *An Inquiry into the Nature and Causes of the Wealth of Nations* (1776; ed. Edwin Cannan, edn. 1937), 501.

tence of craftsmen, the encouragement of population growth, the
protection of domestic shipping—were intended to guarantee and
enlarge power, although they did not exclude a concern for prosperity. In his famous pamphlet, *England's Treasure by Foreign
Trade*, written as far back as the late 1620s, Thomas Mun had already argued that sound commercial policy would benefit not
merely the king, but merchants as well. In 1662, the statistician John
Graunt laid it down that "the art of governing, and the true politiques, is how to preserve the subject in peace, and plenty," and a
little later Sir Josiah Child constructed an appealing and harmonious
cycle: "Foreign trade," he wrote in 1681, "produces riches, riches
power, power preserves our trade and religion."[5] Mercantilists even
suggested that economic power depended on the welfare of the poor
as much as on the prosperity of the merchant: "The Full Employment of All Hands in the Nation," wrote Francis Brewster in 1702,
in his *New Essays on Trade*, "is the Surest Way and Means to Bring
Bullion into the Kingdom."[6] For mercantilist thinkers, wealth was
part of, and a means to, power, and had value in its own right.

But power came first. As long as power and wealth, and even
power and welfare, coincided, there was obviously no need to make
hard choices; but when they came into conflict it was equally obvious that welfare and wealth would give way. Whatever the rhetoric
of mercantilist writers, however humane their sentiments—and their
humanity was cool enough, with its utilitarianism just below the
surface—their view was always that economic units are antagonistic
to one another. Mercantilist policies were the continuation of warfare by other means. "All trade," as Sir Josiah Child candidly said,
is "a kind of warfare."[7]

In an age of brutally competitive statemaking it could hardly
be otherwise. Economists and statesmen alike conceived of power
and wealth as static quantities: there are only so many resources,
their total is fixed. It followed with inexorable logic that one coun-

[5] Both quoted in Jacob Viner: "Power versus Plenty as Objectives
of Foreign Policy in the Seventeenth and Eighteenth Centuries,"
World Politics, I, 1 (October 1948), 12, 15.
[6] Quoted in Charles Wilson: *England's Apprenticeship, 1603–1763*
(1965), 234.
[7] Quoted in William Letwin: *The Origins of Scientific Economics:
English Economic Thought 1660–1776* (1963), 44.

try's gain must be another country's loss, that prosperity can be achieved only at the expense of someone else's misery. "By such maxims as these," judged Adam Smith in his devastating survey of mercantilism, "nations have been taught that their interest consisted in beggaring all their neighbours. Each nation has been made to look with an invidious eye upon the prosperity of all the nations with which it trades," and so, "commerce, which ought naturally to be, among nations, as among individuals, a bond of union and friendship, has become the most fertile source of discord and animosity." The mercantile system, Adam Smith said contemptuously, had sprung from the "spirit of monopoly"; it was a set of "political maxims" derived from "the sneaking arts of underling tradesmen."

Adam Smith was too deeply engaged in his polemics on behalf of *laissez faire* to recognize the historic place of mercantilism: the system was not sheer wickedness or folly, but the product of its day. The philosophes' passion for decency and shrewdness in political economy had their part in overthrowing it, but neither enlightened humanity nor enlightened social science did their work in isolation. They coincided with expanding trade and increasing productivity in a relatively peaceful period, and these commercial and industrial developments invited the conception of a dynamic world economy in which the prosperity of some was the prosperity of all. In economic thought as elsewhere, the ideas of the Enlightenment were firmly anchored in contemporary realities.

II

The shift from the mercantilism of the seventeenth century to the subtler economics of the Enlightenment came in slow, deliberate steps, and on a wide front; it enlisted the abbé Galiani and Pietro Verri in Italy, the school of Physiocrats in France, the Cameralists in Vienna, David Hume and Adam Smith in Scotland. Much as they differed among each other on matters of theory and of policy— there were severe protectionists among them—all contributed to making economics at once more humane and more scientific. Old slogans acquired new meaning; a mercantilist could have accepted Adam Smith's definition of political economy as "a branch of the science of a statesman or legislator"; but he could not have gone on, as Adam Smith did, to say that this science had "two distinct objects: first, to provide a plentiful revenue or subsistence for the people, or more properly to enable them to provide such a revenue or subsistence for themselves; and secondly, to supply the state or commonwealth with a revenue sufficient for the public services. It proposes to enrich both the people and the sovereign." Adam Smith's emphasis would have offended the mercantilists' sense of priorities. To the economists of the Enlightenment, wealth came before power, and even power—the public services—wore a less militant look than before. Adam Smith properly recognized this reversal of priorities when he declared the "sole end and purpose of all production" to be "consumption" and insisted that "the interest of the producer ought to be attended to, only so far as it may be necessary for promoting that of the consumer." This maxim, so "self-evident," had been consistently disregarded in the "mercantile system," in which "the interest of the consumer is almost constantly sacrificed to that of the producer"[8]—a sacrifice Adam Smith thought quite as immoral as it was unscientific.

The clarity of eighteenth-century thinking on economics has long been rather obscured by the uncertain reputation of its best-known school of economists, the Physiocrats. Quesnay, its founder, and his followers, had some formidable opponents among the advanced thinkers of the day, but their most formidable enemy was doubtless their style of writing and their exalted sense of themselves. Quesnay was a powerful person, an ideal father figure for disciples in search of authority. A prominent court physician, he did not turn to economic questions until his sixties, but once he did, he rapidly gathered around himself a group of enthusiastic and docile followers—the elder Mirabeau, Pierre Samuel Du Pont, Mercier de La Rivière, and others—who drank in his words, and called him master, father, "the Confucius of Europe," and, more pointedly perhaps, "the modern Socrates."[9] The spectacle they presented gave abundant material to scoffers in search of material: Voltaire derided their supposed utopianism—"finding themselves at leisure, they gov-

---

[8] *Wealth of Nations*, 460–1, 397, 625.
[9] Thomas P. Neill: "Quesnay and Physiocracy," *JHI*, IX, 2 (April 1948), 154 *n*.

ern the state from the corner of their hearth"[1]—while others dismissed them as a sect.[2] Quesnay's celebrated *Tableau économique*, first circulated in 1758-9, did not help matters: even Mirabeau, Quesnay's most devoted and voluble disciple, could not understand the diagram, with its three columns of figures connected by crisscrossing lines and its laconic comments which only deepened the mystery. At least at first, despite private explanations, Mirabeau was "bogged down in the zigzag,"[3] and others, who had no commitment to physiocracy, found it easy to ridicule what they took no trouble to grasp. For Adam Smith, the *Tableau économique* was the work of a doctrinaire and "very speculative physician" bent on prescribing a rigid diet to a country that did not need it.[4] Other critics, less kindly and less patient, dismissed the *Tableau* as sheer nonsense. To make things worse, some leading Physiocrats, like Mirabeau, wrote badly; others, one may say, wrote too well: they were addicted to portentous phrases and an unfortunate taste for flamboyant slogans; serious critics and witty parodists agreed that physiocracy was mysticism masquerading as science.

One can hardly blame them, but they were wrong. If anything, physiocracy was science masquerading as mysticism. Their puzzling charts, their incomprehensible explanations, their provocative terminology concealed their clear—and, for the science of economics, vitally important understanding of the economy as a system. An economy, Quesnay said, is a "general system of expenditure, work, gain, and consumption," and such a system is open to examination. "In nature everything is intertwined," he argued, and "the fact that these different movements are necessarily interconnected means that things can be understood, differentiated, and examined."[5] The gain for reason was enormous. "With the Physiocrats, for the first time in the history of economic thought," writes Ronald L. Meek in his

---

[1] *L'Homme aux quarante écus*, in *Œuvres*, XXI, 308.
[2] "With the Physiocrats," Ronald L. Meek has said, "for the first time in the history of economic thought, we come face to face with that curious sociological phenomenon which we call a 'school' if we sympathize with it and a 'sect' if we do not." "Introduction," *The Economics of Physiocracy* (1962), 27.
[3] This is what Quesnay candidly told Mirabeau; see ibid., 115.
[4] *Wealth of Nations*, 638.
[5] Article "Corn" in Diderot's *Encyclopédie*; in Meek: *Economics of Physiocracy*, 82; and *Dialogue on the Work of Artisans*, ibid., 204.

authoritative examination of the school, "we find a firm appreciation
of the fact that the 'areas of decision' open to policy-makers in the
economic sphere have certain limits, and that a theoretical model of
the economy is necessary to define these limits. We are unfree, the
Physiocrats in effect proclaimed, so long as we do not understand
the necessities by which we are bound in our society; and we can
understand these necessities, in a society as complex as ours, only if
we use the methods of simplification, selection, and generalization in
our analysis of it."[6] Far from being remote from the facts, the Physiocrats were too close to them: if they lacked anything, it was the
scientific imagination that would have taken them from their immediate observations to the possibilities inherent in mercantile and
industrial developments. Their notorious emphasis on agriculture,
which did them as much damage as anything, only testifies to their
immersion in French realities—Adam Smith, for one, treated it
lightly as a case of the rod having been "bent too much one way,"
now being bent "as much the other way" to straighten it out.[7] In the
France of the old regime, the problem of agriculture was the dominant problem, and the Physiocrats never lifted their eyes from their
world.

For all the narrowness of their concerns, the Physiocrats developed a comprehensive set of ideas, suggestive even to those who did
not share their overwhelming preoccupations. The heart of their
theory was, as I have said, the sense that the economy was a system,
comprehensible because it was subject to laws. "A knowledge of
order and of the natural and physical laws," Du Pont laid it down as
emphatically as he could, "should serve as the basis of economics."
It is only when this "great, fundamental truth" has been recognized
and accepted that prejudice will give way to science.[8] These laws
go beyond the work behind the backs of individuals and their conscious plans: "The whole magic of well-ordered society," the leaders
of the school said, "is that each man works for others, while believing that he is working for himself." This economic order is part of
a larger and higher order: "This magic" is revealed in "the princi-

---

[6] Ibid., 370.
[7] *Wealth of Nations*, 628.
[8] Quoted in Neill: "Quesnay and Physiocracy," 165.

ples of economic harmony," which a fatherly Supreme Being has bestowed on mankind.[9] Prices, values, profits—all are part of this natural, harmonious, rational scheme.

It follows—and here, in characteristic Enlightenment fashion, the humane purpose of economic analysis finally emerges—that the closer a society approximates the laws of nature, the higher its prosperity will be, the larger (to use the Physiocrats' language) its net product. It was the primary task of society to increase its net product, and the primary task of economists to show society how to increase it. The celebrated slogans of the Physiocrats, *laissez faire, laissez aller,* were demands on statesmen to liberate the economy from protection—that host of outworn, long-lived taxes, regulations, and monopolies that crippled individual initiative and social growth. *Laissez faire* would permit agricultural prices to find their natural level, and individuals to follow their own interest, which, after all, they know better than anyone else. The old system had survived for so long, the Physiocrats thought, because it served powerful interests, and because men were all too easily victimized by habit. The new science of economics would make its way once it was known. There was really nothing mysterious about it: "The science of economics," wrote Du Pont, "is nothing but the application of the natural order of government to society."[1] Economics was, therefore, more than a mere science of wealth; it was the science of social justice.

The grossest injustice, the Physiocrats thought, as well as the most striking irrationality in the France of their day was the burden on agricultural enterprise. The Physiocrats saw essentially three classes in society—the productive class, or agricultural laborers and entrepreneurs; the sterile class, or nonagricultural laborers and entrepreneurs, merchants, professionals; and the proprietors' class, or the owners of land, clerical, noble, and common, who derived income from land by various means, mainly in rent. In regarding agricultural entrepreneurs and laborers as the only productive class,

---

[9] Quesnay and Mirabeau: "Rural Philosophy," in Meek: *Economics of Physiocracy,* 70.
[1] Quoted in Neill: "Quesnay and Physiocracy," 164. For the consequences of these ideas for political theory, see below, 493–6.

the Physiocrats did not wish to stigmatize the others as drones in society. "The unproductive class," as Adam Smith correctly read physiocratic doctrine, "is not only useful, but greatly useful."[2] The Physiocrats' argument was complex: they saw agriculture as the sole sector in the economy capable of yielding a surplus which would enhance the net product. Obviously, the Physiocrats' call for a single tax on land rent was intimately connected with this analysis: it would sweep away imposts, free entrepreneurs to improve land and thus increase the net product, and secure income to the state from the sources that could best pay it—the owners of land—in the most rational possible way.

Physiocratic doctrine did not fare well. Philosophes who might have been its supporters were its opponents. Voltaire mercilessly lampooned it in *L'homme aux quarante écus;* Hume thought its advocates incurably doctrinaire: "I hope," he wrote to the abbé Morellet, who was proposing to write a *Dictionnaire de commerce,* "that in your work you will thunder them, and crush them, and pound them, and reduce them to dust and ashes! They are, indeed, the set of men the most chimerical and most arrogant that now exist, since the annihilation of the Sorbonne."[3] Worse, Adam Smith, a decent controversialist, discredited the Physiocrats with deadly condescension. Physiocracy, he wrote, is "with all its imperfections," perhaps "the nearest approximation to the truth that has yet been published on the subject of political œconomy," but he found it necessary to add that it was "a system, which never has done, and probably never will do any harm in any part of the world."[4] What intellectual construction can survive such praise?

Among the most damaging attacks on the Physiocrats was doubtless Galiani's *Dialogues sur le commerce des blés* of 1769, which Diderot helped to revise and prepare for publication; among other things, it converted Diderot, who had been for some time an admirer of the school. Galiani, "the little Neapolitan," as Diderot affectionately called him,[5] who became a great favorite among the philosophes of Paris for his wit, his cheerfulness, and his learning,

---

[2] *Wealth of Nations,* 633.
[3] Hume to Morellet, July 10, 1769. *Letters,* II, 205.
[4] *Wealth of Nations,* 642, 627.
[5] Diderot to Grimm, February 9, 1769. *Correspondance,* IX, 22.

attacked the Physiocrats in their most vulnerable spot—their dogmatism. If the Physiocrats understood that the economy is a system of interacting parts, Galiani understood, better than they, the complexities of that system. Galiani did not object to placing a high value on agriculture, or to free trade as such; but, as a good pragmatist, he demanded that the claims of each group and each policy be substantiated in reality. There were times when economic conditions called for government controls, others when the flow of grain could be left to the market. "The Economists," wrote Diderot after he enlisted in Galiani's camp, advance "general principles with the most marvelous intrepidity. But not a single one of these is not subject to an infinite number of exceptions in practice."[6] These objections were all the more cogent since Galiani himself had once been sympathetic to physiocracy, and had undergone conversion as a result of near-famine and unrest in the France of 1768: his call to practicality had a practical cause.

But in the end, what finally defeated the Physiocrats was not the flaws in their doctrine but the great economic crisis that predated, and helped to bring about, the French Revolution. The problems of the old regime were even more serious than the Physiocrats knew, and they knew much. They deserve sympathy; where failure is unavoidable, it is not discreditable. After 1776, when Turgot was dismissed, no one could have saved the old regime. What matters about the Physiocrats is not their liabilities but their assets: with all their pretentiousness and mystification, all their stubborn parochialism, they grasped what a moral science should be: secular—for their Supreme Being was as absent as a socially prominent landlord in their France, and largely a metaphor for the ideal—comprehensive, scientific at least in intent, and bent upon welfare. In addition, it is not the least of their merits to have had a hand in shaping the mind, or at least confirming the intuitions, of Adam Smith.

---

[6] Arthur M. Wilson: "The Development and Scope of Diderot's Political Thought," *VS*, XXVII (1963), 1885. For earlier expressions on physiocracy, see Diderot to Damilaville (June or July 1767). *Correspondance*, VII, 75–80; and the fascinating transitional statement to Falconet (May 1768), ibid., VIII, 27–46, where Diderot argues that while most Physiocrats might be enthusiastic missionaries and fanatics, Mercier de la Rivière at least should probably be exempted from this charge.

III

Between 1764 and 1766, when physiocracy was at its height, Adam Smith visited France and met its leading proponents. He was ready for them; he already shared many of their ideas, and, as his *Wealth of Nations* was to show in 1776, he was willing to acquire more. But he was not their disciple. He did not need to be: he had developed the leading conceptions of *The Wealth of Nations*—the existence of a natural order and the beneficent effects of economic freedom—a quarter of a century before. "Projectors disturb nature in the course of her operations in human affairs," he had said in lectures as early as 1749, "and it requires no more than to let her alone, and give her fair play in the pursuit of her ends that she may establish her own designs." He had even drawn the political consequences of this position: "Little else is requisite to carry a state to the highest degree of opulence from the lowest barbarism, but peace, easy taxes, and a tolerable administration of justice; all the rest being brought about by the natural course of things. All governments which thwart this natural course, which force things into another channel or which endeavour to arrest the progress of society at a particular point, are unnatural, and to support themselves are obliged to be oppressive and tyrannical."[7] When Adam Smith expressed these views, Quesnay had not yet written a line on economics.

But others had, both in England and Scotland, and notions of an economic science, and of economic freedom, were becoming familiar. "Trade," David Hume observed in 1742, "was never esteemed an affair of state till the last century,"[8] but when he wrote, it had become an important affair for statesmen, and for theorists who wrote less for statesmen than for one another. In 1740, Joseph Massie, who assembled an impressive library of books on economic affairs—itself testimony to the development of the discipline—noted that while there were a few writers who "considered Commerce as a science," and others who "treated it as a branch of history," both groups had "made only light essays" on "elementary" matters. And

---

[7] "Introduction," *Wealth of Nations*, xliii.
[8] "Of Civil Liberty," *Works*, III, 157.

the third class of writers, the most numerous, had indiscriminately mixed history and policy, to the benefit of neither. The time for a serious treatise was at hand.[9] Adam Smith would respond to Massie's invitation in 1776.

He had had long, sound preparation through the conversation and the writings of his friends, most notably David Hume. Hume addressed economic questions as he addressed all questions in the social sciences—as an intelligent amateur. The informality of his presentation and the lucidity of his reasoning suggested what culti-vated men in his century liked to suggest—that a man of letters, any man of letters, could apply himself profitably to all subjects what-ever. It was a false impression: to write Hume's essays on economics required Hume's intelligence, and that was rare.

When Hume published his seven essays on economics in 1752, he lacked even a proper name for them; he called them "Political Discourses," and mixed them in with essays on demography and political theory. They are short, suggestive rather than exhaustive, and anything but systematic. But they take up, one by one, the issues central to eighteenth-century economic thought; their world is modern—the world of classical economics—and their tone hostile to the tribal philosophy of the mercantilists. The foundation of eco-nomic theory, Hume argues, drawing freely on all his thought, is psychology: "Our passions are the only causes of labour,"[1] and the student of economics, like the statesman, must know these passions. The "natural bent" of men's minds is toward consumption, maxi-mization of income—as he put it, toward luxury; and the best system is the one that complies with this inclination. Sparta is not a model but a warning. Cultivation and prosperity, which are linked, are inestimable benefits; they make life worthwhile, and it is the task of the statesman to encourage and protect them. Fortunately, wealth and power are in general allies: "The greatness of the state, and the happiness of its subjects, how independent soever they may be sup-posed in some respects, are commonly allowed to be inseparable with regard to commerce; and as private men receive greater secu-rity, in the possession of their trade and riches, from the power of the public, so the public becomes powerful in proportion to the

---

[9] Quoted in Letwin: *Origins of Scientific Economics*, 219.
[1] "Of Commerce," *Works*, III, 293.

opulence and extensive commerce of private men." As Hume notes
with relief, the ancient maxim that the sovereign should consult his
interest rather than the happiness of his subjects is now unenforce-
able: "Ancient policy was violent, and contrary to the more natural
and usual course of things"; modern doctrine strives toward nature.[2]

Now, according to the "most natural course of things," it is
"industry and the arts and trade" that "encrease the power of the
sovereign as well as the happiness of the subjects"[3]; a flourishing
economy, resting on a high standard of living widely diffused, has
beneficent effects in all spheres, including the political: "Laws, order,
police, discipline; these can never be carried to any degree of perfection, before human reason has refined itself by exercise, and by
an application to the vulgar arts, at least, of commerce and manu-
facture."[4] Significantly, Hume has kind words not merely for the
vulgar arts but for the vulgar multitude as well; economists in the
Enlightenment wanted the poor to have a share in the general well-
being. "A too great disproportion among the citizens," Hume reasons, "weakens any state. Every person, if possible, ought to enjoy
the fruits of his labour, in a full possession of all the necessaries, and
many of the conveniences of life. No one can doubt, but such an
equality is most suitable to human nature, and diminishes much less
from the *happiness* of the rich than it adds to that of the poor."[5]
Such benevolence, to be sure, is at least partly utilitarian: this policy,
Hume insists, "also augments the *power of the state*, and makes any
extraordinary taxes or impositions be paid with more chearfulness.
Where the riches are engrossed by a few, these must contribute very
largely to the supplying of public necessities. But when the riches
are dispersed among multitudes, the burthen feels light on every
shoulder, and the taxes make not a very sensible difference on any
one's way of living." Besides, radical inequality only tempts the rich
to oppress the poor, which is, at the very least, uneconomic; it leads
"to the discouragement of all industry."[6] On the other hand, a general prosperity, which allows peasants to become "rich and independent" and tradesmen to "acquire a share of the property," will

---

[2] Ibid., 295, 288–9, 291.
[3] Ibid., 292–3.
[4] "Or Refinement in the Arts," *Works*, III, 303.
[5] "Of Commerce," ibid., 296–7.
[6] Ibid., 297.

increase the number and power of the middle classes—"that middling rank of men"—so conducive to public order, being, as they are, the "best and firmest basis of public liberty."[7] The philosophes always enjoyed clothing their humane impulses in economic and political justifications.

As Hume recognized, this view of the good society affronted a whole catalogue of well-entrenched prejudices. There was, first of all, the fear of luxury. This, Hume argued, was quite unfounded: "the arts" do not destroy what is valuable about the "martial spirit"—the vigorous love of country and of freedom. They do not enervate "either the mind or body. On the contrary, industry, their inseparable attendant, adds new force to both."[8] Trade and industry flourish best in a world market; both draw strength from peaceful international exchange. "Foreign trade, by its imports, furnishes materials for new manufactures; and by its exports, it produces labour in particular commodities, which could not be consumed at home. In short, a kingdom, that has a large import and export, must abound more with industry, and that employed upon delicacies and luxuries, than a kingdom which rests contented with its native commodities." In free trade everyone wins. "The individuals reap the benefit of these commodities, so far as they gratify the senses and appetites. And the public is also a gainer, while a greater stock of labour is, by this means, stored up against any public exigency."[9] That much for the fear of civilization. The fear of foreigners was equally myopic. The mercantilists strive for a favorable balance of trade, seek to hoard money, all because they are jealous of their neighbors. Hume himself was not wholly free from protectionist notions; he was too flexible, too skeptical, to trust any theory all the way. But the general direction of his thought is toward recognition of the "natural course of things." Money, he insists, "is none of the wheels of trade: It is the oil which renders the motion of the wheels more smooth and easy"; indeed, considering one country by itself, "the greater or less plenty of money is of no consequence," since it is, after all, simply a measure, an indicator, "the representation of labour and commodities," serving only "as a method of rating or

---

[7] "Of Refinement in the Arts," ibid., 306.
[8] Ibid., 304.
[9] "Of Commerce," ibid., 295.

estimating them."[1] True, the flow of money in one direction or another may cause dislocations, and Hume veers between deflationary and inflationary moods. But his point remains: a fixation on money, so typical of the mercantilists, is absurd in theory and pernicious in practice. Money is "chiefly a fictitious value"; "all real power and riches," after all, consist in "the stock of labour," in "men and commodities."[2]

As the value of money is largely a fiction, a favorable balance of trade is wholly so. Only nations "ignorant of the nature of commerce" will prohibit certain exports, or obstruct the outward flow of money, or place customs duties on all foreign goods. "The Author of the world," Hume writes in an access of poetic piety, has intended nations to exchange goods "by giving them soils, climates, and geniuses, so different from each other." There might be some reasonable import duties: certain domestic industries need to be encouraged, colonies deserve protection. But these are exceptions based on particular policies, justified by certain social or political consequences. The general rule is clear enough: let each nation contribute to the world what it can produce best. British jealousy and hatred of France have "occasioned innumerable barriers and obstructions upon commerce," but the bargain has been an unwise one. "We lost the FRENCH market for our woollen manufactures, and transferred the commerce of wine to SPAIN and PORTUGAL, where we buy worse liquor at a higher price." Imports, after all, bring about exports: "There are few ENGLISHMEN who would not think their country absolutely ruined, were FRENCH wines sold in ENGLAND so cheap and in such abundance as to supplant, in some measure, all ale, and home-brewed liquors: But would we lay aside prejudice, it would not be difficult to prove, that nothing could be more innocent, perhaps advantageous. Each new acre of vineyard planted in FRANCE, in order to supply ENGLAND with wine, would make it requisite for the FRENCH to take the produce of an ENGLISH acre, sown in wheat or barley."[3] What Hume derisively calls the "jealousy of trade" is thus stupid and inhumane at once. "I shall therefore venture to acknowledge," he concludes in a magnificent peroration, "that, not only as a

---

[1] "Of Money," ibid., 309, 312.
[2] "Of Interest," ibid., 321, 315, 319.
[3] "Of the Balance of Trade," ibid., 343, 336.

man, but as a BRITISH subject, I pray for the flourishing commerce of GERMANY, SPAIN, ITALY, and even FRANCE itself. I am at least certain, that GREAT BRITAIN, and all those nations, would flourish more, did their sovereigns and ministers adopt such enlarged and benevolent sentiments towards each other."[4]

What is remarkable about these views is not merely their largeness and benevolence, but their shrewdness, their fund of good sense, their delight in civility, their clearsighted effort to tie economics to psychology, and, perhaps most important of all for the future of the science, their attempt to get beyond mere words to actual transactions, to the realities that lie concealed behind appearances. Adam Smith paid tribute to these qualities in his masterpiece when he hailed Hume as "by far the most illustrious philosopher and historian of the present age."[5]

IV

Hume was in his last illness when he read this compliment, but he roused himself to respond to it. "Euge! Belle!" he wrote to Adam Smith on April 1, 1776, upon the publication of *The Wealth of Nations*. "Dear Mr Smith: I am much pleas'd with your Performance; and the Perusal of it has taken me from a State of great Anxiety. It was a Work of so much Expectation, by yourself, by your Friends, and by the Public, that I trembled for its Appearance; but am now much relieved." He expressed doubts on some minor points, but on the whole he was more than satisfied; the book, he wrote, "has Depth and Solidity and Acuteness." Though requiring much attention and thus unlikely to win immediate popularity, it "is so much illustrated by curious Facts, that it must at last take the public Attention."[6]

Hume's praise was justified; his anxiety was not. Adam Smith's *An Inquiry into the Nature and Causes of the Wealth of Nations*

---

[4] "Of the Jealousy of Trade," ibid., 348. See above, 40–1.
[5] *Wealth of Nations*, 742.
[6] *Letters*, II, 311. The letter that immediately precedes this one in Hume's collected correspondence is the one thanking Gibbon for volume I of *The Decline and Fall of the Roman Empire*. It was Hume's last spring, but what a spring!

was an instant success. It appeared in March 1776; a second edition
was called for less than two years later, and the fifth edition, the
last in Adam Smith's lifetime, in 1789. When he died a year later,
his fame and influence were wholly secure. Far beyond Scotland, in
the German states and in the American republic, economists wrote
treatises and statesmen made policies in his name.

The reasons for this power are not far to seek. *The Wealth of
Nations*, part analysis, part prophecy, came at a supremely opportune
moment; it told men what they wanted to hear and needed to know
about nascent industrial society. Moreover, as Adam Smith himself
candidly acknowledged with his parade of footnotes: his predecessors had done much valuable work. But this is not all. *The Wealth
of Nations* is a thoroughly satisfying book in its own right; it is a
triumph of reason and clarity, of systematized humanity.

Curiously enough, its very greatness has obstructed the sympathetic understanding of Adam Smith's philosophy. Adam Smith was
not the man of one book; nor was he simply an economist. His work
demonstrates, as clearly as anything in his time, how incomplete the
division of labor among intellectuals still was. He was a moral
philosopher, the independent disciple of Hutcheson, the student of
the Stoics and of modern natural lawyers like Grotius and Pufendorf,
the attentive reader of Shaftesbury and Montesquieu. *The Wealth of
Nations* was Adam Smith's most important book: he worked on it
longer and harder than on anything else he did. But its portrait of
man as a trading animal, exercising his "propensity to truck, barter,
and exchange one thing for another,"[7] is firmly embedded in Adam
Smith's sociology, and that sociology in a general view of man's nature, purpose, and possibilities. *The Wealth of Nations* fully deserves
its reputation as a signal contribution to the science of economics, but
its total intention was more comprehensive than that, and wholly
consonant with the philosophes' preoccupation with moral science:
it was to exhibit the nature of wealth, but, in addition to that, the
possibilities of individuality in the economic system, and the relation of opulence and character.

These concerns were foreshadowed in Adam Smith's lectures
on justice, police, revenue, and arms, and in his first book, *The Theory of Moral Sentiments*, published in 1759, when he held the chair

---

[7] *Wealth of Nations*, 13.

of moral philosophy at Glasgow. The *Theory* is a judicious survey of philosophical ethics, both its nature and its psychology; it seeks to determine what men should, and what men actually do, approve. It is an eclectic work, at once appreciative and critical of classical systems, inclined to stress benevolence as a value and sentiment as a motive, but alert to the finer shades of moral conduct and to the difficulty of translating rational principles into action: "The man who acts according to the rules of perfect prudence, of strict justice, and of proper benevolence, may be said to be perfectly virtuous. But the most perfect knowledge of those rules will not alone enable him to act in this manner; his own passions are very apt to mislead him—sometimes to drive him, and sometimes to seduce him, to violate all the rules which he himself, in all his sober and cool hours, approves of."[8] The guarantor of moral action, therefore, its essential though not its sufficient condition, is self-command, regulated by a well-developed conscience, the "impartial spectator" in man's breast. It is this spectator, with his detachment and objectivity, who will prevent excessive pride and excessive timidity, and permit man to see through his self-deception, whether self-flattery or self-abasement. Adam Smith was a modern, moderate Stoic.

He was also something of a cosmic optimist who trusted unintended consequences. The "benevolence and wisdom" of the "divine Being" have "contrived and conducted the immense machine of the universe" in such a way that man may follow his private inclinations and obey his most powerful passions, and yet benefit the social order. By taking care of his own happiness, man is led to promote the happiness of others—this is the notorious "invisible hand" which leads men to "advance the interest of society" without intending it, without even knowing it.[9] All is for the best in the only possible world that God could have made.

In *The Wealth of Nations*, Adam Smith keeps these philosophical concerns alive, but with greater subtlety than before, with far greater respect for harsh truths and for the exceptions that modify all rules, and with an impressive command of social realities. Like Diderot, Adam Smith learned much in the 1760s; like Diderot, he did not discard his essential philosophy, but complicated it.

---

[8] *The Theory of Moral Sentiments* (1759; edn. 1966), 349.
[9] Ibid., 264–6.

To say that *The Wealth of Nations* is more than a work of economics is not to minimize the economics it does contain. Adam Smith himself unambiguously emphasized its importance in the full title he gave the book: he intended it as an inquiry into the nature and causes of the wealth of nations. The plan of the work, which Adam Smith outlines in the Introduction and faithfully carries out in the text, confirms the impression that while his economics is part of a wider social science and social theory, it is economics that will hold the center of the stage here: the book begins with a study of the "productive powers of labour"—the causes of its improvement and nature of distribution; it then turns to the capital stock that regulates the number of productive laborers. These first two books contain the theoretical principles that have secured Adam Smith's fame as an economist: the analysis of the division of labor, the labor theory of value, and his account of the accumulation of capital. Book Three then analyzes national policies that have led to the rise of cities and the decay of agriculture; in Book Four, having made his theoretical and historical survey, Adam Smith launches into his celebrated attack on mercantilism and the equally celebrated examination of physiocracy, and he concludes, in Book Five, with practical questions of economic statecraft—the sources available, and the expenditures essential, to the state. *The Wealth of Nations* is as perspicuous as a French garden—far more French indeed than, say, Montesquieu's *De l'esprit des lois*, which is a Romantic wilderness compared to it. This clarity yields more than aesthetic pleasure: it gives the impression that economic relationships, economic developments, and economic policies, manifold as they are, are yet open to rational study and complete mastery.

Far from discounting the complexity of his subject, Adam Smith appears to glory in it: his famous analysis of the division of labor, which begins Book One, impressively demonstrates that economics operates within a social framework; and it demonstrates something else—the law of compensation so cherished by Hume and Wieland and the other philosophes.[1] The division of labor is the source of progress and of suffering. To begin with, Adam Smith argues, it is the most significant cause of the "improvement in the productive powers of labour, and the greater part of the skill,

---

[1] See above, 100–6.

dexterity, and judgment with which it is any where directed, or applied." The reason for this is plain: one workman could scarcely make one pin in a day, but with each doing his minute share, one drawing out the wire, another straightening it, a third cutting it, a fourth adding its point, a fifth grinding its top, still others putting on the top and putting the pins into paper, a small factory of ten men, though relatively ill equipped, could still make twelve pounds of pins—about forty-eight hundred—a day.[2] What is true in pin-making is true everywhere: the specialization that the division of labor imposes vastly increases productivity by improving dexterity, saving time, and encouraging inventiveness by introducing new tools and machinery. All advanced civilizations owe their opulence to the division of labor, in which self-interest works to the advantage of society: look at the coats men wear and the ships they sail, all the combined products of many hands! And this holds for all types of this division, including the trade of town with countryside: in such trade, "the gains of both are mutual and reciprocal, and the division of labour is in this, as in all other cases, advantageous to all the different persons employed in the various occupations into which it is subdivided." Yet there is also a darker side. "In the progress of the division of labour," Adam Smith concedes, sounding in this quite as ready to confront grim facts as Ferguson, and even more pessimistic, "the employment of the far greater part of those who live by labour, that is, of the great body of the people, comes to be confined to a few very simple operations, frequently to one or two." All this has disastrous psychological consequences: after all, men's understandings are formed by their day-to-day occupations, hence the man who has no need to use his mind or exercise his inventiveness must lose "the habit of such exertion," and generally "becomes as stupid and ignorant as it is possible for a human creature to become." Adam Smith's acount of his dehumanization is as explicit and clear-eyed as any modern account of fragmentation and alienation in industrial society: "The torpor of his mind renders him, not only incapable of relishing or bearing a part in any rational conversation, but of conceiving any generous, noble, or tender sentiment, and consequently of forming any just judgment concerning many even of the ordinary duties of private life," to say nothing of the "great

---

[2] *Wealth of Nations*, 3–5.

and extensive interests of his country." He loses all possible interest in politics, his patriotism is corrupted, even his body is enfeebled. "His dexterity at his own particular trade seems, in this manner, to be acquired at the expence of his intellectual, social, and martial virtues." Adam Smith was not a metaphysician avid for paradox; he reported what he so perceptively saw. "In every improved and civilized society this is the state into which the labouring poor, that is, the great body of the people, must necessarily fall, unless government takes some pains to prevent it."[3]

Unless government takes some pains to prevent it: the reservation is critical. Broadly speaking, between the alternatives of a state-regulated economy and a free economy regulated by competition, Adam Smith vastly preferred the second to the first. His stress on the division of labor as the primary source of opulence is evidence of this choice: the division of labor was both a result and a cause of individualism. On the whole, Adam Smith found government regulation of the economy distasteful, advantageous to a few special interests alone, politically, socially and economically counterproductive. The invisible hand is still part of Adam Smith's intellectual arsenal; he still thinks highly of the unintended consequences of selfishness. "As every individual," he writes in a much-quoted passage, "endeavours as much as he can both to employ his capital in the support of domestic industry and so to direct that industry that its produce may be of the greatest value, every individual necessarily labours to render the annual revenue of the society as great as he can. He generally, indeed"—and here is the echo from his earlier book—"neither intends to promote the public interest, nor knows how much he is promoting it. By preferring the support of domestic to that of foreign industry, he intends only his own security; and by directing that industry in such a manner as its produce may be of the greatest value, he intends only his own gain; and he is in this, as in many other cases, led by an invisible hand to promote an end which was no part of his intention. Nor is it always the worse for the society that it was no part of it. By pursuing his own interest he frequently promotes that of the society more effectually than

---

[3] Ibid., 356, 734–5.

when he really intends to promote it. I have never known much good done by those who affected to trade for the public good."[4] The fame of this passage is unfortunate; its careful qualifications— "nor *is it always the worse* for the society . . . he *frequently* promotes" the interest "of society . . ."—are clues to new discriminations: Adam Smith now sees the operation of the invisible hand as much less prominent than he had in *The Theory of Moral Sentiments*, much less certain in its consequences, much more in need of aid and correction by visible hands than had seemed necessary in the 1750s.

What Adam Smith now recognized was that the free play of self-interest led to enduring, often harmful conflict, did not maximize resources, and made victims; in fact, the interests of some powerful groups directly contradicted the public interest. Tradesmen and industrialists are in no way Adam Smith's heroes: he speaks with superb disdain of the "mean rapacity, the monopolizing spirit of merchants and manufacturers, who neither are, nor ought to be, the rulers of mankind," and he is ready to countenance public control of their viciousness, which cannot, perhaps, be corrected, but may "very easily be prevented from disturbing the tranquillity of anybody but themselves." Merchants and manufacturers hate and fear competition; their "wretched spirit of monopoly" induces them to seek import duties, or to prevent the founding of a rival establishment in their neighborhood, or to export goods for high profits when they should be selling them for moderate profits at home. In the setting of wage scales, manufacturers and men are in inevitable and often insoluble conflict, and Adam Smith is on the side of the men, who are less powerful and far more desperate than their masters. "We rarely hear, it has been said, of the combinations of masters, though frequently of those of workmen. But whoever imagines, upon this account, that masters rarely combine, is as ignorant of the world as of the subject. Masters are always and every where in a sort of tacit, but constant and uniform combination, not to raise the wages of labour above their actual rate. To violate this combination is every where a most unpopular action, and a sort of reproach to a master among his neighbours and equals. We seldom,

---

[4] Ibid., 423.

indeed, hear of this combination, because it is the usual, and one
may say, the natural state of things which nobody ever hears of."
Sometimes masters do even worse: they combine to depress wages
below current rates. If workers oppose the masters by combining
in turn, their combinations are merely defensive and, Adam Smith
strongly implies, wholly justified. In fact, he describes the "utmost
silence and secrecy" of the masters with a mixture of relish and
contempt, and notes, in language that nineteenth-century populists
could have adopted without change: "People of the same trade
seldom meet together, even for merriment and diversion, but the
conversation ends in a conspiracy against the public, or in some
contrivance to raise prices." To raise prices, or depress wages unduly, is not simply a wicked proceeding, it is imprudent as well, for
an economically progressive society is one characterized by "that
universal opulence which extends to the lowest ranks of the people";
after all, "what improves the circumstances of the greater part"—
which is to say, "servants, labourers and workmen of different
kinds"—can "never be regarded as an inconveniency to the whole.
No society can surely be flourishing and happy, of which the far
greater part of the members are poor and miserable." Characteristically, Adam Smith offers humane as well as economic reasons for
his position: "It is but equity, besides, that they who feed, cloath and
lodge the whole body of the people, should have such a share of the
produce of their own labour as to be themselves tolerably well fed,
cloathed and lodged." Yet economic reasons are never far from his
mind: high wages pay for themselves by enabling workmen to keep
their children alive, and to increase their own productivity. "The
liberal reward of labour, therefore, as it is the effect of increasing
wealth, so it is the cause of increasing population. To complain of it,
is to lament over the necessary effect and cause of the greatest public
prosperity." Unfortunately, manufacturers and merchants do not
often recognize these obvious truths: in economic affairs, there is
an invisible hand—secret combination and conspiracy—that seems
like a vicious caricature of the invisible hand of beneficent providence. Political institutions are, in a sense, the public expression of
these private arrangements: "Civil government," Adam Smith concludes, almost cynically, "so far as it is instituted for the security of
property, is in reality instituted for the defence of the rich against

the poor, or of those who have some property against those who have none at all."[5]

But precisely because the providential economic order is imperfect, government ideally has other roles to play. Of course, it was Adam Smith's purpose to get government out of, not into, economics, and the prevailing temper of his polemic is against surviving mercantilist regulations. Nor was it merely a question of polemics; fundamental values—Enlightenment values—were involved in the issue of economic freedom, most notably man's right to determine his own fate, his right to be treated not as the ward of a supremely wise government but as an autonomous being. "It is the highest impertinence and presumption," he wrote, "in kings and ministers, to pretend to watch over the œconomy of private people, and to restrain their expence, either by sumptuary laws, or by prohibiting the importation of foreign luxuries." Kant could have said the same thing. Are not the great themselves "always, and without any exception, the great spendthrifts in the society"? Is it not true that "The violence and injustice of the rulers of mankind is an ancient evil," for which there is probably no remedy?[6] But at the same time Adam Smith did not envisage the government as wholly passive; the night-watchman state of nineteenth-century liberals was not his ideal. It was the primary task of the state to defend the country against foreign enemies, and to maintain security and justice at home, and these roles exacted certain kinds of government interference; in a clash of values between military defense and economic freedom, the latter might have to yield. Beyond this, the weak deserved some protection against the strong: the state should do something to protect ignorant consumers against fraudulent producers, defenseless laborers against all-powerful employers, slaves against their masters: like national defense, common humanity should prevail over *laissez faire*. Finally, the state should undertake the kind of public works—some forms of transportation, some forms of education—which are essential, yet too expensive or onerous for private enterprise to carry on. Not being a system-maker, Adam Smith was not precise—on principle; the casualness and openness of his recom-

---

[5] Ibid., 460, 428, 68–9, 128, 11, 78–81, 674.
[6] Ibid., 329, 460.

mendations for government action may be a flaw, but they were a policy, and a policy that flowed quite directly from the Enlightenment's desire for flexibility and its distrust of metaphysics.

Indeed, in its total intellectual style, *The Wealth of Nations* is a cardinal document of the Enlightenment: it is secular in its perception of the world, devoted to facts, confident in its search for scientific generality, intent on translating knowledge into beneficent action, comfortable in its expectation that humanity and utility often coincide, yet alert to the conflict of interests and the need for intervention in behalf of values higher than those of getting and spending. Adam Smith, after all, could even see some justice in arguments for a progressive income tax. There was at least one disciple, Jeremy Bentham, who after years of rumination accused Adam Smith of a kind of sentimental aversion to government intervention; Smith, he wrote, had talked of "invasion of natural liberty" in order to forestall the kind of necessary government action to which, on pragmatic grounds, Bentham came to have no objection. For egalitarian reasons, Bentham wanted the state to take charge of public health, education, and transport, even though, on the whole, the individual knew his own interests best.[7] But Adam Smith was not so remote from Bentham's view as Bentham came to think. However political economy would change in the hands of the classical economists of the nineteenth century, with their comfortable pessimism concerning the perpetual and necessary misery of the working classes, for Adam Smith economics was not yet a dismal science.

4. HISTORY: SCIENCE, ART, AND PROPAGANDA

I

SOCIOLOGY and political economy were young disciplines in the eighteenth century, and in shaping them the philosophes took all the risks and gathered all the glory of innovators. It was different with history. As cultivated men with long memories, the philosophes

---

[7] T. W. Hutchison: "Bentham as an Economist," *The Economic Journal*, LXII, 262 (June 1956), 299.

well knew that history was a genre as old as the Greeks. It needed not foundations but a revolution, and a revolution is what the philosophes made: the map they drew of the past seems today partly incomplete, partly distorted, but it is recognizable and usable—in many respects our map.

In drawing it, the philosophes were not alone. The leading historians of the age were by and large leading philosophes, but the passion for history was quite general. "I believe," David Hume said confidently in 1770, "this is the historical Age and this the historical Nation,"[8] and while non-Scots would have questioned the second half of Hume's assertion, everyone, Scot and non-Scot alike, would have accepted the first. The eighteenth century was in fact an age of consuming interest in history. History was a craft, a discipline, and an entertainment. Addison spoke with high appreciation of the historian's "most agreeable Talent," which puts his readers into "a pleasing Suspense" as he unfolds his colorful tale[9]; half a century later, Gibbon noted that "History is the most popular species of writing, since it can adapt itself to the highest or the lowest capacity." Gibbon's own history, obviously suited to readers of most if not all capacities, secured a vast admiring public upon its first appearance. "My book was on every table," Gibbon recalled about the first volume, "and almost on every toilette; the historian was crowned by the taste or fashion of the day; nor was the general voice disturbed by the barking of any profane critic."[1] Hume used similar language: history, he wrote, is "suited to every capacity."[2] Amateur historians of great individuals like Boswell diligently collected documents so that their biographies might be copious and accurate. There was a growing feeling that the past, faithfully recaptured, gave rise to worthy feelings and thoughts. In 1709, long before the invention of romantic nostalgia, Vanbrugh urged the preservation of the old manor house at Woodstock; men value ancient buildings, he argued, because "they move more lively and pleasing Reflections. . . . On the persons who have Inhabited them; On the Remarkable things which have been transacted in them; On

---

[8] To William Strahan (August 1770). *Letters*, II, 230.
[9] *Spectator*, No. 420; III, 574.
[1] *Autobiography*, 175.
[2] *My Own Life*, in *Works*, III, 4.

the extraordinary Occasions of Erecting them."[3] Later, especially after Winckelmann's erudite and imaginative re-creation of the history of Greek art, the interest in historical precision became nothing less than fastidious. When in the second half of the eighteenth century the Gothic *Liebfrauenkirche* in Frankfurt was fitted out with rococo altars, this mixture of periods displeased at least one local citizen, who complained that this lovely church had been ruined by being rebuilt in two incompatible styles.[4] Historical consciousness, it seems, animated philosophers and ordinary men alike.

The prestige of historians matched the interest in history. True, Samuel Johnson thought that "great parts" are not "requisite for a historian" since in the writing of history "all the greatest powers of the human mind are quiescent,"[5] but this crusty observation was uncharacteristic of the age, and even of Johnson. By 1752, a year after its publication, Lord Chesterfield had read Voltaire's *Siècle de Louis XIV* four times and had expressed his admiration to the author in adulatory letters. The most distinguished philosophers and poets of the age wrote history confident that as historians they were neither betraying their vocation nor lowering their dignity. Montesquieu pursued his historical studies after he had been elected to the *Académie française;* for him, as for the age of the Enlightenment in general, the company of Thucydides and Tacitus was respectable enough. William Robertson took delight in distinguished readers as varied as Garrick and Catherine of Russia. Between 1759 and 1777, he brought out highly accomplished and widely read histories of Scotland, Charles V, and America, but his lifelong concern with history and his impressive productivity neither compromised his prominent position in the Scottish Presbyterian Church nor slowed his majestic ascent toward the principalship at the University of Edinburgh. Robertson's friend David Hume, who began and ended his career as a philosopher, did not abandon that career when he turned toward history; as early as 1747, while he was in the midst

---

[3] Quoted in Pevsner: *The Englishness of English Art*, 50.
[4] See Voelcker: *Die Stadt Goethes*, 296.
[5] Recorded by Boswell: *Boswell's London Journal, 1762–1763* (1950), 293.

of philosophical and theological studies, he expressed a strong interest in "historical projects" and confessed his long-standing "intention, in my riper years, of composing some History,"[6] and when he published his *History of England*, beginning in 1754 at the end with the Stuarts, and ending in 1762 at the beginning with early Britain, he worked on his vast undertaking without forgetting his philosophy. That, one might say, was one of its problems, but it was not a problem for Hume. Similarly, Voltaire was happy to be a historian. It is likely that one of his motives for writing the *Siècle de Louis XIV* (1751) and the *Essai sur les mœurs* (1756) was to outdo his rivals and gain fame, but then, this was one of his motives for doing everything. In his own time, Voltaire was celebrated first as a poet and playwright, and later as a humanitarian and polemicist, but thinking and writing about history helped to shape both these phases. Voltaire's plays and poems involved him in a certain amount of historical research: the *Henriade*, his audacious and unsuccessful bid for immortality as an epic poet precipitated him into the history of sixteenth-century France, while his first history, the *Histoire de Charles XII*, published in 1731, reads much like a tragedy in prose. And later, conversely, the polemical passages in his great histories show him to be the serious historian always mindful of his self-imposed duties as propagandist for Enlightenment. Gibbon, finally, experienced the need to write history as nothing less than a vocation; it would be inappropriate to call it sacred, but it was irresistible. Gibbon might speak a little slightingly about his efforts being crowned by "the taste and fashion of the day," but his work, and the best work of the other historians, survived the vagaries of taste and the amnesia of fashion; they were, in a word, masterpieces. Works of history, like all of men's works, are part of history and must be judged as such; whatever defects subsequently emerged, Voltaire's *Siècle de Louis XIV*, Hume's *History of England*, Roberston's *History of America*, and Gibbon's *Decline and Fall of the Roman Empire* were monumental achievements in their day and for their discipline; they stand, if not as proof, at least in support, of Hume's claim that his was the historical age.

---

[6] Hume to Henry Home (1747). *Letters*, I, 99. And Hume to the same (1747). Ibid., 109.

II

Whatever the philosophes might claim for their work and their age, their claims were not honored by their successors: nineteenth-century historicist (and not the historicists alone) judged their historical writings with extraordinary severity. Insisting that historical epochs are all different and all worthy, that they are all, in Ranke's famous formulation, "immediate to God," Ranke and the others refused to extend their own sympathetic doctrine to Voltaire and Hume and Gibbon: the philosophes, they suggested, had written not bad history so much as mere literature—not history at all. Had the Enlightenment not defamed scholarship, turned its back on the wealth of historical experience with its doctrine of the uniformity of human nature, and judged the past instead of entering it?

The nineteenth-century critique of the philosophes' historical work was as partisan and time-bound as the philosophes' treatment of Christianity—it was unsympathetic to the philosophes' achievement and alert mainly to their failures—but like that treatment, it was not without merit. The philosophes managed their inheritance from the the seventeenth century like brilliant, willful and not wholly responsible heirs, safeguarding some of their legacy, improving some of it, and squandering the rest.

The style of historical writing the Enlightenment found in the preceding century was a curious mixture of credulity and realism, pettiness and patience, tough-minded reporting and brazen partiality. In the Renaissance, Humanists had joyfully embraced antique models in their horror at the tedium and superstitiousness of medieval chroniclers, and had begun to liberate history writing from its subservience to theology, dependence on miracles, mythopoeic schemes of periodization, and apocalyptic expectations. Yet Humanist historians had been imprisoned by the instruments of their liberation; they unearthed devices from the ancients that they might best have left buried, filling their books with sonorous, appropriate, but wholly imaginary speeches, spinning out their material into interminable narrations, and putting tiresome stress on the moral function of history. Besides, they did not completely secularize historical writing: in 1681, Bossuet published his famous *Discours sur l'histoire universelle* which divided the past into periods governed by religious events, and portrayed the course of human history as the realization of a divine plan. For all its touches of modernity, the intellectual world of Bossuet's *Discours* was medieval, and Bossuet's style, like his world, lived on into the eighteenth century in the historical-theological writings of Charles Rollin in France and Jonathan Edwards in America.[7]

The literal-mindedness and devotion of seventeenth- and even eighteenth-century historians kept alive a tribe of extreme skeptics, the Pyrrhonists, who snapped at the heels of the dogmatists with their inconvenient questions. In mid-seventeenth century La Mothe le Vayer aggressively stated the Pyrrhonist case with an essay instructively entitled *Du peu de certitude qu'il y a dans l'Histoire*, while some decades later the well-known Jesuit scholar Jean Hardouin turned Pyrrhonism into paranoia with his scandalous assertions that the accounts of Church councils before Trent were spurious and that nearly all classical works had been forged by medieval monks.

The Pyrrhonists were scholars—*érudits*—intent on using their scholarship for destructive purposes. But there were scholars among the devout historians as well, great scholars, who were the glory of their profession. The philosophes knew their work well and used it freely: the traditional portrait of the indolent philosopher-historian —Hume writing his *History of England* with his feet on the desk, Voltaire skimming a few authorities to lend substance to his malicious witticisms—cannot survive the testimony of the philosophes' historical writings or of their correspondence, filled as it is with requests for books, information, criticism. Parts of his English history, Hume reported, were a "Work of infinite Labour & Study," a labor, he added, which he did not grudge, "for," after all, "I have nothing better nor more agreeable to employ me."[8] He read assiduously, above all the seventeenth-century English medievalists, wrote away for books, consulted the library of the British Museum as soon as it opened in 1759, and worked (though not systematically) in archives. Voltaire struggled through the compilations and diction-

---

[7] See *The Rise of Modern Paganism*, 75–8.
[8] Hume to Andrew Millar, March 22, 1760. *Letters*, I, 321. This letter (322–4) contains an instructive list of books that Hume wanted Millar to get for him.

aries of Christian scholars: he cursed them and mocked them in comic despair, but he was intelligent and detached enough to use their work in his own, and his histories reflect his reading, much to their benefit. He read the documents collected by the Bollandists, the chronicles of medieval annalists, the accounts of recent historians, and, in his modern histories, eye-witness reports and unpublished memoirs. While he read them, as he read everything, rapidly and often carelessly, and while his labors were not, like Hume's, infinite, they were at least persistent and wide-ranging, more persistent and wide-ranging in fact than appeared in his finished product—much to the disappointment of Robertson and other admirers, he did not cite the authorities he used.[9] But he used them, profusely and proficiently.

While Hume and Voltaire worked hard at being historians, Robertson and Gibbon worked, if anything, even harder. In his long preface to the *History of America*, Robertson announced that he had "endeavoured to authenticate whatever I relate," and added his credo as a historian: "The longer I reflect on the nature of historical composition, the more I am convinced that this scrupulous accuracy is necessary. The historian who records the events of his own time, is credited in proportion to the opinion which the Public entertains with respect to his means of information and his veracity. He who delineates the transactions of a remote period, has no title to claim assent, unless he produces evidence in proof of his assertions. Without this, he may write an amusing tale, but cannot be said to have composed an authentic history." Robertson devotes the bulk of his Preface to record his efforts at making his *History of America* not an amusing tale—no one would accuse Robertson of being amusing—but an authentic history: he used the good offices of the British ambassador to Spain to secure him access to archives, and the aid of the chaplain of the embassy to procure rare sixteenth-century Spanish and other valuable manuscripts; he consulted or had friends consult the Imperial Libraries in Vienna and St. Petersburg, sent detailed queries about Indians to Portuguese officials and colonial governors—Governor Hutchison of Massachusetts, himself a meritorious historian, was only one of his valuable and well-con-

---

[9] See Momigliano: "Gibbon's Contribution to Historical Method," 46–7.

nected helpers—and borrowed books from specialized libraries. Like all scholars, he had his frustrations: the Spanish archives, reputed to hold "eight hundred and seventy-three large bundles" relating to America, were closed, but he tried to gain access to them—in vain. "Conscious of possessing, in some degree, the industry which belongs to an historian," he writes, "the prospect of such a treasure excited my most ardent curiosity." But, he sadly adds, "the prospect of it is all that I have enjoyed."[1] The point is that he tried.

In writing his credo and expressing his sentiments as a historian, Robertson noted, he had "been confirmed by the opinion of an Author, whom his industry, erudition, and discernment, have deservedly placed in a high rank among the most eminent historians of the age."[2] That author was Gibbon, and Gibbon's erudition is deservedly proverbial. Unlike other philosophes, he did not deplore erudition and regretted philosophic attacks on scholars. He loved books, especially scholarly books, with the passion with which other men love women or success. He was steeped in the classics—like Hume, who read over all the Greek and Roman classics to prepare his great essay on the populousness of ancient nations, Gibbon had read the ancient writers again and again—in the writings of seventeenth-century *érudits*, and in those of his contemporaries. His appetite for the written word was inexhaustible; he started his splendid private library with the *Mémoires* of the Academy of Inscriptions: "I cannot forget the joy," he recalled many years later, "with which I exchanged a bank note of twenty pounds for the twenty volumes of the Memoirs," nor "would it have been easy, by any other expenditure of the same sum, to have procured so large and lasting a fund of rational amusement." And this was only a beginning.[3] The footnotes to his *Decline and Fall of the Roman Empire* record his dependence on Beausobre's history of the Manicheans, Mabillon's magnificent study of diplomatics, and many others, above all Tillemont's copious and dependable histories of the early church. If the quality of Gibbon's masterpiece declines when he reaches the

---

[1] "Preface," *The History of America*, in *The Works of William Robertson*, 12 vols. (1820), VIII, i–xvii *passim*.
[2] Ibid., XIV. Robertson goes on to observe that it was Gibbon who had suggested that he publish the catalogue of the Spanish books he had used, a suggestion that Robertson adopted.
[3] *Autobiography*, 121; see *The Rise of Modern Paganism*, 369.

sixth century, this is less a reflection of his unconquerable prejudice
against medieval civilization than a tribute to Tillemont's work,
which breaks off at this point: "And here," Gibbon records, in a
characteristically ungracious acknowledgment, "I must take leave
forever from that incomparable guide—whose bigotry is overbal-
anced by the merits of erudition, diligence, veracity, and scrupulous
minuteness."[4] In this list, Gibbon summarized the ideal of the
érudits, and his own.

Yet, when this has been said, it must be added that it was an ideal
the other philosophes rarely realized. The kind of history they encountered when they began to write was immensely useful to them:
historical piety offered splendid instances of what to avoid; historical skepticism, though excessive, remained serviceable—Pyrrhonism,
Gibbon said, was "useful and dangerous"[5]—because, after all, previous historians had erred on the side of belief rather than unbelief;
and scholarly research could be mined for recondite facts. But the
philosophes were too embattled to do justice to the whole range of
their predecessors' work. They grandly patronized the *érudits* as
learned idiots who had done some good work, mainly in spite of
themselves, and who deserved nothing better than to be pillaged and
denigrated by the clever historians who came after them. "History
must be written by philosophers," Grimm pronounced, "whatever
our pedants say."[6] Doubtless there was real point in seeking to avoid
pedantry—the major histories written by the philosophes are distinguished works of literature—but the dismissal of scholars as pedants
was less a prescription for stylishness than a failure of vision; the
érudits had established a valuable tradition of documentary research
and scrupulous detective work that must falter if it was not kept up.
The philosophes did not keep it up; even Gibbon, who never joined
the popular Enlightenment sport of pedant-baiting, was only a consumer without being a producer of scholarship. It was certainly
healthy to be skeptical of medieval sources or antique legends masquerading as history: "To penetrate into the obscure labyrinth of
the Middle Ages," Voltaire argued in a typical passage, "we need

---

[4] *The Decline and Fall of the Roman Empire*, V, 132 *n*; see *The
Rise of Modern Paganism*, 370.
[5] Momigliano: "Gibbon's Contribution to Historical Method," 44.
[6] Quoted in Carl Becker: *The Heavenly City of the Eighteenth-
Century Philosophers* (1932), 91.

the aid of archives, and there are hardly any. A few old monasteries have preserved charters and diplomas which contain donations whose authority is highly suspect."[7] Such methodological talk was all very well; Voltaire's adroit allusion to "donations," which recalls celebrated monkish forgeries, coupled as it is with a shrewd appeal to archives, touched upon a sensitive spot in Christian historiography. As Voltaire and his fellow historians said over and over again, historians, whether fanatical monks or servile Romans, had inundated the world with fables and forgeries. But in recent decades it had been precisely the "pedants" who had discredited the fables and unmasked the forgeries; Voltaire's contempt for Christianity kept him and his fellows imprisoned in the erroneous assumption that Christian chroniclers, Christian scribes, and Christian historical critics had lied and continued to lie, from habit or from vocation, almost from second nature. "If the philosophers are not always historians," the young Gibbon smoothly said, "it would at least be desirable if historians were philosophers,"[8] an observation that describes his own hopes and implies the conclusion that piety and history were incompatible. Later, Gibbon would bestow that grandiose title—"our philosophical historian"[9]—on a most obviously anti-Christian historian, David Hume. Voltaire took the same position: in several well-known passages he demanded that history be written *en philosophe*, he himself wrote it *en philosophe*, and argued that Christians, lacking that essential capacity, could not write good history: "Count Boulainvilliers," he wrote, "is quite right when he claims that a Jesuit cannot write history accurately"[1]—and if even the urbane Jesuits could not write it, what of "fanatical" Jansenists or other, equally "fanatical" sectarians?

Scholarship itself was not the central issue. Some of the philosophes might express irritation with "mere" scholarship and impatience with what they were pleased to call minutiae and verminous details. They might take a high, New Historian's line, and declare

---

[7] Quoted in J. H. Brumfitt: *Voltaire Historian* (1958), 133.

[8] *Essai sur l'étude de la littérature*, in *Miscellaneous Works*, IV, 66.

[9] *Decline and Fall of the Roman Empire*, VII, 215; that this notion was a commonplace in the age of the Enlightenment is evident from Hume's casual and minor essay "Of the Study of History" (*Works*, IV, 388–91), in which he makes great claims for the philosophical importance of history.

[1] *Essai sur les mœurs*, II, 540.

that they could not be bothered with "scrupulously examining" whether "some piece of nonsense that happened six centuries ago" took place "on the 25th or the 26th of a certain month"[2]—a philistine reproach to the fact-grubbing specialist that has long been the stock in trade of literary men. But their performance was often better than their ill-tempered declarations, and their ambition was nothing less than to turn history into a science—*la science de l'histoire*.[3] History was to become one of the sciences of man, less precise than the physical sciences, perhaps, but no less scientific for all that. Conceding that in history certitude could never be so great as in logic or physics, Turgot still suggested that history be added to the "physical sciences."[4]

History, the philosophes thought, could become a science because it was now subject to philosophy—that is, to method—and because it sought for the truth alone. Of course, the claim that history is a search for pure truth was an ancient commonplace, endlessly reiterated and rarely credited; the philosophes said it again, with honest conviction and a good deal of confidence. "No doubt," Diderot wrote, "one must be truthful both in eulogy and in history."[5] Voltaire wholly agreed: "We need the truth in the smallest things." Writing from Prussia to the Jacobite writer Richard Rolt in 1750, he said it again: "j must hunt again after my favourite game, truth, in foreign cowntries. J travel like Polibus to see the different teaters of war. J do consult both friends and ennemys. . . . History must be neither a satir nor an encomium."[6] Voltaire's English spelling was uncertain, but his meaning was clear.

The scientific ideal—the historian who studies his material without praise or reproach—was in the philosophes' mind not a utopian wish but a reality. David Hume, for one, Voltaire suggested, had

---

[2] Voltaire to the Duchess of Saxe-Gotha, September 27 (1753), *Correspondence*, XXIII, 203; see Brumfitt: *Voltaire Historian*, 134.
[3] *Remarques pour servir de supplément à 'L'Essai sur les mœurs,'* in *Essai sur les mœurs*, II, 900. It is important to keep in mind that Voltaire did not conceive of this science in any dogmatic way; he was too sympathetic to Pyrrhonist doubts about the past to become a doctrinaire positivist.
[4] *Tableau philosophique des progrès*, in *Œuvres*, I, 310–11.
[5] Diderot to Madame d'Épinay (September 1771). *Correspondance*, XI, 183.
[6] *Le siècle de Louis XIV*, in *Œuvres historiques*, 878 *n.*; Voltaire to Richard Rolt, August 1, 1750. *Correspondence*, XVIII, 108.

realized it: Hume's *History of England* was "perhaps the best ever written in any language." And what made its merit was its impartiality: "Mr. Hume, in his *History*, is neither parliamentarian, nor royalist, nor Anglican, nor Presbyterian—he is simply judicial." Partisan rage, which has for so long deprived England of a good historian, is absent here: in this "new historian we find a mind superior to his materials; he speaks of weaknesses, blunders, cruelties as a physician speaks of epidemic diseases."[7] The medical metaphor, always a favorite with the philosophes, emphatically suggests that Voltaire wanted his praises taken seriously. David Hume himself, wryly confessing to the universal unpopularity of his volume on the early Stuarts, unwittingly claimed scientific status for his work: "I thought that I was the only historian, that had at once neglected present power, interest, and authority, and the cry of popular prejudices," but found himself "assailed by one cry of reproach, disapprobation, and even detestation; English, Scotch, and Irish, Whig and Tory, churchman and sectary, free-thinker and religionist, patriot and courtier, united in their rage against the man, who had presumed to shed a generous tear for the fate of Charles I and the Earl of Strafford."[8] This was all to the good: since the sixteenth century, unpopularity with one's own side had been accounted a sign of historical objectivity.

What turned the philosophes against the scholars, then, was less that they were scholars than that they were Christians. But whatever the reason, it was a judgment that compromised their own hopes for turning history into a science. The philosophes were serious historians and read the *érudits* to better purpose than they themselves admitted, but precisely because they were serious craftsmen, their disdain for what they called pedantry prevented them from applying the kind of open-minded self-criticism they needed to detect and correct their own biases.

---

[7] Quoted in Mossner: *Life of David Hume*, 318.
[8] *My Own Life*, in *Works*, III, 4–5.

III

What I have said about the philosophes' attitude toward scholarship applies in a rather different way to their belief in the uniformity of human nature. In itself it did not prevent them from writing good history; it was the conjunction of their psychology with their antireligious bias that produced the difficulties. To begin with, the assumption of uniformity helped to guarantee the reliability of historical assertions: "What would become of *history*," David Hume inquired rhetorically, "had we not a dependence on the veracity of the historian, according to the experience, which we have had of mankind?"[9] History was usable as sociology, and understandable as history, only insofar as the past was in some significant sense like the present. It is true that while the philosophes' historical perception was wider and deeper than the perception of their predecessors—even the great Mabillon had been, after all, cloistered and confined in his historical understanding—the idea of uniformity kept the philosophes' vision relatively flat: it encouraged them to make comparisons with the Middle Ages or Chinese civilization mainly for the sake of scoring political points. Somehow the philosophes' historical comparisons always turned out to be invidious comparisons. Yet, as I have insisted before, the doctrine of unity in no way foreclosed the possibility of variety. If Hume found that the study of history, even remote history, taught him nothing "new or strange" about human nature, the "revolutions of human kind, as represented in history," surprised him with their "prodigious changes," and offered a "spectacle full of pleasure and variety."[1] It was only the fundamental passions that were uniform and universal; customs, religions, institutions, forms of social organization, and styles of life were susceptible to almost infinite, almost unimaginable variety. As

---

[9] *Enquiry Concerning Human Understanding,* in ibid., IV, 73. There is an apparent circularity here: the assumption of uniformity prepares the historian to find in history the uniformity he is looking for, which, in turn, guarantees the correctness of his assumption. But this is only apparent: for Hume, experience was primary, providing highly probable evidence that man's nature was in fact uniform through time and place.
[1] For my earlier use of these quotations, see above, 168–9.

Voltaire put it, agreeing with the historians of his age, while the essential principles of human life are and remain the same, *mœurs* and culture produce "different fruits." While all men "are formed by their age" and "very few rise above the *mœurs* of their day," ages and *mœurs* differ vastly one from the other; climates and even more than climates, forms of government, insure these differences.[2] Saint-Évremond, modern Epicurean and proto-philosophe, had said it late in the seventeenth century, in his own urbane way: "If we were to make love like Anacreon and Sappho, nothing would be more ridiculous; like Terence, nothing more bourgeois; like Lucian, nothing cruder. Every age has its own character."[3] For the Enlightenment, the past was not a monochrome.

The philosophes' capacity to appreciate historical individuality mirrored and produced a relativist conception of the past, a certain willingness to suspend judgment and to see other epochs from the inside. In 1751, David Hume put the still fairly rudimentary relativism of the little flock into an amusing dialogue. He describes a nation that rewards ingratitude, brutality, incest, homosexuality, suicide, and murder—and it turns out to be the classical Greeks, and he then plays the same cunning game with Frenchmen, who welcome cruelty to children as long as it is the Bastille for a disobedient son, and murder as long as it is an honorable duel. An Athenian of merit, though civilized and intelligent, would be execrated by modern Frenchmen; a modern Frenchman, though equally civilized and intelligent, would have been execrated by the ancient Greeks. It is true that fundamental moral principles have changed little, but their expression and application differ enormously. What remains, then, is to apply the internal standards that a nation would apply to itself. "Would you try a GREEK or ROMAN by the common law of ENGLAND? Hear him defend himself by his own maxims; and then pronounce." Indeed, "there are no manners so innocent or reasonable, but may be rendered odious or ridiculous, if measured by a standard, unknown to the persons."[4] The germs of historicism are in these views: the historians of the Enlightenment were not quite so different from Ranke as Ranke and his followers liked to believe.

---

[2] *Essai sur les mœurs*, I, 774, and II, 416.
[3] Quoted in Vyverberg: *Historical Pessimism*, 31.
[4] *A Dialogue*, in *Works*, IV, 289–305; quotation on 294.

Hume's historicist sentiments were neither isolated nor insignificant. "When I have summoned up antiquity," Montesquieu wrote in the Preface of his *De l'esprit des lois*, "I have sought to adopt its spirit, that I might not regard as similar situations that are really different, and not overlook the difference in those that appear to be similar."[5] In the body of his book he applied this principle faithfully, warning his readers that "we must not separate the laws from the circumstances in which they were made,"[6] and that "to apply to remote centuries all the ideas of the age in which we live is among sources of error the most fruitful."[7] In his first book, the young Gibbon argued that while the philosophic spirit is a gift of nature, it can be cultivated by cultivating a historicist attitude: "The study of literature, the habit of becoming in turn Greek, Roman, the disciple of Zeno or Epicurus, is extremely useful for developing and training it." In general, the philosophes prescribed the practice, and regretted the rarity, of this kind of relativism. In 1758, Nicolas Lenglet du Fresnoy, a widely respected historian and methodologist, complained that too many of his contemporaries were writing about the past in accord with their "own standards rather than in the spirit of the age which we seek to portray. We attempt to make everything conform with our present-day habits and nature."[8] Voltaire, who knew the work of Lenglet, said the same thing: "Here," he wrote, speaking of Muslim culture, "are *mœurs*, customs, facts, so different from everything we are used to that they should show us how varied is the picture of the world, and how much we must be on guard against the habit of judging everything by our customs."[9] The philosophes knew the road to historical objectivity—they knew it, mapped it, and recommended it highly to others and to themselves.

[5] "Préface," *De l'esprit des lois*, in *Œuvres*, I, part 1, ix. In a *pensée*, Montesquieu notes: "To judge the beauties in Homer, it is necessary for us to place ourselves into the camp of the Greeks and not into a French army." *Œuvres*, II, 42.
[6] *De l'esprit des lois*, book XXIX, chap. xiv, chapter heading, *Œuvres*, I, part 1, 281.
[7] Ibid., book XXX, chap. xiv, *Œuvres*, I, part 1, 315.
[8] *Plan de l'histoire générale et particulière de la monarchie française*, I, ix–x, quoted in Lester A. Segal: "Nicolas Lenglet Du Fresnoy (1674–1755): A Study of Historical Criticism and Methodology in Early Eighteenth Century France" (Columbia University Ph.D. dissertation, 1968), 39–40.
[9] *Essai sur les mœurs*, I, 259–60.

Yet, while the philosophes advocated the ideal of relativism, they generally neglected it. They were in fact uneasy about their own performance. As Montesquieu said, in an observation that the critics of Enlightenment history have often quoted: "Voltaire will never write a good history. He is like the monks who write not for the subject they are dealing with, but for the glory of their order. Voltaire is writing for his monastery."[1] Certainly the criticism is overstated: even Voltaire was often disinterested in his historical work; even Voltaire did not see the Christian Middle Ages as a time of unrelieved and undifferentiated darkness. The other philosophic historians were still more detached than Voltaire. Robertson wrote a remarkably judicious survey of medieval culture; Gibbon conceded that "the darkness of the middle ages exhibits some scenes not unworthy of our notice."[2] Among the philosophes, hostility to an era dominated by organized religion was relieved by the sheer interest in the past and delight in portraiture. Beyond this, however, Montesquieu's remark about Voltaire carries conviction: benign condescension, isolated stabs at objectivity, and a certain inventiveness in varying the charges against the Middle Ages were the best the Enlightenment could muster in the face of its Christian past. Relativism was swamped by polemical passion.

It is this political context that made the philosophes' insistence on judging the past—aided by their assumption that human nature was always the same—so risky. The very idea of the historian as censor or builder of morale was a heritage from classical antiquity; history had always been an adjunct to ethics or politics, it had always been called upon to point a moral, enlist loyalties, improve its readers. In the time of Voltaire and Gibbon this notion was still very much alive. In 1763, James Boswell noted in his journal, "I employed the day in reading Hume's *History*, which enlarged my views, filled me with great ideas, and rendered me happy. It is surprising how I have formerly neglected the study of history, which of all studies is surely the most amusing and the most instructive."[3] This was the philosophes' view as well; as classicists, as radicals, and as men of their time, they sought to amuse and instruct, like everyone else. Each

---

[1] *Pensées*, in *Œuvres*, II, 419.
[2] *Decline and Fall of the Roman Empire*, VII, 210; see *The Rise of Modern Paganism*, 209.
[3] *Boswell's London Journal* (under February 20, 1763), 197.

did his work in his own way, and each history had its own mixture of scholarship and propaganda—Gibbon's propaganda differs from Voltaire's propaganda, the propaganda in Voltaire's *Essai sur les mœurs* differs from that in Voltaire's *Histoire du parlement de Paris*—and besides, the philosophes saw nothing wrong in their propaganda. They were confident that their treatment of Christianity was not mere vindictiveness, self-serving partisanship, or a failure of understanding, but a wholly truthful report: to omit the attack on Christianity would have been not an exercise of historical sympathy, but a suppression of unpalatable facts. Was it the philosophes' fault if the Middle Ages had been, on the whole, a time of wickedness and stupidity? If enlightened historians found it necessary to "fall upon *l'infâme*," that was because *l'infâme* had given them so much material to work with, and because *l'infâme*, at the same time, history showed that to expose vice was to advance virtue, to fix the contours of unreason was to help the cause of reason. It was necessary, Voltaire told his confidant Damilaville, to "make people see how we have been deceived in everything; to show how much of what is thought ancient is modern; how much of what has been given out as respectable is ridiculous."[4] At least one of the tasks of history was to make propaganda, but it must be propaganda in behalf of the truth, and it would be effective propaganda only if it were the truth. The philosophes therefore saw no reason to be apologetic about their didacticism: "Other historians," Diderot wrote to Voltaire, "tell us facts in order to teach us facts. You do it in order to excite in the depth of our souls a strong indignation against mendacity, ignorance, hypocrisy, superstition, fanaticism, tyranny; and that indignation remains when the memory of facts has gone."[5] This, as Diderot obscurely sensed, produced some intellectual difficulties. He celebrated Raynal's aggressive, radical history of the Two Indies as a magnificent weapon in the hands of humanity: "Raynal is a historian of a sort we no longer see; so much the better for him and so much the worse for history. If from the beginning history had seized, and dragged by the hair, both political and religious tyrants, I don't suppose they would have been better men,

---

[4] Quoted in J. H. Brumfitt: "History and Propaganda in Voltaire," *VS*, XXIV (1963), 272.
[5] (November 28, 1760). *Correspondance*, III, 275; see *The Rise of Modern Paganism*, 188.

but they would have been more thoroughly detested, and their unhappy subjects would have perhaps become less patient with them."
But then a doubt arose: was such bellicose history still history? "All
right," Diderot added, "efface the word 'history' from his book, and
be silent. The kind of book I like is the one that kings and their
courtiers detest, it is the kind of book that give birth to Brutuses—
give it whatever name you please."[6]

The historicists would extend Diderot's doubt into a system,
and deny to history the function he had so vigorously yet so uneasily assigned to it. Yet it was not the philosophes' commitment to
moral judgment—made, after all, in the name of truth—that made
for inadequate historical writing, but the kind of judgments they
made. What limited the value of their history and compromised its
very historical nature was the historical position in which they were
compelled to write it. What the philosophes' critics forgot was that
the philosophic historians could do nothing else. It is easy to be
above the battle only when the battle is over.

IV

It was precisely their irreligiosity that enabled the philosophes
to make their decisive contribution to the craft of history; their
position, one might say, had the virtues of its vices. If the historical
masterpieces of Voltaire and the others have faded into museum
pieces, what makes them still magnificent and in any event historically important museum pieces is the vigor with which they attacked the very presuppositions of Christian history writing. The
philosophes made their revolution in history by secularizing its
subject matter.

Doubtless the philosophes were wrong in their persistent insinu-
ations that Christians cannot write good history. The Christian
"superstition" made room for strenuous inquiry and truthful reporting. When the Reformation brought competition for the Christian
past, the efforts to unmask the lies of heretics acted as a stimulus
for further research. Long before Voltaire, devout monks had un-

---

[6] Quoted in Hans Wolpe: *Raynal et sa machine de guerre: 'L'Histoire des deux Indes' et ses perfectionnements* (1957), 43–4.

derstood that the truth is excellent propaganda, and the quarrels between Protestants and Catholics over the antiquity of their respective churches had called forth careful editions of documents and equally careful scholarly work in ancient languages. Even intramural conflict had its uses: stung by Jesuit charges that the Merovingian documents housed in the Benedictine monastery of Saint Denis were forgeries, Mabillon had rescued the reputation of the documents in the possession of his order, and by the way laid down his now classic rules for the study of historical documents.

At the same time, the philosophes' charge contained a valid and important point. As long as God played an active part in the world, the historian had no way of subjecting historical events to independent critical examination. If one king prospered because he had prayed and another was overthrown because he had sinned, or (since God's decrees were inscrutable) if a devout king was overthrown because it pleased God to overthrow him, if battles were won or lost in accord with divine interventions that had nothing to do with terrain, the morale of the troops, or the wit of generals, if empires rose and fell because it was God's will—if, in short, the course of history was the fulfillment of a mysterious divine plan, then the historian must direct his inquiry to theological questions and equip himself with knowledge not of geography or psychology or even the course of history itself, but of the Scriptures and its commentators. The philosophes' view that history was pervaded by struggles between virtue and vice, reason and unreason, philosophy and superstition, has come to seem naïve, but it was a purely human struggle, open to scientific inquiry and criticism. The struggle the Christian saw dominating history had its origins and pursued its course in the shadow of the supernatural. Wherever history was enacted—in the minds of men or on the fields of battle—it was somehow a reenactment of the very beginning of history, which was the seduction of Eve by the serpent; it was the working out, in myriad forms, of the war of Satan against God and His children. More than merely seeing history as justification for their particular version of Christianity, Christian historians saw it as part, and proof, of the supreme truths enshrined in religion. Events were on the one hand foretastes or repetitions of transcendent religious moments in the life of the world—the expulsion from Paradise, the Incarnation of Christ, the Second Coming—or on the other hand demonstrations of divine power, no matter which way they went: if heretics swarmed across Europe, this was a sign of God's anger at the faithful; if they retreated, it was a sign of His good will. However gravely the philosophes sinned in converting the events of history into a usable past, Christian historians had anticipated and in every way outdone them in this dubious enterprise.

It is true that Christian historians were coming to visualize God as acting not directly, by intermittent personal appearances, but indirectly, through human instruments. But inevitably, in their histories, the most significant human shapers of history were mere marionettes; they fulfilled God's designs without wishing to, or knowing it. Despite his attempts to portray divine action in history as indirect, the most influential, eloquent, and, to the philosophes, most provocative of Christian historians—Bossuet—regarded the Bible as more authoritative than the most reliable of secular histories, Moses as the first historian, the Creation, the Deluge, or worldly events with religious implications (like the reign of Constantine) as the decisive events in the past. Bossuet was not alone, and by his time no longer wholly typical, but the most philosophical of Christian historians were, like Bossuet, compelled to give religious—which is to say, incomplete, incorrect, inadequate, and often irrelevant— answers to questions men were beginning to ask about historical causation.

The philosophes changed all this, and their act is a decisive moment in the history of history. Barely emerged from the chrysalis of credulity, the philosophes were themselves sometimes credulous enough; they would ascribe great importance to world-historical individuals and the rational plans of statesmen rather than the confluence of historical forces, and they liked to attribute large events to trivial causes. D'Alembert traced the Renaissance to the Greek scholars whom the Fall of Constantinople had driven to Italy,[7] and Voltaire took a dramatist's delight in small incidents productive of

---

[7] R. G. Collingwood has used this particular piece of naïveté (in his *The Idea of History* [1946], 80) to convict the Enlightenment of lacking the historical conception of origins or processes. He has at least a point: see Condillac: "Often the slightest causes (*moyens*) are the principle of great revolutions." *Traité des systèmes*, in *Œuvres*, 208. But as I have shown in *The Rise of Modern Paganism*, 277 *n.*, both Gibbon and Voltaire had a far more sophisticated interpretation of the origins of the Renaissance than d'Alembert.

vast consequences: the messenger who, during the disorders of 1651, reaches the Prince de Condé too late and thus plunges France into civil war is a characteristic figure in Voltaire's histories, and in other Enlightenment histories.

But the philosophes did not make this kind of pragmatic history into a system. They had no system. The list of causes that Gibbon offers for the decline and fall of the Roman Empire—scattered through his book and revealed in isolated pronouncements and asides—is impressively diverse: as Gibbon sees it, the long period of peace induced torpor, effeminacy, and a decline in public spirit; the vast territory of the empire and the lack of real freedom froze institutions into rigidity; economic exploitation produced a populace reluctant to defend a Rome in which it had no stake—and all these conditions, reinforcing one another, made the incursions of the German barbarians and the spread of Christianity, the two decisive causes of the fall, irresistible.

Gibbon's list of causes, like lists of causes adduced by other philosophic historians for other events, was incomplete and uncoordinated; the philosophes had no overriding explanation of historical change that would have permitted them to show how causes interacted or how they could be arranged in a hierarchy of importance. Their theory of society was too primitive, and their idea of history as sheer battle too deeply engrained, to permit them to discover a really convincing theory of development. Uncertainty marks much of their work. It is instructive to see Voltaire's treatment of the Glorious Revolution of 1688: as he interpreted the event, it had been largely determined by the characters of James II and William III, and he offered it as a good example to those "who like to see the cause of events in the conduct of men."[8] But while this one event gave support to this particular theory of historical causation, Voltaire's language makes it plain that he cannot commit himself to it in explaining other events. In fact, elsewhere Voltaire shows himself to be a supporter of the larger view that historical changes arise from an interaction among massive impersonal forces: in his *Lettres philosophiques* he traces the splendor of England to a happy congruence of prosperity, freedom, and the dominance of

---

[8] *Siècle de Louis XIV*, in *Œuvres historiques*, 768.

commercial values; elsewhere he argues that the motive power of history must be sought in changes of religion or forms of government. Other Enlightenment historians offered similar causes; in his *De l'esprit des lois*, Montesquieu suggests that "men are governed" by "several things"; he lists them as "climate, religion, the laws, the principles of government, the example of the past, manners, and fashions," and adds that one or two of these causes will take prominence in the history of one society or another, depending on its general state of culture.[9] The philosophes had a sense that history is more than a drama of towering individuals. Yet their sociology is likely to be impressionistic; they had no way of converting their intuitions into formal arguments. Face to face with great historical questions, the philosophes often seem to be at play; they describe an event, list some plausible causes with an air of confidence, and move on.

This cavalier evasion of analysis or, rather, this substitution of literary elegance for analysis, which is often irritating, should not obscure the magnitude of their achievement. In offering a secular alternative to the theological determinism of Christian historians (whether in its rationalist version showing God clearly at work, or its mystical version according to which God manipulates events shrouded in mystery), the philosophes, whatever the inadequacies of their own analyses, opened the possibility for an all-embracing causal understanding of historical events and historical change. Their character sketches, the great set pieces about Luther or Cromwell, and their extended comparisons between William III and Louis XIV, are often psychologically improbable; accounts of great moments in history—the decline of the Roman Empire, the ascendancy of Louis XIV, the Spanish conquest of the New World—often suffer from a certain rationalism, and a disturbing if unconscious refusal to see the issues in all their complexity. But the expulsion of God from the historical stage remained an enormous gain for historical science. History became what Lenglet du Fresnoy called *érudition profane*,[1] with no reserved precincts, no privileged subjects, no figures exempt from criticism. Historians could now address them-

---

[9] *De l'esprit des lois*, book XIX, chap. iv, *Œuvres*, I, part 1, 412.
[1] Lester A. Segal: "Lenglet Du Fresnoy," 89.

selves, without reserve and without fear, to what Montesquieu called
"general causes, whether moral or physical."[2] God's disappearance
left a vacuum that the secular intelligence was called upon to fill.

The effect of this secularization was striking in all areas of history, but it was most notable in the philosophes' historical treatment
of religion and politics. To move from proving religion to be true
to proving it to be false might seem a petty gain, but the secular
attitude permitted, in fact demanded, an entirely new set of inquiries. The philosophes cheerfully conceded to the Christians that religion was indeed a powerful motive force in history, but they
insisted on redefining that force in what seemed to believers a
scandalously free and utterly subversive manner. Beginning with
Montesquieu's *Dissertation sur la politique des Romains*, continuing
with Hume's provocatively entitled *Natural History of Religion*,
and culminating in Gibbon's brilliant and aggressive chapters on
pagan government and Christian religion in the *Decline and Fall of
the Roman Empire*, the philosophes analyzed the psychological
causes and the historical influence of the religious impulse. In the
hands of these disenchanted historians, the two great sacred subjects,
religion and politics, became, for all practical purposes, one; religion, the philosophic historians demonstrated, was a form of politics, and, in many cultures, politics was a form of religion. The
priest concealing the "sentiments of an atheist under the sacerdotal
robes," emperors cynically exploiting the superstitions of the populace, Church Fathers persecuting one another with intolerant zeal
for the sake of power, the false miracles adroitly reported and
credulously believed, the base motives of emperors and bishops
masquerading as generosity and piety—all these elements in Gibbon's work described with well-placed adjectives, dramatized by
carefully selected detail, and made plausible through painstaking
scholarship, are more than the ebullitions of one man's talent. They
are a collective product, the triumph of the Enlightenment's secular
comprehension of the world. Gibbon piously announced that he
was restricting himself in his history to "secondary causes," to the
merely "human causes" that attend the fortunes of religion in this
world, presumably taking the sacred truth of Christianity for
granted. He "flattered" himself, he said in mock-indignation in his

---

[2] *Considérations sur les Romains*, in *Œuvres*, I, part 3, 482.

Autobiography, that "an age of light and liberty would receive, without scandal, an inquiry into the *human* causes of the progress and establishment of Christianity."[3] Such disclaimers were intended to deceive no one. Gibbon knew, and hoped his readers would discover, that there *were* only human causes.

The philosophes' secularization of historical cause enabled them to enlarge historical space. The world once circumscribed by faith grew wider, older, more varied in their hands than it had been in the hands of Christian historians. Much though by no means all of the Enlightenment's hostility to the Jews of the Bible had its roots in this enlargement. Bossuet, Voltaire argued, had mistaken a pious retelling of Hebrew tales for the history of the world: "His socalled *Universal History*" is "nothing but the history of four or five peoples, and above all of the little Jewish nation, either ignored or justly despised by the rest of the world."[4] Bossuet, Voltaire reiterated in the Preface to his own attempt at universal history, the *Essai sur les mœurs*, "seems to have written for the sole purpose of insinuating that everything in the world was done for the sake of the Jewish nation: that if God gave hegemony over Asia to the Babylonians, it was tó punish the Jews; if God had Cyrus reign, it was to avenge them; if God sent the Romans, it was, once again, to chastise the Jews. That," he added drily, "may be; but the greatness of Cyrus and the Romans also had other causes."[5] True universal history must proceed differently; it must begin with the Oriental nations which were civilized when the West was still sunk in primitive barbarity. Voltaire carried out the program of his Preface in the body of his book: the *Essai sur les mœurs* opens with chapters on China, moves on to India, and then to Persia, a provocative instance showing history as philosophy preaching by examples.

In assigning such unmistakable prominence to Oriental cultures in the most ambitious of his histories, Voltaire had, as usual, several purposes in mind at once. In his pointed admiration for the religion of the Chinese and the Indians, with their advanced conception of a single deity enjoining a pure morality and demanding no superstitious worship, Voltaire was obviously aiming at his own Christian

---

[3] *Decline and Fall of the Roman Empire*, II, 2, 32, 175.
[4] Quoted in Brumfitt: *Voltaire Historian*, 32.
[5] *Essai*, I, 196.

culture, with its idolatry, its incredible tales, its persecutions. In referring, just as pointedly, to the great age of Asiatic civilizations, Voltaire was throwing doubt on the Biblical account of early history, to which Christian historians still stubbornly clung. In keeping Bossuet quite explicitly at the center of his stage, Voltaire was gratifying his ambition to excel Bossuet even at his best. But whatever his polemical purposes and private urges, Voltaire was also making propaganda in behalf of universal history, of an attitude toward the past that embraced all civilizations in the world without prejudice or parochial purpose, partly at least for their own sake, and in their own place. The philosophes were certain that authentic universality became possible only through unmasking the fraudulent universality of Christian historians—that myopic parochialism masquerading as world history.

Unfortunately, in dissipating the parochialism of Christian historians, the philosophes reintroduced a parochialism of their own, for familiar reasons: their relativism was not disinterested but in the service of absolutes. In this sense at least the widespread charge against the Enlightenment, that it took the ideology of Christianity and turned it upside down, is justified; as Christians had used non-Christian nations to make a case for Christianity, the philosophes used them to make a case against Christianity.

Still, the less-than-universal universal history of the philosophes remains a significant advance over the history of their pious predecessors, in practice and in potential alike. Defective as his chapters on the Orient may be, Voltaire wrenched the center of history away from the Christian or the European world, and if, seeking to redress the balance, he introduced a new imbalance of his own, he showed how it might finally be securely established by historians better informed and less embattled than he. Voltaire's fellow historians, it might be added, traveled as widely as he did to construct their historical universe: Robertson treated India, Spanish America, and medieval Europe with nearly as much objectivity as he treated his native Scotland; Gibbon concentrated on the Roman Empire, but he was alert to the remote world beyond its frontiers. It was an exhilarating expansion of vistas and a great act of liberation.

Not content with widening the area of historical inquiry, the philosophes moved deeply into culture itself, with unprecedented boldness and unprecedented dividends: cultural history in its modern sense is an invention of the Enlightenment. The philosophes' impatience with trivia, their rejection of the aristocratic ideal, and their insistent secularism all played their part here. What had been covered over by superficial anecdotes, worshipful accounts of heroic individuals, and layers of devotion was now laid open to exploration and analysis, and could be incorporated into a new, comprehensible entity of historical study—culture. As the scientists of the seventeenth century had unified their world, demolishing the hierarchies of celestial and terrestrial motion and bringing all physical events into a single system, so the historians of the eighteenth century made their revolution by opening access to all historical phenomena and by placing them on the same level, into the same system. As was customary, their intentions were better than their performance—in Gibbon, and even more in Hume, culture is segregated into separate sections and the interaction of cultural phenomena—of political, economic, literary, religious forces—is far from complete, but their performance was at least a clue to future historians. Like their conquest of time or of objectivity, their conquest of culture was magnificent and revolutionary less in what they did—though, I insist, that was magnificent and revolutionary enough—than in what they said must be done, and what they made it possible for others to do.

Certainly the whole program of cultural history, if not modern cultural history itself, can be found in the pronouncements of the philosophes. "A lock on the canal that joins the two seas, a painting by Poussin, a fine tragedy," wrote Voltaire, the most programmatic among Enlightenment historians, "are things a thousand times more precious than all the court annals and all the campaign reports put together."[6] He insisted that this kind of history was the only kind to deserve the name philosophical: "People are very careful to report on what day a certain battle took place," he wrote in 1744, reasonably enough, "and they are right to do so. They print treaties, they describe the pomp of a coronation, the ceremony of receiving the Cardinal's hat, and even the entrance of an ambassador, forgetting neither his Swiss soldiers nor his lackeys. It is a good thing to have

---

[6] Brumfitt: *Voltaire Historian*, 46.

archives on everything, that one might consult them when necessary; and I now look upon all these fat books as dictionaries. But
after I have read three or four thousand descriptions of battles, and
the terms of some hundreds of treaties, I have found that fundamentally I am scarcely better instructed than I was before. From
these things I learn only events." By reading reports on the victory
of Tamerlane over Bajazet, Voltaire goes on, he did not learn to
know the Tartars and the Turks; by reading the memoirs of the
Cardinal de Retz, he found out only what the queen mother said,
word for word, to her attendants, but this was hardly instructive.
All these are "little miniatures," which live for a generation or two,
and then die forever; and it is for their sake that more important
knowledge has been neglected. "I should like to learn just what was
the strength of a country before a war, and if the war had increased
or diminished it. Was Spain richer before the conquest of the New
World than today?" Why did the population of Amsterdam grow
within two hundred years from twenty thousand to two hundred
and forty thousand? How did the arts and manufacturing establish
themselves in one country, and move from one to another? These
are the questions historians should ask, but have failed to ask: "I
read the annals of France in vain: our historians are silent on these
details." Voltaire had recourse to the popular antique cliché from
Terence to make his revolutionary point: "None of these historians
has taken for his motto, *Homo sum, humani nil a me alienum puto*.
Yet it seems to me that one must skillfully incorporate this useful
kind of knowledge into the tissue of events."[7] In the famous programmatic opening words of *Le siècle de Louis XIV*, Voltaire said
it again, briefly: "It is not merely the life of Louis XIV that we
claim to write; we have set ourselves a larger objective. We want
to attempt to paint for posterity, not the actions of a single man,
but the spirit of men in the most enlightened century that ever
was."[8] The book itself seeks to realize the program of this daring
first paragraph: it reduces court anecdotes to four short chapters,
opens its account of the political and military events of the reign of

---

[7] *Nouvelles considérations sur l'histoire*, in *Œuvres historiques*,
46–8.
[8] *Œuvres historiques*, 616.

Louis XIV with a survey of Europe, and, quite symmetrically, concludes that long section of the book with another survey of Europe during the last year or two of the king's reign; it then disposes of its anecdotes and moves into domestic affairs, the sciences, the arts, and literature, to conclude with a polemical section—some chapters on religious quarrels, and on the Jesuits' penetration of China. "But if God had wanted China to be Christian, would he have been content with putting crosses in the air? Would he not have put them into the hearts of the Chinese?"[9] These are, strikingly enough, the last sentences in a book ostensibly devoted to the reign of a French king; a reminder that for a historian as professional as Voltaire, in the age of the Enlightenment, political concerns, indeed political obsessions, were never very far from the surface.

It is this element—politics—that gave Enlightenment history its flavor, made possible its radical achievements and saddled it with its difficulties. In the other social sciences of the eighteenth century, the inclination of the philosophes to translate description into prescription raised no strenuous intellectual difficulties; sociology and political economy, after all, were what we have come to call "policy sciences," whose very purpose it was to convert facts into values. For the philosophes, history was a policy science as well, but it was also, as they rather obscurely saw, something different; it was a discipline in which too much insistence on policy would compromise the science.

Yet, to repeat, they could not escape their situation. Near the end of his life, frightened by the "disorders in France," Gibbon professed his admiration for Burke's antirevolutionary philosophy, and, characteristically enough, sought to blame others for what he too had been responsible for. "I have sometimes thought of writing a dialogue of the dead in which Lucian, Erasmus, and Voltaire should mutually acknowledge the danger of exposing an old superstition to the contempt of the blind and fanatic multitude."[1] Gibbon, it is true, had never addressed the multitude, but his notorious chap-

---

[9] Ibid., 1109. The text of *Le siècle de Louis XIV* is, of course, followed by those famous catalogues, which include lists of the royal family of France, sovereigns of Europe, and short biographies of "celebrated" writers and artists.

[1] *Autobiography*, 203.

ters on early Christianity in the *Decline and Fall of the Roman Empire* had been part of the great and unappeasable debate of the eighteenth century. Not even Gibbon—and if not Gibbon, then who else?—could avoid the realities of his time, or the force of Rousseau's observation that everything is at bottom connected with politics.

CHAPTER EIGHT

The Politics of Decency

THE MEN of the Enlightenment had no doubts about their political aims. With few hesitations and only marginal disagreements, they called for a social and political order that would be secular, reasonable, humane, pacific, open, and free, and their firm consensus gives sturdy support to the idea of a philosophic family, sometimes divided and contentious, but essentially united in its view of the world and perception of its ideals. It was different with political methods; as I shall show, the road to the realization of their political demands was difficult and devious, and often seemed impassable: the problems of politics were intractable and led the philosophes into agonizing perplexities. Yet, however divergent and difficult these problems turned out to be, the philosophes faced them with the same spirit and the same program; they agreed that it was essential to give humanitarianism organized form and effective force.

In their own day, the philosophes' strident advocacy of their social and political ideals was widely publicized. Contemporaries did not agree on just what all this activity meant: detractors disparaged it as nothing more than a brash, noisy version of widespread and increasingly popular attitudes; admirers celebrated it as the philosophes' signal merit, delighted in their propaganda in behalf of toleration, peace, legal reform, and the emancipation of slaves, and enjoyed retelling, over and over again, Voltaire's splendidly disinterested behavior in the Calas case.

In a way, both detractors and admirers were right. As I have said, in the age of the Enlightenment the temper of civilized men was evolving from overt brutality toward sober self-restraint, shifting from violence to debate. But the philosophes were more than chips on a rising tide of humanitarianism: they were the perfectionist conscience of their day, propagandists for, if by no means the sole inventors of, the politics of decency.

1. TOLERATION: A PRAGMATIC CAMPAIGN

I

SINCE THE PHILOSOPHES' efforts at defending and disseminating humanity are so familiar and so diverse—there was so much to be humane about!—it is less important to catalogue their interventions than to discover their reasons. These reasons are implicit in their conviction that if anything will change man's lot it is the scientific method (which is to say, *their* method) and in their passionate and hopeful observation of the social changes in their time. Montesquieu listing the rights of accused persons, Lessing advocating tolerance of Jews, Beccaria constructing a humane jurisprudence, Rousseau defending the claims of the child, Voltaire rehabilitating the victims of judicial miscarriage, Kant analyzing the preconditions for world peace, all were elaborating a single view of man and of politics—a single view of man *in* politics—which offers no surprises, since it follows with inescapable logic from their general way of thinking. Of course, Christians, both before and during their time, had been, and were, humane; they were far more humane, in fact, than it was comfortable for the Enlightenment to admit or even to believe. But theirs were different grounds.

The philosophy of the Enlightenment insisted on man's essential autonomy: man is responsible to himself, to his own rational interests, to his self-development, and, by an inescapable extension, to the welfare of his fellow man. For the philosophes, man was not a sinner, at least not by nature; human nature—and this argument was subversive, in fact revolutionary, in their day—is by origin good, or at least neutral.[1] Despite the undeniable power of man's antisocial passions, therefore, the individual may hope for improvement through his own efforts—through education, participation in politics, activity in behalf of reform, but not through prayer. In consequence, the philosophes saw society no longer as a family of God's children dependent on paternal direction and approval which must anxiously

---

[1] See above, chap. iv, section 1.

appease the divinity by maintaining uniformity of religious practice and fidelity of observance. In the older, tribal view, the blasphemer, the heretic, the unbeliever, the outsider of any description endangered the whole and had to be purged from a society he tainted by his very presence. The philosophes saw the offender not as a scourge or an enemy but as a victim, usually of society itself.

The most prominent casualty of this attack on tradition was the idea of hierarchy, the idea that society is divinely, eternally ordered in ranks. To be sure, few of the philosophes ventured to adopt a full-fledged democratic position in which hierarchies are purely functional and wholly temporary; but the preponderant political thought of the Enlightenment, a kind of snobbish liberalism, at least envisioned the possibility, and proclaimed the desirability, of a society open to talents, in which commoners, even from poor circumstances (especially if they were men of letters) might rise to positions of influence, wealth, and status. Reason, ability, even luck, rather than birth, were the criteria by which the philosophes wanted men to be judged in society.

The demand for the toleration of religious minorities, philosophical dissenters, and sexual deviants was the practical correlative of these propositions about man and society, reinforced by the philosophes' characteristic view of philosophy—skeptical, empiricist, a little cynical, and heavily concentrated on social ethics. Montesquieu and Diderot, Wieland and Beccaria, Voltaire and Lessing all sound the same note, first sounded in the sixteenth and early seventeenth centuries by Montaigne and the Christian Stoics: to kill others for their ideas is to exaggerate the importance of ideas. Since men are all hopelessly ignorant of the ultimate mysteries shrouding the universe, it would be the utmost in barbarity and absurdity to constrain, let alone persecute, those who hold views divergent from the dominant one: certainty is the mother of intolerance, disdain for metaphysical construction is an inducement to toleration. The philosophes enlisted even their cynicism and their anticlericalism in the good cause: the man who shrugs his shoulders at the foolishness of the world or rails at the persecuting spirit of priests will never become a fanatical assassin of dissenters.

Since philosophy, for the philosophes, was constructive as well as critical, they had good humanitarian, ethical, and even religious reasons for toleration: it is distasteful to expose men to constraint, compel them to silence, or condemn them to death for their political, social, or religious opinions, since all men are brothers. As Lessing rather touchingly put it: "Little children, love one another," a doctrine all the philosophes accepted—with some wry reservations, for there were many whom it was hard to love.

In fact, on the whole the philosophes found *Schwärmerei* highly suspect, and they based their demand for tolerance largely on practical grounds. "I'm an odd person, don't you think, my dear Fritz?" Wieland wrote to friend. "But that's how I am and, according to my philosophy I say, let everything be just as it may. What good is all the enormous mass of enthusiasm we have for one another, if we don't learn to stand one another?"[2] This was the point: men must learn to stand one another, and tolerance as embodied in institutions was a significant step in that direction. Since societies are not families or tribes but complex totalities composed of individuals, clans, groups, classes with diverse histories and conflicting interests, differences in opinions and behavior are to be expected and, indeed, encouraged: "If there were only one religion in England," Voltaire noted in his famous report on the philosophes' favorite country, "one would have to fear despotism; if there were two, they would cut each others' throats; but they have thirty, and they live happy and in peace."[3] As the toleration of diversity seemed an indispensable prerequisite for the effective pursuit of knowledge—it is only open debate, even the spouting of error, that will permit the critical mind to operate and enable men at least to approach an acceptable philosophy of life—it seemed equally indispensable for politics: it uncovered injustices committed by entrenched powers, and, as Locke had already argued in his first *Letter Concerning Toleration*,

---

[2] Sengle: *Wieland*, 299.
[3] Lettre VI, *Lettres philosophiques*, I, 74. To reiterate a formula I advanced in the first volume of this essay: "Relativism, Eclecticism, and toleration are so intimately related that they cannot be strictly separated even in thought. Relativism is a way of looking at the world, the recognition that no single set of convictions has absolute validity; Eclecticism is the philosophical method consequent on relativism—since no system has the whole truth, and most systems have some truth, discriminating selection among systems is the only valid procedure. Toleration, finally, is the political counterpart of this world view and this method: it is a policy for a large and varied society." *The Rise of Modern Paganism*, 163.

far from fostering seditious factions it alone makes for social peace.

This line of reasoning thrust heavy responsibilities on the individual. It demanded rational conduct from citizen and government alike; within the state, it exacted the sublimation of hostility, and in the relation of states to one another, it substituted, for automatic mutual hostility, the ideal of a peaceful worldwide community in which the struggles among individual members take the form of debates over ideas and competition for markets. As the philosophes' conception of man was (in the Enlightenment's sense of that word) rationalist, their conception of the state was utilitarian: governing authorities and institutions justify themselves not by an appeal to religious or historical sanctions but by the effectiveness with which they perform their assigned task, which is to minimize pain and maximize pleasure.[4] The philosophes' revulsion against the traditional heroic code of aristocratic societies, a revulsion that placed Newton above Louis XIV and merchants above generals, splendidly complemented this shift toward service, decency, and peace.

II

The philosophes' writings on peace—the extension of tolerance to the international stage—testifies to their struggle, on the whole successful, in behalf of humane realism against utopian fantasies. These writings are crowded with denunciations of war: war is, for the philosophes, the most devastating of disasters, which only irresponsible kings can initiate, fanatical priests can encourage, cruel soldiers can love, and the foolish rabble can admire. Diderot derided the military hero as a butcher who continues to flourish in modern culture only because the mob loves him. In a similar vein, Holbach insisted that war has remained an instrument of national policy simply because the military caste has retained its influence, and for no other—that is, for no good—reason. War, Lessing wrote a little picturesquely, drives away the muses: "Peace will return without them; a sad peace, accompanied by a single melancholy pleasure"—weeping over loss and destruction. The warrior-king covers his

---

[4] See below, 459-60.

people "with laurels and with misery." Glory is not worth the price:
"What costs blood is not worth blood."[5] Voltaire veers between
lamentation and analysis, with lamentation in command: priests bless
the colors while hapless conscripts go to an unnecessary death;
princes reap undeserved glory by devastating innocent provinces;
patriotism is another word for mass murder; untutored soldiers are
brutish simply because they are brutes, but their cultivated com-
manders are often quite as brutish, from vanity or from other,
equally dubious, motives. Voltaire insists that war has many causes:
superstition, greed, credulity, ambition, all powerful ingredients in
human nature, all discreditable. Christian pacifists like the Quakers
had argued and continued to argue that war was probable because
men were not Christians; Voltaire, far more pessimistic, argued that
war was probable precisely because they were. Montesquieu early
and Condillac, Mably, Wieland, and others later in the eighteenth
century return to this depressing theme again and again. Reading a
report on the Isle de France, an island off Madagascar that the
French had occupied, Diderot finds his humanity offended and his
sensibilities outraged: "Ah! my friend," he reported to his mistress
in 1769, "tears came to my eyes a hundred times. Is this how you
treat men? You have no idea what an intendant is really like, or a
commander they send to these poor islanders; what a tribunal of
justice is in a colony; what a businessman is. A businessman is a
soul of bronze to whom the life of his fellow man means nothing,
whose aim is to starve a whole country for the sake of getting a good
profit for his wares. . . . The commander and the intendant are
atrocious proconsuls, like those among the ancient Romans, sent to
the provinces of the empire to desolate them, devastate them, and
enrich themselves."[6] Clearly war and conquest were profitable—to
some—but that did not commend them to the men of the Enlightenment.

Even those profits were at best problematical: most of the
philosophes who addressed themselves to the phenomenon of militant
imperialism found it not merely vicious, but stupid as well. Montesquieu, who shrewdly described conquerors as driven men, out of

---

[5] See Paul Rilla: *Lessing und sein Zeitalter* (1960), 74–5.
[6] To Madame de Maux (?) (beginning of November 1769). *Correspondance*, IX, 196–7.

control and often self-destructive, exposed the baleful effects of warlike expansion on the ancient Romans; Raynal offered the same diagnosis for modern Europeans. Voltaire argued that for all its prominence in human affairs, war solves nothing: it spreads untold and unnecessary suffering, it perpetuates and in fact intensifies the very evils that pious preachers had promised it would solve. There were, to be sure, militant minority voices in the philosophic family: Adam Ferguson thought of war as a builder of morale and internal unity; Adam Smith extolled the martial virtues as manly virtues; and Rousseau had much good to say for passionate love of country. Yet even Ferguson thought that war was often nothing better than "rapine,"[7] and that modern governments, having established a certain tranquillity at home, indulged their predatory impulses abroad: war itself "may be made the subject of traffic," and "often human blood is, without any national animosity, bought and sold for bills of exchange."[8] While in itself war was not, for Ferguson, a corrupt institution, he acknowledged that it could often be corrupted. Adam Smith, studying the economic effects of war, sardonically noted that those who felt the war least enjoyed it most: "In great empires the people who live in the capital, and in the provinces remote from the scene of action, feel, many of them, scarce any inconveniency from the war; but enjoy, at their ease, the amusement of reading in the newspapers the exploits of their own fleets and armies," and he drily suggested that if these spectators were made to pay for the war, they might make peace more speedily and undertake to make war less wantonly—hardly a passionate stand, but still a plea for peace.[9] Rousseau, finally, sufficiently curbed his patriotism and his admiration for bellicose virility to decry military expansion and military conquest in language familiar to his fellow philosophes: "Whoever wants to be free," he told the Poles, "should not wish to be a conqueror."[1] When Voltaire contemptuously lampooned the Anglo-French conflict over Canada as a quarrel over a few acres of snow, he was a bad prophet but a good philosophe.

---

[7] *An Essay on the History of Civil Society*, 103.
[8] Quoted in Kettler: *Social and Political Thought of Adam Ferguson*, 207–8.
[9] *Wealth of Nations*, 872, 878.
[1] *Considérations sur le gouvernement de Pologne et sur sa réformation projetée*, in *Œuvres*, III, 1013.

Pacific as they were in their inclinations, the philosophes were not pacifists in the modern sense: they neither advocated resistance to war nor expressed confidence that war would ever disappear. Their analysis of the causes of war—economic rivalry, the inherently unstable state system, and the aggressive aspects of human nature—inclined them to pessimism, and therefore many of them preached peace in the candid expectation that their preachments would go unheard; like other pessimists, they expressed their views less to convert the world than to soothe their disquiet. Their response to the abbé de Saint-Pierre's *Projet de paix perpetuelle*, published from 1713 to 1717 and widely publicized through later abridgments, is a measure of their gloom: Rousseau, who was interested enough in Saint-Pierre's ideas to edit and publish his posthumous manuscripts, was not persuaded by Saint-Pierre's hopes for the future. He professed affection for the abbé's ideas but found them inapplicable to man as he is. Statesmen make war, whether wisely or not, because they need it to advance their careers; rulers make war because they want to consolidate or to expand their power. War, Rousseau sadly concluded, is simply the "consequence of a mutual, constant, and palpable disposition"[2] to destroy or weaken hostile states. Voltaire, in his turn, was even less inclined than Rousseau to be seduced by Saint-Pierre's glittering schemes; his sardonic comments on inevitable war are the outbursts not of the detached cynic but of the disappointed humanitarian. He even allowed his disillusionment, coupled as it was with his intense aversion for Rousseau, to distort his reading of Rousseau's edition of Saint-Pierre's fragments: attributing to him an unworldly pacifism that Rousseau had in fact called unrealistic, Voltaire denounced the fantasies of projectors, the perversity of human conduct, and the foolishness of Jean-Jacques in the same outburst: "They said peace, peace," he wrote in 1761, "and there was no peace, and this mad Diogenes of a Rousseau proposes perpetual peace."[3] A philosophe's lot was far from easy; one of his most difficult and most necessary duties, it seemed, was to discipline his desires under the insistent pressures of reality.

The best known among the philosophes' efforts to find the

---

[2] "Que l'état de guerre naît de l'état social," a fragment in ibid., 607.
[3] Quoted in Merle L. Perkins: *Voltaire's Concept of International Order*, VS, XXXVI (1965), 104. Despite these reservations, Voltaire thought well of the abbé's humanitarianism (see above, 37).

conditions of perpetual peace, Kant's *Zum ewigen Frieden*, is just such a combat between realism and hope. *Zum ewigen Frieden*, published in 1795 in the midst of war and revolution, is one of Kant's last works, and one of the last words of the waning Enlightenment. The inquiry, Kant warns his readers at the outset, is in no way guaranteed success: "To eternal Peace," was, after all, a satirical inscription that a Dutch innkeeper had put on his signboard; it was the legend accompanying the picture of a graveyard.[4] Yet, for all its obvious difficulties, no subject deserves more earnest consideration than this. To be sure, nature with her dark, mysterious plans, acting rather as Adam Smith expected the invisible hand to act, compels men to behave in ways that may produce unexpected results—even peace. But in general, the achievement of peace depends on careful self-analysis, on a willingness of practical politicians to listen to theorists, and on a deliberate policy designed to disarm, slowly, the most potent causes of war. In search of this course, Kant carefully differentiates between what he calls the preliminary and the permanent articles of peace. What Kant had said of goodness, he now said of peace: it can be conquered only step by step, with infinite labor.

The preliminary articles have a single object: to produce a new climate of opinion which alone will make possible the far-reaching changes needed for perpetual peace, and they include the willingness of statesmen to deal candidly with one another; to eschew acquisitions of territory; gradually to dissolve standing armies, which are, by their very existence, a threat to peace; to undertake never to meddle in the internal affairs of other states; and to conduct future wars, if they should after all be unavoidable, with so much humane restraint that later accommodation will be possible: "A war of extermination" will permit perpetual peace only, as it were, metaphorically, in "the great cemetery of the human race."[5] Of course, as long as statesmen continue to equate practical wisdom with the policy of perpetually increasing their power, peace is impossible, and these preliminary articles will appear "schoolmasterly and pedantic."[6] War, Kant concedes in good Hobbesian fashion, is natural; peace,

---

[4] Kant: *Zum ewigen Frieden*, in *Werke*, VI, 427. "*Zum*" in *Zum ewigen Frieden* means both "to" and "at the."
[5] Ibid., VI, 431.
[6] Ibid., 428.

therefore, must be *made;* and it can be made only after practical men have been convinced that their supposed realism is not practical after all.

Kant's preliminary articles, therefore, are moves to reduce the temperature of international relations; confidence breeds confidence. The definitive articles of eternal peace can then be drawn up with some possibility of realization. They are three: the civic constitution of every state must be republican (by which Kant means that it must be a government of law, responsible to its citizens through representative institutions); since peace can be assured only under law, states must freely band together in a federation; this federation must guarantee a rule of general hospitality, enabling strangers to visit freely but also requiring guests to conduct themselves with politic restraint. It is in these three articles that the tough-mindedness of the Enlightenment appears at its most impressive: what Kant asks for is difficult and may be impossible, but then the achievement of peace is at best difficult, and to propose simple solutions, to expect that a mere change of mind or a mere piece of institutional machinery will perform miracles, is to betray the cause they are designed to advance. Peace can come only when these hard conditions are met, not before. Republicanism, for one, is a far-off goal, but, Kant argues, it is essential not merely because the republican form is a pure form in its origins, but also because it permits those whom war affects most intimately to decide their own fate: in other states, where the ruler is not "a fellow citizen in the state but the owner of the state—*nicht Staatsgenosse, sondern Staatseigentümer*—that ruler, precisely the one who will lose nothing of his "banquets, hunts, châteaux, court entertainments" in wartime, treats war as a "kind of pleasure party."[7] This is the doctrine of autonomy in action: let those whose stake in foreign policy is greatest participate in its making, and reason may prevail.

In an appendix to his essay, Kant added a "secret article," suggesting that statesmen should take advice from "the maxims of philosophers." It may be too much to "expect kings to philosophize, or philosophers to become kings." Nor would it be desirable: power inevitably corrupts judgment. "But that kings or royal nations (that

---

[7] Ibid., 436.

is, self-governing nations acting under egalitarian laws) will not permit the class of philosophers to shrink away or fall silent, but let them speak publicly, is indispensable to them both for the clarification of their work."[8] This secret article is what Kant might have called a maxim of hope; it is the political philosophy of the Enlightenment at its most poignant. In general, the philosophes did not expect, and only rarely hinted, that it was their task to guide rulers. Yet they were convinced that if not their persons, at least their philosophy should have—*must* have—influence over public affairs. But they had experienced too many disappointments to believe in their own prescription fully. They doubted not its efficacy but its palatability: it was salutary, in fact the only salutary prescription available, but the patient seemed resistant and was, to his own misfortune, more powerful than these physicians of civilization could ever hope to be. And so, in the cause of peace, the philosophes were men of good will, though scarcely of good hope.

2. ABOLITIONISM: A PRELIMINARY PROBING

I

THE PURSUIT OF POWER and profit in the world took many forms, most of them obnoxious. But most obnoxious of all was the institution of slavery, which came to arouse benevolent men in the eighteenth century, especially after the 1750s, to displays of eloquent indignation. Slavery, it would seem, was coeval with organized society: Voltaire thought it as old as war and human nature itself, and it became, for the Western conscience, a peculiar institution in more ways than one. A few philosophers among the ancients, notably those cosmic cosmopolitans, the Stoics, had deplored slavery; but inclined as they were to accept the course of the world with dignified resignation, they argued not for its abolition in law, but, as it were, in men's minds. They taught that the slave is free if he learns

---

[8] Ibid., 456.

to disdain cruel fortune, freer indeed than his master, driven by the anxieties and crushed by the burdens that society imposes on a man of wealth and rank. Such teachings may have done something for the morale of educated slaves; they did not lead to the abolition of slavery. The Roman law described slavery as contrary to the laws of nature and solely sanctioned by the laws of men, the *ius gentium;* Christianity, with its doctrine of individual salvation, contained and concealed a kind of "latent egalitarianism."[9] But for centuries, the tensions that the reasonings of Roman lawyers and doubts of Christian theologians introduced into the discussion of slavery were repressed, or, rather, resolved, in favor of the slaveholder. In the sixteenth century, Jean Bodin, the great theorist of sovereignty, reopened the debate, arguing that there were sound, in fact compelling moral and legal, arguments against an institution that positive law had condoned for centuries; in the seventeenth, and in the philosophes' own century, a sense of moral outrage over slavery, even of guilt, spread to a certain number of Quakers and other Protestant Dissenters, and to a handful of Anglicans and Catholics who took the virtue of Christian charity seriously. "The Quakers of Pennsylvania," John Millar noted in 1771, "are the first body of men" who have "discovered any scruples" and who "seem to have thought that the abolition of this practice is a duty they owe to religion and humanity."[1] Quakers like William Penn had still owned slaves; with his descendants, conscience, and (as both the abbé Raynal and Adam Smith noted) the relative insignificance of slaves to the economy in Pennsylvania, induced them to abolish slavery among themselves and to petition for general emancipation. Earlier, as early as 1702, Daniel Defoe, as usual one of the first to discern, applaud, and encourage dawning humanitarian impulses, had vigorously satirized the slave trade. And by mid-century, Horace Walpole began to punctuate his correspondence with energetic denunciations of slavery in general, and of the slave trade in particular. In 1773, when the commercial interests in the British West Indies successfully beat

---

[9] The phrase is David Brion Davis's: *The Problem of Slavery in Western Culture* (1966), 294.
[1] *The Origin of the Distinction of Ranks* (2d edn., 1779, reprinted in its entirety in William C. Lehmann: *John Millar of Glasgow, 1735–1801* [1960]), 311.

back an inquiry, Walpole raged to Sir Horace Mann: "Caribs, black Caribs, have no representatives in Parliament; they have no agent but God, and he is seldom called to the bar of the House to defend their cause; 206 to 88 gave them up to the mercy of their persecutors; and as the Portuguese call *their* negroes, the Caribs are deemed *disaffected*. Alas! dare I complain of gout and rheumatism, when so much a bitterer cup is brewed for men as good as myself in every quarter of the globe! Can one be a man and not shudder at all our nature is capable of! I welcome pain: for it gives me sensibility, and punishes my pride. Donatello loses his grace when I reflect on the million of my fellow creatures that have no one happiness, no one comfort!"[2] This was the new, still small voice of eighteenth-century humanity, a prey to conscience, and if a trifle precious still uncompromising. Walpole's outrage at slavery even forced him into ambivalence about the rebellious American colonists and into unconscious wishful prophecy of future racial troubles: "If all the black slaves were in rebellion," he wrote in 1774, "I should have no doubt in choosing my side, but I scarce wish perfect freedom to merchants who are the bloodiest of all tyrants. I should think the souls of the Africans would sit heavy on the swords of the Americans."[3] Obviously the philosophes, who agreed that slavery was detestable, were not alone.

But while the philosophes, as so often, did little more than to express advanced opinion in their own time, they were in its vanguard. The denunciations of slavery by Horace Walpole and Samuel Johnson, by Granville Sharp and the marquis de Lafayette, came half a century after Montesquieu first vented his antislavery sentiments in the *Lettres persanes*. Before Montesquieu, certainly, objections to slavery had been comfortably unspecific. It is true that John Locke had assailed the very idea of slavery in the first sentence of his *First Treatise*: "Slavery," he had written there, "is so vile and miserable an estate of man, and so directly opposite to the generous temper and courage of our nation, that it is hardly to be conceived that an Englishman, much less a gentleman, should plead for it." But then, this energetic declaration was really directed against Filmer's pa-

---

[2] February 17, 1773. *Letters*, VIII, 241.
[3] Walpole to Rev. William Mason, February 14, 1774. Ibid., 423.

ternalistic theory of government; and besides, Locke's part in the
establishment of the Carolina colonies, and his investments in the
slave-trading monopoly, the Royal African Company, shows plainly
enough that actual slavery did not trouble his conscience. It may
be charged that it was easy for Montesquieu and his fellow philosophes to detest slavery: they had no financial stake in it; after all,
when one of them, Thomas Jefferson, did have such a stake, he
might denounce it vigorously but could still live with, and off it.
But, at least, except for those philosophes who happened to be
Virginians, their conduct did not compromise their pronouncements.

II

The philosophes' view on slavery are predictable and anything
but systematic: they are generally exclamations, rarely thoroughgoing analyses. Well-meaning, often vague, they read rather like an
automatic response to human misery that speaks well for the philosophes' intentions but hardly amounts to a crusade; indeed, advocates
of slavery sometimes borrowed the philosophes' imprecise pronouncements or deliberately misread their sarcasms for their own
purposes. In general, though, the men of the Enlightenment helped
to change men's thinking on the subject; early in the field and
eloquent in their revulsion, they swelled antislavery sentiment from a
trickle to a respectable stream of opinion that would grow, at the
end of the century, with their help, into the torrent of abolitionism.
That this torrent prominently included conscientious judges and
evangelical enthusiasts heedless of the economic costs of emancipation does not lessen the philosophes' share in the campaign and
underscores, once more, the alliance among enlightened forces in
eighteenth-century civilization.

When Montesquieu first addressed himself to the issue of slavery
in his *Lettres persanes*, opposition to slavery was almost unknown
in France. Slaves in French territories, of whom there were somewhat less than one million, were governed under the so-called Code
Noir, promulgated by Louis XIV in the fateful year 1685, the very
year in which he deprived French Huguenots of all protection.
The Code Noir recognized, and rewarded, the slave trade as an eco-

nomic necessity; it was extraordinarily severe—toward the slave, of course—but its promulgation marked the beginning of some constraint on the masters. In 1712, near the end of his reign, Louis XIV added one of several codicils to the Code, with an edict prohibiting the torture of slaves by masters—a sure sign that torture had in fact been employed. Slavery was woven into the fabric of the French economy; the slave trade benefited the traders, the shippers, the planters directly, and, less directly but no less obviously, a host of industries connected with colonial products. Leading commercial families in port cities like Le Havre and Bordeaux discovered and cherished the slave trade as the avenue to local prestige, enormous wealth, and—most coveted distinction—noble status. Not surprisingly, historians have called Nantes the city of the slave trade, and the eighteenth century in Nantes, the age of the slave trader. Local slavers were prominent in cultural affairs and powerful in the city government, and in the reign of Louis XV, most of Nantes' slave traders secured titles; in the very age of the Enlightenment, slave merchants were made counts for their services to the state. Understandably enough, feeling themselves indispensable to the French economy as a whole, the port cities were extraordinarily sensitive to any threat that might imperil their profitable livelihood, and remarkably effective in their lobbying. They used influence with highly placed personages; they launched official protests against interference; they hired scribblers to defend their cause. As late as 1789, in the midst of widespread antislavery agitation, the Chambre de Commerce of Bordeaux declared: "France needs its colonies to sustain its commerce," and, until an alternative system of efficient agricultural labor can be discovered, France "consequently" needs "slaves."[4]

When Montesquieu launched a handful of sarcasms against this dominant view of things in 1721, his criticism stung, out of all proportion to its quantity or its intensity, because Montesquieu knew Bordeaux intimately, knew its merchants and the chief source of its impressive wealth. Christian princes, Montesquieu writes in his *Lettres persanes*, freed their slaves in Europe because it was profitable for them to do so—it allowed them to enlist the masses in their efforts

---

[4] Henri Sée: *La France économique et sociale au XVIIIe siècle* (5th edn., 1952), 121.

to undermine the powerful nobility; but the same Christian princes continue to encourage slavery in the colonies because there it was slavery, rather than emancipation, that was profitable. "What shall I tell you?" is Montesquieu's cynical conclusion. "Truth in one age, error in another."[5] But the slave trade is not merely a matter for jokes: untold numbers of human beings are being sacrificed on the altar of commercial rapacity. The slaves, transported from Africa to America, to a strange and unsalubrious climate, "perish there by the thousands. The work in the mines . . . the malignant vapors that issue from them, the mercury they must use constantly—these destroy them irretrievably. Nothing is so extravagant as to have innumerable men die in digging gold and silver from the depths of the earth."[6]

In *De l'esprit des lois*, Montesquieu gave the question more extensive treatment. In his best sociological manner, he finds some situations in which slavery might actually be less intolerable than it generally is, but Montesquieu's concessions to relativism concede almost nothing. Slavery may be bearable in despotisms, but then in such states everyone is a slave: if Muscovites readily sell themselves into slavery, he observes, that is quite simply because their freedom is worthless. Again, one cause of the peculiar institution had been, paradoxically enough, the feeling of pity: slavery was a humane substitute for the ancient practice of killing all prisoners of war. Finally, slavery is less irrational in extremely hot climates than elsewhere, for in the tropics masters and slaves alike are condemned to sloth, and nothing at all would get done unless some are forced to work.

Slight as these concessions are, Montesquieu takes care to surround and overwhelm them with fervent denunciations, aggressive aphorisms and damaging sarcasms. "Sugar would be too expensive," he noted in a draft, "if the plant that produces it were not cultivated by slaves, or if one treated them with some humanity."[7] All the legal rationalizations in behalf of slavery, ancient and modern, are invalid: slavery is evil by its very nature, unlawful, morally corrupting for the master quite as much as for the slave. Anticipating a favorite

---

[5] *Lettres persanes*, No. 75, in *Œuvres*, I, part 3, 155–6.
[6] Ibid., No. 118, in *Œuvres*, I, part 3, 236–7.
[7] See Shackleton: *Montesquieu*, 237.

technique of Voltaire's, Montesquieu lists arguments that could be advanced in behalf of slavery which are so absurd that they turn into indictments of racial snobbery, aesthetic parochialism, and Western greed: "Having exterminated the American nations, European nations had to enslave those of Africa, to use them for clearing all that land. . . .

"The people in question are black from head to toe; and their nose is so flat that it is practically impossible to pity them.

"It is impossible to believe that God, who is a very wise Being, should have put a soul, especially a good soul, into a body that is black all over.

"One proof that the Negroes lack common sense is that they make more of a glass necklace than of gold which, among civilized nations, is of such consequence.

"It is impossible for us to suppose that those creatures are men; because if we suppose them to be men, one might begin to think that we ourselves are not Christians.

"Small minds greatly exaggerate the injustice committed against the Africans. For, if it were as reported, would it not have occurred to European princes, who conclude so many useless treaties with one another, to conclude a general one, in favor of mercy and compassion?"[8] Arguments in behalf of slavery were, in Montesquieu's transparent caricature, a reflection on the self-centered and self-satisfied manner in which Europeans perceived the world.

Montesquieu's polemical virtuosity and his shrewd conflation of two arguments, moral and legal, made the other philosophes into his disciples: most later antislavery writings in the Enlightenment added detail and vehemence, but little that was new. The pitifully mutilated Negro in *Candide*—the victim of economic imperialism—might have come out of the pages of the *Lettres persanes;* indeed, in the 1770s Voltaire cheerfully acknowledged Montesquieu's leadership: "If anyone has ever battled to restore liberty, the right of nature, to slaves of all kinds, surely it was Montesquieu. He pitted reason and humanity against all kinds of slavery," against the enslavement of Negroes bought on the Gold Coast to harvest sugar in

---

[8] *De l'esprit des lois,* Book XV, chap. v, in *Œuvres,* I, part 1, 330–1.

the Caribbean Islands, and against serfdom in Europe.⁹ Earlier, the *Encyclopédie* had celebrated Montesquieu's antislavery writings and propagated his sentiments in his spirit, with his arguments.

The inhumanity of slave drivers furnished the philosophes with much gratifying material for moral outrage: it permitted them to attack Christians who had refused to denounce slavery, kings who permitted it, conquerors who spread it. "Even imaginary misfortunes wring tears from us in the silence of our study and, even more, in the theater," wrote Raynal in his *Histoire des deux Indes*, which, with its well-documented historical and political chapters, amounts to a sustained indictment of slavery and a call to conscience. "Only the fatal destiny of miserable Negroes fails to interest us. They are oppressed, they are mutilated, they are burned, they are stabbed— and we hear it coldly, without emotion. The torments of a people to which we owe our pleasures never reach our hearts."¹ Diderot, who had a large share in Raynal's massive *Histoire*, luxuriated in such rhetoric, with its peculiar mixture of sincere revulsion and adroit propaganda: "We have reduced them," Diderot said about Negro slaves, "I won't say to the condition of slaves, but to that of beasts of burden. And we are reasonable! and we are Christians!"² And so the evils of slavery became one more weapon in the philosophes' crusade for secularism: obviously it was preferable not to be a Christian— one had a better opportunity to be humane, it seemed, as an atheist.

While these moral tirades lent fervor to the philosophes' de- nunciation of slavery, their legal arguments gave it solidity. When Voltaire argued, in the *Questions sur l'Encyclopédie*, that slavery is an innovation that violates man's original free nature, he was say- ing what Montesquieu and others had said before him. But then he went beyond Montesquieu: partisans sometimes suggest that a poor laborer would rather be a pampered slave, but ask the laborer—he will cling to his freedom. And a slave, in turn, will choose freedom over slavery, even if he must leave the kindest of masters to face unforeseen hardships. Lawyers like Grotius and Pufendorf may say

---

⁹ *Commentaire sur quelques principales maximes de l'Esprit des lois* (1777), in *Œuvres*, XXX, 445.
¹ Quoted in Hans Wolpe: *Raynal et sa machine de guerre*, 155.
² Arthur M. Wilson, who quotes this passage from the *Encyclo- pédie* article "Humaine espèce," says that it is "probably" by Diderot. See "The Development and Scope of Diderot's Political Thought," *VS*, XXVII (1963), 1883.

what they like, if they hold that slavery is ever legal they are wrong and, Voltaire insists, it is nature that proves them wrong.[3]

Other philosophes also pitted the law of nature against the natural lawyers. Jaucourt argued in the *Encyclopédie* that a Negro cannot divest himself of his natural right, which is freedom, and that no one else can legally deprive him if it.[4] Rousseau argued the same case in the first book of his *Contrat social*: it is true, as Aristotle and other defenders of slavery since his time have said, that some men are born slaves, but they have mistaken the effect for the cause— men born into slavery, knowing nothing else, may lose the desire for freedom and love their chains. "So if there are slaves by nature, that is because there have been slaves against nature. Force made the first slaves, their cowardice perpetuated their slavery."[5] But force, Rousseau insists, does not create rights. A man who gives himself away is insane, and even if one actually could enter slavery voluntarily, he cannot commit his children: "They are born men, and free."[6] Grotius claims to derive his argument from international law: the conqueror may spare his prisoners in return for their selling their own freedom. But this, Rousseau objects, is a misreading of that law: war is a conflict between states which in no way entitles the victor to kill the vanquished. Grotius's supposed legal argument is nothing better than a sophism; slavery rests on a gigantic illogicality that touches man in his very essence. "To renounce one's liberty," Rousseau concludes in an emphatic paragraph, "is to renounce one's humanity, one's human rights, and even one's duties—*sa qualité d'homme, aux droits de l'humanité, même à ses devoirs.* There is no possible reparation for the one who renounces everything. Such a renunciation is incompatible with the nature of man; it is to remove all morality from his actions and all freedom from his will."[7] By making his particular case against slavery a special instance of his general case for freedom, Rousseau supplied abolitionism with arguments of absolute universality.

---

[3] "Esclave," *Questions sur l'Encyclopédie*, in *Œuvres*, XVIII, 599–606.
[4] "Traité des Nègres," *Encyclopédie*, quoted in Davis: *Problem of Slavery in Western Culture*, 416.
[5] *Du Contrat social*, in *Œuvres*, III, 353.
[6] Ibid., 356.
[7] Ibid.

III

I have suggested that after Montesquieu the Enlightenment's denunciations of slavery yield little that is new. But there was at least one other argument, the utilitarian, that gained prominence, fittingly enough, in the second half of the eighteenth century, in tune with the Enlightenment's shift of temper from natural law to utility. Like war, the argument runs in brief, slavery is, in addition to all its other palpable and irreparable vices, a bad bargain.

Among the first to develop this line of reasoning was David Hume. Though publicly on record with his conviction that Negroes are racially inferior to whites, a conviction that he shared with most men of his time, Hume inveighed against slavery for its cruelty, its barbarity, its sheer inhumanity; but more than being offensive and, indeed, disgusting, it was also self-defeating. Elaborating a contention advanced earlier by Montesquieu,[8] Hume rejected the claim of proslavery propagandists that, since masters breed slaves as they breed cattle, slavery is a spur to population. On the contrary, Hume found overwhelming evidence that populousness is the necessary attendant of decency rather than cruelty: "Wherever there are most happiness and virtue, and the wisest institutions," he wrote, "there will also be most people,"[9] and populousness in turn encourages productivity, cultivation, and high consumption. Slavery, in a word, is uneconomic.

While the Physiocrats employed the utilitarian argument in the 1760s, the Scottish economists made it into a kind of specialty, as though its cool, practical humanity, implied rather than pronounced, was a congenial temperature for them. In 1771, in a sociological analysis of power relations between men and women, fathers and children, states and subjects, John Millar devotes one long chapter, the last, to "The Authority of a Master over his Servants." Slavery, Millar argues, had arisen in primitive days, when the helpless and indigent sold themselves to their more fortunate and opulent neigh-

---

[8] See *Lettres persanes*, Nos. 115 and 122, in *Œuvres*, I, part 3, 229–30, 244–5.
[9] "Of the Populousness of Ancient Nations," *Works*, III, 384; for Hume's general discussion of slavery, see 384–97.

bors, when captives taken in war were allotted to their conquerors, and when judges consigned convicted criminals to servitude. Domestic slavery appears to be very ancient, and to have been practically universal, and Millar judged it a perfectly comprehensible institution in rude ages. But now, with changed times, slavery appeared supremely inappropriate: "When a people become civilized, and when they have made considerable progress in commerce and manufactures, one would imagine they should entertain more liberal views, and be influenced by more extensive considerations of utility."[1]

Millar's views on slavery are in the mainstream of enlightened opinion. He expresses the usual doubts about its present-day legality, and the usual horror at its brutalizing consequences, which, he is shocked to note, affect even "persons of the weaker sex," and this "in an age distinguished for humanity and politeness." There can be no question: slavery is "inconsistent with the rights of humanity."[2]

While these sentiments were irreproachable, Millar's persistent emphasis on the economic disutility of slavery is rather more original. That its unprofitable nature has not been generally recognized, Millar suggests, is a tribute to human conservatism, to "that blind prepossession which is commonly acquired in favour of ancient usages: its inconveniences are overlooked, and every innovation, with respect to it, is considered as a dangerous measure." Once this psychological resistance has been overcome, it will become apparent that slavery is not merely pernicious, but also "contrary to the true interest of the master."[3] Slavery is unprofitable, first of all, because slaves have never been encouraged to acquire either skills or discipline; hence they are wholly unfitted for any but the crudest labor. It is unprofitable, in the second place, because slaves are turned into resentful beasts of burden who will submit sullenly, revolt on occasion, and never work efficiently. "No conclusion seems more certain than this, that men will commonly exert more activity when they work for their own benefit, than when they are compelled to labour for the benefit merely of another. The introduction of personal liberty has therefore an infallible tendency to render the inhabitants of a

---

[1] *Distinction of Ranks*, in Lehmann: *Millar*, 299.
[2] Ibid., 303, 302.
[3] Ibid., 302.

country more industrious."[4] Slavery is unprofitable, finally, because
it prevents the introduction of labor-saving devices and depresses
productivity in general. While he cautiously admits that the matter
has never been properly examined, Millar finds "ground to believe
that the institution of slavery is the chief circumstance that has prevented those contrivances to shorten and facilitate the more
laborious employments of the people, which take place in other
countries where freedom has been introduced,"[5] a belief directly
contradicting the current view that slavery was the only way of
forcing men to cultivate the soil in an untoward climate.

Millar's book was a success: it had a second edition in 1773,
and a third in 1779, under its new and better-known title, *The Origin
of the Distinction of Ranks*. Millar's conviction that slavery is
"equally inconvenient and pernicious"[6] thus found a sizable audience.
But it was Adam Smith, Millar's teacher, friend, and colleague, who
gave the utilitarian argument its final form and widest hearing.
Smith only glances at the institution of slavery, but his *Wealth of
Nations* was so avidly read, its formulations seemed so authoritative,
that a few sentences on the subject were incontrovertible *obiter
dicta*, at least to those not blinded by what Millar had called "blind
prepossession" in behalf of ancient usages. In harmony with, and,
indeed, as part of, his general argument in favor of "the liberal reward of labour," Smith asserts that a slave costs his master more
than a free laborer. Both need subsistence pay, enough to perpetuate
their kind; but a slave is likely to be in the hands of a "negligent
master or careless overseer," that is of men who waste the precious
resource in their keeping, while a free man, managing himself, is
likely to waste himself less. "It appears," Smith concludes, and from
"the experience of all ages and nations, I believe, that the work done
by freemen comes cheaper in the end than that performed by slaves.
It is found to do so," he adds, with that insistent urge toward specificity that was part of his persuasiveness, "even at Boston, New
York, and Philadelphia, where the wages of common labour are so
very high."[7] Slavery is a special case of protectionism, a prominent
instance of that supreme piece of bad reasoning that has for so long

---

[4] Ibid., 316–17.
[5] Ibid., 320.
[6] Ibid., 316.
[7] *Wealth of Nations*, 81.

crippled economic growth. To reinforce this point, Smith advances the ironical paradox that slaves are better protected in despotisms than in free states, for the despot can intervene in the private affairs of the great planters and prevent the grossest cruelties. But this is no proof that the modern world needs despotism; it is proof rather that the modern world needs emancipation. The irony of slavery does not stop here. Adam Smith concedes that the profits of the sugar plantations in the West Indies are high, and those of the tobacco plantations, though smaller, still impressive, but this only means that these industries can "afford the expence of slave cultivation"—they are, economically speaking, wasteful and peculiar luxuries. For, as Smith reiterates, "the work done by slaves, though it appears to cost only their maintenance, is in the end the dearest of any."[8]

Smith's supporting arguments for this position are a mixture of economic analysis and deductive psychology: "A person who can acquire no property, can have no other interest but to eat as much, and to labour as little as possible. Whatever work he does beyond what is sufficient to purchase his own maintenance, can be squeezed out of him by violence only, and not by any interest of his own." Slavery has been given up in Europe because it was palpably uneconomic; if it persists elsewhere, this is less for economic than for psychological reasons: "The pride of man makes him love to domineer, and nothing mortifies him so much as to be obliged to condescend to persuade his inferiors. Whenever the law allows it, and the nature of the work can afford it, therefore, he will generally prefer the service of slaves to that of freemen."[9] Obviously, the economy cannot afford to gratify the power drives of wealthy merchants.[1]

In the long run, though, it was humanity, an irresistible alliance of religious with secular enthusiasm, that brought the slave trade and, after that, slavery itself to its end. The change of temper was measur-

---

[8] Ibid., 365.
[9] Ibid.
[1] In his *Theory of Moral Sentiments*, 299–300, Adam Smith sentimentalized the African, singled him out for his "magnanimity," and spoke of African slaves transported to American as "nations of heroes," subjected to "sordid masters," to "the refuse of the gaols of Europe, to wretches who possess the virtues neither of the countries which they came from, nor of those which they go to."

ably aided by the shifting interests of merchants and industrialists, but this shift was at least in part a supple response to antislavery agitation, and the most eloquent spokesmen for abolition were, by and large, tenacious philanthropists like Granville Sharp, persistent philosophes like Condorcet, and obsessive evangelicals like Wilberforce. The utilitarian argument, at least in the eighteenth century, suffered visible liabilities; it was vastly offensive to potent vested interests, and it was, at least in its sweeping, generalized form, demonstrably false. Prudently, Adam Smith had admitted that slave industries like the sugar plantations were highly prosperous, but he, like his fellows, neglected to add that slavery showered profits on many related industries as well. In the middle of the eighteenth century, the three great ports, London, Bristol, and Liverpool, sent out about four hundred slave ships a year, and it was not slaves alone that guaranteed the prosperity of these harbor towns: shipbuilders, importers from the colonies, and furnishers of supplies for the vessels and their crews all shared in the blessings of the triangular trade. The agreement that gave the British a monopoly over the supply of slaves to the Spanish colonies imposed on Spain at the Peace of Utrecht, the much-debated *asiento*, had its drawbacks as a commercial instrument, but it underscores the importance of the slave trade to the British economy and in the British mind. Humanity was not at issue for anyone; the rivalry among the port towns, from which Liverpool eventually emerged triumphant, centered around the price of slaves, and Liverpool shippers, most of them hardened smugglers, managed to supply the goods—that is, African slaves—to the British West Indies at several pounds less than its rivals. Profits on each voyage could be as high as several thousand pounds sterling and several hundred per cent, although in the aggregate, what with commissions, costs, and inevitable losses, the profit amounted to a mere thirty to forty per cent—a return high enough to encourage the most determined defense of the trade. Not that such defense was needed, at least not until the 1770s or so. Slave traders were highly respected; besides, the slave trade was popular and thought vital to the British economy, just as it was thought vital to the French economy. In 1764, the prominent Bristol slave trader John Pinney expressed his conviction, and sought to convince others, that "Negroes," which is, of course, to say, slaves, "are the Sinews of a Plantation, and it is as impossible for a Man to make Sugar without the assistance of Negroes, as to make Bricks without Straw."[2] There was no need for him to labor the point; others were as convinced as he was. A few years before, Malachy Postlethwayt, a prolific, thoroughly unoriginal publicist on economic matters who specialized in demonstrating the surpassing value of the slave trade to the British economy, said out loud what almost everyone in his time believed: the slave trade is "the first principle and foundation of all the rest, the mainspring of the machine which sets every wheel in motion."[3] Scruples—and many, even Postlethwayt, were not total strangers to scruples—melted away in the face of this reality.

While some abolitionists were later to complain that enlightened men of the eighteenth century had failed to make abolition into a crusade, they underestimated the radicalism of the philosophes' writings for their time, and the persistence, the sheer strength of traditional opinion. As late as the 1770s, while the voice of antislavery agitation was rising in Britain, it was still the voice of a distinct and not particularly potent minority; in France the sustained and furious assaults by the abbé Raynal was a rare and, it seemed to most, a cranky outburst.[4] The rather peculiar debate between Johnson and Boswell—if debate it can be called—shows that the hold of the complacent, self-serving proslavery position on even informed opinion remained strong. Samuel Johnson was a passionate adversary of slavery. Boswell, much to his regret, was constrained to report that Johnson, "upon one occasion, when in company with some very grave men at Oxford," had offered the toast: " 'Here's to the next insurrection of the negroes in the West Indies.' "[5] Johnson deeply resented the clamor of American colonists for freedom as nothing less than revolting hypocrisy: "How is it," he asked, "that we hear the loudest *yelps* for liberty among the drivers of negroes?"[6] But British colonials elsewhere were no better; their rapacity and callousness toward their black victims made them nothing better than

---

[2] Quoted in C. M. MacInnes: *A Gateway to Empire* (1939), 193.
[3] Quoted in Eric Williams: *Capitalism and Slavery* (1944), 51.
[4] "In our country, the abbé Raynal remains a far more isolated figure than the group of English antislavery advocates." Gaston-Martin: *Nantes au XVIIIe siècle: L'ère des Négriers (1714-1774)* (1931), 427. On the other hand, Raynal's *History* was widely read in England, and seems to have had considerable effect there.
[5] *Life of Johnson*, III, 200. Under September 23, 1777.
[6] *Ibid.*, 201.

"English barbarians."[7] With all his passion for travel and exploration, Johnson even professed fear of new discoveries since they always seemed to "end in conquest and robbery."[8]

   Johnson's abolitionism rose above a humane and angry sympathy
for particular victims to general principles, and his expression of
those principles sounded practically like a plagiarism from a writer
whom he detested almost as much as he detested slavery: Jean-
Jacques Rousseau. In 1777, joining in the legal struggle initiated by
Granville Sharp to have slavery declared illegal in Britain, Johnson
dictated a memorandum to Boswell in which he expressed his doubts
"whether slavery can ever be supposed the natural condition of man.
It is impossible not to conceive that men in their original state were
equal." The legal situation of slaves everywhere is deplorable and
itself illegal under higher law; it is intolerable to see that in Jamaica,
for example, the laws "afford a Negro no redress. His colour is considered as a sufficient testimony against him." Yet, even if the slave's
lot were less wretched, it would be no less unnatural: "An individual may, indeed, forfeit his liberty by a crime; but he cannot by
that crime forfeit the liberty of his children. What is true of a
criminal seems true likewise of a captive." There may have been
a time when slavery was the justified condition of one Negro, but
this condition cannot be handed down to his descendant: "He is
certainly subject by no law, but that of violence, to his present
master." Slavery, in a word, is both lamentable and against the
"rights of nature."[9] Nothing, Johnson thought, could be plainer than
this.

   Boswell did not think it plain at all. Ever the faithful biographer,
he recorded Johnson's opinions, but he stoutly refused to be instructed by his master on this vital question; he treated Johnson's
reasoning against slavery with a kind of respectful condescension,
convinced that they must be "owing to prejudice, and imperfect or
false information." The attempt to "abolish so very important and
necessary a branch of commercial interest" was nothing less than
"wild and dangerous"; it constituted not merely "*robbery* to an

---

[7] Quoted in Donald J. Greene: *The Politics of Samuel Johnson*
(1960), 270.
[8] See *Life of Johnson*, II, 477, where this letter of March 4, 1773,
is quoted.
[9] Ibid., III, 202–3. Under September 23, 1777.

innumerable class of our fellow-subjects," not merely an assault on a "*status*, which in all ages GOD has sanctioned," but also "extreme cruelty to the African Savages, a portion of whom it saves from massacre, or intolerable bondage in their own country, and introduces into a much happier state of life." As Boswell poetically concluded, quoting from Gray's *Elegy* in a breathtaking display of moral earnestness and confusion: "To abolish that trade would be to '— shut the gates of mercy on mankind.' "[1]

In treating abolitionist sentiment as uninformed, irresponsible, immoral, almost a kind of treason, and in rationalizing imperialism as a divine dispensation, Boswell was speaking for the well-meaning respectable majority in his time. Placed within its historical context, the debate between Boswell and Johnson was less a debate between callousness and decency, or darkness against light; it was a debate between the present and the future. Slavery as an institution seemed so natural, so normal, so inevitable to most that the slave-holders among the philosophes like Thomas Jefferson—who was a persistent and troubled advocate of abolition—lived with slavery and traded in slaves as though nothing else were possible. It is plausible to charge that the philosophes did not do enough to secure the future for which Johnson and Raynal and Condorcet spoke so movingly; it is likely that they could have done more; and it is certain that there was much to do.

3. JUSTICE: A LIBERAL CRUSADE

I

WHILE THE PHILOSOPHES' EFFORTS to aid victims of Western civilization in remote parts of the world were compromised by a certain tepidness of will, their indignation against injustices closer to home was less ambivalent and more effective. The philosophes' crusade for legal reform bears all the marks of their splenetic

---

[1] Ibid., 201–4.

empiricism, their urge to exploit incidents and translate discontent into action; satisfied neither with rescuing this or that victim of judicial injustice, nor with proposing improvements in this or that procedure, the philosophes embodied in their legal writings all their political ideals. Strangely enough, the philosophes discovered the horrors of the criminal law rather late. Had they been alert to them, they would have found spectacular instances of injustice everywhere at all times. But then, they were men of their day as well as prophets of a new day, and, in obedience to the economy that compels reformers to concentrate on some grievances at the expense of others, they simply accepted for decades the legal systems under which they lived. Once they saw, they acted as if they had never been blind— insights are great amnesiacs—and fell on the defects of the criminal law with nothing less than a convert's ferocity, anticipating by two centuries Marc Bloch's dictum that the most reliable touchstone of a social system is the manner in which men are judged in court.[2]

In the age of the Enlightenment, the criminal law of civilized countries everywhere was ferocious, and, in direct conflict with new notions of philanthropy, humanity, and good sense, generally grew more ferocious decade by decade. Here and there the law responded to the demands of the new philosophy; upon his accession in 1740, Frederick of Prussia confirmed the good name which, as crown prince, he had acquired among the philosophes: he ordered an end to torture in cases of high treason and mass murder and by 1755 he had suppressed torture altogether. In 1743, acting on the same impulse, he abolished the death penalty for theft and eliminated a series of humiliating and brutal punishments, such as mutilation. But in general, the new humaneness worked, where it worked at all, in the interstices of the written law and bent the old letter to the new spirit: in 1774, Frederick instructed his courts that "*in criminalibus*" sentences should be "too lenient rather than too strict."[3] In France, although the *parlements* would hand the philosophes some splendid cases of stubbornness, stupidity, and sheer sadism, the courts were often inclined to be moderate in their sentences, especially if the convicted person was a member neither of that hunted minority, the Huguenots, nor of that silent majority, the poor. In the Dutch Re-

---

[2] See *La Société féodale*, 2 vols. (1939–40), II, 117.
[3] Quoted in Leon Radzinowicz: *A History of English Criminal Law and Its Administration from 1750*, 3 vols. (1948–56), I, 288 n.

public, torture was not officially suppressed until 1798, but the practice of torture was abandoned at the beginning of the eighteenth century. In England, accused persons found guilty and in fact obviously guilty were sometimes allowed to escape the rigor of the law: judges could recommend a reprieve, an act that stayed and often prevented execution; the king could—and in hundreds of cases did—exercise his prerogative by commuting the death sentence, usually to transportation; lawyers could save defendants (with the connivance of the judge) by discovering some technical flaw in the indictment; juries, appalled at the sentence that would follow conviction, sometimes insisted on acquitting a guilty defendant or (once again with the connivance of the judge) find him guilty of a lesser offense than the one for which he was being tried. The old severity had many champions, but they found formidable adversaries in the ingenuity of decent men.

These instances of humanity, though, common as they were, were like flashes of lightning that illuminated, for a few dazzling moments, the bleak landscape of criminal procedure. In most civilized countries—Prussia was a notable exception—laws became more vindictive than ever. Human life was still cheap, especially if it was the life of the lowly, and men were executed without qualms and with dispatch, normally after rapid and perfunctory proceedings:

> The hungry judges soon the sentence sign,
> And wretches hang that jurymen may dine.[4]

It was property that was worth a court's time.

Like the law's haste in criminal cases, the law's delay in cases involving property was a source of injustice. Only those with adequate resources could afford the cost of litigation. By the time cases were decided in the German Imperial Court (as Goethe recalled with some amusement), the original cause had disappeared, the parties had changed their minds, or had died. Goethe found nothing untoward in this situation; he was, after all, speaking for those for whom this system seemed to be expressly designed: "The state is interested only in seeing that property is certain and secure; whether it is lawfully held concerns it less."[5] In the absence of effective police forces, the possessing orders protected their property by adding to the list of

---

[4] Alexander Pope: *Rape of the Lock*, III, 21–2.
[5] *Dichtung und Wahrheit*, in *Gedenkausgabe*, X, 576.

crimes and increasing the severity of punishments. In continental states, with their powerful aristocracies, courts rendered class justice and readily suffered their verdicts to be overturned by edicts from above: a nobleman in favor at court or with a duke's mistress was, if not always immune from prosecution, usually safe from punishment, while peasants or poor laborers had no recourse against savage prosecutions or capricious and cruel penalties. In France, eighteenth-century courts proceeded under Colbert's Criminal Ordinance of 1670, which was a timidly modernized version of the Code of 1539. Its only modern feature was its severity with crimes against property; for the rest it read much the earlier code from which it was derived. Its catalogue of crimes was long, the identification of sin and crime was left untouched, torture remained a permissible method of interrogation, everything—the mode of investigation, the role of the judge, the limitations on the accused, the favor shown to the most dubious testimony—conspired to make a French trial an inquisition that seemed like a predictable gladiatorial contest in which one combatant holds all the weapons: the defendant appeared like an outcast from society; to have incurred sufficient suspicion to be prosecuted was almost enough to make one a criminal. This Ordinance was sometimes evaded, but normally it was enforced: once Voltaire and other critics of the French law began their crusade for reform, they could draw material to support their cause from hundreds of lurid trials.

The history of the British law in the eighteenth century is one of the most unpleasant paradoxes in the age of the Enlightenment. British procedure seemed to continental reformers worthy of envy and imitation: did it not permit the defendent counsel? did it not give him the protection of trial by his peers? do without torture? allow for appeals? manipulate a whole elaborate machinery of mercy? Yet even Britain—in fact, especially Britain—participated in the widespread eighteenth-century tendency to make repression more repressive. The position of a defendant was anything but enviable: persons under arrest often languished in jail until their cases came up for trial, and even after acquittal the poor found themselves back in detention until they could raise the money to pay their fees. This was bad enough; what was worse was the progressive aggravation of penalties for crimes against property. The list of death penalties for such crimes grew, in the age of the Enlightenment, with astounding rapidity. In the mid-1760s, Blackstone estimated the number of capital crimes at 160, of which more than a hundred had been added to the books since the Glorious Revolution; around 1820, the number had risen to perhaps 220. This luxuriating jungle of retribution was increasingly made up of painstaking and piecemeal statutes against theft, highway robbery, pickpocketing, forgery, and similar assaults on the comfortable orders. This list is an instructive guide to new industries, new sources of prosperity, new luxuries. Roads and canals were protected by a series of enactments imposing the death penalty for the destruction of locks, floodgates, bridges, and turnpikes; respectable importers, by similar laws against smuggling; farmers, manufacturers, shop keepers, and householders, by statutes exacting the death penalty for grand larceny (which was defined as stealing an object worth more than twelve pence), for thefts of cattle or merchandise, forgery of bank notes, embezzlement of funds. Every year, perhaps more than once a year, the wall around property was raised still higher.

These statutes were a reliable guide to practice: it is significant that while in Prussia, between 1775 and 1778, two executions out of forty-six were for crimes against property, in London and Middlesex, in 1785, at least 89 out of 97 executions were for such crimes, including two for "personating others to obtain prize money."[6] As I have said, it seemed a little strange, and more than a little depressing to men of good will, but in the age of Enlightenment, in the teeth of a prospering movement toward humanity, the law grew more stringent, religiously safeguarding property—or, rather, safeguarding property as though it were a new religion. What was true of the slave trade was true, with quite as much force, of the law: there was a great deal to do.

II

Montesquieu, showing the Enlightenment the way once again, rejected this prevailing conception of law in detail and in principle early, in his first book. As everyone knows, the *Lettres persanes* is a frivolous book, a fragile vessel to carry so much heavy freight,

---

[6] Radzinowicz: *History of English Criminal Law*, I, 148.

and important precisely for that reason: with its urbane tone and
light touch, it was a singularly apt vehicle for serious propaganda.
One of its letters is devoted to a principled and, significantly enough,
wholly utilitarian defense of leniency: the most reasonable, most
perfect government, Montesquieu argues, is the one that "reaches
its goal with a minimum of cost." Since people are just as docile
under a mild as under a harsh regime—"In countries where penalties
are moderate, they are feared as much as they are in those where
they are tyrannical and horrible"—a lenient code of laws is to be
preferred to a harsh one.[7] Really drastic punishments should therefore be reserved for really great crimes. In other letters, he calls for
the incorporation of religious toleration in the laws of the land, and
expresses his sympathy with the victims of persecution: to "torment
the conscience of others" is, quite simply, inhuman.[8]

In *De l'esprit des lois*, notably in book XII, which has been
called, with understandable enthusiasm, "the Magna Carta of the
citizen,"[9] Montesquieu codified these generalities. Political liberty—
this is his fundamental principle which he elaborates with lawyer-
like specificity—"consists in security," or, at least, in the feeling of
security, and security in turn "depends on the good quality of the
criminal laws."[1] The most insidious enemies of security are "public
or private accusations"[2]; hence trials must give the accused a hearing, false witnesses should be punished, informers are to be discour-
aged, no one should be condemned to death on the deposition of a
single witness, and specific punishments should be prescribed for
specific crimes, so that legal and judicial caprice are eliminated. With
these few simple but far-reaching proposals, Montesquieu sought to
convert trials from a one-sided, largely ritualistic combat into a
humane inquiry for truth and search for justice.

From his radical attack on court procedure Montesquieu moves
to the definition of crime. Traditionally, he writes, lawyers have
divided crimes into four kinds: crimes against religion, morals, public tranquillity, and the security of the subject. But some of these
"crimes" are not crimes at all: sacrilege that remains locked within a

---

[7] *Lettres persanes*, No. 80, in *Œuvres*, I, part 3, 164.
[8] Ibid., No. 85, in *Œuvres*, I, part 3, 174.
[9] Franz Neumann: "Introduction," to Montesquieu's *Spirit of the Laws*, lix.
[1] *De l'esprit des lois*, book XII, chap. ii, in *Œuvres*, I, part 1, 251.
[2] Ibid.

man's mind, for one, is not a concern of the state—it is between man and God. Some people have the idea that "one must avenge the Deity. But one must honor the Deity, and never avenge it." Montesquieu lends force to this dictum with a characteristic story: "A historian of Provence relates an incident which gives us an excellent idea what effect this notion of avenging the Deity can have on weak minds: a Jew, accused of having blasphemed the Holy Virgin, was sentenced to be flayed alive. Then some masked gentlemen climbed on the scaffold, knife in hand, and drove the executioner away, that they themselves might avenge the honor of the Holy Virgin. . . . I do not want to anticipate the reflection of the reader."[3] Again, the man who commits sacrilege publicly may be expelled from his religious community either for a time or permanently, he may be shunned and cursed, but, once again, none of this concerns the judicial arm of the government. The separation of church and state, and the subjection of church to state, are implied in these few impassioned paragraphs.

Montesquieu is willing to describe crimes against morals as true crimes, but of a lesser order, to be repressed, partly as blasphemy should be repressed, by symbolic action, private disapproval, and ostracism, and partly by fines or exile imposed by the state. Crimes against public tranquillity are more serious still, but the only class of crimes to which, Montesquieu thinks, really drastic punishments are ever appropriate, are large-scale thefts, and, above all, murder. Yet even here, as always, Montesquieu insists that distinctions and degrees of punishment should be "founded in nature." Punishment of felonies is "a kind of retaliation" by which "society refuses security to a citizen who has deprived, or intends to deprive, another of it. This punishment is drawn from the nature of the thing, drawn from reason and the very sources of good and evil. A citizen deserves death when he has violated security to the point of taking life, or having undertaken to take life. This death penalty is, so to speak, like the remedy of a sick society." Theft is another matter: the death penalty may sometimes be appropriate then, but "perhaps it would be better, and closer to nature, to punish crimes against the security of property by loss of property."[4] In a bold and enlightened departure from prevailing standards, Montesquieu dares to

---

[3] Ibid., book XII, chap. iv, in *Œuvres*, I, part 1, 254.
[4] Ibid., 255–6.

place a higher value on life than on property, a transvaluation hardly welcome to a society in which the repression of the property-less furnished the propertied with *their* sense of security. But to advocate leniency was, for Montesquieu, more than a daring foray into novelty, more than the expression of a private taste for humanity. "Everything I have said," he noted with some pride, "is drawn from nature and highly favorable to the liberty of the citizen."[5]

"Drawn from nature" meant "intertwined with the rest of my philosophy." In fact, Montesquieu places his call for leniency squarely into his political sociology; he has no hesitation in connecting modes of punishment with forms of government. "The severity of punishment suits despotic governments, whose principle is terror, better than monarchies and republics, whose inner springs are honor and virtue."[6] Severity, which is merely a euphemism for cruelty, is natural in a form of government which is, in Montesquieu's political thought, vicious by its very nature: severity is evil in its own right and, at the same time, a revealing and depressing symptom of the system with which it is so properly associated. Montesquieu claims that liberty and leniency vary in direct proportion to one another: as one flourishes the other flourishes, as one decays the other decays; the more virtuous a nation, the fewer and milder can the authorities permit penalties to be. Besides, the habit of leniency brings its own rewards: "Experience suggests that in countries where punishments are mild, the citizen there is affected by them quite as much as he is elsewhere by greater severity." Men should be managed not by extreme, but by moderate, methods. "When we examine the causes of all moral laxity, we will discover that it springs from the impunity of the criminal, not from the moderateness of punishment."[7] Of course—Montesquieu insists on this—crimes vary in degree; hence punishments must vary with them. Developing a hint which he had first thrown out in the *Lettres persanes* and which was to emerge as a principal point in the philosophes' case for legal reform, Montesquieu called for a "just proportion between punishment and crime." It is essential, he wrote, "that punishments maintain a cer-

---

[5]. Ibid., 256.

[6] Ibid., book VI, chap. ix, in *Œuvres*, I, part 1, 109.

[7] Ibid., chap. xii, in *Œuvres*, part 1, 113–14.

tain proportion with one another, because it is essential to avoid a greater crime rather than a smaller one"—if all penalties are Draconian, men would rather hang for a murder than for a theft.[8] Montesquieu's humanity was part of his rationalist analysis of society.

All these were safeguards for the innocent, for defendants guilty of crimes smaller than the crimes of which they had been accused, or for criminals who deserved milder punishments than was customary. But Montesquieu was not content with placing only one fence around ever-endangered human life; he found it important to surround this line of defense with additional bulwarks. One inexhaustible source of mischief, he noted, was the rage to punish, whether motivated by religious zeal, or by sadism, or by the desire for advancement in an administrative or judicial career. The classification of crimes, therefore, must be supplemented with an earnest warning to prosecutors and judges to be extremely circumspect in finding that a crime has been committed, for many "notorious" crimes never took place at all. Witchcraft is one of those imaginary crimes; heresy is another—a vague accusation untenable in court, since almost anything can be called heretical; and the felonies supposedly committed by despised outsiders are nearly always pure invention. "Under the reign of Philip the Long, the Jews were expelled from France, accused of having poisoned the wells with lepers. This absurd accusation should make us doubt all those accusations founded on public hatred."[9] Acts openly admitted but actually not criminal, like "the crime against nature," deserve the same care.[1] Montesquieu professes all the proper abhorrence for homosexuality which, he concedes, is condemned with equal severity by religion, morality, and law. It should be proscribed, but society should entrust educational institutions like the family with discouraging such a detestable habit; to punish it with the customary cruelty is to act in excess. This was not an abstract argument: in 1750 two Parisian workers were publicly executed for homosexuality. "The *parlement* of Paris," Raynal reported, "which rarely makes examples of severity in certain genres, has had two men burned for the sin of noncon-

---

[8] Ibid., chap. xvi, in *Œuvres*, part 1, 121.
[9] Ibid., book XII, chap. v, in *Œuvres*, part 1, 257–8.
[1] Ibid., chap. vi, in *Œuvres*, part 1, 258.

formity, and, in the same week, seven or eight women publicly whipped for the contrary sin."[2] As with stealing, so with special tastes in sex: only the privileged could indulge themselves with impunity.

There was one offense on the statute books that seemed to Montesquieu to epitomize the defects of all existing codes—high treason. Like the poisoning of wells, treason was usually an imaginary crime; like buggery, it was sometimes a real crime of relatively minor importance, magnified into a vicious felony. The very word "treason," Montesquieu warned, was being used far too loosely: counterfeiting coins is not treason. In their frantic search for traitors, suspicious rulers often manage to create what they tremble to find. They employ *agents provocateurs* to stir up treacherous talk and hound their courtiers into discovering disaffection in high places. Treason, in short, must be defined with statesmanlike self-restraint: "If the crime of *lèse-majesté* is vague, that is enough to have the government degenerate into despotism."[3] Once again Montesquieu ties his analysis of the criminal law to the dynamics of his political sociology.

Montesquieu's treatment of treason is instructive because it emphasizes and specifies the distinction between public and private, which Montesquieu had already drawn in his treatment of sexual deviation, private blasphemy, and religious heterodoxy. Thoughts are not treason: to punish men for thinking treacherous thoughts is characteristic only of despotism. "The laws undertake to punish only overt acts."[4] Speech, even an indiscreet utterance, is not treason: it lies open to the most varied interpretations and often has no influence on action at all. Wherever words are converted into the crime of *lèse-majesté*, "not only liberty, but its very shadow, is no more."[5] Even words reduced to writing are not treason: most states repress satires, even criticism of the government, severely, but if the written word does not actually prepare the way for treason, treason is not what it should be called. True, words, whether spoken or written, may be direct incitements to treacherous actions, and then they must be punished. But then—and the distinction may

---

[2] *Correspondance littéraire*, I, 450.
[3] *De l'esprit des lois*, book XII, chap. vii, in *Œuvres*, I, part 1, 260.
[4] Ibid., chap. xi, in *Œuvres*, I, part 1, 264.
[5] Ibid., chap. xii, in *Œuvres*, I, part 1, 265.

seem a quibble but is actually of the highest importance—the crime lies not in the words but the actions. Montesquieu was not yet ready to draw an absolute distinction between public and private; in his writings the separation of church and state and the toleration of sexual deviance are, as I have said, incomplete, partially rather than wholly explicit. But in delimiting thoughts from words and words from acts, Montesquieu was translating the old ideal of the private sphere in which no public agency, neither guild nor church nor state, has any business, into the modern form that it has had ever since in liberal political thought.

III

Montesquieu's *De l'esprit des lois* aroused immediate controversy, and its pious critics did not overlook Montesquieu's legal ideas: one objected to Montesquieu's demand that men cease to try avenging the deity; another, that his legal, like his political principles, must lead to toleration, that most unfortunate of social consequences. Not unexpectedly, the philosophic family welcomed these very principles and treated them with respect, but they had no immediate effect on its work or its preoccupations. I have said that the philosophes turned legal reformers because they were empiricists, because they found the need for reform appallingly apparent in their immediate experience—that is, once it was apparent. They had to be educated by spectacular cases before their latent, rhetorical humanity would become manifest and practical. The Calas case—endlessly described, yet worth describing just once more—is a critical moment, for Voltaire, for French justice, and for the Enlightenment, precisely because it was the dramatic event that supplied the needed specificity, and the needed timeliness, for Montesquieu's generalizations on the law. It made the letter spirit.

Voltaire first heard about the Calas case in the middle of March 1762, when it was too late to do anything about it—at least about Jean Calas. Voltaire was nearing sixty-eight, he was rich and famous, he was still writing furiously, and he had just begun to publish, after decades of concealment and careful preparations, his outrageous attacks on Christianity in all its forms. The story about Calas, which a French visitor told him at Ferney, propelled him into still another career: he had said a few perfunctory things in favor of justice and leniency before this, he would say many passionate things about both from now on, to the end of his life sixteen years later.[6]

From his visitor's report, and from inquiries he promptly undertook on his own, Voltaire gathered these facts: on the evening of October 13, 1761, Marc-Antoine Calas, eldest son of Jean Calas, a Huguenot cloth merchant in Toulouse, had been found hanged in his father's shop. At first the Calas family had claimed that the young man must have been murdered by a stranger; upon further interrogation, all of them changed their story and insisted that he had actually committed suicide. The case captured the imagination of Toulouse: though normally the Huguenots there found the dominant Roman Catholic majority tolerant and even indulgent, in times of war and distress—and 1761 was a year of both—economic and political anxieties were distorted into paranoid suspicion of "outsiders." The old, repeatedly discredited charge of ritual murder was now revived against Jean Calas: the rumor went about the town that Marc-Antoine had been about to convert to the True Faith, and that his fanatical father, to prevent this defection, had killed him. The authorities did their utmost to find the truth. They questioned scores of witnesses, interrogated the accused Calas family with all the methods at their disposal, involved the church in the investigations by having local clergymen read from the pulpit a *monitoire*—a public admonition to all who had information to come forward and testify. A leading local magistrate, David de Beaudrigue, pursued the case with zealous diligence. The conclusion was as predictable as the end of a well-planned tragedy: on March 9, 1762, the *parlement* of Toulouse, in its capacity of appellate court, condemned Jean Calas to death at the stake, and on March 10, in accord with regular procedures, Jean Calas was put through what was euphemistically known as the "ordinary question" and the "extraordinary question"—that is, torture of several kinds—designed to extract the

---

[6] On May 25, 1778, five days before his death, when the end was obviously near, Voltaire received word that one of his many legal battles, this one in behalf of General Lally, whose name he had struggled to clear for ten years, had been won at last. The old man roused himself from his dying torpor for a final effort to congratulate the general's son; now, he wrote, he was ready to die content. It was his last letter. See May 26 (1778). *Correspondence*, XCVIII, 247.

confession he had stoutly refused to make, and to inculpate his accomplices. The question produced no answers: through his entire ordeal, even when he was broken on the wheel, Jean Calas continued to profess his innocence; when Beaudrigue entreated his victim to confess at the last moment, in the presence of death, Calas turned his head away without a word. A few minutes later, he was strangled by the executioner.

The case was horrible but, for Voltaire, perfect. His response was characteristic: here was a riddle worthy of the most avid intelligence, and, better, it represented a concatenation of events discrediting *l'infâme* which he had just begun to belabor in print. If Calas had murdered his son, this was a splendid specimen of Protestant fanaticism; if the authorities had murdered Calas, this was a splendid specimen of Catholic fanaticism: in either case, the philosophes could only profit. "Was he guilty or innocent?" Voltaire inquired soon after he had heard of the case, with a mixture of fascination, enjoyment, and rage. "One way or the other, this is the most horrible fanaticism in the most enlightened century. My tragedies are not so tragic."[7]

But his humanity soon won out over the desire to parade evidence of human wickedness and stupidity for the sake of scoring points against *l'infâme*. Calas obsessed Voltaire. He begged for information; he made inquiries in Toulouse and Paris; he disregarded the well-meaning warnings of his friends to stay away from a case that had been decided correctly, and, moreover, in accord with the legal code. Voltaire became convinced that Calas had been innocent and that the case had been nothing less than a monstrous miscarriage of justice. With the energy that characterized him to the last, he threw himself into the effort of rehabilitating Calas's memory, and the good repute of the Calas family. He was doing what he had learned to do incomparably well: to move men by the written word, with his inimitable combination of clarity, oversimplification, and a kind of witty fury. In his hands, the Calas case became the most celebrated case in Europe. His reputation did not suffer. In August 1762, Diderot accorded to Voltaire the reformer the praise he usually reserved for Voltaire the dramatist: "It's Voltaire who is writing in behalf of this unhappy family," he wrote to Sophie Volland. "Oh!

---

[7] Voltaire to Camp, March 27 (1762). Ibid., XLVIII, 173.

my friend, what a splendid use of genius! That man must have spirit, sensibility; injustice must be revolting to him; he must feel the charms of virtue. For what are the Calas to him? What is it that can interest him in them? What reason has he to suspend labors he loves, to occupy himself in their defense? If there were a Christ, I assure you that Voltaire would be saved."[8] It was a warm but deserved tribute. Voltaire felt unable to continue work on a tragedy of his own, he said, until the tragedy of Toulouse had been resolved; and he importuned his friends to help him. "Shout everywhere, I beg you, for the Calas," he wrote to d'Alembert in September 1762, "and against fanaticism, for it's *l'infâme* that has caused their misery."[9] His success was rapid and dramatic: aided by fellow philosophes and by others of good will, including those whose Christian faith was unimpeachable but whose names are little known, Voltaire managed to reverse the verdict of the *parlement* of Toulouse, and to reunite and rehabilitate the scattered members of the Calas family. On March 9, 1765, on the third anniversary of Jean Calas's conviction, a royal tribunal declared the victim innocent, and ordered his conviction, as well as the convictions of other members of the family, stricken from the record. It was now official: Marc-Antoine Calas had committed suicide.

"It's *l'infâme* that has caused their misery"—this was Voltaire's first conclusion. Not unexpectedly, he was inclined to dwell on the religious causes of this terrible miscarriage of justice. Yet, as other cases were brought to him, now that he was becoming *l'homme aux Calas,* and as he studied the memoranda that prominent lawyers submitted to him at his request, it dawned on him that it was the French legal system as such that was on trial. Every aspect of the Calas case disclosed a glaring defect in the Criminal Ordinance of 1670. Why had the Calas family lied at first, denying that Marc-Antoine had committed suicide? Because under French law, a suicide was a felon who was subjected to an ignominious mock trial, dragged through the streets naked by the heels, and hanged. Why had the judges lent credence to so much improbable testimony? Because the Ordinance permitted the most outrageous rumors, hearsay upon hearsay, to be accepted into the record. Why were there so few who

---

[8] (August 8, 1762). *Correspondance,* IV, 97.
[9] See ibid., 97 *n.*; and Voltaire to d'Alembert, September 15 (1762). *Correspondence,* L, 29.

had come forward in behalf of Calas? Because the intervention of the church in the case with its inflammatory language had spurred on witnesses for the prosecution and intimidated witnesses for the defense. Why had highly placed judges resorted to the abomination of torturing an old man? Because this was the accepted legal method of extorting confessions from an obdurate but obviously guilty defendant, and of discovering the accomplices he hoped to shield by his professions of innocence. To be sure, the Calas case had implications outside the law itself: in his moving *Traité sur la tolérance* of 1763, written in the midst of his efforts in behalf of the Calas family, Voltaire pleaded for toleration of religious minorities as a policy both humane and practical. "Doubtless," he wrote, as usual hitting two targets with one shot, "like us, the Huguenots have been intoxicated with fanaticism and sullied with blood; but is the present generation as barbarous as its parents? Time, reason which is making so much progress, good books, the decent manners of society—have they not penetrated at all among those who guide the souls of these people? And do we not see that almost all of Europe has changed its face during the last fifty years or so?"[1] But even this tract, so eloquently directed against persecution, begins with a long, typically tendentious account of the Calas case: the French legal system was now in the center of Voltaire's attention.

IV

In the fall of 1765, in the mood for generalizations and in search of principles, Voltaire was singularly fortunate to encounter an eloquent general treatise on the criminal law, Beccaria's *Dei delitti e delle pene*. This powerful little book is a characteristic product of the free trade in ideas so widespread in the Enlightenment, and would have been unthinkable without it. Beccaria, the Milanese aristocrat who ascribed his "conversion to philosophy" to Montesquieu's *Lettres persanes* and who had erased what he regarded as the baleful effects of his "fanatical" Jesuit education by studying Helvétius, Buffon, Diderot, Hume, d'Alembert, Condillac, and

---

[1] *Traité sur la tolérance* ... (1763), in *Œuvres*, XXV, 31.

VIII: THE POLITICS OF DECENCY

Rousseau, now repaid his masters, with interest.[2] He developed their hints into ideas, their ideas into sustained arguments, and influenced some of the very men who had liberated him. He was deeply indebted to the Enlightenment; the Enlightenment came to be deeply indebted to him.

Nothing in *Dei delitti e delle pene* is new; its governing ideas had been formulated, though often in tentative or fragmentary shape, by the teachers whom Beccaria so freely acknowledged; the legal philosophy of "the immortal Montesquieu,"[3] the libertarian passion of Rousseau's *Contrat social*, the rationalist yet humane calculations of Helvétius are the visible raw materials of his book. Yet *Dei delitti e delle pene* impressed its readers as a splendid innovation and earned its author the kind of extravagant epithet of which the eighteenth century was so fond: Beccaria was, for Voltaire, a laborer "in behalf of reason and humanity,"[4] and, for the German *Aufklärer* Hommel, the "Socrates of our epoch."[5] What lent Beccaria's treatise the appearance of an originality he never claimed for it was the energy of its language, the cumulative logic of its case, the economy of its formulations, and the apparent singlemindedness of its author.[6] *Dei delitti* was like a drawing by a master: every line counted and every line was right. Diderot, highly sensitive to the music of language, noted a kind of rhythm in Beccaria's treatise which led the author, and with him the reader, from calm reflection to passionate sympathy and back again, a "melody of sentiment"[7] that revealed, and by revealing induced, enthusiasm for its enlightened teachings.

While the appeal of Beccaria's treatise was in the main emotional, Beccaria hoped that it was scientific; he presents *Dei delitti* as a product of the science of man. The laws under which men live in the eighteenth century are "the dregs of the most barbarous of

---

[2] See my earlier discussion of Beccaria in *The Rise of Modern Paganism*, 10–22.
[3] See above, 325.
[4] Voltaire to Beccaria, May 30, 1768. *Correspondence*, LXIX, 159.
[5] Quoted in *Dei delitti*, 623.
[6] That singlemindedness was more apparent than real; Beccaria had to be driven into his achievement by his close associates, the Verri brothers. See below, 444–5.
[7] See Diderot: *Œuvres*, IV, 60; in *Dei delitti*, 405.

centuries"[8]; their fatal flaw lies not so much in their specifically medieval origins as in their slavish dependence on tradition. These laws were first made by caprice and fortune, generally in favor of the very men and groups whose interest it is to set themselves against rational or progressive legislation; and these laws have been changed, when they have been changed at all, through half-blind trial and error, and in response to the demands and needs of the powerful. Men need a dispassionate study of human nature, but precisely what they need they have not had. Yet it is in their grasp: the modern science of government has at its disposal the principle by which all law must be judged: "*La massima felicità divisa nel maggior numero* —the greatest happiness divided among the greatest number."[9]

It is evident from Beccaria's rhetoric, his appeal to a single principle and its corollaries, and his infatuation with geometry that his science of law was rather less empirical and more deductive than the comparative sociology of Montesquieu and of the Scottish school. Indeed, Beccaria relied more heavily on logical coherence and verbal vehemence than on detailed case histories; not that he invented judicial cruelty, indifference, irrationality—they were all there, in abundance—but he offered partial observations as total history. And Beccaria's science was less than scientific in another respect. Like the other philosophes, Beccaria sought to make his legal science objective without making it indifferent to man; its very objectivity was to guarantee its humanity. But in actuality, when Beccaria found objectivity and humanity in conflict, humanity won out. Beccaria's emotions are never in doubt; they inform every page of his work and guide his most theoretical questions: is torture just and effective? Is the death penalty necessary and useful to an orderly society? How do we prevent crime? What is the influence of punishment on behavior? What is a reasonable scale of penalties? These questions, Beccaria insists, deserve not metaphysics, "sophisms," or "seductive eloquence," but "geometric precision."[1]

Since one man's right to punish another is by no means self-evident, Beccaria seeks the basis of that right in the nature of political organization and the nature of man himself. His discoveries are,

---

[8] *Dei delitti*, 31.
[9] Ibid., 9.
[1] Ibid., 30.

if not simpleminded, at least simplistic, but what they lose in subtlety they gain in clarity: in political theory, Beccaria belongs to the social contract school; in psychology, among the hedonists. Yet his simplicity does not lead him into naïve optimism: he refuses to believe that men voluntarily surrendered their freedom for the common good. "That chimera exists only in romances."[2] Quite the contrary: men, especially the multitude, excited by prospects of short-range advantages and private profit, often seek to escape the obligations that an ordered society must impose on them, and to plunge it back into the chaos of the state of nature. Hence punishments are absolutely indispensable, a conclusion Beccaria obviously adopts with reluctance, in obedience to his self-proclaimed realism. Let others write "romances"; he aspires to writing the science of justice.

But while punishment is an indispensable element in all societies, it must be minimal for the objective it is intended to achieve. "Every act of authority of man over man which does not derive from absolute necessity," Beccaria writes, generalizing a dictum of Montesquieu's, "is tyrannical"[3]; penalties justify themselves, as it were, to the degree that the sovereign guarantees his subjects liberty and security. Here is the counterpart of Beccaria's utilitarian principle prescribing the greatest happiness for the greatest number: the law must parcel out for the smallest possible amount of suffering for the smallest possible number.

Having established the right to punishment in, and through, a rational and enlightened jurisprudence, Beccaria in effect draws two corollaries, each of them an aspect of what we have come to call the rule of law. Punishment can be decreed only by the law and judges have no right to interpret the law under which they decide a case; and if the severity of a certain punishment can be shown to be useless, then it is irrational, contrary to justice, fit not for happy free men but for a "herd of slaves."[4] These corollaries shape the rest of Beccaria's treatise; they appear and reappear as leading themes with recognizable, well-disciplined variations.

---

[2] Ibid., 12.
[3] Ibid.
[4] Ibid., 15. While Beccaria speaks of "four corollaries," I have combined them into two for the sake of clarity.

First: the rule of law in a state produces the life of reason for the citizen, and Beccaria devotes much effort to discovering the conditions under which such a life can flourish. Reason depends on prediction. It follows that the laws must be written in the ordinary language of the country; they must be clear and open, a "solemn and public book" rather than a private possession. In full agreement with the other philosophes, Beccaria rejoiced in the invention of printing, which, he thought, had been responsible for the decline of superstition and barbarity. Publicity and accessibility reduce crime as, and because, they increase the range of reason: "The larger the number of those who understand, and hold in their hands, the sacred code of the laws, the rarer crimes will become, for there can be no doubt that ignorance about, and uncertainty of, punishments enhance the eloquence of the passions."[5]

Inevitably, of course, in the best-regulated and most humane legal systems, some men will find themselves in court, and the life of reason must function there as well. Since it is essential that men be enabled to calculate the consequences of their actions, only that conduct specifically prohibited by law can draw penalties of any sort, penalties must be specified in the law, and judges must be restricted to finding facts. To give them greater leeway than that, to permit them to imprison accused men, set penalties, or interpret the laws on their own authority is to make them into tyrants who subject their victims to their moods, their prejudices, their changes of opinion. Judges are not legislators and must not become legislators; conversely, the sovereign is not a judge and must not become a judge; he must restrict himself to framing general laws that bind all citizens alike. When all these conditions have been observed, "citizens acquire personal security, just, because it is the reason why men are in society, and useful, because it allows them to calculate with precision the inconveniencies attaching to a misdeed."[6]

To find facts on a rational basis, the judge must be guided by rational procedures. In this sensitive region, procedure, Beccaria finds the courts of Europe sadly wanting, and his dismay leads him to some of his most pointed observations. They are even more

---

[5] Ibid., 18.
[6] Ibid., 17.

pointed than they appear to be: a judge in Beccaria's Lombardy, or elsewhere in the Italian states, or across the civilized world, could recognize his remarks as directed against himself. Beccaria was too sweeping in his indictment, severe with the lapses and forgetful of the merits of current practice. Yet his enthusiastic and, to his opponents, ungenerous criticisms were not a fantasy; they directly contradicted the legal assumptions and courtroom procedures of his day. A defendant must be presumed innocent until he is proved guilty—generally, he was presumed guilty until he was found innocent and not free of suspicion even then; judicial inquiries must be short—they were long; imprisonment before trial must count as part of the sentence—it was normally ignored after conviction; self-incrimination, extorted confessions, and torture are as inhumane as they are unreliable—both were perfectly standard everywhere; the more atrocious the crime, the more reliable the testimony must be—current practice, in its avidity to find culprits, became less and less stringent in its demands for truthfulness or even probability the more heinous the alleged offense; accusations and trials must be public—the use of secret informers and trials behind closed doors were widespread. The very abuses to which Beccaria most fiercely objected as most manifest—the extortion of confession, the free employment of secret calumniators, the caprice of incompetent judges whose only qualification was that they had bought their place, and, worst of all, torture, to which Beccaria devotes a brilliant, vehement, wholly uncompromising chapter—were the very props of justice in Beccaria's time. When Beccaria laments "the moans of the weak, sacrificed to cruel ignorance and opulent laziness; the barbarous torments, multiplied with lavish and useless severity, for crimes either not proved or imaginary; the squalor and horrors of a prison, increased by that cruellest tormentor of the miserable, uncertainty,"[7] he was addressing the men who ruled his Lombardy; the liberalism of Count Firmian, the Hapsburg governor, and of his chief, Count Kaunitz, did not reach into the courts and the prisons.

Beccaria's second corollary, that punishment must be rational, is the counterpart to the first, that criminal law and procedure must be rational: reasonableness is, for Beccaria, the pervasive, dominant ideal. The sole purpose of punishment, he argues, is to reduce the

---

[7] Ibid., 10.

harm to which society is exposed by crime; in a radical break with older conceptions and in wholehearted agreement with Montesquieu, Beccaria sees punishment not as a measure of vengeance but as a measure of prevention. "It is better to prevent crimes than to punish them,"[8] better to educate people and give them greater liberty than to seek conformity by repression. The logic of leniency follows from these considerations without strain: a crime is an act that harms society; the more harmful the act the greater is the stake of society in its prevention; hence "there must be a proportion between crimes and punishments."[9] The only proper test of a penalty is a pragmatic one: if it deters crime at minimum expense to all, it is justifiable—all else is tyranny. And the only proper guide to a penalty is man's psychological make-up: since man seeks pleasure and shuns pain, the legislator must, in laying down his scale of punishments, proportion pain to the pleasure that a crime would give the potential offender. Once again following Montesquieu, Beccaria insists that if punishments are all equally savage, men will prefer the greater crime to the lesser one. Proportionality and its chosen companion, leniency, are desirable because they work. With all his cautious estimate of human nature, Beccaria never wholly freed himself from the optimistic expectation that men reason about consequences and will permit themselves to be deterred from a criminal act by appropriate punishment. Yet his rationalism is far from facile or complete: "It is impossible," he noted with some caution, "to prevent all disorders in the universal combat of human passions. They increase in a ratio compounded of population and the conflicts of private interests, which it is not possible to turn with geometric precision in the direction of public utility. For mathematical exactitude we must substitute, in the arithmetic of politics, the calculus of probabilities."[1] Like the other philosophes, Beccaria thought of the science of society as less exact than the science of nature.

In repeatedly defining a crime as an act that does harm to society, Beccaria took "harm" quite literally. What matters is not the intention of the offender, but his effect on society. The rank of the criminal is irrelevant: an aristocrat must be punished for his crimes

---

8 Ibid., 96.
9 Ibid., 19.
1 Ibid., 19–20.

quite as much as a commoner. The state has limited interest in injuries to honor, little interest in sexual offenses, and no interest in suicide; like Montesquieu, Beccaria finds it essential to reduce not merely the severity of punishments but the list of offenses by redefining the very nature of crime. Once again, he resorts to the principles of the rule of law: any act not explicitly interdicted is permitted; a vague word like "vice" must never be invoked to punish an individual for doing what no one has forbidden.

While the humane intentions of this utilitarian philosophy are obvious on every page of *Dei delitti*, they are nowhere more dramatically in evidence than in Beccaria's passionate attack on the death penalty. This chapter is, with the chapter on torture, the longest chapter in his treatise. The death penalty, Beccaria argues, is not a right but a usurpation; it is, in his felicitous phrase, "the war of a nation against a citizen because it has judged that the destruction of his being is necessary or useful."[2] But the death penalty, presumed to be both, is neither. The only possible exceptions are a time of anarchy, or a time of national peril when a prominent citizen, even in prison, can continue his dangerous machinations. At all other times, there can be no excuse for it. Setting aside his rationalism, Beccaria now insists that the death penalty is not a deterrent: it is so extreme, so quickly over with, that a potential criminal will not be frightened by its specter. Besides, it is a mere entertainment for some and a source of mixed contempt and compassion for others: witnesses do not experience the beneficial fear that it is supposed to arouse. Finally, the death penalty gives the public an example of barbarity; it is a crime committed by dignified public officials, it induces disrespect for law and a cynical estimate of public policy, and invites imitation. There must be an end to such needless and repulsive cruelty.

Beccaria had some sense of his cause, but limited confidence in his effectiveness: "A philosopher's voice is too weak for the tumults and the shouting of so many men guided by blind habit. But the few wise men scattered over the face of the earth will echo me in their hearts."[3] It was for these wise men that Beccaria professed to write, but diffident, often depressed, always reluctant to enter public

---

[2] Ibid., 62.
[3] Ibid., 69.

controversy, he wrote, it seems, mainly for himself. In an autobiographical passage, he poured out once again the passion that had really driven him—not science but humanity: "If I have no other merit than to have been the first to offer Italy, with some good evidence, what other nations have dared to write and are beginning to practice, I should consider myself fortunate; but if, by upholding the rights of man and of unconquerable truth, I should contribute to saving, from the spasms and agonies of death, some miserable victim of tyranny or of equally fatal ignorance, the thanks and tears of one innocent man in his transports of joy would console me for the disdain of all mankind."[4]

V

Beccaria's timid aspiration was touching but needlessly self-deprecating. His book aroused immediate attention and caused widespread controversy in Italy; only two years after its publication it was in its sixth printing. It was greeted in France, especially by the philosophes, with authentic and unreserved applause; it was extensively and enthusiastically reviewed in both learned and popular journals. Grimm hinted in the couse of an extensive exposition that it would be most desirable "if all the legislators of Europe would take M. Beccaria's ideas into consideration."[5] D'Alembert, for whom Beccaria in his turn professed the highest esteem, let it be known that he was "enchanted" and "enthusiastic," and that he had spread news of the book, "which should give its author an immortal reputation," among a number of philosophes.[6] Voltaire supplied *Dei delitti* with a commentary in which he accepted Beccaria's reform program point by point, and applied it to France. It was a good time for such application: Voltaire was in the midst of another *cause célèbre*, the case of the adolescent chevalier de la Barre, tortured and executed

---

[4] Ibid., 30–1. John Adams was apparently so deeply impressed with this formulation that he used most of it (omitting, of course, the references to Italy) when he defended the British soldiers involved in the Boston Massacre. See Henry Paolucci's translation and edition of Beccaria's *On Crimes and Punishments* (1963), xxi.

[5] See *Dei delitti*, 320.

[6] See ibid., 313.

for blasphemy. Morellet's French translation of late 1765 was widely criticized for its arbitrary reshuffling of Beccaria's chapters, but it made the book accessible to those who did not read Italian. In Great Britain, Jeremy Bentham credited Beccaria for setting him "on the principle of utility" and for suggesting the calculus of pleasures.[7] Other British legal reformers admired his humanity, copied his reasoning, and made it relevant to their domestic legal scene. In the American colonies, where young Jefferson copied passages from *Dei delitti* by the page and became an outspoken opponent of the death penalty, it was the same story: wide popularity and largely uncritical admiration. Catherine of Russia professed herself a follower: her famous *Nakaz* of 1768, the instructions to her Commission to draw up a legal code, reproduced substantial portions of *Dei delitti*.

Much of this shower of adulation may be discounted as a product of the eighteenth-century capacity for facile enthusiasm. Talk was cheap: Catherine of Russia, for one, received credit for reforms she did not intend to carry out; nothing at all came of Catherine's well-advertised enterprise of reforming the legal code, and it is notorious that the peasants, the vast majority of Russians, found themselves more deeply in slavery during, and after, than before, the reign of that philosophical Tsarina, admirer of Montesquieu, friend of Voltaire, patron of Diderot but servant, first and last, of her own pleasures and her own power. Everywhere, men found it easier to praise Beccaria than to put his program into action. Still, Beccaria's practical impact remained gratifying and extensive. He educated prolific and influential reformers like Bentham and Eden and Romilly in England, and through them his ideas gradually but drastically reformed the English law. His vast reputation and the many editions and translations of his book made the idea of reform popular, palatable, respectable, almost fashionable.

Nor is this all. When in 1772 Gustavus III abolished torture in Sweden—the very year that the Lombard Senate voted to retain it—

---

[7] See Mary P. Mack: *Jeremy Bentham: An Odyssey of Ideas* (1963), 104; Beccaria was, to be sure, in good company, including among others Montesquieu and above all Helvétius, but Beccaria's importance to Bentham remained great: he did not scruple to call Beccaria "My master, first evangelist of reason, who hast raised thy Italy so much above England and also France. . . ." Coleman Phillipson: *Three Criminal Law Reformers: Beccaria, Bentham, Romilly* (1923), 92.

he explicitly credited Beccaria's influence; whatever slow, halting improvements were made in the Austrian lands under Maria Theresa and Joseph II at least indirectly reflected Beccaria's work. But the finest monument to Beccaria is the Tuscan code promulgated in 1786 by Beccaria's declared disciple, Archduke Leopold. In its Preamble, Leopold claimed that he had been interested in legal reform since his accession in 1765, and he reminded his people that he had already abolished torture and the death penalty by special edict. But whatever the origins of Leopold's concern, the code mirrored the mind and followed the prescriptions of Beccaria. It reiterated, in grave and general language, Leopold's earlier edicts: it prohibited torture, eliminated the crime of *lèse-majesté* from the statute books, removed confiscation as an unjust burden on the family of a convicted criminal, and confirmed the abolition of the death penalty. In obedience to Beccaria's philosophy, the code directed itself at the prevention rather than the avenging of crime, sought to proportion punishment to offense, and to protect accused persons from irresponsible denunciation and inquisitorial procedures. Doubtless, the code reflected not simply the theories of Beccaria, but Leopold's successful experiments with leniency, and his humane and reformist temper as well. But precisely this combination of philosophical theory, administrative experience, and royal temperament suited the philosophes' political ideas to perfection. That such a combination was desirable was a point on which the men of the Enlightenment could agree without hesitation, as they could agree on the contents of their political program. But such a combination was rare; it was, in fact, uniquely embodied in Archduke Leopold of Tuscany. What was to be done in the other countries? That was a question on which the philosophes found that no agreement was possible.

CHAPTER NINE

The Politics of Experience

I. THE VARIETIES OF POLITICAL EXPERIENCE

I

"THE SCIENCE OF POLITICS," wrote Alexander Hamilton in 1787, like "most other sciences has received great improvement."[1] Hamilton had some right to his self-assurance; the *Federalist* papers, in which his dictum appears, were in themselves impressive evidence of how great that improvement had been. Yet everywhere shadows clouded certainties, and the philosophes found themselves often baffled and silent, often wavering between contradictory prescriptions, too often desperately satisfied with superficial solutions that were no solutions at all.

Differences of opinion, of course, were to be expected: they emerged quite naturally from the variety of the philosophes' political experience at home and abroad, and they fed on the philosophes' highly individual, sometimes idiosyncratic manner of interpreting their experience.[2] In addition, perception was obstructed by sheer novelty; the kind of politics the philosophes' thought implied, in fact demanded, was only in its rudimentary stage in the eighteenth century. The men of the Enlightenment sensed that they could realize their social ideals only by political means, and, with their verbal facility, with their partisan pamphlets, tendentious histories, and semi-public letters, they set the stage for the kind of politics they needed. As professional men of the word, the philosophes did

---

[1] *The Federalist*, No. 9, 51. Other philosophes like the marquis d'Argenson, and allied reformers like the abbé de Saint-Pierre, also speak of a "science of politics."
[2] See also below, 465–6.

more than feed political discussion; in some countries they did nothing less than to bring it into being. Yet, the very idea of politics by discussion, on which they staked so many of their hopes, was untried, precarious, and in many states, impossible. The public airing of public issues is a social habit like any other, subject like all habits to development and decay, and responsive like all habits to encouragement or inhibition. If, in the German states, there was little talk about politics, that silence sprang less from fear than from lack of practice and indifference; Germans were simply unaccustomed to such talk, and found other issues, notably religious controversy, far more rewarding subjects for the exercise of their contentiousness. As one *Aufklärer*, the Berlin journalist G. N. Fischer, rather pathetically complained as late as 1788: "Many people think *only* of religion when they hear of *Aufklärung*." Fischer acknowledged that "*Aufklärung* is of course of the greatest importance in the field of religion," but he insisted, obviously running against the mainstream, that it should extend "far beyond the comparatively narrow field of religion."[3] Politics here was only implied, not specifically mentioned. In such model states as Weimar, with its impressive collection of poets and thinkers, resident intellectuals won the right to hold unconventional ideas about personal morals and religion by tacitly surrendering their rights in the political arena, and by sublimating whatever political discontent they felt by writing melodramas.

In some countries, of course, debate on political issues was a well-established tradition; while there were firm limits on the innovations one could safely advocate in Great Britain, preachers and lawyers, vocally seconded by educated amateurs, had long put their political thoughts and passions into accessible printed form. The French situation was more complicated: it was officially fettered but actually fairly free, though, at least in the philosophes' view, in need of a steady growth of freedom. The *Encyclopédie* said that countries were "enlightened" by the "continual discussion" of such affairs,[4] but this was the formulation of a wish masquerading as a statement of fact, and the most prominent French philosophes la-

---

[3] Quoted in Klaus Epstein: *The Genesis of German Conservatism* (1966), 35.
[4] "Intendants," in *The Encyclopédie*, 121. See above, chap. ii, section 1, and below, chap. ix, section 2.

bored long to make that wish into a fact; both Diderot, with his devoted service to the *Encyclopédie,* and Voltaire, with his dogged scribbling of pamphlets, eloquently testify to the philosophes' high expectations for that new, still shapeless phenomenon, public opinion. They thought it possible to mobilize that opinion, and possible that that opinion would have power over policy. At the end of a century of Enlightenment it was by no means certain that they had been right.

The obstructions in the way of the politics of discussion pointed to some fundamental difficulties. As the philosophes understood it, the science of politics was a supremely practical science with two related tasks: to provide intelligent, humane administration, and to discover forms of government that would establish, strengthen, and maintain rational institutions in a rational political atmosphere.[5] There was trouble with both of those tasks, more with the second than the first: the state within, and the state system as a whole, appeared to have aims incompatible with enlightened ideals; the most flexible and decent of ruling groups fell short of the philosophes' demand. Enlightened politics is modern liberal politics, and such politics requires forums for the debate and formulation of policies, some degree of responsibility of governors to the governed, some measure of participation by the governed in the government, unofficial channels for the generation of opinion and for its translation into policies—in short, parliamentary regimes, political parties, widespread literacy, and a free press. As I have suggested, in the age of the Enlightenment such institutions were scarce, and in many places unimaginable. The persistence of habit, the burden of deference, the difficulties of communication, the enormous social distance between rulers and ruled—these were the enemies of modern liberalism. The state, it seemed, functioned simultaneously as the subverter of traditional institutions and as a bulwark against liberalism. Almost everywhere, it had weakened the old deliberative bodies; in some states, it had dismantled them altogether. While provincial estates

---

[5] It was admittedly hard to define practicality: one man's realism was another man's wishful thinking. Thus the marquis d'Argenson criticized the abbé de Saint-Pierre for his inexperience: "He is often mistaken, because he has never held public office, and neither men nor affairs may be understood when viewed only from one's library." (I owe this reference to Gerald J. Cavanaugh.)

or *parlements* had for centuries been predominantly and fiercely devoted to the interests of the privileged orders—of plutocracies of urban notables or landed nobles—they had at least acted as restraints on centralized power and as arenas for debates or quarrels. In Prussia, the diets that survived in a few provinces met mainly to ratify the tax demands of the king; in France, the *parlements*—that is to say, the great courts which claimed a share in the law-making power—and the provincial estates, did little more than to obstruct royal policies.[6] Most European states had no representative institutions at all; their only constraints on power were custom and the good will, laziness, or intelligence of the ruling house. Poland, the most dramatic exception to this pervasive concentration of power, only offered convincing arguments for the proponents of absolutism: the country was an anarchy of self-willed and unruly aristocrats, the standing joke of Europe, a chaos that no one envied and no one wished to reproduce.

Fortunately for the philosophes, Poland was unique, and the Prussian pattern was not universal. Great Britain and the Dutch Republic proudly displayed parliamentary institutions that were more than memories or impotent debating societies, and, with equal pride, gave relatively free reign to public discussion on touchy issues. Both were oligarchies, governments by and for the rich, the gently born, or the well-connected; fond as the philosophes were of them, they were realistic enough to see that. But compared to the rest of the civilized world, these two countries were veritable models of public responsibility, free speech, open circulation of the elite, and political participation. With all their imperfections, therefore, Great Britain and the Dutch Republic functioned as models for the Enlightenment; they demonstrated that liberal regimes were not fantasies but possibilities.

This meant a great deal to the philosophes, for they took institutions seriously: Montesquieu's political sociology and Hume's quarrel with Pope's view that only fools argued about forms of government are only two instances of their alertness to the decisive impact that the political order exercises on the substance of policy. This is why the establishment of a "*science du gouvernement*," of a "divine science" of politics, of the "principles of political architec-

---

ture"[7] seemed such urgent business to them: perhaps the most important way to improve the world was to improve political institutions. Their very demand for a political climate in which debate would be possible and meaningful was a radical demand for new, or at the very least, drastically reformed, types of government.

At the same time, the constricted repertory of political possibilities and the untried quality of political debate imposed severe limitations on the philosophes' political thinking and compelled many of them, more in despair than in hope, to subordinate their appetite for fundamental change to the satisfaction of concrete demands that might be realized in, and through, the institutions they found around them. For many of the philosophes, enlightened absolutism was a refuge, a response to overpowering realities rather than a first preference, an imposed rather than a free choice. Philosophes in Berlin and Milan, Vienna and St. Petersburg, hedged in by censors, awed by the presence of power, and depressed by the general illiteracy, widespread destitution, and total absence of responsive institutions, could either advocate a new regime (which was a risky, and at best a utopian, venture), withdraw from politics as the arena of futility (which was a seductive temptation), or work for specific changes without alienating the powerful (which appeared to many of them the most promising course). But whatever their choice, with their besetting uncertainty over political means, their frequent silences in the midst of political agitation, their support of rulers they did not trust, the philosophes demonstrated to the sheer novelty of modern politics as such.

II

While the philosophes' political opinions ranged from the democratic radicalism of Rousseau to the relativism of Voltaire and the absolutism of Beccaria, there is one philosophe who seems to stand outside this wide spectrum, David Hume.[8] Hume posed, and often wrote, as an urbane conservative. The portrait is familiar: the corpu-

---

[7] See *The Federalist, passim.*
[8] For Rousseau, see below, chap. x, section 3.

lent, good-humored Epicurean indifferent to the reforming passions
of his brethren; the skeptical psychologist intent on vindicating the
powers of habit and the rights of belief against the claims of reason;
the reactionary historian who found sympathetic words for Charles
I; the contented man of letters looking back to the Revolution of
1689 rather than forward to the Revolution of 1789—in short, the
ancestor not of Robespierre but of Burke. But this portrait, to which
Hume contributed a good deal of material, is nothing better than a
plausible caricature. Like the other philosophes, Hume was deeply
engaged with the world around him; he had, if anything, fewer
illusions and needed fewer fictions than the rest of the philosophic
flock. He commanded the political writings of Plato and Machiavelli
and Montesquieu, but the energy animating his political thinking
stems from what he saw around him. The general and the particular
nourished one another in his mind. As a philosophe he defined what
he called superstition and fanaticism as the supreme threats to civilized life; as an unbeliever of Presbyterian origins, he was inclined to
identify superstition with Roman Catholicism and fanaticism with
the Puritans. As an educated man, he was, like his fellow philosophes,
hopeful of diffusing enlightenment and uncertain just how much
light the untutored common man could bear; as a Scot, he welcomed
the burgeoning Scottish Enlightenment and the booming Scottish
economy and despised the Scottish Kirk. The great political event
of his life was the last serious threat to the Hanoverian dynasty,
the famous Forty-Five, this "miserable war,"[9] Hume called it, which
ended, as it had to end, with the rout of the ragged forces of the
Young Pretender by the British army. "When the shock was over,"
H. R. Trevor-Roper has written, "all parties in Britain were determined that no such thing should happen again. One step taken to
prevent it was the abolition, in 1747, of the feudal jurisdiction of the
Scottish nobility. Another was the repudiation by the English tories
of the last relics of their jacobite loyalty."[1] This meant that Hume
could afford to repudiate the Whiggish notions of the "social compact" without seeming disloyal to the British crown and without
being compelled to adopt the reactionary Tory notions of "passive

---

[9] Hume to Sir James Johnstone of Westerhall, October 31 (1745).
Letters, I, 66.
[1] H. R. Trevor-Roper, reviewing Giuseppe Giarrizzo: *David
Hume. Politico e Storico*, in *History and Theory*, III, 3 (1964), 385.

obedience"; he could, in short, contentedly enjoy the blessings of his government while criticizing the elaborate if useful lies on which it was based.

Contentment is normally a prop for conservatism; it invites acceptance of things as they are. David Hume (although in his later years he looked upon the conduct of domestic affairs with some alarm), in the main found his experience of Britain a source of real satisfaction: the country was prosperous, more prosperous than other countries; its social structure gave room to talent, more room than other societies; its government extended freedom of speech even to infidels like himself, more freedom than other governments. Had he lived in France or Prussia, Hume might have been a consistent radical—it is impossible to know. But the point after all is that he lived in Britain, a country that already enjoyed what others still longed for. The Anglomania widespread among continental philosophes was a tribute to British institutions. Moreover, Hume's epistemology and psychology reinforced the lessons of his immediate experience. In Hume's view, knowledge, though adequate to the conduct of human affairs, always remained ultimately uncertain; behavior was governed by belief and habit—men inclined to do what they did because they had done it before; the passions and the imagination generally prevailed over the constructions of reason and even the calculations of self-interest. Such a theory of knowledge made most programs for reform look rash, unrealistic, downright foolish, and offered support for existing institutions that had proved themselves workable simply by existing. It was in character for Hume to have little use for revolutions, to admire long-lived institutions for the wisdom they enshrined, and to urge that change, if change must come, be slow.

But while Hume believed all this, he did not profess it with the ideological purity and the almost religious intensity that Burke would profess similar ideas two or three decades later. Hume, the critic of human stupidity, knew perfectly well that while custom may be the accumulation of man's best knowledge, it may also be a repository of foolishness. Christianity—an example always in Hume's mind—was an institution which, despite its longevity, demanded not passive acceptance, let alone worship, but alert, continuous, skeptical examination. Hume thought that revolutions often destroy what is valuable and produce what is pernicious, but he admitted that some revolutions are inevitable, others plainly a good thing. Plans go wrong, designs do not work, experiments are unsuccessful, but men, to the extent that they can muster intelligence and self-criticism, must continue to make plans, designs, and experiments. In his best conservative style, Hume warned that "an established government has an infinite advantage, by that very circumstance of its being established," and he thought it wisdom in a magistrate to "adjust his innovations, as much as possible, to the ancient fabric."[2] At the same time, his writings on economics sharply rejected prevailing policies, and he even indulged himself in constructing a perfect commonwealth, which turns out to be a responsible, representative republic equipped with a moderately wide franchise, safeguards for property, and provisions for exhaustive debate. It was not a dream or a game; Hume explicitly designed his personal utopia as a possible basis for future large-scale reform. If he was not a radical, he was not a conservative either; Hume was as skeptical of immobility as he was of revolution. It was only that the generally satisfactory course of events in Great Britain made moderate demands on his capacities for devastating criticism; Hume did not believe in expending more effort than was necessary.

III

However averse to revolutions in general, in one area of political theory Hume's thought was beyond doubt revolutionary, and marks an epoch in the internal history of the Enlightenment. Hume had no use for the "mere philosophical fictions"[3] that underlay current political philosophy. His most conspicuous target was "the suppos'd *state of nature*," the "fallacious and sophistical" theory of the social contract,[4] and with it the whole school of natural law. He piously insisted that he was in wholehearted agreement with the liberalism of the natural lawyers; he professed to share their aims and to reject only their reasoning. Despite these reassurances, however, Hume's attack on natural law remains an ambiguous venture;

---

[2] "Idea of a Perfect Commonwealth," *Works*, III, 480.
[3] *Treatise of Human Nature*, 493.
[4] Ibid., 549.

it was part of the Enlightenment's general attack on fictions, but it exposed the attackers to considerable risks. After all, natural law, almost from its emergence among the Greeks and codification among the Romans, had served ends to which the philosophes also subscribed. Reformers found arguments from natural law extraordinarily convenient: the distinction between nature and convention that lay at its heart, a distinction, it was argued, that was easy to discover in the hearts of good men everywhere and therefore universal in its application, made it a potentially devastating critic of existing laws and institutions. It gave rational men good reasons for disapproving and perhaps disobeying positive law. Aristotle had already said that an unjust law is not a law, and Roman lawyers had drawn the implication from this distinction by arguing that while the positive law depends quite simply on man's will, the natural law rests firmly on his noblest endowment, his reason. Slavery, as we know, was legal in the courts of men, but not in the court of nature.

For the Stoics and other natural lawyers in antiquity, these claims had metaphysical, even religious status; the appeal from positive law to natural law, from *lex scripta* to *recta ratio*, was an ethical injunction: as a participant in the universal right reason which he often violates but to which he is still subject, man has a duty to discover what he ought to do. In the Christian era, natural law had been overshadowed by higher laws; compared to divine edicts manifesting themselves in revelations, to Scriptures and the decrees of the church, it was humble enough. But humble things had their place in the Christian scheme of the world, and natural law served effectively in the pious endeavor to discover the legal order in which Christian men should live. Then, in the seventeenth century, when natural-law doctrines like the state of nature, the social contract, and natural rights became staples of political argumentation, natural law was secularized. Grotius, the greatest among the founders of modern natural law and a widely read if controversial author in the Enlightenment, was anything but impious, yet he insisted that the law of nature would retain its universal validity, and should still be obeyed, even if there were no God. Early in the Enlightenment, Montesquieu said precisely the same thing: "Even if there should be no God, we should always love justice"; indeed, "though we might be freed from the yoke of religion, we should never be free from the yoke of equity," for in truth, "justice is eternal and does not depend on human conventions."[5] Montesquieu's beloved Cicero had not put it any differently.

In the hands of the philosophes, natural law was, in effect, secular, a modern version of classical pagan speculation: there are eternal immutable principles of morality that stand as critics of positive law, for they often contradict it. "In vain do the civil laws make chains," said Montesquieu, "natural law will always break them."[6] The *Encyclopédie* devoted several articles to natural law— Boucher d'Argis's "Droit de la nature," Jaucourt's "Loi naturelle," Diderot's own "Hobbisme"—and all of them took Montesquieu's position: there are laws independent of, and superior to, human enactments; they are engraved in men's hearts, eternal, immutable, universal, and they impose moral obligations on the ruler and give moral rights to the ruled. Casually, occasionally, these writers would speak of God as the author of the natural law and as the source of its authority, but in actuality they all derived its origin and binding quality from the nature of man, the agreement of wise men across the world and through history, the testimony of reason, man's natural sense of justice, and, as Diderot put it in a revolutionary if still tentative way in the *Encyclopédie*, the infallible general will of men.[7] No wonder that orthodox Christian apologists took such small comfort in the religious tatters in which these secular thoughts were clothed. "I grant legislative power neither to the individual nor to the species . . .," André Chaumeix wrote in his attack on the *Encyclopédie*. "I recognize a Superior, above humanity, and it is to his tribunal that I refer my case."[8] The philosophes recognized no such Superior; their highest tribunal was humanity itself.

By claiming standards independent of positive law and professing that they had found them in man, history, reason, or the general will, those philosophes who still used natural-law rhetoric embroiled themselves in a dilemma that they resolved with a characteristic compromise. Natural law is essentially a rational and a rationalist

---

[5] *Lettres persanes*, No. 83, *Œuvres*, I, part 3, 169–70.

[6] Ronald Grimsley: "Quelques aspects de la théorie du droit naturel au siècle des lumières," *VS*, XXV (1963), 728.

[7] See especially Diderot to Falconet (September 6, 1768). *Correspondance*, VII, 117.

[8] Grimsley: "Droit naturel," *VS*, XXV, 736.

construct. As historians and sociologists, the philosophes recognized differences in men's ways; as reformers, they insisted on the imperfections of positive laws. Now these very differences and imperfections proved the assertions of natural law to be organized wishes rather than current realities, moral imperatives rather than generalizations from experience. True, the philosophes called upon factual evidence to make their generalizations; Diderot in particular, with his appeal to the practice of nations and the universal passions of men, sought to give the natural law an empirical grounding. Just as the philosophes had repudiated objective laws in aesthetics but argued for a consensus on works of art, so in their political writings the philosophes thought they possessed good grounds for asserting the existence of laws that were higher than the laws in the statute books.

It was a brave but unsuccessful attempt to rescue what the philosophes should not have tried rescue. Yet, while they were destroying the logic of natural law with their epistemology, their sociology, and their history, they continued to use its language as a support for their social criticism and guide for their reform program. Natural law appears in their writings as a commonplace, a kind of shorthand on which all educated, and many uneducated men, may be presumed to agree, or, with Kant, as an aim toward which mankind should strive. It is no accident that natural-law phrases should figure prominently in the pamphlets of the American and French Revolutions: they were appealing battle cries, slogans of reform, humanity, and constitutionalism. As pragmatists, many of the philosophes preferred effectiveness to consistency, and they persisted in proclaiming what their own thought made implausible.

But this is only one side of a complicated history. While philosophes continued to profess that they saw eternal standards independent of positive legislation, they dismissed the essential fictions intimately associated with that position, notably the state of nature or the social contract, with contempt or in silence; with rare exceptions, they overlooked or ridiculed the professional lawyers who continued the great seventeenth-century tradition of Grotius and Pufendorf into the eighteenth century. While in authoritarian central and eastern Europe natural-law doctrines continued to furnish the rationale for legal and administrative reforms, in the West the philosophes gave Wolff and Burlamaqui and Blackstone a harsh reception. Diderot could still commend Burlamaqui's *Éléments du droit* to Catherine of Russia, but Voltaire, who derided Grotius, Pufendorf, Vattel, and other natural lawyers as bores, mediocrities, and imitators, was far more characteristic of the Enlightenment's dominant view. As the century went on, the philosophes' attitude toward natural law became more and more skeptical, their relation to it more and more tenuous: the variety of the Enlightenment's political experience was a variety not of space alone, but of time as well. In France, utilitarian doctrines began to compete with natural law in the late 1750s, with the fertile suggestions of Maupertuis and the bald utilitarian account of political origins and political obligation offered by Helvétius in his *De l'esprit*. In Britain, Bentham took the ideas of Hume, Helvétius, and Beccaria to their logical conclusions in his first book, the polemical *Fragment on Government* of 1776: "*It is the greatest happiness of the greatest number that is the measure of right and wrong.*"[9] This, Bentham said, is the fundamental axiom of public life.

Utilitarianism, which dominates the second half of the Enlightenment, as natural law had dominated the first, was less dramatic than natural law but in all other respects a proper foundation for enlightened political thought: it professed to base its propositions on the science of man, and to dispense with the fictions on which earlier generations had lived. In this way, it brought the philosophes' theory of knowledge into line with their political program. Increasingly (though, it is worth repeating, by no means exclusively), the philosophes came to legitimize the state on the ground of its utility, rather than on tradition or an original contract. This justification was a test of governmental conduct and if necessary a call to revolution: Bentham complained that Blackstone's natural-law doctrines were actually a defense of conservatism, and insisted that utilitarianism alone, with its persistent questioning, was consistently progressive. It gave the philosopher the freedom to judge governments by their works and to condemn them if they failed to do their obvious duty. Only that government is acceptable, and deserves to survive, that devotes itself to the general happiness; the state exists not for its own sake, not by divine command or historical prescription, but

---

[9] P. 93. Italics in the original. For Beccaria's use of this phrase see above, chap. viii, section 4.

quite simply because it has a task to perform that private individuals, large families, and even gathered clans cannot perform.

By the 1770s, these arguments were widely repeated, but most of them go back to David Hume's critique of Locke's political ideas. Government, Hume argues, establishes social stability by guaranteeing peace, the security of private property, and ease of mutual intercourse. There are always reasons, or passions, that lead men to indulge in "fraud or rapine"; hence some kind of government is inevitable. "Men must, therefore, endeavour to palliate what they cannot cure."[1] It is not probable that government was instituted by some legal contract—Locke is simply wrong. "Reason, history, and experience shew us, that all political societies have an origin much less accurate and regular."[2] It is far more probable instead that government arose during time of war, when the superiority of one man over another, as well as the need for an arbiter, became glaringly apparent. Like everything else, the state is the fruit of experience; like everything else, it persists because men are creatures of habit. Hume urges "reasoners" to "look abroad into the world"[3]; it is there that they will find the realities that should govern their philosophizing. The point of Hume's argument is not to vindicate authority at all costs; on the contrary, he constructed it to show that while the doctrines of natural law are untenable in logic and history alike, their disappearance in no way implies a return to religious or traditionalist doctrines of authority. The point was to move from fiction, no matter how comfortable, and metaphysics, no matter how grandiose, to realities, no matter how trying, to justify authority by arguments that were historically, logically, sociologically sound. This meant, once again, that authority was not automatically justified simply by its existence, but by its actions. Politics, Hume said, is a difficult science, but it can become a science, and it can do so only if men see the real tensions within society rather than the imagined harmonies of which philosophers have always dreamed. "In all governments, there is a perpetual intestine struggle, open or secret, between AUTHORITY and LIBERTY; and neither of them can ever absolutely prevail in the contest. A great sacrifice of liberty

---

[1] "Of the Origin of Government," *Works*, III, 114.
[2] "Of the Original Contract," ibid., 450. I have already quoted this passage above, 335.
[3] Ibid., 446.

must necessarily be made in every government; yet even the authority, which confines liberty, can never, and perhaps ought never, in any constitution, to become quite entire and uncontroulable."[4] This was Hume's general view of politics, realistic in its awareness of conflict, hard-headed in its call for order, but, at the same time, liberal in its insistence on a domain of freedom, and, above all, flexible in its very generality. It was an invitation not to this system or that, but, within the secure bounds of reason and humanity, an invitation to a civilized, tolerant relativism.

IV

As consistent eclectics in their philosophical style, the philosophes found relativism in politics sensible, attractive, perfectly natural. Their relativism, to be sure, did not lead them to superb indifference to forms of government: David Hume, after all, was at once a relativist and a partisan of constitutional government; Montesquieu, who encouraged a whole century to think comparatively about forms of government, condemned despotism, as we know, as always and absolutely evil. The political relativists of the Enlightenment were, so to speak, relativists about their relativism; they firmly retained their respect for certain values that transcended all differences and remained valid in all climates. Their relativism amounted essentially to the recognition that political experiences varied because realities varied from country to country and that therefore different states at different stages of development would flourish best under different institutions.

Jeremy Bentham put the case with perfect lucidity. Relativism is both rational and practical: "I should think myself a weak reasoner and a bad citizen," he wrote, "were I not, though a Royalist in London, a republican in Paris."[5] Less dramatically, but to the same end, the chevalier de Jaucourt argued that taxation must be analyzed state by state rather than in general terms: "But how shall taxes be raised? Should they be laid on persons, land, consumption, merchan-

---

[4] "Of the Origin of Government," ibid., 116.
[5] See *The Rise of Modern Paganism*, 170.

dise, or other things? Each of these questions . . . calls for a profound treatise which would, moreover, be adapted to different countries, in accord with their circumstances, size, government, products, and commerce."[6] Even Rousseau, despite his uncompromising love of equality and insistence on universal participation in the good state, showed himself relatively indifferent to specific forms of government, and thought that these forms should depend, as Montesquieu had said they should, on physical factors such as size and climate. If there was any principle to which the majority of the philosophes subscribed in politics, it was not absolutism no matter how enlightened, but this restricted relativism—relativism was, quite simply, good sense.

The representative political relativist in the Enlightenment, impressive alike in the range of his political information and the flexibility of his political preferences, was doubtless Voltaire. Voltaire's politics displays the politics of the Enlightenment at its best, and at its worst as well. Even in his early years, in his most exclusively literary phase, Voltaire was a thoroughly political animal; when his experience was still rather confined, his gifts of observation and absorption were already highly developed. When he talked nonsense about politics, he talked nonsense because he was inadequately informed or because he kept himself inadequately informed on purpose. When he wanted to flatter a despot with at least a semblance of good conscience, ignorance was the best possible equipment. Thus Voltaire induced himself to believe that Catherine of Russia had not had her husband murdered, and that she had invaded Poland for the sake of securing religious liberty there—specimens of willed credulity nothing less than astonishing in an observer as intelligent and as cynical as he was. Yet, Voltaire's political writings abound in shrewd appraisals; the spectrum of his political ideas mirrors the spectrum of the political possibilities of his time, and the wide range of his ideas testifies not to irresponsibility or an inclination to abstract thinking, but, quite the contrary, to his clear-sightedness and his realism. As I shall show, in his own country he supported the monarchy against the claims of the aristocratic coalition concentrated in the *parlements*. In England, which he loved from his youth for being a country "where one obeys to the laws only and to

---

[6] "Impôt," in *The Encyclopédie*, 111.

one's whims,"[7] he welcomed the growing power of the House of
Commons because, he thought, it represented "the most numerous,
even the most virtuous, and consequently the most respectable
class of men, consisting of those who study the law and the sciences,
of businessmen, of artisans."[8] In the Dutch Republic, he spoke approvingly of parties, "necessary in a republic,"[9] and of the egalitarianism and simplicity of the ruling oligarchy. It was different with
Frederick of Prussia and Catherine of Russia: with both, self-interest
dulled his judgment; they had too much of what he wanted. He
thought it a good thing, as he himself admitted, to have a crowned
head up his sleeve, and he was reluctant to jeopardize his cozy arrangements with the King of Prussia and the Empress of all the
Russians—though, as his quarrel with Frederick shows, he was too
irrepressible, and he had, although he valiantly tried to deny it, too
much self-respect to be consistently servile.

While Voltaire's dealings with reigning monarchs are too self-
serving to make pleasant reading, his intervention in Genevan
politics offers a welcome contrast and, besides, a splendid example of
his political empiricism. Voltaire had settled on Genevan soil, at
Les Délices, in the winter of 1775–6, and his natural associates were
the patrician families that had, for a century or more, subverted the
republican constitution of the little state by engrossing all political
power in their hands through intermarriage, bribery, nepotism, and
threats of violence. These patricians were the French-educated elite
of Geneva who came to visit Voltaire and enjoyed his private theatrical parties despite the pious disapproval voiced by the Calvinist
pastorate. For some years, in fact, Voltaire's relations with this plu-
tocracy were excellent, but in the early 1760s, when a bourgeois
party around Rousseau demanded its constitutional right to participate in the political process, Voltaire moved to the left under the
pressure of his experience, and found himself, to his surprise, Rousseau's ally, although by then he thought Rousseau nothing better
than a treacherous madman. In 1765, after Rousseau himself had re-
tired from Genevan politics, Voltaire became the active spokesman
for his party and developed, almost incidentally, a general liberal

[7] April 11, 1728. *Correspondence*, II, 67, in English.
[8] Lettre IX, *Lettres philosophiques*, I, 101.
[9] See Voltaire to the marquis d'Argenson, August 8 (1743). *Correspondence*, XIII, 32–3.

position applicable to situations beyond Geneva itself. "To burn a rational book," he wrote, "is to say 'We do not have enough intelligence to reply to it.' . . . In a republic worthy of its name, the liberty to publish one's thoughts is the natural right of the citizen. . . . A criminal code is absolutely necessary for citizens and magistrates. . . . The magistrates are not the masters of the people; the laws are masters. . . . We have the right, when we are assembled, to reject or approve the magistrates and the laws that have been proposed to us. . . . Civil government is the will of all, carried out by a single person or by several, in accord with the laws that all have supported. . . . When a law is obscure, all must interpret it, for all have promulgated it. . . . It is to insult reason and law to pronounce these words: *civil and ecclesiastical government*. We must say, *civil government and ecclesiastical regulations*, and these regulations can only be made by the civil power. . . . It is perhaps useful to have two parties in a republic, because then one watches over the other."[1] There is not a word here in which advocates of despotism or absolutism could take comfort. These dicta, firm, clear, and consistent, contain the essence of modern liberalism: secular government, popular sovereignty, the rule of law, the need for free speech, and the advantage of party. While these principles are general in language, each sentence goes back to the Geneva of the 1760s and recalls a particular incident or a particular demand. It was prudent of Voltaire to clothe a partisan position in universal form; but his disguise adds up to a philosophy of politics.

The spectacle of Voltaire the political ally and political heir of Rousseau is odd enough, but by 1766, Voltaire had moved to the left of Rousseau, and taken a position that the great democrat had never even considered. Once again he was learning. In that year, to avert civil war, the Genevan oligarchs called in outside powers to mediate. At this point the political pariahs, the so-called Natives, gathered up their courage to address the mediators and ask for redress of their pressing grievances. The Natives made up three quarters of the population; most of them were third- and fourth-generation Genevans, respectable watchmakers and property owners, yet all of them were kept out of higher grades in the army and the liberal profes-

---

[1] *Idées républicaines*, in *Œuvres*, XXIV, 414-26, *passim*.

sions, hampered by burdensome and humiliating taxes and regulations, denied citizenship and thus deprived of the vote. Now Voltaire,
the flatterer of kings, the friend of aristocrats, the snobbish landed
gentleman, found it possible to assist the Natives' cause. He was
not, and would never become, a consistent democrat; his convictions were a lasting mood without becoming a doctrine. But he
discovered late in life that there were some among the *peuple*, more
in the city than in the country and more in Protestant than in Catholic lands, but *peuple* still, who had taste, knowledge, and judgment:
"But let us distinguish," he told Linguet in 1767, "in what you call
peuple, between the professions that demand a decent education and
those that call only for the labor of one's arms and daily fatigue."[2]
He could not have written this five years before: the Natives, well-
informed and responsible, had taught him much. Nothing came of
the protests of the Natives; the government harshly repressed them,
and Voltaire could do little more than give them refuge on his extensive property and rail against the oppressors. But the point is
that despite his advanced age—and by the time the Natives entered
Genevan politics, Voltaire was over seventy—his old habit of listening to the evidence had not atrophied. The politics of experience,
the counterpart of his relativism, never deserted him.

2. THE BATTLE FOR FRANCE

I

THE PHILOSOPHES' DEVOTION to empiricism did not guarantee
unanimity. In France, where the concentration of philosophes
was densest and the political struggle least concealed, the philosophes'
experience pointed in conflicting directions; the intellectual contest
among them faithfully mirrors the political contest for France in the
eighteenth century. The old saying that if two men see the same
thing they do not see the same thing applies to this contest with

---

[2] (March 15, 1767). *Correspondence*, LXV, 47. See also below,
chap. x, section 2.

special force: just as Diderot's and Voltaire's Frederick II appear to be two different kings, Montesquieu's and Voltaire's France appear to be two different countries, while Diderot's France changed its shape with bewildering rapidity, like a landscape in a dream.

The battle for France was rationalized and in many ways exacerbated by two competing positions which political and legal theorists had first seriously stated in the sixteenth century, the *thèse nobiliaire* and the *thèse royale*. The "noble thesis," upheld and in the course of the eighteenth century imaginatively elaborated by parliamentary and aristocratic publicists, amounted to the historical claim that the French kingdom had been a constitutional monarchy from its beginning, when the Franks had invaded Gaul. Royal assertions of a monopoly of legislative, judicial, and executive power were therefore usurpation; absolutism was tyranny. The separation of executive and judicial functions, as Montesquieu put it in a famous phrase, had "come from the German forests,"[3] and must be preserved at all costs. Some parliamentary ideologists went so far as to describe the *parlements* as the successors of the feudal lords who had made legislation in open and free assemblies. "It is a fundamental law," wrote the anonymous author of the tract *Judicium Francorum*, published in 1732, "that nothing can be imposed on the subjects of the king, and that no officer can be created, no new title can be granted, without the consent of parlement, which represents the general consent of the people. That is the essential form of the French government."[4] While nobles of the robe and nobles of the sword disagreed on much, while each inclined to exaggerate the importance and inflate the authority of their own ancestors, both accepted this version of the French past and this interpretation of its contemporary import.

It was a fanciful theory. It was bad history and bad law, a transparent defense of privilege in the guise of constitutional principles; it had wider application only because it came to be expressed in universal terms as the eighteenth century went on. At once self-serving and inaccurate, it deserved, and would have found, little sympathy

---

[3] *De l'esprit des lois*, book XXX, chap. xviii, in *Œuvres*, I, part 2, 327.
[4] Franklin L. Ford: *Robe and Sword: The Regrouping of the French Aristocracy after Louis XIV* (1953), 93.

among the philosophes except for its articulate advocacy on the part of Montesquieu.

Montesquieu was far more than an ideologist. His sympathy was comprehensive; as we know, it included slaves and Jews and victims of the courts quite as much as the courts themselves, and his sociological generalizations about the institutions that guarantee freedom applied to many political systems. Montesquieu, as his critics did not fail to point out, came from a robe family, had for some years been a judge, had long associated with robe nobles and enjoyed the company of spokesmen for the *thèse nobiliaire*, but his intelligence, his detachment, his catholic reading and extensive travels had enabled him to enlarge his ideas beyond the confined sphere of aristocratic ideology. Yet, though not confined, Montesquieu was pervasively indebted to the philosophy that dominated all segments of the French aristocracy; it was the distinction of his mind, the scholarly appearance of his work, and the philosophical tone of his theories that did much to rescue the *thèse nobiliaire* at mid-century. For when his *De l'esprit des lois* appeared in 1748, this aristocratic position had been severely damaged by historical and legal criticism, most effectively by the abbé Dubos. In 1734, fifteen years after he had published his bulky work on aesthetics,[5] Dubos published an even bulkier work, *Histoire critique de l'établissement de la monarchie Française*, which, for all its immense size was an immense success. Challenging the *thèse nobiliaire* in its most dubious position, its account of early history, Dubos argued that the Franks had come to Gaul as allies and followers of the Romans and had brought with them essentially Roman, not Germanic, institutions, including kingship. If there had been usurpation in French history, it was the work of feudal lords; the centuries-long attacks on the nobility by the crown had been defensive actions, designed to restore a legitimate and traditional order. As Dubos's public well knew, this historical argument had contemporary political bearing: it legitimized Louis XIV's silencing of the *parlements* and his insistence that their only task was the prosaic one of presiding over law suits, and it justified Louis XV's claim to a monopoly of legislative as well as executive authority.

Dubos's argument impressed the public because it was con-

---

[5] See above, 298-9.

tentious and exhaustive; it also happened to be largely sound. Montesquieu's "refutation," which came fourteen years later in his *De l'esprit des lois*, impressed the public even more because it was aphoristic and brilliantly evasive. Montesquieu covered his right flank, as it were, by criticizing Boulainvilliers's extreme feudal interpretation of early French history; then, under the cover of independence, he concentrated his fire on Dubos. "It is true," Franz Neumann has justly said, that Montesquieu "seemed to reject Boulainvilliers's views as a conspiracy against the third estate, and Dubos's as one against the nobility; but in reality, he followed Boulainvilliers closely. He thus identified himself with the reactionary trend of French politics, that trend which ultimately produced the French Revolution. No contemporary of Montesquieu was in doubt about Montesquieu's position and his effect upon the scene of French politics."[6] Montesquieu had learned much from Dubos, and he adroitly acknowledged his good qualities: "If that great man has erred, what must I not fear?"[7] But in two circumstantial though somewhat demagogic chapters, Montesquieu overcame his fear and demonstrated to his own satisfaction that Dubos had erred.

With all their political overtones, these historical excursions were in themselves interestingly and evidently relevant. But Montesquieu went beyond them; his whole theory of freedom stands as a long critique of Dubos and the *thèse royale*. Monarchies, Montesquieu holds, need "intermediate powers" for their well-being: "Intermediate, subordinate and dependent powers constitute the nature of monarchical government."[8] The "most natural" of these powers is the nobility as it enters "in some fashion" into the very "essence of monarchy"—whence the maxim, *"no monarch, no nobility; no nobility, no monarch."*[9] And *nobility* here included the nobility of the robe: the *parlements*. Other intermediate powers like the church,

[6] Franz L. Neumann: "Introduction" to Montesquieu: *Spirit of the Laws*, xxvii.
[7] *De l'esprit des lois*, book XXX, chap. xxv, in *Œuvres*, I, part 2, 358.
[8] Ibid., book II, chap. iv, in *Œuvres*, I, part 1, 20. In the manuscript the formulation is even stronger: "The intermediate powers constitute the nature of monarchical government, that is to say of that in which one single man governs by fundamental laws." Shackleton: *Montesquieu*, 279.
[9] *De l'esprit des lois*, book II, chap. iv, in *Œuvres*, I, part 1, 21.

or privileged bodies like the cities, also had their part to play in the protection of freedom, but Montesquieu never doubted that the nobility was the principal safeguard of the healthy monarchical state. It followed that monarchy is poisoned at its source when the monarch deprives the intermediate powers of their privilege—*there* is the road to despotism. With commendable consistency, Montesquieu saw much good in the well-entrenched French practice of treating public office as private property; the buying, selling, trading, and bequeathing of judgeships and most other official positions, which critics derided as "venality," struck him as a massive counterpoise against the concentration of power in royal hands. Actually, the trade in offices was a grave abuse; it led to the multiplication of offices, the installment of incompetents, and the dictatorship of the rich. Accordingly, proponents of the *thèse royale* were appalled at Montesquieu's defense of venality. But venality fitted smoothly into Montesquieu's logic: it was precisely because the holding of office was a large and valuable investment that it must lead to restrictions on the crown's range of action.[1]

Montesquieu's celebrated and influential interpretation of the British Constitution forms part of the same logical fabric. Power tends to corrupt; power undivided cannot escape this tendency, hence power divided is the only realistic protection freedom can call upon. In France, power was divided between the king and the owners of office; in Britain, power was divided among the executive, legislative, and judicial branches of government, above all the executive and legislative branches. The two systems, the French and the British, then, sought the same effect with similar methods; what made them all the more comparable was that British freedom, precisely like the French, had come out of the German forests.[2] To keep

---

[1] "The vested interests created by venality were enormous. They naturally sought protection for their investments. A strong monarchy must, of necessity, appear to them the greatest danger. Support for this investment could come only from groups and theories that made the king subject to effective controls by the privileged. A new theory of feudalism corresponded to the growing process of infeudation." Neumann: "Introduction" to Montesquieu: *Spirit of the Laws*, xxii.

[2] *De l'esprit des lois*, book XI, chap. vi, in *Œuvres*, I, part 1, 207–22 *passim*. See above, 466.

his own countrymen vigilant, Montesquieu acknowledged that Great Britain was actually superior to France in its constitutional arrangements: Britain, Montesquieu said flatly, is the one country in the world whose constitution directly aims at political liberty.[3]

From the day Montesquieu published his admiring, tendentious analysis of the British Constitution to our own time, critics have called attention to its obvious defects: Montesquieu had taken the partisan cant of the opposition to Walpole, especially of Bolingbroke, for political reality. In actuality, the executive met and mingled with the legislature in the House of Commons; the peers exercised judicial as well as legislative functions; and there were other mutual invasions of presumably reserved territory that compromised the neatness of Montesquieu's model. The fabric of freedom in England, such as it was, consisted less of formal devices than of slowly emerging habits and a dawning sense that Britain was secure enough, both against domestic and foreign enemies, to afford the luxury of a certain measure of dissent. Montesquieu did not see it that way. "The love of power is natural," he noted in 1730, during his English visit, characteristically borrowing the idea from Bolingbroke's *Craftsman*. "It is insatiable almost constantly whetted never cloyed by possession." Almost twenty years later, though long removed from the circle of Walpole's detractors, Montesquieu translated this observation into a famous maxim: "To prevent the abuse of power," he wrote in his *De l'esprit des lois*, it is necessary to "have power check power."[4] Stated this comprehensively, it is a tough-minded principle; it admirably faces the realities of political society. But Montesquieu's justified fear of power drew in its wake (or, shall I say, used as its fuel?) an unjustified claim to power on the part of privileged orders that received without giving, craved influence without responsibility, and denounced reforms as tyranny. Voltaire, whom Montesquieu little liked and only grudgingly respected, saw things more clearly. Just as Voltaire's England, with its increasing influence of the House of Commons, was closer to facts than Montesquieu's fanciful balancing act, so was Voltaire's France.

---

[3] Ibid., chap. v, in *Œuvres*, I, part 1, 207.
[4] Ibid., chap. iv, in *Œuvres*, 206; and Shackleton: *Montesquieu*, 300.

II

Through his long career as a political publicist, from the day he entered public controversy to his death over sixty years later, Voltaire was a loyal and outspoken partisan of the *thèse royale* in France. He recognized, and often reiterated, that Parliament and *parlement*, though the same word and indeed designating institutions with similar origins, were by no means the same thing: the instrument of freedom, reason, and middle-class participation in England was the instrument of repression, cant, and aristocratic privilege in France. "It is ridiculous to say," Voltaire noted about the *parlement* of Paris, "that it represents the nation. The very word 'parlement' makes up part of its power."[5] In France, therefore, Voltaire was convinced, "the cause of the king is the cause of the philosophes."[6]

This was a political judgment, aimed at the struggles of Voltaire's own time; it was also a judgment on French history. As early as 1723, three years before he first saw England, Voltaire advocated the *thèse royale* in *La ligue*, the first version of his epic poem celebrating Henri IV. In addition to staking Voltaire's claim to being the Vergil of France, in addition to being an appeal for toleration and a broadside against the clergy, *La ligue*, like its better-known final version, *Henriade*, is a spirited defense of royal sovereignty. Voltaire portrays Henri IV, the French king he most admired, as a reasonable political leader who brings a measure of toleration and stability to his country only because he has subdued the League, that insolent troop of superb feudal lords. This is the political message of Voltaire's epic: certainly in France the road to freedom and political sanity had always been the road leading away from "feudal anarchy" toward the unity of powers. Dubos's masterly *Histoire critique*, whose publication in 1734 coincided with the publication in France of Voltaire's book on England, offered copious historical justification for the ideas that Voltaire, the youthful royalist, had

---

[5] *Notebooks*, 94. See Voltaire's lucid comparative analysis of Parliament and *parlements* in his *Essai sur les mœurs*, I, 787.
[6] Voltaire to d'Alembert, October 16 (1765). *Correspondence*, LIX, 125.

held for over a decade: it gave Voltaire good reasons for arguing that what was true in the early eighteenth century under Louis XV and had been true at the turn of the seventeenth century under Henri IV had been true from the very inception of the French state. Voltaire warmly thanked Dubos for having "so ably disentangled the chaos"[7] of French origins, asked Dubos's assistance with the *Siècle de Louis XIV*, and continued his historical explorations in Dubos's spirit. His royalist convictions find ample room for play in his two historical masterpieces; in *Le siècle de Louis XIV* Voltaire examines a French reign whose end he had witnessed and whose shadow still hung over French politics decades after its close; in the *Essai sur les mœurs*, which takes a generous, world-wide sweep across history, he devotes ample space to the growth and travail of the French monarchy through the centuries.

The very title of Voltaire's earlier work is freighted with political significance: the second half of the seventeenth century and the first decades of the eighteenth are the *age of Louis XIV;* it was a French king who had put his stamp on a century. Yet, though precise and meaningful, this title also has its less felicitous side; it seems to imply, and has often been taken to be, a panegyric on the Sun King. In fact, despite its reputation, *Le siècle de Louis XIV* is often extremely critical of its illustrious protagonist; the age was the age of Louis XIV for ill quite as much as for good. Voltaire's Louis XIV is in love with war, so enamored of glory, territory, revenge that he conducts inhuman campaigns, neglects the poor at home, and forgets that a good king must above all bring peace. Worse than this, in addition to his fatal love of glory, Louis XIV is cursed, especially in his later years, by a sinister piety which leads him to countenance, and even instigate, acts of shocking intolerance against religious minorities. One could hardly expect Voltaire, as a self-proclaimed champion of tolerance, to find excuses for a king who revoked the Edict of Nantes, especially since this edict of toleration bore the imprint of that greatest of French kings, Henri IV. For Voltaire, Louis XIV stands condemned as a monarch who missed some of his greatest opportunities: he failed to do all the good it had been in his power to do.

Granting all this, Voltaire had no doubt that Louis XIV was also

---

[7] Voltaire to Dubos, October 30, 1738. Ibid., VII, 424–7.

a great king. It was in his reign, and with his active participation, that France became the cultural center of the Western world. This, for Voltaire, the conscious heir of Corneille and Racine, weighed heavily in the balance of judgment. But his most unreserved praise for Louis XIV often comes indirectly, through comparisons with his domestic rivals. The glory of Louis shines at its brightest against the gloomy background of seditious nobles, obstructive judges, and bigoted clerics. If the King failed to do all the good in his power, his adversaries did all the harm in theirs. They instigated civil war; they failed to criticize, let alone correct, the viciously inequitable tax structure that worked in their favor; they were blind to starvation, resisted progress in science and administration, and generally turned their faces toward the past. They supported the crown only when it legislated intolerance; Voltaire found it incomprehensible that anyone should regard the magistrates as the fathers of the country or as bulwarks of freedom. It was a puzzle that would agitate liberal reformers and hard-working public servants like Turgot throughout the eighteenth century.

The history of France could not be reduced to a single issue, but the one thread running through it all was the fortunes of royal power. "France a poor thing up to Louis XIV," Voltaire laconically said in one of his notebooks. "Kings without power before Louis XI. Charles VIII and Louis XII unlucky conquerors. Francis I beaten, civil wars up to Henri IV, under Louis XIII feebleness and faction."[8] In its chapters on France, the *Essai sur les mœurs* traced this often pathetic history down to Louis XIII; in some later, more overtly polemical historical essays, Voltaire would bring it up to date, to feebleness and faction under Louis XV.

The *Essai sur les mœurs*, as I have said before, is far more than a tendentious tract; it is pioneering social history, generous in scope and remarkably catholic in judgment. Nor are its chapters on France mere propaganda: Voltaire finds the justification of the *thèse royale* in the events themselves; the thesis is more than an ideology: it is a historical judgment. Yet Voltaire never denied his passionate involvement in the political controversies of his own time, and it would have been pointless to deny it, for it emerges in his sarcastic treatment of the antiroyalist forces. When in the 1470s Louis XI humbles the

---

[8] *Notebooks*, 110.

nobility, "about fifty families" deplore his policy, but "more than five hundred thousand had cause to celebrate."[9] It had been that way before and would be that way after Louis XI: the interest of the French people lay in the assertion of royal power.

In the early 1750s, when Voltaire's two great histories appeared, he was no longer in France; in the nearly thirty years that remained to him, he observed the vicissitudes of the royal cause from Potsdam, Geneva, and Ferney. During the previous decade, Voltaire had wasted much time at the French Court, pursuing his career with a thick-skinned singlemindedness that dismayed some of his warmest admirers. But if he had fantasies of shaping the policies of Louis XV, his writings, both published and unpublished, give no evidence of it: he traveled with the royal entourage, wrote slight comedies, composed mediocre poems, and turned servile compliments to further not the cause of France but his own. He had his rewards: in 1745 he was appointed Royal Historiographer; in the following year he finally won his seat in the *Académie française*, which he had coveted for over a decade. In some of his moments of lucidity and self-awareness, he complained that he was acting the part of a poor buffoon,[1] and his writings of those years show traces of restlessness, disappointment, and occasional self-disgust. Zadig, the reasonable man in an unreasonable society, is Voltaire: hard-working, public-spirited, utterly vulnerable to the capricious favor of the powerful: "Zadig said, 'At last, then, I am happy!' But he was deceived."[2]

Zadig was written in 1748. In the following year, Machault d'Arnouville, the *contrôleur général des finances*, imposed his five-per cent income tax, the *vingtième*, on all orders. It was a brave attack on privilege in a country built on privilege: money was, of

---

[9] *Essai sur les mœurs*, II, 8. Anyone who thinks that Voltaire was an indiscriminate supporter of strong kings should read his pages on Louis XI in the *Essai;* they show Voltaire to be a most discriminating historian.

[1] "Don't scold a poor devil who is the buffoon of the king at fifty, and who is more burdened with musicians, decorators, actors, actresses, singers, dancers, than are the eight or nine German electors to make themselves a German Caesar. I run from Paris to Versailles, I write verses in post chaises. I must praise the king loudly, madame la dauphine discreetly, the royal family very delicately; I must satisfy the court and not displease the town." Voltaire to Cideville, January 31, 1745. *Correspondence*, XIV, 103.

[2] *Zadig*, in *Œuvres*, XXI, 45.

course, the perennial problem of the French monarchy, and the two first estates almost entirely escaped any fiscal obligations whatever— the nobility paid few taxes, and the first estate, the church, immensely rich, clung to its traditional right of granting the state a "voluntary gift" assessed at its quinquennial assemblies, a substantial sum but a pittance still. The *vingtième* was a tax that Voltaire wholeheartedly approved of, and he entered the controversy at the very start. Two weeks after Machault had issued the decree, Voltaire sent him a long memorandum expressing his support both on the general principle that tax burdens should be equal and on the concrete economic consideration that France could afford the tax and should pay for the costs of war in times of peace. Resistance to the impost varied: the *parlements* accepted it with surprising meekness, and after courteous remonstrances, registered the tax decree. The clergy, on the other hand, put up a spirited fight; it was defending both the principle of voluntary self-taxation and its wealth: the *vingtième* would roughly have doubled its contribution to the treasury. Bishops protested and in early 1750, the Assembly of the Clergy reiterated its traditional position: the church is not of this world, and its property, which is the property of the poor, must not be touched by profane hands—a love offering must not be degraded into a forced tribute.

These pious arguments both amused and enraged Voltaire, and he replied with some witty fables and an aggressive pamphlet, *La voix du sage et du peuple*, probably Voltaire's first political polemic. In one of these fables, Voltaire has an Indian philosopher visiting Turkey; there he sees "about twenty beautiful two-footed animals" pass by, evidently priests. He asks a Turkish palace guard just how many of these "well-made big fellows" there are in Turkey. "Nearly a hundred thousand of different kinds," the Turk replies. They would be fine workers, the Indian muses: "How I would like to see them, spade, trowel, square rule in hand!" The Turk agrees but adds: "They are too great saints to work." What, then, do they do? the Indian asks. "The sing, they drink, they digest," the Turk replies. "How useful to the state!" says the Indian.[3] In another invention Voltaire imagines a decree from the Papal Inquisition in the proper pompous language of officialdom: "Antichrist has already come;

---

[3] *Des embellissements de la ville de Cachemire*, in ibid., XXIII, 478.

said Antichrist already has sent several circular letters to the bishops of France, in which he has had the audacity to treat them as Frenchmen and subjects of the king," and tried to prove that "the clergy form part of the body politic, instead of affirming that they are essentially its masters." Never averse to a little hyperbole, Voltaire has the Inquisition continue: Antichrist suggests "that those who have a third of the revenue in the state owe at least a third in contributions; he seems to forget that our brethren are made to have everything and to give nothing."[4]

La voix du sage et du peuple translates these playful pinpricks into serious political discourse. The broadside draws upon the thèse royale in all its guises: it calls upon French history, the logic of political theory, and the practical demands of the day in about equal degree. "There ought not to be two powers in the state" is a maxim, Voltaire writes, propounded by sound political thinking and confirmed by history: "The happy years of the monarchy were the last years of Henri IV, the years of Louis XIV and Louis XV, when these kings governed by themselves." As ready to pose as a good Christian as he was to oversimplify French history, Voltaire argued that the clergy deserved respect, but not authority; unfortunately the French church has abused "the distinction between spiritual power and temporal power." Precisely like any other public body, the church in France must subordinate itself to the sovereign: "The prince must be absolute master of all ecclesiastical regulations, without any restriction, since those ecclesiastical regulations are a part of the government; and just as the father of a family prescribes to the preceptor of his children the hours of work, the kind of studies, etc., so the prince may prescribe to all ecclesiastics, without exception, all that has the least bearing on the public order." This meant, in 1750, that the clergy must "contribute to the expenditures of the state in proportion to its revenues."[5]

Voltaire got little thanks for writing La voix du sage; its political effect apparently was negligible. In 1750 Louis XV reaffirmed his tax edict, but in 1751 he withdrew it, overborne by his timidity, his indolence, and his fear of damnation. As Voltaire pathetically wrote

---

[4] Extrait du décret de la sacrée congrégation de l'Inquisition de Rome, à l'encontre d'un libelle intitulé 'Lettres sur le vingtième,' ibid., 463.
[5] La voix du sage et du peuple, ibid., 466–71.

in August 1750, from Potsdam: he had tried "to sustain the rights of the king. But the king hardly cares to have his rights sustained."[6] As other royalists would discover over and over again, this was only a slight exaggeration, but Voltaire could not abandon his feeble and inconstant ally; the king might be a small hope, but he was also, as far as Voltaire could see, the only hope for France.

Voltaire's specific application of the *thèse royale* to the recalcitrant clergy in 1750 suggests its pragmatic, and in a sense, defensive, role in his political thought. During the 1750s and 1760s, in isolated pamphlets and in the *Dictionnaire philosophique*, Voltaire applied it wherever it seemed applicable: to the combat between Jesuits and their post-Jansenist enemies in the early 1760s, to the conflict between provincial estates and the crown a few years later. It was not until the mid-sixties that he could apply it once again to the central target of his scorn, the *parlements*. In 1766, after two years of watching an obstructive alliance of provincial *parlements* and estates paralyze royal administration in Brittany, Louis XV had another access of courage: on March 3, 1766, he confronted the *parlement* of Paris and read it a stern lecture that has become known to history, a little melodramatically, as the *séance de flagellation:* "Sovereign power," the king said, restating the *thèse royale* with all the vigor at his speech-writer's command, "resides in my person alone," and "Legislative power belongs to me alone," and "My courts derive their authority from me alone." Voltaire responded to this lecture with unabashed euphoria: "It's been a long time," he wrote to a Paris correspondent, "since I have read anything so wise, so noble, and so well written."[7]

This time the king held firm: in 1768 he elevated René-Nicolas de Maupeou, an ambitious, hard-working, abrasive official and ruthless adversary of the *parlements*, to the chancellorship, and Maupeou developed a program for reducing the magistrates to obedience. As with Machault nearly two decades before, so now again Voltaire plunged into the battle without hesitation. He did not need to generate any new ideas: his interpretation of French politics served him in the late 1760s as it had in the early 1720s. The king was still in the

---

[6] Voltaire to the duc de Richelieu (*c.* August 31, 1750). *Correspondence*, XVIII, 144.
[7] Voltaire to Damilaville, March 12 (1766). Ibid., LX, 152.

right. So was his minister, even though Maupeou detested the philosophes and tried, though without success, to stifle free expression in France: in moments of crisis, Voltaire chose allies not on the basis of affection or congeniality, but of utility.

In the spring of 1769, Voltaire delivered his support for the *thèse royale* by placing his talent for history into the service of politics: his *Histoire du Parlement de Paris*, though filled with accurate facts and often quite objective, is wholly partisan in intent. Lying or distortion would not have served Voltaire's cause: there were too many alert lawyers and historians about for that. Hence he wrote of the *parlement* soberly, with few overt allusions to current controversy, and with generous paragraphs on its occasional good sense. The truth, especially with Voltaire's irony playing over the whole spectacle, was damaging enough. And that truth, as every intelligent reader could piece together for himself, buttressed Maupeou's enterprise. Clearly, the *parlement* was not now, as it had rarely been, in a position to make sound policy; in 1768, as before, it was reactionary, selfish, divisive, irresponsible, superstitious, and intolerant. Voltaire amply documented each of these adjectives. Had it not obstructed the establishment of the *Académie française* and the distribution of the *Encyclopédie?* Had it not served the interests of a small minority with the affecting rhetoric of popular rights? Had it not instigated religious, civil, and class war through the centuries? Had it not capriciously tried the dauphin Charles in 1420 without a shred of legal authority? Had it not condemned the first printers in France and applauded the massacre of Saint Bartholomew? And had it not, over and over, harassed men of letters, persecuted Huguenots, and victimized the innocent? Moreover, the *parlement* had acquired no new rights at any time: its task was to try court cases, not royal ministers; its foundation was separate from that of the other *parlements*, hence all attempts to establish a union of *parlements* so as to better resist the crown were temerarious and illegal. Finally, its right to act as a depositary of the laws was now, as always, a purely administrative act rather than an authorization to participate in the making of the laws. Voltaire's conclusion was inescapable: in the present crisis, the *parlements* could do only one thing—obey.

Oddly enough, at least one philosophe, Diderot, thought that Voltaire had handled the *parlement* rather too gently. Unlike Montesquieu and Voltaire, Diderot had come to politics almost reluctantly, drawn into the arena mainly by intense likes and dislikes, an editor's troubles with censors, and humane impulses. As a young writer, in 1747, he had complained mildly about the prohibitions that impeded authors from touching upon religion and politics—but this was an evident response to the banning of his own philosophical debut, the *Pensées philosophiques*, in the previous year. But during the early 1750s, in the midst of noisy, prolonged disputes over Machault's tax program, Diderot had very little to say, unless his article "Autorité politique" may be taken as an oblique comment on them.[8] But if it is one, that comment is ambiguous; it mixes some audacious remarks on the necessary limits on power with a call for obedience. Just which of the parties these generalities were designed to support remains obscure.

"Autorité politique" appeared in 1751, in the first volume of the *Encyclopédie*. Later in the decade, and in the 1760s, Diderot occasionally spoke about politics, mostly in theoretical terms which, unlike Voltaire's, had little relevance to France. The great events that moved Europe in those years, like the Seven Years' War, did not move him—at least not visibly. Diderot was a humanitarian and a libertarian, and his observations on authoritarian regimes abroad mark a deepening of his political awareness. But in France his ambiguities remained unresolved. His brief flirtation with the Physiocrats in the late 1760s demonstrates his uncertainty over political methods; for two or three years he embraced enthusiastically what he was to repudiate with equal enthusiasm after Galiani and other critics had shown him the error of the Physiocrats' ways.

Diderot's response to the *parlements* demonstrates his uncertainty, if anything, even better. In June 1769, Diderot correctly identified Voltaire as the author of the pseudonymous *Histoire du parlement de Paris*, and warmly praised its style, its organization, its assembly of information, and its logic: "Voltaire clearly proves," he thought, that the *parlements* are "merely simple salaried courts of law whose supposed privileges are only a sort of usurpation founded on fortuitous, sometimes quite frivolous circumstances." But

---

[8] As Professor Arthur M. Wilson has pointed out, it may of course be true that Diderot did comment on political questions in some of the numerous letters of the period that obviously have been lost.

then, surprisingly enough, Diderot complains that Voltaire had treated the subject rather too superficially. Taking the line that Voltaire had followed all his life and using some of Voltaire's very words, Diderot now argues that had Voltaire been more thorough he would have been even more critical of the magistrates than he was in this book. Had he gone back all the way to the origins of the *parlement* of Paris, he would have shown the *parlement* displaying *esprit de corps* at its worst. "We would have seen that body having itself exiled, refusing to deal out justice to the people, and bringing about anarchy when its chimerical rights were involved but never when it was a question of defending the people. We would have seen its intolerant, bigoted, stupid, preserving its gothic and vandal privileges and proscribing good sense. We would have seen it burning to meddle in everything: religion, government, war, finance, the arts and sciences, and mixing up everything with its ignorance, its self-interest, and its prejudices. We would have seen it too bold under feeble kings, too feeble under firm kings. We would have seen it further behind the times, less in touch with intellectual progress than the monks locked in the cells of Chartreux." Moreover, "we would have seen it sold to authority; most of its members pensioned by the court, and the most violent enemy of all liberty, be it civil or religious," and so on, through a whole catalogue of misdeeds. For the Diderot of this letter, no criticism seemed strong enough: pretending to reform the laws, the magistrates had left the laws in chaos; sworn to uphold justice, they had only pursued privileges and wealth at any price; perhaps worst of all, they had been the eager servants of "sacerdotal fury": at the instance of fanatical priests, they had "lit the stakes and prepared the instruments of torture."[9]

One should have thought that no fate, surely not dismissal, would be too harsh for such entrenched, deliberate, habitual criminals. Voltaire certainly thought so. When in the midst of winter in 1770–1 Maupeou exiled the magistrates to their estates in the country and replaced them by new courts, Voltaire approved. "You seem to be afraid," Voltaire warned the *parlements*, "that tyranny might some day take the place of reasonable power. But let us be even more afraid of anarchy, which is only a tumultuous tyranny." Seeking to

---

[9] Diderot to Grimm (June 1769). *Correspondance*, IX, 64–5.

stem the popular tide of sympathy for the magistrates, Voltaire harangued his readers, once again, on the limits of parliamentary authority: they are, or rather ought to be, "respectable organs of the laws, created to follow and not to make them."[1] This view was perfectly consistent with Voltaire's lifelong position, and with Diderot's critique of the *parlements,* but suddenly Diderot found much to admire in the magistrates. "Surely," says Rameau's nephew, speaking this once for his creator, "surely you would never have written *Mahomet,* but then, you wouldn't have written the panegyric on Maupeou either."[2] It was logical and understandable for a philosophe to detest both the *parlements* and the chancellor: both were open enemies of the new ideas and equally intent on hobbling, if not crushing, their advocates. But Diderot's position, far from being subtle, was simply inconsistent. By early 1771 he regarded the royal policy on the *parlements* as an attack on liberty: the magistrates, those enemies of reason, humanity, and freedom had somehow been transformed in his mind into their greatest champions. His much-quoted remark, "Every century has its spirit that characterizes it; the spirit of our century seems to be that of liberty,"[3] is part of a long letter in which he excoriates Maupeou's destruction of the *parlements.* He notes that Maupeou's action had aroused widespread emotion "among all the orders of the state"; princes, tribunals, nobles are showering remonstrances on the king. Men grow heated, and he approved of this emotion: "This fire is spreading by degrees; the principles of freedom and independence, hitherto hidden in the hearts of a few thinking men, are at present establishing themselves, and are openly professed."[4]

This, of course, was true enough; one of the unintended consequences of Maupeou's *coup d'état* was the efflorescence of libertarian rhetoric. But Diderot did not see this bold talk as a fortunate accident; he thought it appropriate to the occasion and the *parlements* as objects worthy of his solicitude. "We are at the point of a crisis that will end in slavery or freedom; if it is to be slavery, it will be a

---

[1] *L'Équivoque,* in *Œuvres,* XXVIII, 424; *Les peuples aux parlements,* ibid., 413.
[2] *Le neveu de Rameau,* 15.
[3] Diderot to Princess Dashkoff (April 3, 1771). *Correspondance,* XI, 20.
[4] Ibid., 19.

slavery similar to that now existing in Marocco or Constantinople. If all the parlements are dissolved and France is inundated with little .tribunals composed of magistrates without conscience and without authority, and subject to dismissal at the first sign of their master, then farewell to all the privileges of diverse estates which form a corrective principle preventing monarchy from degenerating into despotism."[5] Diderot had displayed great admiration for Montesquieu, an admiration that seems to have waned with the years. In fact, not long after he had written the letter I have just quoted, he told Catherine of Russia that he simply could not understand Montesquieu's affection for feudalism: what is good about the feudal form of government, he said, can be summed up in ten pages, while its defects would take up a thousand.[6] Yet here in 1771, the advocate of the open society, the radical, the near-democrat Diderot sounded like one of Montesquieu's most loyal disciples.

In the light of events, of course, it is possible to argue that Diderot's new-found *thèse nobiliaire* was hardly more irrelevant to France than Voltaire's consistent advocacy of the *thèse royale* was to become. It is true that the battle of the early 1770s, though exhilarating and for some years promising, was in its denouement, pathetic. "I shall never change," Louis XV proclaimed, and for the last four years of his life he remained true to his word; the new courts did their work, if not without scandal, at least with some effectiveness. Then, in 1774, Louis XV died, and Louis XVI dismissed Maupeou and recalled the *parlements*. But the young king also gave power to Turgot, a public servant who seemed to embody the *thèse royale* at its best. Like others, the aged Voltaire took new hope at the appointment; if ever reform from the top had a chance in his country, it was now. But then in May 1776 Louis XVI dismissed Turgot, and Voltaire, now within two years of his death, collapsed as the *thèse royale* collapsed around him. As late as September 1776 he lamented to Condorcet: "Since that fatal day, I have not followed anything, I have asked nobody for anything, and I am waiting patiently for someone to cut our throats."[7] It was cold comfort to the old man that Montesquieu's position had always been bad history

---

[5] Ibid., 20.
[6] *Diderot et Catherine* II, ed. Tourneux (1899), 105.
[7] September 7, 1776. *Correspondence*, XCV, 46.

and bad politics, and that Diderot's divagations were a sign of confusion rather than subtlety: his own position, good history always and good politics for decades, had now become simply pointless. In a revolutionary situation, it seemed, empiricism was not enough.

3. ENLIGHTENED ABSOLUTISM:
FROM SOLUTION TO PROBLEM

I

FOR A PHILOSOPHE to support the king in France was a natural thing to do; it raised neither logical nor moral difficulties. For a philosophe to support other kings further east might seem just as natural, but in fact it raised difficulties both logical and moral. These central European rulers were powerful and ambiguous figures. Far more visibly than Louis XV, they embodied the possibilities and the problems of enlightened absolutism; Frederick II of Prussia in particular engaged the imagination of his time and stirred up questions about the political philosophy of the Enlightenment. Frederick was a philosopher and a king: if anyone might fill the role of modern philosopher-king with éclat, it was he. D'Alembert was only one among the little flock to call him *roi philosophe;* from his youth, Frederick had appeared to the philosophes as the fulfillment of a cherished wish.

It was in 1736, while he was still crown prince, that Frederick had begun a correspondence with Voltaire, and as Voltaire never failed to tell his friends, it was significant that it was Frederick who had taken the initiative. In his long and uncomfortable intercourse with the Prussian king, Voltaire, always ready with a pleasing comparison, found many synonyms calculated to please; as one patient scholar[8] has discovered, Voltaire likened Frederick to Caesar, Augustus, Marcus Aurelius, Trajan, Antoninus Pius, Titus, Julian,

---

[8] Adrienne D. Hytier. See her "Frédéric II et les philosophes récalcitrants," *The Romanic Review,* LVII, 3 (October 1966), 161.

Vergil, Pliny, Horace, Maecenas, Cicero, Catullus, Homer, La Rochefoucauld, La Bruyère, Boileau, Solomon, Prometheus, Apollo, Patroclus, Socrates, Alcibiades, Alexander, Henri IV and Francis I— a rather miscellaneous but shrewdly conceived list. Yet, however grossly Voltaire would later shower his facile adulation on his royal admirer, their peculiar friendship began with the prince adulating the poet. In his malicious *Mémoires*, Voltaire acknowledges that he had found the King attractive both for his private and his public virtues: "He had wit and charm and," Voltaire added candidly, "what is more, he was king, which, given human weakness, is always a great seduction." But this seduction had been reinforced by Frederick's eagerness to court a mere writer: "Ordinarily, we men of letters flatter kings; this one praised me from head to toe."[9] Then, in 1740, when Frederick ascended the throne, he rapidly took a series of actions that further ingratiated him with philosophes other than the uniquely privileged Voltaire. As king, Frederick restored the Berlin Academy and practically handed it over to French savants; he proclaimed freedom of conscience and proved his good intentions by recalling the philosopher Christian Wolff from the exile that his father, Frederick William I, had imposed on him; he sent his architect Knobelsdorff abroad to gather experience; took an active, comprehensive, salutary interest in the economic affairs of the state; and, as I have said, reduced the savagery of punishments. Prussia under Frederick II seemed on the verge of a cultural, political, legal, and economic renaissance, destined to become, in Voltaire's hyperbole, the Athens of the North. That the philosophes should have high expectations of such a king requires no explanation; idealization was a response to palpable realities: to compare Frederick with that bullying, coarse, single-minded drill sergeant, his father, or with that interesting but ultimately disappointing lot, his contemporaries, made admiration and hope plausible attitudes rather than a delusion or the consequence of principled devotion to the doctrines of enlightened absolutism.

The philosophes discovered soon enough that the Athens of the North was only a frigid Sparta after all; the philosopher-king was more the militarist king than the pacific philosopher. Frederick's

---

[9] *Mémoires*, in *Œuvres*, I, 17.

cynical invasion of Silesia, his patent unreliability as an ally, his reimposition of censorship, his shabby and, whatever the provocations, brutal treatment of Voltaire after their friendship began to pall in 1752, his disheartening failure to overhaul the laws and humanize the army, his low estimate of man (which even Voltaire found troublesome), and his principled refusal to take the philosophes' advice on anything besides his verses—all this decisively outweighed his ostentatious affection for French men of letters, his irreligiosity, and his diligence. Voltaire's visits to Prussia culminating in that disastrous stay of 1750–3 and d'Alembert's suave letters to Frederick are in the long run less significant than the philosophes' reserve, their refusal of pressing invitations, and their outright hostility.

Some of the philosophes' most weighty reservations were, to be sure, nonpolitical: they did not want to settle in Prussia because they were happy in France or calculated that, even though occasionally persecuted, they would be happier in Paris than in Potsdam. They did not want to leave their mistresses, especially for a court that had no women. They disliked the raw Prussian climate and the crude provinciality of Berlin society. They were dissatisfied with the skimpy terms that Frederick had to offer them. But personal reasons shaded into political ones. The philosophes simply liked their freedom too well. That is why Voltaire allowed his relations with Frederick to deteriorate at the very time that his return to Paris was cut off. That is why d'Alembert, a foundling, a bastard, a commoner, a man with no means, would give the King of Prussia nothing more than soothing letters and a visit of three months.

The philosophes' preference for freedom to this kind of servitude is in itself a commentary on their political thought, but beyond that, it was a commentary on Frederick's conduct. Rousseau spoke for the philosophes in 1758 when he called himself an "admirer of the talents of the King of Prussia, but in no way his partisan"—a meaningful distinction. "I can neither esteem nor love a man without principles, who tramples on all international law, who does not love virtue, but who considers it as a bait with which to amuse fools, and who began his Machiavellianism by refuting Machiavelli."[1]

---

[1] Quoted in Hytier: "Frédéric II et les philosophes récalcitrants," 176.

With the passage of time the philosophes' distrust grew stronger, but it was not until the 1770s that Diderot gave final expression to them. As a self-respecting man of letters and a good bourgeois, Diderot rightly judged that he would never be happy at court. His odd friendship with Catherine II in no way contradicts this sense of himself: his kindly feelings for her were compounded of gratitude for her delicate generosity, susceptibility to her personal charm, and inadequate information about Russia, and punctuated in any event by candid criticisms of all the aspects of her regime he understood. Diderot kept himself rigorously independent of Frederick: he refused to visit Potsdam even when it would have been convenient for him to do so; he refused to lavish praises on the Prussian king in his published writings, the kind of coy, indirect message that the philosophes generally liked to send because monarchs generally liked to receive them. He never even wrote to Frederick; his only "letter" was a cold little essay of 1771 which, far more than a personal message, goes quite directly to the critical problems of political thought in the Enlightenment.

Diderot's *Lettre* to Frederick is the tailpiece of a debate, a rejoinder to a reply.[2] Early in 1770 there appeared an anonymous treatise, *Essai sur les préjugés*, a highly characteristic product of the Holbachian factory: it denounced with all the customary vehemence, all the customary dogmatism, the vices of the priesthood and the absurdity of Christian belief. But the unknown author also ventured into politics, a field that Holbach and his friends had so far left untouched. As doctrinaire here as in its assaults on religion, the *Essai* denounced absolute princes as "despots," and characterized despots as the scourges of their country, the victims of poisonous flatterers, war-loving criminals, and oppressive impostors who mislead the world with their dubious academies that are in reality nothing better than slave societies. Frederick read the treatise with unfeigned disgust soon after it appeared, and correctly applied its heavy-handed sarcasms to himself. What troubled him most was the largely implicit but fundamental thesis of the *Essai* that man is made for the

---

[2] The manuscript is dated 1771, and entitled *Lettre de M. Denis Diderot sur l'examen de l'Essai sur les préjugés*. It has become better known by the title that Franco Venturi gave it in 1937: *Pages inédites contre un tyran*. See Diderot: *Œuvres politiques*, 129–33. And see below, chap. x, section 1.

truth, and should be told the truth; cynical and self-protective, Frederick in his refutation squarely took the opposite position: "Man is made for error"; lies to the people, in political and religious matters, are essential to sound government.[3]

Diderot entered the discussion at this critical point, spurred on by his passion for truth and aversion for the Prussian king. He had probably read the *Essai* in draft and discussed it with Holbach; it is significant that Voltaire, normally well-informed in such matters, thought that Diderot might actually have written it.[4] In fact, Diderot's own effort was more economical, less turgid, and if possible even more aggressive: The world may be full of errors, but that is the fault not of man but of "the villainous preachers of lies" who crowd the world; man is born for truth, needs the truth, flourishes on the truth. Like the other sociologists in the Enlightenment, Diderot was happily free from the illusion that men do the good once they know it: powerful lying villains "deliver to their dupes eulogies to the truth." There are so many enemies of truth and goodness in the world! so many corrupt laws! so many bad governments! so many men whose interest lies in evil![5]

"So many" meant "one"—Frederick of Prussia, whom servile men had already begun to call "The Great." Unfortunately, Diderot's letter never reached the address for which it was intended; it was not published until the 1930s, when a far more vicious regime than Frederick's held power in Germany. It seems a pity: one wonders how much Stoicism the King of Prussia could have mustered in the face of Diderot's characterization of him as a mediocre thinker, poor poet, disappointing king, in a word, bad sovereign. The royal author had written in the transparent disguise of a philosopher. "May God preserve us," Diderot piously concludes his riposte, "from a sovereign who resembles that kind of philosopher."[6] Frederick, obviously enough, was too much the despot and not enlightened enough to deserve more than the most perfunctory and the most self-interested support from the philosophes.

---

[3] See Diderot: *Œuvres politiques*, 138–9 *n*.
[4] See ibid., 131. Voltaire's other candidates were Damilaville or Helvétius.
[5] Ibid., 136.
[6] Ibid., 148.

II

Sheer passion, no matter how well intentioned or fiercely phrased, could not dispose of absolutism; it was and remained the most prominent political system for theorists and practitioners of government alike. I have already commented on the history of eighteenth-century states: with the partial exception of Great Britain and the Dutch Republic and the ludicrous exception of Poland, the tide was running toward absolutism, and absolutism was in decisive ways more modern, more efficient, and to the surprise of some philosophes, more "enlightened" than the older political systems it was attacking. Absolutism was aggressive in part because it felt itself on the defensive; rather than calling the eighteenth century the century of the rising bourgeoisie, we might call it the century of the rising aristocracy. In Poland the nobility was wholly, in Russia largely, in France fatally, triumphant, and everywhere monarchs did battle with recalcitrant privileged orders, or struck uneasy alliances with them. Where representative forms were not dead or moribund, they were reactionary, and in these countries reformers found their choice restricted to an authoritarianism that took pride in its modernity and a traditionalism that took pains to reject modernity.

In the German states—Prussia, the smaller southern regimes, and the Hapsburg Empire—this limited choice was at its most clear-cut. There, specialists in the science of government, the Cameralists, found their proper place in administration. They pressed for efficient bureaucracies, intrigued against obstructive aristocrats, and drafted reforms for the benefit, but without the participation, of the masses. Christian Wolff in Halle, Joseph von Sonnenfels in Vienna, J. H. G. von Justi in Vienna and Göttingen, are only the three best known among a tribe of authoritarian rationalists whose ideas and ideals all seem cast from the same mold or copied from one another. Their aims were ambitious, though, and from their point of view, realistic: they sought to produce and increase happiness by reasonable enactments. Their political theory constitutes an escape from politics into management, the tactful evasion of a challenge to real power that would have been hopeless.[7] Without a historical, social, or educational basis for liberalism, liberalism seemed to them Utopia, paternalism the only way to general betterment.

As the Cameralists understood it, the prerequisite for successful paternalism is a correct grasp of human motives that the legislator then translates into administrative action. Sonnenfels and the others were eager to subordinate pity or other commendable emotions to sober calculation, in the service of the benevolent manipulation of the people. "A properly constituted state," wrote Justi in a characteristic passage, "must be exactly analogous to a machine in which all the wheels and gears are precisely adjusted to one another; and the ruler must be the foreman, the mainspring, or the soul—if one may use the expression—which sets everything in motion."[8] Sonnenfels's metaphors were, if anything, even more picturesque: "We perceive society," he wrote, "we perceive ourselves as part of it in the sovereign, in this permanent oracle of general intelligence—of which he is the symbol, the mirror, the awe-commanding image."[9] The word *Polizei*, like the word *police*, had a generous meaning in the eighteenth century: it meant the rational superintendence of domestic affairs, and for the Cameralists, political theory was exhausted in the work of *Polizei*. It seemed self-evident to these writers that the single purpose of government is to diffuse happiness. But their definition of happiness did not include the freedom of the subject; the subject had other, well-defined duties. As the ruler must make his people happy, the subject must, by God, obey and *be* happy: "All the duties of people and subjects," wrote Justi, "may be reduced to the formula: to promote all the ways and means adopted by the ruler for their happiness, by their obedience, fidelity and diligence."[1] The Cameralists were very fond of formulas; Rous-

---

[7] "Rationalist politics, like any politics orientated towards the achievement of a single end or even of a few closely linked ends, rather than towards the harmonization of a wide variety of ends, tends inevitably to lose its political character and become a matter of implementation and administration." Geraint Parry: "Enlightened Government and its Critics in Eighteenth-Century Germany," *The Historical Journal*, VI, 2 (1963), 182.
[8] Quoted in ibid.
[9] Quoted in Robert A. Kann: *A Study in Austrian Intellectual History: From Late Baroque to Romanticism* (1960), 170.
[1] Quoted in Leo Gershoy: *From Despotism to Revolution, 1763–1789* (1944), 53.

seau's caricature of their style of thinking was deadly in its accuracy.

This view of government had absolute monarchy as its most plausible corollary. To do his duty adequately, the ruler must have at his disposal a perfectly obedient bureaucracy, all the knowledge it is possible for him to gather, and unlimited authority to translate his programs into law. Popular participation in such a scheme was not so much impious or impudent as simply irrelevant. If the ruler was the physician of his country, supremely knowledgeable and uniquely wise, there was no reason why he should consult his ignorant and superstitious patients; Plato had made that point long ago, and authoritarians made it again in the eighteenth century. Frederick II, deeply imbued with this rationalism, said flatly that men are governed by two mainsprings of action—"fear of punishment and hope for reward."[2] Hence the system of guidance that the ruler must devise for his subjects is simple, as simple as their psychology; it would only be obstructed by such nonsense as representative institutions or a free press.

Since there was no tradition of liberalism in the German states, opposition to this kind of paternalism came from conservatives dismayed by the vanishing of beloved and time-honored institutions, and by the ease with which closet philosophers and their princely disciples thought society could be improved. Society, these conservatives argued, is not a watch but an organism, incorporating through its long, slow growth the accumulated wisdom of the ages; to reshape it by means of a few simple rules drawn from academic psychology and administrative technology is to destroy what makes life worth living for the sake of a chilling nightmare. "These *idées simples et uniques*," wrote Justus Möser, "mark the clear path to monarchical (and, in the same way, also to democratic) despotism."[3]

Though in many details eminently just, these criticisms lost much of their force and their disinterested quality by being yoked to a reactionary ideology; the argument in behalf of moving slowly all too often took the form of an argument in behalf of not moving at all. Yet in their insistence on the variety of human experience,

---

[2] Friedrich der Grosse: *Die politischen Testamente*, tr. Friedrich von Oppeln-Bronikowski (1922), 37 (testament of 1752).
[3] Quoted in Parry: "Enlightened Government and its Critics in Eighteenth-Century Germany," 187.

the difficulty of reform, and the respect that men owe to history, Möser and his allies also laid bare the essentially unenlightened character of the so-called enlightened reform in the Hapsburg lands and elsewhere and thus laid bare the problem the philosophes faced: the philosophes wanted reform for other reasons and, for the most part, with other means, yet in most of Europe there *were* no other means, at least not in sight.

III

The theories of the Cameralists enjoyed success at least in this: they were put into practice. In the second half of the eighteenth century, breaking down the determined resistance of principle, inertia, and self-interest, a number of European rulers took the advice of their "enlightened" tutors and undertook often far-reaching reforms in institutions and policies. These rulers, summarily labeled "Enlightened Despots" by nineteenth-century historians, make up an extensive but inconclusive list: Catherine II of Russia, Frederick II of Prussia, Charles III of Spain, Gustavus III of Sweden, Emperors Joseph II and Leopold II have undisputed claim, Maria Theresa of Austria, Louis XV of France, Joseph I of Portugal a somewhat uncertain claim to membership.

This collection of monarchs was something more than an accidental collocation.[4] Their reigns coincided, and they knew and watched one another; they often admired the same ideas, competed for the same celebrities, and mouthed the same slogans; their education and their cultural milieux were strikingly similar: "The courts where they grew to manhood and rulership in many cases already reflected much of the secularism, wit, and cultural cosmopolitanism that were so much the earmarks of the polite intellectual world of the salons and the philosophes of the eighteenth century."[5] Moreover, the repertory of reform was of necessity restricted, and therefore the efforts of all these rulers bear a certain family resemblance; they were all essentially efforts to establish effective government in

---

[4] For the whole question of "Enlightened Despotism," the current status of controversy and scholarship, see Bibliographical Essay below.

[5] John G. Gagliardo: *Enlightened Despotism* (1967), 21.

their realm. These emperors, kings, czarinas, and grand dukes worked to clear up a morass of regulations, to lighten the financial burdens on trade, to make more or less sincere moves toward humanizing the criminal law, to aid the education of farmers and craftsmen—in a word, as much as their talents and their opposition would let them, to rationalize their states.

Yet such resemblances fade in the face of dissimilarities. None of these rulers was a visionary; each was intent above all to solve real problems for the eminently practical purpose of surviving in the jungle of international relations. Hence each found his own way of rationalizing government and neutralizing opposition. In Vienna, Maria Theresa and her son, co-regent, and successor Joseph II, greatly expanded the authority of the central administration over the provinces and supervised bureaucrats through a pervasive system of espionage. In Potsdam, Frederick II employed the same method of control, and, in addition, kept all threads of government in his own hands by demanding written reports from officials on which he acted alone, but, precisely that he might retain sole power, he distributed bureaucratic authority among widely scattered offices: unlike the Hapsburg system, his system combined the tightest personal supervision with administrative decentralization. Leopold of Tuscany, for his part, followed yet another direction: like Frederick, he decentralized his administration; unlike Frederick, he gave his officials wide powers. Charles III of Spain centralized and decentralized his government at once, by increasing the duties of local governments and those of his royal cabinet.

Dissimilarities pile on dissimilarities. While Catherine II burdened Russia's peasants with new exactions and drove them into unprecedented slavery, the Hapsburg rulers practically abolished serfdom; where Joseph II timidly restricted the use of torture, his brother Leopold and Frederick II abolished it altogether. Even the role of the nobility, obviously a matter of the highest importance, varied from enlightened state to enlightened state: Catherine depended strongly on the support of her aristocracy and cemented it by granting it ever more privileges; Frederick II reversed his father's relatively liberal policy and restored the Prussian nobility to its exclusive status, which gave it extensive power over its hapless dependents. In contrast, both Joseph II and Leopold II attacked the privileges of the privileged estates, sometimes with undisguised disdain and overt hostility.

The philosophes thus came by their political disagreements honestly; their debates over Catherine II or Frederick II reflect not simply a difference in their temperament or in their expectations, but real bafflement at princes who were doing so many different things in so many different ways with such similar rhetoric. The policies even of a single prince often left his most benevolent observers confused. Du Pont's ambivalence over Joseph II is an almost poignant illustration of the philosophes' dilemma: "The Emperor is hard to judge," Du Pont complained. "When one observes what he has done and is doing daily for his country, he is a prince of the rarest merit." On the other hand, in international affairs, in his "avidity for war," his "desire for aggrandizement," his "disrespect for old treaties" and his "inclination to decide everything by force" he appeared not as a "noble-minded eagle" but as a "terrible bird of prey."[6] Other rulers were just as puzzling. There can be little doubt: this so-called group of so-called Enlightened Despots was not what the philosophes were—a family.

And the so-called theory of Enlightened Despotism was not even a theory, at least not for the philosophes. Voltaire's friendship with Frederick, Diderot's visits to Catherine on the one hand, and the princes' moves against the Jesuits and against torture on the other, suggest a certain natural affinity; philosophes and princes could use one another to their own profit, and philosophes and princes could agree, in very general terms, on the advantages of reason over superstition, order over chaos, humanity over cruelty. But then all educated men in the eighteenth century, Christians and atheists, writers and rulers, agreed on these matters: Boswell defended the slave trade on the ground that the British colonies were more humane than the African states. Where the autocrats and the philosophes parted company, though they often did so politely, was on the critical issue of freedom.

Even the political thought of the Physiocrats, which comes closer than any other system in the West to an apology for "despot-

---

[6] Quoted in Heinz Holldack: "Der Physiokratismus und die Absolute Monarchie," *Historische Zeitschrift,* CVL (1932), 533.

ism," contains a pervasive and ultimately dominant libertarian strain. The Physiocrats' political theory was an adjunct to their economic theory; property came before the state, both in time and in importance. They were monarchists; as French writers concentrated on France, haunted by their vision of obstructions in the way of the natural laws of social life, they could hardly be anything else. But much of their writing on forms of government reads like a prosaic restatement of Pope's poetic relativism: forms of government are largely irrelevant; that government is best which best administers the natural laws that the Physiocrats have discovered.[7] This superb pose was bad enough; the Physiocrats' fatal love for pithy formulations, on which I have commented before, was worse. Turgot, who was himself half a Physiocrat, saw the danger clearly: the Physiocrats' favorite political slogan, "legal despotism," far from clarifying their views, only obscured them. "That devil 'despotism,' " he wrote to Du Pont, "will forever stand in the way of the propagation of your doctrine."[8]

Forever is a long time, but for two hundred years Turgot has been right. The term "despotisme légal" caused an immediate and inconclusive debate. Its father, Le Mercier de la Rivière, who in 1767 used it prominently in his authoritative exposition of physiocratic politics, dropped it as soon as its dangerous potentialities became apparent. By then it was too late: slogans have a life of their own and a tenacity that permits them to survive the most convincing explanations and conclusive refutations; they subsist, it seems, on a level too deep for reason to penetrate. In its own day, though, the phrase "despotisme légal" stood in the Physiocrats' way because it testified not so much to their aversion to freedom as to their inability to think. While Mably attacked it as a chimera that must lead to tyranny and barbarism, that view largely anticipated later fears.[9]

---

[7] While I have not seen the passage quoted by any Physiocrat, the Cameralist Sonnenfels does quote it, and with emphatic approval. See Kann: *A Study in Austrian Intellectual History*, 170.

[8] Michel Lhéritier: "Rapport général: le despotisme éclairé, de Frédéric II à la Révolution française," *Bulletin of the International Committee of Historical Sciences*, No. 35, vol. IX (1937), 188.

[9] See Mably's *Doutes proposés aux philosophes économistes sur l'ordre naturel et essentiel des sociétés politiques* (1768), conveniently summarized in Edmund Richner: *Le Mercier de la Rivière: Ein Führer der physiokratischen Bewegung in Frankreich* (1931), 80–2.

In the 1760s the characteristic criticism was that of Rousseau: "Stop talking to me about your legal despotism," he candidly told Mirabeau. All he could see, he wrote, was "two contradictory words which, put together, mean nothing to me."[1] And it is significant that Diderot, whose alertness to any trace of authoritarianism was marked, found Le Mercier's book a marvel of lucidity and logic. This was during his brief, passionate infatuation with physiocracy, to be sure, but when he turned against it he did so, as we know, only because Galiani had persuaded him that it was too doctrinaire on the grain trade.[2] That physiocratic devil "despotism" was never a devil for Diderot.

If it became a devil for others, the Physiocrats had only themselves to blame. They were too singleminded, too fanatically attached to their economic laws, too confident in their "philosophical discoveries," to develop an autonomous or flexible theory of politics. Some of their political pronouncements, though awkwardly formulated, made good sense: their insistence that sovereignty must be united rather than dispersed was a critique of privileged castes that they regarded, not without justice, as special interest groups hostile to essential economic reforms; this was their way of supporting the *thèse royale* in France. But other pronouncements were bound to arouse skepticism: Le Mercier offered Euclid as the model of the perfect despot whose decrees had found universal obedience.[3] To the Physiocrats this must have seemed a brilliant comparison: the laws of nature, they argued, impose themselves with such force that no rational man can refuse them their assent. The other philosophes were ready to accept the proposition that there are no parties in science, and that once its truth has become evident a scientific law will enlist a unanimous following. But Le Mercier's unhappy analogy between intellectual and political authority hinted at an authoritarian streak in his thinking and strongly suggested that the Physiocrats were contemptuous of freedom in their infatuation with order and the security of private property.

---

[1] Rousseau to Mirabeau, July 26, 1767. *Correspondance générale*, XVII, 158.

[2] Diderot to Falconet (July 1767). *Correspondance*, VII, 94—a paean of praise for Le Mercier. For Diderot and physiocracy, see above, 352–3.

[3] This choice example is quoted in Geoffrey Bruun: *The Enlightened Despots* (1929), 28.

This was partially, but only partially, just. The political thought of the Physiocrats, however glib, ambiguous, manipulative, and incomplete, in essence seeks to overcome authoritarianism, at least the capricious authoritarianism of arbitrary rulership. One day the dauphin, the father of the future Louis XVI, grumbled to Quesnay that monarchy was hard work. "Monsieur," replied the doctor, "I don't think so." "Really!" said the dauphin, "and what would you do if you were king?" "Monsieur," said Quesnay, "I would do nothing." "Who would govern, then?" the dauphin asked. "The laws," said Quesnay.[4] Admittedly a conversation is not a theory, but this conversation points to a theory. The Physiocrats' ideal was an efficient government unhampered by privileged groups, governing with a minimum of regulations and a minimum of interference in the life of the citizen, subject to the rule of law, checked by an independent judiciary, and directed by public opinion. Like most of the philosophes, the Physiocrats came, especially in their later writings, to profess great respect for public opinion; in the accepted style, Mirabeau called it *la regina del mundo*. But on this point the Physiocrats went beyond commonplaces: public opinion, they argued, must be made meaningful through the support of free and universal education, and by a free press. Here, too, the Physiocrats are not above criticism: they certainly expected to make the new educational institutions into vehicles of propaganda for their doctrine. But this much remains: Their belief in the elimination rather than the proliferation of regulations, a kind of negative government that was the political counterpart of Rousseau's negative education, their insistence on safeguards for the rights and the privacy and the property of the subject, and their fertile ideas on public opinion led the Physiocrats to advocate a constitutional absolutism, which was an incomplete form of liberalism. Only one hard question remained: how to create liberalism in an illiberal world.

---

[4] This instructive story has been reported many times, most authoritatively by G. Weulersse; see *Les Physiocrates* (1931), 187.

CHAPTER TEN

The Politics of Education

I. THE LOGIC OF ENLIGHTENMENT

I

I THINK IT IS now apparent that politics presented the Enlightenment with a dilemma of heroic proportions. The philosophes stood for reform; they stood, at the same time, for freedom in its many guises—freedom of thought, speech, and the press, freedom to participate in the shaping of public policy, to pursue one's career and realize one's talents. Reform and freedom were for them two faces of a single hope: freedoms were among the reforms to be accomplished, reforms were among the happy consequences of freedom. But the realities tore this alliance apart: with the overpowering presence of the illiterate masses and the absence of the habit of autonomy, freedom and reform were often incompatible. Libertarians seemed to have no way of initiating reforms; the most effective among the royal reformers were self-willed paternalists who made improvements in their own way and for their own sake. The road to the realization of the philosophes' political program thus led through the devious and embarrassing detours of repression and manipulation that were a denial or a mockery of the world they hoped to bring into being; the very methods used to distribute the fruits of enlightenment seemed calculated to frustrate enlightenment itself.

One way of escaping the dilemma was to deny that it was there, or that it was grave: this is the tendency of Voltaire's conformist pronouncement about Prussia and Russia. Voltaire implied with his casual but pointed silences that the ordinary Prussian or Russian was so far below being a political animal that there was no need to take him into account except as the passive recipient of humane enactments. Voltaire did not want Frederick to have his recruits beaten to death, but it did not occur to him that Frederick might train them to be voters.

This was a comfortable kind of theory, a complacent empiricism content to take things as they were. It was also, and for these reasons, a wholly inadequate escape from the philosophes' dilemma, one that made Voltaire himself, in his better moments, quite uneasy. A more courageous way out was proposed by some of the radicals of the Enlightenment, notably Diderot and Rousseau, who generalized their observation of Frederick II into opposition against absolutism as such. Both tried to dissolve the incompatibility of freedom and reform by insisting that reform without freedom was no reform at all. Rousseau placed his distrust of beneficent paternalism into the heart of his political theory in the *Contrat social*, while Diderot made it a prominent theme of his political writings in the 1770s. "One of the greatest disasters that could befall a free nation," Diderot wrote to Catherine, "would be two or three consecutive reigns of a just and enlightened despot."[1] Such despots, were they the best of men, would "habituate the nation to blind obedience; in their reigns the people would forget their inalienable rights; they would fall into a fatal trust and apathy; they would no longer experience that continual uneasiness that is the necessary guardian of liberty."[2] Such despots were like good shepherds who reduce their subjects to animals; they would "secure them a happiness of ten years for which they would pay with twenty centuries of misery."[3] If England had had three Queen Elizabeths in succession, Diderot told Catherine, the country would have fallen into slavery.[4]

These observations amounted to the recognition of the power that means have over ends; what Rousseau and Diderot were saying in effect is that men who are treated as children will always remain children. But the dilemma remained: the illiterate *were* illiterate; no administrative machinery, however ingenious, could transform silent subjects into self-reliant citizens. There was only one realistic

---

[1] *Diderot et Catherine II*, ed. Tourneux (1899), 144.
[2] *Observations sur le Nakaz*, in *Œuvres politiques*, 354-5.
[3] *Diderot et Catherine II*, 144.
[4] *Observations sur le Nakaz*, in *Œuvres politiques*, 355.

way of accepting the world of the present without sacrificing the possibilities of the future—education. This was the logic of enlightenment: if most men are not yet ready for autonomy, they must be *made* ready for it. The great political dilemma of the Enlightenment could be resolved only through time.

If eighteenth-century rulers refused to see, or refused to act on, this logic, that was only human. Education formed an indispensable part of their reform schemes: peasants needed to be instructed in the use of new implements, merchants and manufacturers to be acquainted with new techniques or products, public servants to be trained to new tasks. But civic education was something else again. After all, like all good education, good civic education aimed at making the educator unnecessary, and this required a degree of self-abnegation that the princes—all but one—could not muster.

The only ruler who understood the logic of Enlightenment and almost realized it in his state was Archduke Leopold of Tuscany, the prince I have already had occasion to describe as the most consistent and most enlightened reformer of the age. From the year of his accession, 1765, Leopold had imposed on his astonished and often reluctant subjects one progressive reform after another: unprecedented freedom of commerce, reconstitution of local government, improvements in the police and the military establishment, and a radical, humane legal code. As he proceeded, his enactments began to disclose a certain inner logic. They impressed him as parts of a large, coherent purpose: the gradual but comprehensive civic education of the Tuscan people. All earlier reforms, he wrote in 1782, had served the purpose of "awakening in men's hearts the feeling of an honorable civic freedom, and the habits of devotion to, and zeal for, the public good."[5] In 1779, Leopold acted on this insight, and began to draft a constitution that would be at once the climax of and the reward for that education. He put into his successive drafts all that he knew: what he had learned about Tuscany in his inspection trips, about political theory from the philosophes, about political possibilities from the American Revolution. Even his aversions played a part in these drafts: he abhorred what he called the "despotism" of

---

[5] See Adam Wandruszka: *Leopold II. Erzherzog von Österreich, Grossherzog von Toskana, König von Ungarn und Böhmen, Römischer Kaiser*, 2 vols. (1963–5), I, 370, 385.

his brother Joseph II (which he took to be the opposite of the Physiocrats' "*despotisme légal*"),[6] and he determined to avoid all its traits in the Tuscan regime of the future.

Despite superficial resemblances with traditional mixed constitutions, Leopold's drafts were thoroughly modern. They emphatically insist on the natural rights of the citizen and the constitutional duties of the ruler, on his continuous accountability. As he later summed up his principles: "I believe that the sovereign, even if hereditary, is only the delegate of his people"—a view radically different from Frederick II's famous dictum that the king is the first servant of his people. Frederick meant to say that the king is the hard-working dutiful master of the political machine; Leopold, that the ultimate power lies with the nation. "Every country should have a constitution or a contract between the people and the sovereign which limits the authority and the power of the latter." If the sovereign breaks this law, "he has in effect renounced his position," and all "obligation to obey him" ceases. In other words, "the executive power belongs to the sovereign, but the legislative power belongs to the people"—constitutionalism pure and simple. In another pointed departure from Frederick's practice, Leopold laid it down that "the sovereign cannot interfere, directly or indirectly, in civil or criminal proceedings, or change its forms or its penalties," and all arrests and convictions must follow due process. Even taxes, that most sensitive of all questions, were a matter to be resolved amicably between the ruler and his people. After giving a precise annual accounting and reporting on the state of public finance, the sovereign must leave it to the people and its representatives to vote the taxes, and then only for one year. Indeed, no regulations, no grants of pensions, can have binding force until the people and its representatives have voted for it. Nor should the people be terrorized by any arbitrary acts on the part of the sovereign or the military. "I believe," Leopold wrote, "that the sovereign must govern through law alone," and that the people can never renounce its fundamental rights, "which are the rights of nature." These fundamental rights are the ground on which the people had accepted a sovereign ruler in the first place; "it granted him preeminence that he might bring about its happiness and its well-being, not as he wants it, but as they themselves want it

---

[6] Ibid., 371.

and feel it—*nicht wie er es will, sondern wie sie selbst es wollen und empfinden.*" This, of course, was the point of Leopold's great educational enterprise: to make ordinary men feel competent to judge their real needs and participate in making the environment in which they choose to live.[7] Happiness, these principles suggested, was not something a man received, but something he made.

With all the expected restrictions on the franchise, and all the necessary elaborations of detail, these principles had actually found their way into the final draft of 1782. But time and circumstances were unpropitious; a combination of domestic resistance, administrative sabotage, and undesired foreign troubles kept the draft from becoming anything more than that, and so the single effort of a single eighteenth-century ruler to hand over most of his powers to his enlightened people came to nothing. It seems a pity: it would have been a splendid constitution.

II

The philosophes were well aware that education was of strategic importance for their political and social thought; after all, some of their favorite intellectual forebears—Seneca, Rabelais, Montaigne—had devoted serious attention to pedagogy, and besides, was it not highly significant that the admirable John Locke should have written a whole book on it? Nor was Locke's *Some Thoughts Concerning Education* a casual performance; it was a pioneering essay of vital interest to reformers partly because it advocated far-reaching reforms, but mainly because it was an evident offspring of Locke's major work, the *Essay Concerning Human Understanding*. To its many approving readers in the eighteenth century, *Some Thoughts Concerning Education* was the new philosophy in action; Locke's philosophy of education deserved a hearing and demonstrated the importance of its subject, because it was Locke's philosophy *in* education. In this area, as in others, the philosophes were pleased to be Locke's pupils.

They were pupils that they might become preceptors. All the

---

[7] Ibid., II, 217-18.

philosophes, more or less consciously, thought of themselves as educators, and enlightenment was what they taught. Diderot said as much: he wanted to change men's way of thinking with his *Encyclopédie;* Voltaire was less explicit, perhaps, but just as didactic with his polemical pamphlets; Lessing rarely stepped out of his chosen part as preacher of peace, tolerance, and humanity; the Physiocrats lectured the general public incessantly with their journals and their popular tracts; Beccaria, modest as his expectations were, hoped to convert princes to his principles of jurisprudence. For some of the philosophes, especially those who had at some time borne public responsibility, education had a kind of desperate urgency: both the marquis d'Argenson and Turgot, during and after their periods of office under the French crown, entreated their master to enlist the public behind his program. "The king is badly advised," wrote d'Argenson, as dismayed in the fifties as Turgot was to be in the seventies, by the popularity that the *parlements* enjoyed. "In this enlightened and philosophic age of ours he is slowly being discredited. If Henri III was obliged to place himself at the head of the League, Louis XV should place himself at the head of philosophy, justice, and reason."[8] Education here was a two-stage process: the philosophes had to educate the king in the need for educating his people.

But education was more than a theory or a hope for the philosophes; it was also an experience—in fact, it lies at the heart of their experience *as* philosophes. I have defined that experience as a dialectical struggle in which the philosophes first pitted classical thought against their Christian heritage that they might discard the burdens of religion, and then escaped their beloved ancients by appealing to the science of nature and of man; this pursuit of modernity was the essential purpose of their education. Indeed, their experience was an education in the most specific possible sense. Each philosophe recapitulated in his private development the course that the Enlightenment was prescribing for mankind in general; each first sensed his opportunity for engaging in this liberating and exhilarating struggle, and equipped himself for it, in his school.

---

[8] See Gerald J. Cavanaugh: "Vauban, d'Argenson, Turgot: From Absolutism to Constitutionalism in Eighteenth-century France" (Columbia Ph.D. dissertation, 1967), 140–1.

When the philosophes went to school—run, practically all of them, by clerics—the old synthesis of Christianity and classicism, devised centuries before, was breaking down. Schools are notoriously conservative institutions, but the pressures of the eighteenth century could not be ignored; however muffled, they invaded the sanctuary of religious instruction and demonstrated the teaching of the classics to be excessive in its demands and ineffective in its results—or, at times, too effective in its results. Eighteenth-century criticism, all in all, amounted to the charge that the schools could do no right: the pious complained that the schools taught too little religion and the classics too well; the philosophes, on the contrary, that they taught too much religion and the classics not well enough. Gibbon records that at Oxford, "even the study of an elegant classic, which might have been illustrated by a comparison of the ancient and modern theatres, was reduced to a dry and literal interpretation of the author's text."[9] Diderot vividly remembered "the pain students endured in explaining Vergil, the tears with which they soaked the pleasant satires of Horace," and he warned that such disagreeable instruction had disgusted pupils "with these authors to such a degree that they later looked at them only to shudder." The French curriculum, he thought, produced graduates who are "thoroughly tired, thoroughly bored, thoroughly chastened, and thoroughly ignorant, to say nothing of the disgust they have acquired for sublime authors whom they will return to only rarely."[1] Voltaire summed up these charges in a famous phrase about the educational standard in his day: "I learned Latin and nonsense."[2]

There was much truth in these charges, but not the whole truth: the philosophes themselves are splendid testimony that the schools taught the classics pleasantly enough to attract pupils to unbelief, and memorably enough to permit them later to read, cite, and use the classics they had mastered. The schools, even though they were justly under attack, served better than the philosophes, as ungrateful pupils, liked to remember.

The Christian scholars of the Renaissance, Protestant and Catholic alike, had taken a calculated risk, forced upon them by a flour-

---

[9] *Autobiography*, 78–9.
[1] "Plan d'une université pour le gouvernement de Russie," in *Œuvres*, III, 471.
[2] "Éducation," *Questions sur l'Encyclopédie*, in *Œuvres*, XVIII, 471.

ishing, irrepressible scholarship, the invention of printing, and the growth of a literate public. These scholars had steadily enlarged the range of Christian learning; they attempted to assimilate what they could not suppress. Nor were these simply the tactics of desperation: sixteenth-century educators found the classics less a menace too strong to ignore than a delight too great to renounce. For two centuries or more, Christian civilization continued to swallow increasing doses of anticlerical or pagan learning without gagging. But for eighteenth-century men, more and more aware of the sciences, stimulated by technology, skeptical of miracles, and eager to enjoy the world of the senses, pagan doctrines acquired new and dangerous vitality. The old charge that the Jesuits taught paganism, even by implication, is just as invalid as the charge that the Jansenists abetted materialism by emphasizing science. By their lights, these religious orders, and all the others, did their Christian duty. They taught what they had taught for centuries: a taste for pagan writers. It was not the schools that changed, but the times.

The schools, in fact, had changed very little. The Jesuit *collèges* still proceeded under the *ratio studiorum* devised in the sixteenth century by the founder of the Jesuit order and by his immediate successors. Ignatius Loyola, born at the height of the later Renaissance, had been thoroughly aware of the skeptical, impious implications of Renaissance humanism. It had been his aim to establish schools that would detach the great acquisitions of that humanism, the classics, from impiety, and weld them firmly to Christian doctrine. The first plan of study was drawn up under Loyola's supervision in 1541 and revised several times later in the sixteenth century. It stressed leniency, urged that pupils' ambition be fostered through competition, and proclaimed the central importance of the classics.

The principles of the *ratio studiorum* were tenaciously retained through two centuries of criticism. When the philosophes went to Jesuit schools in the eighteenth century—and in the Catholic countries most of them did—they still read a Martial cleaned up in 1558 at Loyola's orders, an emasculated version of Horace's *Odes*, some Vergil (carefully omitting Book IV of the *Aeneid*, which describes Dido's suicide), selections from Cicero's speeches, and the more harmless poets. Jesuit teachers, often respectable classical scholars, stressed linguistic drill, not pagan doctrine; they sought to form Christians with good taste. Saint-Lambert, a minor poet who held the unique distinction of seducing Voltaire's mistress while preventing Rousseau from seducing his own, celebrated the urbane compromises of his Jesuit teachers in a neat verse:

> Indulgente Société,
> Ô vous, dévots plus raisonnables,
> Apôtres pleins d'urbanité,
> Le goût polit vos mœurs aimables.
> Vous vous occupez sagement
> De l'art de penser et de plaire
> Aux charmes touchants du Bréviaire
> Vous entremêlez prudemment
> Et du Virgile et du Voltaire.[3]

Jesuit *collèges*, then, sweetened the Christian message with worldly poetry. Their celebrated *collège Louis-le-grand* in Paris, which produced a host of pagans from Voltaire to Robespierre, prescribed edifying Latin dramas as part of the curriculum. Nearly all the French philosophes were products of this fashionable classical education. At *Louis-le-grand*, Voltaire met the marquis d'Argenson, who became foreign minister and a royalist political theorist; his brother the comte d'Argenson, who had a distinguished career under Louis XV and somewhat ungraciously protected Diderot's *Encyclopédie;* the comte d'Argental and the provincial aristocrat Cideville, who belonged to that intensely useful group of allies without whom the philosophes could not comfortably exist—often rich, always loyal, amateur poets, lovers of the theater, ready to smuggle subversive manuscripts, speak to a minister in behalf of a philosophe in trouble, advance *lumières* and impede *l'infâme* in any way the leading spirits thought appropriate.[4] Malesherbes, Helvétius, and Turgot all went through *Louis-le-grand;* Diderot attended the Jesuit *collège* at Langres; Buffon and his close friend and collaborator Daubenton, Hénault, Vauvenargues, Marmontel, and Condorcet all had a Jesuit education. Throughout Catholic Europe, the Jesuits trained their most intransigent enemies.

---

[3] André Schimberg: *L'Éducation morale dans les collèges de la Compagnie de Jésus sous l'Ancien Régime* (1913), in "Additions et Errata," not paginated.
[4] For this group, see *The Rise of Modern Paganism*, 19.

While other orders drastically modified the Jesuit curriculum, the essential recipe—Christian edification made palatable through classical literature—remained intact. Montesquieu, educated at the Oratorian *collège* at Juilly, acquired his overpowering admiration for antiquity there; d'Alembert, who was turned toward mathematics by his severe Jansenist masters, nevertheless became a good Latinist at the *collège* Mazarin.

Protestant education was little different. Here too piety came first, classics second; here too the ancients stalked about like aged lions in the zoo, their ideological fangs drawn, noble, decorative, and innocuous. In Lessing's *Gymnasium* in Meissen, prayer and the study of religion preceded Latin and Greek, and the ancient languages were imparted as exercises in philology. At the University of Edinburgh, Hume read Cicero and Marcus Aurelius and heard lectures filled with Newtonian Christianity; in England, with its inchoate conglomeration of schools, discipline was harsh, learning mechanical, instruction pedantic, and politics a demoralizing intrusion. Latin and Greek were taught, but in England, as elsewhere, the object was not to produce pagans, but Christians fit to live in polite society.

This system was not fatal to the classics largely because the love of the classics was in the air. Today we assume, and Diderot suggested it then, that a taste for higher things is ruined by bad education. But schooling has this baleful result mainly when cultivation is no longer prized by the culture as a whole. In the age of the Enlightenment, the kind of tiresome or hateful preceptors of whom Gibbon and Diderot complained did not poison the taste for the classics; they merely postponed its gratification. If the incentive to master them did not come from the school—though, as I have said, often enough it did come from there—it would come from the great world. Gibbon was his own tutor, and so was Rousseau; what Nicolai missed in one school he got in another.

Still, however adequate traditional schooling was here and there, dissatisfaction with accepted modes of pedagogy had been lively since the seventeenth century, and reformers had persistently demanded that the educational process modernize itself both by improving the teaching of the classics and by diversifying the curriculum as a whole. When the philosophes began to call for educational reform, they pushed, as they so often did, at an open door.

It was John Locke who anticipated many of the reforms that later reformers would embrace, usually in his name. Locke denounced the traditional method of teaching by rote, and thought it wholly inappropriate to beat children for the sake of dead tongues. He did not object to Latin; he objected rather to its disproportionate importance in the curriculum and the mechanical manner in which it was taught. Sound learning, Locke argued, must build on sound character, just as a sound mind needs a sound body—this famous line from Juvenal, indeed, is the first line of Locke's treatise—but, Locke complained, the schools of his day reversed and perverted the natural sequence: they ruined character by imposing a deadening and often cruel routine. Latin should be taught, but only after French, and be taught through simple grammar and conversation. After the pupil has mastered some easy texts, he can work up his way gradually to the masterpieces of antiquity, "the most difficult and sublime of the Latin authors, such as are Tully, Virgil, and Horace."[5] With a boldness rare in his day, Locke urged that education be somehow made relevant to the future career of the pupil; let him learn history, geography, and anatomy if the Latin classics will not have any importance to him later: "Can there be anything more ridiculous than that a father should waste his own money, and his son's time, in setting him to learn the Roman language, when, at the same time, he designs him for a trade, wherein he, having no use of Latin, fails not to forget that little which he brought from school, and which it is ten to one he abhors for the ill usage it procured him?"[6] Locke was not a philistine; he recognized the intrinsic value of cultivation, but he had no sympathy with the organized flogging of remote classics into reluctant schoolboys who would hate what they learned and promptly forget it.

Locke's ideas found a sympathetic hearing in France, where reforming pedagogues had already experimented with less repulsive methods of imparting the classical tongues. The Oratorians and Port Royal simplified the old grammars and made them more interesting and less cumbersome than before; Port Royal even tried out Latin grammars written in French. The Jansenists and Oratorians emphasized mathematics and science, just as some of the Dissenting schools

---

[5] *Some Thoughts Concerning Education* (1693), para. 184.
[6] Ibid., para. 164.

in England tried to prepare their pupils for the world of business by modifying the traditional curriculum. Educators were beginning to notice that there was more to learn than ever before. The study of history, the knowledge of geography, the domain of the natural sciences had enormously widened and deepened since the sixteenth and seventeenth centuries, and it seemed—at least to reformers—essential to have these advances reflected in the curriculum. But the travail of classical learning began here: more time for science meant less time for Greek—it was as simple as that.

In addition to the pressure of technical subjects, the schools also began to experience pressure from vernacular literatures. The British and the French especially were building up collections of plays and poems that had every right to claim the time-honored title of "classic," hitherto jealously reserved for works in Latin and Greek. It was essential for the educated man to know these modern classics; it even seemed likely that he would love them more than the old classics. In any event, the advent of impressive modern literature demanded a new attitude toward the staples of literary taste. In the seventeenth century, this problem was not yet serious. One day, the story goes, someone asked the great Arnauld of Port Royal what was the best way to form style. "Read Cicero," he replied. "I am not asking about writing in Latin, but in French." "Ah," said Arnauld, "in that case, read Cicero."[7]

By the eighteenth century, such advice came to seem reactionary. But it could still be heard: in his *Réflexions critiques sur la poésie,* which, though written in the 1720s, found readers as late as the 1770s, the abbé Dubos argued that Latin was infinitely preferable to French as the language of poetry.[8] But then, as the century went on, this became a distinct minority view. Bossuet modeled his style on the Greeks and Romans; his successors modeled their style on Bossuet. Racine was indebted to Euripides; Voltaire was indebted to Racine. Shakespeare studied Seneca; Dryden studied Shakespeare. While French and British reformers demanded that schoolboys master their language because they could take pride in their literature, German reformers demanded that their schoolboys master their lan-

---

[7] See Augustin Sicard: *Les Études classiques avant la Révolution* (1887), 200.
[8] See in Geoffroy Atkinson: *Le sentiment de la nature et le retour à la vie simple (1690–1740)*, (1960), 20.

guage so that they might *create* a literature in which they could take pride. In 1747, the rector of the *Gymnasium* at Görlitz asked, "Why should we not have *autores classicos* in our mother tongue as well as in that of the Romans?"[9] The question, with its Latin phrase, was still a little pathetic, but it pointed to the future. In 1774, the *Aufklärer* Basedow, an enthusiastic disciple of the deist theology of Reimarus and the radical pedagogy of Rousseau, published his *Elementarwerk*, a vast program for educational reform on modern lines; in the same year he found sufficient support to found a school in Dessau, the *Philanthropin*, designed to make his ideas reality. Also in 1774, innovation had gone far enough in England to alarm the defenders of traditional classical learning, and prompt them to a touching lament, portraying Vergil displaced by mathematics and Horace by Newtonian popularizers:

> See Euclid proudly spurns the Mantuan muse,
> While gentle Horace wipes Maclaurin's shoes.
> There Homer learns the theory of light,
> And tortured Ovid learns to sum and write.[1]

Things were far from this fearful stage; in some countries the classical schools retained their prestige and power through the nineteenth century. But modernity was on the way.

These reformist notions readily found their way into philosophic literature. The Encyclopedist Dumarsais, a disciple of Locke who had acquired a considerable reputation among the philosophes with his progressive proposals for the study of Latin, went so far as to suggest the elimination of grammars entirely; other reformers, lamenting years of wasted drill and arid memorization, sought to speed up the acquisition of Latin and Greek and to make both easier to learn and more pleasant to remember. D'Alembert wrote a trenchant critique of the prevailing system for the *Encyclopédie;* his article "Collège," influential and controversial, was obviously aimed at Jesuit-dominated secondary schooling and provoked some outraged replies, but even d'Alembert sufficiently overcame his hostility

---

[9] Quoted in Friedrich Paulsen: *Geschichte des gelehrten Unterrichts auf den deutschen Schulen und Universitäten* (1885), 396.
[1] Quoted by Sir Charles Mallet: "Education, Schools and Universities," *Johnson's England,* II, 227.

to the Jesuits and his preoccupation with science to admit at least some classics into the curriculum of his ideal school: "In philosophy, logic should be limited to a few lines; metaphysics to an abridgment of Locke, purely philosophical ethics to the works of Seneca and Epictetus, Christian ethics to Christ's sermon on the mount. . . ."[2] A truncated and impoverished classical curriculum, to be sure, but not without its Stoics.

These drastic prescriptions were codified in the widely read *Essai d'éducation nationale* of 1763, by La Chalotais. Attorney general to the *parlement* of Brittany, La Chalotais seemed an unlikely person to be popular with philosophes, but he had ingratiated himself among them with his noisy campaign against the Jesuits, and his acceptance had been sealed by the accolade of a correspondence with Voltaire. His most far-reaching proposal was that the educational system be secularized and nationalized, but he also found much to criticize in the curriculum. "Our education," he wrote with the severity common to inventors of projects, "everywhere shows the effects of the barbarism of past centuries. Except for a little Latin, which he has to study all over again if he wants to use that language, the young man on entering the world must forget almost all he has been taught by his so-called instructors."[3] Instead, he urged that French and Latin be taught simultaneously, and that the student grow proficient in both through constant comparison of the two literatures.

The philosophes found such plans admirable but troublesome; with many uneasy glances back at their beloved classics, they joined the movement toward modernity. They saw the value of scientific training, but they loved liberal learning too much to discard it as useless or to patronize it as a mere luxury. Diderot pointedly asked Catherine II: "What is it that particularly distinguishes Voltaire from all our young writers? Learning. Voltaire knows a great deal, and our young poets are ignorant. The work of Voltaire is full of material; their works are empty."[4] A writer, in any event, must have

---

[2] "Collège," in *The Encyclopédie*, 30.
[3] See François de la Fontainerie: *French Liberalism and Education in the Eighteenth Century; The Writings of La Chalotais, Turgot, Diderot and Condorcet on National Education* (1932), 48–9.
[4] "Plan d'une université pour le gouvernement de Russie," in *Œuvres*, III, 444. I have quoted this passage in *The Rise of Modern Paganism*, 197; see also above, 215.

the classics at his command: "If he wishes to excel, he absolutely needs an intimate acquaintance with Homer and Vergil, Demosthenes and Cicero."[5] There was one way of resolving the conflicting claims of classical and scientific education—by assigning the classics to a narrow elite and modern technical subjects to all the other pupils. This was in fact the way that Diderot proposed. Still, a certain ambivalence remained in all the philosophes wrote about education: they were committed to modernity and professed to love the sciences, but they knew that they loved the ancients as well. And so, in pronouncements that were, if not logical, all too human, they sought to preserve in the educational system the best of two worlds.

III

To believe in the importance of education was to believe, at least implicitly, in its power. Of course, from the perspective of their philosophy, the philosophes were almost compelled to believe in that power: it supported their position on original sin. Christians, too, believed in education, and were, down to the philosophes' time, the leading educators, but the most optimistic Christian was not free to assert that education, no matter how thoroughgoing, could ever erase the effects of Adam's Fall. The myth of original sin, which the philosophes thought they had exploded, made much of man's incapacity to change fundamentally through his own efforts: education could not do the work of grace. Conversely, the philosophes' doctrine of man's original innocence, though it did not necessarily imply, persuasively testified to the efficacy of education in man's renewal. Locke had seen this clearly: "The crucial importance of Locke's *Some Thoughts Concerning Education*," as J. A. Passmore has suggested, lies "not so much in its rejection of innate ideas as in its rejection of original sin."[6]

Rejection of original sin and the general recovery of nerve

---

[5] "Plan d'une université," in *Œuvres*, III, 473.
[6] "The Malleability of Man in Eighteenth-Century Thought," in Earl R. Wasserman, ed.: *Aspects of the Eighteenth Century* (1965), 22.

combined to make the philosophes into pedagogical optimists. Locke had already insisted that "men's happiness or misery is part of their own making," and that constitutional differences are insignificant compared to the effect of education. "I think, I may say, that, of all the men we meet with, nine parts of ten are what they are, good or evil, useful or not, by their education."[7] In support of such optimistic doctrine Montesquieu had devoted a whole book of his *De l'esprit des lois* to education, and singled out "the laws of education," the "first we receive," as being of decisive importance because "they prepare us to be citizens." Hence, "every family should be governed on the principles of the great family that comprehends each of them."[8] A little later, in the 1750s, Helvétius explicitly drew the political implications of these views: "In every country," he wrote in *De l'esprit*, "the art of forming man is so closely linked to the form of government, that it may not be possible to make any considerable change in public education without making changes in the very constitution of the state."[9] Diderot, who much admired Helvétius, reiterated these sentiments in the 1770s, more in what he implied than in what he chose to assert: "To instruct a nation is to civilize it,"[1] he told Catherine of Russia. There is no indication that she had any intention of following his hint; after all, to civilize a nation would be to make autocrats like her obsolete.

But granted that education could do much, how much could it do? This was the vexed question concerning the relative strength of nature and nurture, hackneyed today, but fresh and meaningful in the age of the Enlightenment. It too was in essence a political question, for the more thoroughly the educator could change his pupils, the easier the work of the legislator, and the closer the work of the legislator to that of the educator: the Physiocrats were by no means the only philosophes to notice this connection. Fired by the radical possibilities of the new secular view of education that Locke had hinted at, one prominent philosophe, Helvétius, thought that education could do everything. Other philosophes were not quite so sanguine. To judge from the utopian world he set up for Émile,

---

[7] *Some Thoughts Concerning Education*, para. 1.
[8] Book IV, chap. i, in *Œuvres*, I, part 1, 39.
[9] *De l'esprit* (1758; edn. 1769), Discourse IV, chap. xvii, 472.
[1] "Plan d'une université pour le gouvernement de Russie," in *Œuvres*, III, 429.

Rousseau thought that education could do a great deal only after a great deal had been done about education first. Still other philosophes, like Diderot, thought it best to be moderate: their faith in education, though powerful, was not unlimited. The spectrum of enlightened opinion on this delicate matter emerges most perspicuously in a strange private debate that Diderot held with the shade of Helvétius early in the 1770s. Helvétius was not the most famous of the philosophes; he was only the most notorious. In 1758, he had published *De l'esprit*, a materialistic and utilitarian treatise that epitomized the most radical views of the most radical philosophes with a kind of clumsy candor. The book, passed for publication by an inattentive censor, produced a reverberating scandal: authorities from the *parlement* of Paris to the Papacy thundered condemnations, and the philosophes' enemies exploited the uproar by tarring Diderot's *Encyclopédie* with Helvétius's brush.

De *l'esprit* was a treatise on human motives, and as such prominently a treatise on education. Helvétius was a psychological egalitarian and extreme environmentalist. Men (as long as they are healthy specimens) are essentially equal; in explicit opposition to Montesquieu's theory that "physical causes" greatly influence human character, Helvétius insists that the differences that do arise spring from "moral" cause alone.[2] From Locke's sensationalism and La Mettrie's materialism Helvétius constructed a picture of man that is stark in its simplicity; even tough-minded contemporaries found his almost gloating insistence on universal, unrelieved egotism a little repulsive. Men, Helvétius argues, are the recipients of sensations and the centers of passion. Thus equipped, each man acts to realize his desires in the world by following his self-interest with a kind of iron consistency. This is a profoundly pessimistic view of man's nature, but it is relieved by Helvétius's optimistic view of man's possibilities. What man thinks, believes, even what he feels, is open to the most extensive modifications through the social environment—man, in other words, can be educated to be almost anything, even a good citizen.

Helvétius was often naïve, but he was not naïve enough to equate education with schooling. Men's education, taking the word "in its true and more extensive signification," differed far more than

---

[2] *De l'esprit*, Discourse III, chap. xxvii, 329.

their schooling did, hence the vast observed differences among them. "I say, no one receives the same education" as anyone else: "Everyone, if I may put it this way, has for his preceptors the form of government under which he lives, his friends, his mistresses, the men by whom he is surrounded, his reading, and, finally, chance, that is to say, an infinite number of events whose causes and connections our ignorance does not permit us to perceive." In fact, Helvétius says with emphasis and seeks to prove with two unfortunate examples, "chance plays a larger part in our education than we think." Chance led Galileo to that Florentine garden where gardeners "piqued" the "brains and the vanity of that philosopher" with their baffled questions about the water that would rise only to a certain height. Similarly, chance led Newton, thinking of nothing else, to the avenue of apple trees where, seeing some apples drop to the ground, the theory of gravitation sprang into his mind. Offering a psychological version of the pragmatic theory familiar from the philosophes' histories, Helvétius suggested that small events often have enormous consequences. "How many men of parts remain lost in the mass of mediocre men, for want either of a certain tranquillity of mind, or of meeting a gardener, or of the fall of an apple!"[3] In the light of such coarseness, the only thing that surprises us is the high esteem in which Helvétius was held by Diderot.

We have come to dread the menace posed by this environmentalism—the distortion of education through propaganda, the manipulation of public opinion through the organization of lies and the mobilization of hatreds. But Helvétius saw only its positive possibilities. This was not because he thought well of despotism but, on the contrary, because he thought so little of it. In his contemptuous chapters on despotic regimes he describes them as too vicious, too corrupt, too ignorant, and too feeble to use education for their own purposes. Only the responsible legislator, it seems, can recognize the essential truth that the sciences of legislation and of education are really one and the same. Himself educated in true philosophy, and legislating for a well-informed public that has shed the baleful vices of ignorance and superstition, the legislator-educator will work for the general well-being: "It is solely through good laws that one can form virtuous men. Thus the whole art of the

---

[3] Ibid., chap. i, 188–9.

legislator consists of forcing men, by the sentiment of self-love, to be always just to one another." Obviously, "to make such laws one must know the human heart, and to know first of all that men, responsive to themselves, indifferent to others, are born neither good nor bad, but ready to be the one or the other."[4] Despite Helvétius's pronounced distaste for despotism, this was dubious doctrine, both as educational and as political theory, especially since he did not consider Frederick of Prussia to be a despot, but quoted him with full approval: "There is nothing better than the arbitrary government of princes who are just, humane, and virtuous."[5]

If nothing else, this passage alerted Diderot to the dangerous implications lurking in the educational views of Helvétius, and he addressed himself to them in 1773 and after. Helvétius had died, still relatively young, in 1771, and left behind a book, *De l'homme*, which was if anything more explicit on the wonders of education than his earlier *De l'esprit* had been. Diderot saw "the posthumous Helvétius" on his way to Russia, and studied it with considerable care. The book, he thought, was full of good ideas that only a few writers could have had, and a number of errors that everyone could easily correct. This was a family argument: for Diderot, Helvétius remained a brother, even if occasionally misguided. At least, unlike Rousseau, Helvétius did not constantly contradict himself: "The difference between you and Rousseau," Diderot apostrophized his dead acquaintance, "is that Rousseau's principles are false, and the consequences true, while your principles are true and the consequences false. In exaggerating his principles, Rousseau's disciples will be nothing but madmen; yours, moderating your consequences, will be wise men."[6]

The judgment is too beautifully balanced to be entirely trustworthy, but in any event Diderot envisioned his task to be fairly simple: it was to moderate Helvétius's consequences. The result is a series of reasonable objections to Helvétius's bold pronouncements, designed not so much to refute Helvétius as to "restrain" him: "*He says:* Education does everything. *Say:* Education does a great deal. *He says:* Constitution does nothing. *Say:* Constitution does less than

---

[4] Ibid., Discourse II, chap. xxiv, 176–8.
[5] Quoted by Diderot: *Réfutation suivie de l'ouvrage d'Helvétius intitulé l'Homme*, in *Œuvres philosophiques*, 619.
[6] Ibid., 576.

you think." And again: "*He says:* Character depends entirely on circumstances. *Say:* I think that they modify it. *He says:* One gives a man the temperament one wants to give him. . . . *Say:* Temperament is not always an invincible obstacle to the progress of the human spirit."[7] Everywhere, Diderot seeks to rescue Helvétius's principles from the exuberance of their author. It is only when Helvétius moves from implicit to explicit politics that Diderot's refutation acquires a certain warmth: quoting Helvétius's reference to Frederick of Prussia, Diderot bursts out in disappointment and with rage: "And you, Helvétius, quote this tyrant's maxim in high praise! The arbitrary government of a just and enlightened prince is always bad. His virtues are the most dangerous and the most certain of his seductions: they insensibly habituate the public to love, respect, serve his successor, evil and stupid as he may be." And he says again what he has now come to believe firmly: "One of the greatest misfortunes that can happen to a nation would be two or three reigns of a power that is just, mild, enlightened, but arbitrary: the people will be led by happiness to the complete forgetfulness of their privileges, and into perfect slavery."[8]

It is an appealing outburst: Diderot remains an optimist in education but warns against the seductions of passivity. Yet no one in the Enlightenment, not even Diderot, fully faced, let alone resolved, the problems raised for political theory by the dangers and opportunities of education. The philosophes at best glimpsed the logic of Enlightenment and proclaimed it, but they did not see it clearly enough to work it through to the end. And there is a good reason for their failure: the canaille stood in their way.

---

[7] Ibid., 601.
[8] Ibid., 619–20.

2. A FAITH FOR THE CANAILLE

I

THE QUESTION of the lower orders is the great unexamined political question of the Enlightenment. It is not that the philosophes preserved silence on the issue; they never preserved silence on any issue. Their writings and, even more, their private correspondence, abound in references to the common people, the *gemeine Pöbel*, the *peuple*, the canaille, the vulgar. What is missing is a serious attempt at working out the logic implicit in the philosophes' view of Enlightenment, which, as I have said, was in essence pedagogic. There is snobbery in these casual remarks and a certain failure of imagination. There is also something else: a sense of despair at the general wretchedness, illiteracy, and brutishness of the poor, which appeared by and large incurable.

It is easy to grow impatient with the superb sneer that most of the philosophes directed, most of the time, at their less fortunate fellow beings; even the show of despair was, after all, at least in part a comfortable excuse for doing nothing, or doing nothing to disturb existing social arrangements. The kindly spirits that sent the children of the poor to the charity schools in England, for example, had no intention of permitting these pupils to rise above their station: the point of this schooling was to produce piety and insure deference; when some attempt was made to teach the most intelligent of these children something more than reading, petty tradesmen objected to this potential competition with their own children.[9]

Yet the despair of the philosophes was also something better than a self-protective ideology. If the idea of hierarchy had been expelled from the heavens, it continued to have its place in the society of men. The ladder of ascent everywhere was steep and narrow; differentiations among orders and even within orders were carefully marked and universally acknowledged; the gap between

---

[9] See Dorothy Marshall: *English People in the Eighteenth Century* (1956), 161.

the noble and the peasant or the rich and the poor was a vast gulf
across which the one stared at the other almost with disbelief. Far
too many men and women remained in the eighteenth century what
they had been through all the centuries before: beasts of burden,
"two-footed animals," as Voltaire said not without compassion, "who
live in a horrible condition approximating the state of nature."[1] The
metaphor of a hierarchy came to the pens of eighteenth-century
writers so casually that it is obvious how real the phenomenon was,
and how entrenched. "Opinions, like fashions," wrote Swift, "always
descend from those of quality to the middle sort, and thence to the
vulgar"[2]; and some decades later Samuel Johnson said: "All foreigners remark that the knowledge of the common people is greater than
that of any other vulgar. This superiority we undoubtedly owe to
the rivulets of intelligence which are continually trickling among
us, which anyone may catch."[3] Evidently, there was real advantage
to an open society: anyone might catch a drop of civilization. But
even that kind of society still preserved fences that only a few could
leap, and still condemned the majority to hopeless indigence and
permanent exclusion from the political public.

The educational plans of the age took these realities into account, without much analysis and without any apology. As early as
1681 John Locke had explained why class distinctions mattered
fundamentally: "The three great things that govern mankind are
reason, passion and superstition. The first govern[s] a few; the two
last share the bulk of mankind and possess them in their turns; but
superstition most powerfully, and produces the greatest mischiefs."[4]
This was the condition the educator confronted: the vulgar were,
and would doubtless forever be, prey to passion and superstition;
reason was beyond them. Accordingly, Locke confined his educational program—the study of Latin and other ornaments of gracious
civilization—to gentlemen, and recommended that the children of
the poor be sent to special "working schools" where they would
learn "spinning or knitting, or some other part of woollen manu-

---

[1] See above, 4.
[2] Quoted in James Sutherland: *A Preface to Eighteenth Century
Poetry* (1948), 61; from Swift: *An Argument Against Abolishing
Christianity*.
[3] *The Idler*, No. 7, May 27, 1758. Samuel Johnson: *The Idler and
The Adventurer*, eds. W. J. Bate *et al.* (1963), 23.
[4] Quoted in Richard H. Cox: *Locke on War and Peace* (1960), 33.

facture," and such edifying matters as "some sense of religion."[5]
For Locke, education was designed not to subvert, but to confirm,
the class system. By and large, the philosophes moved away from Locke's analysis with very deliberate speed. Hume thought "the bulk of mankind"
governed "by authority, not reason," and he doubted that most men
could discard superstition. "When will the people be reasonable?"
he asked; not, he was sure, in the foreseeable future.[6] Rousseau, the
great democrat, said flatly in *Émile*, "The poor have no need of education"[7]; and while this was not a recommendation, it was an acceptance of things as they were. Kant, Rousseau's disciple, who
owed to Rousseau, he said, his respect for the common man, evidently did not carry that respect very far: the "*Volk*," he wrote,
"consists of idiots."[8] Diderot sounded much the same way; his writings offer a depressing anthology on the theme of the mob as a fact
of life. Diderot calls the poor "*imbécile*" in matters of religion[9];
while the "national superstition is declining," that welcome development will stop short of embracing the populace: the *peuple* is "too
idiotic—*bête*—too miserable, and too busy" to enlighten itself.
There is no hope here: "The quantity of the canaille is just about
always the same." The multitude needs a religion filled with ritual
and with ridiculous fables, and always will.[1] Reason is too cool; it
presents none of the surprises, none of the wonderment, that the
populace wants.[2] "The general mass of the species is made neither to
follow, nor to know, the march of the human spirit."[3] Enlightenment is confined to a small troop, an "invisible church," capable of
looking intelligently at works of art and literature, capable of re-

---

[5] These passages are from a plan Locke drew up in 1697 to revise
the Elizabethan Poor Law in the light of the increase in pauperism.
The proposal is reprinted in H. R. Fox Burne: *A Life of John
Locke*, 2 vols. (1876), II, 337–91.
[6] "Idea of a Perfect Commonwealth," *Works*, III, 480; *The Natural History of Religion*, in ibid., IV, 349.
[7] *Émile, ou de l'éducation* (edn. 1939), 27.
[8] *Der Streit der Fakultäten*, in *Werke*, VII, 328.
[9] Pensée LIII, *Pensées philosophiques*, in *Œuvres philosophiques*,
43.
[1] To Sophie Volland (October 30, 1759). *Correspondance*, II, 299,
310–11.
[2] To the same (July 25, 1762). Ibid., IV, 71.
[3] "Encyclopédie"—a strategic place to make such a remark. *The
Encyclopédie*, 54.

flecting, of speaking calmly; that little flock, rather than the canaille, will prevail in the long run.[4] These are not merely the views of a young man or a part-time cynic: in his very last and most solemn book, the essay on Seneca, Diderot returns to the charge and denounces the masses for their perversity, their crudity, their stupidity.[5] They have not changed and will not change.

At the same time, in the midst of this apparently unrelieved pessimism about the capacities of the canaille, and the capacity of education to permit the canaille to become something better, some of the philosophes could see countervailing forces at work. Diderot came to understand, if fleetingly, that the ignorance of the masses was not an inescapable condition, but a result deliberately produced by the holders of power and privilege: he invited Falconet to look at the "fear they have of the truth," and at "the efforts they have made at all times to stifle it, and to keep the people in a state of ignorance and stupidity."[6] When in the 1770s, he devised an educational program for the realm of Catherine II, he told the czarina that there should be education for all: "From prime minister down to the last peasant, it is good for everyone to know how to read, write, and count." The objection of aristocrats that education made peasants litigious and the objection of men of letters that it made the lower orders discontented with their station were nothing better than special pleading: it has always been in the interest of the privileged orders to keep the lower orders illiterate—it makes oppression so much easier. Of course, while all schools including the universities should be in principle open to all without distinction of rank, not everyone needed the same, or a higher, education. Nor should all study the classics: they should be reserved to those who really needed them—poets, scholars, men of letters. These suggestions are just that: suggestions. But they show Diderot at least groping for a principle: an aristocracy of education emerging from a democracy of opportunity.

Even Voltaire showed tendencies in the direction of liberalism.

---

[4] See Diderot's fragment "L'église invisible," in Dieckmann: *Inventaire*, 233; and Diderot to Falconet (September 1766?). *Correspondance*, VI, 306.
[5] See *Œuvres*, III, 161, 263–4, 331. I owe one of these references to Mrs. Matile Poor.
[6] Diderot to Falconet (May 1768). *Correspondance*, VIII, 41.

Unfortunately for his reputation among the reformers, throughout his life he expressed his contempt for lesser breeds in quotable formulations. In his earlier literary work he denounced the "people" as vacillating, emotionally unreliable, unjust, cruel, and fanatical.[7] In his histories, he took the unqualified position that "the populace is the same nearly everywhere."[8] Like Hume and Diderot, he saw no improvement likely: "As for the canaille," he wrote to d'Alembert, "I have no concern with it; it will always remain canaille."[9] Logically enough, Voltaire was inclined to argue that efforts at enlightenment must be restricted to the orders that can profit from it. Those who live by manual labor alone probably will never "have the time and the capacity to instruct themselves; they will die of hunger before they become philosophers."[1] Flippantly, Voltaire told d'Alembert: "We have never pretended to enlighten shoemakers and servants; that is the job of the apostles."[2] The consequences were plain: "Natural religion for the magistrates, damn'd stuff for the mob."[3] This was an early view; but in the 1760s, he was still of the same opinion: "I commend *l'inf* . . . . to you," he wrote to Diderot; "it must be destroyed among respectable people and left to the canaille large and small, for whom it was made."[4] When La Chalotais sent him his educational plan, Voltaire was delighted to see that it explicitly excluded the *peuple:* "I thank you for proscribing study among day-laborers," he wrote in acknowledgment. "I, who cultivate the earth, petition you to have laborers, not tonsured ecclesiastics."[5]

But the same man who could cynically put down manual laborers as canaille who would always go to mass and to the tavern, because they could sing in both places, also championed the Genevan Natives in the mid-1760s, and learned, in those years, to discriminate among various types of canaille. With the years, Voltaire became less disdainful, more optimistic about the capacities of ordinary men. There were countries, notably England, the Dutch Republic, and

---

[7] *Œdipe* and *La mort de César*, in *Œuvres*, II, 83; III, 330.
[8] *Siècle de Louis XIV*, in *Œuvres historiques*, 720.
[9] June 4 (1767). *Correspondence*, LXVI, 6.
[1] Voltaire to Damilaville, April 1 (1766). Ibid., LXI, 3.
[2] September 2 (1768). Ibid., LXX, 45.
[3] Quoted in Walter L. Dorn: *Competition for Empire, 1740–1763* (1940), 211.
[4] September 25 (1762). *Correspondence*, L, 53.
[5] February 28 (1763). Ibid., LI, 204.

Geneva, where common men were avid readers and reasonable political beings. When Linguet warned him that all would be lost once the people should discover that it has intelligence, Voltaire demurred: some people, those who did nothing but toil, were doubtless beyond the pale of light. "But the more skilled artisans who are forced by their very profession to think a great deal, to perfect their taste, to extend their knowledge, are beginning to read all over Europe." No, he protested to Linguet, "all is not lost when one gives the people the chance to see that it has intelligence. On the contrary, all is lost when one treats it like a herd of cattle, for sooner or later it will gore you with its horns."[6] This was written in 1767, when Voltaire had done a great deal to educate himself about the potentialities of the lower orders. Like Diderot's perceptions of the 1770s, Voltaire's perceptions of the 1760s were promising beginnings; they were the prerequisites for a comprehensive liberal theory of politics that would connect the logic of education as enlightenment with the practical needs of the poor, give room to the dimension of time by recognizing that those who were illiterate now might become literate later, and exercise the philosophes' favorite device, criticism, on the self-interest of the ruling orders who kept the canaille in its place not because that place was natural but because it was convenient—for the ruling orders. But the philosophes stopped with these perceptions, and perceptions are not a theory. Their failure is the central weakness in the philosophes' political thought; it lends a certain weight to the widespread charge that the philosophes were after all superficial thinkers.

II

To speak about the masses in the eighteenth century is to speak about the social religion. While the question goes back to the ancients, it was of consuming interest to the men of the Enlightenment and, since they were all passionate classicists, they did not hesitate to draw on classical literature when they considered their own times. The case for a social religion, in short, is this: the masses, prey to passion and inaccessible to reason, must be frightened out of anti-

---

[6] (March 15, 1767). Ibid., LXV, 48.

social behavior with tremendous threats of supernatural punishment, and tempted into docility by promises of supernatural rewards. This cynical, calculated religiosity, preached by rulers who do not believe it, is a kind of auxiliary police, more effective than any mere temporal restraining force. The mob, Juvenal had disdainfully said, wants only *panem et circenses;* but others added that it needed not merely tangible rewards and distracting amusement, but the whip of fear as much as the lure of reward: the rabble inspires fear only as long as it is not itself afraid, Tacitus said; once it has been intimidated by superstitions, it may be safely despised.[7]

As comparative sociologists eager to use historical materials for their generalizations, the philosophes were delighted to discover that Roman rulers in particular had inculcated superstitions for the sake of controlling the populace, and that Roman writers had understood and applauded that policy. Montesquieu, in his *Sur la politique des Romains dans la religion,* and Gibbon, with elegant sophistication and evident enjoyment in his *Decline and Fall of the Roman Empire,* noted that Roman statesmen had manufactured religious notions, forged religious documents, piously celebrated religious rites they secretly despised, all to keep the lower orders in check: Augustus, said Gibbon, was "sensible that mankind is governed by names," and so, to preserve social peace, he gave the Romans names, both glorious and frightening. "The policy of the emperors and the senate, as far as it concerned religion," Gibbon noted with relish, "was happily seconded by the reflections of the enlightened, and by the habits of the superstitious, part of their subjects. The various modes of worship which prevailed in the Roman world were all considered by the people as equally true, by the philosopher as equally false, and by the magistrates as equally useful."[8] It seemed an interesting policy and, some of the philosophes thought, one worth imitating in a modern version in the eighteenth century. If the masses really were hopelessly mired in their passions and their superstitions, if attempts to make them reasonable were simply utopian, the social religion offered a cheap and effective means of social control. To deprive the masses of religion was a risky business, even, Voltaire thought,

---

[7] See Tacitus: *Annales,* I, 29.
[8] For further details and references see *The Rise of Modern Paganism,* 152–7.

the "thinking masses"; unable to discriminate between true and false religion, they might take a legend that has been exposed to stand for religion itself, and then terrible consequences might follow: "Then they will say, 'There is no religion,' and will abandon themselves to crime."[9] By the middle of the eighteenth century, this view was a commonplace in advanced circles—even among liberal clergymen.

It was a seductive, apparently impeccable line of reasoning. But it ran afoul of the philosophes' prized desire to spread enlightenment in general, and to crush l'infâme in particular. It was of course possible to argue, as Voltaire had argued, that one must educate some but not all, enlighten some but not all, écraser l'infâme for some but not all. But this involved a kind of selective lying that appeared too clever to be comfortable, and downright disagreeable. Moreover, as the philosophes knew, throughout history there had been a respectable minority party of scholars and thinkers who rejected the social religion: in the sixteenth century, Pietro Pomponazzi had argued in a famous essay that men who doubted the immortality of the soul could still be moral; late in the seventeenth century, Bayle had argued that a society of atheists could flourish and live in peace. Obviously the argument that ordinary men freed from the check of religion will simply run riot and give their antisocial impulses full play did not impress Bayle; he was concerned far more with the baleful effects of superstition. "The ancient paradox of Plutarch," wrote Gibbon, one of Bayle's admirers, "that atheism is less pernicious than superstition, acquires a tenfold vigour when it is adorned with the colours of his wit, and pointed with the acuteness of his logic."[1] Since the philosophes took Bayle with the utmost seriousness, his reasoning, which ran wholly counter to all arguments in behalf of a social religion, entered the mainstream of enlightened speculation and caused some debate. Voltaire, moved in part by his suspicion of atheism, took occasion to disagree with his great model: a society of atheists could function, he wrote late in life, only if it is a small colony of philosophers.[2]

This was a concession, and it suggests that the whole notion of

[9] Notebooks, 313.
[1] Autobiography, 89. See The Rise of Modern Paganism, 292.
[2] See Voltaire: "Athée, Athéisme," Questions sur l'Encyclopédie, in Œuvres, XVII, 461-3.

religion as policeman caused the philosophes a good deal of uneasiness. Frederick II had no doubts: the mob needs the deception of religious lies for the sake of society as a whole. But then, Frederick was not a philosophe. Those who were treated the subject with hesitations, and they experienced sudden reversals. D'Alembert, for one, thought that in view of the irrationality of the multitude a social religion was a logical policy, yet he had doubts whether it would be effective: "In general the multitude is vividly moved only by the fear of an evil or the experience of a present good. Sad experience, unfortunately only too true, proves, to the shame of mankind, that the crimes punished by the laws are committed more rarely than those of which the Supreme Being is the sole witness and the sole judge, although divine law prohibits both the one and the other equally. Thus, on the one hand, the penalties with which faith threatens us are by nature the most formidable curb on crime; on the other hand, the blindness of the human spirit prevents this curb from being as general as it might be."[3] Here was a genuine perplexity: men were even too superstitious, it seemed, to listen to the voice of religion. In a letter to Frederick of Prussia, d'Alembert pours out his perplexity and his uncertain hope that a rational religion, a kind of ritualistic deism, might work after all: he was inclined to agree with the Prussian king, he wrote, that the "people needs a creed other than a reasonable religion." Yet then he goes on, "If the Peace of Westphalia would permit a fourth religion in the Empire, I should beg Your Majesty to have a very simple temple constructed in Berlin or in Potsdam; there, God should be honored in a manner worthy of Him, and there one should preach nothing but humanity and justice. And if the crowd would not come to this temple after a few years (for one really must allow reason a few years to win its cause), Your Majesty would clearly be victorious—it would not be the first time."[4] This is the hesitant philosophe face to face with the self-confident cynic, hoping, almost against hope, that reason will slowly, slowly come to prevail even among the

---

[3] *"Morale des législateurs,"* in *Éléments de philosophie.* For Frederick and the need for lies, see above, 486–7.
[4] D'Alembert to Frederick II (February 1771). *Œuvres complètes,* V, 308. I owe this reference, and the previous one, to Mr. Ronald I. Boss.

common people, and seeking a *culte* which, however unnecessary it might be for a philosophe, would not contain anything that would make a philosophe ashamed.

D'Alembert's hesitations point the way to a principled rejection of any prudential lying whatever. In the Enlightenment there was a party of honesty, including not merely Kant, who thought lying unacceptable under all circumstances whatever, but philosophes like Holbach and Diderot, who had even less confidence in the powerful than they had in the poor. Holbach objected to even the most reasonable religion as nothing better than a trick imposed on the subject by the ruler for his own selfish purposes; besides, religion never prevented crime but often caused it. Diderot for his part was convinced that a nation relying on God to keep men from stealing and murdering must be backward indeed; the existence of God, he wrote, is like marriage: it is a notion useful for three or four people, but disastrous for the rest of the world. "The vow of indissoluble marriage makes, and must make, almost as many unhappy people as there are husbands. Belief in a God makes, and must make, almost as many fanatics as there are believers." Wherever there is belief in God, "the natural order of moral duties is reversed, and morality is corrupted."[5] Honesty was the only good policy.

Even Voltaire, the notorious cynic, gradually moved in the direction of a candid liberalism. Everyone knows the anecdote about Voltaire entertaining fellow philosophes at Ferney: as they frankly talk about atheism, he silences them, sends the servants out of the room, and then justifies his precaution: "Do you want your throats cut tonight?" It is a dubious story, but the feeling is authentic enough. Repeatedly, Voltaire called for a social religion that would sustain the social order by holding out the warning of a God who watched the world, punished sinners, and rewarded the good. This was certainly not the God in whom Voltaire himself believed, but it was also not the God of Christianity. The social religion Voltaire called for was a relatively rational religion that reduced nonsense, observances, manipulation, and priestly power to a minimum: deism for the mob. "The simpler the laws, the more the magistrates are respected; the simpler the religion, the more its ministers will be

---

[5] To Sophie Volland (October 6, 1765). *Correspondance*, V, 134.

revered. Religion can be simple. If the Protestants have got rid of twenty superstitions, they can get rid of thirty. . . . When enlightened people will announce a single God, rewarder and avenger, no one will laugh, everyone will obey."[6] Unfortunately, priests and politicians through the ages had imposed other kinds of religion, filled with terror, superstition, incredible fables, and enforced by inquisitors, "torch in hand."[7] That kind of religion had been both intellectually despicable and politically unsound; worse, it had burdened the world with misery and crime instead of relieving the one and controlling the other.

But Voltaire went further than this. "I want my attorney, my tailor, my servants, even my wife to believe in God, and I think that then I shall be robbed and cuckolded less often."[8] For Voltaire, the social religion embraces members of respectable classes. It embraced even royalty; Voltaire was as afraid of a king's atheism as of a servant's atheism, perhaps more. "An atheist king is more dangerous than a fanatical Ravaillac."[9] Except for the philosophes, who needed no lies to orient themselves in the world and who could sustain morality through philosophy alone, everyone could use the spur of hope and the specter of fear.

But in the 1760s, while he continued to voice the old doubts, Voltaire went beyond this position to approach the categorical stand of Holbach and Didcrot. His surprising and pleasing experiences with ordinary Genevans helped to shape his growing misgivings about any sort of social lie. It was, after all, a matter of time and education. "The pure worship of the Supreme Being is today beginning to be the religion of all respectable people; it will soon descend to the sound part of the masses."[1] Religion will be purified by thinking men; the others will follow. Reason had already made inroads in

---

[6] *Notebooks*, II, 381.
[7] Ibid.
[8] "A,B,C," in *Philosophical Dictionary*, II, 605.
[9] *Histoire de Jenni*, in *Œuvres*, XXI, 573—a strong thing to say, since Voltaire regarded the assassin of Henri IV as the greatest criminal in history. Incidentally, Voltaire obviously here is thinking of Frederick II of Prussia, but Frederick was not an atheist; he was a cynic about men and wholly unashamed about exploiting what he regarded to be their weakness.
[1] *Le dîner du comte de Boulainvilliers*, in *Œuvres*, XXVI, 555.

superstition, it will make further inroads with the passage of time. It was certain that throughout history the most avid advocates of a social religion had been men whose aims ran counter to the aims of philosophical minds; it was at least possible, therefore, that the philosophes might strike an alliance with ordinary men and uproot superstitions together with them. Mankind had been dominated by the "deceiving party"; perhaps it was time to trust the "deceived party" at last.[2] The elimination of the social religion presented itself to Voltaire at least as a possibility. "Perhaps," he wrote, and the caution is obvious, "there is no other remedy for the contagion" of fanaticism "than finally to enlighten the people itself."[3]

One thing, though, he thought absolutely clear: whatever social religion might finally be devised, it must include no compulsion. That is why Voltaire responded so vehemently to the notorious chapter on social religion in Rousseau's *Contrat social*. Rousseau had urged a civil profession of faith that everyone in the community must subscribe to; anyone who, having publicly accepted this profession, then acted as though he did not believe it, must be put to death. Voltaire found this notion nothing less than outrageous: "All dogma is ridiculous, deadly," he noted in the margin of his copy; and again, "All coercion on dogma is abominable. To compel belief is absurd. Confine yourself to compel good living."[4]

It scarcely matters that Voltaire did not fully understand Rousseau's purpose; his anger does credit to his liberalism. It suggests, once again, that he and most of the other philosophes were unwilling to force even their most cherished convictions on men not ready to accept them. They were not fanatics, even if they were often condescending and cynical about those who had not had their advantages. Yet even that condescension and cynicism were open to revision in their minds; it was just that the lot of the poor seemed so hopeless. But was it hopeless? The philosophes—and here they agreed with Rousseau—were always reluctant to give up hope.

---

[2] *Jusqu'à quel point on doit tromper le peuple*, in ibid., XXIV, 71. The whole essay is worth reading, along with the article "Fraud" in the *Philosophical Dictionary*, I, 279–83.
[3] *Précis du siècle de Louis XV*, in *Œuvres*, XV, 394.
[4] George R. Havens: *Voltaire's Marginalia on the Pages of Rousseau: A Comparative Study of Ideas* (1933), 68. On the question of Rousseau's social religion, see below.

3. JEAN-JACQUES ROUSSEAU: MORAL MAN
IN MORAL SOCIETY

I

ROUSSEAU was not wholly in the Enlightenment, but he was of it. The course of his life was one long estrangement from his fellow philosophes; his intimacy with Diderot, his admiration for Voltaire, his dependence on Hume, all ended in mutual hostility and public recriminations. While in his later years, his judgment clouded by paranoia, Rousseau greatly exaggerated the malice and the range of the "conspiracy" that the "Holbachian clique" had launched against him, he was right to suspect them of rancor and not wholly wrong to fear their machinations. Yet in some sense Rousseau always remained a member of the family he would not have and that would not have him. They needed each other in friendship as in enmity; they never stopped thinking and writing about one another, and some philosophes, like Hume and d'Alembert, who had good grounds for complaint against him, continued to treat Rousseau with compassion, and as a philosophe: in the mid-1760s, when Voltaire was incensed at Rousseau's indiscretions, d'Alembert urged him to be calm: it is annoying, he told Voltaire, "that there should be discord in the camp of philosophy at the very moment when it is going to capture Troy."[5]

The quarrels that divided Rousseau from his fellows are highly instructive. They were partly the fault of his style, an instrument much admired in his day, even by his critics, but a sharp knife that could cut in two directions. His writings, as David Hume noted in 1766, were "full of Extravagance"[6]; they are marked by a vehemence of expression, an almost forced spontaneity, a fatal addiction to lapidary phrases that veiled their essential meaning despite all of

---

[5] Grimsley: *D'Alembert*, 145.
[6] Hume to Jean-Baptiste-Antoine Suard, November 5, 1766. *Letters*, II, 103.

Rousseau's desperate attempts to make them perspicuous. The philosopher who talked of forcing men to be free, or who defined the "thinking man" as a "depraved animal," could hardly be surprised if his critics called him an authoritarian or an irrationalist, though he was neither. Rousseau came to discover that each of his clarifications invited new misunderstandings, and his life—that melodramatic vagabondage punctuated by angry letters—only focused attention on the paradoxes in his thought. As his former associates were to complain: Rousseau was a playwright who inveighed against the theater, a moralist who abandoned his children, a religious philosopher who changed his confession twice for dubious reasons, a libertarian who could not get compulsion out of his mind, a deist who accused his fellow deists of irreligion, a professional celebrant of friendship who broke with everyone.

Those of Rousseau's ideas that were clear produced quite as much estrangement as those that seemed mere paradoxes. His devastating critique of culture, his unprecedented candor, his imaginative history of reason, his passion for politics set him apart from his fellow philosophes. Yet, in themselves, these ideas should have caused little trouble: other philosophes found it possible to disagree with one another across a wide range, and on matters they took very seriously, without raising their voices. Rousseau alone aroused aversion amounting at times to hatred, and alone invited retaliation. Moreover, while Rousseau's ideas made him an isolated figure among the men of the Enlightenment, they also made him a member of their party. True: by offering a solution to the dilemma between freedom and reform that beset the others, Rousseau had entered a new era, for men who solve the problems that their contemporaries merely state have stepped, by that very act, beyond them. But if Rousseau's solutions presented glimpses of a future not wholly palatable, offering some new possibilities and many new dangers, his problems, his interests, and in most essential respects his philosophical style anchor him firmly in the soil of the Enlightenment.

Nor can mere personal causes fully explain Rousseau's isolation. His touchiness and impulsive gestures were disagreeable in the extreme; he permitted himself indiscretions that threatened to endanger writers intent on hiding their authorship of radical pamphlets, and he interfered in the cozy amorous arrangements of his friends with his middle-aged passions. By the 1760s he often moved beyond the boundaries of sanity, spreading false and ridiculous accusations against well-meaning and innocent acquaintances. On the other side, Rousseau's very way of life grated on his former associates as though it were a reproach. But this too does not account for the philosophes' sense that they were dealing with a demonic figure. There was something in him not to be explained by his style, his ideas, or his eccentricities alone, but compounded of all three, a strange element, that made his contemporaries uneasy.

This element is easy to identify but hard to define. It emerges in Rousseau's almost voluptuous retelling of repulsive anecdotes about heroic Spartans who would rather have a fox eat out their insides than show a moment's distress, his self-righteous attack on the theater as an immoral institution, his evident infatuation with the impossibly self-important heroine of his *Nouvelle Héloïse*, and his humorless ideal of the good man as exemplified in young Émile, a combination of Spartan muscularity, Genevan philistinism, and the bourgeois ethic of utility. Beyond this, Rousseau is all too often inclined to play God with his characters. One might argue, of course, that a writer may do with his characters as he chooses, but Rousseau sometimes sounds like a caricature of the enlightened despot about whom he had said some cutting things. It is as though Rousseau, fearful of his powerlessness, compensates by dreaming his dreams of omnipotence in public. Such conduct is always inappropriate, but especially so in *Émile*, his pedagogic masterpiece, designed after all to show the road to human autonomy. Young Émile repeatedly finds himself the victim of his manipulative tutor who takes some satisfaction in his capacity to get Émile to think and do what the tutor wants him to, while Émile mistakenly thinks that he is really free. When, at the end, Émile has married and reached his goal of independence, the tutor ostentatiously takes his leave to retire. But Émile is as much a dependent boy as before, perhaps more: "Up to now I have done my best to fulfill my duty to you," the tutor tells Émile and his wife; "at this point my long task is over, and that of another begins. Today I abdicate the authority you have entrusted to me, and here," pointing to Émile's wife, "is your guardian from now on." Even after the tutor has left them, the young couple continue to consult him and ask him to "govern" them: "We shall be docile,"

Émile promises. "As long as I live, I shall have need of you."[7] Having constructed his bold ideal, Rousseau is afraid to take hold of it.

This fear, I think, reappears in another area of Rousseau's concern, and one of critical importance: his urgent, sometimes frantic longing for community. The most acutely alienated among the philosophes, and the one most acutely aware of alienation as a cultural as well as personal malaise, Rousseau was also, and largely for that reason, impatient with frivolity and diversity. His models were simple civilizations, legendary Sparta and a Genevan republic idealized out of all recognition. He longed for a small society of equals in which each was candid with all, political participation was a universal feast of reasonable discussion and passionate fraternity, civic loyalty eclipsed all partial loyalties, and social utility governed all public deliberations. The pleasures, the diversions, the cultivation he prescribed for his good society are intensely purposeful, designed never to entertain but always to teach, to inculcate moral ideals, encourage respectable marriages, and stoke the fires of patriotic fervor.

This peculiar mixture of antique moralizing and political Calvinism pervades Rousseau's polemical and prescriptive writings. In his famous *Lettre à d'Alembert sur les spectacles*, which I have discussed before, Rousseau argues that Geneva had escaped the corruption of Paris by prohibiting a theater within its boundaries, for even at its best, the theater is a diversion in the literal sense: an activity that seduces men from the straight path of thinking on, and doing, their duty. His diatribe makes depressing reading, but it is perfectly comprehensible considering Rousseau's fear of pleasure and of effeminacy.[8]

Rousseau's advice to the Poles concerning their state, written in 1771 at the invitation of a Polish nobleman, transfers his search for community from his own to a foreign country. Education, Rousseau writes, is crucial, for it is "education that must give souls their national form, and so direct their opinions and their tastes that they will be patriots by inclination, by passion, by necessity."[9] By education Rousseau obviously means more than schooling: he calls for the glorification of patriotic virtues through honors and public rewards,

---

[7] *Émile*, 614. For instances of manipulation, see ibid., 120–7, 412–15.
[8] See above, 258–9.
[9] *Considérations sur le Gouvernement de Pologne et sur sa réformation projetée*, in *Œuvres*, III, 966.

suggests that a small country can succeed in being free because there "all the citizens know and watch one another," and proposes sumptuary legislation that will stifle greed and the lust for luxury. While there shall be "military luxury" conducive to the martial spirit, it is "necessary to abolish (even at court, to set an example) the ordinary amusements of courts like gambling, theaters, comedies, opera; everything that makes men effeminate, everything that distracts them, isolates them, makes them forget their country and their duty; everything that makes them enjoy themselves as long as they are being entertained."[1]

The most familiar and most widely discussed instance of Rousseau's craving for wholeness appears in his chapter on the social religion in the *Contrat social*. Since the mid-1750s, when he had asked Voltaire to write the catechism of a civil profession of faith, Rousseau had considered the question of social cohesion. In the *Contrat social* he set out how such cohesion could be guaranteed: the state needs a "purely civil profession of faith," whose articles were fixed "not precisely as dogmas of religion but as sentiments of sociability, without which it is impossible to be a good citizen or a faithful subject." To be sure, no one should be compelled to accept these articles, but the sovereign can banish those who do not believe them, "not as impious, but as antisocial, as incapable of sincerely loving the laws and justice, and of immolating their life to their duty if necessary." Finally, if someone, having publicly acknowledged these dogmas, "behaved as though he did not believe them, he should be put to death; he has committed the greatest of crimes, he has lied before the law." Rousseau insisted that the dogmas be clear and few in number, limited to belief in an intelligent and beneficent God, a life to come, the happiness of the just, the punishment of the wicked, the sanctity of the social contract and the laws, and outlawing only one thing: intolerance.[2] Rousseau evidently did not believe that either atheists or fanatics could ever be good citizens.

All this was deeply disturbing to the other philosophes, not to Voltaire alone. Yet Diderot and Rousseau have been called "hostile brothers," and with some restrictions the same name applies to Voltaire and Rousseau, d'Alembert and Rousseau. And philosophes like

---

[1] Ibid., 970, 962.
[2] *Du contrat social*, in *Œuvres*, III, 468–9.

Kant, who enjoyed the advantage of not knowing Rousseau in person, did not hesitate to acknowledge him as their master, just as the archbishop of Paris, quite as unhesitatingly, stigmatized him as an impious philosopher. Later history has given undue prominence to what was a disturbing undertone in Rousseau and converted an organic but subdued element into a dominant concern of political speculation. But the estimates of Rousseau's contemporaries remain just, while the terms current in the vocabulary of our day lead to misunderstandings. Rousseau was not a totalitarian; he was not even a collectivist. If he was anything, he was, with his fervor for freedom, what his earliest readers called him: an individualist. But, then, none of these names reach the heart of Rousseau, for looking beyond politics Rousseau was above all a moralist, and, as a moralist, an educator.

II

To fix Rousseau the man and thinker with a label is to impoverish him, for one prominent characteristic he shared with the other philosophes was versatility. Like Diderot, Hume, and Lessing, Rousseau was competent in many areas, and active in areas in which his competence was at best limited. Rousseau was for a time a popular composer and widely known for his writings on music; he won fame with an unmeasured assault on civilization, and kept it alive with an enormously successful novel and an enormously influential book on pedagogy; he participated in political polemics in Geneva, offered political advice to Corsicans and Poles, and devoted some of his best efforts to political theory; he was an innovating autobiographer and psychologist. Almost from the beginning of his life to the very end he had a genius for catching the imagination of the public; even his solitude was well publicized, and he succeeded in making himself into a center of controversy as much for what he was and even what he wore as for what he wrote.

Rousseau was by no means so scattered and impulsive as he appeared to be. His reports of his sudden dramatic inspirations are too well known; they have eclipsed his other reports of slow, deliberate reflection. If historians have come to visualize him seizing the secrets of the universe under a tree, bathed in tears, this is largely his own doing. Many of his most important ideas, in fact, he pondered for years and subjected to severe logical scrutiny. I have said before that all his attempts at clarifying his thought only resulted in further confusion, but he stubbornly told the world that he was consistent in his work and operated with a small store of ideas, well thought out. "All that is daring in the *Contrat social*," he said in the *Confessions*, "had previously appeared in the *Discours sur l'inégalité*; all that is daring in *Émile* had previously appeared in *Julie*."[3] No one believed him: his life and, it seemed, his work showed him to be a man torn and confused, a man guilty proclaiming his innocence. He was all of that, but he sought wholeness and clarity, and his conception of himself as an educator, a role that the other philosophes also liked to claim, gave his work a center of gravity. Like his favorite philosopher, Plato, he sought to discover and produce the moral man who would make the moral society, and a moral society that would foster the moral man.

Rousseau often insisted on the critical importance of education. Throughout *Émile* he scatters hints that education and life and, in particular, education and politics, belong together. He refers those interested in education to his history of culture in the *Discours sur l'origine de l'inégalité*; he sends them to his political writings to learn the political bearing of his educational ideas; he lays it down that "We must study society through individuals, and individuals through society: those who want to treat politics and morals separately will never understand anything of either."[4] Most instructive of all, he appeals to Plato: "If you want a good idea of what public education is, read Plato's *Republic*. This is by no means a work on politics, as those who judge books only by their titles like to think: it is the finest treatise on education ever written"[5]—an injunction that invites us to perform the opposite operation with *Émile* and see it as a great book on politics masquerading as a treatise on education. Occasional diversions apart, Rousseau's work stands under the sign of civil education—*paideia*.

Plato had seen learning as the recovery of what had been lost: the trauma of birth had deprived man of what he had always known,

---

[3] *Œuvres*, I, 407.
[4] *Émile*, 279.
[5] Ibid., 10; see also, 70, 223.

and his education must restore to him what was rightfully his. Rousseau saw education as a recovery in a somewhat different sense. He often came back to it: his leading theme was man's tragic departure from his essential nature, and his great task, to find the way that would enable man to reclaim it. Appropriately, Rousseau announces this theme in the very first line of *Émile:* "All is good as it leaves the hands of the Author of things, all degenerates in the hands of men,"[6] a famous sentence echoed in the equally famous sentence that opens the first chapter of the *Contrat social:* "Man is born free, and everywhere he is in chains."[7] While Rousseau's account of man's essential character varies, it always remains faithful to the idea that man is originally without sin, that he comes into the world a free being, and that he is equipped with the capacity for decency, public-spiritedness, candor, authentic rationality. History, then, is for Rousseau a depressing commentary on man's failure to realize his potentialities.

Rousseau did not launch his career as a philosopher with a life's program; yet if most modern critics have found a profound coherence in his thought and an orderly development, this is not of their making. It is there, in his writings. Rousseau's books of the 1750s are diagnostic and critical. They lay bare the damage. Rousseau's trio of masterpieces, published between 1760 and 1762, move from diagnosis to prescription: they outline the remedy. Even the painful books of his last years perform a didactic task, though more indirectly.[8] His three autobiographies are an appeal to a world that will not understand. They do not invite imitation—Rousseau knows that he is inimitable. But these brilliant and pathetic apologies, unprecedented in their grasp of the dark side of men's motives, make a case for the one man among modern men who could have done the pedagogic work he had done: "Whence could the painter and apolo-

---

[6] Ibid., 5.
[7] *Œuvres*, III, 351.
[8] This division between critical, constructive, and confessional phases in Rousseau's writings has become familiar to scholars of his work. They are, of course, not to be strictly divided in this way, since, for example, the *Discours sur l'économie politique*, which, dating from 1755, belongs to the first phase chronologically, foreshadows the constructive proposals of the *Contrat social*, which is of 1762.

gist of human nature have taken his model, if not from his own heart? He has described this nature just as he felt it within himself. The prejudices which had not subjugated him, the artificial passions which had not made him their victim—they did not hide from his eyes, as from those of all others, the basic traits of humanity, so generally forgotten and misunderstood. . . . In a word, it was necessary that one man should paint his own portrait to show us, in this manner, the natural man."[9] The autobiographies are the pleas of the physician of civilization falsely accused of being its poisoner; they assert the uniqueness of his competence and the accuracy of his prescription.

From his first discourse, then, to his last reminiscence, Rousseau traversed a long but unbroken road; the claims of the latest works are implicit in the criticisms of the earliest. Rousseau's *Discours sur les sciences et les arts* suffers all the disadvantages of a first work: it is strident, argumentative, a debater's speech marshaling all the evidence on one side while suppressing all the evidence on the other. Rousseau himself later came to distrust this discourse, and with some justification: he scolds a great deal in it, and analyzes little. But as a first try at his great theme—man's departure from his nature—it is perfectly satisfactory. "Our souls have been corrupted to the degree that our arts and sciences have advanced toward perfection."[1] His second book, the *Discours sur l'origine de l'inégalité*, is far more ambitious than the first, and far more discriminating, but it pursues the same theme; it delineates a hypothetical history of man to discover how he has come to be what he is: snobbish, heartless, indifferent to elemental passions, and a stranger to true morality. In the original state of nature, men had been torpid, pacific, and equal; then the invention of private property, social distinctions, and the state introduced complications. "The first man who, having enclosed a piece of land, thought of saying, *This is mine*, and found people simple enough to believe him, was the true founder of civil society. How many crimes, wars, murders, miseries and horrors, might mankind not have been spared, if someone had pulled up the stakes or filled in the ditch, and shouted to his fellow-men: 'Beware of listen-

---

[9] "Dialogue Troisième," *Rousseau juge de Jean-Jacques*, in *Œuvres*, I, 936.
[1] *Œuvres*, III, 9.

ing to this impostor; you are ruined if you forget that the fruits of the earth are everyone's, and that the soil itself is no one's.' "[2]

His first readers impatiently repudiated the discourse on inequality as an invitation to primitivism: Voltaire covered the copy Rousseau had sent him with uncomplimentary remarks, and acknowledged it with a burst of facile jokes: he thanked Rousseau sarcastically for his "new book against the human race" and suggested that it would tempt men to walk on all fours.[3] But this was not the case Rousseau intended to make. The vices of modern civilization may be glaring, but since cultivated men share in them, and profit from them, they need a powerful, shocking demonstration of the betrayal they have perpetrated on their true nature. Instead of collaboration, there is social strife; instead of benevolence, hostility; instead of justice, injustice; instead of equality, inequality; worst of all, instead of the recognition of reality, the deliberate cultivation of appearance—this is the world Rousseau wanted men to see clearly for the first time. But the cure for modern civilization is not return to the savage state; it is, rather, the construction of a higher civilization. "We must not call Rousseau a liberal," John Plamenatz has said, "because others have called him a totalitarian."[4] Just so; and we must not call Rousseau a primitivist because he attacked modern civilization. The original state of nature, and the several stages of prepolitical society that followed upon it, are ineligible as an option and unsuitable as an ideal. Their single use now is to hold a mirror up to society, that men may learn to despise and to reform it. Mankind cannot go back—on this point Rousseau always insisted, though, perhaps, in this early stage, less forcefully than was necessary to secure understanding of his thought. In all his writings, Rousseau said of himself late in life, he saw "the development of his great principle that nature has made man happy and good but that society depraves him and makes him miserable. *Émile* in particular, that book that has been so much read, so little understood, and so poorly appreciated, is nothing but a treatise on the original goodness of man." In his earliest writings, he had "concentrated most of all on

---

[2] Ibid., 164.
[3] Voltaire to Rousseau (August 30, 1755). *Correspondence*, XXVII, 230. See above, 95.
[4] John Plamenatz: *Man And Society*, I, *Machiavelli Through Rousseau* (1963), 436.

destroying that illusion that gives us a foolish admiration for the instruments of our unhappiness, and to correct that misleading evaluation that makes us honor pernicious talents and despise useful virtues. Everywhere he shows us mankind better, wiser, and happier in its primitive condition, blind, miserable, and wicked to the degree that it has departed from that condition." But, he emphatically adds, "human nature does not turn back. Once man has left it, he never returns to the time of innocence and equality"—this was another principle on which Rousseau "insisted most strongly." Rousseau repudiates the widespread and "obstinate" accusation that he had wanted "to destroy the arts and sciences, the theater, and the academies, and to plunge the world into its original barbarism." Quite the contrary: "He always insisted on the preservation of existing institutions, arguing that their destruction would only remove the remedies but leave the vices intact, and to substitute plunder for corruption."[5]

This is explicit, clear, and almost wholly accurate: if Rousseau is a doubtful witness to his life, he is a perceptive and dependable commentator on his writings. His explication requires only one correction: in the *Discours sur l'inégalité* Rousseau displays primitive man as anything but wise; he is neither good nor bad, he is torpid, stupid, given over to his simple passions. For Rousseau, man is superior to the animals in a single regard—his capacity for perfection. But primitive man cannot take advantage of this unique endowment; he may be happy, but he is not a moral being. Only civilized man can realize his potentialities. Rousseau's recognition that in fact man has not realized them leads him to the conclusion that there is a desperate need for a thoroughgoing, fundamental reformation that will substitute a good for an evil civilization. "The passing from the state of nature to the civil state produces a very remarkable change in man by substituting in his conduct justice for instinct, and giving his actions the moral quality they had lacked before. It is then only, with the voice of duty succeeding physical impulse and right succeeding desire, that man, who has up to then thought of himself alone, finds himself compelled to act on other principles, and to consult his reason before he listens to his inclinations. Although in

---

[5] "Dialogue Troisième," *Rousseau juge de Jean-Jacques*, in *Œuvres*, I, 934-5. See above, 94-6.

that state he deprives himself of several advantages which he has from nature, he gains in return others so great, his faculties are so stimulated and developed, his ideas so extended, his feelings so ennobled, and his whole soul so elevated, that if the abuse of his new condition did not often degrade him below the one from which he had emerged, he would endlessly bless the happy moment that tore him from it forever, and which, in place of a stupid and narrow animal, made him an intelligent being and a man."[6] This famous passage is from the *Contrat social,* but it grows directly out of Rousseau's earlier critique of culture, and acts as a commentary upon it: his first two discourses were not exercises in nostalgia but in criticism. The work of construction depended upon, and could only follow it.

III

Rousseau developed his constructive ideas at the end of the 1750s with three important books which, dissimilar as they appear to be, belong together in conception and execution. *La Nouvelle Héloïse,* the *Contrat social,* and *Émile,* the first a novel, the second an essay on political theory, the third a treatise on education, complement and clarify one another; remove one and the other two remain incomplete and partially incomprehensible.

If the mutual relevance of the *Contrat social* and *Émile* is easy to perceive, the place of a novel in this earnest company is at first glance a little surprising. But only at first glance. On the surface, *La Nouvelle Héloïse* is a sentimental epistolary novel of the sort popular in Rousseau's day. Julie, unimpeachably aristocratic, articulate, a born lecturer, and distressingly perfect, falls in love with her middle-class tutor, Saint-Preux, who loves her for her perfections but then, being only human, for her physical charms as well. Passive, delirious with desire but anxious to sin without having to feel guilty, Saint-Preux actually has Julie seduce him; but then she sends her lover away, repents, endlessly discusses the state of her soul with her adoring friend Claire, and marries an older man, the cool, all-

---

[6] *Contrat social,* book I, chap. viii, in *Œuvres,* III, 364.

knowing atheist Wolmar, who purifies her once again through marriage, and with whom she leads a calm and fulfilling life. Saint-Preux returns, and with him the danger, but all ends, as it were, happily, with the triumph and apotheosis of Julie: she dies after rescuing one of her children from drowning, and leaves behind her an inconsolable community of widower, lover, and friend who unite in worshipping her memory. All the elements are here to make the novel a popular triumph: the slow dawning of sexual love, an affair across class lines, a daughter disobeying her father, scenes of rapture and anguish. But there is more to *La Nouvelle Héloïse* than its mechanical plot and embarrassing exclamations; its scenario, mainly the Swiss countryside and sophisticated Paris, permits Rousseau to develop some of his favorite themes. He sings hymns to the beauties of nature, has Saint-Preux experience all the corruption and viciousness and deplore all the alienation from one's true being consequent on metropolitan life, compels his characters to confess endlessly to one another and thus pay homage to his favorite cult: the cult of sincerity. But beyond that, Rousseau paints, in Julie's married life with Wolmar, a social utopia. It is a small idyll, a community reduced to its essentials and thus suitable for observation. Life in the Wolmar household, for masters and servants alike, is a model of mutual candor, general respect, kindly government, rational discourse, silence that is deeper than words. The religion the leading characters debate is a first draft of the *Profession de foi*, the education Julie's children receive is a first draft of the rest of *Émile*. *La Nouvelle Héloïse* began as an outlet for Rousseau's erotic fantasies; it ended as a didactic demonstration, aiming, like *Émile* and the *Contrat social*, at constructing a world that must be if man is to become man.

The most explicitly pedagogic of these three books is, of course, *Émile*, which Rousseau himself more than once called his best and most important work. *Émile* parades as a rational, carefully planned program designed to produce a true man, worthy of living in a good society and capable of producing such a society; its subtitle proclaims it a work on education. But soon doubts arise: the very extravagance of its governing device—the solitary boy, brought up by a single tutor, removed from his family and abstracted for years from the outside world—suggests that Rousseau is concerned with large principles rather than with a realistic scheme of education that

pedagogues might apply in life. Rousseau himself insisted on the theoretical character of his book: in 1764, he acknowledged to a correspondent that "it is impossible to make an Émile," but, he added, "can
you believe that this should have been my aim and that the book
bearing this title is a true treatise on education? It is a relatively
philosophical work on a principle that its author has advanced in
other writings: that man is naturally good."[7] *Émile* is a thought experiment in which Rousseau strips man of all that is adventitious and
of all that has corrupted other men; young Émile is of a piece with
Condillac's statue devised to demonstrate the growth of the senses.[8]
False values have dominated and distorted man's life and perceptions
for so many centuries that the very memory of authentic values has
grown dim; even the philosopher must be suspected of complicity in
the civilization he pretends to purify. This is why Rousseau employs
his extraordinary device and invents the improbable situation into
which he places Émile: the deepest study of contemporary modes of
life alone can only reveal what is wrong, but not what is right, nor
what must be done to set it right.

Some of Rousseau's contemporaries were inclined to be amused
by his educational "novel," and saw only its surface. No doubt, Rousseau gave ammunition to these critics with his strained dialogues,
unfortunate gift for provocative pronouncements, and irritable, aggressive asides to his readers. But *Émile* is a thoroughly logical and
wholly serious book; some of its notions are odd, some of its proposals outlandish, some of its implications unpleasant, but the whole
exhibits a consistent development of a few coherent central ideas.
The key to *Émile* is the Stoic injunction that man must live according to nature; it was Rousseau's genius to harness this idea, derived
from Seneca, to the idea of human development. Other pedagogues,
Rousseau notes in his Preface, "always seek the man in the child,
without thinking of what he is before he becomes a man."[9] Precisely
the opposite course is the correct one: "We must view the man as a

---

[7] Rousseau to Philibert Cramer, October 13, 1764. Quoted in *Émile*,
vi *n.*
[8] This has also been noticed by Ernst Cassirer: *The Question of
Jean Jacques Rousseau*, 113.
[9] *Émile*, 2.

man and the child as a child"[1]—to do this is to follow the indications that nature gives, and to prepare human beings to live in obedience to its commands.

The idea that children deserve respect was not in itself a new one; Juvenal, whom Rousseau paraphrases, had already said, *Maxima debetur puero reverentia*.[2] Moreover, it had been obvious for centuries that growing children pass through a set of characteristic phases; a few educators in fact, notably Locke, whom Rousseau much admired and often quotes, had passed beyond conventional talk about "the seven ages of man." But no one before Rousseau had drawn the consequences implicit in the idea of human development. The child, Rousseau forcefully argues, is not an imperfect or incomplete adult; he is a full human being with his own capacities and limitations. This is why Rousseau demands that the intellect be cultivated last—not from some innate hostility to reason, but from his estimate of the place of reason in the rhythm of human growth. "Of all man's faculties, reason, which is, so to speak, a compound of all the others, is the one that develops last and with the greatest difficulty." To reason with children, therefore, is futile, a cruel reversal of the process that nature has so obviously prescribed; it is, Rousseau notes sarcastically, "to begin at the end." If "children understood reason, they would have no need to be pupils."[3] Rousseau is in no hurry to teach Émile how to read; the boy will learn to read late because he learns to think late. For the same reason, Émile will learn history or foreign languages only after he is ready for them. "People will be surprised to see that I count the study of languages among the futilities of education; but it must be remembered that I am here speaking only of the studies of the earliest years."[4] Here, as always, Rousseau is intent on matching desires with capacities as closely as possible; it is only when the child's capacities are at full employment, neither frustrated by insensate demands nor idle through the tutor's laxity, that he can be truly happy.

While childhood is "the sleep of reason," it is also the age when

---

[1] Ibid., 63.
[2] Ibid., 102; Juvenal, XIV, 47.
[3] *Émile*, 76.
[4] Ibid., 105.

the senses are keen and the body is vigorous; this is the time when one should train the first through observation and the second through exercise. The child must not study geography out of books: he should wander in the fields, across streams and hills, get lost with a few instructions and apply what he has learned on his rambles that he may find his way home to lunch; this is how Émile will learn the geography that matters, in a way that he will always remember and always use properly. Not "words, more words, still more words," Rousseau exclaims, but "things, things!"[5] Émile is being educated in the only way that education can work: by making his experience his own.

This dogma about the late growth of reason with its attendant delay in the training of the mind is dubious doctrine, anti-intellectual in its consequences if not in its intent. Like most of Rousseau's thought, his educational ideas have proved to have the most divergent results. They have served to liberate pupils from deadening routine and in the course of two centuries have raised important questions about the meaning of education, but they have also spawned mindless platitudes about learning by doing and induced educators to mistake lack of discipline for authentic freedom. But all this was in the future. Rousseau took his view of reason as a sound observation, based firmly on the salient facts of human nature. It was "natural education," or, also in Rousseau's words, "negative education," designed to avoid the mistakes of the past and to keep Émile from absorbing the vices of his culture. Eighteenth-century education, Rousseau argues, makes children into parrots who repeat what they do not understand, or into monsters who turn into premature, hypocritical sages, skilled at parading their learning but badly crippled by a pedagogy that has given them a permanent distaste for the things that matter and false standards they will not escape as long as they live. Émile will be different; ignorant for years, he will remain pure, and as he grows, become wise without becoming superior, learned without becoming pedantic, sociable without becoming snobbish.

With adolescence comes advanced learning, at the right time and on the right foundation. The emphasis of Émile's later education will remain utilitarian, but it will include the sciences and literature. The walk in the fields that prepared Émile for geography is only the be-

[5] See ibid., 104, 203.

ginning of his scientific education; it will be followed by instruction in the use of instruments, in rudimentary applied mathematics, a practical trade, and finally—on his way to fifteen—reading.

Rousseau sounds grudging about this part of his educational program: "I hate books," he exclaims, "they teach us only to talk about things we do not know."[6] But there must be books, and so the tutor chooses as appropriate reading for the young Émile's "first book" and "for a long time his whole library"—*Robinson Crusoe*. It is an obvious choice: the adventures of Robinson Crusoe are a kind of thought experiment much like the education of Émile—Crusoe is man naked, free of accidental trappings, free of society, face to face with nature, alone. Rousseau uses *Robinson Crusoe* as a treatise on natural education; it teaches the real utility of things.[7] But while this utilitarian handbook is Émile's first reading, it is not his last: by the time he is a young man of eighteen who has experienced true friendship, authentic sociability, and the first stirrings of sensual passion, he is ready to read widely—history, biography, religion, and later, at twenty, the Latin classics. Now Émile is grown, responsible and ready for marriage.

IV

The cultural ideal implicit in this course of education is congruent with the cultural criticism of Rousseau's discourses: Rousseau's good man is in all respects the opposite of the Rococo man of eighteenth-century urban civilization. Émile has no false politeness, no egotism, no guile; he is healthy, clear-thinking, cultivated without regard to fashion, sturdy, self-reliant, public-spirited, and capable of giving and accepting affection. It is, as I have said, a humorless ideal and a little unattractive, but it has a nobler side: Rousseau has intended Émile to grow up as no one before him had grown up: into an autonomous man. Kant's affection for *Émile* was not an accident.

It is at this point, autonomy, that the *Profession de foi du Vicaire savoyard* justifies its place in *Émile*. The *Profession de foi* appears to be a lengthy digression, feebly justified by Rousseau's professed

---

[6] Ibid., 210.
[7] Ibid., 211–12.

intention to discuss Émile's religious instruction. But the digression is not an intrusion; it is necessary to explicate the first sentence and fundamental position of *Émile*—that man is born good but has somehow spoiled his natural heritage—and to show the way to his worldly redemption.

Like the rest of Rousseau's religious writings, the *Profession de foi* is drenched in emotion. Rousseau had always imported his needs into his thoughts on religion: when, in 1756, Voltaire gave vent to a profound pessimism in response to the catastrophic and, it seemed to Voltaire, senseless Lisbon earthquake, Rousseau had almost tearfully insisted on his continuing belief in Providence—not because the proofs for Providence were convincing, but because he needed his belief in Providence to live: "No," he exclaimed to Voltaire, "I have suffered too much in this life not to expect another. All the subtleties of metaphysics will not make me doubt the immortality of the soul for a moment; I feel it, I believe it, I want it, I hope for it, I shall defend it to my last breath"[8]—a moving outburst, but hardly an impressive demonstration in view of Voltaire's persistent denigration of "the subtleties of metaphysics." With Rousseau, for all his logic and critical acumen, the will to believe was prelude to belief.

Despite its passionate passages, its apostrophes to the deity and to conscience—"divine instinct"[9]—the *Profession de foi* is an exercise in philosophical theology; it is significant that among all of Rousseau's writings, this was the only one to gain Voltaire's enthusiastic approval. No wonder: it was an essay that, occasional hyperbole apart, any one among the deists in the Enlightenment would have been proud to write. It outlines a natural religion appropriate to the natural education Émile is receiving. Its very placement is important: Rousseau exposes Émile to the monologue of the Savoyard vicar when his young charge is about eighteen—when he has full command of his reason.

For the *Profession de foi is,* in its heated way, a celebration of reason. "The highest ideas of the divinity come to us from reason alone."[1] Rousseau, to be sure, maintains that reason needs the assist-

---

[8] Rousseau to Voltaire, August 18, 1756. *Correspondance complète*, ed. R. A. Leigh (1965 ——), IV, 81.
[9] *Émile*, 354.
[1] Ibid., 361.

ance of sincere emotion: he always insisted that man must establish an alliance between the rational and the passionate elements in his nature. But reason, unaided autonomous reason, is its own best authority, and the only reliable test of religious truth. Doctrines, books of exegesis, tradition, clerical establishments, priestly authority are like so many veils before the divine being. "How many men between God and me!" the Savoyard vicar exclaims, and it is Rousseau's voice we hear. God needs no intermediary, no interpreter, particularly since most, if not all, of his self-appointed spokesmen have done the divinity grievous injusice. Many of their statements are false, other are circular: "After proving the doctrine by the miracle, they then prove the miracle by the doctrine."[2] To be sure, there is a God; we have solid evidence of his existence and his transcendent goodness both through inner certainty and rational argument—Rousseau was a constructive as well as a critical deist. But the point is that man needs no external authority to prove that divine existence; to rely on others is to betray one's vocation as a man. As the Savoyard vicar tells his rapt listener: "I closed all my books. There is one book open to all eyes, that of nature. It is in this great and sublime book that I learned to serve and worship its divine author." There is no excuse for closing one's eyes to that book, for it is intelligible to all men. Suppose, the vicar suggests, "I had been born on a desert island, seen no other man, never heard what took place long ago in some corner of the world; still, if I use my reason, if I cultivate it," and make good use of the faculties with which God has endowed all men, "I should learn on my own to know him, to love him, to love his works, to want the good he wants, and to fulfill all my duties on earth to please him. What more than that could all the learning of men teach me?"[3] There is a touch of anti-intellectualism here that is familiar from Rousseau's other writings; Rousseau was always quick to ask his readers to close their books. But the dominant element here is his call for independence of judgment, for self-reliance. Since man alone is responsible for the evil in the world, man alone must strive to overcome it. In a short staged dialogue between reason and inspiration, Rousseau gives reason

[2] Ibid., 366.
[3] Ibid., 378; note the phrase "some corner of the world," which is a typical deist's reference to the origins of Christianity.

all the good lines. "No one is exempt from the first duty of man, no one has the right to depend on the judgment of another."[4] It is pronouncements such as these that made his fellow philosophes treat Rousseau like a lost brother rather than a Christian enemy, and, in the midst of their irritation, regret his desertion.

V

The *Profession de foi* is part of Rousseau's scheme to make a moral man fit to live in a moral society. Morality is private, but its stage is public. Doubtless the debate between solitude and sociability was a sensitive point for Rousseau: his first serious quarrel with Diderot, never wholly repaired, was over what he took to be Diderot's insulting reference to Rousseau's "personal reformation" in the 1750s, which included his withdrawal from Parisian society. Diderot tactlessly said that "only the evil man is alone"; Rousseau believed that he had withdrawn only to be strengthened for return. Once again, the quarrel is more than a quarrel; Rousseau's conduct is a kind of paradigm for the rhythm of Émile's education: "Wanting to form the natural man, I have no intention of making him into a savage and sending him back to the woods." The tutor intends to strengthen him for social existence by making him capable of detachment and independence: Émile must not "allow himself to be carried away by passions or by the opinions of men. Let him see with his eyes, let him feel with his heart, let him be governed by no authority but his own reason."[5] To make the social and political significance of education, if anything, even plainer that that, Rousseau includes an extensive discussion of political questions in book V of *Émile*, a book ostensibly devoted to the education of women. This book, the last, is the bridge to the *Contrat social*. *Émile* has shown the making of moral man; the *Contrat social* shows the making of moral society.

In form as in substance, the *Contrat social* is a treatise on political theory in the classical tradition. Its announced purpose is to establish a sound theory of obligation. "One thinks himself the master of others, which still leaves him more of a slave than they. How did

---

[4] Ibid., 377.
[5] Ibid., 306.

this change come about? I do not know. What can make it legitimate? I think I can resolve that question."[6] It is an ancient question, but Rousseau's solution is modern, and inextricably intertwined with his educational program. The society that makes obedience lawful, and lawful obedience practicable, is a society of Émiles.

Force does not create right. But then, what can? Men must remain free; otherwise organized society is not worth having. But men must obey; otherwise organized society cannot function. This is Rousseau's overriding problem: "To find a form of association which defends and protects with the whole common power the person and property of each associate, and in which each, uniting himself to all, yet obeys himself alone, and remains as free as before."[7] Rousseau's solution is the social contract, by which each surrenders all his powers to the general will; but since each is the general will, he has lost nothing essential and rather gained what he needs most: civic freedom. The *Contrat social* takes up where Rousseau's first two discourses had left off: it is a demonstration that the exchange of natural freedom for civic freedom is worth making, for it is this exchange that elevates man into a moral being capable of realizing his potentialities.

Man surrenders his natural rights to society, not to the state. Like other philosophes a moderate relativist, Rousseau was not doctrinaire about forms of government, and thought responsible aristocracies and elective monarchies legitimate; like other philosophes a disciple of Montesquieu, Rousseau did not think all forms suitable to all regions: freedom can subsist in many types of states and is wholly unattainable in others. But in any event, governments are only agents of society, never its master, and whatever the state may be, it must arise out of a society governed by the general will. Thus Rousseau envisions his good society as a society of free men, served rather than dominated by their government, freely obeying the laws that they themselves have made.

Political theorists have always sought to delimit the respective spheres of public authority and private freedom, and the dominant liberalism of political thought in the Enlightenment treated the two as in perpetual combat. But Rousseau eliminated the boundaries al-

---

[6] *Du contrat social,* book I, chap. i, in *Œuvres,* III, 351.
[7] Ibid., book I, chap. vi, in *Œuvres,* III, 360.

together; he was, after all, not a liberal. Rousseau's citizen is at once
ruler and ruled, lawgiver and subject. The general will, which both
underlies and expresses rational public policy, is, in the good society,
the voice of all, or nearly all, and the ruler of all. The general will is
absolutely general: "To be general, it is not always necessary for the
will to be unanimous, but it is necessary that all votes be counted; any
formal exclusion breaches generality."[8] If Rousseau was not a liberal,
he was a democrat.

Rousseau insisted that his democracy was not merely formal; it
cannot function without certain social conditions, among them
moral, legal, and relative economic equality. Other philosophes, including Holbach and Hume and Morelly, had seen the social utility
of substantial equality, but Rousseau built equality into his theoretical system. No man, in his view, should be so poor that he must
sell himself to another; no man so rich the he can buy others. Thus
liberty and equality, far from competing or being incompatible with
one another are actually, for Rousseau, indispensable allies, each giving substance to the other. There are other preconditions necessary
before the general will can function: it works best in a small country,
in a society without partial associations and pressure groups, and
equipped with institutions embodying direct participation: it is notorious that Rousseau saw nothing but harm in representative government. But the most important of these preconditions, the one that
brings the education of Émile quite directly to bear on Rousseau's
political thought, is the prevalence of the civic spirit.

The general will is always right, by definition. But how is it to
be discovered? The state itself is to be founded by an almost super-
human being, the legislator, who stands above human frailty and
manipulates his human material, much as Émile's tutor stands above
common humanity and manipulates his charge for his own good. But
this charismatic figure retires from the scene once his work of construction is done. Men can discover the general will only by listening
to the voice of the sovereign people. The man who has voted with
the minority is not merely bound by the majority decision, but he
also discovers, after the fact and through the very majority vote, that
his own view has been mistaken all along. Rousseau offers two signs
of the general will at work: pacific assemblies and near-unanimity.

---

[8] Ibid., book II, chap. ii, in *Œuvres*, III, 369 *n*.

"Long debates, discord, tumult, announce the ascendancy of particular interests and the decline of the state." But then Rousseau takes back what he has just granted; quiet assemblies and near-unanimity are good signs only as long as "all the qualities of the general will are still to be found in the majority; when they cease to be there, whatever side one may take, there is no more freedom."[9] Slaves, too, are subdued and united. The majority, in other words, is right as long as it is right.

This, I submit, is a fruitful tautology; it calls attention to Rousseau's distinction between the general will and the will of all, and to his persistent demand that the voter in the good state be a moral being. The will of all is the sum of private interests; the general will emerges as men consider the common interest. It is true that Rousseau prescribes the preconditions for the general will with care, but in a selfish, corrupt, anomic society none of these—equality, absence of pressure groups, and the like—will have much effect. Once again: Rousseau's society can function only if all its citizens are Émiles. Diderot had already noted in the *Encyclopédie*, and Rousseau had repeated it after him in the first version of the *Contrat social:* the general will should be "a pure act of the understanding which reasons in the silence of the passions" about the demands a man may make of his fellows, and his fellows of him.[1] It was an exacting standard, for men thought of themselves first, and disinterestedness was rare. It was especially rare in eighteenth-century civilization, which, it seemed, celebrated the vice of selfishness *(amour propre)* in the mistaken belief that it was the virtue of self-regard *(amour de soi)*. Of course, disinterestedness was rare; of course, the good state was only a hope and might not ever become reality. Rousseau, with all his optimism about man's original condition, was a pessimist about his capacity to reform himself. But if reform was possible at all, it must come in the way in which the *Nouvelle Héloïse, Émile,* and the *Contrat social* outlined it. All three books, converging from different starting points —family, individual, society—aim at the same target: the citizen, responsible and free.

---

[9] Ibid., book IV, chap. ii, in *Œuvres*, III, 441.
[1] See Diderot's article "Droit naturel" for the *Encyclopédie*, in *Œuvres politiques*, 34; and Rousseau's first version of the *Contrat social*, in *Œuvres*, III, 286.

VI

One should not ask of Rousseau what he cannot give. He was not a representative figure for the Enlightenment: his thought was at once too ancient, with its reminiscences of classical philosophy, and too modern, with its anticipation of future problems, to make him into a typical philosophe. But then he was not a typical anything. With a mixture of pride and indignation, he advertised himself to be unique and repudiated the very thought that he might be doing what others were doing. "I am not made like any other man I have seen," he proclaimed in the opening paragraph of the *Confessions*, and he lived and wrote as if he fully believed it.

Yet, with all his hunger for community, Rousseau urged men on in the direction that the Enlightenment as a whole wanted mankind to go. If his language is feverish, the substance of his thought is free of fanaticism; his great political work, the *Contrat social*, is amply equipped with safeguards for the individual against the pressures of the community. He said over and over again, with the pathos of the man who does not think anyone will believe him, that freedom was more valuable to him than anything else. We may believe him: solitary and often despised, he did the work of the Enlightenment, and gave substance, more than any other pholosophe, to the still youthful, always precarious, science of freedom.

FINALE

The Program in Practice

I

The science of freedom was intended as a practical science, and in the 1770s and early 1780s a series of events in the British colonies of North America roused hopes among the philosophes that this intention might be realized. The Enlightenment was at the height of its influence; its leading ideas had been explored and its great debates had been settled. The Old Guard in the philosophic family was moving from the scene: Hume died in 1776, Rousseau and Voltaire in 1778, Turgot and Lessing in 1781, d'Alembert in 1783, and Diderot in 1784. But the American Revolution brightened the last years of these philosophes; while some of the British brethren were torn between demands of loyalty to empire and devotion to freedom, all the others felt unreserved delight in the events overseas. The splendid conduct of the colonists, their brilliant victory, and their triumphant founding of a republic were convincing evidence, to the philosophes at least, that men had some capacity for self-improvement and self-government, that progress might be a reality instead of a fantasy, and that reason and humanity might become governing rather than merely critical principles.

The philosophes had long taken an interest in the British settlements in America. European ideologues used them for varied, often contradictory purposes: partisans of simplicity and the primitive appealed to them quite as often as partisans of civility and refinement. This is why Benjamin Franklin was such an impressive spokesman for the colonists' cause: his astonished admirers in the European salons found that he embodied the virtues of nature and the triumphs of urbanity at the same time and with equal ease. Franklin greatly enjoyed playing the colonial as philosopher, the sage as backwoodsman. Even the critical minority, who thought the American climate unpropitious to the development of advanced civilizations, were converted by Franklin's imposing performance. Raynal, highly regarded as a specialist in the New World, was one of these converts: after making some derisive remarks about the American colonists, he came to expect great things of them. The Americans, he said, might produce new Homers and new Anacreons, and, even better, "perhaps there will arise another Newton in New England."[1] In the age of the Enlightenment there could be no compliment more trite, or more extravagant, than that.

As the form of Raynal's tribute indicates, European philosophes were regarding British America as a land of potential allies, even of leaders, in the march of human enlightenment. David Hume was among the first to give expression to this view. In 1762, when Benjamin Franklin was making ready to return to America from England, Hume eloquently regretted his imminent departure: "I am very sorry," he wrote to Franklin, "that you intend soon to leave our hemisphere. America has sent us many good things, gold, silver, sugar, tobacco, indigo, etc.; but you are the first philosopher, and indeed the first great man of letters, for whom we are beholden to her."[2] Hume was as ready as anyone in his age to write a graceful letter, but his appreciation of Franklin was authentic enough: he recognized him as a fellow philosophe. In later years, as the troubles with the American colonies became serious, Hume drew the logical consequence: a land of philosophes deserved independence.[3]

The philosophes on the Continent had no doubts—especially by 1778, after the colonists' first impressive victories. America, wrote Turgot in that year, was bound to prosper, for the American people were "the hope of the human race; they may well become its model."[4] About the same time, Diderot interrupted his essay on the reigns of Claudius and Nero with a fervent aside: "After centuries of

---

[1] Quoted in Durand Echeverria: *Mirage in the West: A History of the French Image of American Society to 1815* (1957), 31.
[2] May 10, 1762. *Letters*, I, 357.
[3] In several letters (see for example, Hume to the Earl of Hertford, February 27, 1766. *Letters*, II, 18–23; and to William Strahan, October 26, 1775. Ibid., 300–1), Hume expressed his energetic hope for the independence of the colonies, although his reasoning in these letters is normally entirely pragmatic: Britain cannot afford to subjugate the colonies.
[4] Quoted in Echeverria: *Mirage in the West*, 69.

general oppression," he burst out, "may the revolution which has just occurred across the seas, by offering all the inhabitants of Europe an asylum against fanaticism and tyranny, instruct those who govern men on the legitimate use of their authority! May these brave Americans, who would rather see their wives raped, their children murdered, their dwellings destroyed, their fields ravaged, their villages burned, and rather shed their blood and die than lose the slightest portion of their freedom, prevent the enormous accumulation and unequal distribution of wealth, luxury, effeminacy, and corruption of manners, and may they provide for the maintenance of their freedom and the survival of their government!" In Diderot's frenzied vision, untroubled, it seems, by factual information, rustic American philosophes were facing decadent British barbarians, and enjoying unprecedented opportunities coupled with unprecedented obligations. They must jealously guard their freedom and always remember how they came to be what they now are: "May they defer, at least for a few centuries, the decree pronounced on all the things of this world; the decree that has condemned them to have their birth, their time of vigor, their decrepitude, and their end! May the earth swallow up those of their provinces powerful enough, and mad enough, one day to seek the means of subjugating the others!"[5] A few months before Diderot wrote these words, Voltaire, the arch-philosophe, had come back to Paris to be deified and to die, and among his carefully staged final performances was a highly emotional meeting with Benjamin Franklin in mid-February: twenty spectators, "shedding tender tears," were present to see Voltaire embrace Franklin and bless Franklin's grandson in English with these charged words: "God and liberty."[6] By now God had become the guide to American philosophes, and liberty an American specialty.

The elevation of Benjamin Franklin to mythical status was eminently useful to those who wished the Enlightenment well, for it supported their claim to a practicality that its critics had often refused to grant. It was generally thought one of Franklin's chief virtues that he was an eminently practical man, an experimental scientist, a propagandist in behalf of the dissemination and application of theoretical

---

[5] Œuvres politiques, 491.
[6] See Voltaire to the abbé Gaultier, February 20, 1778. Correspondence, XCVIII, 110.

knowledge through scientific societies, a man of the laboratory who did his duty as a citizen, and a worldly philosopher who brought thinking to bear on action with his collected maxims, which were perhaps as widely read in France as they were back home. After the colonies had won their independence and the colonists had shown their capacity to survive, the myth that Franklin embodied appeared to acquire a good deal of substance. The liberty that the Americans had won and were guarding was not merely an exhilarating performance that delighted European spectators and gave them grounds for optimism about man; it was also proving a realistic ideal worthy of imitation. "Men whom the reading of philosophic books had secretly converted to the love of liberty," Condorcet wrote in his eulogy to Franklin, "became enthusiastic over the liberty of a foreign people while they waited for the moment when they could recover their own, and they seized with joy the opportunity to avow publicly sentiments which prudence had prevented them from expressing."[7] Condorcet composed this tribute in 1790, when the French Revolution was well under way and looked, to all but Burke and emigré nobles, like a blissful dawn. The Americans, it seemed, had returned the intellectual investments that Europeans had made in them, with interest.

II

The American Revolution converted America from an importer of ideas into an exporter. What it exported was, of course, mainly itself, but that was a formidable commodity— the program of enlightenment in practice. Before the 1770s, the American colonists had been chiefly consumers: it was significant that Hume should not merely praise Franklin as a philosopher but also implicitly criticize the colonies by calling him the first. In the mid-1760s, when the efflorescence of the American Enlightenment began and came to the attention of Europeans, the intellectual structure of the Enlightenment was practically complete. Not all colonial thought was a mere copy of Europe; like all others, the American philosophes developed

---

[7] Quoted in Echeverria: *Mirage in the West*, 42.

their particular intellectual style by responding to domestic developments in Boston or Philadelphia or Richmond or the frontier that
lay just beyond. But the substance of their ideas came from a handful of European thinkers.

Traces of this discipleship mark the leading figures in the American Revolution. Benjamin Franklin confessed that he had formed his
style on Addison's *Spectator;* he had worked his way into deism by
devouring the tracts of English controversialists and perfected his
knowledge of modern science by studying the English Newtonians.
He greatly admired Voltaire early and late for his good sense, sound
reasoning, and amusing wit. Even in his amorous inclination he
turned to Europe: in France, he met the widow of Helvétius, and
proposed to her what he thought would be a logical match—after all,
he said, he and Helvétius had loved the same studies, "the same
friends, *and the same wife.*"[8] John Adams, though outspoken and
ungracious in his contempt for what he was pleased to consider the
"naïve optimism" of Helvétius and Rousseau—his own optimism,
though less extravagant in expression was quite as strong in substance
—made it no secret that his defense of "lawful" revolution owed
much to Grotius, Pufendorf, Barbeyrac; his political outlook much
to Harrington, Locke, Montesquieu; his view of human nature much
to Hutcheson, Ferguson, Bolingbroke. Adams liked to think by
fighting opponents, and he freely expressed his distaste for European
"dreamers." But if he rejected some European philosophes, he rejected them in the name, and with the aid, of other European philosophes. Even more than Adams, Thomas Jefferson was European to
the bone. When Adams still felt malicious about the man who would
later become his favorite correspondent, he remarked that Jefferson
"drank freely of the French philosophy, in religion, in science, in
politics." But this is less than just, and less than complete; Jefferson
listened to his Virginian experience quite as much as he did to the
writings of French philosophes, and he drank more freely from English than he did from French thought and literary models. Like his
British brethren, Jefferson was a Francophile; at the same time, like
his French and German brethren, he was an Anglomaniac. He loved
the classics but also used them, as the European philosophes had used

---

[8] Alfred Owen Aldridge: "Benjamin Franklin and the Philosophes,"
VS, XXIV (1963), 44, 58.

them, to free itself from the burdens of belief; he worshipped the three giants—Bacon, Newton, and Locke—whom Voltaire, d'Alembert, Hume, Lichtenberg, and Kant also worshipped, as the trinity of the three greatest men the world had ever seen.[9]

James Madison's intellectual development followed similar paths. Madison imitated Addison's style and found Voltaire congenial. Locke and Dubos, Montesquieu and Hume shaped his political thought and, with that, the Constitution of the United States. Finally, whatever the ultimate reasons for Alexander Hamilton's eventual estrangement from this group, it was not caused by any disagreements about the European Enlightenment. True, Hamilton thought better of monarchy and (if we may believe Jefferson) of Julius Caesar than did most of his fellow delegates at the Constitutional Convention or his fellow authors of the *Federalist* papers, but he too had studied the style of *Spectator* to perfect his own, and when as a young revolutionary he debated Samuel Seabury on the merits of the Continental Congress, he showed a thorough grasp of Pufendorf and Burlamaqui, Locke and Montesquieu. His reservations about the masses and advocacy of energetic government are softened by generous and sincere pronouncements in behalf of reason and humanity.

Even George Washington, though less of an intellectual than his colleagues, did not escape, and almost automatically adopted, their enlightened philosophy. When he addressed the governors of the American states in June 1783, shortly after victory, his circular letter breathed pride in his philosophical century: "The foundation of our Empire," he said, "was not laid in the gloomy age of Ignorance and Superstition, but at an Epocha when the rights of mankind were better understood and more clearly defined, than at any former period; the researches of the human mind after social happiness, have been carried to a great extent, the treasures of knowledge, acquired by the labours of Philosophers, Sages, and Legislators, through a long succession of years, are laid open for our use, and their collected wisdom may be happily applied in the Establishment of our forms of Government."[1] Never in the history of man had a

---

[9] Dumas Malone: *Jefferson and His Time*, I, *Jefferson the Virginian* (1948), 101.
[1] Quoted in Douglass Adair: " 'That Politics May Be Reduced to a Science': David Hume, James Madison, and the Tenth *Federalist*," *The Huntington Library Quarterly*, XX, 4 (August 1957), 343.

statesman so confidently recommended the application of social science to human affairs, or so confidently expected widespread happiness as a consequence of their application. If George Washington thought so well of the Enlightenment, who could deny that the labors of the philosophes had entered the mainstream of eighteenth-century life?

Not unexpectedly, the enlightened, Europe-centered ideology of the Founding Fathers was shared by less celebrated Americans. The radicals who early in the 1760s began to wonder out loud whether the British colonies could continue to live under a monarchy increasingly corrupt and increasingly tyrannical adapted their reading for their own uses, but that reading was European. Whether it was James Otis or Jonathan Mayhew or John Dickinson, the proto-revolutionaries sprinkled their inflammatory writings with ideas, arguments, and phrases—and at times simply plagiarized extensive passages—from Voltaire and Beccaria, Scottish and English moralists, and English common lawyers to whom the Loyalists also turned for comfort and support. The main source of revolutionary logic was the work of English republicans of the late seventeenth and early eighteenth centuries, Milton and Harrington and Sidney, Trenchard and Gordon, and that much maligned, much underestimated Latitudinarian prelate, Bishop Hoadly; these English radicals were to the American rebels the very sum of modern political wisdom.[2] England, it was clear from America, had the best constitution men had ever devised—the mixed constitution—and if it was now becoming necessary to rebel that was only because England was shamefully departing from this glorious invention: England must be rescued from herself, with English and with Continental weapons.

In new hands, and in different circumstances, these weapons acquired new functions. While the formal institutions of the American colonies were all British in origin and management, their political operation was quite distinct from that in Great Britain. In the homeland, noisy opposition orators charged the government with despoiling the magnificent constitution that was the pride and protection of all free Britons, deplored the decay of freedom, painted hideous portraits of corruption, and forecast the collapse of all orderly gov-

---

[2] Bernard Bailyn: *The Ideological Origins of the American Revolution* (1967), chap. ii, "Sources and Traditions."

ernment in universal tyranny; they aroused fears and suspicions, and could even, at times, thwart the will of ministers. But in the face of this rhetoric the system worked uncommonly well; the bonds of influence and of shared interests held together what the orators and pamphleteers threatened to pull apart. In the colonies, on the other hand, this opposition literature found a wide response even before serious unrest began in the 1760s. The powers of the colonial governors—the executive—were far more extensive in the colonies than those of the crown in Britain; they included the veto, the right to dissolve the legislatures, and control over the judiciary. Yet these "tyrannical" powers were more apparent than real: the supposedly omnipotent governors had little patronage to dispense, faced an uncommonly large body of voters, and were persistently obstructed by orders from overseas. The colonists perceived this incongruity, but far from congratulating themselves on the honesty of their officials, the extent of their franchise, and the impotence of their masters, they looked back to Britain with fears for the future. It was this incongruity between expectations and realities that made them so receptive to the Jeremiads of the British opposition. "Swollen claims and shrunken powers," as Bernard Bailyn has observed, "especially when they occur together, are always sources of trouble, and the malaise that resulted from this combination can be traced through the history of eighteenth-century politics."[3]

This dictum holds true elsewhere in the age of the Enlightenment—it applies aptly to France—but it applies most forcefully to the American colonies, for in true British fashion the colonists were highly articulate, passionately engaged in political arguments, and ready to see the need for change. There might be silence in Prussia or Russia but there was never silence in the colonies. "Whatever deficiencies the leaders of the American Revolution may have had"—to quote Bernard Bailyn one again—"reticence, fortunately, was not one of them."[4] The colonists poured out broadsides, pamphlets, and books by the hundreds; voluble preachers printed sermons touching on high principles of political obligation; ambitious lawyers and aspiring politicians denounced intolerable corruption, confiscatory taxation, oppressive vetoes, tyrannical ministers, and invoked heroes

[3] *The Origins of American Politics* (1968), 96.
[4] *Ideological Origins*, 1.

of antique and modern times—Cato, Cicero, Machiavelli, Locke, Trenchard and Gordon, and Montesquieu—with the ease of educated men knowing that they have an educated audience. When the colonists decided, regretfully but irrevocably, that it had become necessary to dissolve their political bonds to the British crown, and to assume, among the powers of the earth, the separate station to which they thought the laws of nature and of nature's God entitled them, they found that the world was listening.

III

As the Revolution took its course and the Founding Fathers established the American Confederation, debate did not slacken. There were new things to talk about in this time of troubles and expectations, and it was in this excited atmosphere that Madison, Hamilton, and Jay wrote the eighty-five articles that were to become *The Federalist*. It was a supremely practical piece of polemics, addressed not to posterity but to the moment, the work of three active politicians with one purpose: to persuade the voters of New York to accept the proposed constitution of the United States. But the *Federalist* has achieved, and fully deserves, immortality as a classic in the art of politics. It is also a classic work of the Enlightenment, a worthy successor to Montesquieu's *De l'esprit des lois* and a worthy companion to Rousseau's *Contrat social*.

The three authors of *The Federalist*, known by their collective signature, "Publius," sound all the great themes of the Enlightenment, if often by implication only: the dialectical movement away from Christianity to modernity; the pessimistic though wholly secular appraisal of human nature coupled with an optimistic confidence in institutional arrangements; the pragmatic reading of history as an aid to political sociology; the humane philosophy underlying their plea for the proposed constitution; the commitment to the critical method and the eloquent advocacy of practicality. The elements of *The Federalist* are thoroughly familiar; it is made of Hobbes and Harrington, Locke and Montesquieu, Hume and the *Encyclopédie*. What is new in the book is its particularly happy fusion of well-worn aspects of enlightened thought—psychology, history, political science, ethics—into a coherent and lucid whole, and its powerful sense that America is somehow different and certainly worth observing. With a certain modest pride, the authors of *The Federalist* accept the invitation to display America as a model for Europe: the Americans are "framing a Government for posterity as well as ourselves."[5] and for the world as well as for North America. "It has been frequently remarked," Hamilton notes in the very first paragraph of the book, "that is seems to have been reserved to the people of this country, by their conduct and example, to decide the important question, whether societies of men are really capable or not, of establishing good government from reflection and choice, or whether they are forever destined to depend, for their political constitutions, on accident and force." The struggle for the union of the American states, Hamilton confidently asserts, involves an empire which is "in many respects, the most interesting in the world."[6] The terms in which Hamilton—and Madison—saw the issue justified their claim: particularly to men of the eighteenth century nothing could be of greater interest than a contest in which, perhaps for the first time in history, reason might triumph over necessity.

In eighty-five papers on a system presumed to be of surpassing importance to all of civilization, the three authors of *The Federalist* drew on the intellectual resources common to educated men in the age of the Enlightenment, referring, freely and familiarly, to the history of Greece, Venice, medieval Europe, and Great Britain, to eighteenth-century struggles, and to colonial experience, and reinforcing these appeals to history, ancient, modern, and contemporary, with attacks on utopian dreamers and arguments from human nature. For them, history is recorded experience, experience material for history, the science of man the systematic explanation of history and experience together, and the science of politics their systematic utilization. The "lessons of history," to which they allude over and over again,[7] are so relevant to the formation of the American Union because they give clear expression to man's essential nature in the

---

[5] Alexander Hamilton: *The Federalist*, ed. Jacob E. Cooke (1961), No. 34, 213.
[6] Ibid., No. 1, 3.
[7] See James Madison: "This melancholy and monitory lesson of history," ibid., No. 20, 128; Hamilton: "History furnishes us with so many mortifying examples," ibid., No. 22, 142. And many other instances.

remote or the recent past. Like the other philosophes, Madison, Hamilton, and Jay rejoice in the variety of human conduct but insist on the unity of human nature.

The most instructive lesson history has to teach is that men need institutions to master their passions and regulate their conflicts. Man is not all bad, but a mixture of many qualities: "As there is a degree of depravity in mankind which requires a certain degree of circumspection and distrust: So there are other qualities in human nature, which justify a certain portion of esteem and confidence"; in fact the kind of regime Madison is advocating for America, "republican government," is itself an expression of moderate optimism, since it "presupposes the existence of these qualities in a higher degree than any other form."[8] *The Federalist* in its own way, though it persistently employs reasoned argument and addresses the reason of its readers, does not disdain what it regards as the higher passions: pride, humanity, and patriotism. But on balance the passions are anti-social; men, Hamilton writes, are dominated by "ambition, avarice, personal animosity, party opposition," by resentment, vindictiveness, rapacity, and the love of power.[9] The cause of faction, that great enemy of ordered society and rational policy, Madison concurs, is "sown in the nature of man," and the "propensity of mankind to fall into mutual animosities"[1] is overwhelming. And it is because man's vices overbalance his virtues that government is essential. "It may be a reflection on human nature, that such devices should be necessary to controul the abuses of government. But what is government itself but the greatest of all reflections on human nature? If men were angels, no government would be necessary. If angels were to govern men, neither external nor internal controuls on government would be necessary. In framing a government which is to be administered by men over men, the great difficulty lies in this: You must first enable the government to controul the governed; and in the next place, oblige it to controul itself."[2]

The problem that Madison raises here is ancient in lineage: *Sed quis custodiet ipsos custodes?* Juvenal had asked seventeen centuries

---

[8] Ibid., No. 55, 378.
[9] See ibid., No. 1, 5; the same, ibid., No. 6, 28, and often elsewhere.
[1] Ibid., No. 10, 58–9.
[2] Probably Madison, ibid., No. 51, 349.

before. But for the men of the Enlightenment, Juvenal's old question had particular urgency; it was not simply a matter for them of cowing passionate and factious men, for then an oppressive government would have suited them far better than the law-abiding, reasonable, and mild government they were proposing: the authors of *The Federalist* wanted freedom quite as much as they acknowledged the need for order. Like all political theorists in the Enlightenment, therefore, they called for vigorous government not to stifle, but to protect liberty.

Much of this libertarianism is implicit: *The Federalist* does not develop a formal catalogue of values. It does not need to, for values were not a problem; the kind of qualities necessary to the good society—humanity, public happiness, protection against arbitrary government, popular sovereignty, enlightened policies—seem almost self-evident. But the question of how the government may "controul itself" is more difficult, and this justifies the concentration of *The Federalist* on the institutions proposed for the United States: the bulk of the papers deals with the presidency, Congress, the courts, with foreign and domestic policies and the federal system. The aim of these practical papers is never in doubt: to advocate a government that will guard the passions of individuals for the sake of order and guard the guardians for the sake of freedom.

A political system constructed on distrust of human nature and hostile to utopian optimists is bound to have its conservative side. But this side, though prominent, did not dominate *The Federalist;* the book is a document of the Enlightenment in its hopeful realism. The Founding Fathers, Madison wrote, "accomplished a revolution which has no parallel in the annals of human society: They reared the fabrics of governments which have no model on the face of the globe," and now they were ready to move beyond the achievement of the Confederacy to the still greater achievement of a Union. Again and again "Publius" used the word "experiment" as a word of self-praise: the Americans had made singular and unprecedented experiments, because they had trusted themselves, and experience had proved them to be right. It was Madison's proudest boast that the Americans, though respectful to antiquity, had been pioneers of modernity. Why, he asks, "is the experiment of an extended republic to be rejected merely because it may comprise what is new? Is it not the glory of the people of America, that whilst they have paid a decent regard to the opinions of former times and other nations, they have not suffered a blind veneration for antiquity, for custom, or for names, to overrule the suggestions of their own good sense, the knowledge of their own situation, and the lessons of their own experience? To this manly spirit, posterity will be indebted for the possession, and the world for the example of the numerous innovations displayed on the American theater, in favor of private rights and public happiness."[3] Nothing could epitomize the spirit of the Enlightenment more beautifully than this oratorical flight, with its declared openness to experiment undeterred by its respect for the past, its disdain for authority, and its reliance on autonomous reason, good sense, and experience, all for the sake of freedom and happiness.

The very magnificence of the passage makes it disquieting reading today. This is not a good time to appreciate the claims of enlightened men. Even America, the hope of civilized men everywhere in the eighteenth century, has given and continues to give its most benevolent well-wishers grounds for grave anxiety. If historians have dealt too unkindly with the Enlightenment, history itself has been far from gentle with its hopes and predictions. The world has not turned out the way the philosophes wished and half expected that it would. Old fanaticisms have been more intractable, irrational forces more inventive than the philosophes were ready to conjecture in their darkest moments. Problems of race, of class, of nationalism, of boredom and despair in the midst of plenty have emerged almost in defiance of the philosophes' philosophy. We have known horrors, and may know horrors, that the men of the Enlightenment did not see in their nightmares. Yet, though few are today inclined to believe it, none of this impairs the permanent value of the Enlightenment's humane and libertarian vision, or the permanent validity of its critical method, any more than the philosophes' failure to live up to their own prescriptions or realize their own ideals compromises the worth of those prescriptions and those ideals. It remains as true today as it was in the eighteenth century: the world needs more light than it has, not less; the cure for the shortcomings of enlightened thought lies not in obscurantism but in further enlightenment. Our recognition of human irrationality, self-centeredness, stupidity beyond the philosophes' most pessimistic appraisals demands not surrender to such

<hr>

[3] Ibid., No. 14, 88–9.

forces, but battle against them. In the light of recent history and to-day's headlines, this may appear to be a truly utopian prescription. It will perhaps appear less quixotic if we recall that there was a time when tough-minded men looked to the young republic in America, saw there with delight the program of the philosophes in practice, and found themselves convinced that the Enlightenment had been a success.

BIBLIOGRAPHICAL
ESSAY

GENERAL

This bibliographical essay, like the volume it serves, is independent of the bibliographical essay I appended to the first volume, and, at the same time, tied to it. Inevitably I used, in *The Rise of Modern Paganism*, many of the books I used again here, and this put me into a dilemma: to repeat the full evaluation I gave in the first volume would have made this essay too long and partly redundant. On the other hand, to supply only a cross-reference would have compelled the reader to engage in a time-consuming hunt for titles in another book. I have therefore adopted a compromise which, I trust, will be acceptable: whenever a title discussed in any detail in *The Rise of Modern Paganism* reappears in the present essay, I have confined myself to giving essential bibliographical information and added, in square brackets, a cross-reference to the first appearance of the title in the first volume.

I need hardly emphasize that this essay, like its earlier companion, is subjective and incomplete; ranging as it does over many areas, many of them interesting to scholars and replete with controversy, it could hardly be anything else. I have had many teachers, and this essay, I hope, reflects my many obligations with some accuracy. I have in the main cited books and articles that supplied me with facts or interpretations, gave me ideas, or aroused me to dissent. One other preliminary point: in this volume, as in the first, I am deeply indebted to the philosophical writings of Ernst Cassirer, particularly to his distinction between critical and mythical thinking [I, 423-4].

CHAPTER ONE

The Recovery of Nerve

I . PRELUDE TO MODERNITY:
THE RECOVERY OF NERVE

THE CENTRAL PROPOSITION of this chapter, that in the eighteenth century the West experienced a "recovery of nerve," an unprecedented sense of confidence of which the Enlightenment was expression, consequence, and partly the cause, rests of course on the aggregate of my reading. This includes biographies of, and monographs on, the philosophes in all countries, as well as their collected correspondence [I, 429–49]. Such journals as James Boswell's, beginning with *Boswell's London Journal, 1762–1763*, ed. Frederick A. Pottle (1951), and its sequels, and E.-J.-F. Barbier: *Journal historique et anecdotique du règne de Louis XV*, ed. A. de la Villegille, 4 vols. (1847–56) [I, 435], have been invaluable. I have also relied on such modern biographies as J. H. Plumb: *Sir Robert Walpole*, 2 vols. so far (1956, 1960), which takes Walpole's career to 1734. A fresh, interesting approach through the social sciences has been offered by Arthur M. Wilson: "The *Philosophes* in the light of present-day theories of modernization," *VS*, LVIII (1967), 1893–1913.

Books on social history exist in profusion; I can mention only a few. For England, see A. R. Humphreys: *The Augustan World: Society, Thought, and Letters in Eighteenth Century England* (1954), which intelligently offers a full set of "reading lists" (261–9). The best books on the change in the English temper are Charles Wilson: *England's Apprenticeship, 1603–1763* (1965), and Asa Briggs: *The Age of Improvement, 1783–1867* (1959), both fine, unorthodox general histories; the "Introduction" to the latter supplies splendid instances of the English recovery of nerve. G. M.

Trevelyan: *Illustrated English Social History*, III, *The Eighteenth Century* (edn. 1951), though justly celebrated for its lucidity, is relatively superficial. Dorothy Marshall: *English People in the Eighteenth Century* (1956), has some instructive materials on food riots and rural discontent. The well-known collection of essays, *Johnson's England: An Account of the Life and Manners of his Age*, 2 vols. (1933), ed. A. S. Turberville [I, 432], deserves to be consulted. Turberville's own *English Men and Manners in the 18th Century* (2d edn., 1929), is amusing, full of detail, but hardly searching. In contrast, Dorothy George: *London Life in the Eighteenth Century* (2d edn., 1930), and her brief set of B.B.C. lectures, *England in Transition: Life and Work in the Eighteenth Century* (Penguin edn., 1953), are tough-minded and informative, though in some respects now somewhat out of date. Max Beloff: *Public Order and Popular Disturbances, 1660–1714* (1938), is a pioneering essay in the social history of the poor. G. E. Mingay skillfully analyzes property and social relations in *English Landed Society in the Eighteenth Century* (1963), as does also J. D. Chambers and Mingay: *The Agricultural Revolution, 1750–1880* (1966). (See also below, 577–8, for the Industrial Revolution in England.)

French society, for all the abundance of monographs, still needs further study. Among general histories of France, I found chaps. xi and xii of Georges Duby and Robert Mandrou's *History of French Civilization from the Year 1000 to the Present* (1958; tr. James Blakely Atkinson, 1964),[1] a characteristic product of the *sixième section*, exceptionally rich in insights. Extensive biographies of philosophes to which I have alluded, like, say, Desnoiresterres's exhaustive eight-volume study of Voltaire, *Voltaire et la société française au XVIIIe siècle* (1867–76), [I, 435], remain informative for all their relative antiquity. Typical of superficial "social" history is Charles Kunstler: *La vie quotidienne sous Louis XV* (1953). Far better are the detailed studies of individual cities, like Louis Trénard's superb *Lyon, de l'Encyclopédie au Préromantisme*, 2 vols. (1958), immensely rich in relevant detail. Pierre Goubert: *Beauvais et le Beauvaisis de 1600 à 1730*, 2 vols. (1960), is a magnificent social

---

[1] As in the first volume, I have here adopted the following convention with translations: I give the English title, followed by the original date of publication, the name of the translator, and the date of the translation.

history in depth of a small area, partly relevant to this chapter. Franklin L. Ford: *Strasbourg in Transition, 1648–1789* (1958), is modern social history at its best. For the French aristocracy, Henri Carré: *La noblesse de France et l'opinion publique au XVIIIᵉ siècle* (1920) remains very useful; J. McManners: "France," in A. Goodwin: *The European Nobility in the Eighteenth Century* (1953), is lucid. I have already singled out McManners: *French Ecclesiastical Society Under the Ancien Regime* (1960), a brilliant study of eighteenth-century Angers, for praise [I, 545]. A handful of specialized monographs, like Robert Forster: *The Nobility of Toulouse in the Eighteenth Century: A Social and Economic Study* (1960) offer insights into social morale far beyond their announced subject. Constantia Maxwell: *The English Traveller in France, 1698–1815* (1932) collects some valuable foreign impressions. Conservative attempts at rescuing the Ancien Régime, notably Pierre Gaxotte: *Le siècle de Louis XV* (edn. 1933), and Franz Funck-Brentano: *The Old Regime in France* (1926; tr. Herbert Wilson, 1929), offer some slight corrective to radical denunciations of the Old Regime, and have much information, but they say more about the French Right in the Third Republic than about the events that led to the First Republic.

France was, of course, a rural country, and no generalization about a French recovery of nerve can omit the peasants. Here we have at least two superb works: Marc Bloch's *Les caractères originaux de l'histoire rurale française* (1931; edn. 1952–6, 2 vols., with a supplement by Robert Dauvergne), and Georges Lefebvre's vast authoritative dissertation, *Les paysans du Nord pendant la Révolution* (1924). Bloch's work is now available in a translation by Janet Sondheimer (1966). See also Elinor Barber: *The Bourgeoisie in 18th Century France* (1955), [I, 434]. The social historian of eighteenth-century France has at his disposal a library of monographs compiled by A. Babeau, books now old but filled with information: *Le village sous l'ancien régime* (1891), *La ville sous l'ancien régime*, 2 vols. (2d edn., 1884), *La vie rurale sous l'ancien régime* (1885), *Les bourgeois d'autrefois* (1886)—to mention only the four best known. Douglas Dakin: *Turgot and the Ancien Regime in France* (1939), [I, 437] has a fascinating analysis of a province and its government in the mid-eighteenth century. I have used other books as well, but I agree with Alfred Cobban that

Philippe Sagnac's well-known *La formation de la société française moderne*, 2 vols. (1945–6), shows by its very generality of treatment, that "the fundamental research has still not been done, to provide a satisfactory synthesis." (Cobban: *A History of Modern France*, I, *Old Regime and Revolution, 1715–1799* [1957], 268, itself an authoritative survey.)[2]

If there is incomplete knowledge of eighteenth-century French society, the societies of the German states, large and small, remain for the most part unexplored; what we mainly have are chatty volumes of court reminiscences. Hence Karl Biedermann's old *Deutschland im achtzehnten Jahrhundert*, 2 vols. in 4 (1854–80), W. H. Bruford: *Germany in the Eighteenth Century* (1935), *Culture and Society in Classical Weimar, 1775–1806* (1962), and Hajo Holborn: *A History of Modern Germany, 1648–1840* (1963), [all I, 440], remain indispensable. There is much of value in Otto Hintze: *Die Hohenzollern und ihr Werk* (1915), critical despite its official character and very shrewd on Frederick II's "state socialism." Hans Gerth: *Die sozialgeschichtliche Lage der bürgerlichen Intelligenz um die Wende des 18.-Jahrhunderts* (1935) is a pioneering essay in a neglected field. H. Brunschwig: *La Crise de l'état Prussien à la fin du XVIIIᵉ siècle et la genèse de la mentalité romantique* (1947) is often brilliant but also tendentious, pointing (doubtless not without justice) to perpetual crisis and the eventual "betrayal" of their vocation by the ruling groups; its bibliography is discriminating. Heinrich Voelcker, ed.: *Die Stadt Goethes: Frankfurt am Main im 18. Jahrhundert* (1932) has a number of informative essays on social customs. Rudolf Stadelmann and Wolfram Fischer have ventured into a relatively unexplored area with their modern sociological study, *Die Bildungswelt des deutschen Handwerkers um 1800: Studien zur Soziologie des Kleinbürgers im Zeitalter Goethes* (1955); more such studies are badly needed.[3]

For Italy consult the volumes by Franco Valsecchi, *L'Italia nel settecento dal 1714 al 1788* (1959), Mario Fubini, ed.: *La cultura illuminista in Italia* (1957), and Franco Venturi, ed.: *Illuministi Italiani*, III (1958), and V (1962), [all I, 441], and VII (1965). While

---

[2] For the economic history of France—Labrousse, Sée and others—see below, 581–2.

[3] For other titles on German social history, see the chapters on politics, especially 676–7.

Venturi's magisterial synthesis, *Settecento riformatore, Da Muratori a Beccaria* (1969), reached me too late to affect this volume, I can safely predict that it will affect all future attempts to write the social-intellectual history of eighteenth-century Italy.

The social history of the American colonies has been fully explored, often, though by no means always, in antiquarian and trivial ways. L. B. Wright: *The Cultural Life of the American Colonies, 1607–1763* (1957), [I, 442], is a reliable summary with an eminently serviceable bibliography; Carl Bridenbaugh has put the profession in his debt with a collection of informative studies, most notably, *Cities in the Wilderness: The First Century of Urban Life in America, 1625–1742* (2d edn., 1955), *Cities in Revolt: Urban Life in America, 1743–1776* (1955), and *Rebels and Gentlemen: Philadelphia in the Age of Franklin* (1942).

The question of the recovery of nerve—how real, how deep, how widespread—is of course intimately related to the question of the industrial revolution, and the associated question of living standards in the eighteenth century. Ever since Friedrich Engels exposed the misery of the poor in *The Conditions of the Working Class in England in 1844* (1845; trs. and eds. W. O. Henderson and W. H. Chaloner, 1958), social historians—not all of them socialists—have generally portrayed the worker as victim, while economic historians have on the whole pointed to the industrial revolution as an unprecedented blessing. Indeed, the very extent and nature of the industrial revolution remain a matter of relatively heated argument, though, it seems, a consensus is emerging. As Paul Mantoux points out, it was Karl Marx, in volume I of *Kapital,* who first offered a "systematic description" of the "industrielle Revolution" (see Mantoux: *The Industrial Revolution in the Eighteenth Century: An Outline of the Beginnings of the Modern Factory System* [2d. edn., 1927; tr. Marjorie Vernon, 1928], itself a learned and reasonable contribution to the great debate). The term entered the consciousness of historians largely through the celebrated set of lectures by Arnold Toynbee, *Lectures on the Industrial Revolution in England,* published posthumously in 1884. For Toynbee, the revolution began in the 1760s and was indeed a revolution. In our century, the revisionists began to question both his claims: thus John U. Nef, in *Industry and Government in France and England, 1540–1640* (1940), in some chapters of *Cultural Foundations of Industrial Civilization*

(1958), and in a series of articles, notably "A Comparison of Industrial Growth in France and England from 1540 to 1640," *Journal of Political Economy*, XLIV, 3 (February 1936), 643–66, and "The Industrial Revolution Reconsidered," *Journal of Economic History*, III, 1 (May 1943), 1–31, argued that there was no revolutionary change in the eighteenth century, and that if there was a revolution at all, it must be seen in an earlier period, at the end of the sixteenth and the beginning of the seventeenth century. At the other extreme, J. H. Clapham has argued that the revolution was far from complete in the nineteenth century (*An Economic History of Modern Britain*, 3 vols. [1932–9]). The revisionists have usefully pointed to the inevitable complexities of industrial development, and the dangers of uncritically employing general names, but they have not, in my judgment, disproved the Marx-Toynbee contention that there was a revolutionary change in the economic sphere—the employment of steam power, the organization of labor and industry, the conscious cumulation of invention, associated changes in agriculture, public administration, health, and so forth—in England after the mid-eighteenth century. Indeed, recent historians have returned to the old verities. With deliberate naïveté, T. S. Ashton entitled his masterly popularization *The Industrial Revolution, 1760–1830* (1948), while L. S. Presnell has edited a series of papers, *Studies in the Industrial Revolution* (1960). Phyllis Deane has summarized the debate with admirable lucidity, and remained with the idea of a revolution in *The First Industrial Revolution* (1965), an extremely helpful survey on which I have relied. W. W. Rostow's original *The Stages of Economic Growth* (1960), with its now famous though facile notion of "take-off," supports this new consensus. So do the various contributors to the massive sixth volume (in two parts) of *The Cambridge Economic History of Europe*, eds. H. J. Habbakuk and M. Postan (1965); I shall note some individual contributions to these volumes in the course of this essay. The most substantial and adventurous contribution to the work is David S. Landes: "Technological Change and Development in Western Europe, 1750–1914," 274–601, which fortunately begins in the mid-eighteenth century.

Industrial change in eighteenth-century Scotland is of particular interest in view of the brilliant Scottish Enlightenment that flourished in its midst. See T. C. Smout: *Scottish Trade on the Eve of Union, 1660–1707* (1963), for the earlier period, and for the eighteenth century, two books by Henry Hamilton: *An Economic History of Scotland in the Eighteenth Century* (1963), and the older but still valuable *The Industrial Revolution in Scotland* (1932).

If there was a revolution, was it a good thing? The suffering of the many, the brutality of masters to men and women and children, the dislocation of rural poor, the rise of new diseases incident on crowding—all this remains real enough and cannot be apologized away. But it may have received excessively emotional attention, notably in the writings of J. S. and B. Hammond, passionate, informed, but rather one-sided: see their *The Village Labourer, 1760–1832* (1911), *The Skilled Labourer, 1760–1832* (1919), *The Town Labourer, 1760–1832* (1920), and *The Rise of Modern Industry* (1925). J. S. Hammond has explicitly defended the views advanced in these volumes in "The Industrial Revolution and Discontent," *Economic History Review*, II, 2 (1930), 215–28. The Hammonds' indictment has had enormous influence, and is not without justice; it has retained enough validity to be quoted with approval by such critics as T. S. Ashton. In recent years, radical English historians have in fact revived the Hammond thesis, contradicting Ashton, with impressive documentation. See above all Eric J. Hobsbawm: "The British Standard of Living, 1790–1850," *Economic History Review* (second series), X, 1 (1957), 46–61. A series of revisionist essays, *Capitalism and the Historians* (1954), ed. F. A. Hayek, has helped to right the balance, but badly overstates the case for capitalism and thus introduces an imbalance of its own. Of more solid value and less polemical are the magisterial works of T. S. Ashton: (with J. Sykes), *The Coal Industry of the Eighteenth Century* (1929); by himself, *Iron and Steel in the Industrial Revolution* (2d edn., 1951); *An Economic History of England, The Eighteenth Century* (1955); "The Standard of Life of Workers in England, 1790–1830," *Journal of Economic History*, Supplement IX (1949), 19–38. Ashton has drawn on E. W. Gilboy: *Wages in Eighteenth-Century England* (1934), which demonstrates a surprising stability of wages. Phyllis Deane's summary (chap. xv of *First Industrial Revolution*) is lucid, as usual; her bibliography lists other specialized articles. An interesting and by no means unimportant sidelight on the issue of economic progress is revealed by the growing failure of traditional gilds to control their members; see J. R. Kellett: "The Breakdown of Gild and Corporation Control Over the Handicraft and Retail Trade in London," *Economic History Review* (second series), X, 3 (1958), 381–94. What survives, I think, is the portrait I have briefly sketched in my text: widespread suffering but ultimate amelioration, and vast differences among groups, crafts, and cities. On the whole, there was spectacular long-range progress, achieved at enormous cost.

Strict economic history is not the only way to answer the riddle of progress. Historians of social structure have much to contribute. For England, the works of George Rudé, who has made the "mob" his own, is of decisive importance. For a general statement see his "The Study of Popular Disturbances in the 'Pre-Industrial' Age," *Historical Studies* [Melbourne], X, 40 (May 1963), 457–69. Rudé's *Wilkes and Liberty* (1962) is exceptionally well-supplied with material on social groupings and social unrest in mid-eighteenth century England. See also his " 'Mother Gin' and the London Riots of 1736," *The Guildhall Miscellany*, No. X (September 1959); "The London 'Mob' of the Eighteenth Century," *The Historical Journal*, II, 1 (April 1959), 1–18. For corroborating evidence, E. J. Hobsbawm: "The Machine Breakers," *Past and Present*, No. 1 (February 1952), 57–70, and R. B. Rose: "Eighteenth Century Price Riots and Public Policy in England," *International Review of Social History*, VI, part 2 (1961), 277–92, are of value. R. W. Wearmouth: *Methodism and the Common People of the Eighteenth Century* (1945) has, in addition to a striking analysis of the relation of religion to social policy in England, good material on riots, especially in the provinces. Elie Halévy's classic *England in 1815* (1913, trs. E. I. Watkin and D. A. Barker, 2d edn., 1949), sets the riots in perspective. E. P. Thompson's massive *The Making of the English Working Class* (1963), which, though mainly on the early nineteenth century, looks back at the eighteenth century often enough to be valuable to me here, is both learned and contentious. Its theme is the rise of working-class consciousness, the objective experience and subjective perceptions of English working men during the decisive decades of the industrial revolution. It is a vigorous specimen of radical English history; perhaps the most judicious appraisal I have seen is by R. K. Webb: *The Massachusetts Review*, VI, 1 (Autumn–Winter 1964–5), 202–8. The opening essays in E. J. Hobsbawm: *Labouring Men: Studies in the History of Labour* (1964), have controversial interpretations of the Luddites and on the social bearing of Methodism. See also R. K. Webb: *Modern England from the 18th Century to the Present* (1968), chaps. i-iii, a synthesis masquerading as a textbook; and *Man Versus Society in 18th-Century Britain: Six Points of View*, ed. James L. Clifford (1968), which contains essays of varying value; the first, by J. H. Plumb, "Political Man," is particularly instructive. Countries other than Great Britain cannot match its rate and intensity of change, and I have avoided the term "industrial revolution" when speaking of them. Still, there was drastic economic change and development. Henri Sée: *La France économique et sociale au XVIIIe siècle* (1925) is small but based on comprehensive knowledge and informed by a magnificent synthetic sense. See also the relevant chapters in his *Histoire économique de la France*, 2 vols. (1939). The painstaking writings of Ernest Labrousse and his students are justly famous for their authoritative character. Labrousse's own survey, *Esquisse du mouvement des prix et des révenus en France au XVIIIe siècle* (1934) was the indispensable preliminary to his great analysis of the decline in French economic conditions before the Revolution: *La crise de l'économie française à la fin de l'ancien régime et au début de la révolution* (1944). Shelby McCloy registers French technical progress in his *French Inventions of the Eighteenth Century* (1952); Roland Mousnier's lectures, *Progrès scientifique et technique au XVIIIe siècle* (1958), informal, rather fiercely anti-Marxist, and though comprehensively European devoting much space to France, is another testimony to progress in the midst of economic crisis. W. O. Henderson has devoted his attention to comparing British with continental trends; his *Britain and Industrial Europe, 1750–1870* (1954), is a general comparative survey; more particular is "The Genesis of the Industrial Revolution in France and Germany in the 18th Century," *Kyklos*, IX (1956), 190–207, but it must, by the nature of the case, confine itself to beginnings. Landes's long article (and vast bibliography) cited above, 578, says the essential. On the decline of the reactionary gilds, see E. Martin Saint-Léon: *Histoire des corporations de métiers* (1897).

In its early sections, George Rudé's *The Crowd in the French Revolution* (1959) supplies a wealth of information in economical scope on urban riots and working-class conditions in general *before* the Revolution. Rudé has also dealt with grain riots in the time of Turgot's ministry, "La taxation populaire de mai 1775 à Paris et dans la région parisienne," *Annales historiques de la révolution française*, No. 143 (April–June 1956), 139–79. Finally, since the Huguenots remained a significant element in French culture (as well as the French economy) after their "expulsion" in 1685, their eighteenth-century history in France has meaning for the French "recovery of nerve." See Warren C. Scoville: *The Persecution of Huguenots and French Economic Development, 1680–1720* (1960).

The most useful general survey of German economic history I have found is Friedrich Karl Lütge: *Deutsche Sozial- und Wirtschaftsgeschichte: Ein Überblick* (2d edn., 1960). W. O. Henderson has studied *The State and the Industrial Revolution in Prussia, 1740–1870* (1958); its early chapters are relevant here. See also his *Studies in the Economic Policy of Frederick the Great* (1963), and his volume on the relation of Britain to Europe (cited above, 581). Friedrich Schnabel's magisterial *Deutsche Geschichte im neunzehnten Jahrhundert*, III, *Erfahrungswissenschaften und Technik* (1934), glances back at the eighteenth century, especially in section IV, "Die Technik." Gustav Schmoller's old articles, "Studien über die wirtschaftliche Politik Friedrichs des Grossen und Preussen überhaupt, 1680–1786," *Schmollers Jahrbuch*, VIII (1884), 1–61, 345–421, 999–1091, for all their age, remain informative.

For American economic history in the eighteenth century see chaps. i, iii, and iv in Harold F. Williamson, ed.: *The Growth of the American Economy* (1944); Victor S. Clark: *History of Manufactures in the U.S., 1607–1860*, 3 vols. (1929); J. R. Commons, ed.: *The History of Labour in the U.S.*, I (1936); I and II of *The Economic History of the United States*, 9 vols., eds. Davis *et al.*; J. I. Falconer: *History of Agriculture in the United States Before 1860* (1925); Richard B. Morris: "Labor and Mercantilism in The Revolutionary Era," in Morris, ed.: *Era of the American Revolution* (1939); Arthur M. Schlesinger's classic *The Colonial Merchants and the American Revolution* (1918); and Stuart Bruchey: *The Roots of American Economic Growth, 1607–1861: An Essay in Social Causation* (1965).

For Italy in this period see Antonio Fossati: *Lavoro e produzione in Italia dalla meta del secolo XVIII alla secondo guerra mondiale* (1951), especially chaps. i and ii; Luigi Dal Pane: *Storia del Lavoro in Italia dagli inizi del secolo XVIII al 1815* (1944); Arrigo Serpieri: *L'Agricoltura nell'economia della nazione* (1940); and G. Prato: *Problemi monetari e bancari nei secoli XVII e XVIII* (1916).

Every history that touches in any way on social questions reports continuing brutal exploitation, misery, and occasional uprisings. There were serf-risings in eighteenth-century Bohemia (H. G. Schenk: "Austria," in Godwin: *European Nobility*, 107); in Sweden wages were systematically depressed by legislation (Michael Roberts: "Sweden," in ibid., 142); while B. J. Hovdc reports the clashes of class against class in the same country in *The Scandinavian Countries, 1720–1865*, I (1948), 179–80. A good discussion of the desperate lives of the poor in one big city—Prague—their sense of being trapped, for instance, in times of epidemic, when those better off could leave the infected areas, is Oskar Schürer: *Prag: Kultur, Kunst, Geschichte* (1930), 186, 191, 218.

Still, although evidence remains rather inconclusive, it seems plausible that there were many among the poor, especially among the self-respecting artisans, who had a sense of real possibilities in their time. Certainly their political activities suggest something other than passive despair. A mere look at histories of earlier periods shows how far the eighteenth century had progressed. (To mention only two books: Marc Bloch's *Feudal Society*, 2 vols. [1939–40; tr. L. A. Manyon, 1961], [I, 500], I, 98–9, 116 ff. has a brilliant analysis of the precariousness of medieval life; while Roland Mousnier discusses the famine cycles of the seventeenth century in his synthetic *Les XVIᵉ et XVIIᵉ siècles: Les progrès de la civilisation européenne et le déclin de l'orient, 1492–1715* [1954], 145–51, although the final word on these cycles has not yet been said.)

In conclusion I mention some special topics discussed in this section. For Bacon and Descartes, see the bibliographical entries in I, 528–9. The saying, "Man is the architect of his fortune," is analyzed in Rexmond C. Cochrane: "Francis Bacon and the Architect of Fortune," *Studies in the Renaissance*, V (1958), 176–95. Franklin's scientific optimism is well accounted for in Brooke Hindle: *The Pursuit of Science in Revolutionary America, 1735–1789* (1956). Raymond Trousson: *Le Thème de Prométhée dans la littérature européenne*, 2 vols. (1964), is a fascinating survey of the Prometheus theme; chaps. v and vi are applicable here, to which should be added Dora and Erwin Panofsky: *Pandora's Box* (1956). On the striking increase in the taking out of patents, see the figures in Archibald and Nan L. Clow: *The Chemical Revolution: A Contribution to Social Technology* (1952), 2–3; Watt and his role are discussed in F. J.

Forbes: "Power to 1850," in Charles Singer *et al.*, eds.: *A History of Technology*, IV, *The Industrial Revolution, c. 1750–c. 1850* (1958), 148–67; H. W. Dickinson: "The Steam-Engine to 1830," in ibid., 168–98; Dickinson: *James Watt: Craftsman and Engineer* (1936); and Charles C. Gillispie, in his persuasive "Introduction" to *A Diderot Pictorial Encyclopedia of Trades and Industry*, 2 vols. (1959), xi–xxx, which emphasizes the part steam power must play in our definition of "industrial revolution." For Diderot's "Baconianism" see Herbert Dieckmann: "The Influence of Francis Bacon on Diderot's *'Interprétation de la nature,'*" *Romanic Review*, XXXIV, 4 (December 1943), 303–30. In general, the volume of Charles Singer's *History of Technology*, just mentioned, has a number of informative brief articles on a variety of pertinent subjects. I have also made use of Abbott Payson Usher's well-known *A History of Mechanical Inventions* (2d edn. 1954), *passim*, but especially chaps. xii, xiii, and xiv, dealing with precision instruments, power, and machine tools. Technology is of vital importance to my case since, clearly enough, the technological revolution was the agent through which scientific discoveries were translated into the recovery of nerve.

2. ENLIGHTENMENT: MEDICINE AND CURE

Since the history of medicine has aroused the interest of excellent scholars, and since its records are relatively ample, the supply of general surveys and specialized monographs is impressive. Among several histories of medicine, I have found Richard H. Shryock's lively and scholarly interpretation, *The Development of Modern Medicine: An Interpretation of the Social and Scientific Factors Involved* (1947) most congenial and most helpful. Shryock's lectures, *Medicine and Society in America: 1660–1860* (1962), are lucid and suggestive. There is a good brief discussion of medicine in early America in Bridenbaugh: *Cities in Revolt* (chap. v, section 8). Lester S. King's *The Medical World of the Eighteenth Century* (1948) is a collection of separate essays, on medical ethics, on empirics and quacks, on the classification of diseases; it is especially good on

Hermann Boerhaave. Boerhaave again appears briefly in King's *The Growth of Medical Thought* (1963). G. A. Lindeboom: *Hermann Boerhaave* (1968), a fine study, came too late for me to utilize it in this book. There is much interesting information on Boerhaave in Haller's diary; see *Albrecht Hallers Tagebücher seiner Reisen nach Deutschland, Holland und England, 1723–27*, ed. Ludwig Hirzel (1883). Henry E. Sigerist: *The Great Doctors: A Biographical History of Medicine* (1933) is, as its subtitle suggests, a collection of biographies chronologically arranged; they are slight. English medicine is adequately if briefly treated in Sir D'Arcy Power: "Medicine," in Turberville, ed.: *Johnson's England*, II, 265–86; for the all-important contribution of Dutch physicians to the diffusion of "Newtonian" medicine, see, in addition to King, Sigerist: "Hollands Bedeutung in der Entwicklung der Medizin," *Deutsche Medizinische Wochenschrift*, LIV, 36 (September 7, 1928), 1489–92. German medicine is thoroughly treated in Alfons Fischer: *Geschichte des deutschen Gesundheitswesens*, 2 vols. (1933), a book that also deals with the philosophical basis and propagandistic expressions of eighteenth-century medical thought in the German-speaking area. For French medicine, see P. Delauney: *La vie médicale aux XVIe, XVIIe, XVIIIe siècles* (1935). A variety of special monographs have been instructive to me: Arthur Newsholme: *Evolution of Preventive Medicine* (1927) touches on a subject important to eighteenth-century reformers; David Riesman's article "The Rise and Early History of Clinical Teaching," *Annals of Medical History*, II, 2 (June 1919), 136–47, traces the significant development of simply *looking* at the patient, from its first practice in sixteenth-century Padua, to the great Boerhaave, who practiced in a twelve-bed clinic at Leyden, and taught all Europe—and America. Bernice Hamilton: "The Medical Professions in the Eighteenth Century," *Economic History Review* (second series), IV, 2 (1951), 141–69, has valuable details on the liberation of surgeons from barber gilds, and professional infighting. On the surgeon's struggle for status and independence, see also the volumes by King. Maurice Daumas: *Les instruments scientifiques aux XVIIe et XVIIIe siècles* (1953) deals with medical instruments, while John F. Fulton briefly traces the history of a medical academy, in his "The Warrington Academy (1757–86) and its influence upon Medicine and Science," *Bulletin of the Institute of the History of Medicine*, I (1933), 50–80. Goethe has some observations on the growing importance of the medical profession in his time—(*Dichtung und Wahrheit,* in *Gedenkausgabe,* X, 305).

The subject of mental illness is beginning to receive serious attention; the philosophes, to their credit, were among the first to regard it as a natural affliction rather than a divine punishment or devilish invasion. Michel Foucault: *Madness and Civilization: A History of Insanity in the Age of Reason* (1961; tr. [but somewhat cut] Richard Howard, 1965), is often brilliant and filled with startling facts, but ridden with a metaphysical thesis and the gloomy conviction that the modern world of "normal" men is really the madhouse; its rather hostile treatment of Freud is indicative of its bias. (See my review of the book in *Commentary,* XL, 4 [October 1965], 93–6.) Richard Hunter and Ida McAlpine: *Three Hundred Years of Psychiatry, 1535–1860* (1963), is substantial, and less metaphysical than Foucault's work.

Despite this wealth of material, the intimate relation of Enlightenment to medicine can still be profitably explored. Pierre Brunet: *Les Physiciens hollandais et la méthode expérimentale en France au XVIIIe siècle* (1926) is economical and impressive; I have learned much from it. The last chapters of Gerald J. Gruman: *A History of Ideas About the Prolongation of Life: The Evolution of Prolongevity Hypotheses to 1800* (1966), review the ideas of Franklin, Condorcet, and others on the important theme of lengthening the life span. John F. Fulton: "The Rise of the Experimental Method, Bacon and the Royal Society of London," *Yale Journal of Biology and Medicine,* III, 4 (March 1931), 299–320, is useful. Fulton has also considered "Some Aspects of Medicine Reflected in Seventeenth-Century Literature With Special Reference to the Plague of 1665," in R. F. Jones *et al.: The Seventeenth Century; Studies in the History of English Thought and Literature from Bacon to Pope* (1951), [I, 526], 198–208. Walter Pagel: "The Religious and Philosophical Aspects of van Helmont's Science and Medicine," *Supplements to the Bulletin of the History of Medicine,* No. II (1944), illuminates the relations of science to medicine, medicine to philosophy, and philosophy to religion in the age just preceding the Enlightenment. John Locke's medical philosophy has recently aroused widespread interest. Maurice Cranston's *John Locke, A Biography* (1957) has some material on Locke and Sydenham; Patrick Romanell has gone through "Some Medico-Philosophical Excerpts from the Mellon Collection of Locke's Papers," *Journal of the History of Ideas*, XXV, 1 (January–March 1964), 107–16, and Kenneth Dewhurst has written an informative book on *John Locke (1632–1704), Physician and Philosopher: A Medical Biography* (1963). Until recently, the best biography of Sydenham was David Riesman: *Thomas Sydenham, Clinician* (1926). Now there is Kenneth Dewhurst: *Dr. Thomas Sydenham (1624–1689): His Life and Official Writings* (1966), an essay with a useful anthology attached. For medicine in the *Encyclopédie*, see Maxime Laignel-Lavastine: "Les médecins collaborateurs de l'*Encyclopédie*," *Revue d'Histoire des Sciences*, IV (1951), 353–8; Pierre Astruc: "Les sciences médicales et leurs représentants dans l'*Encyclopédie*," ibid., 359–68; Proust: *Diderot et l'Encyclopédie*, 35–6; and Arthur M. Wilson: *Diderot, The Testing Years, 1713–1759* (1957), 52–3, 93 [I, 436]. Diderot's interest in medicine receives attention in A. Bigot: "Diderot et la médecine," *Cahiers haut-marnais*, No. 24 (1951), 42–3; while Charles G. Cumston: *An Introduction to the History of Medicine* (1926) gives some pages (351–6) to Diderot's celebrated physician-friend Théophile de Bordeu. Herbert Dieckmann has devoted an important article to Bordeu: "Théophile Bordeu und Diderots Rêve de d'Alembert," *Romanische Forschungen*, III (1938), 55–122. Amusingly, and instructively, La Mettrie refers to Diderot as a "Médecin" (*L'homme machine* [ed. Aram Vartanian, 1960], 177). "Voltaire's Relations to Medicine" have been explored extensively though rather superficially in Pearce Bailey's article, in *Annals of Medical History*, I (1917), 54–72; Renée Waldinger: "Voltaire and Medicine," *VS*, LVIII (1967), 1777–1806, is far more useful. M. S. Libby: *The Attitude of Voltaire to Magic and the Sciences* (1935) has some useful pages (240–60) on the same subject. Voltaire's celebrated physician has had his own biography; see Henry Tronchin: *Un médecin du XVIIe siècle, Théodore Tronchin (1709–1791), d'après des documents inédits* (1906). Denis Diderot, it seems, on behalf of his father, also consulted Tronchin; this emerges from the extended note by Jean-Daniel Candaux: "Consultations du docteur Tronchin pour Diderot, père et fils," *Diderot Studies*, VI (1964), 47–54.

I have quoted the long, moving passage from David Ramsay's review of the state of eighteenth-century medicine from the original edition; the little pamphlet is now available once more, together with other works and letters, in the convenient edition by Robert L. Brunhouse: *David Ramsay, 1749–1815: Selections from his Writings* (1965).

Both to the men of the eighteenth century, and to historians today, the advance of medicine and the state of population were, and are, inseparable. General histories of population to be consulted are Marcel Reinhard: *Histoire de la population mondiale de 1700 à 1948* (1949), and the important collective work by D. V. Glass and D. E. C. Eversley, eds.: *Population in History: Essays in Historical Demography* (1965), which has a number of valuable articles on demography all over Europe.

The fact of eighteenth-century population growth is universally accepted, but the causes of the demographic revolution remain controversial. The available facts (for England) and the current state of the controversy have been summarized ably in Deane: *First Industrial Revolution*, chap. ii. The older argument, offered in M. C. Buer's informative *Health, Wealth and Population in the Early Days of the Industrial Revolution* (1926), that population grew because the death rate fell as a result of improvement in many areas of life, long regarded as obvious, has now been challenged; it must be at least refined and probably modified. The careful researches of H. J. Habbakuk show that the fall in the death rate was marked only after 1780, but that earlier population increases may have resulted from earlier marriages and improved nutrition, which produced higher birth rates. See Habbakuk: "English Population in the Eighteenth Century," *Economic History Review* (second series), VI, 2 (1953), 117–33, and "Population Problems and European Economic Development in the Late Eighteenth and Nineteenth Centuries," *American Economic Review*, LIII, 2 (May 1963), 607–33. His views have been supported in J. T. Krause's authoritative though still cautious "Changes in English Fertility and Mortality, 1781–1850," *Economic History Review* (second series), XI, 1 (1958), 52–70. Other valuable contributions to the debate in England have been offered, again by Krause, in a helpful survey, "Some Implications of Recent Work in Historical Demography," *Comparative Studies in Society and History*, I, 2 (January 1959), 164–88; T. McKeon and R. G. Brown: "Medical Evidence Related to English Population Changes in the Eighteenth Century," *Population Studies*, IX, 2 (November 1955), 119–41; D. V. Glass: "The Population Controversy in Eighteenth

Century England," ibid., VI, 1 (July 1952), 69–91, and the earlier but still helpful article by John Brownlee, "The Health of London in the Eighteenth Century," *Proceedings* of the Royal Medical Society, XVIII, part 2 (1925), 78–85, which has figures on the London Lying-In Hospital.

On demographic information for countries other than England, see, in addition to the general histories of population already cited, H. Gille: "The Demographic History of the Northern European Countries in the Eighteenth Century," *Population Studies*, III, 1 (June 1949), 3–65, to be supplemented by an extremely informative essay by E. F. Heckscher, "Swedish Population Trends before the Industrial Revolution," *Economic History Review* (second series), II, 3 (1950), 266–77.

For France, see Philippe Ariès: *Histoire des populations françaises et leurs attitudes devant la vie depuis le XVIIIe siècle* (1948), and Pierre Goubert: "En Beauvais: problèmes démographiques du XVIIe siècle," *Annales*, VII, 4 (October–December 1952), 453–68, which, though concerned with the seventeenth century, shows the improvement in life-expectancy in the second half of that century, which was the taking-off point for the eighteenth. See also François de Dainville: "Grandeur et population des villes au XVIIIe siècle," *Population*, XIII, 3 (July–September 1958), 459–80; A. Sauvy and Jacqueline Hecht: "La population agricole française au XVIIIe siècle et l'expérience du marquis de Turbilly," ibid., XX, 2 (March–April 1965), 269–86; Jean Meuvret: "Les crises de subsistances et la démographie de la France d'ancien régime," ibid., I, 4 (October–December 1946), 643–50; Anita Fage: "Les doctrines de population des Encyclopédistes," ibid., VI, 4 (October–December 1951), 609–24; Fage: "Économie et population: les doctrines françaises avant 1800," ibid., IX, 1 (January–March 1954), 105–10; and P. E. Vincent: "French Demography in the 18th Century," *Population Studies*, I, 1 (June 1947), 44–71.

In addition to relying on the titles just mentioned, I have drawn figures for the text from Ashton: *The Eighteenth Century*, 9; Jacques Godechot: *La Grande Nation*, 2 vols. (1956), I, 44; J. L. and Barbara Hammond: "Poverty, Crime, Philanthropy," in Turberville, ed.: *Johnson's England*, I, 308; and G. E. Mingay: "The Agricultural Depression, 1730–1750," *Economic History Review* (second series), VIII, 3 (1956), 323–38.

The history of nutrition is of great significance for my theme. The French journal *Annales* has been running some important articles since 1961. Radcliffe N. Salaman: *The History and Social Influence of the Potato* (1949) is a justly famous pioneering work; large but by no means extravagant claims for the part of the potato in changing life in Europe have been made by William L. Langer, in his "Europe's Initial Population Explosion," *American Historical Review*, LXIX, 1 (October 1963), 1–17. For other histories of various foods, including bread and wine, see the bibliography in Robert Mandrou: *Introduction à la France moderne, Essai de psychologie historique, 1500–1640* (1961), 372, which I have found useful. Lord Ernle: *English Farming Past and Present* (edn. 1961) connects nutrition to the agricultural revolution. For that revolution, especially in England, see chap. iii in Deane: *First Industrial Revolution*, and Ashton: *The Eighteenth Century* (chap. ii). See also G. E. and K. R. Fussell: *The English Countryman: His Life and Work, A.D. 1500–1900* (1955). Enclosures, in addition, are treated in E. C. K. Gonner: *Common Land and Enclosures* (1912), which should be read in conjunction with H. G. Hunt: "Landownership and Enclosure, 1750–1850," *Economic History Review*, XI, 3 (1959), 497–505, as well as the earlier essay by J. D. Chambers, "Enclosure and Labor Supply," ibid., V, 2 (1952), 319–43, which, together with the revisionist work of major economic historians, suggests the economic and social advantages of enclosures.

Other countries experienced agricultural and nutritional changes of great importance as well. They are taken into account in Olga Beaumont: "Agriculture: Farm Implements," in Singer, ed.: *History of Technology*, IV, 1–12; and G. E. Fussell: "Agriculture: Techniques of Farming," ibid., 13–42. See also E. Soreau: *L'agriculture du XVIIe siècle à la fin du XVIIIe siècle* (1952).

3. THE SPIRIT OF THE AGE

If the material for the first two sections of this chapter is rich, it is overwhelming for this section; I shall confine myself to items of central importance.

The sociological perception of civilization as an interacting totality of interdependent sectors is best, if most informally, expressed in some of Voltaire's Notebook entries, some of them cited in the text, and in Voltaire's *Lettres philosophiques*, best read in the great edition of Gustave Lanson, 2 vols. (1909). Carl Bridenbaugh reports on an American instance of such sociological perception; in 1773, an unidentified gentleman in Baltimore wrote:

> Liberty, science and commerce, the great friends of man, are sister adventurers. They are intimately, indeed, inseparably linked together, and always take up their residence in the cities. Thither, the greatest geniuses of the age generally resort, and incited by emulation or fired by ambition, they stimulate each other to successful exertions of native talents; which might have otherwise lain dormant and forever deprived mankind of much useful instruction. To them repair the patriots, the men of letters, and the merchants who become the guardians of the people's rights, the protectors of learning, the supporters of their countries' trade. Thus, free cities, considered in this light are the repositories, preservatives, and nurseries of commerce, liberty and knowledge. *Cities in Revolt*, 215.

For the rise of reason in the eighteenth century, I offer in evidence *The Rise of Modern Paganism*, with its Bibliographical Essay [esp. I, 505–46]. Roland N. Stromberg: *Religious Liberalism in Eighteenth-Century England* (1954), [I, 550] is good for England; Leslie Stephen: *English Thought in the Eighteenth Century*, 2 vols. (1876), [I, 431] remains so. See E. Préclin and E. Jarry: *Les Luttes politiques et doctrinales aux XVIIe et XVIIIe siècles*, 2 vols. (1955–6), [I, 546], for France; Karl Aner: *Theologie der Lessingzeit* (1929), [I, 440, 536], for Germany, although the subject invites further monographic work. I have traced the rise of rationalism in New England through a study of Puritan historians in my *A Loss of Mastery: Puritan Historians in Colonial America* (1966), which contains a full and argumentative bibliography; here I single out Conrad Wright: *The Beginnings of Unitarianism in America* (1955), and Joseph Haroutunian: *Piety Versus Moralism: The Passing of the New England Theology* (1932). Hugh Trevor-Roper: "The Scottish Enlightenment," *VS*, LVIII (1967), 1635–58, is a wicked, witty, and persuasive essay on the rise of reason in a backward Calvinist society.

The best book on touching is Marc Bloch's magnificent and exhaustive analysis, *Les Rois Thaumaturges: Étude sur le caractère surnaturel attribué à la puissance royale particulièrement en France et en Angleterre* (1924), fully documented and superbly controlled. In an English notebook, incidentally, Voltaire notes (in English): "My footman touched for the King's evil till he was seven years of age" *(Notebooks, 59).*

The literature on humanitarianism[4] is large though not always very good. But see David Owen: *English Philanthropy, 1660–1960* (1964): its first five chapters concentrate on the eighteenth century, tracing the change of spirit concretely in charitable institutions. M. Gwladys Jones: *The Charity School Movement* (1958) is a full, judicious, tough-minded account of a complex subject. See also W. K. Lowther Clarke: *A History of the S.P.C.K.* (1959), and R. H. Nichols and F. A. Wray: *The History of the Foundling Hospital* (1935). Samuel C. McCulloch has edited a collection of essays, *British Humanitarianism, Essays Honoring Frank J. Klingberg* (1950), which contain much useful detail but are, in general, rather mediocre. A. W. Coats has an interesting article on "Changing Attitudes to Labour in the Mid-Eighteenth Century," *Economic History Review* (second series), XI, 1 (1958) 35–51, on which I have drawn. For Hume's humaneness, see Eugene Rotwein's *David Hume: Writings on Economics* (1955).

Shelby T. McCloy has written a comprehensive survey of *The Humanitarian Movement in Eighteenth-Century France* (1957), full of information but rather lacking in discrimination and decisive judg-

---

[4] For the philosophes' humanitarian ideas—on toleration, peace, abolition of slavery, and judicial reform—see below, 669–74.

ment (I accept the strictures of Elinor Barber in her review of this book, *Journal of Modern History*, XXX, 2 [June 1958], 144–5. Still, the book is informative. It may be supplemented by McCloy's own *Government Assistance in Eighteenth Century France* [1946].) For Germany, see Hans M. Wolff: *Die Weltanschauung der deutschen Aufklärung in geschichtlicher Entwicklung* (2d edn., 1963), and Holborn: *A History of Modern Germany, 1648–1840,* especially 238, 270–1. Leo Gershoy: *From Despotism to Revolution, 1763–1789* (1944) has a good survey of the advance of welfare, coupled with the secularization of charity (chaps. viii and x).

That all was far from well can be seen from the expulsion of the Jews from Prague (Schürer: *Prag,* 225–9); and the fate of the Norwegian figure Christian Lofthuus (1750–97), who spent the last ten years of his life chained to a block (Hovde: *The Scandinavian Countries,* 201). It would be all too easy to multiply the instances. Let me call attention to my pages on Catherine of Russia in my *Voltaire's Politics: The Poet as Realist* (1959), 171–84, and the bibliographical notes (384–5); Catherine is of special interest because she masked brutality, especially toward the helpless serfs, behind the guise of enlightened rhetoric. On the Russian serf, Geroid T. Robinson's scholarly *Rural Russia under the Old Regime* (1949) is conclusive.

Doubtless, the best place to study the other side of the eighteenth century—the victory of stagnation and clerical conservatism—is Spain, and here we have the magnificently detailed, observant survey by Jean Sarrailh: *L'Espagne éclairée de la seconde moitié du XVIIIe siècle* (1954), a brilliant essay on social rigidity; it may be read in conjunction with Richard Herr: *The Eighteenth-Century Revolution in Spain* (1958).

For all its obvious importance, the history of the Western family remains to be written, though there has been some pioneering work in recent years. Philippe Ariès: *Centuries of Childhood: A Social History of Family Life* (1960; tr. Robert Baldick, 1962), is a masterly survey of the idea of childhood beginning in the late Middle Ages and moving into the modern period; it skillfully employs family portraits, intimate diaries, and scholastic programs. *Studien über Autorität und Familie*, ed. Max Horkheimer (1936), is the celebrated collective report from the Institut für Sozialforschung; it displays that curious mixture of philosophical Marxism and orthodox psychoanalysis typical of the work of that Institute. It begins with a psychological article by Erich Fromm, a theoretical article by Max Horkheimer, and a historical article by Herbert Marcuse; offers detailed interpretations of questionnaires and long, immensely useful reviews of available literature. For England, see the recent effort by Peter Laslett: *The World We Have Lost* (1965), pioneering, tentative, and controversial. (The review of this book in the *Times Literary Supplement* of December 9, 1965, though shrewd, is excessive in its hostile zeal.) The best book on the New England family is by Edmund S. Morgan: *The Puritan Family: Religion and Domestic Relations in Seventeenth-Century New England* (2d edn., 1966). Curt Gebauer has written two informative articles on family structure and moral training in eighteenth-century Germany: "Studien zur Geschichte der bürgerlichen Sittenreform des 18. Jahrhunderts," *Archiv für Kulturgeschichte*, XV (1923), 97–116; and "Studien zur Geschichte der bürgerlichen Sittenreform des 18. Jahrhunderts: Die Reform der häuslichen Erziehung," ibid., XX (1930), 36–51. Friedrich Sengle: *Christoph Martin Wieland* (1949), [I, 441], 17, has a significant comment on the new, less patriarchal father in German society.

For France, in addition to Ariès, see Roger Mercier: *L'Enfant dans la société du XVIIIᵉ siècle, avant l'Émile* (1961), and Edmond Pilon: *La vie de famille au XVIIIᵉ siècle* (1941). Changes in family structure and ideals of marriage from seventeenth- to eighteenth-century France can be glimpsed from the relevant chapter on "La mystique du mariage," in H. Brémond: *Histoire littéraire du sentiment religieux en France*, IX (1932), 289–330. A model of what this kind of social history must be—imaginative yet firmly wedded to fact, sociological and psychoanalytical at once—is Marc Raeff: "Home, School, and Service in the Life of the Eighteenth-Century Russian Nobleman," *The Slavonic and East European Review*, XL, 95 (June 1962), 295–307, which makes much of the absent father and the migratory habits of noble families; we need more articles of this sort in all areas of Western civilization of the eighteenth century. See also Raeff's important *Origins of the Russian Intelligentsia: The Eighteenth-Century Nobility* (1966). Lawrence Stone: "Marriage among the English Nobility in the 16th and 17th Centuries," with comment by William J. Goode: *Comparative Studies in Society and History*, III, 2 (January 1961), 182–215, is very valuable on arranged marriages, and suggestive for my text although it regrettably stops short of the age of the Enlightenment. Stone's theme is taken up by a valuable unpublished article by J. Jean Hecht on rational love and mate selection in eighteenth-century England. Paul Kluckhohn's monograph, *Die Auffassung der Liebe im 18. Jahrhundert und in der Romantik* (2d edn., 1931), is highly suggestive on the relation of Pietism, "*Empfindsamkeit*," and rationalism to literature. On the "mysterious" subject of women, to which Diderot devoted an essay-review, "Sur les femmes," (1772) reviewing Antoine-Léonard Thomas's *Essai sur le caractère, les moeurs et l'esprit des femmes* . . . (1772), (see *Œuvres*, II, 251–62), and which was the subject of ruminations by Hume, Wieland, Voltaire, and other philosophes, much further work is needed. For a psychoanalytical investigation into the notion of the "dangerous woman" as the source of vice, see H. R. Hays: *The Dangerous Sex* (1964). On Defoe, the pioneering feminist, see Bonamy Dobrée: *English Literature in the Early Eighteenth Century, 1700–1740* (1959), [I, 538], 37–8. Jean Elizabeth Gagen: *The New Woman: Her Emergence in English Drama: 1600–1730* (1954) is a useful dissertation.

The translation of Christian charity into secular generosity is well observed in Owen: *English Philanthropy* (see above, 592), and Ernst Troeltsch: *Protestantism and Progress* (1912; tr. W. Montgomery, 1912), 109 ff. George Sherburn: "Fielding's Social Outlook," in James L. Clifford, ed.: *Eighteenth Century English Literature* (1959), 251–73, says the essential. See also Donald J. Greene: *The Politics of Samuel Johnson* (1960), [I, 450].

This is not the place to assess the validity of Max Weber's conception of the Protestant Ethic. Certainly his celebrated essay, *The Protestant Ethic and the Spirit of Capitalism* (1904–5; tr. Talcott Parsons, 1930), has been enormously stimulating, and has invited not merely controversy but also valuable research. While, I think, its central proposition has been severely damaged by Kurt Samuelsson: *Religion and Economic Action: A Critique of Max Weber* (1957; tr. E. Geoffrey French, 1961), the latest in a long series of controversial essays called forth by Weber's famous essay (which also lucidly reviews the history of the controversy in the first chapter), Weber's portrait of hard-working, ascetic Western man remains valuable for an understanding (among other things) of the problematic relation of duty to pleasure in the Enlightenment. The working out of this ethic in eighteenth-century Germany occupies a central place in Wolff: *Weltanschaung der deutschen Aufklärung* (see above, 593). Sengle: *Wieland* (above, 594) has some good pages on the same subject (203 *ff.*, 302, 317–18). The tension between profits and humanity in industrialists has been well observed in Mantoux: *Industrial Revolution* (see above, 577), 464–7.

My comments in the text on the transvaluation of values—the high estimation of work and low estimation of heroism—are clearly only a beginning. I found some instructive hints in Dieckmann: *Cinq Leçons sur Diderot* (1959), [I, 436], 21–2. Early instances of the trader's mentality are noted in Hans Baron: *The Crisis of the Early Italian Renaissance* (2d edn., 1966), [I, 511], *passim.*

The Spectator has now been given a splendid new edition, equipped with variants, reliable notes, and an informative introduction, by Donald F. Bond, 5 vols. (1965); I have published an appreciation of this edition, and the cultural meaning of the magazine, "The Spectator as Actor: Addison in Perspective," *Encounter*, XXIX, 6 (December 1967), 27–32. It may be supplemented by Calhoun Winton: *Captain Steele: The Early Career of Richard Steele* (1964); and Peter Smithers: *The Life of Joseph Addison* (1954), the best biography.

The point made by d'Alembert, that mid-century is decisive both in the eighteenth century and in other centuries, has been noted before me, by Cassirer: *Philosophy of the Enlightenment*, 3–4, and Wilson: *Diderot*, 95.

CHAPTER TWO

Progress: From Experience to Program

I HAVE BRIEFLY DISCUSSED Voltaire's naïve political conduct at the court of Frederick II in my *Voltaire's Politics*, 151–2; see also the germane volumes of Besterman's *Correspondence* of Voltaire (X–XV), and Fernand Caussy: "La mission diplomatique de Voltaire (1743–5)," *La Grande Revue*, LXV, 2 (February 1911), 547–63. Kant makes his simple but brilliantly persuasive argument that theory and practice cannot contradict one another in "Über den Gemeinspruch: Das mag in der Theorie richtig sein, taugt aber nicht für die Praxis," *Werke*, VI, 355–98. The famous quotation from Laurence Sterne comes from *Tristram Shandy*, book I, chap. xxiii.

1. THE REPUBLIC OF LETTERS

Much of the material I used to construct my argument that men of letters experienced their own recovery of nerve in the age of the Enlightenment I have of course used before, in the first chapter of this volume, and in *The Rise of Modern Paganism*. Here I shall confine myself to the essential titles. For Scotland, see Henry Grey Graham: *Scottish Men of Letters in the Eighteenth Century* (1901), Gladys Bryson: *Man and Society: The Scottish Inquiry in the Eighteenth Century* (1945), E. C. Mossner: *The Life of David Hume* (1954), W. R. Scott: *Adam Smith As Student and Professor* (1937), and C. R. Fay: *Adam Smith and the Scotland of His Day* (1956), [all I, 430–1].

For England, see Leslie Stephen: *English Literature and Society in the XVIIIth Century* (1907), R. W. Chapman: "Authors and

Booksellers," in Turberville, ed.: *Johnson's England*, II, 310–30, Alexandre Beljame: *Men of Letters and the English Public in the XVIIIth Century* (2d edn., 1897; tr. E. O. Lorimer and corrected by Bonamy Dobrée, 1948), J. A. Cochrane: *Dr. Johnson's Printer: The Life of William Strahan* (1964), J. M. Saunders: *The Profession of English Letters* (1964), David M. Low: *Edward Gibbon, 1737–1794* (1937), and A. S. Collins: *Authorship in the Days of Johnson* (1927), [all I, 431–8]. Collins, in addition, has informative material in his *The Profession of Letters* (1928); he has dealt with the unsolved, perhaps unsolvable question of the reading public in "The Growth of the Reading Public during the Eighteenth Century," *Review of English Studies*, II, 7 (July 1926), 284–94. On this same question, see also James Sutherland: "The Circulation of Newspapers and Literary Periodicals, 1700–1730," *The Library* (fourth series), XV, 2 (February 1934), 111–13. K. Ewart has analyzed a difficult and important question in *Copyright* (1952). The complex and on the whole heartening evolution of a free press in England is traced by Laurence Hanson: *Government and the Press, 1695–1763* (1936), W. H. Wickwar: *The Struggle for the Freedom of the Press* (1928), and Fredrick Seaton Siebert: *Freedom of the Press in England, 1476–1776: The Rise and Decline of Government Control* (1952), especially chaps. xii–xviii. The older article by Douglas M. Ford: "The Growth of the Freedom of the Press," *English Historical Review*, IV, 2 (1889), 1–12, and the book by F. Knight Hunt: *The Fourth Estate*, 2 vols. (1850), remain useful. I have drawn some figures and quotations from Ian Watt: *The Rise of the Novel: Studies in Defoe, Richardson and Fielding* (1957), which is really social more than it is literary history, especially from chap. ii. For English circulating libraries, see Hilda M. Hamlyn: "Eighteenth Century Circulating Libraries in England," *The Library* (fifth series), I, 3 (December 1946), 197–222. Stanley Morison: *The English Newspaper* (1932) is informative; see also Walter Graham: *The Beginnings of English Literary Periodicals, 1665–1715* (1926).

Among the writers Richardson is perhaps most instructive, since he was both a publisher and an author. The best studies are probably A. D. McKillop: *Samuel Richardson: Printer and Novelist* (1936), and William Merritt Sale: *Samuel Richardson, Master Printer* (1950). The sociological exploration of the new reading public has been undertaken, still rather impressionistically, by Watt, and in a long article by Leo Lowenthal and Marjorie Fiske: "The Debate over Art and Popular Culture in Eighteenth Century England," in Mirra Komarovsky, ed.: *Common Frontiers of the Social Sciences* (1957), 33–112. R. K. Webb's *The British Working Class Reader, 1790–1848: Literacy and Social Tension* (1955) is a serious attempt to analyze the relation of reading, class, and politics. There is a good new edition of Moritz's *Travels:* translated and edited by Reginald Nettel (1965).

The French situation, like the English, has been thoroughly canvassed. To mention only the best: Lucien Brunel: *Les Philosophes et l'académie française au dix-huitième siècle* (1884), Jacques Proust: *Diderot et l'Encyclopédie* (1962), Daniel Mornet: *Les Origines intellectuelles de la révolution française* (1947), Pierre Grosclaude: *Malesherbes: Témoin et interprète de son temps* (1961), Kingsley Martin: *French Liberal Thought in the Eighteenth Century* (1929), Ira O. Wade: *The Clandestine Organization and Diffusion of Philosophic Ideas in France from 1700 to 1750* (1938), Maurice Pellisson: *Les Hommes de lettres au XVIII siècle* (1911), a major work, and above all, David T. Pottinger: *The French Book Trade in the Ancien Régime, 1500–1789* (1958), which is indispensable [I, 434–5]. Pottinger's book does not fully supersede his own informative articles, "Censorship in France during the Ancien Régime," *Boston Public Library Quarterly*, VI, 1, 2 (January–April 1954), 23–42, 84–101. J.-P. Belin: *Le commerce des livres prohibés à Paris de 1750 à 1789* (1913) takes up where Albert Bachman: *Censorship in France from 1715 to 1750: Voltaire's Opposition* (1934) leaves off. Paul Dupont: *Histoire de l'imprimerie*, 2 vols. (1854) is excellent on the book trade, with appended documents; it can be supplemented with Gabriel Peignot's *Essai historique sur la liberté d'écrire* (1832), which prints excerpts from government decrees. Paul Mellottée: *Les transformations économiques de l'imprimerie sous l'ancien régime* (1905) has a significant economic analysis of the book industry. The government's opening of mail, a source of great annoyance to the philosophes and a real danger, is well discussed by Eugène Vaillé in *Le Cabinet noir* (1950). I have discussed Voltaire's publishing tactics in *Voltaire's Politics, passim*, especially 66–87; and in *The Party of Humanity*, chaps. i–iii. The critical controversy over Helvétius's *De l'esprit* is best examined in D. W. Smith: *Helvétius: A Study in Persecution* (1965), [I, 437], and Wilson: *Diderot*. Dieckmann has convincingly shown that Diderot's hesitation to publish was not caused solely by fear (*Cinq leçons sur Diderot*, 18–19). At the same time (and the two views are compatible) Frank A. Kafker has demonstrated the consequences of censorship for Diderot and his great enterprise in "The Effect of Censorship on Diderot's Encyclopedia," *The Library Chronicle*, XXX, 1 (January 1964), 25–6. To these may be added Douglas H. Gordon and Norman L. Torrey: *The Censoring of Diderot's Encyclopédie and the Re-established Text* (1947), [I, 434]. J. Lough has suggested ("The Encyclopédie: Two Unsolved Problems," *French Studies*, XVII, 2 [April 1963], 126–34), that the interference of the publisher may have been even more drastic than Gordon and Torrey have found. On social rigidity and mobility that includes the careers of writers, once again, Barber: *Bourgeoisie in 18th Century France*. The interesting career of Pierre Rousseau, who evaded French censors by operating from the relatively free soil of the Duchy of Bouillon, throws much light on eighteenth-century French publishing conditions; it has been explored by Raymond F. Birn in "The *Journal Encyclopédique* and the Old Regime," *VS*, XXIV (1963), 219–40; and in "Pierre Rousseau and the 'Philosophes' of Bouillon," *VS*, XXIX (1964). The seizure of the *Académie française* by the philosophes can be traced in Brunel, cited above, in Ronald Grimsley: *Jean D'Alembert, 1717–83* (1962), [I, 436], in the relevant volumes of Grimm's *Correspondance littéraire*, in François Albert-Buisson: *Les quarante au temps des lumières* (1960), which though brief and vulgarly chatty is surprisingly informative, and in the older survey by Émile Gassier: *Les cinq cents immortels: Histoire de l'Académie Française, 1634–1906* (1906), especially 70–114, and the documents, 390 ff. *Trois siècles de l'Académie française, 1635–1935* (1935) is a collection of essays on various aspects of its history by the forty Immortals of 1935. But a full analysis of strategies and counterstrategies, which uses the surviving records and the discreet—sometimes indiscreet—hints in the philosophes' correspondence, remains a desideratum. In general we may conclude, as I conclude in the text, that Tocqueville's cozy conclusion—"authors were harried to an extent that won them sympathy, but not enough to inspire them with any real fear. They were, in fact, subjected to the petty persecutions that spur men to revolt, but not to the steady pressure that breaks their spirit," *The Old Regime and the Revolution* (1856; tr. Stuart Gilbert, 1955), 152-3—cannot withstand careful examination. Biedermann: *Deutschland im achtzehnten Jahrhundert*, II, part I, 484 *n.*, has the figure on the shift from Latin to German; he discusses the tribulations of German "political" journalism in I, 112 *ff.* Leonard Krieger: *The German Idea of Freedom: History of a Political Tradition* (1957), especially 43, analyzes what social consequences that journalism did have. While Albert Köster: *Die deutsche Literatur der Aufklärungszeit* (1925), [I, 440], is primarily a work of literary history, it discusses Prussian censorship on 207-8. Bruford's *Germany in the Eighteenth Century* is explicitly directed (as its subtitle makes clear) at the "social background of the literary revival" and is particularly useful for this section. Two books, though now old, remain informative on the history of the German book trade—Karl Buechner: *Beiträge zur Geschichte des deutschen Buchhandels*, 2 vols. (1873-4), and Johann Goldfriedrich: *Geschichte des deutschen Buchhandels*, 3 vols. (1908-13), of which I and II are particularly relevant to the age of the Enlightenment.

For the survival of illiteracy among nobles and persistence of patronage in other countries, see J. M. Roberts: "Lombardy," in Goodwin: *European Nobility*, 70, and Michael Roberts: "Sweden," ibid., 152. That the so-called Westernization of the Russian mind under Peter the Great amounted to very little has been proved once and for all by L. R. Lewitter: "Peter the Great, Poland, and the Westernization of Russia," *JHI*, XIX, 4 (October 1958), 493-506.

The literature on American freedom of the press is largely one of self-congratulation, although modern studies have introduced some complications into the picture. Leonard W. Levy's rather astringent criticisms in *Legacy of Suppression* (1960) are refreshing and an essential corrective, but they remain a dissenting voice. A different view is taken by Zechariah Chafee, Jr.: *Free Speech in the United States* (1948). See also the standard treatment, Arthur M. Schlesinger: *Prelude to Independence: The Newspaper War on Britain, 1764-1776* (1958), and Livingston Schuyler: *The Liberty of the Press in the American Colonies before the Revolutionary War* (1905).

2. FROM PAST TO FUTURE:
THE GREAT REORIENTATION

The question of life styles, of attitudes toward death, toward past and future, and toward civilization, has not yet been fully treated. The *locus classicus* for antique pessimism is in Nietzsche's great essay, *Die Geburt der Tragödie aus dem Geiste der Musik* (1872; tr. several times, most recently by Francis Golffing, 1956). Modern scholarly examinations of Greek antiquity have not destroyed, even if they have modified, Nietzsche's portrait; see above all Werner Jaeger: *Paideia: The Ideals of Greek Culture*, 3 vols. (1936; tr. Gilbert Highet, 2d edn., 1945), E. R. Dodds: *The Greeks and the Irrational* (1951), A. D. Nock: *Conversion: The Old and New in Religion from Alexander the Great to Augustine of Hippo* (1933), H.-I. Marrou: *A History of Education in Antiquity* (1948; tr. G. R. Lamb, 1956), [all, I, 466-9]. For Roman pessimism, Sir Ronald Syme: *Tacitus*, 2 vols. (1958), and *The Roman Revolution* (1939), [I, 476, 479], are decisive. I have also discussed Lucretius in *The Rise of Modern Paganism*, 98-105; I have, on both occasions, learned much from Santayana's *Three Philosophical Poets* (1910), [I, 475]. Jean Seznec: *The Survival of the Pagan Gods* (1940; rev. edn., tr. Barbara F. Sessions, 1953), [I, 493], has treated classical classicism as a form of nostalgia (p. 322); but Ernst Robert Curtius: *European Literature and the Latin Middle Ages* (1948; tr. Willard R. Trask, 1953), [I, 477], has shown (165-6) that the ancients also defended themselves against the overwhelming pressure of ancestor worship.

For medieval attitudes, Marc Bloch: *Feudal Society*, is indispensable (see above, 583). Millard Meiss: *Painting in Florence and Siena after the Black Death: The Arts, Religion and Society in the Mid-Fourteenth Century* (1951), [I, 513], is a fascinating monograph. It may be supplemented by Helmut Rosenfeld: *Der Mittelalterliche Totentanz* (1954). Johan Huizinga's famous *The Waning of the Middle Ages* (2d edn., 1921; tr. and rev. by the author and F. Hopman, 1924) has often been taken as a corrective for Jacob Burckhardt's *Die Kultur der Renaissance in Italien: Ein Versuch* (1860),

[I, 506], erroneously so, for Huizinga and Burckhardt do not deal with the same region; besides, Burckhardt's view of the profound, indeed tragic ambivalence of Renaissance life and attitudes toward life is far from optimistic. I have analyzed Burckhardt's ambivalence in "Burckhardt's *Renaissance*: Between Responsibility and Power," in Leonard Krieger and Fritz Stern, eds.: *The Responsibility of Power: Historical Essays in Honor of Hajo Holborn* (1967), 183–98.

A book of principal importance to this section has been Erwin Panofsky's *Tomb Sculpture: Its Changing Aspects from Ancient Egypt to Bernini* (1964), which develops with masterly erudition the crucial distinction between retrospective and prospective attitudes toward death; chap. iv traces the gradual conversion of death into a symbol designed to terrify rather than purify. Alberto Tenenti: *La vie et la mort à travers l'art du XVe siècle* (Cahiers des Annales, No. 8, 1952), and his larger *Il senso della morte et l'amore della vita nel Rinascimento* (1957), are pioneering studies which I found most useful; I only wish there were similar studies for the eighteenth century. See also Robert Mandrou: *Introduction à la France moderne (1500–1640): Essai de psychologie historique* (1961), [I, 505]. Theodore Spencer: *Death and Elizabethan Tragedy* (1936) shows that while in the Middle Ages sudden death was feared as cutting off the possibility of pious preparation and repentance, by the time of Montaigne it was coming to be thought desirable. A. J. Krailsheimer: *Studies in Self-Interest from Descartes to La Bruyère* (1962), [I, 524] has interesting passages on the all-too-un-Christian love of fame in the sixteenth and seventeenth centuries. Brémond's chapter on "L'art de mourir," in *Histoire Littéraire*, IX (see above, 594), is instructive, especially for comparative purposes.

The seventeenth century is, of course, the century when ancients battled moderns, a combat that has been much examined. The best known and in many respects the best book on the combat in England is Richard Foster Jones: *Ancients and Moderns: A Study of the Rise of the Scientific Movement in Seventeenth Century England* (2d edn., 1961), a magisterial work; my only reservation is that it tends to see the Puritans as rather more modern in their ideas, let alone their consequences, than I should tend to see them. I have criticized this tendency to modernize Puritanism in *A Loss of Mastery: Puritan Historians in Colonial America*, passim. Jones's "The Background of 'The Battle of the Books,'" in Jones et al.: *The*

Seventeenth Century, 10–40, is very interesting in this context. For the combat in France, the standard work is H. Gillot: *La Querelle des anciens et des modernes en France* (1914). I have indicated Voltaire's view of the combat in the text; his general attitude has not been fully explored. If it is to be, the Notebooks offer rich materials; it was in one of these that he wrote, quite simply: "Those who read only the ancients are children who never want to talk to anyone but their nurses" *(Notebooks, 193)*.

All these books lay the groundwork for an understanding of eighteenth-century attitudes toward life. Here the bulky dissertation by Robert Mauzi: *L'idée du bonheur au XVIIIe siècle* (1960), well surveys the field. Mauzi's critical edition (with a long Introduction) of Madame du Châtelet's *Discours sur le bonheur* (1961) is extremely illuminating. Bernard Groethuysen's *Die Entstehung der bürgerlichen Welt- und Lebensanschauung in Frankreich*, 2 vols. (1927–30), [I, 545], should be contrasted with Brémond's chapter, just cited, on the art of dying.[5] Lester G. Crocker has useful indications on attitudes toward life and death, both in *An Age of Crisis: Man and World in Eighteenth Century Thought* (1959) (chaps. i–iii) and *Nature and Culture: Ethical Thought in the French Enlightenment* (1963), (chaps. v and vi), [both in I, 428]; see also his article on "The Discussion of Suicide in the Eighteenth Century," *JHI*, XIII, 1 (January 1952), 47–72. As should appear from the text, my interpretation of Diderot's remark about posterity is quite different from that offered by Carl Becker in his *Heavenly City*, 119 ff. The remarkable correspondence between Diderot and Falconet can now be read in George Roth's edition of Diderot's *Correspondance*, V and VI. Herbert Dieckmann and Jean Seznec have made this correspondence their own; see their partial edition, *Diderot et Falconet, Correspondance* (1959) and their article, "The Horse of Marcus Aurelius: A Controversy between Diderot and Falconet," *Warburg Journal*, XV (1952), 198–228 [I, 437]. Anne Betty Weinshenker's excellent dissertation on Falconet, which, I said in my first volume, should be published, has now appeared—*Falconet: His Writings and His Friend Diderot* (1966).

The classic study of primitivism is A. O. Lovejoy and George

---

[5] The text of this work has now been translated into English by Mary Ilford: *The Bourgeois: Catholicism vs. Capitalism in Eighteenth-Century France* (1968).

Boas: *Primitivism and Related Ideas in Antiquity: A Documentary History of Primitivism and Related Ideas*, I (1935), from which grew other studies by the authors and their numerous students; it makes the central distinction between "soft" and "hard" primitivism—the commitment to nostalgia or to cultivation. The first result of their collective studies, appearing even before their major work, was Lois Whitney: *Primitivism and the Idea of Progress in English Popular Literature of the Eighteenth Century* (1934), which is dependable and informative, with an instructive Foreword by Lovejoy. Among other Johns Hopkins dissertations on the subject, Edith Amelie Runge: *Primitivism and Related Ideas in Sturm und Drang Literature* (1946), was one of the few to be printed; in its bibliography (298) it conveniently lists the others. Thomson, the poet of Newtonianism, forms a special and interesting specimen; he has been studied in Raymond D. Havens: "Primitivism and the Idea of Progress in Thomson," *Studies in Philology*, XXIX, 1 (January 1932), 41–52. One fascinating early product of the Hopkins group's studies was George Boas's amusing and informative *The Happy Beast in French Thought of the Seventeenth Century* (1933). But we may go back further than this, to the writings of another Johns Hopkins scholar closely associated with Lovejoy and Boas, Gilbert Chinard, whose *L'exotisme américain dans la littérature française au 16ᵉ siècle* (1911) set the tone; his *L'Amérique et le rêve exotique dans la littérature française au XVIIᵉ et XVIIIᵉ siècle* (1913), [I, 485], took the story to the seventeenth and eighteenth centuries. In addition, see also Geoffrey Atkinson: *The Extraordinary Voyage in French Literature from 1700 to 1720* (1922); and Durand Echeverria: *Mirage in the West: A History of the French Image of American Society to 1815* (1957), which traces French views of America [both in I, 485]; Chauncey B. Tinker: *Nature's Simple Plan* (1922), and Hoxie N. Fairchild: *The Noble Savage* (1928). Scholars, it seems, have long been fascinated by the primitive.

There are good critical editions of Montesquieu's *Lettres persanes* by Antoine Adam (1954) and Paul Vernière (1960), and of Diderot's *Supplément au voyage de Bougainville* by Gilbert Chinard (1935), and above all, Herbert Dieckmann (1955). I have once again found James Doolittle: *Rameau's Nephew: A Study of Diderot's "Second Satire"* (1960), helpful. G. L. van Roosbroeck: *Persian Letters Before Montesquieu* (1932) places Montesquieu in the tradition [all in I, 485].

Rousseau the "primitivist" has long occupied the attention of the popular writer and, fortunately, the careful scholar. George R. Havens's critical edition of Rousseau's first *Discours* (1946), [I, 485–6], which analyzes Diderot's share in the work should be read in conjunction with Lovejoy's justly celebrated article "The Supposed Primitivism of Rousseau's *Discourse on Inequality*" (1923), in *Essays in the History of Ideas* (1948), 14–37. If a full study of the tension between "primitivism" and reformism in Rousseau is to be made, it will have to include his minor political writings, especially the essays on Poland and Corsica. For China, a target of long-distance admiration among the philosophes, an anti-Christian, though hardly primitivist ideal, see Virgile Pinot: *La Chine et la formation de l'esprit philosophique en France, 1640–1740* (1932), Walter Engemann: *Voltaire und China* (1932), and, above all, the exhaustive study by Basil Guy: *The French Image of China Before and After Voltaire, VS, XXI* (1963), [all in I, 454–5].

3. THE GEOGRAPHY OF HOPE

The literature on the theory of progress is sizable and valuable, but to my knowledge the broad context into which I have placed the idea of progress—including the general recovery of nerve and the fortunes of literary men—has not been explored before. The standard discussion of progress remains J. B. Bury: *The Idea of Progress: An Inquiry Into Its Origin and Growth* (1920), which, for all its narrowness of concern and occasional superficiality, has in its easygoing way much penetrating analysis.[6] Jules Delvaille: *Essai sur l'histoire de l'idée de progrès jusqu'à la fin du XVIIIᵉ siècle* (1910) is comprehensive but shares with other studies of progress the fault of seeking out, and finding, clues to a theory of progress everywhere. Morris Ginsberg's stimulating essay, *The Idea of Progress: A Revaluation* (1953), and René Hubert: "Essai sur l'histoire de l'idée de progrès," *Revue d'Histoire de la philosophie et d'histoire générale de*

---

[6] Ludwig Edelstein's posthumous *The Idea of Progress in Classical Antiquity* (1967) came to my attention too late for me to use it; its evidence, though interesting, seems to me less than conclusive.

la civilisation (new series), II (October 15, 1934), 289–305, and III (January 15, 1935), 1–32, serve as excellent correctives. Charles Frankel: *The Faith of Reason: The Idea of Progress in the French Enlightenment* (1948) is a stimulating essay perhaps unduly neglected. I found R. V. Sampson: *Progress in the Age of Reason* (1956) a sensible survey with some apt quotations, but hardly profound. Charles Vereker: *Eighteenth-Century Optimism* (1967) particularly stresses the theological (or pseudo-theological) side of "redemptive optimism." Frederick John Teggart, ed.: *The Idea of Progress: A Collection of Readings* (1949) is an adroit anthology. There are useful hints in Georg G. Iggers: "The Idea of Progress: A Critical Reassessment," *American Historical Review*, LXXI, 1 (October 1965), 1–17. Lovejoy's masterly *The Great Chain of Being: A Study of the History of an Idea* (1936) has some very important chapters on the "temporalization of the chain of being" as an instrument for the construction of a theory of progress. That we must interpret the evidence with deliberate care becomes obvious when we find as well-informed a historian as Sir Isaiah Berlin writing: "The third great myth of the eighteenth century was that of steady progress, if not inevitable, at least virtually certain; with consequent disparagement of the benighted past . . ." ("Herder and the Enlightenment," in Earl R. Wasserman, ed.: *Aspects of the Eighteenth Century* [1965], 82). Readers of my first volume know that I think the second part of Sir Isaiah's statement must be modified; readers of chap. ii of this volume know that I think the first part must be rejected.

The literature on primitivism cited before naturally contains much material on progress as well. For the Christian theory of progress, which partly accompanied, partly competed with the secular idea of progress, see the pioneering articles by R. J. Crane: "Anglican Apologetics and the Idea of Progress, 1699–1745," *Modern Philology*, XXXI, 3 (February 1934), 273–306; and 4 (May 1934), 349–82. Ernest Lee Tuveson makes the important point that the idea of progress had deep Christian roots in *Millennium and Utopia: A Study in the Background of Progress* (1949). A subtle yet important contributing factor in Christian optimism was the illogical but powerful assumptions that Christian doctrine, though eternal and eternally valid, somehow evolved; Owen Chadwick has explored this notion with his customary astuteness in *From Bossuet to Newman:*

The Idea of Doctrinal Development (1957). Georges Hardy has connected the church fathers with seventeenth-century Christian optimistic views of history in *Le "De Civitate Dei," source principale du "Discours sur l'histoire universelle"* (1913). Norman Cohn has pursued Christian millenarianism through the Middle Ages in his brilliant but still controversial *The Pursuit of the Millennium* (2d edn., 1961). Theodor E. Mommsen's important article on "St. Augustine and the Christian Idea of Progress," *JHI*, XII, 3 (July 1951), 346–74, which I have cited before [see I, 495], deserves to be cited again.

While I have long pursued my own research into philosophical pessimism, I was both encouraged and helped by Henry Vyverberg's *Historical Pessimism in the French Enlightenment* (1958), [I, 449], rich in gloomy quotations, some of which I have borrowed. A good instance of the difficulties confronting the interpreter of the eighteenth-century mood is the confrontation of Gustave Lanson's "Le déterminisme historique et l'idéalisme social dans *L'Esprit des lois*," *Études d'histoire littéraire* (1929), 135–63, which sees Montesquieu as an optimist, with Gilbert Chinard's "Montesquieu's Historical Pessimism," *Studies in the History of Culture* (1942), 161–72, which sees Montesquieu as a pessimist (see Vyverberg: *Historical Pessimism*, 243). It is too easy to say that both are right; of course they are, but it is necessary to be more precise than this. I incline toward a pessimistic interpretation of Montesquieu's ideas—not the absence of hope for energetic reformist activity to be sure, but a firm, rather grim conviction that all effort will leave life very imperfect indeed. Montesquieu's pessimism is supported by Franz Neumann's splendid "Introduction" to *The Spirit of the Laws* (1945), [I, 436], and René Hubert's "La Notion du devenir historique dans la philosophie de Montesquieu," *Revue de Métaphysique et de morale*, XLVI, 4 (October 1939), 587–610. Diderot is interesting and, as always, extremely complicated; see Lester G. Krakeur (Lester G. Crocker): "Diderot and the Idea of Progress," *Romanic Review*, XXIX, 2 (April 1938), 151–9. For Diderot's pessimism and warnings against philosophical naïveté, see especially his correspondence—for example his letter to Sophie Volland, October 20 (1760), *Correspondance*, III, 164–82, especially 171–2, and other letters to her, especially of this period; as well as *Pages Contre un Tyran*, in *Œuvres politiques*, 135–48.

One interesting and confusing aspect of the debate over progress is the cyclical theory of history. In Europe, Swift (see Ricardo Quintana: *Swift: An Introduction* [1955], [I, 537], 79, 153–5), and Wieland (see Wolffheim: *Wielands Begriff der Humanität* [1949], [I, 439], especially 29–32) are prominent representatives. For cyclical theories among colonial historians in America, see Stow Persons: *American Minds* (1958). Indeed, Adam Ferguson's call for caution, uttered in *An Essay on the History of Civil Society* in mid-eighteenth century, remains valid: "We are often tempted into these boundless regions of ignorance or conjecture, by a fancy which delights in creating rather than in merely retaining the forms which are presented before it; we are the dupes of a subtlety, which promises to supply every defect of our knowledge. . . ." (quoted in Sampson: *Progress in the Age of Reason*, 91).

For Turgot, see the essay in Frank E. Manuel: *The Prophets of Paris: Turgot, Condorcet, Saint-Simon, Fourier and Comte* (1962), which is lucid, learned, suggestive, though perhaps a little too intent on making the public servant into a prophet. Dakin: *Turgot* I have cited above, 575; useful as it is on Turgot's public career, its account of his philosophy is less satisfactory. Alfred Neymarck: *Turgot et ses doctrines*, 2 vols. (1885), is a comprehensive survey. See below, 680, for Turgot's political ideas.

Manuel's chapter on Condorcet in his book just cited is excellent, resting on much unpublished material. J. Salwyn Schapiro's *Condorcet and the Rise of Liberalism* (1934) is orderly though rather simplistic. Léon Cahen: *Condorcet et la révolution française* (1904), [both I, 436], shows rather convincingly (537–41) that it is highly unlikely that Condorcet committed suicide, although the evidence must remain of necessity inconclusive. Alexandre Koyré: "Condorcet," *JHI*, IX, 2 (April 1948), 131–52, is excellent. See also the brief study by Alberto Cento, *Condorcet e l'idea di progresso* (1956).[7]

---

[7] For Condorcet the "social mathematician," see below, 66.

CHAPTER THREE

The Uses of Nature

I. THE ENLIGHTENMENT'S NEWTON

THIS CHAPTER, more than any other, is a response to a challenge —to Charles C. Gillispie's original and provocative formula that the philosophes loved nature and hated science. Gillispie argues that the men of the Enlightenment (with the notable exception of Voltaire) had a romantic, anthropomorphic conception of the place of science in their philosophical scheme: see his "The *Encyclopédie* and the Jacobin Philosophy of Science," in *Critical Problems in the History of Science*, ed. Marshall Clagett (1959), 255–89; "Science in the French Revolution," *Behavioral Science*, IV, 1 (January 1959), 67–73; and his chapter on "Science and the Enlightenment," in *The Edge of Objectivity: An Essay in the History of Scientific Ideas* (1960). I regard this idea as the most interesting contribution to the study of the Enlightenment offered in recent decades. As my chaps. iv to viii suggest, I do not wholly accept it; the philosophes found a way out of the dilemma that "value-free" science posed.

A critical figure in Gillispie's account of the rise of "romantic science" is Goethe. Barker Fairley: *A Study of Goethe* (1947) is indispensable to an understanding of Goethe's search for scientific objectivity as a search for health. Rudolf Magnus: *Goethe as a Scientist* (1906; tr. Heinz Norden, 1949) is a comprehensive, well-informed, and admiring survey of Goethe's wide range of scientific activities. Karl Viëtor, a celebrated Goethe specialist, has a section on "The Student of Nature," in his *Goethe the Thinker* (1950; tr. Bayard Q. Morgan, 1950). See also René Berthelot: *Science et philosophie chez Goethe* (1932). But the particular emphasis on the "romantic" bearing of Goethe's scientific inclinations is largely Gillispie's contribution.

The language of science and its influence on poetry and culture generally has been thoroughly investigated. I am indebted to W. K. Wimsatt, Jr.: *Philosophic Words* (1948), Donald Davie: *The Language of Science and the Language of Literature: 1700–1740* (1963), William Powell Jones: *The Rhetoric of Science* (1966), Alan Dugald McKillop: *The Background of Thomson's "Seasons"* (1942), and Marjorie Hope Nicolson: *Newton Demands the Muse: Newton's "Opticks" and the Eighteenth Century Poets* (1946), all highly instructive, all demonstrating that science did not kill eighteenth-century poetry. Hoxie Neale Fairchild: *Religious Trends in English Poetry*, I, *1700–1740: Protestantism and the Cult of Sentiment* (1939), has indispensable material on the relation of Newtonianism to poetic performance. For d'Alembert's view of metaphysics as a form of science, see Grimsley: *D'Alembert* (see above, 600), 226–7.

For the style and organization of eighteenth-century science a close look at seventeenth-century science is essential; here Martha Ornstein: *The Rôle of Scientific Societies in the Seventeenth Century* (3rd edn., 1938), [I, 525], remains the indispensable monograph. Chap. vii of Hall: *The Scientific Revolution* (1954), and chap. v of Hall: *From Galileo to Newton, 1630–1720* (1963), are excellent studies of scientific organization. Thomas Sprat's famous *History of the Royal Society*, first published in 1667 as a tract in behalf of the new learning, has recently been edited by J. I. Cope and H. W. Jones (1958); it may be supplemented, but has not been superseded, by recent popular accounts of the Royal Society like Dorothy Stimson's *Scientists and Amateurs* (1948). See also Sir Henry Lyons: *The Royal Society, 1660–1940* (1944). For the French academy of science the old book by J. Bertrand: *L'Académie des Sciences et les Académiciens de 1666 à 1793* (1869) is still useful; it is to be read in conjunction with Harcourt Brown: *Scientific Organizations in Seventeenth-Century France* (1934).

The general character of eighteenth-century science is laid out in the contributions to Allan Ferguson, ed.: *Natural Philosophy Through the Eighteenth Century and Allied Topics* (Anniversary Number of the *Philosophical Magazine*, 1948), and A. Wolf: *A History of Science, Technology and Philosophy in the 18th Century* (2d rev. edn. by D. McKie, 1952), which is very comprehensive and remains useful, although it often degenerates into a mere catalogue of names, books, and specific experiments. The Voltaire letter of 1735 I quote in the text is often cited; I had drafted this chapter when I came upon it once again in an interesting essay by Henry Guerlac: "Where the Statue Stood: Divergent Loyalties to Newton in the Eighteenth Century," in Earl R. Wasserman, ed.: *Aspects of the Eighteenth Century* (1965), 317–34. Diderot as scientist has been discussed by Dieckmann, Proust (for both, see above, 587), and in great detail by Jean Mayer: *Diderot: Homme de science* (1959); for Diderot's competence in mathematics, see his *Correspondance*, IX, 198 and *n*. On the whole question of "humanism" in the scientific thinking of philosophes like Diderot, and its relation to antiquity, my *Rise of Modern Paganism* offers plentiful evidence.

The fullest life of Sir Isaac Newton is by Louis Trenchard More: *Isaac Newton, A Biography* (1934), [I, 529]. It has been highly praised, and has great merit, exploiting as it does much unpublished material, but it is sometimes grossly inaccurate in its historical detail (thus, for example, it places the beginning of Voltaire's visit to England a year too early, in 1725, and the publication of Voltaire's *Lettres philosophiques* in 1765 instead of 1734), and must therefore be used with caution. The great edition of Newton's *Correspondence* now under way, eds. H. W. Turnbull *et al.*, I–IV (1959–67), covering the years 1661 to 1709, will make possible a new comprehensive biography soon. Meanwhile, Frank E. Manuel: "Newton as Autocrat of Science," *Daedalus* (Summer 1968), 969–1001, is an interesting study of Newton in a position of dominance, while Manuel: *A Portrait of Isaac Newton* (1968) offers a penetrating analysis of Newton's personality in relation to his work from a psychoanalytical point of view. Ferdinand Rosenberger: *Isaac Newton und seine physikalischen Principien: Ein Hauptstück aus der Entwicklungsgeschichte der modernen Physik* (1895) is an excellent general survey of Newton's achievement and influence. I first learned about Rosenberger's book through a reference in Alexandre Koyré's posthumous *Newtonian Studies* (1965), a splendidly informative collection of essays emphasizing Koyré's opposition to both the Marxist and the sociological interpretations of the scientific revolution. For the same point, see the recent collection of six essays by Koyré: *Metaphysics and Measurement: Essays in the Scientific Revolution* (tr. R. E. W. Maddison, 1966). Koyré's set of lectures, *From the*

Closed World to the Infinite Universe (1957), [I, 525], is a moving and suggestive essay on the philosophical meaning of the scientific revolution. A very important, though still controversial, corrective to the traditional notion that Newton and Newton alone governed eighteenth-century science, insisting that the Bernoullis, Euler, and others made important independent contributions, especially in mechanics, is C. Truesdell: "A Program toward Rediscovering the Rational Mechanics of the Age of Reason," *Archive for History of Exact Sciences,* I, 1 (1960), 3–36. The best representative of the sociological school remains Robert K. Merton: *Science, Technology, and Society in Seventeenth-Century England* (1938), while the most persuasive (though obviously to me not persuasive) representative of the Marxist school is Franz Borkenau: *Der Übergang vom feudalen zum bürgerlichen Weltbild* (1934). *Sir Isaac Newton, 1727–1927: A Bicentenary Evaluation of His Work* (1928), is a collection of papers, most of them—on Newton's *Opticks,* dynamics, experiments, chemistry, alchemy, and so forth—helpful but not extensive enough to be really searching or profound. The general histories of science, above all by Hall (just cited), and E. J. Dijksterhuis: *The Mechanization of the World Picture* (1950; tr. C. Dikshoorn, 1961), naturally give abundant space to what Hall has felicitously called "The Principate of Newton." Hélène Metzger: *Newton, Stahl, Boerhaave et la doctrine chimique* (1930) may be read in conjunction with her earlier treatment of chemistry in France: *Les Doctrines chimiques en France du début du 17e à la fin du 18e siècle* (1923). To these may be added H. W. Turnbull: *Mathematical Discoveries of Newton* (1945); G. N. Clark: *Science and Social Welfare in the Age of Newton* (1949), an original brief essay; A. R. and M. B. Hall: *Unpublished Scientific Papers of Isaac Newton* (1962); and A. C. Crombie: "Newton's Conception of Scientific Method," *Bulletin of the Institute of Physics* (November 1957), reprinted in Norman Clarke, ed.: *A Physics Anthology* (1960), 80–104. I. B. Cohen *et al.*: *Isaac Newton's Papers and Letters on Natural Philosophy, and Related Documents* (1958), makes available a number of Newton's hitherto inaccessible writings. I have also learned from J. E. McGuire: "Body and Void and Newton's De Mundi Systemate: Some New Sources," *Archive for History of Exact Sciences,* III, 3 (1966), 206–48; and a fascinating reading of the meaning of Newton's work by McGuire and P. M. Rattansi, "Newton and the 'Pipes of Pan,'" *Notes and Records of the Royal Society of London*, XXI, 2 (December 1966), 108–43. Newton's leading contemporaries have also been studied with care; among the best volumes are A. E. Bell: *Christian Huygens and the Development of Science in the Seventeenth Century* (1947); E. F. MacPike: *Hevelius, Flamsteed and Halley* (1937); and Margaret 'Espinasse: *Robert Hooke* (1956). Marie Boas: "The Establishment of the Mechanical Philosophy," *Osiris*, X (1952), 412–541, is an instructive general survey. Fontenelle's *Éloge* to Newton is an important document, showing Fontenelle's sympathetic awareness of Newton (reprinted in *Œuvres de Fontenelle*, II [1825], 181–207). Leonard M. Marsak has demonstrated Fontenelle's openness to Newtonian doctrines in his "Bernard de Fontenelle: The Idea of Science in the French Enlightenment," *Transactions of the American Philosophical Society*, IL, 7 (December 1959), and his conclusive *Two Papers on Bernard de Fontenelle* (1959), [both I, 530]. Roger Hahn's little pamphlet, *Laplace as a Newtonian Scientist* (1967), is an intelligent introduction. Cassirer has well discussed Kant's Newtonianism in his *Kants Leben und Lehre* (1918), (especially 23); so has A. D. Lindsay in his *Kant* (1934), (15–24), [both I, 441]. For Newton in Scotland, see Gladys Bryson: *Man and Society* (see above, 597), 7–8, 18.

The students of scientific language in the age of Newton have also paid close attention to the literary worship of Newton—largely because the two phenomena were substantially the same. In addition to Thomson, Prior was another poet in whom the Newtonian strain can be traced without difficulty; see the new edition of his poetry, *The Literary Works of Matthew Prior*, eds. H. Bunker Wright and Monroe Spears, 2 vols. (1959). Ruth Murdock has continued Marjorie Nicolson's researches for France in her "Newton and the French Muse," *JHI*, XIX, 3 (June, 1958), 323–34, to which I am indebted. See also Murdock's dissertation, "Newton's Law of Attraction and the French Enlightenment" (1950). For Haller and Newton, see Howard Mumford Jones: "Albrecht von Haller and English Philosophy," *PMLA*, XL, 1 (March 1925), 103–27. I learned that the knighting of Newton the scientist was unprecedented in England from More's *Newton*, p. 522.

The diffusion of Newton's ideas in England and on the Continent is of such importance to the history of science that all general histories devote ample space to it. Rosenberger is excellent, as are Koyré: *Newtonian Studies*, and Hall: *From Galileo to Newton* (cited above, 611). E. W. Strong: "Newtonian Explications of Natural Philosophy," *JHI*, XVIII, 1 (January 1957), 49–83, is a comprehensive article. For the spread of Newtonianism to the Dutch physicians and to France, the work of Pierre Brunet is indispensable. See *Les physiciens hollandais* (above, 586); *La vie et l'œuvre de Clairaut (1713–1765)*, (1952), and, of course, *L'Introduction des théories de Newton en France au XVIIIe siècle* (1931), [I, 530], which takes the struggle down to 1738, the year that Voltaire published his influential book on Newton (see immediately below). Grimsley: *D'Alembert* is also most helpful here. Among the continental Newtonians was the Genevan mathematician Gabriel Cramer; Condillac's letters to him have been edited by Georges Le Roy in *Condillac, Lettres inédites à Gabriel Cramer* (1953). Brunet's work on the Dutch Newtonians can be supplemented with an interesting short article by C. A. Crommelin: "Die holländische Physik im 18ten Jahrhundert mit besonderer Berücksichtigung der Entwicklung der Feinmechanik," *Sudhoffs Archiv für Geschichte der Medizin und der Naturwissenschaften*, XXVIII, 3 (December 1935), 129–42. I have already lamented in *The Rise of Modern Paganism* (443) that Gustav Zart: *Einfluss der englischen Philosophie auf die deutsche im 18ten Jahrhundert* (1881) is little more than a catalogue; here is a fascinating subject calling for a good monograph. See for now, Erich Adickes: *Kant als Naturforscher* (1924–5). For the American colonies, I. B. Cohen: *Franklin and Newton* (1956) is of value. As for Voltaire's gradual appropriation of Newton, see Henry Guerlac's article cited above (612), Brunet, as well as Léon Bloch: *La philosophie de Newton* (1908). See Robert L. Walters: "Chemistry at Cirey," *VS*, LVIII (1967), 1807–27, for a judicious study of Voltaire's scientific collaboration with Madame du Châtelet. On the same subject, see also Sir Gavin de Beer: "Voltaire et les sciences naturelles," in *The Age of the Enlightenment: Studies Presented to Theodore Besterman*, eds. W. H. Barber *et al.* (1967), 35–50. Charles Gillispie's account (in *The Edge of Objectivity*, 157–9) of Voltaire's uncertainty in the *Lettres philosophiques* of 1734, followed by his unqualified adoption of Newtonianism four years later, in the *Éléments,* is perceptive as always, but in view of the last part of Lettre XV, which is highly critical of Descartes's method, a little too schematic; even in the early 1730s, I am convinced, Voltaire was far more a Newtonian than a Cartesian.

That this should have been so (as I indicate in the text) was largely the work of Maupertuis, a remarkable scientist who was long unduly neglected, thanks in part to Voltaire's witty malice. This has now been rectified by some excellent monographs, especially Pierre Brunet: *Maupertuis,* 2 vols. (1929), and some recent articles—Harcourt Brown: "Maupertuis–*philosophe:* the Enlightenment and the Berlin Academy," *VS,* XXV (1963), 255–69; and Marie Louise Dufrenoy: "Maupertuis et le progrès scientifique," ibid., 519–87 [see I, 437–8]. Émile Callot: *Maupertuis: Le Savant et le philosophe, présentation et extraits* (1964), has an introduction and collection of texts. (See also below, section 3, on Maupertuis as biologist.)

The *Encyclopédie* was, of course, filled with articles on the sciences, and their collective attitude is of great interest. They have been analyzed by students of Diderot, like Proust; there are also articles by Gerard Vassails on "L'*Encyclopédie* et la physique," *Revue d'histoire des sciences,* IV (July–December 1951), 294–323 (from a Marxist perspective); by Charles Bedel on "L'avènement de la chimie moderne," ibid., 324–33; by Maurice Daumas on "La chimie dans l'*Encyclopédie* et dans l'*Encyclopédie méthodique,*" ibid., 334–43.

While it is undeniable that Newton was a "modern," his ties to antiquity remain close and deserve to be even more carefully traced than they have so far; see *The Rise of Modern Paganism,* chap. v. In his *The Newtonian System of the World,* the prolific popularizer J. T. Desaguliers wrote: "The System of the Universe, as taught by Pythagoras, Philolaus, and others of the Ancients, is the same, which was since reviv'd by Copernicus, allowed by all the unprejudiced of the Moderns, and at last demonstrated by Sir Isaac Newton." (Quoted in McKillop: *Background of Thomson's "Seasons,"* 35.) Voltaire certainly knew this: "Newton," he wrote in the first book of his *Éléments de la philosophie de Newton,* "followed the ancient views of Democritus, Epicurus, and a crowd of philosophers corrected by our celebrated Gassendi" (*Œuvres,* XXII, 410). There is room for exploration here.

2. NEWTON'S PHYSICS WITHOUT NEWTON'S GOD

For the general background to Newton's religion, E. A. Burtt: *Metaphysical Foundations of Modern Physical Science* (2d edn., 1932), [I, 529], is indispensable. E. W. Strong has dealt with Newton's religion in a series of articles, most notably in "Newton and God," *JHI*, XIII, 2 (April 1952), 146–67; and "Newton's 'Mathematical Way,'" ibid., XII, 1 (January 1951), 90–110; see also "Newtonian Explications" cited above (615). Richard S. Westfall: *Science and Religion in 17th Century England* (1958) is a sensible general survey, while Westfall's brief discussion, "Isaac Newton: Religious Rationalist or Mystic?," *Review of Religion*, XXII, 3–4 (March 1958), 155–70, concentrates on the point at issue here. Hélène Metzger: *Attraction universelle et religion naturelle chez quelques commentateurs anglais de Newton* (1938) is a splendid survey of Newtonian religious and scientific thought from Bentley and Toland to Derham and Priestley. There is much of value on Newton's religion in Frank Manuel: *Isaac Newton Historian* (1963). For Newton's Unitarianism, see Herbert McLachlan: *The Religious Opinions of Milton, Locke, and Newton* (1941). Herbert H. Odom: "The Estrangement of Celestial Mechanics and Religion," *JHI*, XXVII, 4 (October–December 1966), 533–48, surveys the gradual secularization of science intelligently but with no surprises.

The controversy between the Newtonians and Leibniz over natural religion has been much discussed, and the correspondence printed several times, most recently and most adequately by H. G. Alexander: *The Leibniz-Clarke Correspondence* (1956), [see I, 530]. Among several instructive discussions of this controversy, see above all Koyré: *From the Closed World to the Infinite Universe* (cited above, 612–13), chap. xi; Koyré and I. B. Cohen: "Newton and the Leibniz-Clarke Correspondence," *Archives Internationales d'histoire des sciences*, XV (1962), 63–126; and Ernst Cassirer: "Newton and Leibniz," *Philosophical Review*, LII, 4 (July 1943), 366–91.

The precise influence of Descartes on the Enlightenment (especially in France) remains a matter of debate. Aram Vartanian, himself a participant in that debate, has lucidly delineated the competing parties: Francisque Bouillier: *Histoire de la philosophie cartésienne*, 2 vols. (3rd edn., 1868), was among the first to argue that

the French philosophes were in no way the heirs of Descartes, but
rather the followers of Bacon, Newton, and Locke (a view rather
generally accepted today); the view has the prestige of Cassirer's
Philosophy of the Enlightenment. The opposing camp was led by
Hippolyte Taine, whose *Les Origines de la France contemporaine:
L'Ancien régime*, 6 vols. (1884–94), portrays the philosophes as the
unhappy inheritors of a mixture of classicism and Cartesian rationalism. There is a third, compromise, party, led by Fernand Brunetière:
see especially his "Jansénistes et Cartésiens," in *Études critiques sur
l'histoire de la littérature française* (fourth series), (1889), 111–78,
followed and carefully documented by Gustave Lanson in several
essays, most notably "Origines et premières manifestations de l'esprit
philosophique dans la littérature française de 1675 à 1748," *Revue
des cours et conférences*, XVII (1908–9), 61–74, 113–26, 145–57,
210–23, and 259–71; and the important early article, "L'influence de
la philosophie cartésienne sur la littérature française," *Revue de
métaphysique et morale*, IV (1896), 517–50, which holds that the
philosophes accepted only part of Descartes's philosophy—his radical skepticism—but rejected the rest; this school, Vartanian notes,
takes the word of the philosophes without question (see Aram
Vartanian: *Diderot and Descartes: A Study of Scientific Naturalism
in the Enlightenment* [1953], chap. i). Vartanian belongs to a fourth
school: he holds that the French philosophes who all imbibed Cartesianism early and thoroughly were far more deeply in his debt
than they found it politic to say, for polemical reasons, and especially
the important materialist strain in French Enlightenment philosophy
is largely Cartesian. I do not accept Vartanian's thesis, though I
hasten to add that I have learned much from his refreshing and
contentious book; it is rich in apt quotations and suggestive ideas.
I agree in principle that one should not take one's sources on trust;
as I say in the text, the philosophes were "ungenerous in acknowledging, and hasty to minimize" the power of Descartes's ideas (146).
But, as Vartanian himself shows with abundant quotations, the philosophes quite openly acknowledged the merits of at least parts of
Descartes's thought; besides, there is no logical necessity why for
polemical reasons they should have denied Descartes's influence.
Quite the contrary, anxious as they were to acquire respectable
ancestors and to avoid trouble with the authorities, it would have
been far more logical for them to adopt and even exaggerate Descartes's influence than to deny it. It seems to me unquestionable that

the discrediting of Descartes's physics dragged Descartes's philosophical method into disaster, and that Newtonian empiricism struck the philosophes—even the materialists, who were much indebted to Descartes—as the only true philosophy, leading to agreement and action.

For the influence of Descartes in England, see Sterling Lamprecht: "The Role of Descartes in 17th-Century England," in *Studies in the History of Ideas*, III (1935), 181–240, and Marjorie H. Nicolson: "The Early Stage of Cartesianism in England," *Studies in Philology*, XXVI, 3 (July 1929), 356–74, which offers good evidence for the early influence of Descartes, especially among the Cambridge Platonists. On the same subject, the older book by John Tulloch: *Rational Theology and Christian Philosophy in England in the Seventeenth Century*, 2 vols. (1872), especially II, remains valuable. See now Rosalie L. Colie: *Light and Enlightenment* (1957), [I, 534]; Ernst Cassirer: *The Platonic Renaissance in England* (1932; tr. James P. Pettegrove, 1953), [I, 533]; and J. A. Passmore: *Ralph Cudworth, An Interpretation* (1951). For the complexity of what I have called the "victimization" of Descartes, see the excellent pages in Rosenberger: *Isaac Newton* (see above, 612), 224–48, 342–3.

In addition to these titles, I have drawn heavily upon Koyré's independent estimate of the relation of "Newton and Descartes," (in *Newtonian Studies*, 53–114). Koyré quotes (63–4 *n.*) a fascinating passage from William Whiston's *Autobiography* which shows the clash of Newtonian and Cartesian ideas in the English universities.

The retreat of God before science is, of course, one of the Enlightenment's central themes and has been touched upon in all the studies of the philosophes and all major histories of the time. Roger Mercier: *La réhabilitation de la nature humaine (1700–1750)* (1960) is a bulky French thesis, full of good material. A. Dupront: *Les lettres, les sciences, la religion et les arts dans la société française de la deuxième moitié du XVIIIe siècle* (1963) takes up where Mercier left off. Stromberg: *Religious Liberalism in Eighteenth-Century England* (see above, 591), devotes a number of pages, notably 27 *ff.*, to the subject. Sometimes the secularization of ideas is palpable in one man: "In 1762, Linnaeus conjectures that the work of God in the Creation stopped at providing the common source of each genus, or maybe only of each order. . . . In 1766, he omits from the final edition of the *Systema Naturae* his famous dictum that there are no new species. Finally, in 1779, he expresses the view that 'species are the work of time,' and that one of the great scientific enterprises of the future will consist in demonstrating this truth." Bentley Glass: "Heredity and Variation in the Eighteenth Century Concept of the Species," *Forerunners of Darwin: 1745–1859*, eds. Bentley Glass, Oswei Temkin, William L. Straus, Jr. (1959), 150. I trust that nothing I have said in the text, or in this bibliography, will lead anyone to saddle me with the opinion that religion was dead by the end of the eighteenth century; it did not "revive" early in the nineteenth century, for it had always been alive. The final blow probably came with Darwin. On this question, though perhaps inclined to overestimate the power of Christian belief on thought, see the able dissertation by Charles C. Gillispie: *Genesis and Geology; A Study in the Relations of Scientific Thought, Natural Theology, and Social Opinion in Great Britain, 1790–1850* (1951). One excellent instance of deep inner religious conflict suffered by a leading scientist is Albrecht von Haller. See the collection of his essays, reviews, diaries, *Tagebuch seiner Beobachtungen über Schriftsteller und über sich selbst*, 2 vols. (1787); Margarete Hochdoerfer: *The Conflict between the Religious and the Scientific Views of Albrecht von Haller (1708–1777)* (1932), a thoughtful survey; Stephen d'Irsay: *Albrecht von Haller, Eine Studie zur Geistesgeschichte der Aufklärung* (1930), a good general analysis, if a little vulgar in tone; Heinrich Ernst Jenny: *Haller als Philosoph* (1902), short, much too partisan; Hans Stahlmann: *A. v. Hallers Welt- und Lebensanschauung, Nach seinen Gedichten* (1928) does what its title says—it is economical; and Eduard Stäuble: *Albrecht von Haller, "Über den Ursprung des Übels"* (1952), a short dissertation, a critical edition of Haller's poem with extended comment.

3. NATURE'S PROBLEMATIC GLORIES

The development of the biological sciences in the eighteenth century has received much good treatment recently. Jacques Roger: *Les sciences de la vie dans la pensée française du XVIIIe siècle* (1963), [I, 438], is a rich and enormously bulky survey ranging from seventeenth-century French speculation to, and beyond, d'Alembert;

I have used it with great profit. Jean Éhrard: *L'idée de la nature en France dans la première moitié du XVIIIe siècle*, 2 vols. (1963), is also excellent. Once again I found Hall: *The Scientific Revolution* (cited above, 611) most useful, especially chap. x, "Descriptive Biology and Systematics." Philip C. Ritterbush: *Overtures to Biology: The Speculations of Eighteenth-Century Naturalists* (1964) surveys the transfer of "Newtonian" ideas into other sciences, and deals with electricity, speculations on plant generation, and botanical classification. Elizabeth Gasking: *Investigations into Generation, 1651–1828* (1967), is highly instructive; her book lucidly discusses the vehement debates among eighteenth-century biologists over preformation; Gasking should be read in conjunction with relevant articles in Bentley Glass et al.: *Forerunners of Darwin* (cited above, 620), particularly Francis C. Haber: "Fossils and Early Cosmology," 3–29; and Bentley Glass: "The Germination of the Idea of Biological Species," 30–48, and "Heredity and Variation in the Eighteenth Century Concept of the Species," 144–72.

The most remarkable biologist of the century was, of course, "the eloquent and philosophic Buffon," as an admiring Gibbon called him (*Decline and Fall of the Roman Empire*, VII, 308 *n.*). In view of Buffon's versatility and originality, the scarcity of good work on him is surprising. There is Jean Pivoteau's intelligent "Introduction" to Buffon's *Œuvres philosophiques* (1954), a bulky volume that also includes excellent short essays by other scholars on particular aspects of Buffon's work [I, 438]; there are the instructive pages in Roger's *Sciences de la vie* (527–84); and there is Arthur O. Lovejoy's "Buffon and the Problem of Species," in Glass: *Forerunners of Darwin*, 84–113. See also the brief article by Franck Bourdier and Yves François: "Buffon et les Encyclopédistes," *Revue d'histoire des sciences*, IV (1951), 228–32; Otis Fellows: "Buffon and Rousseau: Aspects of a Relationship," *PMLA*, LXXV, 3 (June 1960), 184–96, and "Buffon's Place in the Enlightenment," *VS*, XXV (1963), 603–29 [I, 438]; and Robert Wohl: "Buffon and his Project for a New Science," *Isis*, LI, part 2, No. 164 (1960), 186–99.

For Maupertuis in general, see above, 616, and, in addition, Paul Ostoya: "Maupertuis et la Biologie," *Revue d'histoire des sciences*, VII (1954), 60–78.

CHAPTER FOUR

The Science of Man

1. ENLIGHTENMENT MAN

FOR THE CONCEPTION of "philosophical anthropology," the writings of Bernard Groethuysen are basic. See above all his important theoretical article, "Towards an Anthropological Philosophy," in *Philosophy and History: Essays Presented to Ernst Cassirer*, eds. Raymond Klibansky and H. J. Paton (1936; edn. 1963), 77–89, and *Anthropologie philosophique* (1952), which outlines the history of the philosophy of man from antiquity down to Erasmus and Montaigne, and suggests modern perspectives in a short conclusion.

For Hume, to whom I shall return later in this chapter, see above all Passmore: *Hume's Intentions* (1952), chap. i, "In Defence of the Moral Sciences," and the thoroughgoing scholarly study by John Laird: *Hume's Philosophy of Human Nature* (1932). Kant's view of man is analyzed well if briefly in John E. Smith: "The Question of Man," in *The Philosophy of Kant and Our Modern World*, ed. Charles W. Hendel (1957), 3–24; and George Schrader: "The Philosophy of Existence," in ibid., 27–61. For Rousseau on man the key article is by Arthur O. Lovejoy: "The Supposed Primitivism of Rousseau's Discourse on Inequality" (cited above, 606). The much-debated conflict between Rousseau and Diderot touched on their respective conceptions of human nature; the best analysis is Jean Fabre: "Deux frères ennemis: Diderot et Jean-Jacques," *Diderot Studies*, III (1961), 155–213 [I, 448]. Voltaire's critique of Pascal is of great importance, and has been well discussed, notably by J.-R. Carré in *Réflexions sur l'Anti-Pascal de Voltaire* (1935); see also J. S. Spink: *French Free-Thought from Gassendi to Voltaire* (1960), [I, 524], esp. chap. xvi. Wieland's humanism has been studied by Ludwig Edelstein, in "Wielands 'Abderiten' und der deutsche Humanismus," *University of California Publications in Modern Philology*, XXVI, 5 (1950), 441–71.

There is some useful general discussion on philosophical anthropology in Crocker: *An Age of Crisis* (see above, 604), especially chaps. vii, "The Theory of Human Nature," viii, "Man's Detractors," and xii, "Man's Goodness." Josef Kremer: *Das Problem der Theodizee in der Philosophie und Literatur des 18. Jahrhunderts mit besonderer Rücksicht auf Kant und Schiller* (1909), deals with eighteenth-century man's attempt to justify man by justifying God.

I have dealt with antique humanism in *The Rise of Modern Paganism*, chaps. i–iii; I should like to add only three items here which I found both informative and stimulating: I. Heinemann: "Humanitas," in Pauly-Wissowa: *Real-Encyclopädie*, Supplement vol. V (1931), 282–310; R. Reitzenstein: *Werden und Wesen der Humanität im Altertum* (1907), a splendid essay; and Bruno Snell: "Die Entdeckung der Menschlichkeit und unsere Stellung zu den Griechen," *Geistige Welt*, II, 1 (April 1947), 1–9.

2. NEWTONS OF THE MIND

For psychology in the eighteenth century in general the excellent, searching chapter by Cassirer (chap. iii, "Psychology and Epistemology") in his *Philosophy of the Enlightenment* is basic. Equally excellent is Cassirer: *Das Erkenntnisproblem in der Philosophie und Wissenschaft der neueren Zeit*, II (edn. 1920), books 5 and 6. George Sidney Brett: *A History of Psychology*, II, *Mediaeval and Early Modern Period* (1921) is an indispensable survey. Another helpful short general history is Max Dessoir: *Outlines of the History of Psychology* (1911; tr. Donald Fisher, 1912). Dessoir's *Geschichte der neueren deutschen Psychologie* (1902) is brisk but magisterial. It may be supplemented with the detailed analyses in Robert Sommer: *Grundzüge einer Geschichte der deutschen Psychologie und Aesthetik* (1892).

For the uses of "savages" and animals in eighteenth-century thought, Hester Hastings: *Man and Beast in French Thought of the Eighteenth Century* (1936), a Johns Hopkins dissertation, adds material to the Lovejoy–Boas enterprise; it is informative on travel literature. Lovejoy's "Supposed Primitivism of Rousseau's Discourse on Inequality," once again, and his "Monboddo and Rousseau," (1933), in *Essays in the History of Ideas*, 38–61, are pertinent. For Saunderson, the blind mathematician, see Dugald Stewart's *Memoirs*, as quoted in A. D. Woozley: "Introduction" to Thomas Reid: *Essays on the Intellectual Powers of Man* (1941), viii; and Wilson: *Diderot*, 98–9.

There is a brief analysis of Locke's psychology in Brett: *A History of Psychology*, II, 257–63; Richard I. Aaron: *John Locke* (2d edn., 1955), [I, 531], part II, *passim*, esp. chap. iv, "The Beginnings of Modern Psychology"; James Gibson: *Locke's Theory of Knowledge and its Historical Relations* (1917); and Fulton Henry Anderson: *The Influence of Contemporary Science on Locke's Method and Results* (1923).

For Condillac the psychologist see G. Le Roy: *La Psychologie de Condillac* (1937), and the intelligent examination by Isabel F. Knight: *The Geometric Spirit: The Abbé de Condillac and the French Enlightenment* (1968).

While Hartley and associationism have not been neglected, they could use deeper study. In addition to the general histories by Brett, Dessoir, Sommer, just cited, Howard G. Warren: *A History of the Association Psychology from Hartley to Lewes* (1921) has a short but clear survey of Hartley's thought, and some pages on his precursors and successors. Maria Heider: *Studien über David Hartley (1705–1757)* (1913) is a typical German dissertation: exceedingly short, perfunctory in style, but diligent in research; this book contains some important letters by Hartley to his friend Lister, and reprints an anonymous short treatise of 1741, "An Introduction towards an Essay on the Origins of the Passions . . . ," which is clearly Hartley's draft for his *Observations*. Bruno Schönlank: *Hartley und Priestley, die Begründer der Assoziationspsychologie in England* (1882), and G. S. Bower: *David Hartley and James Mill* (1881), though old, retain some value. The pages on Hartley in G. R. Cragg: *Reason and Authority in the Eighteenth Century* (1964), esp. 216–29, are lucid. Élie Halévy places Hartley and his theory briefly into the utilitarian context in *The Growth of Philosophic Radicalism* (1901–4; tr. Mary Morris, 1928), [I, 432]. For Hume, Laird: *Hume's Philosophy of Human Nature*, once again, and the indispensable Passmore: *Hume's Intentions* (above, 622). On Zanotti, and on continental associationism in general, Luigi Ferri: *La psychologie de l'association* (1878; tr. into French, 1883); also E. Claparède: *L'Association des ideés* (1902), T. A. Ribot: *The Psychology of the Emotions* (tr. J. Fitzgerald, 1889), and the old book by Victor Cousin: *Philosophie sensualiste au XVIIIe siècle* (5th edn., 1866). There is a useful general article by Croom Robertson on "Association of Ideas" in the *Encyclopedia Britannica* (11th edn., 1911), II, 784–6.

The philosophes, as the speculations of Condillac, Rousseau, and others show, were deeply interested in the origins and nature of language. From a growing body of writings on the subject I single out Noam Chomsky: *Cartesian Linguistics: A Chapter in the History of Rationalist Thought* (1966); Paul Kuehner: *Theories on the Origin and Formation of Language in the Eighteenth Century in France* (1944); Ronald Grimsley: "Jean-Jacques Rousseau and the Problem of 'Original' Language," in *The Age of the Enlightenment*, 275–86; and Grimsley: "Some Aspects of 'Nature' and 'Language' in the French Enlightenment," *VS*, LVI (1967), 659–77.

3. THE REVOLT AGAINST RATIONALISM

Of all the labels imposed on the Enlightenment, the label "Age of Reason" has been the most persistent, and the most damaging. It is accurate only if "reason" is read to mean "criticism" and counterposed to "credulity" or "superstition." Unfortunately, historians have gone much further and equated "reason" with coldness; they have caricatured the philosophes as frigid engineers, contemptuous of emotion, blind to poetry, inhabiting an empty universe stripped of all color and love, except for sex. This myth of a prosy, presumptuous precision, of a cold rationalism, was invented by the German Romantics, although Burke had his share in it, and it haunts our estimation of the Enlightenment to this day. If one wants instances of a rigid, geometric rationalism, one might turn to the politics of Peter the Great, or the abbé Siéyès' constitutional schemes, both fine instances of the fancied omnipotence of thought. I am not inclined to deny that the philosophes were sometimes arrogant, sometimes calculating, sometimes cynical, sometimes cold. But none of these characteristics is central to their thought or important to the definition of the Enlightenment; its critical temper was not locked in the laboratory. It was passionate in its own right, and played a part in all irreverence, every call to rebellion, every moral tirade. I have polemicized against this misconception before (see *The Party of Humanity*, 192–4, 269–72); this section of the text is designed to present my view of the philosophes' "rationalism."

There are, of course, signs of change and improvement. To name only a few: in his *In Search of Humanity* (1960), [I, 428] and elsewhere, Alfred Cobban presents a balanced portrait; James Sutherland: *Preface to Eighteenth Century Poetry* (1948), has some splendid pages (71 *ff.*) on the presence of feeling in the age; and it is reassuring to come upon the following statement by Michael Levey in his intelligent *Rococo to Revolution: Major Trends in Eighteenth-Century Painting* (1966), 202–4: "Far from supposing that reason cramps the imagination (a fallacy invented by romanticism and still with us today in most people's attitude to the eighteenth century), Goya felt that without reason imagination was sick." Levey has some fine pages on Goya (especially 9–13, 201–33) on which I have drawn; for Goya see also J. Lopez-Rey: *Goya's Caprichos: Beauty, Reason and Caricature*, 2 vols. (1953).

The rationalist—though not wholly rationalist—psychology of the seventeenth century is well discussed in Brett: *A History of Psychology*, II, 197–256; A. J. Krailsheimer: *Studies in Self-Interest from Descartes to La Bruyère* (1962), and E. B. O. Borgerhoff: *The Freedom of French Classicism* (1950), [I, 524], have observations on the passionate side of seventeenth-century psychological thought. See also the recent monograph by Anthony Levi: *French Moralists: The Theory of the Passions, 1585 to 1649* (1964), which takes the subject down to Descartes's *Traité des passions*.

I have paid some attention to the restoration of pride in the age of Enlightenment in the first chapter of this volume. Arthur O. Lovejoy's set of lectures, *Reflections on Human Nature* (1961) carefully discriminates, in Lovejoy's characteristic manner, various meanings of pride; I found the book chastening and informative. Lovejoy's brief "'Pride' in Eighteenth-Century Thought," (1921), reprinted and expanded in *Essays in the History of Ideas*, 62–8, performs a similar function. La Mettrie's defense of pride is best studied in *L'Homme machine*, ed. Aram Vartanian, and for Hume, see, once again Laird: *Hume's Philosophy of Human Nature*, 192–6. The thought of Rousseau is of great importance here: Rousseau carefully distinguished between *amour de soi* (natural self-love) and *amour propre* (egotism), a distinction discussed by many of his interpreters, notably Ernst Cassirer, in *The Question of Jean-Jacques Rousseau* (tr. Peter Gay, 1954), [I, 439], 45.

On sensuality the material is abundant but on the whole superficial and titillating. As I suggest in the text, for obvious reasons the history of sexual behavior has not been fully written, though often attempted. The old German *Sittengeschichten* are not really satisfactory. More recently we have had Wayland Young: *Eros Denied: Sex in Western Society* (1964), a passionate plea in behalf of Eros disguised as a history. Nina Epton: *Love and the English* (1960), and *Love and the French* (1959), as well as Morton M. Hunt: *The Natural History of Love* (1959), are characteristic of what the historian must work with in this area: chatty, indiscriminating in their anecdotes, superficial in their analysis, but filled with usable material. For the history of sex, see Marrou: *A History of Education in Antiquity* (above, 602), which has valuable chapters on pederasty; Thomas Gould: *Platonic Love* (1963) is a serious attempt, not wholly successful I think, to distinguish various kinds—Platonic, Christian, Romantic, and Freudian—of love; it mainly concentrates on Plato's and Aristotle's teachings. E. R. Dodds: *The Greeks and the Irrational* (1951), [I, 466], is brilliant on eros in Greece, as well as on the rational psychology of the ancients. For the turn of Christian love away from eros, the exhaustive but controversial *Agape and Eros* by Anders Nygren (1930, 1936; tr. Philip S. Watson, 2d edn., 1953), is a splendid starting point. Nygren's conclusion, that pagan and Christian love have nothing in common but their incessant conflict, has been challenged by Father M. C. D'Arcy: *The Mind and Heart of Love* (2d edn., 1956), which seeks to reconcile the two. Denis de Rougemont: *Love in the Western World* (1939; 2d edn., tr. Montgomery Belgion, 1956), has much fascinating material on, but an extravagant interpretation of, the conception of love current among the troubadours; C. S. Lewis: *The Allegory of Love: A Study in Medieval Tradition* (1936), deals with the same subject, sanely and brilliantly—I have learned much from the book. Curtius: *European*

Literature and the Latin Middle Ages (see above, 602), especially chap. vi, has informative treatment of medieval treatments of love, including homosexuality, in literature. Sir Kenneth Clark: *The Nude: A Study in Ideal Form* (1956), [I, 503], includes fascinating discussions on the medieval estrangement from the body in art (11–12, 24–5, 53, 69). For the "violent tenor of life," including the life of the passions, in the period of the Renaissance, two classics, Burckhardt: *Civilization of the Renaissance in Italy*, and Huizinga: *The Waning of the Middle Ages* (see above, 602) are indispensable. Their findings are confirmed for sixteenth-century France in Mandrou: *Introduction à la France moderne* (above, 603), 80 *ff*., and for seventeenth-century France by Ariès's pioneering *Centuries of Childhood* (above, 593). For what I have called the unpuritanical sexual ideas of the Puritans, see especially Perry Miller: *The New England Mind: The Seventeenth Century* (1939), and *The New England Mind: From Colony to Province* (1953), [I, 536], two difficult but always immensely stimulating books that deal, despite their specialized titles, with far more than mind. I am also indebted to Edmund S. Morgan's perceptive essay, *The Puritan Family: Religion and Domestic Relations in Seventeenth-Century New England* (see above, 594).

In my view of sexuality, both its meaning and its history, I have been guided by Freud. In one of his boldest conjectures, Freud suggested that sexual development could be correlated with the historical scheme of Comte: the animistic phase would be equivalent to narcissism both in time and content; the religious phase would correspond to the early stage when the child is attached to his parents; while the highest, scientific phase would correspond to the maturity of the individual, who has succeeded in renouncing the pleasure principle and turns to the outside world to gratify his desires. See *Totem and Taboo* (1923), *Standard Edition*, 24 vols. (1953——), XIII, 90. From this point of view, the sexual ideal of the Enlightenment may be said to have been the genital personality. Among the many commentaries on Freud, Philip Rieff: *Freud: The Mind of the Moralist* (1959), though a little more moralistic than the Freudians—and I—like, has been helpful.

Freud's delight at Diderot's anticipation of the Oedipus complex is to be found in *Introductory Lectures on Psychoanalysis* (1916–17), *Standard Edition*, XVI, 337–8. Other anticipations of Freud's doctrine of the unconscious are noted in Lancelot Law Whyte: *The*

Unconscious Before Freud (1960), which, though little more than a shallow compilation, has its uses.

I am also indebted to Steven Marcus: *The Other Victorians: A Study of Sexuality and Pornography in Mid-Nineteenth-Century England* (1966) which deals, as the title shows, with a period later than that covered in this book, but its Freudian and literary-critical analysis of the subliterature of pornography was useful for my treatment of eighteenth-century sensuality. David Foxon's articles (to which *The Other Victorians* called my attention), "Libertine Literature in England, 1660–1745," *The Book Collector*, XII, 1, 2, 3 (Spring, Summer, Winter 1963), 21–36, 159–77, 294–307, are mainly a bibliographical analysis of dirty books, but end with some instructive speculations on the place of pornography in social development. More, much more work is clearly needed.

For the philosophes most deeply involved in this revaluation of sensuality see the familiar works listed before. Add, for Diderot, Leo Spitzer: "The Style of Diderot," in his *Linguistics and Literary History: Essays in Stylistics* (1948), 135–91, a brilliant essay on the sensual qualities of Diderot's writing. Franz Neumann's "Introduction" to *The Spirit of the Laws* (1945), [I, 436] has a penetrating and highly relevant analysis of Montesquieu's view of life, including sexuality. Hans Wolffheim: *Wielands Begriff der Humanität* (1949), [I, 439] discusses Wieland's attempt to reconcile reason and passion in, and through, *Humanität* (pp. 76–9); see also Sengle: *Wieland*, 90–1. D'Alembert has some significant pages on the passions in his *Réflexions sur l'usage et sur l'abus de la philosophie dans les matières de goût* in *Mélanges*, IV, 315 ff. For Greuze, see Louis Hautecœur: *Les peintres de la vie familiale* (1945) and see the book by C. Mauclair, and the articles by Anita Brookner cited below, 646. Greuze was, if not a great painter, an instructive figure.

4. THE CAREER OF IMAGINATION

A most important book for this section, lucid and judicious, from which I have borrowed a good deal, is Margaret Gilman: *The Idea of Poetry in France from Houdar de la Motte to Baudelaire* (1958). There is no need for me to repeat already familiar titles dealing with Diderot's, and Hume's, and Voltaire's conception of the imagination; in addition to Gilman, the standard monographs on these writers, like Laird for Hume, are by now well known to readers of these volumes. I should only add Harold Taylor: "Hume's Theory of Imagination," *The University of Toronto Quarterly*, XII (1942–3), 180–90, a cool, competent survey; and David Funt: *Diderot and the Esthetics of the Enlightenment, Diderot Studies*, XI (1968), which suggests a place for Diderot among the proponents of the creative imagination. Addison's theory is well discussed in Clarence D. Thorpe's excellent "Addison's Contribution to Criticism," in R. F. Jones *et al.*: *The Seventeenth Century ... From Bacon to Pope*, 316–29. Great but justified claims for Addison's influence are made in E. F. Carritt: "Addison, Kant, and Wordsworth," *Essays and Studies by Members of the English Association*, XXII (1936), 26–36. Pierre Trahard sheds much light on eighteenth-century sensibility in his *Les maîtres de la sensibilité française au XVIIIe siècle (1715–1789)*, 4 vols. (1931–3), although his judgments must be used with some care.

The background to the eighteenth-century position on, and dilemma concerning, the imagination is sketched by Murray W. Bundy: *The Theory of Imagination in Classical and Medieval Thought* (1927); and Donald F. Bond: "The Neo-classical Psychology of Imagination," *ELH, A Journal of English Literary History*, IV (1937), 245–63. I have relied, as before, on Borgerhoff's *The Freedom of French Classicism* (above, 626).

General discussions of the decline and rise of the imagination in the age of the Enlightenment can be found, in addition to Gilman's book, just praised, in Sutherland's also familiar *Preface to Eighteenth Century Poetry*, and Basil Willey: *The Eighteenth Century Background* (1940), [I, 427]. The first volume of René Wellek: *A History of Modern Criticism* (1955), [I, 456] is thoroughly dependable; his discussion of Johnson's sober view of genius is on 95–6. Wellek's *The Rise of English Literary History* (1941), especially 70–1, discusses the relation of imaginative poetry to religion in the eighteenth century. See also Walter Jackson Bate's crisp survey, *From Classic to Romantic: Premises of Taste in Eighteenth Century England* (1946) which, despite its title, has much to say about Kant's aesthetics. The decline of art, which so obsessed Voltaire and greatly troubled other philosophes, like D'Alembert, has been studied by J.

Ranscelot, in "Les manifestations du déclin poétique au début du XVIIIe siècle," *Revue d'Histoire Littéraire de la France,* XXXIII (October–December 1926), 297–520. Cassirer: *Philosophy of the Enlightenment,* has some valuable pages both in chaps. iii and vii. I have found the opening chapter of Edgar Wind: *Art and Anarchy* (1963), stimulating on the unsettling, subversive character of the artist's imagination (see also below, bibliography to chap. v).

This is not the place for a detailed bibliography of the Romantics' rejection of the Enlightenment's view of imagination. I. A. Richards: *Coleridge on Imagination* (2d edn., 1950), has a valuable discussion of Coleridge's repudiation of Hartley and the other philosophes' psychology. The influence of Kant on Coleridge's decision to reject Hartley is carefully demonstrated in Arthur O. Lovejoy: "Coleridge and Kant's Two Worlds" (1940), in *Essays in the History of Ideas,* 254–76. This essay points to a much-neglected area in intellectual history—a splendid hunting ground for paradoxes: the peculiar influence of Enlightenment thought, and generally eighteenth-century thought, on the Romantics. René Wellek: *A History of Modern Criticism, 1750–1950,* II, *The Romantic Age* (1955), is a sturdy and informative history. Wellek's "The Concept of 'Romanticism' in Literary History," (1949), now in a collection of Wellek's essays, *Concepts of Criticism* (1963), 121–98, and "Romanticism Reexamined," a long postscript in ibid., 199–221, are impressive attempts to rescue the very idea of Romanticism from Lovejoy's famous attack, delivered in 1923, "On the Discrimination of Romanticisms" (1924), now in *Essays in the History of Ideas,* 228–53. M. H. Abrams: *The Mirror and the Lamp* (1953), which, as the subtitle makes plain, analyzes "Romantic Theory and the Critical Tradition," looks back on the eighteenth century from the Romantics' perspective. Marjorie Hope Nicolson: *Newton Demands the Muse* (cited above), has some amusing quotations from the Romantics, revealing real hatred for the works of the scientific philosophers.

CHAPTER FIVE

The Emancipation of Art:
Burdens of the Past

I. ART AND ENLIGHTENMENT

THE HISTORICAL ANALYSIS of the relations between eighteenth-
century art and eighteenth-century society is not yet in a
satisfactory state, although things are improving. Recent monographs by Georges Wildenstein, for example, avoid the old generalities about art and culture, and the severe but exhilarating scholarship
of the Warburg circle and their allies—of scholars like Rudolf Wittkower, Sir Kenneth Clark, Nikolaus Pevsner, Sir Anthony Blunt—
though mainly concentrated on the art of the Renaissance and on the
seventeenth century, has had beneficial effects on eighteenth-century
studies as well. I am, as so often, indebted to Herbert Dieckmann,
notably to his long essay, *Esthetic Theory and Criticism in the Enlightenment: Some Examples of Modern Trends* (1965); it offers
some judicious criticisms of scholars like W. Folkierski and Margaret
Gilman, who treat the eighteenth century mainly as a transition between classicism and romanticism. Walter Jackson Bate's little book
on "Premises of Taste in Eighteenth Century England" (cited
above, 630), is even called *From Classic to Romantic*. Good as such
studies are (and Bate's opening chapters on English neoclassicism
are excellent) they give too little credit to the inner, autonomous
qualities of eighteenth-century aesthetic thinking, which, though it
moved away from neoclassicism, was by no means a mere prelude
to or precursor of romanticism.

Inevitably, thinking about eighteenth-century art leads into
general aesthetics. The field, as aestheticians have long complained,

is a swamp. (J. A. Passmore's astringent essay "The Dreariness of Aesthetics," in *Aesthetics and Language*, ed. William Elton [1954], 36–55, is only one example. Indeed, Elton's whole volume is a collective assault of disenchanted linguistic philosophers on modern aesthetic theorizing—negative but far from useless.) The list that follows is a sampling of the works I have consulted. I have learned from Albert Hofstadter's difficult essay, *Truth and Art* (1965), which surveys the aesthetic theories dominant in our time (notably the ideas of Cassirer, Croce, Collingwood, Maritain, and Heidegger), to arrive at a personal statement. (See also Hofstadter: "Validity versus Value: An Essay in Philosophical Aesthetics," *The Journal of Philosophy*, LIX, 21 [October 11, 1962], 607–17, and "Art and Spiritual Validity," *The Journal of Aesthetics and Art Criticism*, XXII, 1 [Fall 1963], 9–19.) John Dewey: *Art as Experience* (1934) remains an indispensable statement of experimentalism in art; Susanne K. Langer: *Feeling and Form: A Theory of Art* (1935) develops Cassirer's ideas. E. H. Gombrich: "Meditations on a Hobby Horse or the Roots of Artistic Form" (originally in *Aspects of Form*, ed. L. L. Whyte [1951]), now in Gombrich: *Meditations on a Hobby Horse and Other Essays on the Theory of Art* (1936), 1–11, is a brilliant short study of the work of perception in aesthetic judgment. Other essays in this collection worthy of special note are "Visual Metaphors of Value in Art," 12–29, and "Expression and Communication," 56–69, although the other essays, not mentioned here, are just as interesting. Gombrich's *Art and Illusion: A Study in the Psychology of Pictorial Representation* (2d edn., 1965) is a long and eminently suggestive essay in the psychology of art. Among general treatises, I found Monroe Beardsley: *Aesthetics* (1958), most satisfactory. On style, on which Gombrich has also much to say, the well-known essay by Meyer Schapiro, "Style" (originally in *Anthropology Today*, ed. A. L. Kroeber, now conveniently reprinted in *Aesthetics Today*, ed. Morris Philipson [1961], 81–113), is indispensable.

A word on Marxist interpretations of art history. Leo Balet: *Die Verbürgerlichung der deutschen Kunst, Musik und Literatur im 18. Jahrhundert* (1936); Arnold Hauser's extremely well-known volumes, *The Social History of Art*, 2 vols. (tr. Stanley Godman and the author, 1951); and Frederick Antal's learned and often brilliant essays, *Hogarth and His Place in European Art* (1962) and *Clas-*

sicism and Romanticism, with Other Studies in Art History (1966), have gained wide influence, in part because they are so stimulating, in part because the field they have dealt with is still relatively unexplored. Perhaps Antal's most interesting disciple was the English sociologist F. D. Klingender, whose best two books, *Art and the Industrial Revolution* (1947) and *Goya in the Democratic Tradition* (1948), both attempts at a social history of art, repay reading. Gombrich's incisive criticism of Hauser, "The Social History of Art" (1953), now in *Meditations on a Hobby Horse* (just cited), 86–94, is worth reading. Marxist history of art is simplistic and often distorted; it sees early modern Europe, and its art, as a spectacle in which the "middle class" rises at the expense of the aristocracy. In the minds of these scholars, art displays the triumph of bourgeois ideology. But this is manifestly wrong: courtly art continues; "bourgeois" art like, say, Chardin's still lifes finds aristocratic customers; society, and with it the world of art patrons, continues to be subdivided among landed gentry, urban aristocrats, ecclesiastics, professionals, and a handful of merchants. Much work, to be sure, remains to be done; subtle Marxists might, after all, argue that the processes they claim to see go on behind the backs of the actors. But the grand simplicities, even of a learned and scholarly writer like Antal, suggest that Marxism, far from aiding, frequently obstructs, the view of the social historian of art. (See also below, sections 2 and 3 of this chapter.)

The taste of the philosophes needs much further exploration, although on their taste in literature the relevant chapters of Wellek: *History of Modern Criticism*, I (see above, 630), are adequate. For Kant, see A. D. Lindsay: *Kant*, 237. In addition, see Ernst Cassirer: *Kants Leben und Lehre, passim;* René Wellek: Aesthetics and Criticism," in C. W. Hendel, ed.: *The Philosophy of Kant and Our Modern World*, 65–7; and Erich Adickes: "Kant als Aesthetiker," *Jahrbuch des freien deutschen Hochstifts* (1904), 315–38, esp. 320–8. Voltaire's taste has been studied in detail by Raymond Naves, in *Le goût de Voltaire* (1938), although, for all its merits, the book does not exhaust its subject. See also the perceptive pages in Gustave Lanson: *Voltaire* (1906; tr. Robert A. Wagoner, 1966), 75–92, which rightly stress the radicalism of Voltaire's theatrical experiments, a radicalism that frightened many of his contemporaries. The literature on Shakespeare and Voltaire is constantly growing; I have used Thomas R. Lounsbury: *Shakespeare and Voltaire* (1902), dated and oversimple, F. C. Green: *Minuet* (1935), which is much better, as well as Jacques Guicharnaud: "Voltaire and Shakespeare," *American Society Legion of Honor Magazine*, XXVII (1956), 159–69, a helpful summary, and Henning Fenger: "Voltaire et le théâtre anglais," *Orbis Litterarum*, VII (1949), 161–287.

Handel has most recently been thoroughly examined by Paul Henry Lang, in *George Frideric Handel* (1966); chaps. xiii, xiv, xix, and xxii—on Handel's *Messiah*, his secular pagan oratorios, and his religious convictions—chapters which effectively polemicize against the religious interpretation of Handel, were especially instructive to me. For Goya, see above, 626.

The revival of Gothic in the eighteenth century, a complicated story of resistance and adaptation to modernity, is thoroughly investigated in Paul Frankl: *The Gothic: Literary Sources and Interpretations Through Eight Centuries* (1960), especially 370–414, with full bibliographies (the monographs most relevant here are listed on 371). While Frankl's treatment is full, it is not exhaustive—the citations in the text, for example, came out of my own reading. Sir Kenneth Clark's *The Gothic Revival* (1928; latest edn., 1962), is, not unexpectedly, both amusing and informative. René Lanson: *Le goût du moyen age en France au XVIIIe siècle* (1926) is of some help but generally shallow. Arthur Johnston: *Enchanted Ground: The Study of Medieval Romance in the Eighteenth Century* (1964) and W. D. Robson-Scott: *The Literary Background of the Gothic Revival in Germany: A Chapter in the History of Taste* (1965) are—the latter with especially full bibliography—both excellent on the literary revival in their respective countries. Hermann Schmitz: *Die Gotik im deutschen Kunst- und Geistesleben* (1921) broadly sweeps from Gothic to neo-Gothic. René Wellek: *Rise of English Literary History* (above, 630), has important chapters on eighteenth-century views of medieval literature. Wellek's counterpart for Germany is Sigmund von Lempicki: *Geschichte der deutschen Literaturwissenschaft bis zum Ende des 18. Jahrhunderts* (1920), notably part II. For trivial Gothicizing taste, see Osbert Sitwell and Margaret Barton: "Taste," *Johnson's England*, II, 36–7, and the interesting pamphlet by Oliver Sigwart: *The Four Styles of a Decade (1740–1750)*, (1960), which deals with Gothic as one of four options open to Englishmen; it also has good material on Hogarth. (I also refer the reader to I, 489–92, where some of these titles, and others, are cited.)

The eighteenth century was the first to put both art criticism and literary criticism on a modern footing. The fundamental paper on this question is the richly documented survey by Paul Oskar Kristeller: "The Modern System of the Arts: A Study in the History of Aesthetics," *JHI*, XII, 4 (October 1951), 296–327; and ibid., XIII, 1 (January 1952), 17–46. There are many histories of aesthetics; Katharine E. Gilbert and Helmut Kuhn: *A History of Esthetics* (edn. 1953) is a useful though not profound survey. Julius Schlosser: *Die Kunstliteratur* (1924) is a widely appreciated classic. A. Dresdner: *Die Kunstkritik: Ihre Geschichte und Theorie*, I, *Die Entstehung der Kunstkritik* (1915, all that appeared), [I, 486], is, on the other hand, a relatively neglected classic— I am especially in debt to Dresdner. K. Heinrich von Stein: *Die Entstehung der neueren Aesthetik* (1886) retains its use despite its age. Wladyslaw Folkierski: *Entre le classicisme et le romantisme. Étude sur l'esthétique et les esthéticiens du XVIIIe siècle* (1925) remains unsurpassed despite the tendentiousness Dieckmann has criticized. And, once again, Cassirer: *Philosophy of the Enlightenment:* his chapter on aesthetics, the last and longest in the book, is nothing less than magnificent.

The theme of the decline of neoclassical art theory runs through this whole chapter. For the definition of neoclassicism, see René Bray: *La formation de la doctrine classique en France* (1927; edn. 1951), which deals mainly with seventeenth-century France; it should be supplemented with Borgerhoff: *The Freedom of French Classicism* (see above, 626), which, in contrast, stresses freedom, "magic," and *je ne sais quoi*. Erwin Panofsky: *Idea: Ein Beitrag zur Begriffsgeschichte der älteren Kunsttheorie* (2d edn., 1960), takes the idea of "Idea," central to Platonic idealism and its offshoots, from antiquity to the Renaissance; it is immensely compressed and immensely learned. Henri Peyre: *Le classicisme français* (1942) is a good essay in definition, with historical notes on the uses of the term "classic" [see, for all these titles, I, 425, 528]. Short but clear and instructive is René Wellek's chapter "Neoclassicism and the New Trends of the Time," in his *History of Modern Criticism*, I. See also Wellek: "The Term and Concept of 'Classicism' in Literary History," in *Aspects of the Eighteenth Century*, ed. Earl R. Wasserman, 105–28, a diligent listing with exhaustive bibliographical indications. Henry Hawley has edited a well-illustrated and thoroughly annotated catalogue of an exhibition at the Cleveland Museum of Art: *Neo-Classicism: Style and Motif* (1964), with a stimulating though in some respects old-fashioned essay on "Neo-Classicism: Virtue, Reason and Nature," by Rémy G. Saisselin. The classical ideas of genre and separation of styles as they are treated in Western realism have been superbly accounted for in Erich Auerbach: *Mimesis: The Representation of Reality in Western Literature* (1946; tr. Willard R. Trask, 1953) [I, 426]. Rudolf Wittkower's paper, "Imitation, Eclecticism, and Genius," in *Aspects of the Eighteenth Century*, 143–61, is an important survey of leading neoclassical ideas and their fate in the age of the Enlightenment. Edgar Wind has written a stimulating chapter on "The Fear of Knowledge," which deals with the neoclassical idea of didactic art, in his *Art and Anarchy*. Much interesting material on didactic neoclassicism in English poetry is offered in Ulrich Broich: "Das Lehrgedicht als Teil der epischen Tradition des englischen Klassizismus," *Germanisch-Romanische Monatsschrift*, N.F. XIII, 2 (April 1963), 147–63. Sutherland: *Preface to XVIIIth Century Poetry* (above, 626), is particularly informative on the flexibility of neoclassical rules (146 ff.). James William Johnson: *The Formation of English Neo-Classical Thought* (1967) deals instructively with the ancient world and its reception in eighteenth-century England, and culminates in Gibbon. It has a useful bibliography as well. It may be supplemented with A. F. B. Clark: *Boileau and French Classical Critics in England, 1660–1830* (1925). But this gets us from neoclassicism into the reception of the classics in the modern world, a related but not identical theme. I have dealt with this reception in detail in my *Rise of Modern Paganism*. The deservedly famous essay by Rensselaer W. Lee: *"Ut pictura poesis: The Humanistic Theory of Painting,"* *The Art Bulletin*, XXII, 4 (December 1940), 197–269, goes far beyond its title; it is enormously informative on the whole spectrum of neoclassical theorizing.

For the neoclassical revival at the end of the century (to which I return in the third section of this chapter) see Fritz Novotny: *Painting and Sculpture in Europe, 1780–1880* (tr. R. H. Boothroyd, 1960), especially chaps. i to v (its bibliography is exemplary). See also Rudolf Zeitler: *Klassizismus und Utopia: Interpretationen zu Werken von David, Canova, Carstens, Thorvaldsen, Koch* (1954);

Sigfried Giedion: *Spätbarocker und romantischer Klassizismus* (1922); Louis Hautecœur: *Rome et la renaissance de l'antiquité à la fin du XVIIIe siècle* (1912); and Harry Levin: *The Broken Column: A Study in Romantic Hellenism* (1931). Robert Rosenblum's conspectus of painting, sculpture, and architecture at the end of the eighteenth century, *Transformations in Late Eighteenth Century Art* (1967), is a pioneering set of essays, still tentative, but most stimulating, especially on the survival of moralizing tendencies; its illustrations are brilliantly chosen and its footnotes a mine of bibliographical information. Related developments are discussed in J. G. Robertson: *Studies in the Genesis of Romantic Theory in the Eighteenth Century* (1923), and G. McKenzie: *Critical Responsiveness: A Study of the Psychological Current in Later 18th Century Criticism* (1949). Two final notes. Neoclassicism is, of course, a leading theme in many books on specific arts, artists, or countries to be cited below. And the end of neoclassicism will be the main theme of chap. vi, section 2.

2. PATRONS AND PUBLICS

The history of patronage is still very incomplete; there are frequent references to it, of course, in histories of art and books on taste, although the latter are often merely chatty. Geraldine Pelles: *Art, Artists and Society: Origins of a Modern Dilemma. Painting in England and France, 1750–1850* (1963), is a stimulating essay. A model for all others, clear, beautifully organized and argued, is Francis Haskell: *Patrons and Painters: A Study in the Relations between Italian Art and Society in the Age of the Baroque* (1963). It should be read (since it is mainly on the seventeenth and early eighteenth centuries) in conjunction with Rudolf Wittkower: *Art and Architecture in Italy: 1600–1750* (edn. 1965), a splendid survey. One remarkable essay, inviting further work, on the sociology of architects, is Nicolaus Pevsner: "Zur Geschichte des Architektenberufs," *Kritische Berichte zur Kunstgeschichtlichen Literatur*, III, 4 (1930–1), 97–122. Chaps. iv to vii of Frank Jenkins's *Architect and Patron:*

A Survey of Professional Relations and Practice in England from the Sixteenth Century to the Present Day (1961) contain much of interest.

For the rise of artistic individualism there is much in Vasari's *Lives* (I used the edn. by William Gaunt, 4 vols. [1963]). A general study (introductory and rather anecdotal), characterized by its authors as a "documented history from antiquity to the French Revolution" on the "character and conduct of artists" is Rudolf and Margot Wittkower: *Born Under Saturn* (1963). See also Rudolf Wittkower: "Individualism in Art and Artists: A Renaissance Problem," *JHI*, XXII, 3 (July–September 1961), 291–302, which is short but revealing [both I, 513].

One subject that deserves far more research than it has received is the growth of the museum—largely an eighteenth-century phenomenon. There are some details in Dresdner, while Georg Friedrich Koch: *Die Kunstausstellung, Ihre Geschichte von den Anfängen bis zum Ausgang des 18. Jahrhunderts* (1967) has much fascinating material on exhibitions down to the beginning of the nineteenth century.

Among representative seventeenth-century artists wrestling with the problem of patronage, the outstanding ones are Rembrandt, Rubens, Bernini, and Poussin. On Rembrandt, the bibliography is by now almost unmanageable. See above all the general survey, which places him in his culture, by Jakob Rosenberg, Seymour Slive, E. H. ter Kuile: *Dutch Art and Architecture: 1600–1800* (1966); its text is judicious and its bibliographies (like all the bibliographies in the Pelican History of Art) are exemplary. Jakob Rosenberg: *Rembrandt*, 2 vols. (2d edn., 1964) is indispensable; for Rembrandt's possible borrowing from Italian sources, see the stimulating though essentially speculative essay by Sir Kenneth Clark: *Rembrandt and the Italian Renaissance* (1966). For Rubens, see H. Gerson and E. H. ter Kuile: *Art and Architecture in Belgium: 1600–1800* (tr. Olive Renier, 1960), chap. v, with splendid bibliographical indications. Bernini has been fortunate in his biographers: there is Rudolf Wittkower: *Gian Lorenzo Bernini: The Sculptor of the Roman Baroque* (2d edn., 1966), Howard Hibbard's recent crisp and excellent *Bernini* (1965), and Wittkower's fine brief treatment in his *Art and Architecture in Italy*, 96–129. Sir Anthony Blunt has made Poussin his special subject; he deals with him briefly and brilliantly in *Art and Architecture in France: 1500 to 1700* (1953); and now exhaustively and definitely in *Nicolas Poussin*, 2 vols. (1967).

Anne Betty Weinshenker: *Falconet* is a model monograph from which I have quoted freely. See also Herbert Dieckmann and Jean Seznec: "The Horse of Marcus Aurelius," both cited above, 604; Seznec: "Falconet, Voltaire et Diderot," *VS*, II (1956), 43–59; and Louis Réau: *Étienne-Maurice Falconet*, 2 vols. (1922).

The basic work on academies is Nikolaus Pevsner: *Academies of Art Past and Present* (1940), which begins with the liberation of academies from gilds and has excellent material on the seventeenth and eighteenth centuries (including the dependence and poverty of the Dutch painters). With patronage, as with artists, I naturally have chosen only a few striking instances. I derived the passage on Dr. Mead's collection from the informative essay by Osbert Sitwell and Margaret Barton, "Taste," in *Johnson's England*, II, 1–40, especially 19–20. For an interesting discussion of the taste of a great English patron in the age of the Enlightenment, Sir Robert Walpole, see especially J. H. Plumb: "The Walpoles, Father and Son," in his *Men and Centuries* (1963), 136–43, and Plumb: *Sir Robert Walpole: The King's Minister*, 81–7. G. E. Mingay: *English Landed Society in the Eighteenth Century* (see above, 574), has a valuable brief chapter (ix) on the taste of the landed gentry. The career of Tiepolo is well surveyed in Antonio Morassi: *Tiepolo: His Life and Work* (1955). Among the large literature on Haydn I found particularly useful Karl Geiringer: *Haydn: A Creative Life in Music* (2d edn., 1963); and see also his "Joseph Haydn, Protagonist of the Enlightenment," *VS*, XXV (1963), 683–90. The sociology of Baroque music in general is discussed in Manfred F. Bukofzer: *Music in the Baroque Era from Monteverdi to Bach* (1947), chap. xii, "Sociology of Baroque Music," which is only an introduction, but a helpful one. In general, Paul Henry Lang's pioneering *Music in Western Civilization* (1941) remains a splendid general orientation. Alfred Einstein: *Gluck* (tr. Eric Blom, 1936) deals with Gluck's reform of the opera in accord with enlightened principles. Edward E. Lowinsky: "Taste, Style, and Ideology in Eighteenth-Century Music," in *Aspects of the Eighteenth Century*, 163–205, seeks to connect Bach with Leibniz, Rousseau with Gluck, Rousseau the composer with Rousseau the philosophe; it is a daring, though not, I think, convincing, venture. (For details on arts and the artists, see section 3, below, and chap. vi.)

Gerald Reitlinger: *The Economics of Taste: The Rise and Fall of the Picture Market, 1760–1960* (1961) is filled with fascinating statistics that tell us much about the fashions in pictorial art in the age of the Enlightenment.

3. BURDENS OF THE PAST

The literature on eighteenth-century English art is of course vast. Nikolaus Pevsner: *The Englishness of English Art* (rev. edn., 1964) provides excellent and amusing guidelines; it has a chapter each on Hogarth and Reynolds. A very short but informative survey down to 1760 is in Basil Williams: *The Whig Supremacy: 1714–1760* (1939), chap. xv, "The Arts." John Loftis: *Comedy and Society from Congreve to Fielding* (1959) and his *The Politics of Drama in Augustan England* (1963) are both fairminded essays that seek to link events on the stage to the political life of Walpole's England. The dependence of English artists and art lovers on foreign, especially Italian, art has been thoroughly studied and is mentioned in all the major biographies and surveys; clearly, Hogarth's claim to independence from foreign models cannot stand—even for him. In general see Rudolf Wittkower and Fritz Saxl: *British Art and the Mediterranean* (1948); J. R. Hale: *England and the Italian Renaissance: The Growth of Interest in its History and Art* (1954); Mario Praz: *The Flaming Heart* (1958), a collection of essays that traces literary relations between England and Italy from Chaucer to T. S. Eliot; and Elizabeth Mainwaring: *Italian Landscape in Eighteenth Century England: A Study Chiefly of the Influence of Claude Lorrain and Salvator Rosa on English Taste, 1700–1800* (1925).

The major works on the various arts deal in detail with English taste, as do the better biographies of individual artists. I have also learned from B. Sprague Allen: *Tides in English Taste (1619–1800): A Background for the Study of Literature*, 2 vols. (1937), scattered and informal but informative. Christopher Hussey: *The Picturesque: Studies in A Point of View* (1927) is the standard monograph on an important subject. It may now be supplemented with Walter J. Hipple: *The Beautiful, the Sublime, and the Picturesque in Eighteenth-Century British Aesthetic Theory* (1957). For English criticism see the relevant chapters in Wellek: *History of Modern Criticism*, I, on "Dr. Johnson," and "The Minor English and Scottish Critics." The best special study on Johnson's taste and criticism is, among a large supply, J. H. Hagstrum: *Samuel Johnson's Literary Criticism* (1952). Among specialized treatments I can only list a few: Ernst Cassirer: *The Platonic Renaissance in England* (1932; tr. James P. Pettegrove, 1953), which ends with Shaftesbury; on Shaftesbury see also R. L. Brett: *The Third Earl of Shaftesbury* (1951); for Francis Hutcheson, W. R. Scott: *Francis Hutcheson* (1900) is the standard work. For the development of the novel, which played a major part in the development of taste and of criticism itself, I mention only Alan Dugald McKillop: *The Early Masters of English Fiction* (1956), with fine essays on Defoe, Richardson, Fielding, Smollett, and Sterne, and comprehensive bibliographical indications. Louis I. Bredvold: *The Literature of the Restoration and the Eighteenth Century, 1660–1789* (edn. 1962) is short and dependable; it also has an excellent bibliography (as does Wellek: *History of Modern Criticism*) for those who wish to go further. I shall take up Burke and Hume separately later, in section 2 of chap. vi.

Sir John Summerson: *Architecture in Britain: 1530–1830* (3rd edn., 1958) is a comprehensive and magnificently well-informed survey. (Geoffrey Webb: "Architecture and the Garden," in *Johnson's England*, II, 93–124, should also be consulted.) Other valuable books by Summerson that I have used with profit are his *Georgian London* (rev. edn., 1962); *Christopher Wren* (1953), to be supplemented by his lucid essay, "The Mind of Wren," reprinted in his *Heavenly Mansions and Other Essays in Architecture* (edn. 1963), 51–86; and his *Sir John Soane* (1952). Summerson's "John Wood and the English Town-Planning Tradition," also in *Heavenly Mansions*, 87–110, moves into the heart of that triumph of eighteenth-century architecture—Bath. For the same subject, see W. Ison: *The Georgian Buildings of Bath* (1948).

Rudolf Wittkower has written some important papers on English Palladianism, a subject of great importance to social history. Among these papers, of particular importance are "Pseudo-Palladian Elements in English Neo-Classical Architecture," *Journal of the*

Warburg Institute, VI (1943), 154–64; "Lord Burlington and William Kent," *Archaeological Journal*, CII (1945), 151–64; and *The Earl of Burlington and William Kent* (Occasional Papers of the York Georgian Society, No. 5 [1948]). Summerson's treatment in *Architecture in Britain* (much indebted to Wittkower) is also worth reading. To this should be added Margaret Jourdain: *The Work of William Kent, Artist, Painter, Designer and Landscape Gardener* (1948). The work of James Gibbs is summarized in Bryan D. G. Little: *The Life and Work of James Gibbs, 1682–1754* (1955). On Kent's impertinence to his "betters," see Peter Quennell: *Hogarth's Progress* (1955), 41–4.

For developments in the architecture of the later eighteenth century, the books on the Adam brothers are particularly instructive. John Fleming: *Robert Adam and His Circle in Edinburgh and Rome* (1962) is an excellent study resting on hitherto unpublished material; it is to be followed by a similar study on Robert Adam's later career. Meanwhile we have James Lees-Milne: *The Age of Adam* (1947), and the older A. T. Bolton: *Robert and James Adam*, 2 vols. (1922). A. J. Youngson: *The Making of Classical Edinburgh: 1750–1840* (1966) is scholarly, well illustrated, engaging, and informative. Closely related to architecture, of course, and of vital importance to an understanding of English social ideals and ways of spending money, is the garden. The best introduction doubtless is Dorothy Stroud: *Capability Brown* (2d edn., 1957).

For English painting in the age of Enlightenment, the volume in the Pelican History of Art, Ellis K. Waterhouse: *Painting in Britain: 1530 to 1790* (1953), though of necessity a little crowded, is authoritative. Waterhouse explicitly connects the famous English passion for portraits with the rise of the painters: varied and individualized portraiture, he writes, "contributed more than anything else to raising the status of portraiture and of the painter in England, where the native practitioner had been despised. . . . This raising of the status of the British artist was the political objective of Reynolds's life and the mainspring of his conduct as first President of the Royal Academy" (163). Andrew Shirley: "Painting and Engraving," in *Johnson's England*, II, 41–71, is filled with useful material for the social history of the art. R. and S. Redgrave: *A Century of Painters of the English School*, 2 vols. (1866; edn. 1947), though very old, has much good material and many good anecdotes. W. T. Whitley:

Artists and their Friends in England, 1700–1799, 2 vols. (1928), more up to date, is equally entertaining and informative. William Gaunt: *A Concise History of English Painting* (1964), very concise indeed, has several helpful chapters on the period. C. H. Collins Baker and M. R. James: *British Painting* (1933), is the standard survey history. Edgar Wind: "Humanitätsidee und heroisiertes Porträt in der englischen Kultur des 18ten Jahrhunderts," *Warburg Vorträge 1930–1* (1932), 156–229, is a brilliant attempt to link art and philosophy. On individual painters: Ellis K. Waterhouse's brief *Gainsborough* (1958), includes studies of the painter's character and income. It should be supplemented by Waterhouse's specialized articles, listed in his bibliography (49). The large standard life, *Thomas Gainsborough* (1915), by William T. Whitley, is excellent. Mary Woodall's edition, *The Letters of Thomas Gainsborough* (1961), is scholarly and instructive. For Reynolds, the old life by Charles Robert Leslie and Tom Taylor: *Life and Times of Sir Joshua Reynolds,* 2 vols. (1865), remains indispensable, but must be supplemented with Ellis K. Waterhouse: *Reynolds* (1941), a good modern account, and the splendid specialized studies by Frederick W. Hilles, who has edited the *Letters of Sir Joshua Reynolds* (1929), written a highly informative study on *The Literary Career of Sir Joshua Reynolds* (1936), to which I am deeply indebted, and published some fascinating, hitherto unpublished writings—essays, character sketches, imaginary dialogues, *Portraits by Sir Joshua Reynolds* (1952), from which I have quoted in the text. Hilles quotes Boswell's regret that Reynolds was not a Christian (18). For Reynolds as a writer, see Hilles: "Sir Joshua's Prose," in *The Age of Johnson: Essays Presented to Chauncey B. Tinker,* ed. Frederick W. Hilles (1949), 49–60. The question of Reynolds's originality and borrowing is analyzed by Edgar Wind in "Humanitätsidee und heroisiertes Porträt in der englischen Kultur des 18. Jahrhunderts" (see just above). Reynolds's *Discourses on Art* have been republished often; I have used the best critical edition, by Robert R. Wark (1959). Discourse XIV, incidentally, is a fine appreciation of Gainsborough, written shortly after his death in 1788. One rather neglected painter now coming into his own is Allan Ramsay. See Alastair Smart: *The Life and Art of Allan Ramsay* (1952), and the catalogue by Colin Thompson and Robin Hutchison: *Allan Ramsay (1713–1784), His Masters and Rivals* (1963). The colorful Hogarth has attracted many students. Quennell: *Hogarth's Progress* (just cited), though popular in appearance, is well done; it includes an interesting discussion of Hogarth's "war" with the connoisseurs (139-41), as does Joseph Burke's "Introduction" to his indispensable edition of Hogarth's *The Analysis of Beauty* (1955). Burke's *Hogarth and Reynolds, A Contrast in English Art Theory* (1943) fruitfully pits the aesthetic revolutionary against the majestic neoclassicist. See also R. B. Beckett: *Hogarth* (1949). There have been some splendid recent editions of his output, notably by Ronald Paulson: *Hogarth's Graphic Work*, 2 vols. (1965), which should be consulted. *Lichtenberg's Commentaries on Hogarth's Engravings* (tr. and ed., with an Introduction, by Innes and Gustav Herden, 1966), is an interesting confrontation of German philosophe and English rebel. For Hogarth's dependence on Dutch and Italian sources, see Pevsner: *Englishness of English Art*, 28-30, 209. (For a comment on Antal's *Hogarth*, see above, 633-4.)

English musical life is splendidly mirrored in Paul Henry Lang's biography of Handel (see above, 635). Another valuable source for the social historian is Roger Lonsdale: *Dr. Charles Burney: A Literary Biography* (1965), which places the man in his culture. And see Bruce Simonds: "Music in Johnson's London," *The Age of Johnson*, 411-20.

Garrick, who so impressed Reynolds and Diderot—as he impressed everyone—is portrayed in an informative recent biography by Carola Oman: *David Garrick* (1958). The earlier book by Frank A. Hedgcock: *A Cosmopolitan Actor: David Garrick and His French Friends* (n.d., 1912?) has much useful material on Garrick's influence on the philosophes.

On sculpture in England, the authoritative monographs by Katharine A. Esdaile—"Sculpture," *Johnson's England*, II, 72-92; *Roubiliac's Work at Trinity College, Cambridge* (1924); *Life and Work of L. F. Roubiliac* (1928); and *English Monumental Sculpture* (1937)—can now be supplemented by Margaret Whinney: *Sculpture in Britain: 1530-1830* (1964). J. T. Smith: *Nollekens and His Times*, 2 vols. (2d edn., 1829) remains amusing and very informative.

The development of artistic theories and art criticism in eighteenth-century France has been dealt with ably in three books that have become minor classics in the literature, and from which I have learned much. I have already mentioned two of them—W. Folkierski: *Entre le classicisme et le romantisme* and Dresdner: *Die Entste-*

hung der Kunstkritik. To this I should now add André Fontaine: *Les doctrines d'art en France de Poussin à Diderot* (1909). Kristeller's articles, "The Modern System of the Arts" (cited above, 636), have much valuable material. I am also indebted to Herbert Dieckmann: "Zur Theorie der Lyrik im 18. Jahrhundert in Frankreich, mit gelegentlicher Berücksichtigung der englischen Kritik," in *Immanente Aesthetik-Aesthetische Reflexion* (1966), 73–112; and to Dieckmann: "Die Wandlung des Nachahmungsbegriffes in der französischen Aesthetik des 18. Jahrhunderts," in *Nachahmung und Illusion* (June 1964), 28–59—two splendid essays.

For painting, Jacques Thuillier and Albert Châtelet: *French Painting: From Le Nain to Fragonard* (tr. J. Emmons, 1964), is sensible and realistic; it should be supplemented by Michael Levey: *Rococo to Revolution* (see above, 626), which though it deals with all of Europe concentrates on France. L. Réau: *Histoire de la peinture française au XVIIIᵉ siècle* (1925) and L. Dimier: *Les peintres français du XVIIIᵉ siècle* (1928–30) should also be consulted. Denys Sutton's catalogue of the Winter exhibition at the Royal Academy in London, *France in the Eighteenth Century* (1968), is splendid and rich. A subject of great importance is treated by J. Locquin: *La Peinture d'histoire en France de 1747 à 1785* (1912). Fiske Kimball: *The Creation of the Rococo* (1943), is a scholarly and detailed examination of a style which, Kimball persuasively argues, was not merely a modification or perversion of baroque, but a real style.

There are now fine studies of individual painters. Georges Wildenstein: *Chardin* (edn. 1963) is a model, as is his *The Paintings of Fragonard* (trs. C. W. Chilton and A. L. Kitson, n.d., 1960?). Wildenstein has also done pioneering work on the still obscure question of eighteenth-century French patronage in two valuable articles: "L'abbé de Saint-Non: Artiste et Mécène," *Gazette des Beaux Arts*, LIV (November 1959), 225–44; and "Un Amateur de Boucher et de Fragonard, Jacques-Onésyme Bergeret (1715–1785)," ibid., LVIII (July–August 1961), 39–84. More work needs to be done on the megalomaniacal Greuze, who so interested Diderot; there is, meanwhile, C. Mauclair: *Greuze et son temps* (1926). Anita Brookner: "Jean-Baptiste Greuze, I," *The Burlington Magazine*, LXXXXVIII (May 1956), 157–62, and "Jean-Baptiste Greuze, II," ibid. (June 1956), 192–9, are straightforward biography, helpful but not profound. For Boucher see A. Michel (1907).

For French sculpture, see the titles on Falconet (above, 604, 640), Paul Vitry: *La Sculpture française classique de Jean Goujon à Rodin* (1934), especially part III, and the somewhat older though still useful book by Edmund Hildebrandt, *Malerei und Plastik des 18. Jahrhunderts in Frankreich* (1924). French architecture of the period is introduced in Blunt: *Art and Architecture in France* (cited above, 640), which takes it almost to the end of the reign of Louis XIV. Emil Kaufmann: *Architecture in the Age of Reason: Baroque and Post-Baroque in England, Italy, and France* (1955), though difficult, is an immensely rewarding collection of essays. Louis Hautecœur: *Histoire de l'architecture classique en France*, 7 vols. (1943–57), is already a classic work of reference. See also Wolfgang Herrmann: *Laugier and 18th Century French Theory* (1962), an excellent study of an influential writer on architecture. (For the theater in France, see chap. vi, section 1.)

What I said in *The Rise of Modern Paganism*—that the need for good work on eighteenth-century German cultural history remains great—is just as true now as it was then. For the main titles, see above, 576, and add Eric A. Blackall: *The Emergence of German as a Literary Language, 1700–1775* (1959), a masterly assessment of an important subject. Max von Boehn's heavily illustrated, superficial, excessively patriotic, but not uninformative *Deutschland im 18ten Jahrhundert*, 2 vols. (1921); and Albert Köster's essay *Die deutsche Literatur der Aufklärungszeit* (1925), [all in I, 440], can be consulted with profit. Similar to von Boehn's work, as well illustrated and more sensibly written, is Hermann Schmitz: *Kunst und Kultur des 18. Jahrhunderts in Deutschland* (1922). Another chauvinistic work, again full of useful material, is *Deutsches Barock und Rokoko*, ed. Georg Biermann (1914); and see Georg Steinhausen: *Geschichte der deutschen Kultur* (3rd edn., 1929). Among general histories of German literature, I found F. J. Schneider: *Die deutsche Dichtung zwischen Barock und Klassizismus, 1700–1785* (1924), most substantial and reliable; the difficulty with much recent writing on German literature and art is that it is colored by the Nazi experience—the later editions of works first written in the 1920s often reflect their authors' subservience to the new regime, and books written by older men after 1945 often reflect hasty re-revision of their ideology. For German art in the general, see the splendid survey by Georg Dehio: *Geschichte der deutschen Kunst*, III (2d edn., 1931). While he rather overstates his case, Louis Réau's work is of importance; his titles announce his thesis: *Histoire de l'expansion de l'art français*, 4 vols. (1924–33); and, even more important, *L'Europe française* (1938). France dominated Germany—and to some extent Europe—but not to the extent Réau suggests. I found Nicolas Powell: *From Baroque to Rococo: An Introduction to Austrian and German Architecture from 1580 to 1790* (1959) exemplary among a literature that usually consists of picture books. For the greatest German architect of the century, see Max H. von Freeden: *Balthasar Neumann, Leben und Werk* (1953).

The literature on Weimar, naturally immense, is well summarized in Bruford's *Classical Weimar* (cited above). For a general survey of smaller lands, singling out two, the Duchy of Württemberg and the County of Montbéliard, see Adrien Fauchier-Magnan: *The Small German Courts in the 18th Century* (1947; tr. Mervyn Savill, 1958), which has many telling quotations. The collective volume *Die Stadt Goethes*, ed. H. Voelcker, is very illuminating on local artists and patronage. For Berlin the old but comprehensive book by Ludwig Geiger: *Berlin 1688–1840: Geschichte des geistigen Lebens der preussischen Hauptstadt*, 2 vols. in 4 parts, I (1892–3), remains a mine of information.

This brings me to Frederick's Prussia. Here the material is abundant but must be used with care—I have commented on German adulation of "Frederick the Unique," set off by often unreasoned hostility on the part of French writers, in *The Rise of Modern Paganism*, 544. The most comprehensive biography remains Reinhold Koser: *Geschichte Friedrichs des Grossen*, 4 vols. (4th and 5th edns., 1912), although it too lacks objectivity. [See I, 544, where I also cite the brilliant essay by Wilhelm Dilthey: "Friedrich der Grosse und die deutsche Aufklärung," *Gesammelte Schriften*, III, 81–205.] (The works I shall cite below [654–5] on Lessing, and, after that on Winckelmann, also contain much material.) For Gottsched see above all Gustav Waniek: *Gottsched und die deutsche Literatur seiner Zeit* (1897), and Max Koch: *Gottsched und die Reform der deutschen Literatur im 18. Jahrhundert* (1887). A modern study would be welcome.

There is one vexed question to which all historians of German eighteenth-century culture must address themselves: what was the impact of the Thirty Years' War? See on this topic especially Francis

L. Carsten: "Was There an Economic Decline in Germany Before the 30 Years' War?," *English Historical Review*, LXXI (1956), 240–7; and the judicious historiographical and bibliographical survey by Theodore K. Rabb: "The Effects of the Thirty Years' War on the German Economy," *Journal of Modern History*, XXXIV, 1 (March 1962), 40–51, which sensibly calls for more regional studies.

Italian art has been well dealt with. Wittkower: *Art and Architecture in Italy* (see above, 638) reaches to mid-century, as does Haskell: *Patrons and Painters* (above, 638). See also, amid a large literature, Michael Levey: *Painting in XVIIIth Century Venice* (1959), and G. Lorenzetti: *La pittura italiana del Settecento* (1948). F. J. B. Watson: *Canaletto* (edn. 1954) and G. Fiocco: *Francesco Guardi* (1923) are also helpful. There are two interesting essays on art in the set of lectures delivered to the Italian Institute in 1957–8, *Art and Ideas in Eighteenth-Century Italy* (1960)—Francis Haskell: "Taste and Reputation: A Study of Change in Italian Art of the 18th Century" (83–93), and Michael Levey: "Tiepolo and His Age" (94–113).

CHAPTER SIX

The Emancipation of Art: A Groping for Modernity

1. DIDEROT AND LESSING: TWO RESPECTFUL REVOLUTIONARIES

IDEROT'S AESTHETIC IDEAS have aroused widespread interest.
Works on eighteenth-century aesthetics, notably the histories
by Wellek, Gilbert and Kuhn, Bäumler, Folkierski, and Dresdner—
especially the last two—and Dieckmann's general essays, have important pages devoted to him; I am particularly indebted to Dresdner
and Dieckmann (for all these titles, see above, 632–6).

Paul Vernière has supplied his edition of Diderot's *Œuvres
esthétiques* (1959) with good brief introductions and notes; it is not
quite complete—the Salons, especially, are excerpted, but here we
are fortunate in having them complete, in critical editions, containing
most of the pictures described, in 4 vols., eds. Jean Seznec and Jean
Adhémar: *Salons,* I (1759, 1761, 1763), II (1765), III (1767), and
IV (1769, 1771, 1775, 1781), (published respectively in 1957, 1960,
1963, 1968). I found Joseph L. Waldauer: *Society and the Freedom
of the Creative Man in Diderot's Thought, Diderot Studies,* V
(1964), a modestly useful essay; in contrast, I learned much from
Gilman: *Idea of Poetry in France* (cited above, 629), especially
chap. ii, "A New Vision of Poetry: Diderot," which ranges far more
widely than the title suggests. Two other essays by Margaret Gilman are of considerable interest here: "Imagination and Creation in
Diderot," *Diderot Studies,* II (1952), 200–20; and "The Poet According to Diderot," *Romanic Review,* XXXVII (1946), 37–54. See
also Hubert Gillot: *Denis Diderot: l'homme, ses idées philosophiques,*

esthétiques, littéraires (1937). For his début as a critic, see Paul H. Meyer: "The 'Lettre sur les sourds et muets' and Diderot's Emerging Concept of the Critic," *Diderot Studies*, VI (1964), 133–55, and Meyer's critical edition of the *Lettre*, ibid., VII (1965), which has an interesting prefatory essay by Georges May, "A l'usage de ceux qui lisent la lettre sur le sourds et muets," xiii–xxvi. Pierre Francastel: "L'Esthétique des Lumières," in *Utopie et institutions: Le Pragmatisme des Lumières* (1963), has some informative observations on the comprehensiveness and practicality of Diderot's criticism, which he connects to Diderot's whole view of culture.

The main disagreement among historians is whether Diderot's aesthetic ideas form a single coherent system or not. Felix Wexler: *Studies in Diderot's Esthetic Naturalism* (1922), mainly devoted to Diderot's drama and dramatic theory, holds that it does; so does Yvon Bélaval's more recent and more subtle *L'esthétique sans paradoxe de Diderot* (1950). Lester G. Crocker: "Subjectivism and Objectivism in Diderot's Esthetics," in his *Two Diderot Studies: Ethics and Esthetics* (1952), is more skeptical, and more convincing. Crocker's essay, which systematically if briefly pursues Diderot's aesthetic ideas from subject to subject, is a welcome corrective, although it suffers from a lack of historical sense: "Diderot's most frequent and consistent precept," Crocker writes, for example, "is the use of the 'modèle idéal' " (68), a statement he could not have made had he pursued Diderot's ideas as they developed.

Herbert Dieckmann has two brilliant chapters—"Questions d'esthétique" and "Les Salons"—in *Cinq Leçons sur Diderot* (above, 596), which analyze the slow growth and eventual subtlety of Diderot's aesthetic perception, and its starting point—his experience; he rightly insists that the mature Diderot is a truly *philosophical* critic, embracing theory, transcending subjectivity, including in his vision both the artist's and the public's point of view. My own reading of Diderot is very close to his. In the same connection I should pay tribute once again to Leo Spitzer's fine "The Style of Diderot," in *Linguistics and Literary History* (see above, 629), which sheds light on the connection between Diderot's sensuality and his aesthetic ideas. The chapter on "L'humanisme et l'art," in Jean Thomas's essay *L'humanisme de Diderot* (2d edn., 1938), recognizes his development. I am also indebted, as so often, to Arthur Wilson's *Diderot: The Testing Years* (esp. chaps. xx and xxiv, on the first two plays), from which I have derived much information, and been led to some passages in Diderot's own writings. See also Jacques Proust: "Le paradoxe du *Fils Naturel,*" *Diderot Studies,* IV (1963), 209–20. Roger Lewinter has examined "L'exaltation de la vertu dans le théâtre de Diderot," ibid., VIII (1966), 119–70, an important study. (For the French theater in Diderot's time, see especially H. Carrington Lancaster's encyclopedic *French Tragedy in the Time of Louis XV and Voltaire, 1715–1774,* 2 vols. [1950], and the important revisionist study by John Lough: *Paris Theatre Audiences in the Seventeenth and Eighteenth Centuries* [1957], particularly part III, "From Marivaux to Beaumarchais," which makes two highly significant points: the audience did not markedly shift from aristocracy to bourgeoisie; and Diderot's own first two plays, although they are advertised as bourgeois, have mainly aristocratic characters [250–2], two points I accept. Lough's book corrects, though it does not wholly displace, Félix Gaiffe: *Étude sur le drame en France au XVIIIᵉ siècle* [1910].) For Diderot's own dramatic theories, see the valuable chapter (ii) "Diderot théoricien du drame," in Roland Mortier: *Diderot en Allemagne: (1750–1850)* (1954). Diderot's reliance on, and relation to, Goldoni has been examined in Herbert Dieckmann: *Diderot und Goldoni* (1961). As for his mysterious last play: J. Undank has provided a superb critical edition of, with variants, and a long interesting "Introduction," to *Est-il bon? Est-il méchant?, VS,* XVI (1961).

Diderot's *Paradoxe sur le comédien* belongs here. The dialogue remains, as Vernière puts it (*Œuvres esthétiques,* 291), among Diderot's most widely read, most commented upon, and most argued about works. I have used Vernière's edition, ibid., 299–381. Belaval's *L'esthétique sans paradoxe de Diderot* (cited above, 651), is directed, of course, mainly at the *Paradoxe.* Among the actors and producers who have wrestled with it Louis Jouvet's *Le comédien désincarné* (1954) is perhaps the most interesting. Arthur M. Wilson's "The Biographical Implications of Diderot's *Paradoxe sur le comédien,*" *Diderot Studies,* III (1961), 369–83, firmly connects the work with Diderot's life and also properly insists on Diderot's careful craftsmanship and the evolution of his aesthetic ideas—a point that is central to my section on Diderot in the text. Dieckmann has an important essay on "Le thème de l'acteur dans la pensée de Diderot," *Cahiers de l'association internationale des Études Françaises*, No. 13 (1961), 157–72.

Diderot's art criticism has naturally engaged practically all students of his work; most important among the writers I have already cited are Dieckmann, Spitzer, and Thomas. Seznec's and Adhémar's edition of the *Salons* (cited above, 650) is provided with good, if rather short, Introductions, and with valuable apparatus. The destructive critique of Fernand Brunetière, especially in his *Nouvelles études critiques sur l'histoire de la littérature française* (1882), 295–321, which is only of historical interest, is convincingly refuted in Dresdner: *Entstehung der Kunstkritik*, 244–8. See also Funt: *Diderot and the Esthetics of the Enlightenment* (see above, 630), and several discriminating essays by Gita May: "Diderot devant la magie de Rembrandt," *PMLA*, LXXIV, 4, part 1 (September 1959), 387–97; and "Diderot et la Présentation au Temple de Giotto," *Modern Language Notes*, LXXV, 3 (March 1960), 229–33. Her "Diderot and Burke: A Study in Aesthetic Affinity," *PMLA*, LXXV, 5 (December 1960), 527–39, shows Diderot's wide reading. Jean Seznec has proved that Diderot continued to respect the neoclassical hierarchies in painting, in "Diderot and Historical Painting," *Aspects of the Eighteenth Century*, 129–42. I largely agree with Georges May's stimulating and outspoken essays "Diderot pessimiste" and "Diderot entre le réel et le roman," in his *Quatre visages de Denis Diderot* (1951), 34–99, 156–209; they argue (among other things) that Diderot underwent a kind of crisis around 1760–1, and that part of his recovery—as well as of his self-education away from his early aesthetics—came from the fortuitous and fortunate assignment as art critic that Grimm imposed on him. Diderot's contempt for the *"amateurs"* and *"connoisseurs"*—a fascinating subject which, coupled with Falconet's, Hogarth's, and Reynolds's similar feelings, would make an interesting study in the sociology of art—is well analyzed in Jean Seznec: *Essais sur Diderot et l'Antiquité* (1957), chap. v, "Le Singe Antiquaire [I, 456].

Diderot the novelist has also been widely appreciated. I found Alice Green Fredman: *Diderot and Sterne* (1955) a generally perceptive study in comparative literature; her account of the evolution of Diderot's sensibility seems reasonable to me, although I think, at the same time, that she rather overestimates (in company with Bela-

val) the coherence and consistency of Diderot's aesthetic thought—
Diderot himself knew better. Georges May has made a good case for
one of Diderot's most puzzling productions, in his *Diderot et "La
Religieuse"* (1954), a book also used to advantage by Spitzer in his
brilliant essay on "The Style of Diderot" (see above, 629). See also
Dieckmann's careful textual analysis "The *Préface-Annexe* of *La
Religieuse*," *Diderot Studies*, II (1952), 21–40; and Jacques Proust:
"Nouvelles Recherches sur *la Religieuse*," ibid., VI (1964), 197–214;
and the critical edition of *La religieuse* by Robert Mauzi (1961).[8]

For *Jacques le fataliste*, see J. Robert Loy: *Diderot's Determined Fatalist: A Critical Appreciation of "Jacques le fataliste"*
(1950); Robert Mauzi: "La parodie romanesque dans *Jacques le
Fataliste*," *Diderot Studies*, VI (1964), 89–132; and the essay by
Lester G. Crocker, "*Jacques le fataliste*, an *Expérience morale*," in
ibid., III (1961), 73–99.

Diderot's complicated views on genius have been brilliantly expounded by Herbert Dieckmann, in "Diderot's Conception of Genius," *JHI*, II, 2 (April 1941), 151–82, from which I have borrowed
although I do not quite accept its results—Diderot's view of genius,
I think, developed rather more than Dieckmann shows in this fine
essay. On the same subject see also Otis Fellows: "The Theme of
Genius in Diderot's *Neveu de Rameau*," *Diderot Studies*, II (1952),
168–99.

Rousseau's attitude toward the theater has occupied his biographers, above all Gaspard Vallette, in *Jean-Jacques Rousseau Genevois* (1911), book II, chap. i. M. Fuchs has produced a critical edition of Rousseau's *Lettre à M. d'Alembert sur les spectacles* (1948),
with a helpful introduction; Allan Bloom has translated the *Lettre*
under the title *Politics and the Arts: Letter to Mr. d'Alembert on the
Theatre* (1960), and provided an apologetic Introduction which I,
for one, find unconvincing. Recently, Robert Niklaus has confronted
Rousseau with his old friend Diderot on this issue: "Diderot et Rousseau: Pour et contre le théâtre," *Diderot Studies*, IV (1963), 153–89.

---

[8] Of all the books on the eighteenth-century French novel I have
consulted, two have been most useful to me—Georges May's brilliant *Le dilemme du roman au XVIIIe siècle: étude sur les rapports
du roman et de la critique, 1715–1761* (1963), and Vivienne Mylne's
judicious survey *The Eighteenth-Century French Novel: Techniques of Illusion* (1965).

Two books place Rousseau into the general literary environment— Margaret M. Moffat: *Rousseau et la querelle du théâtre au XVIIIe siècle* (1930), and M. Barras: *The Stage Controversy in France from Corneille to Rousseau* (1933). Finally, see the introductory remarks by Jacques Scherer to the theatrical writings in Rousseau: *Œuvres*, II, lxxx–lxxxix.

Diderot's impact abroad, especially on Germany and Lessing, has been thoroughly and authoritatively explored by Roland Mortier in his *Diderot en Allemagne* (see above, 652). An early essay by Herbert Dieckmann: "Goethe und Diderot," *Vierteljahresschrift für Literaturwissenschaft und Geistesgeschichte*, X (1932), 478–503, traces an important dependence. Diderot's affinity and close resemblance to Lessing has been noticed by several historians, notably Erich Schmidt, in his *Lessing: Geschichte seines Lebens und seiner Schriften*, 2 vols. (2d edn., 1899), I, 300–11; and, following Schmidt, W. H. Bruford: *Theatre, Drama and Audience in Goethe's Germany* (1950), 133; and, independently, Seznec: *Diderot et l'antiquité*, chap. iv, "Un *Laocoön* français." See also Robert R. Heitner: "Concerning Lessing's Indebtedness to Diderot," *Modern Language Notes*, LXV, 2 (February 1950), 82–8, and, for the reverse, Heitner: "Diderot's Own *Miss Sara Sampson*," *Comparative Literature*, V, 1 (Winter 1953), 40–9.

For Lessing's aesthetic ideas see, in addition to the titles I have cited above, also Folke Leander: *Lessing als aesthetischer Denker* (1942), and Benno von Wiese: *Lessing: Dichtung, Aesthetik, Philosophie* (1931), [I, 440]. Ernst Gombrich: "Lessing," in *Proceedings of the British Academy*, XXXXV (1957), 133–56, is a suggestive lecture. I have used the excellent critical edition of *Laocoön* by Hugo Blümner (2d edn., 1880), which has a long Introduction and full annotations. Bruford: *Theatre, Drama and Audience in Goethe's Germany* has a sensible survey of Lessing's work and ideas; Dilthey's essay on Lessing in *Das Erlebnis und die Dichtung* (edn. 1912), [I, 441], is enthusiastic and immensely stimulating. For Lessing's important correspondence with his friends on the subject of tragedy, Robert Petsch's edition, *Lessings Briefwechsel mit Mendelssohn und Nicolai über das Trauerspiel* (1910) is decisive. J. G. Robertson: *Lessing's Dramatic Theory: Being an Introduction to and Commentary on his Hamburgische Dramaturgie* (1939) fulfills the promise of its title; see also, J. Clivio: *Lessing und das Problem der Tragödie*

(1928), and the thoroughgoing, fully annotated study by Robert R. Heitner, *German Tragedy in the Age of Enlightenment: A Study in the Development of Original Tragedies, 1724–1768* (1963). Finally, Bronislawa Rosenthal: *Der Geniebegriff der Aufklärungszeit* (1933), which deals particularly with Lessing and the so-called popular Enlightenment in Germany.

2. THE DISCOVERY OF TASTE

For the revival of neoclassicism, see the titles listed above. The history of the theory of proportions is lucidly laid out in Rudolf Wittkower: "The Changing Concept of Proportion," *Daedalus*, LXXXIX, 1 (Winter 1960), 199–215, and in his earlier briefer essay, "Systems of Proportion," *Architects' Year Book*, V (1955), 9–18, with full bibliographical indications. I have supplemented it with Erwin Panofsky's fascinating "The History of the Theory of Human Proportions as a Reflection of the History of Styles" (1921; now easily available in Panofsky: *Meaning in the Visual Arts* [1955], 55–107).

I owe the reference to Piranesi's eclecticism to Summerson: *Architecture in Britain* (above, 642), 238–9.

The most comprehensive study of Winckelmann, itself a work of art, remains the old biography by Carl Justi: *Winckelmann und seine Zeitgenossen*, 3 vols. (5th edn., 1956), [I, 459]. I have supplemented it with Henry Hatfield's judicious studies, *Winckelmann and His German Critics* (1943); *Aesthetic Paganism in German Literature* (1964), [I, 460], chap. i; and his brief but not unimportant paper, "Winckelmann: The Romantic Element," *The Germanic Review*, XXVIII, 4 (December 1953), 282–9. On Winckelmann's conversion, in addition to Justi, see Werner Schultze: "Winckelmann und die Religion," *Archiv für Kulturgeschichte*, XXXIV (1952), 247–60. E. M. Butler: *The Tyranny of Greece over Germany* (1935) on the hostile side and Walther Rehm: *Griechentum und Goethezeit* (1936) on the adulatory side [see I, 459–60] both need to be corrected by Hatfield. Friedrich Meinecke's celebrated *Die Entstehung des Historismus*, 2 vols. (1936), has some sensitive pages on Winckelmann (313-24), including his erotic epistemology and the strange ambivalence about history; but to my mind Meinecke (here as elsewhere) gravely underestimates the historical urge of the Enlightenment and equally gravely overestimates the contribution of German Protestantism, and German thought in general, to historical ways of thinking. Udo Kultermann: *Geschichte der Kunstgeschichte: Der Weg einer Wissenschaft* (1966), though chatty and superficial, places Winckelmann into a long tradition.

The best book on the abbé Dubos, from which I have learned much, is by A. Lombard: *L'Abbé Du Bos, un initiateur de la pensée moderne (1670-1742)* (1913). See also E. Teuber: "Die Kunstphilosophie des Abbé Dubos," *Zeitschrift für Aesthetik und allgemeine Kunstwissenschaft*, XVII (1924), 361-410. Montesquieu's aesthetic relativism has been analyzed in Charles Jacques Beyer: "Montesquieu et le relativisme esthétique," *VS*, XXIV (1963), 171-82, while Jean Ehrard: *Montesquieu: Critique d'art* (1965) has carefully followed Montesquieu's voyages to analyze the evolution of his taste. Robert Shackleton, whose biography *Montesquieu* (1961) is standard [I, 436], has dealt with "Montesquieu et les beaux-arts," in *Atti del Vᵒ Congresso internazionale di lingue e letterature moderne* (1955), 249-53. Beyer's critical edition of Montesquieu's *Essai sur le goût* (1967) is very useful. Hume's aesthetic ideas have been subjected to massive treatment by Olivier Brunet, in his *Philosophie et esthétique chez David Hume* (1965), which says far more than needs to be said; while it is good to have careful analyses of Hume's aesthetic pronouncements—for they were important, and closely linked to his general philosophical system—there is no need for exegeses of Hume's short articles many times as long as the articles themselves. It is worth noting that both Wellek (*History of Modern Criticism*, I, 107) and Cassirer (*Philosophy of the Enlightenment*, 307) misread Hume's statement of the extreme skeptical case as Hume's own position, which, as I show, it is not. Hugh Blair's *Lectures on Rhetoric and Belles Lettres*, mainly of historical interest now, have recently (1965) been edited, in two volumes, by Harold F. Harding; *Adam Smith's Lectures on Rhetoric and Belles Lettres*, interesting for themselves and fascinating for the light they shed on a great economist, have also been published now (1963), edited by John M. Lothian. For Burke, see above all the excellent critical edition of his *A Philosophical Enquiry into the Origin of our Ideas of the Sublime and Beautiful* by J. T. Boulton (1958), and the old comparative study by Georg Candrea: *Der Begriff des Erhabenen bei Burke und Kant* (1894). And see the pages on Burke (333–6) in J. W. H. Atkins: *English Literary Criticism: 17th and 18th Centuries* (1951). Samuel H. Monk: *The Sublime: A Study of Critical Theories in XVIII-Century England* (1935) is a brilliantly succinct survey of a complex theme that necessarily deals prominently with Burke, and includes in addition to other British critics, like Addison and Lord Kames, non-British writers from Boileau to Kant. It can be supplemented by Monk's elucidation of an important commonplace of Pope's, " 'A Grace beyond the Reach of Art,' " *JHI*, V, 2 (April 1944), 131–50. Among other of her books, Marjorie Hope Nicolson's *Mountain Gloom and Mountain Glory: The Development of the Aesthetics of the Infinite* (1959) is a particularly interesting contribution to thinking on sublime matters.

For Kant's aesthetics, I am indebted to Hermann Cohen: *Kants Begründung der Aesthetik* (1889), to Victor Basch: *Essai critique sur l'esthétique de Kant* (2d edn., 1927), and to H. W. Cassirer: *A Commentary on Kant's Critique of Judgment* (1938). See also R. W. Bretall: "Kant's Theory of the Sublime," *The Heritage of Kant*, eds. G. T. Whitney and D. F. Bowers (1939), 379–402; Theodore M. Greene: "A Reassessment of Kant's Aesthetic Theory," ibid., 323–56; and René Wellek: "Aesthetics and Criticism," in *The Philosophy of Kant and Our Modern World* (above, 634), 65–89, an excellent essay. Giorgio Tonelli has examined "Kant's Early Theory of Genius (1770–1779), part I," *Journal of the History of Philosophy*, IV, 2 (April 1966), 109–31, and "part II," ibid., IV, 3 (July 1966), 209–24. For the place of Kant's aesthetics in his general system, I have relied most on Ernst Cassirer: *Kants Leben und Lehre*; Lindsay: *Kant*; the brief, introductory, but helpful S. Körner: *Kant* (1955); and Adickes: "Kant als Aesthetiker" (see above, 634).

CHAPTER SEVEN

The Science of Society

I. THE FIRST SOCIAL SCIENTISTS

THERE ARE SEVERAL ATTEMPTS at the history of the social sciences, none really satisfactory. The writing of that history has been marred by false perspectives, especially by the notion that all preceding work leads up to and somehow culminates in the present. Against this, J. W. Burrow's impressive *Evolution and Society: A Study in Victorian Social Theory* (1966)—which, despite its title, has much to say on eighteenth-century social inquiry—has issued a timely warning; the book eminently repays close reading. I found a certain amount of useful material in Harry Elmer Barnes, ed.: *An Introduction to the History of Sociology* (1948), and in the relevant chapters of A. Wolf (see above, 611). Raymond Aron: *Main Currents in Sociological Thought,* I, *Montesquieu, Comte, Marx, Tocqueville, The Sociologists and the Revolution of 1848* (1960; tr. Richard Howard and Helen Weaver, 1965), is a rewarding analysis, full of ideas. So is Robert A. Nisbet: *The Sociological Tradition* (1966), an intelligent, systematic investigation into what sociology in fact is. Robert K. Merton: *Social Theory and Social Structure* (1957) offers a brilliant collection of essays on theory, functionalism, and various major sociologists; Merton has revised part of that book and written a suggestive essay, "On the History and Systematics of Sociological Theory," in *On Theoretical Sociology* (1967), 1–37; but, as Merton observes, much historical work needs to be done. Some of it is being done now by the students of Paul F. Lazarsfeld.

Lazarsfeld himself has made a significant beginning on the history of quantification; see "Notes on the History of Quantification in Sociology—Trends, Sources and Problems," in *Quantification: A History of the Meaning of Measurement in the Natural and Social*

Sciences, ed. Harry Woolf (1961), 147–203. For a tendentious, hostile, but not complete perverse view of the rage for numbers in the Enlightenment, see Louis I. Bredvold: "The Invention of the Ethical Calculus," in R. F. Jones *et al.*: *The Seventeenth Century* (1951), 165–80; and *The Brave New World of the Enlightenment* (1961), *passim*, especially chap. ii, "The New Promise of Science," [I, 429]. Gilles-Gaston Granger: *La mathématique sociale du marquis de Condorcet* (1956) is a fascinating monograph; it recounts the attempts of a remarkable philosophe-mathematician to introduce quantitative analysis into social and political questions.

In the eighteenth century, social science and cultural relativism were inextricably intertwined, and travelers' reports formed the raw material for cultural relativism. Here much work is being done. Claude Lévy-Strauss, an eloquent defender of Rousseau as a social scientist, has movingly portrayed Christian man's discovery of other cultures as a "terrible ordeal," unprecedented and never to be repeated, "unless there should one day be revealed to us another earth, many millions of miles distant, with thinking beings upon it." *Tristes Tropiques* (1955; tr. John Russell, 1961, edn. 1964), 78–9. He is right, but only partly: for many, this discovery was a thrilling event. On Rousseau as a founding father of the social sciences, see Lévy-Strauss: "Jean-Jacques Rousseau, fondateur des sciences de l'homme," in Samuel Baud-Bovy, *et al.*: *Jean-Jacques Rousseau* (1962), 239–48.

For accounts of the impact of non-European cultures on the European consciousness, see the entries above (chap. ii, section 2), and add Geoffroy Atkinson: *Les Relations de voyages du XVIIe siècle et l'évolution des idées: Contribution à l'étude de la formation de l'esprit du XVIIIe siècle* (1924); and Pierre Martino: *L'Orient dans la littérature française au XVIIe et au XVIIIe siècle* (1906) for France; and William W. Appleton: *A Cycle of Cathay: The Chinese Vogue in England during the 17th and 18th Centuries* (1951), which has much material, for England. Among the Germans, Leibniz has been studied most carefully; see the now old Louis Davillé: *Leibnitz historien* (1909) and the more recent article by Donald Lach, "Leibniz and China," *JHI*, VI, 4 (October 1945), 436–55. In general, I found Percy G. Adams: *Travelers and Travel Liars, 1660–1800* (1962), a treatment of imaginary voyages served up as realistic reports, highly amusing and highly instructive.

2: SOCIOLOGY: FACTS, FREEDOM, AND HUMANITY

2. SOCIOLOGY: FACTS, FREEDOM, AND HUMANITY

On the possibility of sociology becoming not merely intellectually retrograde but politically reactionary, see Albert Salomon's impassioned attack on Comte, Saint-Simon, and others, prophets of progress who became theocrats, in *The Tyranny of Progress: Reflections on the Origins of Sociology* (1955). Compare the similar indictment of positivism in Herbert Marcuse: *Reason and Revolution: Hegel and the Rise of Social Theory* (1941), from a totally different intellectual orientation (Hegel and Marx, who are the villains of Salomon's book, are the heroes of Marcuse's). Clearly, Salomon and Marcuse cannot both be wholly right; both, I think, overestimate the impact of ideas on events, but their warning that the "science of society" is not always an automatically progressive force is obviously of real value. The problem of the sociologist whose work is used for reactionary purposes that he himself disclaims is summarized in the Introduction by Charles P. Loomis and John C. McKinney to Ferdinand Tönnies: *Community and Society*, the classic of 1887 translated by Loomis in 1957.

For Montesquieu, the true father of sociology, see, in addition to Shackleton's standard biography, cited several times (note especially his chaps. ii, v, x, xii, xiv and xv), Muriel Dodds: *Les Recits de voyages, sources de l'Esprit des lois* (1929) and Arnold H. Rowbotham: "China in the *Esprit des lois:* Montesquieu and Msgr. Foucquet," *Comparative Literature*, II (1950), 354–9. Raymond Aron's chapter on Montesquieu in his *Main Currents in Sociological Thought* (just cited) is excellent; I have depended on it. Franz Neumann's "Introduction" to *Spirit of the Laws* (see above, 629) is incisive and comprehensive; it taught me a great deal. Neumann tends to see Montesquieu—as do I—interested in classical questions concerning the good government; against this must be put Émile Durkheim's important, suggestive, but not persuasive "La contribution de Montesquieu à la constitution de la science sociale," Durkheim's Latin thesis of 1892, translated into French by M. F. Alengry and reprinted in Durkheim: *Montesquieu et Rousseau*,

Précurseurs de la sociologie (1953), which treats him as an early modern positivist. For Montesquieu's relativism, see the article by Charles Jacques Beyer: "Montesquieu et le relativisme esthétique" (cited above, 657), which moves into aesthetics from sociology. Montesquieu's significant intellectual ancestor, the abbé Dubos, has been well treated as a proto-sociologist in A. Lombard: *L'Abbé Du Bos* (cited above, 657), 239–68.

For the Scottish sociologists, though deeply in debt to Montesquieu still an original and significant group, see above all the general, intelligent survey by Gladys Bryson: *Man and Society: The Scottish Inquiry of the Eighteenth Century* (see above, 597), which reports on the transition from moral philosophy to social science. Louis Schneider's anthology, *The Scottish Moralists on Human Nature and Society* (1967), which offers selected passages from eight Scottish writers including Ferguson, Hume, and Adam Smith, is only mildly helpful. Bryson should be supplemented by William C. Lehmann: *Adam Ferguson and the Beginnings of Modern Sociology* (1930); Herta Helena Jogland: *Ursprünge und Grundlagen der Soziologie bei Adam Ferguson* (1959), [both I, 431]; and above all by David Kettler: *The Social and Political Thought of Adam Ferguson* (1965), a thoughtful essay. Duncan Forbes's edition of Ferguson's great work of 1767, *An Essay on the History of Civil Society* (1966), has a comprehensive introduction on which I have relied. The question of why Hume did not like Ferguson's *Essay* is discussed in Kettler: *Adam Ferguson*, 57–60; but lack of evidence makes it impossible to be conclusive. R. B. Oake: "Montesquieu and Hume," *Modern Language Quarterly*, II, 1 (March 1941), 25–41 and II, 2 (June 1941), 225–48, traces the influence of one sociologist on another. On another sociologist, John Millar, see William C. Lehmann: *John Millar of Glasgow, 1735–1801: His Life and Thought and His Contributions to Sociological Analysis* (1960), a sober survey with long selections from Millar's writings thoughtfully appended. There is an important article on him by Duncan Forbes, " 'Scientific Whiggism': Adam Smith and John Millar," *The Cambridge Journal*, VII, 11 (August 1954), 643–70, which shows both philosophers as writing manifestos quite as much as treatises, and concerned (especially Millar, as a "militant Whig") quite as much to change as to explain the world (651).

3. POLITICAL ECONOMY: FROM POWER TO WEALTH

The prehistory of the science of political economy—that is, the history of the discipline before Adam Smith—appears prominently, in the context of economic realities, in T. S. Ashton: *An Economic History of England: The Eighteenth Century*, Phyllis Deane: *The First Industrial Revolution*, and Charles Wilson: *England's Apprenticeship*, all very valuable books (all cited above, 573–9). Douglas Vickers: *Studies in the Theory of Money, 1690–1776* (1959) moves from John Locke to Adam Smith, across the eighteenth century. See also E. A. J. Johnson: *Predecessors of Adam Smith* (1937), and "The Place of Learning, Science, Vocational Training, and 'Art' in Pre-Smithian Economic Thought," *The Journal of Political Economy*, XXIV, 2 (June 1964), 129–44. Among studies of early economists, that by E. Strauss on *Sir William Petty* (1954) is particularly illuminating. The most important source for these pages, however, was William Letwin's informative and well-considered *The Origins of Scientific Economics: English Economic Thought 1660–1776* (1963), from which I have learned much. Letwin's thesis that the thought of Adam Smith rests mainly on his late seventeenth- and early eighteenth-century predecessors has been challenged by Raymond de Roover: "Scholastic Economics: Survival and Lasting Influence from the 16th Century to Adam Smith," *Quarterly Journal of Economics*, LXIX, 2 (May 1955), 161–90, which usefully stresses survivals, but, I think, overstates its case.

The classic study of mercantilism is still Eli F. Heckscher: *Mercantilism*, 2 vols., first published in Swedish in 1931, translated into English by Mendel Shapiro in 1935, and now available in a second edition, revised by E. F. Söderlund. It replaces the earlier, though still interesting, volume by Gustav von Schmoller: *The Mercantile System and its Historical Significance* (1884; tr. W. J. Ashley, 1896). The thesis common to both books, that mercantilism is an economic policy devoted to political ends, and that it determines the shape of foreign and military policy, has been eloquently challenged by Sir George Clark: *War and Society in the 17th Century* (1958), 68 ff.; and their thesis that mercantilism is almost exclusively a system of power has been challenged, just as eloquently, by Jacob Viner: "Power versus Plenty as Objectives of Foreign Policy in the Seventeenth and Eighteenth Centuries," *World Politics*, I, 1 (October 1948), 1–29 (now conveniently in Viner: *The Long View and the Short: Studies in Economic Theory and Policy* [1958], 277–305). I have taken full account of these objections in the text, but the brute fact of seventeenth-century power politics, with power first and welfare second, remains. Charles W. Cole: *French Mercantilist Doctrines before Colbert* (1931) and his comprehensive *Colbert and a Century of French Mercantilism*, 2 vols. (1939), concentrate on one—perhaps the crucial—country.

The book by Albion Small: *The Cameralists: The Pioneers of German Social Polity* (1909), though now old, can still be consulted with profit. George Rosen: "Cameralism and the Concept of Medical Police," *Bulletin of the History of Medicine*, XXVII, 1 (January–February 1953), 21–42, is a fascinating account of the authoritarian German (and Hapsburg) theory of *Polizey* as applied to medicine; see also Rosen: *A History of Public Health* (1958). For the Austrian Cameralists, see L. Sommer: *Die österreichischen Kameralisten in dogmengeschichtlicher Darstellung*, 2 vols. (1920, 1925).

The most significant work in rehabilitating the Physiocrats has been done by Ronald L. Meek: *The Economics of Physiocracy* (1962), which contains a brilliant long Introduction by the editor, an equally brilliant set of apologetic essays, and lengthy excerpts from relatively inaccessible writings of the Physiocrats—an altogether splendid book. It is dedicated to the memory of the great French specialist on physiocracy, Georges Weulersse, whose writings on the subject remain of great value: see his *Le mouvement physiocratique en France (de 1756 à 1770)*, 2 vols. (1910); the posthumous *La Physiocratie sous les ministères de Turgot et de Necker (1774–1781)* (1950); and the brief, popular, authoritative survey *Les Physiocrates* (1930). *François Quesnay et la physiocratie*, 2 vols., published by the Institut national d'études démographiques (1958), is an interesting collection of essays on physiocracy in general, with a fine long Introduction by Mario Einaudi. In the United States there have been several good articles defending Quesnay and his group, notably Norman J. Ware: "The Physiocrats: A Study in Economic Rationalization," *American Economic*

Review, XXI, 4 (December 1931), 607–19; and the recent essay by Thomas P. Neill: "Quesnay and Physiocracy," *JHI*, IX, 2 (April 1948), 153–73. Much light is shed on French economic theories and realities by Marc Bloch's brilliant articles "La lutte pour l'individualisme agraire dans la France du XVIIIᵉ siècle," *Annales d'Histoire Économique et Sociale*, II, 7 (July 15, 1930), 329–81, and 8 (October 15, 1930), 511–56. One much-neglected early economic thinker was Montesquieu, who has been ably rescued by Nicos E. Devletoglou, in *Montesquieu and the Wealth of Nations* (1963). On the influence of China on the Physiocrats, see Virgile Pinot: "Les Physiocrates et la Chine au XVIIIᵉ siècle," *Revue d'histoire moderne et contemporaine*, VIII (1906), 200–14; and the recent notes by Lewis A. Maverick, "Chinese Influence on the Physiocrats," *Economic History*, III (February 1938), 13, and "Supplement," ibid., IV (February 1940), 15.[9]

For British economic thinking before Adam Smith, see the volumes cited above, especially Letwin. Add to these Rotwein's edition of Hume's economic writings, cited above, 592. Adam Smith, though the subject of some first-rate monographic work, still awaits his modern biographer; John Rae: *Life of Adam Smith* (1895), though useful, is dated, and W. R. Scott: *Adam Smith as Student and Professor* (1937), [both I, 431], which has new documentation, does not pretend to be complete. Until we have the complete works, now promised, Edwin Cannan's edition of *The Wealth of Nations* (Modern Library edn., 1937) will remain standard; the Introduction is helpful. The problem of reconciling this masterpiece with the earlier *Theory of Moral Sentiments* has long occupied the scholars; the German theory of a deep split, inevitably called "Das Adam Smith-Problem," has been shrewdly and definitively disposed of by Glenn R. Morrow: *The Ethical and Economic Theories of Adam Smith: A Study in the Social Philosophy of the Eighteenth Century* (1923), [I, 431]. At the same time, a certain tension remains, beautifully captured and summarized in an important article by Jacob Viner: "Adam Smith and Laissez Faire," first published in 1927, now in *The Long View and the Short*, 213–45. In addition, I found useful John Maurice Clark *et al.*: *Adam*

---

[9] For the political thought of the Physiocrats, see below, chap. ix, section 3.

Smith, 1776–1926 (1928) and C. R. Fay: *Adam Smith and the Scotland of his Day* (1956), [both I, 431]. G. S. L. Tucker: *Progress and Profit in British Economic Thought, 1650–1850* (1960) places Adam Smith into the context of a long debate on economic progress, profits, and the rate of interest (see especially chaps. iii and iv). I have learned from the stimulating essay by Lord Robbins: *The Theory of Economic Policy in English Classical Political Economy* (1952), which moves beyond Adam Smith to his successors. The earliest of these successors, especially Jeremy Bentham, remain relevant to this book. Here I found T. W. Hutchison: "Bentham as an Economist," *The Economic Journal*, LXVI, 262 (June 1956), 288–306, a long review of W. Stark's three-volume edition of *Jeremy Bentham's Economic Writings* (1952–4), enormously helpful and stimulating; it details Bentham's gradual disenchantment with *laissez faire*. It should be read in company with J. Bartlet Brebner's important article, "Laissez Faire and State Intervention in Nineteenth-Century Britain," *Journal of Economic History*, supplement VIII (1948), 59–73, which has been reprinted with minor changes in Robert L. Schuyler and Herman Ausubel, eds: *The Making of English History* (1952), 501–10. See also Mark Blaug: "The Classical Economists and the Factory Acts: A Re-Examination," *Quarterly Journal of Economics*, LXXII, 2 (May 1958), 211–26.

The Italian political economists deserve further attention. Domenico Grimaldi, Francesco Longano, and before them, Antonio Genovesi, are little more than names; much of their work has been deservedly rescued from oblivion by the collections of Franco Venturi: *Illuministi Italiani* (cited above, 576). For the most interesting economist in the group, the philosophe Ferdinando Galiani, see now Harold Acton: "Ferdinando Galiani," in *Art and Ideas in Eighteenth-Century Italy* (cited above, 648), 45–63, a pleasant but hardly analytical essay. [See I, 442.]

4. HISTORY: SCIENCE, ART, AND PROPAGANDA

In my bibliographical essay to *The Rise of Modern Paganism*, I had occasion to deal at length with the secondary literature that has grown up around the historical writings and theories of the philosophes. Since my treatment there is very detailed, I can only refer the reader to my pages there [I, 433, 451–5], and add a few titles. My own essay on seventeenth-century historiography in America, *A Loss of Mastery: Puritan Historians in Colonial America*, deals with the prehistory of Enlightenment historiography; I concentrate on the American colonies there, but in the opening I sort out Renaissance historiography, seventeenth-century erudition, and seventeenth-century piety (see also the bibliographical essay, especially the part devoted to chap. i [123–31]). A formidable, but to my mind unconvincing, case against the historical spirit of the eighteenth century is made in R. G. Collingwood: *The Idea of History* (1946), especially 61–85. Arnaldo Momigliano's article on "Gibbon's Contribution to Historical Method" [I, 453] is now conveniently accessible in Momigliano: *Studies in Historiography* (1966), 40–55. He has also reprinted "Ancient History and the Antiquarian" [I, 452] in the same volume, 1–39. Frank E. Manuel: *Shapes of Philosophical History* (1965) lucidly traces two modes of philosophical history—the cyclical and the progressive—through the ages, and includes material on the eighteenth-century historians. Trygve R. Tholfsen: *Historical Thinking: An Introduction* (1967) is an unpretentious history of historical modes of thought, and includes a chapter (iv) on Voltaire and the historiography of the Enlightenment. René Wellek's *Rise of English Literary History* (cited above, 630) contains much that is relevant to this section. George H. Nadel traces the rise and fall of what he calls "the exemplar theory of history," which ended with historicism, in "Philosophy of History before Historicism," (1964), now in *Studies in the Philosophy of History: Selected Essays from "History and Theory,"* ed. George H. Nadel (1965), 49–73. See also the judicious monograph by Thomas P. Peardon: *The Transition in English Historical Writing, 1760–1830* (1933). The evidence for a burgeoning historical spirit in the age of the Enlightenment is everywhere. See, for instance, Shackleton's *Montesquieu*, 44–5, 153, 160 ff., 133, 337 ff., for examples of secularism and historical scholarship; Reynolds: *Portraits*, 18–21, 29, for examples of the historical mentality in Sir Joshua Reynolds's circle—notably Boswell; and Rosenblum: *Transformations in Late 18th-Century Art* (cited above, 638), for the historical spirit in art. There was historicism before historicism.

On Hume's historical work, the substantial anthology by David Fate Norton and Richard H. Popkin: *David Hume: Philosophical*

Historian (1965), with two introductory essays by the editors, one on "Skepticism and the Study of History," the other on "History and Philosophy in Hume's Thought," is worth consulting. Laurence L. Bongie has written a short study on the reception of Hume in France—*David Hume: Prophet of the Counter-Revolution* (1965). See also two sympathetic, accurate articles by Hume's biographer, Ernest Campbell Mossner: "An Apology for David Hume, Historian," *PMLA*, LVI, 3 (September 1941), 657–90; and "Was Hume a Tory Historian? Facts and Reconsiderations," *JHI*, II, 2 (April 1941), 225–36.

There is a new biography of Gibbon—Joseph Ward Swain: *Edward Gibbon the Historian* (1966); it concentrates on the man more than on the historian. H. R. Trevor-Roper (whose devastating review of Swain's biography in *The New York Review of Books*, IX, 11 [December 21, 1967] 31–4, is perhaps rather harsh), has an interesting essay on Gibbon [in addition to those cited in I, 454], "The Idea of the Decline and Fall of the Roman Empire," *The Age of the Enlightenment* (cited above, 615), 413–30. In the same volume (1–14) O. R. Taylor analyzes "Voltaire's Apprenticeship as a Historian: *La Henriade*, 1–14.

For Dubos as historian, see A. Lombard: *Du Bos* (already cited), 257–68. Hans Wolpe: *Raynal et sa machine de guerre: 'L'Histoire des deux Indes' et ses perfectionnements* (1957), [I, 437], is an excellent analysis.

CHAPTER EIGHT

The Politics of Decency

THERE ARE CHAPTERS on the philosophes' political ideas in all general treatments of the Enlightenment, notably Cassirer: *Philosophy of the Enlightenment*, Valjavec: *Geschichte der abendländischen Aufklärung* (1961), Cobban: *In Search of Humanity*, Diaz: *Filosofia e politica nel settencento francese* (1962), Mornet: *La Pensée française au XVIIIe siècle* [all I, 424–7]. For France itself there is, in addition to Diaz and Mornet, especially Kingsley Martin: *French Liberal Thought in the Eighteenth Century* (1929), [I, 435], and the man-by-man survey, economical but generally just, by Henri Sée: *L'Évolution de la pensée politique en France au XVIIIe siècle* (1925). The monographic and biographical literature on Locke, Montesquieu, Voltaire, Hume, Lessing, and others, of course has much on their political thought. This chapter and the two succeeding ones try to show that I do not find these treatments wholly satisfactory; what I have tried here has been to do for the Enlightenment as a whole what I did in 1959 for Voltaire, in my *Voltaire's Politics*: to place the political ideas of the Enlightenment into their environment.

1. TOLERATION: A PRAGMATIC CAMPAIGN

Our suffering century has looked back, with mingled anxiety and hope, to plans for peace in past centuries. Elizabeth V. Souleyman: *The Vision of World Peace in Seventeenth- and Eighteenth-Century France* (1941) has become the standard survey; more general are Sylvester John Hemleben: *Plans for World Peace Through Six Centuries* (1938) and Arthur Ch. F. Beales: *The History of*

Peace (1931). On the closely associated idea of organization for pacific purposes, see Jacob ter Meulen: *Der Gedanke der internationalen Organisation in seiner Entwicklung, 1300–1800*, 3 vols. (1917–40), and Arthur Nussbaum: *A Concise History of the Law of Nations* (1958). Peace is canvassed from an equally pacific position but a different angle of vision in Alfred Vagts: *A History of Militarism: Civilian and Military* (rev. edn., 1959). War as an institution and instrumentality of foreign policy is, of course, a leading theme for political historians of the eighteenth century; Sir George Clark: *War and Society in the 17th Century* (see above, 663), although it concentrates on the preceding century, is a stimulating introduction to the problem. And see Edmund Silberner: *La guerre dans la pensée économique du XVIe au XVIIIe siècle* (1939).

For individual lovers of peace, see Merle L. Perkins: *The Moral and Political Philosophy of the abbé de Saint-Pierre* (1959) and the same author's *Voltaire's Concept of International Order*, VS, XXXVI (1965), both orderly and informative monographs. See also Jean Daniel Candaux: "Charles Borde et la première crise d'antimilitarisme de l'opinion publique européenne," VS, XXIV (1963), 315–44. Kant's "pacifism" is at the center of Carl Joachim Friedrich's *Inevitable Peace* (1948). Rousseau's important comments on Saint-Pierre are conveniently brought together in *Œuvres*, III, 563–682, equipped with splendid notes and introductory remarks. See also the interesting monograph, including the ideas of Rousseau, Kant, and others, on the subject, by Kenneth N. Waltz: *Man, The State and War* (1959); for Rousseau, see Stanley Hoffmann: "Rousseau on War and Peace," *American Political Science Review*, LVII (June 1963), 317–33.

2. ABOLITIONISM: A PRELIMINARY PROBING

For obvious reasons, the subject of slavery is receiving a great deal of attention from historians now, most of it welcome, not all of it disinterested. These titles are only a sampling. I learned much from Kenneth M. Stampp: *The Peculiar Institution: Slavery in the Ante-Bellum South* (1956), which revises much previous work.

Though dealing with the United States alone, it provides a general setting for, and judicious opinions on, a historic crime. See also, amid a rapidly growing literature, the early pages of John Hope Franklin: *From Slavery to Freedom* (1948).

I encountered David Brion Davis: *The Problem of Slavery in Western Culture* (1966) near the end of my researches; the book is a valuable survey of ideas on slavery from antiquity through the eighteenth century. In addition to confirming my estimates of the philosophes' position, it sharpened my perception of the distinction between humane and economic arguments for abolition. Winthrop D. Jordan: *White Over Black: American Attitudes Toward the Negro, 1550–1812* (1968) came too late for me to use it. Edward D. Seeber: *Anti-Slavery Opinion in France during the Second Half of the Eighteenth Century* (1937) does what its title promises: it concentrates on opinions; so does C. L. Locke: *France and the Colonial Question: A Study of Contemporary French Opinion, 1763–1801* (1932). See also Vincent Confer: "French Colonial Ideas Before 1789," *French Historical Studies*, III, 3 (Spring 1964), 338–59. These should be supplemented by such informative monographs as Gaston-Martin: *Nantes au XVIIIᵉ siècle*, II, *L'Ère des Négriers (1714–1774)* (1931); Gaston-Martin: *Histoire de l'esclavage dans les colonies françaises* (1948); André Loisy: *Le rôle économique du port de Bordeaux* (1922); and Jacques d'Welles: *Monsieur le marquis de Tourny, intendant de Guyenne à Bordeaux et son époque, 1743–1757* (1963). For two of the most significant French philosophes concerned with this question, that is, before Condorcet and the *amis des noirs*, see again Shackleton: *Montesquieu, passim*, and Russell Parsons Jameson: *Montesquieu et l'esclavage: étude sur les origines de l'opinion antiesclavagiste en France au XVIIIᵉ siècle* (1911); and, for Raynal, again Hans Wolpe: *Raynal et sa machine de guerre*, a valuable monograph [I, 437]; and Dallas D. Irvine: "The Abbé Raynal and British Humanitarianism," *Journal of Modern History*, III, 4 (December 1931), 564–77, useful mainly to show the number of the British editions of the *Histoire des deux Indes*. For excerpts, topically arranged, from Raynal's *Histoire*, with an Introduction, see Gabriel Esquer, ed.: *L'anticolonialisme au XVIIIᵉ siècle* (1951). Finally, Shelby T. McCloy offers a brief but helpful survey of conditions and opinions in two chapters of his *Humanitarian Movement in Eighteenth-Century France* (above, 592), "Antislavery Sentiment Prior to 1789," and "Exit Slavery and the Slave Trade," which takes the story into the Revolution.

For Britain, see Frank J. Klingberg: *The Anti-Slavery Movement in England: A Study in English Humanitarianism* (1926); and Klingberg: "The Evolution of the Humanitarian Spirit in Eighteenth-Century England" (1942), now in Schuyler and Ausubel, eds.: *The Making of English History*, 450–61; as well as the short authoritative essay by R. Coupland: *The British Anti-Slavery Movement* (1933), and, also by Coupland: *Wilberforce* (1923). On a pioneering eighteenth-century abolitionist, E. C. P. Lascelles: *Granville Sharp and the Freedom of Slaves in England* (1928) is most instructive. For literary evidence—but that alone— Wylie Sypher: *Guinea's Captive Kings: British Anti-Slavery Literature of the XVIIIth Century* (1942) has collected a good deal of material. Eric Williams: *Capitalism and Slavery* (1944) soberly examines the economic realities of the trade; K. G. Davies: *The Royal African Company* (1957) analyzes the slave-trading monopoly and its career in the late seventeenth and early eighteenth centuries. Richard Pares did some splendid studies on the history of the West Indies, notably *War and Trade in the West Indies, 1739–1763* (1936), and his last work, "Merchants and Planters," *The Economic History Review*, supplement No. 4 (1960). For slave-trading cities, C. M. MacInnes: *A Gateway of Empire* (1939) is good on Bristol; and see W. E. Minchington: *The Trade of Bristol in the Eighteenth Century* (1957). C. Northcote Parkinson: *The Rise of the Port of Liverpool* (1952), though marred by some puerile obiter dicta, has excellent statistics and quotations from contemporary sources; see also Averil Mackenzie-Grieve: *The Last Years of the English Slave Trade, Liverpool, 1750–1807* (1941).

3. JUSTICE: A LIBERAL CRUSADE

General histories of the criminal law have a tendency to be too general, almost breathless. Carl Ludwig Von Bar *et al.*: *A History of Continental Criminal Law*, tr. Thomas S. Bell *et al.* (1916), for all its usefulness, suffers from this brevity. In contrast, Leon

Radzinowicz: *A History of English Criminal Law and Its Administration*, 3 vols. (1948–56), especially I, *The Movement for Reform* (1948), is informative and precise, and helpful not for Britain alone. In addition, I used Sir Frank MacKinnon: "The Law and the Lawyers," in Turberville: *Johnson's England*, II, 287–309. Though old, Sir James Fitzjames Stephen's *History of the Criminal Law of England*, 3 vols. (1883), still repays study. James Heath: *Eighteenth Century Penal Theory* (1963) offers an anthology of legal ideas on the reform of the criminal law, with crisp introductions. Two of Coleman Phillipson's *Three Criminal Law Reformers* (1923) are Bentham and Romilly. For Bentham's theory of law, once again the classic work by Elie Halévy: *The Growth of Philosophical Radicalism* is decisive.

The standard histories of French law are on the whole satisfactory; see especially A. Esmein: *Histoire de la procédure criminelle en France* (1882). Albert Du Boys: *Histoire du droit criminel de la France depuis le XVIᵉ siècle jusqu'au XIXᵉ siècle*, 2 vols. (1874), has interesting comparisons with law in other states; see also Robert Anchel: *Crimes et châtiments au XVIIIᵉ siècle* (2d edn., 1933). I refer the reader to my *Voltaire's Politics*, chap. vi, "Ferney: The Man of Calas," which discusses in detail Voltaire's involvement in legal cases and his polemics; the bibliography contains additional titles. David D. Bien: *The Calas Affair: Persecution, Toleration, and Heresy in Eighteenth-Century Toulouse* (1960) intelligently places the most celebrated of French *causes célèbres* into social perspective.

Beccaria still awaits his definitive biographer. For now, see Cesare Cantú: *Beccaria e il diritto penale* (1862), and Carlo Antonio Vianello: *La vita e l'opera di Cesare Beccaria con scritti e documenti inediti* (1938). Franco Venturi has a fine biographical article in the *Dizionario Biografico Degli Italiani*, VII (1965), 459–69; and his edition of Beccaria's *Dei delitti e delle pene* (1965) is splendid—it contains an informative Introduction and a collection of documents illustrating the reception of Beccaria's treatise in the Italian States, France, and elsewhere. The text of this edition, with much abbreviated apparatus, has been translated into French by M. Chevallier (1965). There is a complete edition of Beccaria's *Opera*, 2 vols. (1958), edited by Sergio Romagnoli. Among monographs, see Marcello T. Maestro: *Voltaire and Beccaria as Reformers of Criminal Law* (1942), an unimaginative but accurate comparison of two great reformers. Coleman Phillipson: *Three Criminal Law Reformers*, just cited, has a full essay on Beccaria, which deals with his life, environment, and influence. Although I made my own translation, I consulted the accurate recent version of *On Crimes and Punishments* (1963), by Henry Paolucci. These works all refer to Beccaria's enormous influence at home and abroad; for America, see Paul M. Spurlin: "Beccaria's *Essay on Crimes and Punishments* in eighteenth-century America," *VS*, XVII (1963), 1489–1504; and David Brion Davis: "The Movement to Abolish Capital Punishment in America, 1787–1861," *American Historical Review*, LXIII, 1 (October 1957), 23–46.

CHAPTER NINE

The Politics of Experience

I. THE VARIETIES OF POLITICAL EXPERIENCE[1]

For the "science of politics," as d'Argenson and Saint-Pierre used the phrase, Joseph Gallanar: "Argenson's 'Platonic Republics,'" *VS*, LVI (1967), 557-75, is instructive; see also G. N. Clark: *War and Society in the Seventeenth Century* (cited in the previous chapter), 213-15. Two studies by Sergio Cotta—*Montesquieu e la scienza della società* (1953), and a fine short article, "L'illuminisme et la science politique: Montesquieu, Diderot et Catherine II," *Revue internationale d'histoire politique et constitutionnelle* (new series), XVI (1954), 273-87—throw light on "political science" in the age. For the general political atmosphere in Europe and America in the second half of the eighteenth century, see the controversial, not infallible, but important and insufficiently appreciated work by R. R. Palmer: *The Age of the Democratic Revolution: A Political History of Europe and America, 1760-1800*, 2 vols. (1959-64).

The bibliography on British politics is enormous. The classic structural analysis is Sir Lewis Namier: *The Structure of Politics at the Accession of George III* (2d edn., 1957) and Namier: *England in the Age of the American Revolution* (1930). Among his essays, "Monarchy and the Party System" and "Country Gentlemen in Parliament, 1750-85," are both of great importance; they have been reprinted in *Principalities and Powers* (1955). Namier has been criticized sharply for his hostility to ideas—see Herbert Butterfield: *George III and the Historians* (1957). Moreover, the attempt to transport Namier's dismissal of the party labels Whig and Tory in

---

[1] For French institutions, see section 2; for political institutions as they relate to "enlightened despotism," section 3 of this chapter. For American institutions, see Finale.

1760 back to the beginning of the century (undertaken in a meticulous study by Robert Walcott: *English Politics in the Early Eighteenth Century* [1956]) has not, despite all of Walcott's accumulation of data, proved successful. The labels and the ideas have been
restored by J. H. Plumb, first in his review of Walcott's book, *English Historical Review*, LXXII (1957), 126–9; then in his constructive alternative interpretation, *The Growth of Political Stability in
England, 1675–1725* (1967). I have also learned much from J. H.
Plumb's lucid biography, *Sir Robert Walpole* (see above, 573). For
the early period, Keith Feiling's *A History of the Tory Party, 1640–
1714* (1924) remains worth reading. Betty Kemp: *Kings and Commons, 1660–1832* (1957) has interesting chapters on the growth of
the power of the House of Commons.

For the later period, see the general survey by J. Steven Watson:
The Reign of George III, 1760–1815 (1960), and the fine specialized
study by Richard Pares: *King George III and the Politicians* (1953).
Namierite examinations of short periods, by John Brooke: *The
Chatham Administration, 1766–68* (1956), and by G. R. Christie:
The Fall of North's Ministry (1958), are detailed and dependable.
The critical issue of the growth of party and the acceptance of a
"loyal opposition" has been treated in a massive volume by Archibald
A. Foord: *His Majesty's Opposition* (1964); but Caroline Robbins:
"Discordant Parties: A Study of the Acceptance of Party by Englishmen," *Political Science Quarterly*, CXXIII, 4 (December 1958),
505–29, remains important. Among the mass of detailed studies on
politics, Lucy Sutherland: "The City of London in Eighteenth Century Politics," in *Essays Presented to Sir Lewis Namier*, eds. Richard
Pares and A. J. P. Taylor (1956), 49–74, and her lecture, *The City
of London and the Opposition to Government, 1768–1774* (1959),
stand out; among George Rudé's examinations of the politics of violence, see especially "The Gordon Riots: A Study of the Rioters
and their Victims," *Transactions of the Royal Historical Society*
(fifth series), VI (1956), 93–114, and his illuminating *Wilkes and
Liberty* (cited, with other essays, above, chap. i, section 1). On
public opinion, just gaining prominence, see William T. Laprade:
Public Opinion and Politics in Eighteenth Century England (1936).

For that congeries of states collectively called eighteenth-century Germany, the primary question is the separation of German
development from that of the West (proudly boasted of during

World War I, but treated with much anxiety since), and the emergence of what has come to be called "the unpolitical German." The crucial article is Hajo Holborn's justly influential "Der deutsche Idealismus in sozialgeschichtlicher Beleuchtung," *Historische Zeitschrift*, CLXXIV, 2 (October 1952), 359–84—the starting point of much investigation [I, 440]. It was well utilized in Leonard Krieger's massive and original study, *The German Idea of Freedom*, which deals brilliantly with German "adaptation" and "resignation" (cited above, ch. ii, section 1), and Fritz Stern: "The Political Consequences of the Unpolitical German," *History*, No. 3 (1960), 104–34. For unpolitical politics in a great cultural center, Bruford: *Culture and Society in Classical Weimar* (cited above, chap. i, section 1), is basic, especially 44, 76–7, 97, 111, 113–17. There is much shrewd observation in the late Klaus Epstein's *The Genesis of German Conservatism* (1966), 33 *ff*. Friedrich Meinecke concedes that peculiar penchant of cultivated Germans to eschew the "dirty" and "uncivilized" realm of politics in his *Das Zeitalter der deutschen Erhebung*, *1795–1815* (1906; 6th edn., 1957), *passim*. The views of one contemporary observer, Goethe, himself an eminently unpolitical man, are revealing; see his *Dichtung und Wahrheit*, 584–6.

For the environment of the Italian *illuministi*, see Mario Fubini: *Dal Muratori al Baretti* (1954), and Franco Valsecchi: *L'assolutismo illuminato in Austria e in Lombardia*, 2 vols. (1931–4). See also Fubini, ed.: *La cultura illuministica in Italia*, and Valsecchi: *L'Italia nel settecento dal 1714 al 1788*, and the new book by Franco Venturi, *Settecento riformatore*, chap. i, section 1. (For Leopold of Tuscany, see entries below, in section 3.)

It is generally agreed that in the course, and through the agency, of the Enlightenment, natural law was in decline in the eighteenth century. In his widely used *A History of Political Theory* (3rd edn., 1962) George H. Sabine entitles his chapter on French eighteenth-century thought "France: The Decadence of Natural Law." I have gone beyond that to argue (*Voltaire's Politics*, appendix I, and in this volume) that even philosophes who used the rhetoric of natural law abandoned its logic and remained loyal to tatters of natural-law arguments for convenience's sake only. I am much in debt to an important survey by Ronald Grimsley: "Quelques aspects de la théorie du droit naturel au siècle des lumières," *VS*, XXV (1963), 721–40; and find Ernst Troeltsch: "Das Stoisch-Christliche Naturrecht und das moderne profane Naturrecht," *Historische Zeitschrift*, CVI (1911), 237–67, congruent with my views. Perhaps the most important modern study of an eighteenth-century natural lawyer is by Bernard Gagnebin: *Burlamaqui et le droit naturel* (1944). For the persistence of natural-law language in the Scottish Enlightenment, see Bryson: *Man and Society*, 190–6; but see the unpublished Master's thesis by my student James S. Allen: "Adam Smith's Theory of Knowledge and his Conception of Natural Law" (1967), which shows that though Adam Smith was thoroughly familiar with Grotius and Pufendorf, he was trained as well in the empiricist tradition, which in the end prevailed. For the uses of natural law in Kant, see Leonard Krieger's essay "Kant and the Crisis in Natural Law," *JHI*, XXVI, 2 (April–June 1965), 191–210. Hans von Voltelini: "Die naturrechtlichen Lehren und die Reformen des 18. Jahrhunderts," *Historische Zeitschrift*, CV (1910), 65–104, is a sympathetic study of German natural-law advocates like Wolff, Martini, and others. Among general historical surveys, A. P. D'Entrèves: *Natural Law* (1951) is lucid and elementary; Henrich A. Rommen: *The Natural Law* (tr. T. R. Hanley, 1947), is more substantial. See also Sir Frederick Pollock: "The History of the Law of Nature," in *Essays in the Law* (1922); and H. J. Jolowicz: *Historical Introduction to the Study of Roman Law* (1936). Franz Neumann's slashing analysis, "Types of Natural Law," in *The Democratic and the Authoritarian State: Essays in Political and Legal Theory* (1957), 69–95, with all its hostility, is most penetrating. Donald J. Greene's polemic against those who would make Samuel Johnson into a natural-law conservative, "Samuel Johnson and 'Natural Law,' " *The Journal of British Studies*, II, 2 (May 1963), 59–87, with comment by Peter J. Stanlis and reply by Greene, is illuminating in this context. Incidentally, Robert Shackleton has proved conclusively that an essay on natural law attributed to Montesquieu is not by him; see " 'L'Essai touchant les lois naturelles' est-il de Montesquieu?" in *Mélanges offerts à Jean Brethe de La Gressaye* (1967), 763–75.

While Hume's political theory is normally described as conservative (see Robert McRae's brief appraisal, "Hume as Political Philosopher," *JHI*, XII, 2 [April 1951], 285–90), I find myself agreeing with, and learned from, John B. Stewart: *The Moral and Political Philosophy of David Hume* (1963), which classes him among the liberals. Giuseppe Giarrizzo: *David Hume. Politico e Storico*

(1962), and H. R. Trevor-Roper's review of the book in *History and Theory*, III, 3 (1964), 381–9, say much about his politics [I, 454]. Voltaire's Genevan politics is treated in detail in chap. iv, "Geneva: Calvin's Three Cities," of my *Voltaire's Politics*, as well as in my essay "Voltaire's *Idées républicaines:* From Detection to Interpretation," now in my *The Party of Humanity*, 55–96. I have drawn on both. Of the secondary literature, the most important are Paul Chaponnière: *Voltaire chez les Calvinistes* (2d edn., 1936); Jane Ceitac: *Voltaire et l'affaire des Natifs: Un aspect de la carrière humanitaire du patriarche de Ferney* (1956); the essay by Bernard Gagnebin: "Le médiateur d'une petite querelle genevoise," *VS*, I (1955), 115–223; and that by Paolo Alatri: "Voltaire e Ginevra," in *Ginevra e l'Italia*, ed. Delio Cantimori *et al.* (1959), 613–49.

2. THE BATTLE FOR FRANCE

I have dealt with Voltaire's French politics in my *Voltaire's Politics*, chaps. ii, "France: The King's Party," and vii, "France: Constitutional Absolutism," and, once again, I have borrowed from it here. The "Présentation" introducing René Pomeau's excellent selection of texts, *Politique de Voltaire* (1963), presents a somewhat different point of view. Constance Rowe: *Voltaire and the State* (1955) is worthless. Theodore Besterman's attempt to range Voltaire once more among the advocates of "enlightened despotism," in "Voltaire, Absolute Monarchy, and the Enlightened Monarch," *VS*, XXXII (1965), 7–21, strikes me as unconvincing. The generally authoritative study of another advocate of the *thèse royale*, Dubos, A. Lombard's *L'abbé Du Bos* (cited before several times) is less than exhaustive on the meaning of Dubos's politics. Enzo Caramaschi: "Du Bos et Voltaire," *VS*, X (1959), 113–236, offers a reasoned defense. For the marquis d'Argenson, Jean Lamson: *Les idées politiques du marquis d'Argenson* (1943) is badly misleading; Henri Sée, though brief, is far more accurate in his *L'Évolution de la pensée politique . . .* (cited in chap. viii, section 1). Among general histories of the age, Alfred Cobban: *A History of Modern France*, I, *Old Regime and Revolution, 1715–1799* (above, 576), frankly introductory,

is a marvel of condensation and good sense. Henri Carré: *Louis XV,*
1715-1774 (1911), though inevitably dated in many respects, retains
surprising vitality. For the royalist side, Dakin: *Turgot and the*
Ancien Régime in France (cited above, 575) should be supplemented with the still-to-be-published Columbia University dissertation by Gerald J. Cavanaugh: "Vauban, d'Argenson, Turgot: From
Absolutism to Constitutionalism in Eighteenth-Century France"
(1967); and Cavanaugh's recent article, "Turgot: The Rejection of
Enlightened Despotism," *French Historical Studies,* VI, 1 (Spring
1969), 31-58. The royalist minister Maupeou has been studied in Jules
Flammermont: *Le chancelier Maupeou et les parlements* (1895), and
in the brief essay by J. de Maupeou: *Le chancelier Maupeou* (1942);
but see David C. Hudson: "Maupeou and the Parlements: A Study
in Propaganda and Politics" (Columbia University dissertation,
1967), which contains interesting new material.

The best examination of the *thèse nobiliaire* remains Franz Neumann's "Introduction" to Montesquieu's *Spirit of the Laws,* cited
several times. Franklin L. Ford's fine study of the French aristocracies
in the first half of the century, *Robe and Sword: The Regrouping*
of the French Aristocracy after Louis XIV (1953), ends with an
illuminating chapter on Montesquieu much in Neumann's spirit.
Shackleton's standard biography of Montesquieu is helpful as always,
though not so penetrating on this as on other subjects. The old
controversy between Élie Carcassonne: *Montesquieu et le problème*
de la constitution française au XVIIIe siècle (1926), which tried to
make him into a liberal, and Albert Mathiez, in his review of this
book, *Annales de la révolution française,* IV (1927), 509-13, and in
a longer article, "La place de Montesquieu dans l'histoire des doctrines politiques du XVIIIe siècle," ibid., VII (1930), 97-112, which
"show" him to be a "reactionary," was won by Mathiez, but repays
reading for the critical issues involved. All reasonable interpreters
agree that Montesquieu was far more than an ideologist for the robe
nobles. See, in addition to Neumann, Ford, and Shackleton, Bernard
Groethuysen: "Le libéralisme de Montesquieu et la liberté telle que
l'entendent les républicains," *Europe,* XXXVII (1949), 2-16; and a
useful collection of pieces celebrating the bicentennial of *De l'esprit*
des lois: La pensée politique et constitutionnelle de Montesquieu, eds.
Boris Mirkine-Guetzévitch and Henri Puget (1952). Among recent

estimates, Sir Isaiah Berlin: *Montesquieu* (1956) is concentrated and effective.[2] For the magistrates, there are good new monographs, notably François Bluche: *Les magistrats du parlement de Paris au XVIIIe siècle (1715-1771)* (1960), and J. H. Shennan: *The Parlement of Paris* (1968). R. Bickart: *Les parlements et la notion de souveraineté nationale au XVIIIe siècle* (1932) should also be consulted. On the French nobility in the time of Louis XV, see the old but still useful book by Henri Carré: *La noblesse de France et l'opinion publique au XVIIIe siècle* (1920), to which should be added John McManners: "France" in A. Goodwin, ed.: *The European Nobility in the Eighteenth Century* (1953), 22–42; Robert Forster: *The Nobility of Toulouse in the Eighteenth Century: A Social and Economic Study* (see above, 575), an instructive monograph that corrects many misconceptions; Hedwig Hintze: *Staatseinheit und Föderalismus im alten Frankreich und in der Revolution* (1928), which analyzes the struggle between centralizing and decentralizing forces in French politics; and Martin Göhring: *Weg und Sieg der modernen Staatsidee in Frankreich* (1947), a popular but scholarly account.

The study of Diderot's politics is sharing in the general revival of Diderot studies. Older works, like Jean Oestreicher: *La pensée politique et économique de Diderot* (1936), and even Henri Sée's generally perceptive and very reasonable pages in his *L'Évolution de la pensée politique* (see above, 669), 175–97, suffer from an addiction to system and pay inadequate attention to the growth of his thought. Like Oestreicher, I. K. Luppol: *Diderot, ses idées philosophiques* (tr. into French, V. and Y. Feldman, 1936), and Henri Lefebvre: *Diderot* (1949), are rather constrained by their Marxist perspective. There are useful references to Diderot's political ideas in Eberhard Weis: *Geschichtsschreibung und Staatsauffassung in der französischen Enzyklopädie* (1956); more important are Arthur M. Wilson: "Why Did the Political Theory of the Encyclopedists Not Prevail? A Suggestion," *French Historical Studies*, I, 3 (Spring

---

[2] For Boulainvilliers, a source for Montesquieu's pseudo-historical ideas, see Renée Simon: *Henri de Boulainvillier, historien, politique, philosophe, astrologue* (1942), and Vincent Buranelli: "The Historical and Political Thought of Boulainvilliers," *JHI*, XVIII, 4 (October 1957), 475–94.

1960), 283–94; "The Concept of *mœurs* in Diderot's social and political thought," in *The Age of the Enlightenment*, 188–99; and above all "The Development and Scope of Diderot's Political Thought," *VS*, XXVII (1963), 1871–900, which I used with great profit. For the political articles in the *Encyclopédie*, see in addition to Wilson: *Diderot*, often cited, René Hubert: *Les Sciences sociales dans l'Encyclopédie* (1923), *passim*. Paul Vernière's edition of Diderot's *Œuvres politiques* (1963) is a sensible collection of texts fully and dependably annotated. (For Diderot and the "enlightened despots," see the section immediately below.)

For the political ideas of two philosophes not yet mentioned—Holbach: Pierre Naville: *Holbach* (2d edn., 1968); W. H. Wickwar: *Baron d'Holbach: A Prelude to the French Revolution* (1935), [I, 436]; and the thoughtful article by Everett C. Ladd, Jr., "Helvétius and d'Holbach, 'La moralisation de la politique,'" *JHI*, XXIII, 2 (April–June 1962), 221–38. Helvétius: in addition to Ladd, above all D. W. Smith: *Helvétius: A Study in Persecution* (1965), which supplements but does not wholly supplant A. Keim: *Helvétius, sa vie et son œuvre* (1907), [I, 437].

3. ENLIGHTENED ABSOLUTISM: FROM SOLUTION TO PROBLEM

The survival of the term "enlightened despotism" is a tribute to the tenacity of a cliché. Foisted on the historical profession in the nineteenth century, it has been rejected in recent years by most historians; even historians like Fritz Hartung, who were once addicted to it, have now given it up. Yet it prospers. "Enlightened despotism" is an unfortunate expression in three ways: it yokes together a disparate group of rulers who have far less in common than the collective name implies; it burdens them with the disparaging name of despot, which was already negatively charged in the eighteenth century, thus anticipating what needs to be proved; and it links these rulers, with its adjective, more closely to the Enlightenment than in fact they were. It is not that they had no connection; but it was relatively intimate only in the German-speaking part of Europe, and problematic or imaginary in France, Britain, and America. I am delighted to record my full agreement with the late Professor Alfred Cobban, who argues in his *In Search of Enlightenment*, 161–79, that the term in any event has no meaning for the philosóphes. One way in which the cliché has survived is through anthologies and popular textbooks. A typical offender is the paperback collection by Roger Wines entitled *Enlightened Despotism: Reform or Reaction?* (1967). This title, which implies that not the existence but only the political direction of this type of rulership is in question, and the titles imposed on several selections perpetuate what should be discarded. Wines gives two excerpts from an important article by Fritz Hartung, calls one "A Definition of Enlightened Despotism" and the other "The Typical Enlightened Despot," but the article itself is entitled "Der aufgeklärte Absolutismus" (see *Historische Zeitschrift*, CLXXX [1955], 15–42). I do not want to persecute this little anthology; its selections are intelligently chosen and worth reading, but it is symptomatic of a great confusion. In earlier years, this confusion was represented by Geoffrey Bruun: *The Enlightened Despots* (1929), a popular, by now dated survey. Despite its title, John G. Gagliardo: *Enlightened Despotism* (1967), is a crisp, lucid survey of the notion, the reforms instituted across eighteenth-century Europe, and the meaning assigned to those reforms by practitioners and theorists; I have used it with profit.

The *Bulletin of the International Committee of Historical Sciences* reports the results of the inquiries on "enlightened despotism" undertaken in the late 1920s and the 1930s by a number of specialists; see in particular, I (1928), 601–12; II (1930), 533–52; V (1933), 701–804; and IX (1937), 2–131, 135–225, 519–37. Of particular interest in the last-named is the summary by Michel Lhéritier: "Rapport général: le despotisme éclairé, de Frédéric II à la Révolution française," IX, 181–225. For decades now, the skeptical writings of Heinz Holldack have pointed out diversities among eighteenth-century rulers and ambiguities in the use of a collective name for them; see in particular "Die Bedeutung des aufgeklärten Despotismus für die Entwicklung des Liberalismus," *Bulletin*, V, 773–9; his summary of the literature, with Felix Gilbert, ibid., 779–91; "Der Physiokratismus und die Absolute Monarchie," *Historische Zeitschrift*, CVL (1932), 517–49; and "Die Neutralitätspolitik Leopolds von Toskana," *Historische Viertelsjahrsschrift*, XXX (1935–6), 732–56.

Three important essays must be added—Robert Derathé: "Les philosophes et le despotisme," in Pierre Francastel, ed.: *Utopie et institutions au XVIIIe siècle*, 57–75; Franco Venturi: "Despotismo orientale," *Rivista Storica Italiana*, LXXII (1960), 117–26, now in an English version in *JHI*, XXIV, 1 (January–March 1963), 133–42; and Richard Koebner: "Despot and Despotism: Vicissitudes of a Political Term," *Warburg Journal*, XVI (1951), 273–302. I have also profited from Thadd E. Hall: Thought and Practice of Enlightened Government in Corsica," which I saw in ms (now *American Historical Review*, LXXIV, 3 [February 1969], 880–905); in addition to treating the Corsican situation very intelligently, it surveys the whole controversy. For other discussions, see the Wines anthology and its bibliography.[3]

The most celebrated of these so-called enlightened despots was of course Frederick II of Prussia. I have said something of the curious state of scholarship—adulation by Germans, detestation by Frenchmen and, by and large, by Englishmen—in the bibliographical essay to *Voltaire's Politics*, 379–81. Despite its obvious bias (his contempt for Voltaire is scarcely veiled), Reinhold Koser: *Geschichte Friedrichs des Grossen*, 4 vols. (see above, chap. v, section 3), remains a valuable source for its research and documentation. Among shorter biographies, Pierre Gaxotte: *Frederick the Great* (tr. R. A. Bell, 1941), though hostile, is surprisingly objective and thorough. Otto Hintze: *Die Hohenzollern und ihr Werk* has been cited before, 576. Friedrich Meinecke's famous long chapter in his *Die Idee der Staatsräson* (1924; tr. Douglas Scott under the title *Machiavellianism*, 1957) is excessively metaphysical and tends to excuse what needs to be explained, but it is sensitive on the conflicts within the Prussian ruler. Among Otto Hintze's many important articles, most relevant here is "Die Hohenzollern und der Adel,"

---

[3] In a recent article I came upon the following: "It was no accident that Voltaire was . . . a supporter of benevolent despotism in politics. . . . Benevolent despotism, though it could be derived by analogy from his views on science, was proposed by him as a rationalisation of a political attitude which in fact grew out of his own experience." This fanciful reading of Voltaire is then justified by reference to "P. Gay: *Voltaire's Politics*, pp. 87–116." Colim Kiernan: "Science and the Enlightenment in Eighteenth-Century France," *VS*, LIX (1968), 25–6. I need hardly point out that I wrote my *Voltaire's Politics* to refute precisely the view for which my authority is being claimed.

Historische Zeitschrift, CXII (1914), 494–524. The most searching examination of Frederick's machinery remains Walter L. Dorn: "The Prussian Bureaucracy in the Eighteenth Century," *Political Science Quarterly*, XLVI (1931), 403–23; XLVII (1932), 75–94, 259–73. It must be supplemented with a pioneering and penetrating book by Hans Rosenberg: *Bureaucracy, Autocracy, and Aristocracy: The Prussian Experience, 1660–1815* (1958). Arnold Berney: *Friedrich der Grosse, Entwicklungsgeschichte eines Staatsmannes* (1934) traces Frederick's intellectual development without hero-worship, though with admiration. Among Frederick's own writings, his political testaments are of the greatest importance; both of them are available in a convenient German edition by Friedrich von Oppeln-Bronikowski: *Die politischen Testamente* (1920). Krieger: *The German Idea of Freedom*, which happily does without the term "enlightened despotism," has some instructive pages on Frederick. On Frederick II as reformer see especially M. Springer: *Die Coccejische Justizreform* (1914) and Herman Weill: *Frederick the Great and Samuel von Cocceji: A Study in the Reform of the Prussian Judicial Administration, 1740–1755* (1961).

For Frederick's relation to the world of the Enlightenment, especially to France, in addition to biographies of Voltaire and Diderot and the studies of their political ideas (like Arthur Wilson's), see Theodore Besterman's editorial comments on the correspondence between Frederick and Voltaire (see above, 597) and compare them with the comments of Reinhold Koser and Hans Droysen, in their *Briefwechsel Friedrichs des Grossen mit Voltaire*, 3 vols. (1908–11); the former is objective but hostile to the Prussian, the latter prejudiced and hostile to the Frenchman. Among secondary works, Émile Henriot: *Voltaire et Frédéric II* (1927); Fernand Baldensperger: "Les prémices d'une douteuse amitié: Voltaire et Frédéric II de 1740 à 1742," *Revue de littérature comparée*, X (1930), 230–61; and Werner Langer's excessively pro-Prussian *Friedrich der Grosse und die geistige Welt Frankreichs* (1932), can now be supplemented by some excellent recent works—Charles Fleischauer's critical edition of Frederick's *L'Anti-Machiavel*, VS, V (1958), which shows the collaboration of Frederick with Voltaire; Theodore Besterman's instructive edition of "Voltaire's Commentary on Frederick's *l'Art de la guerre*," VS, II (1956), 61–206; and the important articles by Adrienne D. Hytier: "Frédéric II et les philosophes récalcitrants,"

The Romanic Review, LVII, 3 (October 1966), 161–76; and her equally excellent study "Le philosophe et le despote: histoire d'une inimitié, Diderot et Frédéric II," *Diderot Studies*, VI (1964), 55–87. On other German states, much work needs to be done; Gagliardi rightly calls Helen P. Liebel: *Enlightened Bureaucracy versus Enlightened Despotism in Baden, 1750–1792* (1965) a "pioneering attempt" (in his *Enlightened Despotism*, 107). For Germany in general, see Frederick Hertz: *The Development of the German Public Mind*, II, *The Enlightenment* (1962), and Fritz Valvajec: *Die Entstehung der politischen Strömungen in Deutschland, 1770–1815* (1951), as well as Epstein: *Genesis of German Conservatism*, cited before. I learned a good deal from Geraint Parry: "Enlightened Government and its Critics in Eighteenth-Century Germany," *The Historical Journal*, VI, 2 (1963), 178–92, which develops German political and unpolitical thinking and practice with uncommon lucidity. (On Cameralism, see the titles cited above, chap. vii, section 3.)

Recent studies of "Josephinismus," especially collections of documents, are clarifying the age; see Ferdinand Maass, ed.: *Der Josephinismus*, 5 vols. (1951–61). Among general studies, the most effective is Fritz Valjavec: *Der Josephinismus: Zur geistigen Entwicklung Österreichs im 18. und 19. Jahrhundert* (2d edn., 1945). Saul K. Padover: *The Revolutionary Emperor, Joseph the Second, 1741–1790* (1934), though convenient, is scarcely penetrating. Paul von Mitrofanov: *Joseph II. Seine politische und kulturelle Tätigkeit*, 2 vols. (German tr., 1910), is still very useful. Robert A. Kann: *A Study in Austrian Intellectual History: From Late Baroque to Romanticism* (1960) contains a penetrating examination of Joseph von Sonnenfels, his predecessors and successors. See also Peter Horwath: "Literature in the service of enlightened absolutism: the Age of Joseph II (1780–1790)," *VS*, LVI (1967), 707–34; and Ernst Wangermann: *From Joseph II to the Jacobin Trials: Government Policy and Public Opinion in the Hapsburg Dominions in the Period of the French Revolution* (1959), which, though filled with references to "enlightened despotism," is informative.

On Maria Theresa, herself something of a reforming ruler (in strictly selected areas), the old biography by Eugen Guglia: *Maria Theresa, ihr Leben und ihre Regierung*, 2 vols. (1917), remains valuable. See also Robert J. Kerner: *Bohemia in the Eighteenth Century —with Special Reference to the Reign of Leopold II* (1932), and

Henry Marczali's older but still useful *Hungary in the Eighteenth Century* (1910), which concentrates on Hungary after 1780, in the reign of Joseph II. In addition to the article by Holldack, cited above, there is now an authoritative and exhaustive biography of Joseph's younger brother, Leopold—the only truly enlightened ruler of them all—by Adam Wandruszka: *Leopold II. Erzherzog von Österreich, Grossherzog von Toskana, König von Ungarn und Böhmen, Römischer Kaiser*, 2 vols. (1963–5), on which I have drawn. "Lombardy," by J. M. Roberts, in Goodwin, ed.: *European Nobility*, 60–82; "Austria," by H. G. Schenk, ibid., 102–17; and "Hungary," ibid., 118–35, are succinct and useful. And see John M. Roberts: "Enlightened Despotism in Italy," in Harold Acton *et al.*: *Art and Ideas in Eighteenth-Century Italy*, 25–44, which is duly critical of loose usage.

Catherine of Russia has been as controversial as Frederick of Prussia. A good biography is still needed. Meanwhile see the section on her by A. Kizevetter: "Catherine II (1762–1796)," in *Histoire de Russie*, eds. Paul Miliukov *et al.*, II (1932). It should be supplemented with the short study by Marc Raeff: *Origins of the Russian Intelligentsia* (cited above, 594), and Allen McConnell: *A Russian Philosopher: Alexander Radishchev, 1749–1802* (1964). See also McConnell: "Helvétius' Russian Pupils," *JHI*, XXIV, 3 (July–September 1963), 373–86. In a series of important articles, Georg Sacke disclosed Catherine's political motives behind her "enlightened" proposals for a new legal code—"Zur Charakteristik der gesetzgebenden Kommission Katharinas II. von Russland," *Archiv für Kulturgeschichte*, XXI (1931), 166–91; "Katharina II. im Kampf um Thron und Selbstherrschaft," ibid., XXII (1932), 191–216; "Adel und Bürgertum in der gesetzgebenden Kommission Katharinas II. von Russland," *Jahrbücher für Geschichte Osteuropas*, III (1938), 408–17; and, in general summary, "Die gesetzgebende Kommission Katharinas II.," ibid., Beiheft 2 (1940).

On Catherine's controversial relations with the philosophes see the acidulous attack on the philosophes' naïveté and self-centered mythmaking by Albert Lortholary: *Le mirage russe en France au XVIIIᵉ siècle* (1951), also published in the same year under the title *Les 'philosophes' du XVIIIᵉ siècle et la Russie*, well-documented, impressive, but too splenetic and forgetful of the pressures under which eighteenth-century men of letters were compelled to work;

the earlier book by Dimitri S. von Mohrenschildt: *Russia in the Intellectual Life of Eighteenth-Century France* (1936), not so aggressive or instructive as Lortholary's work, is sounder in judgment. For Catherine's relations with Voltaire, W. F. Reddaway's edition of *Documents of Catherine the Great: The Correspondence with Voltaire and the Instruction of 1767 in the English Text of 1768* (1931), though still useful, must be supplemented by Besterman's great edition of Voltaire's correspondence. For Catherine's exploitation of Voltaire as a kind of unpaid press attaché in the West, see Louis-Édouard Roulet: *Voltaire et les Bernois* (1950); and three articles by Sacke—"Entstehung des Briefwechsels zwischen der Kaiserin Katharina II. von Russland und Voltaire," *Zeitschrift für französische Sprache und Literatur*, LXI (1938), 273–82; "Die Kaiserin Katharina II., Voltaire und die 'Gazette de Berne,' " *Zeitschrift für schweizerische Geschichte*, XVIII (1938), 305–14; and "Die Pressepolitik Katharinas II. von Russland," *Zeitungswissenschaft*, XIII, 9 (September 1, 1938), 570–9. G. P. Gooch: "Catherine the Great and Voltaire," in his *Catherine the Great and Other Studies* (1954), a sunny appraisal, should be compared with my own far more critical view of Voltaire in chap. iii of *Voltaire's Politics*. (For Catherine and other philosophes, see the relevant articles, like Wilson's on Diderot's political thought, cited earlier.)

While I have said little of enlightened rule in other countries, I have kept them in mind. For the "Spanish Enlightenment" the obvious books are the dependable studies by Richard Herr: *The Eighteenth Century Revolution in Spain;* and the brilliant, bulky volume by Jean Sarrailh: *L'Espagne éclairée* (cited above, 593); and Antonio Dominguez Ortiz: *La sociedad espagnola en el siglo XVIII* (1955). Though much older, the social and institutional survey by Georges N. Desdevises du Dezert: *L'Espagne de l'ancien régime*, 3 vols. (1897–1905, reprinted in the *Revue hispanique* with slight changes, 1925–8), remains a mine of information.

Most of the monographs on the Physiocrats cited above (chap. vii, section 3), deal also with their political theory. In addition, I have drawn on Gustave Schelle: *Du Pont de Nemours et l'école physiocratique* (1888), a very thorough intellectual biography; Benedikt Güntzberg: *Die Gesellschafts- und Staatslehre der Physiokraten* (1907); Paul Dubreuil: *Le despotisme légal, vues politiques des Physiocrates* (1908); André Lorion: *Les théories politiques des pre-*

miers physiocrates (1918); the last three theses confirm one another. See also, above all, the excellent study by Edmund Richner: *Le Mercier de la Rivière, Ein Führer der physiokratischen Bewegung in Frankreich* (1931). Finally, Mario Einaudi: *The Physiocratic Doctrine of Judicial Control* (1938) is an important contribution to our understanding of the Physiocrats' dawning political liberalism. While the government of Great Britain is never discussed in the context I have developed in this section, my friend R. K. Webb points out in his *Modern England*, 100 *ff.*, that Britain too was undergoing drastic changes in the conception of politics, the structure of society, and the administration of government. In addition to his own perceptive pages, the titles he cites have been most illuminating—W. R. Ward: *The English Land Tax in the Eighteenth Century* (1953) and J. E. D. Binney: *British Public Finance and Administration, 1775–1792* (1958).

CHAPTER TEN

The Politics of Education

I. THE LOGIC OF ENLIGHTENMENT

FOR THE PHILOSOPHES' difficult choice between reform and freedom, and the solution offered by Leopold of Tuscany, see the entries just above, chap. ix, especially section 3.

The survival and revival of classical studies are dealt with in *The Rise of Modern Paganism*, especially chap. i, section 2, and the bibliographical indications on 455–61, which survey the subject across the main countries of the Enlightenment, including the American colonies. Classical education in France has been well treated in the old, substantial volume by the abbé Augustin Sicard: *Les Études classiques avant la révolution* (1887); for the same subject in England see the relevant chapters in M. L. Clarke: *Classical Education in Britain, 1500–1900* (1959); and Clarke: *Greek Studies in England, 1700–1830* (1945), [all three I, 456]. German classical education, the cherished subject of many *Humanisten*, can be followed in Friedrich Paulsen: *Das deutsche Bildungswesen in seiner geschichtlichen Entwicklung* (4th edn., 1920), [I, 459]. For education in early America, see Robert Middlekauff: *Ancients and Axioms: Secondary Education in Eighteenth-Century New England* (1963), [I, 461]; see also bibliography below, for the Finale.

On the Jesuits, of such critical importance for many of the philosophes, the following titles are instructive: R. R. Bolgar: *The Classical Heritage and Its Beneficiaries* (1958), [I, 493], for the tenacity of the Jesuit curriculum. Sicard, just cited, has excellent material. So does André Schimberg: *L'Éducation morale dans les collèges de la Compagnie de Jésus sous l'Ancien Régime* (1913). For Jesuits in the German-speaking world, see the account by a Jesuit, Bernhard Duhr: *Geschichte der Jesuiten in den Ländern deutscher Zunge im*

18. Jahrhundert, 2 vols. (1928). For the other side—scientific instruction—in the Jesuit schools, see François de Dainville: "L'Enseignement scientifique dans les collèges des Jésuites," in *Enseignement et diffusion des sciences en France au XVIIIe siècle*, ed. René Taton (1964), 27–65. Other authors in this collective volume treat scientific education in the schools of other orders; see especially Pierre Costabel: "L'Oratoire de France et ses collèges," 67–100, and Robert Lemoine: "L'Enseignement scientifique dans les collèges bénédictins," 101–23. Georges Snyders: *La pédagogie en France aux XVIIe et XVIIIe siècles* (1965) is a modern study.

There is a good general survey of education in England by Sir Charles Mallet: "Education, Schools and Universities," in *Johnson's England*, II, 209–42, equipped with an extensive bibliography. It may be supplemented with the relevant chapters (iii–v) in W. H. G. Armytage: *Four Hundred Years of English Education* (1964); and in Nicholas Hans: *New Trends in Education in the Eighteenth Century* (1951), which shows that educational reform was not the monopoly of the dissenting academies. For modernizing trends in general, chap. i in Brian Simon: *Studies in the History of Education, 1780–1870* (1960), C. H. Firth: *Modern Languages at Oxford, 1724–1929* (1929), and J. W. Ashley-Smith: *The Birth of Modern Education. The Contribution of the Dissenting Academies, 1660–1880* (1954), to be read with Hans, just cited. For Catholic education in England, see H. O. Evenett: *The Catholic Schools of England* (1944).

As my text indicates, the philosophes and their much-admired precursors had much to say about education, and their own education has been scrutinized by biographers. In general, I found J. A. Passmore: "The Malleability of Man in Eighteenth-Century Thought," in *Aspects of the Eighteenth Century*, ed. Wasserman, 21–46, most instructive; as also Arthur O. Lovejoy's judicious *Reflections on Human Nature* (1961), which surveys such critical matters as man's view of himself and his passions in the course of the eighteenth century. (Rousseau is treated separately in section 3 of this chapter.) For Locke, see Nina Reicyn: *La pédagogie de John Locke* (1941). I have discussed the relevance of Locke's general philosophy to his educational ideas in my Introduction to *John Locke on Education* (1964), an abridgment of Locke's *Some Thoughts Concerning Education*. James L. Axtell's critical edition, *The Edu-*

cational Writings of John Locke (1968), supersedes all earlier compilations. The best general studies of Locke's thought, like Richard I. Aaron: *John Locke* (2d edn., 1955), [I, 531, where there are additional titles], also deal with his educational thinking. M. G. Mason: "John Locke's Proposals on Work-house Schools," *Research Review*, IV (1962), 8–16, is instructive. For Voltaire, the old study by Alexis Pierron: *Voltaire et ses maîtres* (1866), if hostile, is not without use; but it must be supplemented and corrected with René Pomeau: "Voltaire au collège," *Revue d'Histoire littéraire de la France*, LII (January–March 1952), 1–10. Henri Beaune: *Voltaire au collège* (1867), though its collection of materials is now wholly superseded, and its analysis of Voltaire's religious views is too simple, remains of some help. For Diderot: in addition to the judicious pages in Wilson's biography, Jean Seznec: *Essais sur Diderot et l'antiquité* (see above, 653). Basil J. Guy: "The Chinese Examination System and France, 1569–1847," *VS*, XXV (1963), 741–48, throws some interesting light on a comparative dimension of French educational thinking. F. de la Fontainerie: *French Liberalism and Education in the Eighteenth Century* (1932), which contains educational writings of Diderot, also prints proposals by Turgot, La Chalotais, and Condorcet. For La Chalotais, see Jules Delavaille: *La Chalotais, éducateur* (1911). For Morelly, radical educator and radical political theorist, see the contrasting interpretations by Gilbert Chinard in his edition of Morelly's *Code de la nature* (1950); and by R. N. Coe: *Morelly: Ein Rationalist auf dem Weg zum Sozialismus* (1961).

For German *Bildung* in the eighteenth century, see the familiar titles, cited repeatedly before: Biedermann: *Deutschland im 18. Jahrhundert*, II, part 2, 1152 ff.; Sengle and Wolffheim: *passim*, for Wieland; Bruford: *Germany in the Eighteenth Century*, and *Classical Weimar*, as well as Justi's great biography of Winckelmann, especially I, 29–41, and Aner: *Theologie der Lessingzeit* [see I, 439–41, 459–60]. See also Wilhelm Roessler: *Die Entstehung des modernen Erziehungswesens in Deutschland* (1961). Among German educational reformers, Basedow, the follower of Rousseau, is the outstanding figure. There are two old studies of Rousseau's influence on him: G. P. R. Hahn: *Basedow und sein Verhältnis zu Rousseau* (1885); and Carl Gössgen: *Rousseau und Basedow* (1891). More work is clearly needed.

For Helvétius: Smith: *Helvétius*, cited several times, chaps. xiii–

xv. The best general book is Ian Cumming: *Helvétius: His Life and Place in the History of Educational Thought* (1955). Two articles deal with the so-called debate between Helvétius and Diderot—Jean Rostand: "La conception de l'homme selon Helvétius et selon Diderot," *Revue d'histoire des sciences et de leurs applications*, IV, 3–4 (July–December 1951), 213–22; and Douglas G. Creighton: "Man and Mind in Diderot and Helvétius," *PMLA*, LXXI (1956), 705–24.

2. A FAITH FOR THE CANAILLE

The philosophes' view of the "mob" (as separate from modern historians' research, like Rudé's, on popular movements in the eighteenth century) needs much further research. Merely to find isolated statements in political writings or private correspondence is not enough; the real meaning of these disparaging names—mob, canaille, *Pöbel*, etc.—still must be discovered in the wider context. Meanwhile, there are some useful preliminary studies—Karl J. Weintraub: "Toward the History of the Common Man: Voltaire and Condorcet," in Richard Herr and Harold T. Parker, eds.: *Ideas in History: Essays Presented to Louis R. Gottschalk* (1965), 39–64; Roland Mortier: "Voltaire et le peuple," in *The Age of the Enlightenment*, 137–51, discriminating though, I think, a little harsh on Voltaire; and Werner Bahner: "Le mot et la notion de 'peuple' dans l'œuvre de Rousseau," *VS*, LV (1967), 113–29. Joseph L. Waldinger: *Society and the Freedom of the Creative Man in Diderot's Thought*, (see above, chap. vi, section 1), has a chapter on "Diderot and the Mass Man," but here too more work is needed. Keith M. Baker has an interesting essay on "Scientism, elitism and liberalism: the case of Condorcet," *VS*, LV (1967), 129–65, which neatly captures the philosophes' dilemma concerning the masses, which their trust in education did not wholly resolve.

The related question of the social religion is in the same situation—calling for more study. The biographies and studies of the philosophes' political ideas often mention it, but a comprehensive study, free from customary clichés, would be welcome. Frank E. Manuel: *The Eighteenth Century Confronts the Gods* (1959), has some very instructive pages on the relation of subversive religious ideas and the management of the "people," especially 66–9, 121–5, 208–9, 240–1 [see I, 550–1]. The political testaments of Frederick II of Prussia, already cited, furnish splendid evidence. It is clear that the call of late eighteenth-century radicals like Cartwright—"trust the people" (see J. Holland Rose: *William Pitt and the Great War* [1911], 280—was not widely heard among the philosophes.

3. JEAN-JACQUES ROUSSEAU: MORAL MAN IN MORAL SOCIETY

In "Reading about Rousseau," *Party of Humanity*, 211–61, I put the literature on Rousseau down to 1964 into its historical context and into chronological order. Briefly, I suggested there that for over a century of fervent admiration and even more fervent denunciation, Rousseau was treated by both sides mainly as a prophet, an emotional force rather than as a thinker. Then, in 1912, Gustave Lanson, in a pioneering essay, "L'Unité de la pensée de Jean-Jacques Rousseau," *Annales*,[4] VIII (1912), 1–31, dared to suggest, first, that Rousseau was a thinker, and second, that his thought had a certain essential unity. In the Introduction to his widely used *Social Contract and Discourses* (1913), G. D. H. Cole made the same point. While disagreement continued concerning just what the unity was, the *fact* of unity came to be accepted, notably by Ernest Hunter Wright, in *The Meaning of Rousseau* (1929), which concentrated on Rousseau's view of nature; and Ernst Cassirer's impressive *The Question of Jean-Jacques Rousseau*, which appeared in 1932 as two long articles and which I translated and edited in 1954—it sees the unity of Rousseau's life and thought in a kind of pre-Kantian moralism. Cassirer restated his thesis in "L'Unité dans l'œuvre de Jean-Jacques Rousseau," *Bulletin de la Société Française de philosophie*, XXXII, 2 (April–June 1932), 46–66. Cassirer's essays rightly had considerable influence; for a telling but respectful criticism, see Robert Derathé: *Le rationalisme de Jean-Jacques Rousseau* (1948), 188.

---

[4] Note that the short title *Annales* in this section refers to *Annales de la société Jean-Jacques Rousseau.*

Charles W. Hendel: *Jean-Jacques Rousseau, Moralist*, 2 vols. (1934), in close agreement with Cassirer, stresses Rousseau's Platonism [see I, 438–9]. In the same period, and with the same motives, scholars began to explore various aspects of Rousseau's philosophy. C. E. Vaughan edited his *Political Writings*, 2 vols. (1915), and while Vaughan's long Introduction offers the untenable interpretation that Rousseau's political thought moved from individualism to collectivism, his editorial work was pioneering. Among later sympathetic interpreters laying stress on his political ideas, the most significant were René Hubert, in *Rousseau et l'Encyclopédie: Essai sur la formation des idées politiques de Rousseau* (1928); and Alfred Cobban, in *Rousseau and the Modern State* (1934), which is a spirited defense, and a critique of Rousseau's critics. Rousseau emotional and intellectual debts to Geneva, though obvious, found their first serious historical analysis in Gaspard Vallette: *Jean-Jacques Rousseau Genevois* (2d edn., 1911), John Stephenson Spink: *Jean-Jacques Rousseau et Genève* (1934), and Guglielmo Ferrero: "Genève et le *Contrat social*," *Annales*, XXIII (1934), 137–52. Since the War the same theme has been explored by R. R. Palmer in "A Clash with Democracy: Geneva and Jean-Jacques Rousseau," in his *The Age of the Democratic Revolution*, I, offering an original reading; François Jost, in *Jean-Jacques Rousseau Suisse; étude sur sa personnalité et sa pensée*, 2 vols. (1961), rather presses his case for Rousseau's Swiss roots. And see Marcel Raymond: "Rousseau et Genève," in Samuel Baud-Body *et al.*: *Jean-Jacques Rousseau* (1962), 225–37.

In the early phase of this reappraisal, Rousseau's religious thought was exhaustively analyzed by Pierre-Maurice Masson in *La religion de J.-J. Rousseau*, 3 vols. (1916), which was preceded by Masson's edition of Rousseau's *Profession de foi du Vicaire savoyard* (1914), still indispensable. Masson stressed Rousseau's ties to Catholicism, a view which, despite Masson's stupendous scholarship and impressive insights, has not carried the day. Albert Schinz, in *La Pensée religieuse de J.-J. Rousseau et ses récents interprètes* (1927) and in his comprehensive *La Pensée de Jean-Jacques Rousseau* (1929), sees him as a pragmatist; Karl Barth: *From Rousseau to Ritschl* (2d edn., 1952; tr. Brian Cozens, 1959), as a modern Calvinist. Pierre Burgelin, who agrees with Derathé's important study (just cited) that Rousseau was a rationalist, and who also follows Cassirer, has devoted some instructive chapters to Rousseau's religion in his interesting *La Philosophie de l'existence de J.-J. Rousseau* (1962); see also his brief study, *Jean-Jacques Rousseau et la religion de Genève* (1962). Ronald Grimsley has written an economical, lucid, and persuasive essay, *Rousseau and the Religious Quest* (1968), in which he discovers a Rousseau quite similar to the Rousseau I present in the text: "Seen in retrospect," he writes (138), "Rousseau's religion appears much closer to the general eighteenth-century outlook than he himself was prepared to admit." In addition, the article by Robert Derathé: "Jean-Jacques Rousseau et le Christianisme," *Revue de métaphysique et de morale*, LIII (1948), 379–414, repays study. Jacques-François Thomas: *Le pélagianisme de J.-J. Rousseau* (1956) is philosophical rather than religious, stressing Rousseau's doctrine of original innocence.

Rousseau's political thought deserves a special place. While until the French Revolution Rousseau appeared mainly as a novelist, as an eccentric with a message to his culture, and as a pedagogue, the Revolution converted him into a political force. His real influence has not yet been fully traced; I find J. L. Talmon's reading that Rousseau was a vital source for "totalitarian democracy" unconvincing: it not merely misreads Rousseau, it also misinterprets the uses to which he was put. Talmon's motives for tracing the sources of modern totalitarianism are of the best—horror and disgust—but his much-debated book, *The Rise of Totalitarian Democracy* (1952), will not stand up as history. Talmon's most formidable critic has been R. A. Leigh: see his "Liberté et autorité dans le Contrat social," in *Jean-Jacques Rousseau et son œuvre: problèmes et recherches* (1964), 249–62. Among the first to show that Rousseau's ideas furnished support for a wide variety of political ideas was Cobban: *Rousseau and the Modern State;* this is confirmed by Gordon H. McNeil, in "The Antirevolutionary Rousseau," *American Historical Review*, LVIII, 4 (July 1953), 808–23. Joan McDonald: *Rousseau and the French Revolution, 1762–1791* (1965) is a good beginning, but only a beginning, to be supplemented with two articles by Albert Soboul—"Audience des lumières; classes populaires et rousseauisme sous la Révolution," *Annales historiques de la Révolution française*, XXXIV (1962), 421–38; and "Jean-Jacques Rousseau et le jacobinisme," in *Études sur le Contrat social de Jean-Jacques Rousseau* (1964), 405–24. See also Louis Trénard: "La diffusion du Contrat social, 1762–1832," in *ibid.*, 425–58. For Rousseau's considerable impact on Britain, see the thorough study by Henri Roddier, *J.-J. Rousseau en Angleterre au XVIIIe siècle; l'œuvre et l'homme* (1950), and Jacques Voisine: *J.-J. Rousseau en Angleterre à l'époque romantique* (1956). For Germany, see the first essay in Ernst Cassirer: *Rousseau, Kant, Goethe* (trs. James Gutmann, Paul O. Kristeller, John H. Randall, Jr., 1945); Burgelin: "Kant lecteur de Rousseau," in *Jean-Jacques Rousseau et son œuvre*, 303–15; and George Armstrong Kelly: "Rousseau, Kant, and History," *JHI*, XXIX, 3 (July–September 1968), 347–64. There are some interesting explorations of Rousseau's fate in America, notably R. R. Palmer: "Jean-Jacques Rousseau et les États-Unis," *Annales historiques de la Révolution française*, XXXIV (1962), 529–40; François Jost: "La fortune de Rousseau aux États-Unis: esquisse d'une étude," *VS*, XXV (1963), 899–959; and Jacques Godechot: "Le Contrat social et la révolution occidentale de 1762 à 1789," in *Études sur le Contrat social*, 393–403. What emerges from these studies is that Rousseau's influence was even more varied than the man himself.

In recent years, it seems, the rationality of Rousseau's thought and the unity of his life and work have been so firmly accepted that interpreters have addressed themselves to the tensions that threatened to tear Rousseau apart; they are beginning to construct a subtler, fuller biography than was possible for the pioneers of fifty or even twenty-five years ago. One of the most notable, and most widely cited, of these efforts has been the sensitive essay by Jean Starobinski: *Jean-Jacques Rousseau: la transparence et l'obstacle* (1958), which, brilliantly using the entire range of Rousseau's writings, describes Rousseau's lifelong search for the restoration of the candor and clarity of his childhood. Starobinski has continued to work on Rousseau since then, with equally impressive results. "Jean-Jacques Rousseau et le péril de la réflexion," in his *L'œil vivant* (1961), 91–190, suggests the enrichment that modern psychology has gained from the "tumult of ideas" Rousseau felt free to record; and his essay, "Du Discours de l'inégalité au Contrat social," in *Études sur le Contrat social*, 97–109, finds essential unity despite obvious diversity. Bernard Groethuysen's posthumous essay, *Jean-Jacques Rousseau* (1949), is highly suggestive. Ronald Grimsley's *Jean-Jacques Rousseau: A Study in Self-Awareness* (1961), conceived independently of Starobinski and employing a somewhat different method, arrives at strikingly similar conclusions concerning Rousseau's development as a man and thinker. Georges May: *Rousseau par lui-même; images et textes* (1961) lucidly presents Rousseau's life and writings, skillfully using Rousseau's own words. Among modern biographers, F. C. Green: *Jean-Jacques Rousseau: A Critical Study of his Life and Writings* (1955) predates the most recent work; though generally reliable, and good on Rousseau's importance to modern literature, its account of political and philosophical ideas depends on dated scholarship. Jean Guéhenno: *Jean-Jacques Rousseau*, 2 vols. (2d edn., 1962; trs. John and Doreen Weightman, 1966) is a brilliant effort to retell Rousseau's life without the benefit of hindsight, thus enhancing one's sense of Rousseau's immediate experience. William H. Blanchard: *Rousseau and the Spirit of Revolt: A Psychological Study* (1967) is a clinical psychologist's attempt to glimpse the true Rousseau, especially the rage behind his benevolence; it is honest, well-informed, but, with its parallels to our own time, somewhat tendentious and not wholly convincing. In general, Rousseau has given ample opportunity to psychologists; Grimsley and Starobinski, just cited, and others, seek the explanation of Rousseau through psychological categories; in addition to their writings, see A. Heidenhaim: *Jean-Jacques Rousseaus Persönlichkeit, Philosophie, und Psychose* (1924); Louis Proal: *La Psychologie de Jean-Jacques Rousseau* (1930); and above all the psychoanalytic essays by René Laforgue: "Étude sur Jean-Jacques Rousseau," *Revue française de psychanalyse* (1927), 370–402; and *Psychopathologie de l'échec* (rev. edn., 1950), chap. ix, which offer worthwhile hypotheses. Mario Einaudi: *The Early Rousseau* (1967) is a lucid account that takes Rousseau down to 1756; it uses all the modern scholarship. J. H. Broome: *Rousseau: A Study of his Thought* (1963), is a thoughtful introduction. Among many articles, I found the following the most significant: Robert Osmont: "Contribution à l'étude psychologique des Rêveries du Promeneur Solitaire," *Annales*, XXIII (1934), 7–135; Marcel Raymond: "Jean-Jacques Rousseau, Deux aspects de sa vie intérieure (intermittences et permanence du 'moi')," ibid., XXIX (1941–2), 7–57; and his "Jean-Jacques Rousseau et le problème de la connaissance de soi," *Studi francesi*, VI (1962), 457–72; also Basil Munteano: "La Solitude de Jean-Jacques Rousseau," *Annales*, XXXI (1946–9), 79–168; Jean Wahl: "La Bipolarité de Rousseau," ibid., XXXIII (1953–5), 49–55; and (though all the articles I have listed are important) the particularly instructive essay by

Jean Fabre, "Deux frères ennemis: Diderot et Jean-Jacques," (cited before, chap. iv, section 1)—obviously I agree with Fabre that Rousseau, though hostile, remained Diderot's brother. The recent critical edition of madame d'Épinay's so-called memoirs, which in fact her friends Diderot and Grimm doctored in part, throws much light on Rousseau's claim that he was being persecuted—he seems to have had a point; see Georges Roth, ed.: *Histoire de Madame de Montbrillant: Les pseudomémoires de Madame d'Épinay*, 3 vols. (1951) [I, 448]. The work toward an authoritative biography is being greatly advanced by the splendid collective edition of Rousseau's *Œuvres complètes*, eds. Bernard Gagnebin, Marcel Raymond *et al.* (1959———) of which three volumes have appeared and the fourth at this writing (January 1969) is overdue. Volume I contains the autobiographical writings, II the fictions and literary essays, III the political writings. In addition to instructive, detailed notes, the volumes contain thorough and revealing introductory essays to each work by such skilled interpreters as Starobinski, Derathé, Fabre, and others. Just as welcome is the new authoritative edition of Rousseau's *Correspondance complète*, ed. R. A. Leigh (1965———). Four volumes have appeared so far, taking Rousseau to 1756; two others are announced. This magnificent edition will wholly replace the *Correspondance générale de J.-J. Rousseau*, 20 vols., eds. Théophile Dufour and Pierre-Paul Plan (1924–34).

There are several important recent examinations of Rousseau's political ideas (in addition to R. A. Leigh's refutation of Talmon, cited on 696). See Robert Derathé's impressive *Jean-Jacques Rousseau et la science politique de son temps* (1950), which traces the sources of Rousseau's political ideas and analyzes their meaning in detail. Derathé, for all his sympathy, has shown himself critical of Rousseau's ideas on the social religion: "La religion civile selon Rousseau," *Annales*, XXXV (1959–62), 161–70. In an interesting, if controversial, essay, Franz Haymann finds natural-law teachings in Rousseau: "La loi naturelle dans la philosophie politique de J.-J. Rousseau," ibid., XXX (1943–5), 65–109. John Plamenatz's chapter on Rousseau in his *Man and Society*, I, *Machiavelli through Rousseau* (1963), 364–442, is penetrating, ready to tackle complex issues, and free from partisanship. Plamenatz has also done something to rehabilitate that notorious saying about forcing men to be free: " 'Ce qui signifie autre chose sinon qu'on le forcera d'être libre': A

Commentary," *Annales de philosophie politique*, V (1965), 137–52. Roger D. Masters: *The Political Philosophy of Rousseau* (1968) offers a close reading of the texts, but reads too much between the lines and comes to the unacceptable conclusion (to me) that Rousseau's "most defensible work" is the first discourse. Judith N. Shklar: "Rousseau's Images of Authority," *American Political Science Review*, LVIII (1964), 919–32; and "Rousseau's Two Models: Sparta and the Age of Gold," *Political Science Quarterly*, LXXXI, 1 (March 1966), 25–51, are instructive. The scholarly consensus, then, which I share, is that despite Rousseau's illiberal streak (brilliantly analyzed by Plamenatz), he was not, in intention or effect, a precursor of totalitarianism; the minority view is represented by Lester G. Crocker, especially in "The Relation of Rousseau's Second *discours* and the *Contrat social*," *Romanic Review*, LI (1960), 33–44; and "Rousseau et la voie du totalitarisme," *Annales de philosophie politique*, V (1965), 99–136.

The central point in my section on Rousseau—that he was essentially a civic educator—has been made before. For the impact of the ancients, see Georges Pire: *Stoïcisme et pédagogie; de Zénon à Marc-Aurèle, de Sénèque à Montaigne et à J.-J. Rousseau* (1958); and Pire: "De l'influence de Sénèque sur les théories pédagogiques de Jean-Jacques Rousseau," *Annales*, XXXIII (1953–5), 51–92 [I, 458]. Jean Château: *Jean-Jacques Rousseau: sa philosophie de l'éducation* (1962) is a good monograph. On the political bearing of Rousseau's educational ideas, Henri Roddier: "Éducation et politique chez J.-J., Rousseau," in *Jean-Jacques Rousseau et son œuvre*, 183–93, is excellent; so is Robert Derathé: "L'homme selon Rousseau," in *Études sur le Contrat social*, 203–17; and so is, finally, Pierre Grosclaude: "La politique dans l'œuvre de Jean-Jacques Rousseau," *Revue politique et parlementaire*, LXV (1963), 43–50.

FINALE

The Program in Practice

WHILE I HAVE DRAWN on a large literature about the late colonial and revolutionary period, I am indebted most to Bernard Bailyn, notably the General Introduction to his edition of *Pamphlets of the American Revolution, 1750–1776,* I, *1750–1765* (1965) [I, 447], which has since appeared, revised and expanded, as *The Ideological Origins of the American Revolution* (1967); and to his stimulating and pioneering essay, *The Origins of American Politics* (1968). See also Bailyn's long Introduction, followed by a full bibliography, *Education in the Forming of American Society* (1960), like everything he has done a fine specimen of the social history of ideas and social history in general. I do not, however, fully accept the dichotomies he suggests in his interesting article "Political Experience and Enlightenment Ideas in Eighteenth-Century America," *American Historical Review,* LXVII, 2 (January 1962), 339–51 [I, 446], for reasons I indicate in my exploratory essay in comparative history, "The Enlightenment," in C. Vann Woodward, ed.: *The Comparative Approach to American History* (1968), 34–46.

The American Enlightenment, as Bailyn has shown, needs and deserves further work. Adrienne Koch's anthology, *The American Enlightenment: The Shaping of the American Experiment and a Free Society* (1965), has generous selections from the writings of Franklin, Adams, Jefferson, Madison, and Hamilton; but her introductions, like her collection of essays, *Power, Morals and the Founding Fathers* (1961), are too admiring to be wholly penetrating; these men were too great to need uncritical treatment. Herbert M. Morais: *Deism in Eighteenth-Century America* (1934) has not yet been, but needs to be, surpassed. Conrad Wright: *The Beginnings of Unitarianism in America* (1955) [I, 536], is very useful. Alan Heimert's scholarly *Religion and the American Mind from the Great Awaken-*

ing to the Revolution (1966) argues, *à la* Perry Miller, that the real revolutionaries were the Calvinists, a stimulating but hardly convincing thesis; see the review by Edmund S. Morgan in *William and Mary Quarterly* (third series), XXIV, 3 (July 1967), 454–9.

Among general treatments of the Revolutionary period, I learned most from the succinct Introduction by Edmund S. Morgan: *The Birth of the Republic, 1763–1789* (1956), as well as Edmund and Helen M. Morgan: *The Stamp Act Crisis: Prologue to Revolution* (2d edn., 1963). Richard B. Morris: *The American Revolution Reconsidered* (1967) is a stimulating reassessment, opening with a survey of the historiography. Carl Bridenbaugh: *Cities in Revolt* (cited above, chap. i, section 1), is excellent. Charles McLean Andrews: *The Colonial Background of the American Revolution* (1924), is not out of date. Beard's famous dissection of the Founding Fathers in his *An Economic Interpretation of the Constitution* (2d edn., 1935), has itself been dissected effectively, if with a churlish tone, by Robert E. Brown: *Charles Beard and the American Constitution* (1956); Brown's revisionist *Middle-Class Democracy and the Revolution in Massachusetts, 1691–1780* (1955), offers an alternative to Beard. One other anti-Beard book must be mentioned— Benjamin Fletcher Wright's compact *Consensus and Continuity, 1776–1787* (1958). The whole controversy, which threatens to produce an unmanageably large literature, has been reviewed and judged in magisterial fashion in Richard Hofstadter: *The Progressive Historians: Turner, Beard, Parrington* (1968), chaps. vi and vii. While New-Left American historians are complaining that the anti-Beardians are drowning the real conflicts in American society in the swamp of consensus, it appears rather that Beard failed not only to give all of the right answers but even to ask some of the right questions.

Many of the titles mentioned give space to the intellectual origins of the American Revolution—which were, in large part, the work of the American Enlightenment before 1775. Louis B. Wright: *The Cultural Life of the American Colonies* (cited above, 577), is an articulate summary. The relevant chapters in Merle Curti: *The Growth of American Thought* (2d edn., 1951), are helpful. Charles F. Mullett: "Classical Influences on the American Revolution," *The Classical Journal*, XXXV, 2 (November 1939), 92–104; and Richard Gummere: *The American Colonial Mind and the Classical Tradition* (1963), a fine collection of essays, deal with a subject of particular importance to the Enlightenment [I, 460, and other titles there]. In addition, note H. Trevor Colbourn: *The Lamp of Experience: Whig History and the Intellectual Origins of the American Revolution* (1965); the older but still useful Randolph G. Adams: *Political Ideas of the American Revolution* (1922); and Carl Becker: *The Declaration of Independence: A Study in the History of Political Ideas* (1922) [I, 447]. They should be supplemented by Edward S. Corwin's significant *The 'Higher Law' Background of American Constitutional Law* (1957); and the brief essay by David G. Smith: *The Convention and the Constitution: The Political Ideas of the Founding Fathers* (1965). Clinton Rossiter: *Seedtime of the Republic* (1953) has the facts, but celebrates more than it analyzes. *The Constitution Reconsidered*, ed. Conyers Read (1938; rev. edn. Richard B. Morris, 1968), has dated very little; many of the articles remain immensely interesting, and the comparative dimension (added by such distinguished European historians as Hajo Holborn) makes this a stimulating collection. The relation of Europe to America—both the transmission of ideas in both directions and America as a complex ideology for Europeans—deserves further work, although much is being done. See again Durand Echeverria: *Mirage in the West* (cited above, 605). Among Gilbert Chinard's many contributions to this subject, note "Eighteenth-Century Theories of America as a Human Habitat," *Proceedings of the American Philosophical Society*, XCI (1947), 27–57. Felix Gilbert: *To The Farewell Address: Ideas of Early American Foreign Policy* (1961) puts these ideas into a Western framework [I, 447]. See also Michael Kraus: *Atlantic Civilization: Eighteenth-Century Origins* (1949); and the first volume of R. R. Palmer: *The Age of the Democratic Revolution* (cited before), chaps. vi–ix.

On the Founding Fathers themselves, the biographical material is enormously rich. I have used the early volumes of the Jefferson, Madison, Franklin, and Hamilton papers, all being sumptuously edited. I have space only to mention the volumes I found most useful—Carl Van Doren: *Benjamin Franklin* (1938), to which should be added Alfred Owen Aldridge: "Benjamin Franklin and the philosophes," *VS*, XXIV (1963), 43–65, and Claude-Anne Lopez: *Mon cher Papa* (1966). See Gilbert Chinard: *Honest John Adams* (1933). Dumas Malone: *Jefferson and His Time*, 3 vols. so far, *Jefferson the Virginian* (1948), *Jefferson and the Rights of Man* (1951), *Jeffer-*

son and the Ordeal of Liberty (1962), are all impressive in their scholarship and broad humanity, but need perhaps, for all that, the counterblast of Leonard Levy's *Jefferson and Civil Liberties: The Darker Side* (1963), which strenuously but effectively concentrates on the failings of a national hero. For Madison, see Irving Brant: *James Madison*, 6 vols. (1941–61); for Hamilton, among a particularly rich crop, John C. Miller: *Alexander Hamilton: Portrait in Paradox* (1959).

While the literature on *The Federalist* is growing, a good book on that masterpiece is still needed. I used the reliable critical edition by Jacob E. Cooke (1961). The critical edition by Benjamin Fletcher Wright (also 1961), has a long and impressive introduction. I found Wright's essay, "*The Federalist* on the Nature of Political Man," *Ethics*, LIX, 2, part II (January 1949), 1–31, very instructive. On the most celebrated of the papers, the Tenth, see especially Douglass Adair: "The Tenth Federalist Revisited," *William and Mary Quarterly* (third series), VIII, 1 (January 1951), 48–67, which conclusively refutes Charles Beard's misreading of the paper as an instance of the economic interpretation of history; see also Adair: " 'That Politics May Be Reduced to a Science,': David Hume, James Madison, and the Tenth *Federalist*," *The Huntington Library Quarterly*, XX, 4 (August 1957), 343–60. For Madison, author of the most significant papers in *The Federalist*, see the useful articles by Irving Brant: "Madison: On the Separation of Church and State," *William and Mary Quarterly* (third series), VIII, 1 (January 1951), 4–23. Edward S. Corwin: "James Madison: Layman, Publicist and Exegete," *New York University Law Review*, XXVII (April 1952), 277–98; Ralph L. Ketcham: "James Madison and the Nature of Man," *JHI*, XIX 1 (January 1958), 62–76; and three articles by Neal Riemer—"The Republicanism of James Madison," *Political Science Quarterly*, LXIX, 1 (March 1954); "James Madison and the Current Conservative Vogue," *Antioch Review*, XIV (December 1954), 458–70; and "James Madison's Theory of the Self-Destructive Features of Republican Government," *Ethics*, LXV, 1 (October 1954), 34–43. Hamilton's thought has been neatly captured in Cecelia M. Kenyon: "Alexander Hamilton: Rousseau of the Right," *Political Science Quarterly*, LXXIII, 2 (June 1958), 161–78. On the vexing and important question of disagreements among the authors of *The Federalist*—the "debate" between Madison and Hamilton not wholly concealed by their common pseudonym—see the important article by Alpheus T. Mason: "*The Federalist*—A Split Personality," *American Historical Review*, LVII, 3 (April 1952), 625–43. A general review of the literature is Douglass Adair: "The Federalist Papers," *William and Mary Quarterly* (third series), XXII, 1 (January 1965), 131–9.

INDEX

abolitionist movement, 116 *n.*, 410–11, 419–21, 423; *see also* slave trade; slavery

absolutism, enlightened, 483–96; and political science, 452; theories of, 488–96

Académie des sciences, 129, 136

Académie française, 28, 67, 68, 79–83, 112, 239, 370 474, 478

Académie Royale de Peinture et de Sculpture, 224, 239

academies, 9, 227, 241; *see also* Prussian Academy; Royal Academy

Adair, Douglass, 560 *n.*

Adams, John, 98 and *n.*, 99, 121, 191, 445 *n.*, 559

Adams, Samuel, 311

Addison, Joseph: on contemporary life, 27, 49; and the *Spectator*, 52–3, 55, 57; and his contemporaries, 65, 299, 307, 308, 311, 560; on art and aesthetics, 210, 212, 217, 302, 304; as a dramatist, 251 and *n.*; on history, 369; see also *Spectator*

aesthetics, 219, 220; of Reynolds, 236–7; of German critics, 246–8; of Diderot and Lessing, 249–90; antirationalist, 291–3, 298; of Winckelmann, 293–8; of Dubos, 298–9; of Montesquieu, 299–301; and psychology, 301–3; of Burke, 303–6; of Hume, 306–10; of Kant, 310–18; *see also* art

agriculture, 5; in economic thought, 350, 351–2

Aldridge, Alfred Owen, 559 *n.*

Alembert, Jean Le Rond d': social philosophy of, 25, 67–8, 78, 509–10, 525–6; and the *Académie*, 80, 82, 83 and *n.*; historical thought of, 101, 102, 387 and *n.*; and the philosophes, 112, 128, 155 and *n.*, 209, 239, 258–9, 259 *n.*, 274, 529, 533; and Newtonian science, 128–30, 134,

145, 146, 149, 150, 152, 157, 161, 162, 165; and psychology, 177 *n.*, 177–8; and Frederick of Prussia, 243, 244, 483, 485, 525; education of, 506; death of, 555

Alexander, H. G., 143 *n.*

Algarotti, Conte Francesco, 135, 220 and *n.*

American colonies, 7, 9, 60, 409, 421, 446, 561–2

American Constitution, 560, 573–8; and Montesquieu's influence, 325

American Revolution, 118, 311, 458, 499, 555–8; and the Enlightenment, 558–63

ancients, vs. moderns, 96, 118, 124, 125, 133, 239

Anglicans, Anglicanism, 87, 144, 147, 186, 209, 218, 408

Anglomania, 24–5, 58, 155, 230, 454, 559

Anne, Queen of England, 28, 131

anthropology: philosophical, 168, 172, 174, 194; cultural, 319

anticomaniacs, 221, 222, 241, 250, 269, 297

anti-Semitism: *see* Jews

Arbuthnot, Dr. John, 175

architecture, 27, 220 *n.*, 226, 228, 229, 241, 243, 291 and *n.*

Argens, Jean-Baptiste de Boyer, marquis d', 244

Argenson, Marc-Pierre de Voyer d', comte d', 77, 505

Argenson, René-Louis de Voyer d', marquis d', 448 *n.*, 450 *n.*, 502, 505

Argental, comte d', 505

aristocrats, aristocracy: manners and morals of, 42, 202; and government, 324, 327 *n.*, 426, 488; *see also* patronage

Aristotelians, 109 *n.*, 141

Aristotle, 84, 97, 113, 178, 182; on

A NOTE ABOUT THE AUTHOR

Peter Gay was born in Berlin, Germany, in 1923, and came to the United States as a young man. A graduate of the University of Denver, he took his M.A. and Ph.D. degrees at Columbia University and joined the Columbia faculty in 1947 as a part-time lecturer in government. He switched to the department of history at Columbia in 1956. In 1962 he was made professor of history there. William R. Shepherd Professor of History at Columbia from 1967 to 1969, he is now Professor of Comparative European Intellectual History at Yale. Regarded as one of the leading authorities on the intellectual history of eighteenth-century Europe, Professor Gay has published many articles and several books, including *The Party of Humanity: Essays in the French Enlightenment; The Dilemma of Democratic Socialism; Voltaire's Politics; The Enlightenment: The Rise of Modern Paganism*, which won the National Book Award in 1967 and the Frederic G. Melcher Award; and *Weimar Culture: The Outsider as Insider*. He has also translated Voltaire's *Philosophical Dictionary* and *Candide*.

A NOTE ON THE TYPE

THE TEXT of this book was set on the Linotype in JANSON, a recutting made direct from type cast from matrices long thought to have been made by the Dutchman Anton Janson, who was a practicing type founder in Leipzig during the years 1668–87. However, it has been conclusively demonstrated that these types are actually the work of Nicholas Kis (1650–1702), a Hungarian, who most probably learned his trade from the master Dutch type founder Kirk Voskens. The type is an excellent example of the influential and sturdy Dutch types that prevailed in England up to the time William Caslon developed his own incomparable designs from these Dutch faces.

Composed, printed and bound by
The Haddon Craftsmen, Inc., Scranton, Pa.
Typography and binding design by

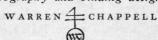
WARREN CHAPPELL